MW00681326

MONEY,

BANKING,

AND

FINANCIAL INTERMEDIATION

GARY SMITH
Pomona College

D. C. Heath and Company
Lexington, Massachusetts   Toronto

Address editorial correspondence to:

D. C. Heath
125 Spring Street
Lexington, MA 02173

Acquisitions Editor: George Lobell
Developmental Editor: Patricia Wakeley
Production Editor: Carolyn Ingalls
Designer: Alwyn Velásquez
Art Editor: Diane Bordow
Production Coordinator: Lisa Merrill
Photo Researcher: Mark Corsey
Text Permissions Editor: Margaret Roll
Cover Designer: Alwyn Velásquez

Cover: © Peter Aaron / Esto

Published simultaneously in Canada.

Printed in the United States of America.

International Standard Book Number: 0–669–21724–7

Library of Congress Catalog Number: 90–83500

10 9 8 7 6 5 4 3 2 1

For my friends,
Joshua and Joanna

The real trouble with this world of ours is not that it is an unreasonable world, nor even that it is a reasonable one. The commonest kind of trouble is that it is nearly reasonable, but not quite.

G. K. Chesterton

TO THE INSTRUCTOR

Banks and other financial intermediaries can be extremely innovative in adapting to government regulations, responding to new opportunities, and offering additional services to their customers. Financial markets are often quite turbulent — sometimes exhilarating, at other times frightening. In this book, I have tried to convey some of this flux and excitement by emphasizing important economic principles and by illustrating these principles with interesting anecdotes and historical incidents.

Recent years have seen the development of many new kinds of monetary assets, and new ones are being introduced all the time. No precise definition of "money" can remain relevant for very long. There are just too many near-moneys and new-moneys. The same is true of banks. Many financial intermediaries, near-banks, now do virtually the same things that traditional banks do. And the list of things that banks do is continually expanding.

This aggressive innovation makes money-and-banking courses exciting, but also very challenging. This book responds to that challenge by taking a broad view of money and banks — looking across a spectrum of financial assets and institutions, emphasizing general principles rather than soon-outdated numbers. Facts are indispensable for understanding the relevance of economic concepts. And this book does have its share of facts. But facts can be overdone, deluging students with technical minutiae. Bewildered and tired, the students struggle to memorize these details or quickly skim over them. In either case, there is a great danger that students will miss the concepts that the facts were intended to illustrate. And, ironically, in a dynamic field like money and banking, many of the "facts" in textbooks are already obsolete.

An emphasis instead on the broad principles of money and financial intermediation can make a book more readable and the course more exciting. The enthusiasm of the professors and, even more importantly, of the students who have read drafts of this book has been extremely gratifying. One student wrote: "Really enjoyed your book a lot. I even read portions of it aloud to people around my house." Another wrote: "Of all the economics textbooks I own (nearly a dozen), this is the only one that I have read twice in one semester. . . . I may even read it again."

Pedagogy

Several pedagogical tools in this book focus attention on the principles of money and banking:

1. **Repetition.** The most important concepts are highlighted in the margin and repeated in summaries at the end of each chapter. In addition, important principles reappear throughout the book for reinforcement. Important terms are boldfaced and reappear in a short list at the end of each chapter and in a full glossary at the end of the text.

2. **Intuitive verbal explanations.** I have tried mightily to explain everything in simple English. Familiar, even homely, examples are used to involve students in the economic reasoning. The principles of money and banking need not use arcane mathematics or tales of an alien culture.

3. **Real-world examples.** Anecdotes and quotations from the financial press are used throughout the book to show the everyday application of economic principles. There are 102 highlighted examples that reinforce this message. They are listed in the table of contents and inside the front cover. The real-world relevance of economic concepts, as illustrated by the Highlights, is much more than tables of soon-outdated numbers.

4. **Interesting exercises.** There are an average of 26 exercises per chapter that allow students to apply the principles they have just learned. Rather than simple recall, many of these exercises require thought and analysis. These exercises ask for interpretation of historical incidents, evaluation of institutional changes, and critique of provocative quotations.

Optional Material

There is an incredible diversity in money-and-banking courses. Students have a wide variety of backgrounds and interests, and instructors place widely varying emphases on economic theory, institutional details, policymaking, economic history, microeconomics, macroeconomics, finance, accounting, and mathematics. Professors freely reshape textbooks to suit themselves and their students. Many instructors will omit certain sections or even entire chapters. Anticipating this, I have identified the optional sections that seem the most likely candidates for omission. These include some historical material, esoteric topics, and more difficult analyses.

Chapters 3, 8, 9, and 10 are particularly flexible. Chapter 3 (International Moneys) introduces the idea of exchange rates early in the book, in response to instructors who want to emphasize the global nature of banking and financial markets. This chapter can alternatively be covered at the end of the course, before Chapter 23 (The Macroeconomics of a Large, Open Economy), or can be omitted entirely. Chapter 8 (Financial Futures and Options) provides a substantial explanation of futures and options, which are increasingly used by financial institutions for speculation and hedging; this chapter can be skimmed or omitted. Chapter 9 (Loans) explains some details about loans, including loan payments, creative financing, and adjustable-rate loans. Students find this material especially relevant and interesting, but much — or all — of this chapter can be omitted. Chapter 10 (The Stock Market) is another nonessential chapter that students enjoy, if there is time for it.

The *IS-LM* model is also a flexible topic. I have written the macroeconomic analysis (Part 5) so that these chapters can be read whenever the instructor wishes, or dropped entirely if the students already know this material or do not need to learn it. One possible course outline is to cover Chapters 1 through 18 (with Chapters 3, 8, 9, and 10 optional). Chapters 16, 17, and 18 cover the major macroeconomic controversies — the quantity theory, monetary targeting, rules versus discretion, rational expectations, and the new classical macroeconomics — without using the *IS-LM* model. If there is time, most of Chapter 22 (Inflation) and Chapter 23 (The Macroeconomics of a Large, Open Economy) can also be covered; those sections requiring knowledge of the *IS-LM* model are at the end of these two chapters and are labeled optional.

An instructor who wants to use the *IS-LM* model can cover Chapters 19, 20, and 21 and the optional sections of Chapters 22 and 23. To allow sufficient time for this material, some of the financial market chapters earlier in the text may be skimmed or omitted: Chapter 6 (Default Risk), Chapter 8 (Financial Futures and Options), Chapter 9 (Loans), Chapter 10 (The Stock Market), and perhaps Chapter 11 (Risk and Return).

Text Supplements

The text is supplemented by an excellent Study Guide for students, written by Nozar Hashemzadeh of Radford University. The text author has prepared an Instructor's Guide with 1,000 examination questions, and computer software that includes financial calculations, macroeconomic modeling, and an instructive banking simulation game.

Acknowledgments

My largest debts, by far, are to William Brainard and James Tobin, who taught me a great deal of economics and much, much more. I have also learned all sorts of things from Dave Backus, Willem Buiter, Jack Ciccolo, Ed Leamer, Ray Fair, Ben Friedman, Gary Fromm, Steve Goldfeld, Michael Kuehlwein, Peter Mieszkowski, Bill Nordhaus, Doug Purvis, Roy Ruffin, John Shoven, Joe Stiglitz, Steve Taylor, and Ed Yardeni. This book was immensely improved by many conscientious, knowledgeable reviewers:

James Barth

Christopher Baum
  Boston College
Dwight Blood
  Brigham Young University
E. Christina Echevarria
  University of Minnesota
Peter Frevert
  University of Kansas
Duane Graddy
  Middle Tennessee State University
Jack Gelfand

Stuart Glosser
  University of Wisconsin, Whitewater
Michael J. Haupert
  University of Wisconsin — LaCrosse
Lora P. Holcombe
  Florida State University
James Kolari
  Texas A&M University

Richard Kinonen

John T. Lee
  Middle Tennessee State University
Chung Pham
  University of New Mexico
Frances Quantius
  Ohio State University
Richard Schiming
  Mankato State University
David Schutte

Larry J. Sechrest
  University of Texas — Arlington
Zena Seldon
  University of Wisconsin, LaCrosse
Alden Shiers
  California Polytechnic State University
Craig Swan
  University of Minnesota — Twin Cities

My students at Yale, Rice, Houston, and Pomona College have been patient and careful readers of various early drafts. Particularly helpful suggestions were made by Pompeyo Aguilar, Decio de Maria, Henry Ehrenhaft, Ken Lin, Manoucher Mokhtari, Bob Parker, Farhad Raseekh, Bill White, and Kathy Williamson.

TO THE STUDENT

Financial institutions are a channel by which the savings of some are loaned to others. This channel between borrowers and lenders is a very important service performed by banks and other financial institutions. But to appreciate this importance fully, we must examine why people borrow and lend, what financial assets are available for borrowing and lending, and why financial institutions are needed to bring borrowers and lenders together. It is the answers to these very questions that you will learn in this book.

I have not drawn artificially precise distinctions between money and other financial assets, nor divorced banks from both their customers and other financial institutions. Your goal is not to memorize 1000 current institutional facts about money and banks. If you focus your attention on these details, you may miss the main theme, which is the overall role of money and banks in an economy. Even worse, with the rapid evolution of financial markets and institutions, many of these "facts" you memorize will be obsolete before the course is over!

In this textbook, I have tried to emphasize general principles that you will find useful after the final exam. I have included some recent numbers, institutional details, historical graphs, and many anecdotes that I think you will find interesting. But these should be viewed as little more than opportunities to apply and test the general principles of money and banking. It is these principles, not the examples, that you should learn.

One of the very best ways to master the principles is to apply them to the exercises at the end of each chapter. You can't become a good soccer player just by watching the World Cup, and you can't learn money and banking just by reading about it. You have to dribble the ball and apply the principles yourself. You will make mistakes at first, but soon you will acquire the necessary skills and experience. The surest way to strengthen your reasoning is to practice on the exercises.

Money and banking is an important and wonderfully interesting topic. I envy the pleasure that you will experience learning about this fascinating subject. And I hope that you enjoy reading this book as much as I enjoyed writing it.

BRIEF CONTENTS

CONTENTS

FINANCIAL INTERMEDIATION

AND

THE ECONOMY

The master-economist must possess a rare combination of gifts. He must be a mathematician, historian, statesman, philosopher — in some degree. He must understand symbols and speak in words. He must contemplate the particular in terms of the general, and touch abstract and concrete in the same flight of thought.

He must study the present in light of the past for the purposes of the future. No part of man's nature or his institutions must lie entirely outside his regard. He must be purposeful and disinterested in a simultaneous mood; as aloof and incorruptible as an artist, yet sometimes as near the earth as a politician.

John Maynard Keynes

A few years from now, you may graduate from college and enter the job market, looking forward to a rewarding and satisfying career. Will jobs be plentiful, as in 1967 when the unemployment rate was 3.5 percent and firms got into bidding wars, offering ever-more-attractive salaries and signing bonuses? Or will the job market be more like that of 1982, when the unemployment rate averaged 9.7 percent and many college graduates ended up flipping hamburgers while they waited for conditions to improve?

After a few more years, you may want to buy a house. You may save some money from your job, and your relatives may contribute a bit more to help you make a down payment. You find a wonderful house, make an offer that is accepted, and go to a bank to apply for a loan. Will mortgage rates be a livable 9 percent, as in 1988, or a crushing 15 percent, as in 1982?

The economic climate is constantly changing. Low interest rates and a strong economy make it easier for businesses to expand and hire more college graduates. High interest rates and a weak economy can wreck the job market and the housing market. This text focuses on why and how these things happen.

Economists, investors, and policymakers have long been interested in the effects of financial events on economic activity, and with good reason. A widely used banking system is crucial to a nation's economic development. Financial booms and busts cause economic expansion and recession. Data on the money supply and banking activity provide clues to the future direction of output, inflation, interest rates, and the stock market. Financial events will affect your job opportunities, the availability of the credit that you need to buy a car and a house, and the purchasing power of your life savings. This is why money, banking, and financial markets are so often in newspaper headlines:

Fed Boss Banking on Housing Slump to Nail Down Inflation
(Chicago Tribune, *April 20, 1980*)

While Congress Fiddles, More Thrifts Burn
(The Economist, *February 27, 1982*)

Closing of Ohio S&L's After Run on Deposits
(The Wall Street Journal, *March 18, 1985*)

Monetary Policy Caused the Crash
(The Wall Street Journal, *October 22, 1987*)

Mortgage Market Goes from Feverish to Sick
(The Wall Street Journal, *March 18, 1989*)

We study money and banking to learn how financial events affect the overall economy and how they affect each of us personally. Every section of every chapter of this book is intended to help you understand monetary events — the reasons behind their occurrence and the economic consequences. If you keep asking How? and Why?, this book will help answer your questions.

WHAT IS MONEY? WHAT ARE BANKS?

Money and banking may seem to be very simple concepts. We use money to buy things. We go to the bank to deposit or borrow money. But there is much more to it than that. Money and banks play crucial roles in our economic life — roles that are both subtle and ever evolving. The competitiveness of financial markets and the innovativeness of financial institutions are continually changing the nature of both money and banking.

What is money? Cash and traveler's checks are evidently money. What about checking accounts and credit cards? Are savings accounts money? Are money-market funds money? Are cash-management accounts at brokerage firms money?

The distinction between money and other financial assets is becoming increasingly fuzzy, making it difficult to settle on a widely accepted definition of money.

No matter how we define *money*, there are other financial assets that are excluded by the definition but that are similar enough to make them "near-moneys" and leave us wondering whether they should be considered part of the money supply. Because the role of money is best explained in relation to and in comparison with the roles of other financial assets, we will study money in this textbook by looking at a spectrum of financial assets. We will look not only at cash and checking accounts but also at savings accounts, money-market funds, and cash-management accounts.

What are banks? The distinctions among financial institutions have also become increasingly blurred as commercial banks have expanded into nontraditional activities and as other financial institutions have encroached on traditional banking. Citibank now sells discount merchandise by phone, Merrill Lynch offers what are, in essence, checking accounts, and AT&T issues credit cards. Commercial banks are no longer unique. Because banking activities now overlap many diverse businesses, we will consider a variety of modern financial institutions — including not only commercial banks but also savings-and-loan associations, brokerage firms, and mutual funds.

There are many types of money and many kinds of financial institutions.

Money and banks are part of an intertwined and ever-changing system of financial markets and agents. To describe this interrelated system, this text employs the following strategy:

Part 1 consists of three chapters that examine different kinds of money: commodity money, paper money, and bank money.

In Part 2, we focus on financial assets and markets — the environment in which financial decisions are made. We will consider loans, bonds, stocks, and interest rates and see why people borrow and lend and how they choose to do so.

In Part 3, we examine the roles of banks and other financial intermediaries. You will learn how banks are managed and how their behavior affects their customers and the economy.

Part 4 is devoted to the federal government's monetary policies — how the government affects the nation's financial markets and institutions and how it chooses its policies.

Part 5 provides a macroeconomic analysis of the influence of monetary events on economic activity.

This introductory chapter gives an overview of the topics we will cover and explains some general concepts and a few institutional details that we will refer to in the chapters ahead. It provides both a preview of what money and banking is about and some useful principles. We will see how financial assets are related to real assets and discuss the distinction between nominal and real rates of return. We will see how the U.S. Treasury finances federal deficits by selling bonds and how the Federal Reserve can alter the money supply by buying or selling these Treasury bonds. You will see that there are a variety of financial institutions — banks and near-banks — that perform several important functions for their customers. We begin by thinking about why households and businesses use banks.

BANK CUSTOMERS

To the casual observer, financial institutions may seem little more than large buildings where well-dressed people shuffle papers. After all, banks don't really produce anything like wheat, steel, or tennis shoes, do they? With this attitude, a student might approach a money and banking course as little more than an offhand look at amusing but harmless curiosities.

That attitude, however, is grievously incorrect. Financial assets and institutions are central to modern economies. They transform the meager savings of cautious families into large investments by bold entrepreneurs. They allow workers to be capitalists, sharing in the profits of industrial giants. They manufacture liquidity and reduce all sorts of risks. Although you can't touch any of these things, they are just as real and important as wheat, steel, and tennis shoes. Money and banks play very important roles in our economy, but it is difficult to understand these roles unless we think about the people who use money and banks. To appreciate fully the services that banks provide to their customers, both lenders and borrowers, we need to look at why people lend and borrow.

Jam Today Versus Jam Tomorrow

In 1989, U.S. households had more than $18 trillion in assets and $3 trillion in liabilities. Their net worth was nearly $60,000 per person, or $240,000 for a family of four. There may be some misers who accumulate wealth for the simple pleasures of counting and admiring it. But for most of us, wealth is a means to an end rather than the end itself.

When we save, we give up some current consumption — food, clothing, entertainment — in order to enjoy more future consumption. You may save to buy a car or a house, take a trip, pay for your children's education, support your retirement, or provide your heirs with the pleasures that you denied yourself. In each case, you are saving — forgoing current consumption — in order to provide for future consumption.

People save to provide for future consumption.

If our income were perfectly synchronized with our spending, we would have little need for saving. Because our spending does not coincide with our income, we must save for future expenditures or borrow against future income. For instance, most people hope to live many years after they stop working and must save during their working years to maintain their accustomed standard of living during retirement. We save for vacations, to buy houses, and to provide for our children's education. We also save a little to bequeath to our children and save some more to protect ourselves against future uncertainties.

Financial and Real Assets

Real assets are tangible physical assets such as houses, automobiles, and televisions; **financial assets** are paper claims including bank deposits, bonds, and stocks. Most financial assets are the financial liabilities of others. Suppose that Joshua has $2,000 and Joanna needs a car to get to her job each day. If Joshua lends Joanna $2,000 to buy a used car, he receives an IOU from Joanna, promising to repay the loan plus interest. This IOU is an asset for Joshua and a liability for Joanna, in that part of her paycheck will go to Joshua, allowing him to buy food with her wages.

This financial arrangement appeals to both: it allows Joshua to invest without stockpiling cars and other real assets and it allows Joanna to buy a car so that she can get to work. If we combine their accounts, Joshua's financial asset and Joanna's liability cancel each other out and their aggregate net worth is the car. In the very same way, a nation's aggregate wealth is its tangible assets. Financial assets and liabilities allow some people to borrow money to buy cars, houses, land, and other real assets and to let other people invest in financial rather than real assets.

Instead of buying a farm, we deposit money in a bank, which lends money to a farmer who buys land and equipment. The farmer hopes to produce a profitable crop, repay the bank loan plus interest, and keep some reward for hard work. The bank, in turn, uses the money it receives from the farmer to repay our deposit plus interest, and keeps a little to pay its bills and earn a profit. Implicitly, we and the bank have invested in the farm, in that we have a claim to part of the profits that it will make. If the crop fails, the bank may foreclose and sell the farm to repay our investment.

Figure 1.1 is a simplified sketch showing three different routes by which the savings of investors are channeled into the acquisition of tangible assets. Savers can buy houses and other real assets directly; they can buy stocks and bonds issued by others who acquire real assets; or they can deposit funds in banks and other **financial intermediaries**, which borrow from savers and lend to those acquiring tangible assets. This sketch is actually oversimplified, because people, businesses, and governments are both borrowers and savers. A household that borrows money from a bank to buy a house may also buy corporate bonds, lending money to businesses. A business that borrows money by issuing corporate bonds may also buy government bonds. The federal government issues bonds and also buys household mortgage notes. Nonetheless, Figure 1.1 is useful because it helps us remember that what ultimately lies behind financial claims — the assets of some and liabilities of others — are real, tangible assets and that financial claims exist to allow investors to own tangible assets indirectly.

Financial intermediaries borrow from some in order to lend to others.

Rates of Return

The return from an investment consists of **income**, the benefits you receive while you own the asset, and **capital gains**, the profits you make when you sell

Investments can provide both income and capital gains.

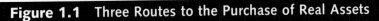

Figure 1.1   Three Routes to the Purchase of Real Assets

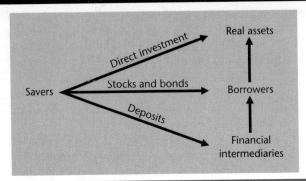

the asset. Income includes the cash flow from the investment — the interest from bonds, dividends from stock, and rent from apartment buildings, and any services the asset provides — as a house provides shelter, an automobile provides transportation, or a television provides entertainment. Rental data can sometimes be used to estimate the value of such services; for example, the value of the services provided by a home can be estimated by the cost of renting a similar home.

The services provided by houses, cars, and other real assets are unseen income that escapes taxation. If you buy bonds and use the interest to rent a house and a car and to wash your clothes at the laundromat, you must pay taxes on the interest. If you instead invest in a house, a car, and a washing machine, then a good deal of your income is asset services, which are unrecorded and untaxed. This tax advantage gives a household a strong incentive to purchase a home and consumer durables. This is one reason that so many rental apartments have been converted to owner-occupied condominiums.

Financial markets affect our investment in physical assets in two ways:

1. Those looking for attractive investments compare the anticipated returns on financial and real assets: when bank deposits, bonds, and other financial assets offer high interest rates, many choose to invest in financial rather than in real assets.
2. Those considering borrowing to buy real assets may be dissuaded by high loan rates. It is much more expensive to buy a house when mortgage rates are above 15 percent, as they were in 1981 and 1982, than when mortgage rates are below 10 percent, as in 1978 and 1988.

High interest rates make financial assets more attractive and also discourage borrowing to buy real assets.

The interest rates on bonds and loans generally move together. When bond yields are high, thereby luring savers away from real assets, loan rates are also high, further discouraging physical investment. At such times, however, consumer loan rates are often sticky and loans rationed; in these cases the observed increase in loan rates understates the difficulty in obtaining credit. In 1981, many savings and loan associations listed their mortgage rates at 16 percent to 18 percent but wouldn't even accept loan applications. Those that did routinely rejected virtually every loan request. They had no money to lend and didn't lend any.

Financial markets influence not only the choice between financial and real assets but also the decision to consume or save. When interest rates are high, some people reduce current consumption, saving more now in order to consume more in the future. It is important to recognize, however, that this trading of present for future consumption depends on both interest rates and inflation, as the next section explains.

Nominal Versus Real

Economic numbers that are recorded in dollars are called **nominal data**. If you are paid $5 an hour for a part-time job, that is your nominal hourly wage rate. If you work full time and earn $20,000 a year, that is your nominal annual income. Your nominal net worth is the market value, in dollars, of the difference between your total assets and liabilities.

A fundamental tenet in economics is that people do not work and save solely for the simple pleasures of counting and recounting their dollars. We work and accumulate dollars in order to buy and enjoy goods and services, and we therefore care about what our dollars will buy. Economic numbers measured in terms of purchasing power are called **real data**. Suppose, for instance, that you are interested only in purchasing hamburgers. Your real income can then be measured in hamburgers, calculated by dividing your nominal income by the price of hamburgers.

Nominal data are in dollars, real data measure purchasing power.

$$\text{Real income (hamburgers/year)} = \frac{\text{Nominal income (dollars/year)}}{\text{Price of hamburgers (dollars/burger)}}$$

If you earn $20,000 a year and hamburgers cost $2, then your real income is 10,000 hamburgers a year. Similarly, at $5 an hour, your real wage rate is 2.5 hamburgers an hour. Your real wealth is your nominal wealth divided by the price of hamburgers.

The underlying economic principle behind the calculation of real data is that it is these real amounts rather than nominal magnitudes that affect people's behavior. A decision to work or play depends on what your wages will buy. Fifty years ago, when a dollar would buy a lot, most people would have been eager to earn $1 an hour. Now, when a dollar buys little, some people would rather watch television than work for $4 an hour.

Similarly, in deciding whether to live like a prince or a pauper, you implicitly think about your real income and real wealth. Someone who behaves differently, who thinks in nominal terms, suffers from an economic nearsightedness that economists call **money illusion**. Anyone who is pleased with a 3 percent increase in nominal income when prices increase by 10 percent is showing definite signs of money illusion.

| Highlight 1.1 | Calculating the Consumer Price Index |

The example in the text used a single price, the price of hamburgers, but we do not live by hamburgers alone. We also buy milk, bananas, clothing, shelter, medical care, haircuts, and football tickets. The purchasing power of our dollars depends on the prices of a vast array of goods and services. People with different tastes attach varying importance to different prices. The well-dressed keep a close eye on clothing prices, and the sickly watch medical costs. People who don't smoke ignore cigarette prices; those who don't care for football games ignore the prices of football tickets.

To get a general, representative picture of real income, real wealth, and real interest rates, the federal government monitors the prices of goods and services and calculates several price indexes that measure the cost of representative commodity bundles. The best known is the **Consumer Price Index (CPI)**, which measures the cost of living for typical U.S. households — the cost of food, clothing, shelter, VCRs, and the other necessities and luxuries we consume.

Every ten years or so, the Department of Labor's Bureau of Labor Statistics (BLS) surveys thousands of households to learn the details of their buying habits — most recently in 1982–1984, when they interviewed more than 140,000 households nationwide. Half were interviewed every three months for five consecutive quarters about their major purchases (cars, televisions, VCRs, and so on). The other half recorded their daily expenses in diaries for two weeks. Based on this survey, the BLS constructed a market basket of 2,000 goods and services. Each month, 250 agents call or visit stores in 56 cities to collect current price data on about 400 of these goods and services.

The resultant price data are used to calculate a price index that measures the current cost of the market basket relative to the cost in a base period,

$$P = 100 \frac{\text{Current cost of market basket}}{\text{Cost of market basket in base period}}$$

Here, for example, are some selected CPI data, using a base period of 1982–1984:

Year	CPI (100 in 1982–1984)
1970	38.8
1980	82.4
1989	123.1

These data allow us to compare consumer prices in the given years with the base year and with each other. For instance, consumer prices more than doubled between 1970 and 1980:

$$\frac{1980 \text{ CPI}}{1970 \text{ CPI}} = \frac{82.4}{38.8} = 2.124$$

and increased by nearly 50 percent between 1980 and 1989:

$$\frac{1989 \text{ CPI}}{1980 \text{ CPI}} = \frac{123.1}{82.4} = 1.494$$

One of the most difficult tasks in constructing price indexes is accounting for changes in the quality of goods and services. When the price goes up 10 percent, but the box says "new and improved," should we believe the claim? If the quality has in fact improved 10 percent, then there hasn't really been any inflation. It's like buying a 10-percent-larger size; you simply paid more to get more. But how do you measure quality? Apple's Macintosh computers are very different from the earlier Apple II computers and cost a lot more, too. What is the percentage change in their quality? Physicians have drugs and equipment that didn't exist 20 years ago; their fees are also much higher, and they don't make house calls. What is the percentage change in the quality of medical services? On the other hand, many products have experienced what economists call "candy bar inflation." For years, candy bar prices were constant, while the bars gradually became smaller and smaller. Many other products and services have similarly deteriorated. Their quality has gone down rather than up. Statisticians try to make quality adjustments in the price indexes, but this task is difficult and subjective.

Inflation

The real value of our income and wealth depends critically on the price level. One reason that we study money and banking is that increases in a nation's money supply tend to cause an increase in its prices. Figure 1.2 shows some evidence of this relationship, using a scatter diagram of money and price data for ten countries during the 1980s. The horizontal axis gives the annual rate of change of M1, a measure of a nation's money supply that includes cash and checking account balances. The vertical axis is the annual rate of change of consumer prices — the annual rate of inflation — in each of these ten countries.

There is a rough positive correlation between money and inflation in that those countries with relatively slow money growth (Switzerland, Japan, and West Germany) had relatively low inflation, while those countries with the fastest money growth (Britain, South Korea, and Spain) had relatively high rates of

Rapid increases in the money supply tend to cause inflation.

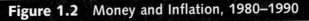

Figure 1.2 Money and Inflation, 1980–1990

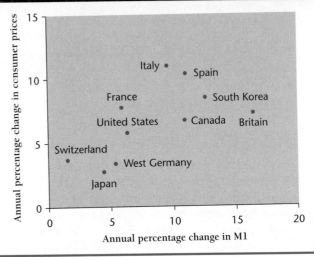

inflation. The correlation is, however, by no means perfect. The money supply grew much faster in Britain than in Italy (16.54 percent annually versus 9.67 percent), yet the annual rate of inflation averaged 11.34 percent in Italy and 7.55 percent in Britain. In later chapters, we will look at how money affects prices and why other factors matter, too.

Real Rates of Return

Another area in which it is important to distinguish between nominal and real values is in the rates of return on investments. The **nominal rate of return** R on an investment is the dollar profit as a percentage of the dollars invested.

$$\text{Nominal return } R = \frac{\text{Dollars earned}}{\text{Dollars invested}}$$

If a $100 investment yields a $10 profit a year from now, then the nominal rate of return is

$$R = \frac{\text{Dollars earned}}{\text{Dollars invested}} = \frac{\$10}{\$100} = 0.10 \text{ (that is, 10 percent)}$$

The **real rate of return** r measures the profit in commodities, as a percentage of the commodities invested:

$$\text{real return } r = \frac{\text{commodities earned}}{\text{commodities invested}}$$

Zero Stroke

The relationship between money and inflation is clearest in countries with extremely high rates of inflation, or **hyperinflation**, in which prices increase at double-digit rates weekly or even daily. In Argentina in the 1980s, the money supply grew at a rate of nearly 200 percent a year; it is no surprise that Argentina also experienced extremely rapid inflation, with prices rising by nearly 300 percent a year. Even more extraordinary increases in the money supply fueled the German hyperinflation of 1922–1923, in which prices increased at a rate of 322 percent a month, and the Hungarian 1945–1946 hyperinflation, in which prices increased by 19,800 percent a month!

To foreign observers, these hyperinflations were a great source of amusing anecdotes. The Hungarian government issued a 1,000,000,000,-000,000,000,000-pengo note, which bought less than one U.S. penny. *The New York Times* told of an American in a Berlin restaurant who asked for all the dinner that a dollar bill would buy. He received a satisfying meal, but, as he was about to leave, the waiter appeared with another bowl of soup and another entree, explaining, "The dollar has gone up again."* Others told of buying beer and receiving more for returning the empty bottle than they had paid for it full. The Associated Press sent out this report:†

"Zero stroke" or "cipher stroke" is the name created by German physicians for a prevalent nervous malady brought about by the present fantastic currency figures.

Scores of cases of the "stroke" are reported among men and women of all classes, who have been prostrated by their efforts to figure in thousands of billions. Many of these persons apparently are normal, except for a desire to write endless rows of [zeros].

---

*The New York Times, October 30, 1923.
†The New York Times, December 7, 1923.

Normally, you don't actually invest or receive commodities. You invest and receive dollars. The logic of a real-yield calculation is that you take into account the purchasing power of the dollars invested and received.

If you are still interested only in hamburgers and these cost $2, then investing $100 is equivalent to giving up 50 hamburgers. A year later, when you are paid $110 (a 10 percent nominal return), you should deflate these dollars according to the prevailing price of hamburgers. If the price of hamburgers has gone up 10 percent, to $2.20, then your $110 buys 50 hamburgers. You have given up 50 hamburgers now for 50 hamburgers later, and your real rate of return is 0 percent. You have run fast but stayed in the same place.

In general, the real rate of return is approximately equal to the nominal rate of return minus the percentage increase, π, in the price level:

$$r = R - \pi \tag{1}$$

If, as in the example, you earn a 10 percent nominal return when the price of hamburgers increases 10 percent, then your real return is zero. If the price of hamburgers rises by only 3 percent, your real return is $10\% - 3\% = 7\%$. If the price of hamburgers increases by 20 percent, your real return is negative, a disappointing -10 percent; you give up 50 hamburgers now for 45 hamburgers a year hence.

Figure 1.3 shows some U.S. data on nominal interest rates, inflation, and real interest rates since 1950. Nominal interest rates tend to increase during inflationary periods, such as the 1970s, but not in lock step — inflation fell much faster and farther than interest rates in the early 1980s, so that real interest rates were unusually high for several years. In later chapters, we will discuss how financial events affect both nominal and real interest rates.

Household Borrowing

Financial institutions make most of the loans that enable households to buy houses, cars, and other physical assets. People expect their incomes to rise throughout their working years. Early in their careers, they want to borrow in order to buy a house and a car and to enjoy a standard of living that is consistent with their anticipated lifetime income, intending to repay these debts with the higher income that they will earn when middle-aged. But it is difficult for people with few tangible assets to borrow, because of the risk that they will declare bankruptcy and default on these loans.

Usually, individuals can borrow only a fraction of the value of their tangible assets, such as securities, real estate, jewelry, and consumer durables. It is very hard to use future labor income as collateral. As the old saying goes, "To borrow money, you must first prove that you don't need it." Individuals who can pledge only their future income are said to be **liquidity constrained**: their future labor income is illiquid in that it cannot be easily converted into spendable cash.

Liquidity constraints provide another channel by which financial markets affect consumer spending. When money is "easy," not only are interest rates low, but it is also easier for weaker credit risks to obtain loans. When money is "tight," interest rates increase and the liquidity-constrained, with only their future income as collateral, are unable to borrow and forced to curtail spending.

The Financing of Business Investment

The economic output of a nation is critically dependent on its capital stock — its buildings, machines, tools, trucks, roads, telephone wires, and so on. A

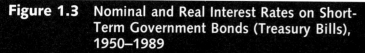

Figure 1.3 Nominal and Real Interest Rates on Short-Term Government Bonds (Treasury Bills), 1950–1989

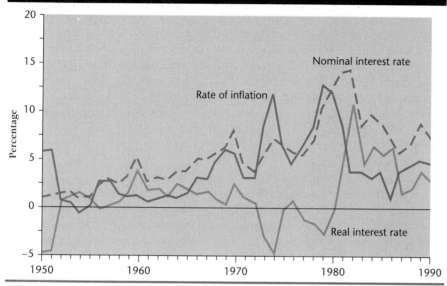

nation's physical capital allows citizens to be more productive and to enjoy more leisure. If there is inadequate capital, people will work harder and produce less.

Governments bankroll some investment projects, such as the construction of highways and airports. But in a mostly capitalist nation such as the United States, private firms make most of the investment decisions. Individual entrepreneurs start businesses, small businesses expand, and giant corporations erect billion-dollar plants. Financial-market events influence all of these decisions.

There are more than 15 million businesses in the United States, of which some 3 million are corporations. A corporation is said to be **publicly owned** when it issues shares that can be bought by any member of the public. The shareholders are the legal owners of the corporation and elect a board of directors that supervises the company's operations. Some privately owned companies are very large (for example, Levi Strauss and United Parcel Service), but most are small "mom-and-pop" businesses.

A corporation is a legal entity that can borrow money from a bank, as you or I would borrow money to buy a car or a house, and it can issue bonds, as the U.S. Treasury does. The difference is in degree. Most corporations are more creditworthy than you or I, but none is as secure as the U.S. Treasury.

Because the shareholders own the company as a group — that is, in common — their stock is said to be **common stock**. Common stock is very different from loans, bonds, and other **fixed-income securities** that specify the amount of money to be paid to the noteholder. A person who buys common stock acquires

Common stock represents equity-ownership of the corporation and a claim on its profits and assets.

partial ownership of the company and is said to own **equity**, a claim on the company's profits after interest and other fixed expenses have been paid and, in the event of liquidation, a claim on the company's assets after its debts have been settled.

Imagine that you own a small business that has assets worth $100,000 but owes $20,000 to a bank. Your claim as owner is equity, and its value is equal to the value of the business in excess of its debts, here $80,000. In the same way, if this business were a corporation, the shareholders would be the legal owners of the business and their stock would be equity, not debt.

Just as a small-business owner spends some of the profits and uses the remainder to expand, so a corporation disburses some of its profits to shareholders as dividends and reinvests the remainder. The size of the dividend is determined by the corporation's directors, who are elected by the shareholders and presumably act in their interest when deciding how to split the company's profits between dividends and reinvestment.

As with households, there are two ways in which financial markets affect business investment in real assets. Firms choose between investing in real and financial assets, and high interest rates make the latter more attractive. In addition, about half of all business investment is financed by borrowing, and this is clearly influenced by the cost and availability of credit.

Corporations can sell additional shares of stock to raise cash, but few do — because the dividends they pay shareholders are not a tax-deductible expense, whereas the interest that they pay banks and bondholders is. In most years, corporate stock repurchases actually exceed sales. During the five years 1984–88, U.S. corporations sold $225 billion in new stock and repurchased $650 billion, a net retirement of $425 billion.

In 1988, for example, U.S. businesses spent $540 billion on plant and equipment, of which $320 billion was for replacement and repair of existing facilities and equipment and $220 billion was new investment. These expenditures were not financed by selling stock. On balance, in 1988, businesses repurchased $110 billion more stock than they sold. Their total spending, $540 billion on capital plus $110 billion to retire stock, was financed by $370 billion in retained profits and $280 billion in bond sales, bank loans, and other debts.

Bonds are an important source of funds for large, well-known businesses. Small and medium-size firms find it difficult and expensive to issue bonds. Denied access to the bond market, they rely on local banks and other financial institutions for loans. Large corporations also borrow from banks, but because they have direct access to financial markets, they demand and get very favorable loan rates. Small and medium-size firms, without this bargaining power, depend on banks.

Some firms, like some households, perceive themselves as liquidity constrained. Their managers are enthusiastic about the firm's future and therefore willing to take substantial gambles. They want to borrow heavily, expand greatly, and repay their loans out of future profits. Lenders are wary of enthusiastic profit projections, and the amount that they are willing to lend may fall far short of

Leveraged Buyouts

A takeover wave hit the United States in the 1980s as a dizzying succession of companies was acquired by corporate raiders. Sometimes the takeovers were approved by the target company's board of directors. Often, the offer was unfriendly, with the raider buying enough stock from shareholders to elect its own slate of directors and replace existing management.

Takeovers are motivated by a belief that the potential value of a company is substantially larger than its current market value. One reason might be that the current management is incompetent. Another reason, illustrated in Table 1.1, is that the company would be able to generate more money each year if it had more debt and less equity, using the tax-deductible interest on its debt as a tax shield to protect profits from taxation.

The company in Table 1.1 could have been financed by (a) selling $1 billion in stock or (b) selling $500 million in stock and $500 million in bonds to the very same investors. Each person who would have bought $10,000 in stock in case (a) buys $5000 in stock and $5000 in bonds in case (b). Either way, the firm's annual before-tax income is $100 million. The after-tax cash flow is very different, though. In case (a), all the firm's annual payments to investors are dividends and cannot be deducted from its taxable income. In case (b), some of the firm's payments to investors are tax-deductible interest. In the example, $17 million in additional annual cash flow is created by avoiding $17 million in taxes each year.

The tax advantage of debt is a primary motivation for the leveraged buyout (LBO) in which, using the target firm's assets as collateral, the

Table 1.1 Annual Corporate Cash Flow With and Without Debt, in Millions

	Financed by $1 Billion in Stock, No Debt (a)	Financed by $500 Million in Stock, $500 Million Debt (b)
Gross income	$100	$100
Interest	0	50
Taxable income	100	50
Taxes (34% rate)	34	17
Dividends	66	33
After-tax cash flow (interest plus dividends)	66	83

takeover group uses borrowed money to buy the target firm's stock. Once the takeover group has control of the firm, there is less equity, more debt, and a larger tax shield. Recognizing that this debt-equity restructuring is the ultimate objective of many takeovers, some target firms have, for self-protection, borrowed heavily, using the proceeds to repurchase their own stock. Once they have created a sufficient tax shield, there is little to be gained from a takeover.

Between 1984 and 1988, U.S. nonfinancial corporations issued $440 billion in corporate bonds and repurchased $425 billion in stock, thereby swapping approximately a half trillion dollars of debt for equity. The danger is that, because of either a recession or overly optimistic profit projections, heavily indebted companies won't make enough money to pay the interest on their massive debts. A wave of corporate bankruptcies could cause a financial crisis in the United States. One remedy would be to treat dividends and interest similarly, allowing firms to deduct either, both, or neither, from their taxable income.

the firm's hopes. Young, unproven companies, with high hopes and few assets, are likely to be liquidity constrained. During credit crunches, funds simply dry up for smaller, less-established firms. Liquidity-constrained, they must abandon investment projects and sometimes even curtail current operations. Later chapters will explain the causes of credit crunches and provide more details about their consequences.

GOVERNMENT SPENDING AND BORROWING

The U.S. Treasury sells securities to finance federal deficits.

The president and Congress determine federal expenditures and tax rates. When the government's outlays exceed its revenue, its budget is in deficit and the U.S. Treasury must sell securities to raise the money needed to pay the government's bills. The Treasury also sells securities regularly to replace old bonds that are maturing (being paid off). If the government's budget is balanced, so that tax revenue covers government expenses (including interest on maturing debt), then the new securities sold just offsets the old ones maturing and the government debt, the total amount of Treasury securities outstanding, remains constant. If the government's budget is in deficit, the amount of new securities sold exceeds the amount maturing, and the government debt increases. Whenever there is a budget surplus, the outstanding debt declines.

The federal government is the nation's biggest borrower. Figure 1.4 shows the annual federal budget deficits as a percentage of gross national product since

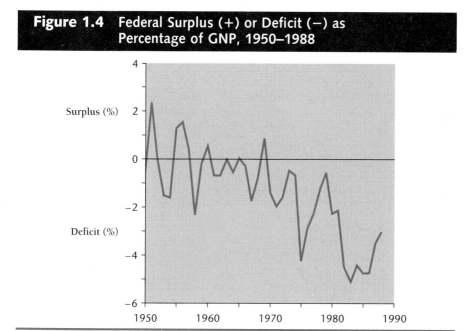

Figure 1.4 Federal Surplus (+) or Deficit (−) as Percentage of GNP, 1950–1988

1950. The deficit generally increases during wartime, as military spending expands dramatically, and during economic recessions, when tax revenue declines. The years from 1985 onward were unprecedented in that there were persistently large deficits during peacetime and prosperity. Many observers lament such deficit spending, believing that federal borrowing "crowds out" private borrowers. In their view, the U.S. Treasury is a 300-pound gorilla that sits where it wants and borrows as much as it pleases — leaving others without chairs or loans. We will examine this argument in later chapters.

The Federal Reserve

There is virtually no chance that the U.S. Treasury will default on its debts, because the federal government has the power to raise taxes and to issue currency to meet its obligations. The **Federal Reserve Board (Fed)** controls the supply of U.S. currency. The Fed can increase the amount of currency by using newly printed paper money — Federal Reserve notes — to buy Treasury bonds. The Fed can, if it wants, reduce the amount of currency by selling some of the Treasury bonds it holds and retiring the Federal Reserve notes it receives for them. The Fed makes its own decisions, but there is no doubt that if the Treasury ever had trouble selling bonds, the Fed would step in and buy as many as needed.

The Federal Reserve's monetary policies affect the availability of credit to household and business borrowers. When the Fed buys Treasury bonds and

The Federal Reserve Board (Fed) controls the supply of currency by buying and selling Treasury securities.

issues new Federal Reserve notes, more money is available for borrowing and spending: credit markets ease. When the Fed sells some of its bond holdings and retires Federal Reserve notes, credit markets tighten because there is less money to lend and borrow.

The Fed uses monetary policy to stabilize the economy, tightening credit when it perceives excessive speculation and easing credit when it wants to avoid a recession or financial panic. In 1979 the rate of inflation was above 13 percent and, in October of that year, the Fed decided that its top priority was to reduce the rate of inflation substantially. Over the next three years, the Fed tightened credit severely and interest rates rose to unprecedented levels. In 1981, interest rates reached 18 percent on home mortgages and were even higher for most other bank loans. The unemployment rate rose above 10 percent in 1982, the highest level since the Great Depression of the 1930s. But the Fed achieved its single-minded objective as the annual rate of inflation fell from 13.3 percent in 1979 to 3.8 percent in 1982.

In the fall of 1982, the Fed decided that the war on inflation had been won and that there were ominous signs of a possible financial and economic collapse. The Fed switched to easy-money policies, supplying funds as needed to fuel the economic expansion that lasted the remainder of the decade.

Clearly, the Fed's monetary policies play a crucial role for financial markets and the economy. In later chapters, we will look at the various policies at the Fed's disposal and at how it implements these policies. We will pay particular attention to a proposal by some economists that monetary policy be taken out of the hands of the Fed and turned over to a computer.

FINANCIAL MARKETS

A market is a means of bringing together buyers and sellers to make transactions. **Financial markets**, for trading bonds, stocks, and other financial assets, come in many different forms and involve a variety of agents.

Primary Versus Secondary Markets

One important distinction is between primary and secondary markets. The **primary market** is where securities are initially issued: a bank lends a household $100,000 to buy a house; the U.S. Treasury raises money by selling a $10,000 bond; a new corporation issues stock. In each case, a financial record of the transaction is created, showing the existence of debt or equity.

Securities are issued in the primary market and resold in the secondary market.

If these records of debt or equity are then sold to others, this subsequent trade is said to occur in the **secondary market.** Examples abound. A business that has acquired a certificate of deposit (CD) by depositing $100,000 in a bank (a primary market transaction) can sell it to someone else (a secondary market transaction), who can either trade it again or hold it until it matures. After a bank lends someone money to buy a house, it can sell the mortgage note to a government agency that packages it with other mortgages and resells it to a pension fund that receives the monthly mortgage payments. The investor who buys a Treasury bond can sell it to another investor; stockholders can sell their shares to others. In each case, the security may pass from hand to hand as one person after another invests for a while and then sells when he or she needs some money or decides that the investment is no longer attractive.

The Stock Exchanges

Some trading in the secondary market takes place on organized exchanges, such as the New York Stock Exchange (NYSE), where brokers meet to trade listed securities. Securities that aren't listed on any organized exchange are said to be traded **over the counter (OTC)**, a reference to the practice long ago of dealers literally trading securities over the counters of their shops. Because this trading is now conducted by telephone, telex, and computer links, a more apt label might be the over-the-phone market.

A commonplace fiction, sometimes promoted by the exchanges themselves, is that the stock exchanges raise capital to finance business investment. In fact, the exchanges are not used by corporations to raise funds. The exchanges are a secondary market in which investors trade securities among themselves. If you buy 100 shares of IBM stock, IBM is not involved in the transaction. You buy shares from Jack, who bought from Jill, and so on through endless trades back to the time when IBM first issued the stock. And so it is with virtually all stock transactions. When a new corporation, or an occasional mature one, sells stock to raise money, it does so through investment bankers, rather than on the exchanges.

The stock exchanges are unquestionably useful. The hundreds of millions of shares traded daily (and the accompanying fees paid to brokers) are ample proof that people value this marketplace. Buyers use the market to find sellers, and sellers to find buyers. Investors would undoubtedly be reluctant to acquire shares if they could not count on using the stock exchanges to find other buyers when they are ready to sell. But the exchanges are not where businesses raise money to finance expansion.

Securities are traded on organized exchanges and over the counter.

FINANCIAL INSTITUTIONS

Financial intermediaries borrow from some and lend to others, thereby channeling funds from savers to borrowers. When you deposit money in a bank savings account paying 5 percent interest, the bank is borrowing this money from you, which it then lends to someone else to buy a car, a house, or a factory. When you buy a life insurance policy, the insurance company is implicitly borrowing your insurance premiums, which it then lends to land developers, the federal government (by purchasing Treasury bonds), or others.

As illustrated by these two very different examples, financial intermediation

Financial intermediaries perform a variety of functions.

involves a variety of functions performed by many different institutions. Figure 1.5 gives a stylized overview of some of the more important roles and participants. It shows nine distinct functions, ranging from checking to insurance. The types of financial intermediaries are divided into three broad groups: deposit institutions, investment intermediaries, and contractual saving, with the X's indicating the primary services of each type of institution.

Deposit Institutions

Deposit institutions offer checking accounts, savings accounts, and other types of deposits that pay specified rates of interest. Savers find these deposits appealing because their money can usually be withdrawn immediately, often by writing a check; the rate of return is known in advance; and the safety of these accounts is generally insured by the federal government. Deposit institutions lend out most of the money that they borrow from their depositors, making a profit on the spread between the interest rates charged on these loans and the interest rates paid on their deposits.

Figure 1.5   Functions of Financial Intermediaries

Functions	Depository institutions		Investment intermediaries			Contractual saving plans	
	Commercial banks	Thrift institutions	Investment banks	Security brokers	Mutual funds	Pension funds	Insurance companies
Checking	X	X		X	X		
Saving	X	X			X	X	X
Consumer lending	X	X					
Business lending	X						
Mortgage lending	X	X					
Security issuance			X	X			
Security trading			X	X			
Money management	X		X	X	X	X	
Insurance		X					X

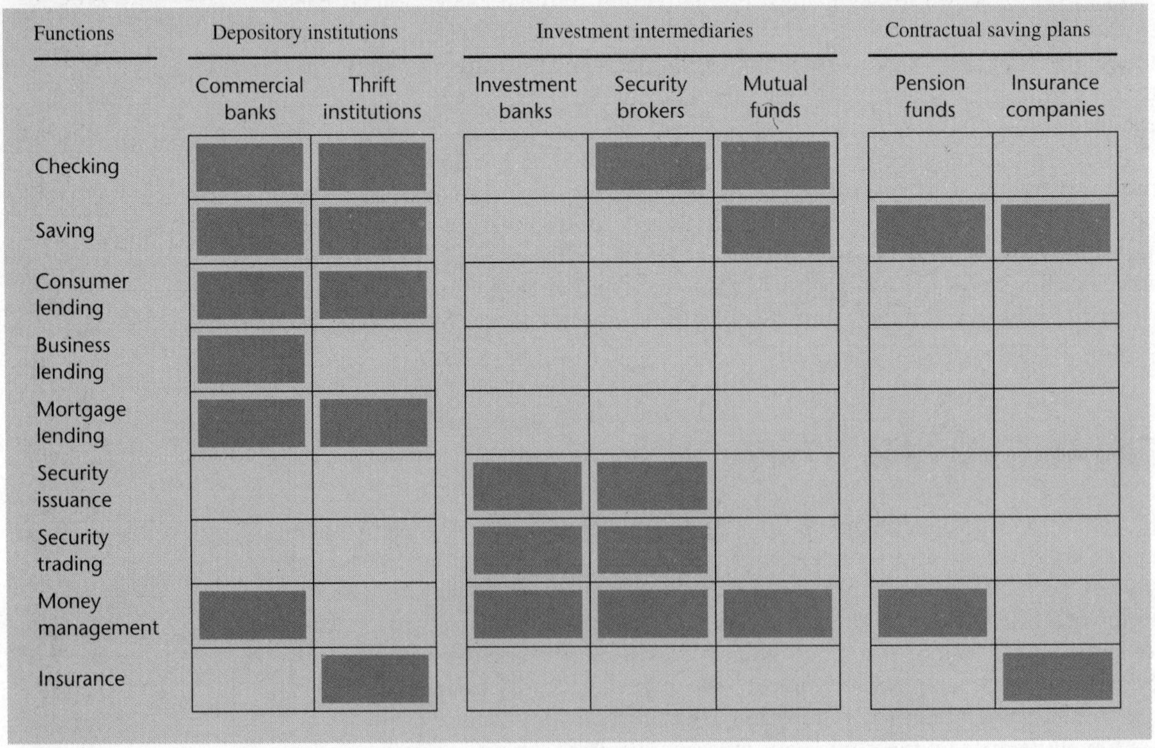

The Glass-Steagall Act of 1933 prohibits a firm from acting as both a **commercial bank** (accepting deposits and making loans) and an **investment bank** (helping businesses and state and local governments issue stocks and bonds). Thus J. P. Morgan, the nation's most prominent bank, was forced to split into two separate companies: J. P. Morgan (commercial banking) and Morgan Stanley (investment banking). Every bank in the United States had to decide whether it would be a commercial bank or an investment bank.

Those that became commercial banks could accept deposits — checking accounts, savings accounts, and so on — and make loans to households and businesses. For nearly 50 years, from 1933 to 1980, commercial banks were the only institutions allowed to offer checking accounts, and they were prohibited from paying interest on these deposits. These provisions protected them from having to compete with other financial institutions and from interest-rate wars among themselves. In return, they were prohibited from purchasing stocks and from acting as investment banks. Many of these legal restrictions have now been removed, and more will soon disappear.

> The Glass-Steagall Act separated commercial and investment banking.

> Commercial banks and other deposit institutions accept deposits and make loans.

The Thrift Debacle

In the 1960s and early 1970s, savings and loans and other thrift institutions paid their depositors interest rates ranging from 2 percent to 5 percent and lent their depositors' money out in 30-year mortgages at 4 percent to 8 percent. When interest rates rose sharply in the 1970s, these thrifts were squeezed. They had to pay double-digit interest rates to hold onto their depositors, but they earned only single-digit interest rates on the mortgages they held. In 1980, the savings-and-loan industry was technically bankrupted when its aggregate net worth became negative.

Eighty-five percent of all thrifts lost money in the second half of 1981. During the two-year period 1981–1982, the industry lost $9 billion and more than 800 thrifts disappeared — mostly through absorption by stronger institutions. In response to this crisis, the Congress moved to deregulate the industry, allowing thrifts to move away from their traditional emphasis on home mortgages and make more business and commercial real estate loans.

Interest rates fell after 1982, but the industry's losses continued. The problem was no longer an interest-rate squeeze but mounting loan defaults — caused too often by excessive risk-taking or outright fraud: depositor money squandered on desert land and lavish bonuses. In 1989, it was widely estimated that the thrift industry had a negative net worth of at least $100 billion and that there would inevitably be a financial meltdown in which as many as 70 percent of the existing thrifts would disappear. In later chapters, we will look more closely at this thrift debacle.

The thrift institutions identified in Figure 1.5 include savings-and-loan associations, mutual savings banks, and credit unions. Historically, they borrowed money, mostly from small savers, by offering savings accounts, and they lent this money primarily to households to buy houses, automobiles, and appliances. Before 1980, they were prohibited from offering checking accounts, and their share of this market is still quite small.

Investment Intermediaries

Investment banks, securities brokers, and mutual funds are primarily investment intermediaries involved, as shown in Figure 1.5, in the purchase and sale of bonds, stocks, and other securities. One of their functions is to help businesses issue securities. Investment bankers study a firm's financial soundness, advise the firm of an appropriate price for the stocks or bonds it wishes to issue, sell the securities to financial institutions and individuals, and monitor the firm's ability and willingness to fulfill the terms of the securities after they have been issued.

Investment intermediaries can also act as securities traders, helping individual and institutional investors to buy and sell stocks and bonds in the secondary market. In this capacity, they help arrange private trades among borrowers and lenders or execute trades on the organized exchanges or in the computerized over-the-counter market.

Investment banks (such as Morgan Stanley, Salomon Brothers, and Goldman, Sachs) have historically emphasized investment banking; brokerage firms (such as Merrill Lynch, Shearson Lehman Hutton, or Charles Schwab) have focused on trading securities. Today, however, there is considerable overlap. Merrill Lynch is one of the nation's five largest investment bankers; Kidder, Peabody began as an investment bank and is now one of the largest brokerage firms.

The third function of investment intermediaries is to help others manage their money. They may advise investors about the selection of stocks and bonds, advise borrowers about their financing alternatives, or take over the money-management task — making decisions rather than merely offering advice.

Mutual funds and other investment companies specialize in managing investors' money for them. Fidelity and Vanguard, two of the largest investment companies, offer dozens of mutual funds with varying objectives. Money market funds buy Treasury bills and other very short-term bonds; most allow limited checking privileges. Other mutual funds buy tax-exempt municipal bonds, growth stocks, or the stocks of small savings-and-loan associations. In each case, these funds pool investor savings and purchase a diversified portfolio of securities. Mutual funds appeal mostly to small investors who don't have enough wealth to amass diversified portfolios on their own and feel that they don't have enough time or expertise to select securities wisely.

Contractual Saving

Pension funds and insurance companies offer yet another type of financial intermediation, in which contractual savings — insurance premiums or retire-

Investment banks help businesses and state and local governments issue and trade securities.

ment contributions — are invested on behalf of savers. In the case of insurance, the timing of the payoff generally depends on an accidental event, such as fire or death, and the size of the payoff is determined by the contract. The premium charged by the insurance company depends on the probability of this event and the company's estimate of how much it can earn by investing the customer's money in bonds, stocks, and shopping malls. Some pension plans base their payoff on the amount of the worker's wages shortly before retirement, so that the retirement benefits will be adequate to maintain an accustomed standard of living. In this case, as with the insurance company, the size of the worker's annual contributions depend on the pension fund's estimate of the rate of return it can earn by investing these contributions. Other pension plans base their payoff directly on worker contributions, crediting the worker with whatever rate of return it earns, less expenses; in this case, the pension fund is really acting as a money manager, investing the workers' savings on their behalf.

Full-Service Intermediaries

Not too long ago, financial intermediaries were pretty specialized. You would go to one for a checking account, to another for a mortgage, to another for a car loan, to another for insurance, and to yet another to buy shares of corporate stock. No more! These artificial distinctions have been permanently breached and are rapidly fading from view. Many of the cells in Figure 1.5 that might once have been left blank now deserve small X's, as intermediaries have spread beyond their traditional roles.

The barriers separating different kinds of financial intermediaries are disappearing.

Specialized financial boutiques are being replaced by financial supermarkets that can handle all your financial needs: checking accounts, mortgages, car loans, insurance, and stocks. The banking giant Citicorp owns a savings and loan, an insurance company, and a credit-card company. So does Sears, Roebuck. Different financial institutions now can compete with each other for your business. Credit unions vie with commercial banks for your checking account. Savings-and-loan associations try to sell you insurance. Money-market funds go after your savings account.

Historically, the differences among banks, credit unions, mutual funds, and other financial intermediaries were due largely to legal restrictions on their operations. They were all financial intermediaries, but they differed in what was permitted and not permitted for each. The dissolution of the barriers between financial institutions has been going on for some time, with fits and starts, corresponding to various victories and setbacks in legislation, regulatory rulings, and court decisions. Many gains were consolidated and broadened in the historic Depository Institutions Deregulation and Monetary Control Act of 1980. It is hoped that these changes will enable financial institutions to better serve their customers, strengthen them by broadening and diversifying their operations, and promote competition among intermediaries. We will discuss all of this and more in the chapters to come.

SUMMARY

Real assets are tangible physical assets such as houses, factories, and automobiles; financial assets are paper claims including bank deposits, bonds, and stocks. What ultimately lies behind financial claims — the assets of some and the liabilities of others — are real, tangible assets.

The return from an investment — financial or real — consists of income (the cash flow and services received while owning the asset) and capital gains (the profits made when the asset is sold). Those considering investing in real assets compare the prospective return with the returns offered on financial assets and with the interest rates charged on loans to finance their purchase. Financial markets affect investment in physical assets through changes in the yields on financial investments and in the interest rates on mortgages and loans. An easing or tightening of financial markets also affects the availability of credit to liquidity-constrained households and businesses.

Real interest rates are equal to the difference between nominal interest rates and the rate of inflation. To get a representative picture of real income, real wealth, and real interest rates, the federal government monitors the prices of goods and services and calculates several price indexes. The best known is the Consumer Price Index (CPI), which attempts to measure changes in the cost of living for typical U.S. households.

Although corporate bonds are debt, common stock is equity, a claim on the corporation's profits after interest and other fixed expenses have been paid. The fact that interest is a tax-deductible expense for corporations, but dividends are not, encourages firms to finance their spending with debt rather than with equity.

The U.S. Treasury sells bonds to finance the federal budget deficit. The Federal Reserve (the Fed) can increase or reduce the supply of currency by buying or selling Treasury bonds. The Fed eases credit when it wants to avoid a recession or financial panic and tightens credit when it perceives excessive inflation and speculation.

The primary market involves the sale of newly created securities. The secondary market is a resale market, in which existing securities are traded. Financial intermediaries are a channel through which the savings of some are lent to others. There are a variety of intermediaries — deposit institutions, investment intermediaries, and contractual saving — which perform a variety of functions, including checking, saving, lending, issuing and trading securities, money management, and insurance.

Competitive, innovative financial institutions have changed the nature of money and banking. The existence of many similar financial assets makes it difficult to settle on a unique, widely accepted definition of money. The distinctions among financial institutions have been blurred by the expansion of commercial banks into nontraditional activities and the encroachment of other financial institutions into traditional banking.

IMPORTANT TERMS

capital gains
commercial bank
common stock
consumer price index (CPI)
equity
Federal Reserve Board (Fed)
financial assets
financial intermediaries
financial markets
fixed-income securities
hyperinflation
income

investment bank
liquidity constrained
money illusion
nominal data
nominal rate of return
over the counter (OTC)
primary market
rates of return
real assets
real data
real rate of return
secondary market

EXERCISES

1. Both young and old people tend to spend more than they earn, while middle-aged people tend to spend less than they earn. How do they do this, and why?

2. Identify each of the following as financial or real assets:
   a. 100 shares of Apple stock.
   b. Money in your checking account.
   c. A home mortgage.
   d. A Macintosh computer.

3. Identify which of the following transactions take place in a primary market and which in a secondary market:
   a. You sell 100 shares of Apple stock.
   b. You deposit money in a bank.
   c. The bank loans money to a home buyer.
   d. The bank sells the home buyer's mortgage note to a federal agency.

4. Identify which of the following are income and which are capital gains:
   a. The price of Apple stock goes up $1.
   b. Apple pays a $1 a share dividend.
   c. You save rent by buying a house.
   d. Housing prices collapse.

5. The Consumer Price Index was 38.8 in 1970 and 123.1 in 1989. What was the percentage increase between 1970 and 1989?

6. What happens to real income if nominal income increases by 5 percent and prices increase by 10 percent? What if prices fall by 5 percent? Assuming that only the price of hamburgers matters, use some illustrative calculations to confirm your reasoning.

7. What is the real interest rate on an investment that yields an 8 percent nominal return during a period when the annual rate of inflation is 3 percent? What if the annual rate of inflation is −3 percent?

8. During the 1800s, there were often years of deflation, in which consumer prices fell. Do you suppose that nominal interest rates were unusually low or high during these deflations? What about real interest rates?

9. The Bureau of Labor Statistics maintains consumer price indexes for several cities and metropolitan areas. Here are the values of some of these price indexes in July 1986 (all indexes are set equal to 100 in 1967):

San Diego	383.1
Denver	358.4
Milwaukee	331.3
Overall average	328.0
Philadelphia	323.0
Detroit	318.4
Chicago	311.1

Do these data show that it it more expensive to live in Milwaukee than in Chicago? Why or why not?

10. It has been alleged that statisticians do not fully take into account quality improvements in what we buy. If so, will their estimates of inflation and real income be too high or too low?

11. Critically evaluate this economic commentary:[1]

When it comes to measuring inflation, the average consumer can do a far better job than the economics experts. . . . Over the years I have been using a system which is infallible. . . . The Phindex [short for the Phillips index] merely requires you to divide the total dollar cost of a biweekly shopping trip by the number of brown paper bags into which the purchases are crammed. You thus arrive at the average cost per bagful.

When I started this system some 10 years ago, we would walk out of the store with about six bags of groceries costing approximately $30 — or an average of $5 per bag. . . .

On our most recent shopping trip, we emerged with nine bagsful of stuff and nonsense, totaling the staggering sum of $114. . . . the Phindex shows a rise from the initial $5 to almost $13, a whopping 153 percent.

12. Explain the error in this interpretation of inflation data:[2]

In the 12-month period ending in December of 1980, consumer prices rose by 12.4 percent after a 13.3 percent increase the year before. Similar measures of inflation over the next three years were 8.9 percent, 3.9 percent, and 3.8 percent. . . . We are certainly paying less for what we buy than we were at the end of the Carter years.

13. Here are some Sotheby Index data, based on auctions affiliated with Sotheby Parke-Bernet:[3]

	1975	1982	1983
Old master paintings	100	199	217
Chinese ceramics	100	460	445
Continental silver	100	134	156

a. Do Chinese ceramics cost more than continental silver?

b. Which of these three would have been the best investment between 1975 and 1982? between 1982 and 1983?

14. United States per-capita gross national product (GNP) was $205 in 1885 and $16,704 in 1985. Prices in 1985 were, on average, 14.17 times 1885 prices. Calculate real per-capita 1885 GNP, in terms of 1985 prices; that is, how many dollars in 1985 did it take to buy what $205 bought in 1885?

15. When a child loses a baby tooth, an old tradition is to put the tooth under the child's pillow, saying that the tooth fairy will leave money for it. A survey by a Northwestern University professor indicates that the tooth fairy paid an average of 12 cents for a tooth in 1900 and $1 for a tooth in 1987.[4] The Consumer Price Index was 25 in 1900 and 340 in 1987. Did the real value of tooth-fairy payments rise or fall over this period? If tooth-fairy payments had kept up with inflation, how large should the 1987 payment have been?

16. The Social Security Administration estimated in 1985 that someone 28 years old, earning $16,000 that year, who worked steadily and retired at age 65 in 2022, would begin receiving annual benefits of about $27,500 in 2023.[5] This calculation assumes that something costing $1.00 in 1985 will cost $4.40 in 2023. If so, how much will this $27,500 buy in terms of 1985 dollars; that is, how much 1985 money will buy as much in 1985 as $27,500 will buy in 2023?

17. The S&P 500 (Standard & Poor's index of 500 stock prices) closed at 92.15 on December 31,

1970, and at 211.28 on December 31, 1985; the corresponding values for the Dow were 838.92 and 1546.67. The Consumer Price Index was at 119.1 in December 1970 and at 327.4 in December 1985. Did stock prices increase by more or less than consumer prices over this 15-year period? If stock prices had increased by just as much as consumer prices, what would the value of the Dow have been on December 31, 1985?

18. Explain why you either agree or disagree with the claim that "the main function of the stock exchanges is . . . to generate funds to be employed in private businesses."[6]

19. Which of these financial intermediaries would you use to help incorporate your small business? Open a checking account? Invest in a diversified portfolio of stocks?
    a. A commercial bank.
    b. An investment bank.
    c. A mutual fund.

20. Which of these financial intermediaries would you use to buy 100 shares of IBM stock? Apply for a home mortgage? Issue bonds to finance the expansion of your small business?
    a. An investment bank.
    b. A savings-and-loan institution.
    c. A securities broker.

PART

1

Money

Optional Chapter

COMMODITY MONEY

AND

GOVERNMENT MONEY

Money is not, properly speaking, one of the subjects of commerce; but only the instrument which men have agreed upon to facilitate the exchange of one commodity for another. It is none of the wheels of trade: it is the oil which renders the motion of the wheels more smooth and easy.

David Hume

Money is such a familiar and pervasive part of our lives that we seldom stop to think about its origins and nature. But we are very much aware that money is important.

As children, we quickly learn that dollar bills are not merely pretty green pieces of paper to be painted, shredded, eaten, or left outdoors in the mud. Dollar bills are special. Dollar bills are important and valuable because dollars are "money" that can be used to buy things. Stores will trade food, clothing, and toys for dollars. Knowing this fact, we, too, are quite willing to work or to sell things for dollars, because we can use this special green paper to buy real things.

It has not always been this way. Not too long ago, real things were used as money. In the United States, gold, tobacco, rice, cattle, and whiskey have been money. In other times and places, people made do without money of any sort. In this chapter, we will see why societies have found money, real and paper, to be a very useful contrivance.

BARTER

A logical place to begin is by imagining an economy without money of any sort. This might be a primitive economy in which little economic trading takes place. Perhaps the citizens are self-sufficient and a bit isolated from one another. When their paths do cross and they make a trade, it is a simple exchange of goods — corn for potatoes, wood for leather, knives for arrows. This kind of economic activity is called **barter**, the trading of goods and services for other goods and services.

Barter can work tolerably well when people are virtually self-sufficient and only make trades occasionally. However, a vital element of economic progress has been the replacement of self-sufficiency with specialization. I teach, consult, do research, and write textbooks on economics. With the fruits of this labor, I can acquire pizza, clothing, a computer, an automobile, and the other necessities of a good life. Other people specialize in making the pizzas that I enjoy. Still others sell the flour for the pizza dough, or turn wheat into flour, or grow the wheat. Through a division of labor, each person can become highly skilled at very specialized tasks. In the aggregate, much more is produced and enjoyed than would be the case if everyone had to be self-sufficient — growing their own wheat, making their own flour, concocting their own pizza, and teaching themselves economics. How long would it take you to make a personal computer and write your own word-processing software?

A necessary accompaniment to specialization is the opportunity to trade one's specialized product for the products of other specialists. And it is here that barter becomes burdensome. In a barter economy, if there is not what W. S. Jevons called a "double coincidence" of wants,[1] each person must make a multiplicity of trades before the desired bundle of goods can be obtained. Too much time and energy are spent swapping goods, and too little time is spent producing and enjoying them.

Suppose that I want a pizza for dinner and my specialization is teaching economics courses. When I go to the pizza maker, hoping for a trade, I may find that he is interested in a transistor radio but not in economics lectures. (For a double coincidence of wants to exist, I would want to trade lectures for pizza and he would want to trade pizza for lectures.) So I trudge off, looking for someone with a transistor radio who would rather listen to economics lectures. With considerable effort, I locate a woman with 100 radios who wants a red boat and knows a man with a boat who is interested in studying economics. Unfortunately, the boat is yellow and worth more than a one-semester economics course (it's a very nice boat). So I have to find someone who will trade a red boat for a yellow one, and then work out another series of deals to acquire something extra to throw in with my lectures. It will be a very late dinner by the time I have it all straightened out.

Some barter is admittedly useful and even enjoyable. Throughout history, the swapping of goods for goods has gone on even where money existed. In a

Barter, the trading of goods and services for other goods and services, can be very cumbersome.

Living Without Money

Money facilitates trade, but it is not absolutely necessary. Within a family, tasks may be highly specialized even without monetary trades. Perhaps the father takes care of the yard and balances the checkbook, the mother buys food and repairs the plumbing, and the son keeps his room clean. Instead of monetary payments, such exchanges can be based on either a communal or totalitarian organization of the family. Similarly, there have been feudal estates and even entire societies whose communal or totalitarian organization made money unnecessary.

On many Polynesian islands, goods are freely provided to poorer inhabitants and even to strangers. It is considered improper to refuse someone's request for goods. In some communities, even the request is unnecessary: it is customary simply to take whatever you desire. There is little need for money in such circumstances. Many small religious groups in North America have attempted to establish similarly moneyless communal societies.

In the Inca empire, money was unnecessary because the citizens' economic lives were thoroughly regulated by a central administration. Each citizen was told what to produce and what fraction of his or her output to give to the central authorities, who then allocated it among all citizens. There was a limited amount of barter in food, but trades of clothing, housing, or land were forbidden. Money was unneeded and unknown before the Spanish conquest.

After the conquest, the Republic of Paraguay was a moneyless totalitarian state established and run by the Jesuits with the intention of protecting the indigenous inhabitants from exploitation. Even after the Jesuits lost their absolute authority, barter continued as the predominant form of exchange in Paraguay. As late as the end of the eighteenth century, taxes and the salaries of religious and government leaders were paid in goods. Although of smaller scale, economic lives within European monasteries and feudal estates during the Middle Ages were also authoritarian and virtually moneyless.

Moneyless societies generally are either composed of self-sufficient citizens or have a communal or totalitarian organization that regulates exchanges of goods and services. In societies with an extensive division of labor, private ownership, and voluntary exchange, however, barter is unworkably cumbersome and inefficient. In most modern nations, specialization and the use of money are so tightly linked that, like the chicken or the egg, it is impossible to say which came first.

simple economy, with substantial inventories of tradable goods, intimate knowledge of the possessions and desires of others, and some zest for the sport, people have bartered successfully. Often, trading is simplified by the use of customary price ratios (one fish for two bananas), which are fixed for years or even generations. In addition, the use of delayed payments lubricates barter by making it unnecessary to find just the right combination of goods at a specific moment. (For example, I could eat my pizza now and pay for it later when I come across a radio.) But in a large, complex, highly specialized society that is neither entirely communal nor entirely totalitarian, some form of money is a virtual necessity.

Commodity Money

Effective barter is easier if everyone maintains an inventory of easily traded goods. If I, the hungry economics lecturer, have accumulated a collection of desirable trinkets, I can give some of these to the pizza maker, and he can trade them to someone else for a radio. Unlike a pure-barter economy, in which trades are made solely for direct consumption, in a mixed-barter economy, some items are accepted in trade not for consumption but so that they can later, in turn, be readily traded for consumables. These traded items that pass from hand to hand are typically goods that are widely recognized and used, so that those who accept them can be confident that they can be traded to someone else. It is also helpful if these items are portable, divisible, and durable — spices, metals, or wood, for example.

This process is self-reinforcing. The more a certain item is used for trades, the more confidence people have in accepting it. The more confidence people have in accepting it, the more it will be used for trade. At some point we can say that this intermediate item has become so popular that it has assumed the status of a **medium of exchange** — something commonly exchanged that the recipients intend to trade for other items. A commodity that becomes a medium of exchange is called a **commodity money**.

A desirable commodity money should possess several characteristics:

1. It should be easily *verifiable*. It is inefficient to use a commodity money that must be continually inspected for its size, weight, or purity. One of the subtle inefficiencies of barter is that both of the items traded must be carefully evaluated.
2. It should be intrinsically *useful*. There is something to be said for using a commodity money that can be consumed if worst comes to worst. A citizenry's readiness to accept an item as a medium of exchange is enhanced somewhat by the perception that the item is intrinsically useful.
3. It should be conveniently *transportable*. If trades take place over a wide geographic area, it is helpful to have a commodity money that can be easily and safely carried about.
4. It should be *divisible*. Trades are simplified when the medium of exchange can be easily divided to purchase exactly the desired amount. Commodity

> A medium of exchange is accepted in trade because it can be used to trade for other things.

moneys that are difficult to divide or that lose their value when split are cumbersome, though the provision for delayed payment eases this problem.

5. It should be *durable*. If you keep an inventory of some medium of exchange that you are always prepared to trade, it is best if the medium does not spoil or rot while you are holding it.

In practice, over the past 4,000 years, the predominant commodity moneys have been precious metals: mostly silver, to a lesser extent gold, and even less frequently copper. However, in generally small, rural communities, the peoples of the world have also used an enormous variety of other commodity moneys. Wampum (strings of shells) was used by native Americans and, for a while, by American colonists from New England to Virginia. In 1641, wampum was made legal tender in Massachusetts (at the rate of six shells to the penny). In Virginia, tobacco was made legal tender in 1642, and contracts payable in gold and silver were outlawed. Tobacco was widely used as a commodity money in Virginia for almost 200 years, in Maryland for about 150 years, and in neighboring states for shorter periods. In various other parts of the United States, rice, cattle, and whiskey have been declared legal tender. Although they lacked legal sanction, musket balls, peas, hemp, furs, and woodpecker scalps were also used as commodity money. Some other selected moneys from around the world are listed below to give you some flavor of the great variety:

A wide variety of commodity moneys have been used as mediums of exchange.

Whale teeth — Fiji
Sandalwood — Hawaii
Fish hooks — Gilbert Islands
Tortoise shells — Marianas
Red parrot feathers — Santa Cruz Islands (as late as 1961)
Rice — Philippines
Salt — many places
Pepper — Sumatra
Sugar — Barbados
Tea bricks — many places in inner Asia
Slaves — Equatorial Africa, Nigeria, and Ireland
Reindeer — parts of Russia
Copper — Egypt
Silk — China
Butter — Norway
Leather — France and Italy
Rum — Australia

These examples come from an interesting book, *Primitive Money,* by Paul Einzig. In 1966, he wrote that there were still "many communities, especially in the Pacific area but also in some parts of Africa and to a less extent in Asia, in which primitive monetary systems are still in operation."[2]

FIAT MONEY

The stone money of Yap is superficially a commodity money. And yet it has no real value as a commodity. A Yap stone is accepted in exchange for useful goods and services solely because its recipients are confident that they will also be able to exchange the stone for goods and services. Its acceptance as a medium of exchange rests on this confidence, nothing more. This is an example of **fiat money**, something that has little value as a commodity but, because of law or tradition, is accepted as a medium of exchange.

The dollar bills used in the United States are fiat money. The paper they are printed on has almost no value. But our government says that these dollars are legal tender, suitable for paying its bills and our taxes. We accept them in trades, confident that they have value because we can exchange them for useful goods and services.

To each person, fiat money has value solely because of laws or tradition, conditioned by many years of successful exchanges. To a society, fiat money has value because it successfully serves as a medium of exchange, thereby allowing society to avoid the inefficiencies of barter. For thousands of years, commodity money was preeminent. Today, fiat money reigns. Let's take a quick look at this gradual but now thorough upheaval.

Fiat money is a medium of exchange that has little value as a commodity.

From Hard Money to Soft Money

Precious metals have many of the desired characteristics of a good commodity money: useful, conveniently transportable, divisible, and durable. The one drawback is that the metals are not easily verified. Every trade requires trusted scales and a reliable assessment of the purity of the precious metal. To avoid this considerable inconvenience, metals can be made into coins of known weight and purity. Thus the British pound was originally a silver coin stamped with a star, with a weight of 240 coins to the pound. Because the Old English word for star was "sterling," these coins came to be called "pounds sterling"; the symbol £ comes from the medieval Latin word for pound, *libra*.

Herodotus noted the use of coins in the ancient kingdom of Lydia around the seventh century B.C. Modern historians believe that coins were independently introduced in China at about the same time, in India a few hundred years earlier, and in Persia a few hundred years later. Coinage flourished in the Greek and Roman empires and then throughout Europe. John Kenneth Galbraith has observed wryly that "after Alexander the Great the custom was established of depicting the head of the sovereign on the coin, less, it has been suggested, as a guarantee of the weight and fineness of the metal than as a thoughtful personal gesture by the ruler to himself."[3]

A recurring difficulty with coins made of precious metal is that people are tempted to make a small profit as the coins pass through their hands by clipping, shaving, or filing bits of metal from the coins. For the governments that press the coins, the temptation is to use cheaper metals so that more coins can be

The Stone Money of Yap

The island of Yap in Micronesia is renowned among economists for using stone money for nearly 2,000 years. The stones are wheel-shaped, each with a hole in the center and often as tall as a person; some are twice this size. The legend is that a wicked god gave stone money to the peaceful people of Yap so that they would have something to fight about; ever since, peace has been replaced by greed and quarreling. The stones themselves were obtained by treacherous expeditions to Palau or, for finer and rarer stones, to Guam, some 400 miles away through frequently stormy seas. Often only one of twenty canoes bound for Guam returned.

In the 1870s, David Dean O'Keffe, an American with a sturdy boat, brought enormous stones into Yap in exchange for coconuts, fish, women, and whatever else he wanted. The largest stone he brought in, said to be 20 feet wide, is at the bottom of the Yap harbor, where it fell while being unloaded from his schooner to a raft. Even though the stone disappeared from view, it was still considered to be part of the possessions of the original owners and then of generation after generation of heirs.

The stones themselves have absolutely no value other than as a medium of exchange. Simple direct barter was traditionally used for most everyday transactions, with debts allowed to accumulate until payment could be made with a large stone. Today, the islanders use stone beads, sea shells, beer, and U.S. dollars for small transactions. The large stones are a store of value used to pay for land, permission to marry, and other large debts. When a large stone changes ownership, a tree can be put through its hole and up to a hundred men roll the stone from its old owner to its new one. Because a broken stone is considered worthless, to avoid the risk of breaking them they are often left in one spot, with the ownership common knowledge. The largest stones are so well known that they even have names. The people pass on, but the stones remain.

In 1944, Willard Price* reported that a waist-high stone was valued at 4,000 coconuts, a five-foot stone was worth many villages, and the largest stones were considered priceless. The largest stones are owned by entire communities and proudly displayed outside community buildings. The smaller, two-foot to five-foot stones are owned by individuals and displayed outside their homes. In 1984, *The Wall Street Journal* reported that an islander bought a building lot with a 30-inch stone, explaining, "We don't know the value of the U.S. dollar."[4] A builder sold a house for $8,700 and a four-foot stone. The value of a stone is determined not only by its size but by the difficulty of bringing it to Yap. The stones acquired before the arrival of O'Keffe are the most valuable; those brought in by O'Keffe are worth half as much; and more recent stones are virtually worthless.

---

*Willard Price, *Japan's Islands of Mystery* (New York: John Day, 1944).

made and spent on wars, monuments, and other royal pursuits. Roman silver coins were reportedly debased until they became 98 percent copper and only 2 percent silver.

With coins of varying authenticity in existence, those who can tell the difference will keep the best ones and spend the lower-quality ones. This is **Gresham's Law**: Bad money drives out good. That is, bad money will circulate while good money is hoarded. (This observation was made by Sir Thomas Gresham in 1558, but Copernicus and undoubtedly others made the point earlier.)

> Gresham's Law says that bad money drives out good.

Gresham's Law implies that money that is more valuable as a commodity than as money will be withdrawn from circulation. For example, in colonial Virginia fine tobacco was smoked while debts payable in tobacco leaves were paid with the scruffiest and foulest tobacco. Similarly, the American Coinage Act of 1792 provided that the gold ten-dollar eagle would contain 247.5 grains of pure gold, and the silver dollar would have 371.25 grains of pure silver. This Act meant that, as a medium of exchange, ten silver dollars, containing 3,712.5 grains of silver, were as valuable as the 247.5 grains of gold in an eagle. Implicitly, the 1792 Coinage Act gave a grain of gold the same value as $3{,}712.5/247.5 = 15$ grains of silver. However, as a commodity, the free-market price of gold was about 15½ grains of silver. In accordance with Gresham's Law, this disparity between the values of gold as a commodity and as a medium of exchange provided an inducement to use silver dollars as a medium of exchange and to hoard the $10 gold eagles — or to melt them and trade the gold as a commodity for $247.5(15.5) = 3{,}836.25$ grains of silver, worth $3{,}836.25/371.25 = \$10.33$.

In 1834, the mint ratio was changed so that a grain of gold had the same value as 16 grains of silver. But as a commodity, the value was still about 15½ to 1 and, consequently, gold eagles circulated while silver dollars were hoarded. More recently, in the 1960s, high silver prices drove silver dimes, quarters, half-dollars, and dollars out of circulation in the United States. In the 1970s copper prices soared and copper pennies were hoarded. The U.S Mint offered a carrot: an Exceptional Public Service Certificate to anyone bringing $25 in pennies to a bank. The Treasury Department tried a stick: a $10,000 fine and five years in prison for melting or exporting copper pennies. Neither the carrot nor the stick repealed Gresham's Law.

Thus adulteration or hoarding often make it difficult to keep full-bodied, precious-metal coins in circulation. One way around this problem is to use a difficult-to-counterfeit piece of paper as a substitute for a full-bodied coin. For each 371.25 grains of silver, instead of coining a silver dollar that can be shaved or melted, the government (or a private bank) can simply hold on to the silver and issue a distinctive piece of paper identified as a "paper dollar," redeemable at any time for 371.25 grains of silver. This is just like a warehouse receipt for tobacco or some other commodity and, except for the effort of redemption, just as valuable as a full-bodied silver dollar.

The early paper notes issued by banks and governments were warehouse receipts of this type and, except for the danger of counterfeiting, alleviated some of the problems of full-bodied coins. In addition, paper is usually less expensive to mint than coins and easier to transport. Convenience is especially important in the substitution of paper for not-so-precious commodity moneys; this is why warehouse receipts for tobacco circulated in the American colonies.

The use of substitute notes presents another opportunity, or danger, that has been repeatedly exploited by both governments and banks: to issue notes for which there is only partial commodity backing or none at all. This was true of the first government paper money (China, starting in the eighth century) and of the notes of the first major public bank (the Bank of Amsterdam, established in 1609) and has tempted governments and banks ever since.

Coins made of precious metal and paper fully backed by metal are often called "hard money." "Soft money" refers to unbacked paper and token coins, which are used as a medium of exchange but have little value as a commodity. Yap stone money is an example of token coins. Since 1853, the U.S. Mint has been authorized to produce token coins, using metal that costs less than the face value of the coins. Congress controls the minting of U.S. coins and, currently, all newly minted U.S. coins are inexpensive alloys made of copper, nickel, aluminum, and the like.

One big advantage of soft money is that, by Gresham's Law, it is kept in circulation and fulfills its destiny as a medium of exchange. Governments generally prefer soft money because it can be produced at a profit, called "seigniorage." In 1974, for instance, it was estimated that switching from copper to aluminum pennies in the United States would save $40 million a year.

Unbacked paper is especially profitable to produce. All paper currency now issued in the United States has no metal backing. If you have a $10 bill, the government will not redeem it for gold, silver, or tobacco. It can be exchanged for two $5 bills, ten $1 bills, or a pocketful of token coins. Nonetheless, like any ordinary commodity, it has a value that is roughly determined by demand and supply.

The value of a $10 bill is measured by what can be obtained in exchange. As with all commodities, there is no absolute price, only innumerable relative prices. Suppose, for instance, that bread trades at $1 a loaf, milk at $2 a bottle, and steak at $5 a pound. What is the value of a pound of steak?

It is worth what can be obtained in exchange: five dollars, five loaves of bread, or 2.5 bottles of milk. Similarly, what is the value of ten dollars? Ten dollars is worth ten loaves of bread, five bottles of milk, or two pounds of steak. In a monetary economy like the United States, prices of goods and services are usually expressed in terms of the medium of exchange, and other relative prices must be calculated. The price label on a bottle of milk says "$2," not "two loaves of bread," because dollars are the medium of exchange.

Thus a dollar has many prices, all of which are relative prices, and all are the inverses of the usual price quotations seen in stores. If the price of milk is $P = 2$ dollars per bottle, then the price of a dollar, measured in milk, is

$$\frac{1}{P} = \frac{1}{2 \text{ dollars/bottle}} = 0.5 \text{ bottles/dollar}$$

| Highlight 2.3 | **What Is Worn-out Money Good For?** |

Paper money doesn't last forever. The average $1 bill wears out in about a year and a half.[5] Larger denominations last a bit longer, perhaps because people take better care of more valuable currency. Bank tellers identify some money that is torn, dirty, or mangled, but most worn-out bills are selected electronically by the machines used by Federal Reserve Banks to sort and count currency. Bills that are ready for retirement are either shredded into strips an eighth of an inch wide or pulverized into confetti.

Each year, the Federal Reserve retires about 3 billion bills, worth $20 billion and weighing more than 3,000 tons. Most of the shredded or confettied currency is buried in landfills. Some is destroyed in special incinerators designed to reduce pollution when paper is burned. And some is recycled. One firm makes an oil-drilling lubricant using confettied currency. A few businesses make novelty items such as pillow stuffings, papier-maché figures, and drinking glasses using readily identified shredded currency. A Salt Lake City entrepreneur buys shredded bills from his local Federal Reserve Bank and makes artificial logs for fireplaces retailing for $2.50 each — a small price to see money burn.

The value of money depends on demand and supply.

In a market economy, these prices of a dollar (along with all relative prices) are simultaneously determined by the demands and supplies of all traded items including bread, milk, steak, and dollars.

Dollars are demanded by private citizens because dollars are useful as a medium of exchange; in later chapters, we will look at the nature of this demand in detail. Dollars are supplied by the government. As with other goods, an increased supply of dollars tends to reduce the price of a dollar, just as the price of peaches falls in the summer when peaches are more plentiful. A fall in the price of a dollar is an increase in conventionally measured prices. If there were an unlimited supply of dollars (like clean air in the good old days), they would be free. If the price of money is zero, then conventionally quoted prices are astronomical. In more familiar terminology, an unlimited expansion of the money supply creates hyperinflation. Conversely, inexpensively produced paper money has value because it is useful as a medium of exchange and is in limited supply.

Money's Roles

So far we have used the term "money" to describe anything used as a medium of exchange. Any money that serves as a medium of exchange will also normally serve in at least two other roles — as a unit of accounting and as a store of value.

Because money is used to buy and sell things, prices are normally quoted in monetary units, thereby making money a unit of accounting. In the United States money is denominated in dollars, and most prices are stated in dollars. So are most laws, regulations, and contracts that require a payment from one party to another. Our economic calculations are simplified by having all prices quoted in dollars, rather than having some prices stated in terms of loaves of bread and other prices in gallons of milk.

Money is also a store of value. When you plan to buy things in the future (and who doesn't?), it makes good sense to hold dollars in anticipation of these transactions. It is inconvenient and expensive to have to sell commodities every time you need dollars to buy other commodities. Even then, we hold dollars as a store of value during the time between the sale of one item and purchase of another. You can hold dollars as a short-term store of value, between the receipt of your paycheck and your purchases of food and the like, or as a long-term store of value, burying $100 bills in your backyard in anticipation of your retirement. The better money stores value, the more it will be held as a store of value. If money earns no interest and prices are rising rapidly, it won't even be worth your effort to dig up those $100 bills when you retire.

Money provides a unit of accounting and a store of value.

Is Hard Money Better Than Soft Money?

With hard money, the denomination of the coin fixes the price of the underlying commodity. For example, when the U.S. ten-dollar eagle contained 247.5 grains of gold, the implicit price of gold was $10/247.5 grains = $0.040404/grain. The quoted dollar price for a commodity is then also a statement about the price of the commodity in gold: if the price of a bottle of wine is $10, then this bottle of wine is worth 247.5 grains of gold. When gold is money, a gold discovery causes inflation — because when gold is more plentiful, its value declines and it consequently takes more gold to buy other goods and services.

A hard money such as gold serves two purposes: it is a commodity and a medium of exchange. Some people believe that the value of hard money relative to other commodities is determined solely by the value of the hard money as a commodity. This belief is false. It is true that the demand and supply for a commodity money as a commodity affect its price. But it is equally and inescapably true that the commodity's price is influenced by its demand and supply as a medium of exchange — by private citizens using the commodity money to conduct business and by governments withholding the commodity for current and future monetary use. Surely, if some commodity were to fall out of fashion as a medium of exchange, thereby freeing large quantities for use as a commodity, its value would drop precipitously.

It follows that the use of a commodity as a medium of exchange artificially raises its price. Less of the commodity is available for use as a commodity, and more time and effort are spent stockpiling it for monetary uses. The people of Yap spent boats and lives bringing in otherwise worthless stones to use as a

When a commodity is used as money, less is available for other purposes.

medium of exchange. Keynes called the use of gold as money a "barbarous relic" that wastes valuable resources. People and equipment are squandered digging holes in the ground, a pointless endeavor known as gold mining. Tongue in cheek, he suggested an easier expedient for increasing the money supply: to put paper currency in empty wine bottles and bury the bottles in existing, easily accessible mine shafts.

Turning this argument around, a prime virtue of a commodity money such as gold is that its limited availability prevents governments from arbitrarily expanding the money supply. With hard money, it is exceedingly difficult to create a hyperinflation. Thus hard money is traditionally advocated by those who favor stable prices.

Creditors, of course, are first in line. For sound personal reasons, they object to debts being repaid with cheapened currency. Established merchants are also generally supporters of hard currency. Trade is easier and less worrisome when you can be confident of what the dollars you accept today will buy tomorrow.

The prices of precious metals, the historically predominant hard moneys, do fluctuate. The extraction of precious metals from the Americas quintupled prices in Spain during the sixteenth century. The California gold discoveries caused inflation in the 1850s, as did increased gold supplies at the turn of the century. The incentive to melt silver coins in the United States in the 1960s arose because sluggish supplies and rapidly increasing commodity demands (for such uses as electronic components and photographic film) pushed silver prices sharply higher. The wild gyrations in gold and silver prices in the 1970s and 1980s were front-page news.

Figure 2.1 shows gold prices since the early 1970s. Figure 2.2 shows that prices in the United States were hardly stable between 1793 and 1915, when its currency was backed by precious metals (usually gold). In fact, short-run price fluctuations in the United States were greater under the gold standard than under the fiat money system used since World War II.[6] On the other hand, there was no long-run upward trend in prices under the gold standard: the price level in 1915 was actually lower than in 1793. With fiat money, the trend of prices has been relentlessly upward, with the level of consumer prices in the United States in 1990 five times the level in 1950.

When the United States was on a gold standard, prices fluctuated considerably, but there was no long-run upward trend.

The fact that three-quarters of the world's gold is produced in a few neighboring mines in South Africa is reason for concern about the future stability of gold production and prices. Silver supplies are more certain, because production is scattered throughout the United States, the Soviet Union, Mexico, Peru, and Canada, but there is considerable uncertainty about the industrial demand for silver. On the criterion of stable supply and demand (and excepting the fling by the American with a good boat), useless Yap stones were a better commodity money than gold or silver.

While admitting that precious-metal prices do fluctuate in unpredictable ways, hard-money supporters argue that this is a lesser evil than trusting governments to produce soft money. In the famous 1811 British debate on the gold standard, David Ricardo[7] conceded that precious metals

Figure 2.1 Month-End Gold Prices

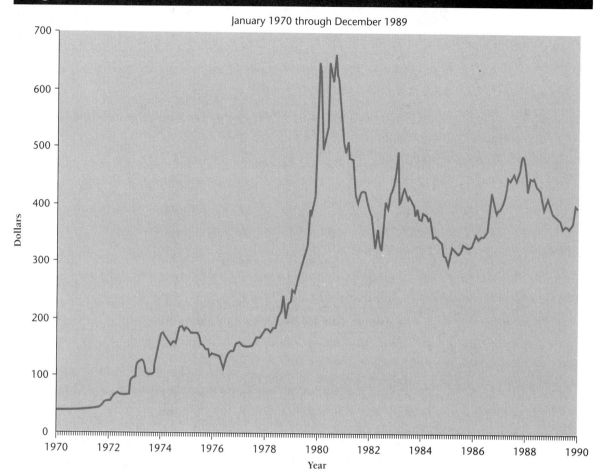

January 1970 through December 1989

source: Data for 1970–1990 were supplied courtesy of
Huntington Advisers, 251 South Lake Avenue, Suite
600, Pasadena, CA 91101.

*are themselves subject to greater variations than it is desirable a standard should
be subject to. They are, however, the best with which we are acquainted. . . .
[Without a precious-metal standard, money] would be exposed to all the fluctuations to which the ignorance or the interests of the issuers might subject it.*

This debate reflects a deep philosophical disagreement over whether governments do things for citizens or to them. On the one side, with Ricardo in the

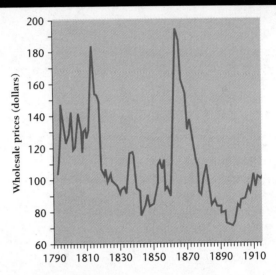

Figure 2.2 Wholesale Prices in the United States, 1793–1915

source: Based on data in George F. Warren and Frank A. Pearson, *Gold and Prices* (New York: Wiley, 1935).

When a society uses fiat money, the supply can be increased greatly, causing inflation.

nineteenth century and with the hard-money enthusiasts today, are those who believe that government officials exploit the citizenry or bungle well-meaning attempts at economic stabilization. On the other side are those who believe that governments can do things for the common good, including an intelligent and beneficial management of the nation's money supply. It is not necessary to divert precious metals from precious uses. It is not necessary to abandon a nation's money supply to the vagaries of commercial demand and discovery. Soft money can be reliably and steadily provided to accommodate commerce and serve as a medium of exchange. Hard-money advocates point to the hyperinflations of history as evidence of government irresponsibility. Soft-money advocates look at the same history and argue that these episodes were infrequent and usually financed wars, including the American and French Revolutions.

A SHORT HISTORY OF U.S. GOVERNMENT MONEY (*Optional*)

In 1690, Massachusetts paid some of its soldiers with paper money redeemable in gold or silver. The colony did not have enough metal on hand to pay off these notes, but hoped that future taxes would raise sufficient revenue. However, the notes multiplied faster than taxes and were eventually redeemed for a fraction of their face value. Rhode Island and South Carolina also issued large amounts of unbacked paper money that eventually had little, if any, value. In contrast, the Middle Colonies — Delaware, Maryland, New Jersey, New York, and Pennsylvania — all successfully introduced moderate amounts of unbacked paper to stabilize prices and stimulate commerce. Unbacked paper was typically used to finance government spending. However, Maryland conducted a successful experimental monetary policy by declaring a one-time dividend of thirty shillings to every citizen.

England disapproved of the colonists' soft money. New issues of paper money were prohibited in New England in 1751 and in the rest of the colonies in 1764. Many fiscally conservative colonists agreed with this prohibition and worried that independence from England would bring the irresponsible and destructive printing of unbacked paper money. As it turned out, the Revolutionary War itself was financed by nearly half a billion dollars of paper money issued by the states and the Continental Congress. Hyperinflation followed. According to Galbraith,[8] a common saying was that "a wagon-load of money would scarcely purchase a wagon-load of provisions." In Virginia, shoes were $5000 a pair, and a suit more than a million dollars. Although eventually redeemed at the generous rate of one cent of hard money to the dollar, the saying "not worth a Continental," meaning a Continental dollar, became part of our national vocabulary.

Despite the indispensable role of paper money in financing the revolution, the disruption caused by the ensuing hyperinflation led to the inclusion of strict monetary regulations in the U.S. Constitution. Only the federal government was permitted to mint coins, and both the state and federal governments were apparently prohibited from issuing paper money. Up until the beginning of the Civil War in 1861, the only paper money in the United States was issued by private banks. During the Civil War, military expenditures were financed by the printing of unbacked "greenbacks" (paper money printed with green ink) in the North and unbacked Confederate notes in the South. With the collapse of the Confederacy, Confederate notes became worthless except as collectors' items.

Before the Civil War, the only paper money in the United States was issued by private banks.

The constitutionality of the Northern greenbacks was debated in prolonged court battles. Ironically, Salmon P. Chase, who as Lincoln's Treasury Secretary asked Congress to authorize the issuance of greenbacks, later as Chief Justice of the Supreme Court spoke for the majority in 1870 in declaring them unconstitutional and vigorously dissented in 1871 when a changed court decided that they were constitutional after all.

The fate of the greenbacks was also a political issue, with various Congresses voting to retire them or to issue more. In 1878, the Greenback Party, organized to promote the issuance of greenbacks, received more than a million votes and elected 14 members to Congress. By 1879, commodity prices had fallen to prewar levels, and Congress made greenbacks redeemable in gold at a fixed price of $20.67 per ounce. (This price was consistent with the quantity of gold in U.S. gold coins since 1834.) In addition, gold certificates were issued, which were fully backed and redeemable in gold.

Earlier, in 1873, Congress had formally stopped the coinage of silver dollars. Because silver prices had been high relative to gold, silver had (by Gresham's

Law) been used commercially rather than coined for many years. The cessation of silver coinage in 1873 was also consistent with the universal gold standard favored by the leading European countries. Not surprisingly, silver prices slumped subsequently, and silver miners in the western states pressed for the resumed coinage of silver dollars at the old rate of 371.25 grains per dollar. Such an action would have given them far more dollars for their silver than could be obtained in commodity markets. Debtors also saw unlimited silver coinage as a way to reverse the post–Civil War deflation. With more dollars being minted than spent to acquire silver, the nation's money supply and prices would expand.

The unlimited-silver advocates founded the Populist Party and sent supporters, Populists and Democrats, to Congress. Congress swung toward soft money, resuming silver coinage in 1878, and then swung back, stopping it in 1893. In the 1896 election, silver coinage was the main campaign issue. The Republican candidate, William McKinley, supported a firm gold standard, arguing that "we cannot gamble with anything as sacred as money." His Democratic opponent, William Jennings Bryan, made an even stronger religious allusion in arguing for the free coinage of silver. He concluded his emotional speech to the Democratic convention with the memorable battle cry:

> We will answer their demand for a gold standard by saying to them: "You shall not press down upon the brow of labor this crown of thorns, you shall not crucify mankind upon a cross of gold."

Despite his stirring oratory, Bryan and silver coinage were soundly defeated in the 1896 election. The Gold Standard Act of 1900 ended the bimetallic standard, affirming what had, in practice, been the case for decades.

During the Great Depression of the 1930s, the gold backing for U.S. money effectively stopped. In 1933, all citizens were required to surrender their gold (other than rare coins and jewelry) to the government at the price of $20.67 an ounce. Gold certificates were also called in and exchanged for unbacked money. The official price of gold was raised to $35 an ounce but, except for legitimate commercial uses, the Treasury sold gold only to foreign central banks and official institutions. From 1933 until 1975, it was illegal for U.S. citizens to own gold.

Gold backing for U.S. currency ended during the Great Depression.

United States silver certificates, which had been issued since 1878, were redeemable for silver dollars (or silver stored at West Point). These silver dollars were usually token coins in that the silver they contained was worth less than a dollar. However, when silver prices rose in the 1960s, silver certificates stopped circulating and were instead hoarded or redeemed (Gresham's Law again).

U.S. currency today is fiat money, almost entirely Federal Reserve notes.

Today almost all of the currency in circulation is in the form of Federal Reserve notes, unbacked paper issued by Federal Reserve banks. Some $300 million, less than 1 percent of the circulating currency, consists of U.S. Treasury notes. These are the old greenbacks, first issued during the Civil War, and these, too, are now fiat money.

On July 15, 1980, the U.S. Treasury began marketing one-ounce and half-ounce gold medallions through post offices. These medallions are emphatically not legal tender. No fixed dollar value is stamped on them. Instead, they are pieces of gold, initially issued at a price about 2 percent above the prevailing market price of gold. As the price of gold fluctuates, so does the market value of gold medallions. These medallions are intended to compete with the gold coins sold by more than 80 governments, including the South African Krugerrand and the Canadian Maple Leaf. The 2 percent premium covers minting costs and gives the government a small profit. In addition, it is hoped that the original buyer's filing of an application form with the government will encourage the payment of taxes on any realized capital gains. Gold enthusiasts hoped that these medallions would be the first step toward the return to a gold standard. In the next chapter we will see that the future is more likely to bring the softest money of all: invisible electronic money.

SUMMARY

Barter may be satisfactory in a small, closely knit community of largely self-sufficient people, or in a communal or totalitarian society. In a large community, however, with specialized labor, private property, and voluntary exchange, barter is very inefficient and trading instead involves a medium of exchange — something that people accept not to use but to trade for something else. Commodity money is intrinsically useful; fiat money is not. The value of money — commodity or fiat — depends on demand and supply. In addition to serving as a medium of exchange, money provides a unit of accounting and a store of value.

Hard money (such as silver coins) can be shaved or debased and may be difficult to keep in circulation; in addition, valuable resources are tied up in the medium of exchange. The value of hard money fluctuates with demand and supply, but a prolonged inflation is unlikely. Unbacked paper money, if its supply is limited, has value because it is useful as a medium of exchange. The danger with soft money is that the government will not manage its supply responsibly.

IMPORTANT TERMS

barter
commodity money
fiat money

Gresham's Law
medium of exchange

EXERCISES

1. Which of the following would you classify as a commodity money and which as a fiat money:
   a. Gold.
   b. Woodpecker scalps.
   c. Yap stones.
   d. Rice.
   e. Federal Reserve notes.

2. Explain why each of the following would make a poor commodity money: oysters, diamonds, wine, sand, 1956 Corvettes.

3. Would you rather be paid your monthly salary in gold, old baseball cards, or paper dollars? Explain your reasoning.

4. Why does barter become less workable as people become more specialized?

5. Why is barter simplified when there is a "double coincidence" of wants? Give an example.

6. Here is a simple four-person economy in which each person produces a single item and now wants to trade some of that commodity for another commodity:

Person	Produces	Wants
Arlene	apples	bananas
Bill	bananas	doughnuts
Carol	coffee	apples
Dave	doughnuts	coffee

If they use pure barter with no medium of exchange, no one can find another person who has what he or she wants and wants what he or she has. What is the minimum number of trades needed for all four to get what they want if they use apples as a medium of exchange?

7. Is the trading of stones by the people of Yap an example of barter or of a medium of exchange? Explain your reasoning.

8. For a hundred years, from 1834 to 1933, the official U.S. price of gold was $20.67 an ounce. If a horse sold for $10, what would have been its price in terms of gold (that is, ounces/horse)? If gold is $1,000 an ounce, how much gold is needed to buy a 25-cent package of chewing gum?

9. Explain why the hoarding of rare coins by collectors is an example of Gresham's Law.

10. Doesn't Gresham's Law imply that fiat money will be driven out of circulation?

11. U.S. Silver Certificates were paper dollars, redeemable in silver dollars that generally contained less than a dollar's worth of silver. What does Gresham's Law predict will happen if the price of silver increases enough that the silver in a silver dollar is worth more than a dollar?

12. If, while the United States is on a gold standard, the growth of the economy causes the demand for gold to grow faster than its supply, will prices in general tend to rise or fall?

13. Between 1873 and 1896, while the United States was on a gold standard, wholesale prices fell by approximately 50 percent in the United States. What happened to the price of gold relative to the price of commodities during this period?

14. In 1834, the U.S. Congress set the official price of gold at $20.67 an ounce and the price of silver at $1.292 an ounce. Consumer prices increased between 1834 and 1989 by a factor of about 12. If the relative price ratios of gold and silver to consumer goods had been the same in 1989 as in 1834, what would have been the 1989 dollar prices of gold and silver?

15. Find the most recent prices of gold and silver by looking in the "Money & Investing" section of the latest Monday edition of *The Wall Street Journal* and locating a box entitled "CASH PRICES." In the precious metals group, there are several gold and silver prices. Use the U.S. dollar spot prices determined in the London Friday PM fixings. How do these current gold and silver prices compare with the hypothetical prices calculated in the preceding exercise? How does the current gold-silver price ratio compare with the 16/1 ratio set in 1834? If the United States were on a bimetallic standard now with a gold-silver price ratio of 16/1, which metal would, by Gresham's Law, be driven out of circulation?

16. Exercise 15 explains how to find some recent commodity prices in *The Wall Street Journal*'s "CASH PRICES" box. Look up the prices of gold, corn, and butter for the last trading day for each of the last 12 months. Graph these price series. Which seems the most stable?

17. Gauge the stability of the three price series in Exercise 16 by calculating the standard deviation of each. Also calculate the standard deviation of the Consumer Price Index during these 12 months, obtaining your data from a source such as the *Federal Reserve Bulletin* or *Survey of Current Business*.

18. In the Mint Act of 1792, the U.S. Congress established a bimetallic standard with the price of gold fixed at $19.39 per troy ounce and the price of silver at $1.292 an ounce — a gold-silver price ratio of 15/1. In 1796, France established a bimetallic standard with a gold-silver price ratio of 15.5/1. Which country do you suppose exported gold and used silver as currency?

19. Name an event that will cause inflation and one that will cause deflation if the United States changes to a monetary system in which all of its money is backed by
   a. Gold.
   b. Buffalo.
   c. Postage stamps produced in 1945.

20. U.S. copper pennies contain $\frac{2}{3}$ of a hundredth of a pound of copper. At what copper price (dollars per pound) can a profit be made by melting pennies?

21. In the 1970s the price of gold increased much faster than the price of most goods and services. If we had been on a gold standard, would there have been inflation or deflation during these years?

22. In the 1960s, the industrial demand for silver grew much faster than silver supplies, sharply increasing the price of silver. If we had been using silver as a commodity money, would there have been an inflation or deflation in the 1960s?

23. An increase in the supply of a commodity generally reduces its price, yet an increase in the money supply usually increases prices. Explain why these two observations are either consistent with each other or inconsistent.

24. When the United States defined a dollar in terms of both gold and silver, the nation was legally on a bimetallic standard. In practice, however, the United States was on either a gold or a silver standard because only one of these metals circulated as money. Will a legal two-metal standard always turn into a one-metal standard in practice?

25. Will a farmer with large debts benefit financially more from inflation or deflation? Explain your reasoning.

3

Optional Chapter

INTERNATIONAL MONEYS

The Bank of England was the instrument of a ruling class. Among the powers the Bank derived from that ruling class was that of inflicting hardship. It could lower prices and wages, increasing unemployment. These were the correctives when gold was being lost; euphoria was excessive. Few or none foresaw that farmers and workers would one day have the power that would make governments unwilling to impose these hardships even in so righteous a cause as defense of the currency.

John Kenneth Galbraith

Many financial transactions crisscross national borders. U.S. investors buy German bonds, Germans buy British stock, and the English buy U.S. hotels. Countries with large trade surpluses, such as Japan and the oil-exporting nations, recycle their excess revenues by investing in the United States, Europe, and elsewhere. Consortia of international banks lend tens of billions of dollars to multinational companies and to governments. These same banks finance much of their lending by issuing international certificates of deposit that are traded in such disparate places as Nassau, Luxembourg, and Hong Kong. Every day, hundreds of billions of dollars' worth of foreign currencies are traded worldwide by individuals, businesses, banks, and governments. The twin centers of this international foreign-exchange market are New York and London. These centers are electronically linked to each other and to other trading areas, and are also interconnected through the international branches of large banks.

Currency prices have real economic effects. A French company that plants grapevines, expecting to export wine to the United States, may find that, by the time the vines mature, the value of the French franc has risen so much relative to the U.S. dollar that the wine cannot be exported profitably. Conversely, a U.S. vintner can make large, unexpected profits simply because the value of the U.S. dollar has fallen. Multinational companies that produce and market products in many countries are continually buffeted by currency revaluations. The 1974 collapse of the Franklin National Bank in the United States was due partly to losses incurred in its foreign-exchange transactions. In 1984, economic difficulties in many debtor nations threatened to topple several U.S. banks.

Another consequence of the linkage of world financial markets is that economic events in one nation have worldwide repercussions. For example, when credit is scarce and interest rates are high in the United States, U.S. banks borrow in Europe, thereby raising interest rates abroad. A stock market panic in one country can have ripple effects on the stock markets in all countries.

In this chapter, we will investigate some consequences of the fact that there are many national currencies. Later chapters will explain more fully how the interrelationships among currencies have important implications for the analysis of financial events and for the conduct of monetary policies.

We will pay particular attention to the gold standard, which once made national currencies commodity moneys and fixed the exchange rates among them. We will look at how the gold standard worked and why it collapsed. In later chapters, when we have the necessary analytical tools, we will return to the question of how exchange rates are determined in the absence of a gold standard.

EXCHANGE RATES

Almost every nation has a domestic currency that is used for transactions within its borders — the U.S. dollar, German deutschemark, Swiss franc, Japanese yen, British pound, and so forth. When transactions cross national boundaries, a currency conversion is usually necessary. For example, consumers in the United States have dollars to spend on wine, but French wine producers want francs to spend at their local McDonald's. Thus, when U.S. citizens buy French wine, their dollars will at some point be exchanged for French francs.

As is true of tomatoes, haircuts, and other goods and services, each foreign currency has a price at which it is bought and sold. The **exchange rate** is the price of one currency in terms of another — for example, the price of a French franc in U.S. dollars or German marks. The exchange rates for currency trades among banks (in amounts of $1 million or more) are reported each day in *The Wall Street Journal*. Table 3.1 shows some of these data for trades made on September 8, 1989. Two prices are given: the number of U.S. dollars needed to buy one unit of the foreign currency and the amount of foreign currency needed

The exchange rate is the price of one currency in terms of another.

Table 3.1 Selected Exchanges Rates, September 8, 1989

Country	U.S. Dollars Per Currency	Currency Per U.S. Dollars
Britain (pound)	1.5395	0.6495
France (franc)	0.1490	6.7095
Japan (yen)	0.006802	147.00
West Germany (deutschemark)	0.5020	1.9920

source: *The Wall Street Journal*, September 11, 1989.

to buy one U.S. dollar. The second price is, of course, just the inverse of the first. For example, a West German deutschemark cost about 0.50 U.S. dollars and, conversely, a dollar cost about $1/0.50 = 2$ marks.

The Wall Street Journal understandably reports all exchange rates relative to the dollar, the currency used by most of its readers. However, from these data, we can calculate other exchange rates, such as the price of the British pound in terms of deutschemarks:

$$\frac{1.5395 \text{ U.S. dollars/pound}}{0.5020 \text{ U.S. dollars/mark}} = 3.0667 \frac{\text{marks}}{\text{pound}}$$

Because it takes about $1.50 to buy a pound and $0.50 to buy a deutschemark, $1.50 will buy either 1 pound or 3 marks; so it takes about 3 marks to buy a pound.

A nation's currency undergoes **depreciation** when foreign currency becomes more expensive; a currency **appreciates** as foreign currency becomes less expensive. Before World War I, a British pound cost $4.76; in 1989, it cost $1.50. Over this period, U.S. dollars appreciated relative to the pound, and the pound depreciated relative to the dollar. Figure 3.1 shows some recent exchange-rate movements. There have been many zigs and zags, but overall, since the early 1970s, the U.S. dollar has appreciated relative to the British pound and Italian lira and depreciated relative to the German mark, Japanese yen, and Swiss franc.

> A currency is said to depreciate when foreign currency becomes more expensive.

The Law of One Price

Exchange rates are important because they determine the domestic price of foreign goods. Suppose that a certain French wine costs 50 francs per bottle. What is the price in U.S. dollars? If a franc costs 15 cents, then the wine implicitly costs $7.50:

$$P = \left(0.15 \frac{\text{dollars}}{\text{franc}}\right)\left(50 \frac{\text{francs}}{\text{bottle}}\right) = 7.50 \frac{\text{dollars}}{\text{bottle}}$$

Figure 3.1   Exchange Rates of Six Currencies Against the Dollar

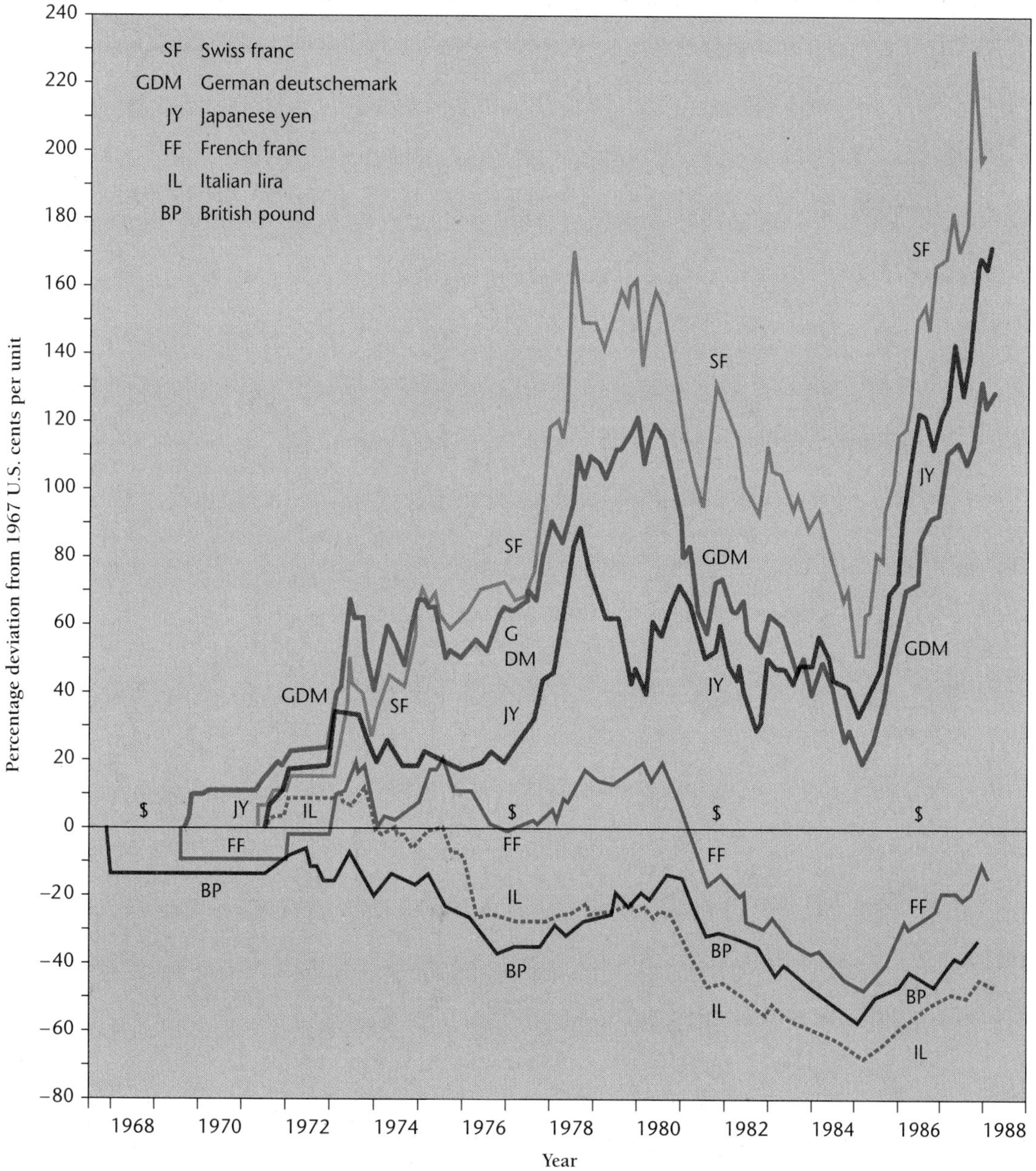

SF   Swiss franc
GDM   German deutschemark
JY   Japanese yen
FF   French franc
IL   Italian lira
BP   British pound

At an exchange rate of 0.15 dollars to the franc, 50 francs cost 0.15(50) = $7.50. Alternatively, we can say that the exchange rate is 1/0.15 = 6.67 francs to the dollar and, therefore, $7.50 costs 6.67($7.50) = 50 francs.

In general, the domestic price of a foreign item is equal to the exchange rate multiplied by the foreign price:

$$\left(\begin{array}{c}\text{Domestic price}\\\text{of foreign item}\end{array}\right) = \left(\frac{\text{Domestic currency}}{\text{Foreign currency}}\right)\left(\begin{array}{c}\text{Foreign price}\\\text{of foreign item}\end{array}\right)$$

These factors — domestic prices, foreign prices, and exchange rates — are roughly linked through what is called the **law of one price**: the domestic price of a foreign item should equal the domestic price of a comparable domestic item. If the U.S. price of the French wine is $7.50, then the U.S. price of a comparable U.S. wine should also be $7.50. Otherwise, people will buy only the wine that is less expensive. In general, the law of one price requires that

$$P_d = eP_f \tag{1}$$

where

P_d = domestic price of domestic item
P_f = foreign price of foreign item
e = exchange rate, domestic currency/foreign currency

In our example, e = $0.15 dollars/franc, P_f = 50 francs, and the law of one price implies a domestic price of

$$P_d = eP_f = (\$0.15)(50) = \$7.50$$

The law of one price does not hold precisely, at least in the short run. For example, when the U.S. dollar depreciated in 1986 and 1987, the dollar price of imported BMWs, Hondas, and Toyotas rose by more than 10 percent relative to the dollar prices of U.S. cars.[1] According to the theory of purchasing-power parity, this should not have happened. The dollar prices of German, Japanese, and U.S. cars should have remained in parity. As the dollars-per-deutschemark and dollars-per-yen exchange rates e increased, the dollar price of U.S. cars P_d should have risen, or the deutschemark price of German cars and the yen price of Japanese cars P_f should have fallen, so as to maintain Equation 1.

One reason for the nonadjustment of prices is that many items, such as automobiles, are traded in imperfect markets with sluggish prices. As the dollar prices of BMWs, Hondas, and Toyotas rose relative to the dollar prices of Chevys and Fords, there was some shift in demand toward U.S. cars. But this demand shift didn't translate into price adjustments. As the demand for U.S. cars rose, it was met by increased production rather than by price increases.

The law of one price works best for products that are relatively homogeneous, like wheat and steel. If buyers perceive unique qualities in what they buy, this uniqueness gives seemingly competitive firms some monopolistic control over prices. This monopolistic competition is true of aspirin, clothes, and automobiles. As the dollar price of BMWs and Toyotas rose relative to U.S. cars,

German Reunification

In the spring of 1990, negotiations began for the historic reunification of East and West Germany. An essential part of German reunification was the adoption of a single currency, and the logical choice was the West German deutschemark, anchor of the European Monetary System. To accomplish this, East Germans would have to trade their ostmarks for deutschemarks. But at what exchange rate?

Before reunification, West Germans could buy ostmarks at the official exchange rate of three ostmarks for one deutschemark, but few of them wanted ostmarks. In East Germany, the black market rate ranged from five to seven ostmarks for one deutschemark. Before negotiations began, West German Chancellor Helmut Kohl suggested, at least for small savings accounts, a generous one-to-one exchange of ostmarks per deutschemark.

However, in April 1990, West Germany's central bank, the Bundesbank, prepared a confidential report recommending an exchange rate of two ostmarks per deutschemark. This report was leaked to the press and set off a storm of protests among East Germans who were hoping for a one-to-one exchange. Much of the ensuing debate was very emotional, with the East Germans arguing that a two-to-one exchange rate made them second-class citizens. And there was understandable self-interest behind the protests of East Germans holding ostmarks.

There were several persuasive economic arguments against a one-to-one exchange rate. Those holding ostmarks or savings accounts, bonds, and other assets denominated in ostmarks would surely benefit by receiving more deutschemarks for their ostmarks. But those with debts denominated in ostmarks would be hurt by having to repay these debts one-to-one with deutschemarks. The Bundesbank estimated that East Germany's internal debts amounted to 400 billion ostmarks, the equivalent of $125 billion at a two-to-one exchange rate and $250 billion at a one-to-one exchange rate. In comparison with a two-to-one exchange rate, a one-to-one exchange rate would effectively transfer $125 billion from debtors to creditors.

The final negotiated agreement required all ostmarks to be deposited in bank accounts by June 30, 1990. On July 1, 1990, depositors were credited with deutschemarks — the first 4,000 ostmarks at a one-to-one exchange rate, the rest at two-to-one. (For children under 14, the first 2,000 were one-to-one; for those over 59, the first 6,000. Other financial assets and debts were converted at a two-to-one exchange rate.)

A more fundamental problem is that East German products would not be competitive if wage rates and prices were converted one-to-one from ostmarks to deutschemarks. The accompanying table compares several preunification West German and East German prices. The East German government's subsidies of basic foods, apartments, and electricity made these bargains at a one-to-one exchange rate, but they didn't intend to subsidize the sale of these products to West Germans. In fact, their intention was the opposite — to eliminate these subsidies and move toward market-determined prices. For unsubsidized products, like coffee and color televisions, the law of one price between East and West Germany required an exchange rate of at least three-to-one.

Comparison of Preunification of West German and East German Prices

	West German Deutschemarks	East German Ostmarks	Law of One Price Ostmarks/deutschemarks
Loaf of rye bread	3.17	0.52	0.16
11 pounds of potatoes	4.94	0.85	0.17
Monthly apartment rent	411	75	0.18
Electricity (per kwh)	0.42	0.08	0.19
Color television	1,539	4,900	3.18
2.2 pounds of coffee	17.86	70	3.92

source: Terence Roth, "East German Winners in Election Now Seek Fast Monetary Union," *The Wall Street Journal*, March 20, 1990.

Unsubsidized East German color television sets, priced at 4,900 ostmarks could not be sold for 4,900 deutschemarks in competition with West German sets priced at 1,539 deutschemarks. If the East German set is comparable to the West German one, then it needs to have a similar price. No matter what the negotiated ostmark/deutschemark exchange rate, the makers of East German television sets inevitably had to price their product at approximately 1,500 deutschemarks and could not make a profit if they paid workers more than 1,500 deutschemarks to produce it.

The underlying problem was that East German wages were too high relative to their productivity for their products to be competitive on world markets at a one-for-one exchange rate. In June 1990, a prominent West German banker stated that "No company in East Germany is ready to be competitive with West German or West European companies" and that fewer than 20 percent would become competitive "any time soon."* To be competitive, East German workers either had to become more productive or be paid far fewer deutschemarks than ostmarks.

---

*Kurt Kasch, quoted in Frederick Kempe, "Merging Currencies of the Two Germanys Will Join Their Fates," *Wall Street Journal*, June 29, 1990.

there was no mass shift in buying habits, because most BMW and Toyota buyers didn't consider U.S. cars to be good substitutes.

Another barrier to the law of one price is transaction and transportation costs, including tariffs, fees, quotas, and other trade barriers. To the extent that these protect domestic industry, they promote price rigidities and disparities. Wine and automobiles can be relatively expensive in France if the French prohibit foreign alternatives or levy high import taxes.

Transaction and transportation costs undermine the law of one price.

The U.S. price of a foreign product is not just the foreign price multiplied by the exchange rate. To this frictionless price, as it is called, must be added all the transaction and transportation costs. If these raise the price 4 percent, then

$$\text{U.S. price of foreign item} = (1 + 0.04)\, eP_f$$

The logic behind the law of one price implies that the U.S. price of a comparable U.S. good cannot exceed this, or else only the foreign good will be bought.

$$P_d \leq (1 + 0.04)\, eP_f \tag{2}$$

Similarly, if transaction costs raise the foreign price of U.S. goods 6 percent, then we divide by the exchange rate to convert dollars into foreign currency.

$$\text{Foreign price of U.S. item} = (1 + 0.06)\, \frac{1}{e} P_d$$

The law-of-one-price logic implies that the foreign price of the comparable foreign good cannot be larger than the foreign price of the U.S. good.

$$P_f \leq (1 + 0.06)\, \frac{1}{e} P_d \tag{3}$$

The combination of Equations 2 and 3 yields the result

$$\frac{1}{1 + 0.06} \leq \frac{P_d}{eP_f} \leq 1 + 0.04 \tag{4}$$

The frictionless price ratio P_d/eP_f need not equal 1. Instead, it can vary over a sometimes wide range, within limits set by import and export expenses.

Many goods and services are said to be **nontraded goods** because import and export costs are prohibitively expensive. U.S. workers may be paid considerably more than British workers as long as commuting from England is infeasible. It can cost much more for a haircut and a round of golf in Japan than in the United States because it is impractical for the Japanese to have their hair cut in Iowa and play golf in Georgia.

The law of one price does not apply to nontraded goods.

The law of one price is most appropriate for raw commodities and for financial assets. Many financial assets are considered good substitutes for one another — indeed, it is because international financial assets are good substitutes and can be traded relatively inexpensively that hectic international financial markets have developed. The law of one price for financial assets means that changes in U.S. interest rates quickly affect the financial markets of other nations and vice versa.

LIBOR measures the interest rate on large Eurodollar loans.

For example, the **London Interbank Offered Rate (LIBOR)** is a measure of what the large international banks charge each other for large Eurodollar loans — loans denominated in U.S. dollars. LIBOR is commonly used as an international benchmark to fix the minimum interest rate charged on Eurodollar loans by bank syndicates, often to foreign governments. In April 1980, LIBOR and the U.S. prime rate (for loans from U.S. banks to the most financially sound U.S. businesses) were both around 20 percent. In June 1980, LIBOR dropped to 9 percent, but the reported U.S. prime rate fell only to 12 percent. Big U.S. corporations, however, demanded and got loans from U.S. banks based on LIBOR rather than on the reported U.S. prime rate. They were able to do this because of the very real threat by the corporations to borrow from foreign banks.

Most international transactions are not for imports and exports of wheat, steel, and automobiles, but are instead financial transactions. Savers today look worldwide, and so do borrowers. Ordinary households may not buy German bonds or British real estate, but banks, insurance companies, and pension funds do so on their behalf. Their profits from such transactions depend not only on foreign interest rates but also on the appreciation or depreciation of foreign currencies. A German bond paying 20 percent won't be profitable for U.S. investors if the value of the deutschemark falls by 30 percent relative to the dollar. We will look at such rate-of-return calculations in more detail in Chapter 7.

Purchasing Power Parity

The law of one price is sometimes applied to the overall price levels in two countries to determine the implied value of the exchange rate. We can rewrite Equation 1 as

$$e = \frac{P_d}{P_f} \tag{5}$$

Where now

P_d = overall level of domestic prices
P_f = overall level of foreign prices
e = exchange rate, domestic currency/foreign currency

Purchasing power parity says the percentage change in an exchange rate is determined by the difference in the two nations' rates of inflation.

According to the theory of **purchasing power parity**, the percentage change in the exchange rate between two currencies is approximately equal to the difference in their rates of inflation:

$$\%e = \%P_d - \%P_f \tag{6}$$

If, for example, U.S. prices increase faster than Japanese prices, then the dollar must depreciate relative to the yen for U.S. products to remain competitive. Specifically, a 10 percent increase in U.S. prices and a 3 percent increase in Japanese prices implies a 7 percent depreciation of the dollar relative to the yen (a 7 percent increase in the number of dollars needed to buy yen),

$$\%e = 10\% - 3\% = 7\%$$

Hamburger Parity

In September 1986, *The Economist,* an influential British periodical, tested the theory of purchasing power parity by surveying the prices of McDonald's Big Mac hamburgers around the world. Some of their data are shown in the accompanying table. For customers, the Big Mac is a non-traded good, because an Australian won't go to Brazil or Canada to buy a hamburger and fries. Nonetheless, the implications of purchasing power parity are interesting.

The Implications of Hamburger Parity

	Local Price P_f	Implied P_d/P_f	Exchange Rate Actual (Sept. 1986)	Exchange Rate Actual (Sept. 1989)	Percentage Change
Dollar overvalued:					
Australia (dollar)	1.75	0.91	0.61	0.76	24.6
Brazil (cruzado)	12.50	0.13	0.07	0.36	414.3
Canada (dollar)	1.89	0.85	0.72	0.85	18.1
Hong Kong (dollar)	7.60	0.21	0.13	0.13	0.0
Dollar undervalued:					
France (franc)	16.40	0.10	0.15	0.15	0.0
Japan (yen)	370	0.0043	0.0065	0.0070	7.7
Sweden (krona)	16.50	0.10	0.15	0.15	0.0
West Germany (mark)	4.25	0.38	0.50	0.51	2.0
United States (dollar)	1.60				

source: "On the Hamburger Standard," *The Economist,* September 6, 1986. © 1986 The Economist Newspaper Ltd. All rights reserved.

According to purchasing power parity, the exchange rate in each country should be determined by $e = P_d/P_f$, where P_d is the U.S. price of a Big Mac, P_f is the foreign price, and e is the U.S. dollar price of the foreign currency. For instance, the price of a Big Mac in 1986 was 12.50 cruzados in Brazil and $1.60 in the United States. The exchange rate required for hamburger purchasing power parity was

$$e = \frac{P_d}{P_f} = \frac{1.60 \text{ dollars}}{12.50 \text{ cruzados}} = 0.13 \frac{\text{dollars}}{\text{cruzado}}$$

At the actual exchange rate of 0.07 dollars per cruzado, the price of a Brazilian Big Mac was only $0.875, about half the cost in the United States.

$$(12.5 \text{ cruzados})\left(0.07 \, \frac{\text{dollars}}{\text{cruzado}}\right) = 0.875 \text{ dollars}$$

Even though Americans weren't about to fly to Brazil for Big Macs, *The Economist* concluded that, by the hamburger standard, the dollar was overvalued against the cruzado, suggesting a prediction that the dollar-to-cruzado exchange rate should increase. As the table shows, this did in fact happen over the succeeding three years, though by more than predicted by hamburger purchasing power parity. For the first four countries in the table, the U.S. dollar seemed substantially overvalued. In three cases, the exchange rate did move in the right direction; in the fourth, Hong Kong, there was no change. The U.S. dollar seemed significantly undervalued relative to the currencies of the last four countries in the table. In three of these cases, there was virtually no change in the exchange rate; in the fourth, Japan, the dollar became even more undervalued.

Although hamburger parity did not predict the exact movements in these eight exchange rates, it did succeed in separating the currencies into two groups, one of which appreciated substantially relative to the U.S. dollar.

Since purchasing power parity is derived from the law of one price, it is subject to the same limitations, including transaction and transportation costs — the extreme case being nontraded goods. Nonetheless, Equations 1 and 5 help us remember the rough relationship among domestic prices, foreign prices, and exchange rates. If, for example, the dollar depreciates relative to the deutschemark, what pressures will be exerted on German and U.S. prices? If e is the dollar price of a deutschemark, then dollar depreciation raises e. According to Equation 1, an increase in e should put upward pressure on U.S. prices while restraining German prices. This makes good sense. When the dollar depreciates, the dollar price of imports rises (and the foreign price of U.S. goods declines), making U.S. goods more attractive and foreign goods less so, and thus tends to increase U.S. prices relative to foreign prices. This price adjustment may be slow and imperfect, but Equation 1 helps us remember the direction in which prices are pushed and pulled.

Let's try another example. If some economic event causes prices to increase in the United States, how will this affect foreign prices and exchange rates? According to Equation 5, as P_d increases, e or P_f should increase also. Thus, U.S. inflation should cause either foreign inflation or depreciation of the dollar. Again, this makes good sense. As U.S. prices increase, demand shifts to foreign goods and people exchange dollars for foreign currencies to carry out these transactions, putting upward pressure on the foreign price of foreign goods and on the dollar price of foreign currencies.

THE GOLD STANDARD

Because exchange rates are a prime determinant of the relative prices of domestic and foreign goods, let's look briefly at how exchange rates are determined. As explained in the previous chapter, the United States adopted a **bimetallic standard** in 1792 with fixed prices for gold and silver. In 1834, the official price of gold was adjusted from $19.39 to $20.67 an ounce, making silver, in comparison with gold, too valuable as a commodity to be used as a medium of exchange.

After 1834, with the exception of the Civil War period and an occasional financial panic, the United States was effectively on a **gold standard**, under which the government bought and sold gold at the fixed price of $20.67 per ounce. Consistent with this commitment, the U.S. twenty-dollar gold piece contained a little less than an ounce of gold and the U.S. ten-dollar golden eagle contained slightly less than a half-ounce of gold.

Most other countries were on a bimetallic standard until the late 1870s, when an international gold standard was established. The British government bought and sold gold at the fixed price of 4.34 British pound notes per ounce of gold. If an ounce of gold could be freely traded for 20.67 U.S. dollars or 4.34 British pounds, then 20.67 U.S. dollars had the same value as 4.34 British pounds. Thus one British pound was worth 20.67/4.34 = 4.76 U.S. dollars, and this was the fixed exchange rate at which dollars and pounds were traded. There were similar fixed exchange rates among all of the currencies issued by gold-standard nations: *an international gold standard fixes the currency exchange rates for all participating nations.*

The enforcement of these fixed exchange rates came from the option of converting one currency into gold and then back into another currency. Suppose, for example, that a U.S. importer needs to exchange dollars for pounds in order to buy British wool and that currency-exchange dealers demand $5 per British pound note. The importer has the option of using dollars to buy gold from the U.S. government, shipping this gold to England, and selling it to the Bank of England. Using the fixed government gold prices, the importer can buy British pounds at the official $4.76 price.

Because shipping expenses raise his total cost to about $4.78 a British pound, currency-exchange dealers could charge up to $4.78, but no more. At a higher price, importers would bypass them. For analogous reasons, currency-exchange dealers must pay at least $4.74 for a British pound if they are to stay in business. Thus, although the official frictionless exchange rate in the late 1800s was $4.76 per British pound, actual exchange rates varied slightly within the range of $4.74 to $4.78. Those pennies do add up, but for all practical purposes the gold standard maintained a fixed exchange rate.

Importers, exporters, and banks that deal in foreign exchange generally favor

The United States adopted a bimetallic standard in 1792.

The official price of gold was raised to $20.67 an ounce in 1834, effectively putting the United States on a gold standard.

In the late 1870s, an international gold standard was established that fixed exchange rates.

fixed exchange rates because these eliminate exchange-rate risk. There are invariably delays between when a deal is struck and when final payment is received. Exchange-rate fluctuations during such a delay can turn a good deal into a bad one — a risk that most merchants would rather not worry about. Just as it is widely believed that price instability impedes domestic commerce, so it is thought that exchange-rate instability hinders international commerce.

Automatic Balance-of-Trade Equilibrium

Most 19th-century economists (the 20th-century English economist John Maynard Keynes called them "classical economists") favored fixed exchange rates because these seemingly made chronic balance-of-trade deficits impossible. Recall the law of one price,

$$P_d = eP_f$$

and let P_d be the U.S. price level and P_f the British price level. The exchange rate e is fixed by the international gold standard.

Now suppose that U.S. prices double, perhaps because of a gold discovery and consequent increase in the U.S. money supply. Then, temporarily, $P_d > eP_f$, so that U.S. items are more expensive than their English counterparts. Both English and U.S. consumers will shift to English goods, and U.S. dollars will flow to the English, who will redeem these dollars for gold at the U.S. Treasury. As the United States loses gold, its money supply will shrink (because, under a pure gold standard, its money consists solely of gold and notes backed by gold), and U.S. prices will presumably fall. Similarly, the larger amount of gold in England will expand the English money supply, thereby increasing English prices. In this way, P_d falls and P_f rises until $P_d = eP_f$ is restored and the balance-of-trade deficit is eliminated. Only when this trade deficit ceases does the flow of gold stop exerting its pressure on prices.

When exchange rates are fixed by the gold standard, the law of one price $P_d = eP_f$ requires a long-run constancy of relative prices among nations:

> The international gold standard automatically offset trade imbalances.

$$\frac{P_d}{P_f} = \text{constant } e$$

Although the price levels P_d and P_f need not be constant, their ratio must be. If prices double in the United States, then prices in the United Kingdom, at least for traded goods, must double, too, to maintain the law of one price.

Table 3.2 shows wholesale price indexes in four countries in selected years during the reign of the gold standard. Relative prices were roughly constant, but the price levels in these countries fell by about 50 percent between 1873 and 1896 and rose by about 50 percent between 1896 and 1913.

One reason 19th-century economists supported the gold standard was their belief that price adjustments are painless. In their view, a doubling of the money supply would double prices with only minor, temporary effects on a nation's employment or output. A halving of the money supply would simply reduce

Table 3.2 Wholesale Price Indexes, 1913 = 100

	United States	United Kingdom	Germany	France
1873	137	130	114	122
1896	64	72	69	69
1913	100	100	100	100

source: Richard N. Cooper, "The Gold Standard: Historical
Facts and Future Prospects," *Brookings Papers on
Economic Activity*, I, 1982, pp. 1–45.

prices by 50 percent. In practice, however, monetary fluctuations caused booms and recessions, speculative binges, and frightened panics.

In our earlier example, when gold flows to England, enlarging its money supply, both output and employment expand along with prices. When gold leaves the United States, employment and output contract, inflicting real economic hardship. The international gold standard broke down because nations became unwilling to tolerate the dislocations of their domestic economies required to achieve balance-of-trade equilibrium. As the epigraph at the beginning of this chapter indicates, some economists believe that the spread of democratically elected governments which must answer to voters is the fundamental reason that the gold standard was abandoned.

The Fall of the Gold Standard

The golden age was undone by three 20th-century calamities: two World Wars and the Great Depression. These catastrophes had both direct and indirect effects on international finance. During World War I, European nations imported massive amounts of food and munitions from the United States and simply did not have enough gold to pay for these war supplies; nor could their economies have held up under the shock of the reductions in the money supply required to match the gold losses that did occur. Instead, these European nations abandoned the gold standard; the governments called in private gold holdings, prohibited gold exports, and stopped selling gold to private citizens.

The international gold standard was abandoned during World War I.

Meanwhile, the United States had accumulated nearly half of the world's monetary gold and had replaced England as lender to the world and champion of the gold standard after World War I. Indeed, the United States was virtually the only nation still on the gold standard. The United States increased its money supply along with its new gold, and the U.S. economy and price levels surged upward.

The 1920s were a tumultuous period for international trade. Some nations, such as Austria and Germany, experienced hyperinflations. Great Britain, under Winston Churchill, tried to engineer a deflation so that it could return to the prewar gold standard with an ounce of gold priced at 4.34 British pound notes. Exchange rates fluctuated wildly in speculative anticipation of future price changes. (According to purchasing power parity, a doubling of the German price level should halve the value of its currency; in 1923, German prices increased a billionfold.) Most European nations longed for a return to the relative tranquillity of a gold standard, and the United States tried to assist this return by inflating its domestic prices and resisting further gold inflows.

Before the war, Britain's gold price had been 4.34 British pounds per ounce of gold and the exchange rate had been 4.76 U.S. dollars per British pound. After the war, with the proliferation of unbacked British pound notes, the free-market price of gold was much higher than 4.34 British pounds, and the exchange rate was much lower than 4.76 dollars per British pound.

To restore the prewar gold price of 4.34 British pounds, the exchange rate had to be driven back up to 4.76 dollars per pound. How? Consider again the law of one price,

$$P_d = eP_f$$

where P_d is the U.S. price level, P_f is the British price level, and the exchange rate e is substantially less than 4.76 dollars/pound. To raise e, the U.S. price level P_d must rise, or the British price level P_f must fall.

The British government's attempts at deflationary policies met with stiff resistance. The continent's less stoic nations wouldn't even consider such masochistic policies. Instead, the European leaders urged the United States to follow inflationary policies. Throughout the 1920s, the U.S. monetary authorities generally obliged, and U.S. easy-money policies pushed up the prices of goods and assets and fueled a booming economy. The increase in U.S. prices discouraged the purchase of U.S. items and slowed the flow of gold to the United States. In addition, the U.S. Federal Reserve lent gold and U.S. dollars to foreign central banks and agreed to lend much more.

By 1927, an international gold standard was close to being reestablished. However, there were two important differences from the prewar gold standard:

1. Many of the official exchange rates were unrealistic and, as a consequence, many currencies traded at unofficial exchange rates and many governments were hard-pressed to satisfy currency transactions at the official rates — typically, such countries would not convert their currencies into gold.

2. Many countries were no longer willing to let their money supplies (and domestic prices) automatically expand and contract with their gold stock. When a nation's gold stock increased, the monetary authorities might withdraw some of the increase from circulation by selling bonds to the public and hoarding the gold received. When gold left a country, the monetary authorities could prop up the nation's money supply by using some of their gold stockpile to repurchase bonds from the public. Governments also borrowed gold from one another to maintain their money supplies in the face of balance-of-trade disequilibria. All of these actions helped to stabilize the domestic economies; however, in so doing, they undercut the price adjustments needed to eliminate balance-of-trade disequilibria.

$$P_d < eP_f$$

To restore price equality with a fixed exchange rate, P_d should rise and P_f should fall. In the prewar years, the international flow of gold would have altered the two nations' money supplies, inducing these equilibrating price adjustments. But in the late 1920s, the inclination was to stabilize the money supplies — in one nation to avoid deflation and in the other to avoid inflation. As a result, P_d remained below eP_f, and the balance-of-trade disequilibria persisted.

As long as the nations resisted a realignment of prices, the only way out of this impasse was for the exchange rate to adjust: e had to decline, making the second nation's currency less expensive. If the governments resisted this adjustment, the situation was exacerbated by speculators who anticipated a future adjustment. Expecting the value of the second currency to decline, speculators traded the second currency for the first. To maintain the fixed exchange rate, the two governments had to accommodate these speculative demands by using their holdings of the first currency to buy up the second. The dam broke when the governments decided that an unrealistic fixed exchange rate was no longer worth saving.

Nations were unwilling to let their money supplies fluctuate with international trade.

During the Great Depression, the shaky international gold standard of the 1920s came crashing down like everything else. Two dozen countries, including England, suspended gold payments in 1930 and 1931. Another dozen followed in the first few months of 1932. The United States held out until Franklin Roosevelt's inauguration in March of 1933. By 1936, virtually every country had greatly modified or completely abandoned the gold standard.

The Gold Reserve Act of January 1934 nationalized all U.S. gold, requiring citizens to turn in their gold and gold coins at the government's new price of $35 an ounce. Gold could be held privately only for "legitimate" nonmonetary uses. The U.S. government no longer sold gold to private citizens, but it did trade gold at the new price with foreign governments and central banks.

During the remainder of the 1930s, gold poured into the United States, much of it due to the export stimulus provided by the devaluation of the dollar. In addition, both people and gold immigrated to the United States, refugees from the political and economic turmoil in Europe. Moreover, the increase in gold prices relative to other commodities stimulated gold production. In all, the U.S. Treasury's gold stock swelled from $4 billion at the beginning of 1934 to $23 billion in 1941.

BRETTON WOODS

As World War II came to an end, an international monetary conference was held in July 1944 at the Mount Washington Hotel in Bretton Woods, New Hampshire. More than seven hundred people from 44 countries came to this small mountain resort to construct a workable international monetary system. As is typically the

Highlight 3.3   Who Can Devalue the Most?

One reason for the collapse of the gold standard in the 1930s was that international lending dried up in the Great Depression. Many governments had borrowed heavily to prop up their overvalued currencies. When these loans were not renewed and new funds could not be found, these governments had no choice but to suspend gold payments at the old prices. In addition, many nations saw their inflated exchange rates as a restraint on foreign sales. With their economies sinking fast, they tried to boost export demand by leaving the gold standard and devaluing their currency. But such actions accomplish little when other nations are also devaluing their currencies. For example, by the spring of 1933, the British pound had been devalued by 30 percent against the U.S. dollar. (Its price had been reduced to $3.40.) But most other currencies had also been devalued against the U.S. dollar by 30 percent or more. Thus the British had gained ground only against the Americans in their efforts to stimulate export demand.

Roosevelt's decision to devalue the dollar was largely intended to offset these earlier devaluations by other nations. He raised the dollar price of gold from $20.67 to $35 an ounce on January 31, 1934, offsetting most of the foreign devaluations and more than offsetting some of them; for example, the dollar price of the British pound was raised from $3.40 to slightly over $5, compared to $4.76 under the old gold standard.

Each nation tried to stimulate its economy by selling its goods to foreigners at bargain prices and found it easier to devalue its currency than to endure a domestic deflation. Even today, many governments have the peculiar idea that instead of encouraging domestic spending, it is better to stimulate output and employment by depreciating their currency.

Similarly, some countries sell products to foreigners for less than their own citizens pay. At the request of U.S. businesses, the U.S. and Japanese governments sampled the prices of 124 Japanese and U.S. products in 1989. They found that 60 percent of the Japanese products could be purchased for less in the United States than in Japan; 10 percent of the U.S.–made products cost less in Japan than in the United States.* For example, a car made in Japan that sold for the equivalent of $16,880 in Tokyo sold for $13,507 in Chicago. In contrast, a car made in the United States that sold for $13,507 in Chicago sold for $25,613 in Japan.

A variation of this logic is the idea that foreign aid benefits a country economically: foreigners will buy more products if given the money. Such subsidized purchases do increase domestic production, but working to produce goods for others is not an economic gain. Foreign aid is a gift.

---

*Art Pine, "Japanese Pay More When the Label Reads 'Made in Japan,'" *Los Angeles Times*, November 8, 1989.

case with such conferences, the plan had been drafted by a few experts and largely accepted beforehand by the principal nations. In this case, England and the United States were the most important participants, and the primary architects were the English economist John Maynard Keynes and an Assistant Secretary of the U.S. Treasury, Harry D. White.

The **Bretton Woods agreement** attempted to restore fixed exchange rates without the domestic disruption caused by the classic gold standard. The participating nations agreed to make whatever currency transactions were necessary to keep exchange rates within 1 percent of the initial fixing. In exceptional circumstances, a nation would be permitted a one-time devaluation of up to 10 percent.

The Bretton Woods agreement restored fixed exchange rates without a classic gold standard.

A central reserve fund, the **International Monetary Fund (IMF)**, was established to lend money to nations that needed to purchase their currency in order to support its value. Instead of the deflationary shock inflicted by the pure gold standard, these loans would give a nation time to take gradual steps to strengthen its currency; an escalation of the fees on these loans was intended to discourage procrastination.

The central reserve fund — $6.8 billion in gold, U.S. dollars, and other strong currencies — was financed by contributions from the members, principally the United States and Britain. The IMF was given a home in Washington, D.C., and a staff to administer the reserve fund and to advise and prod nations with weak currencies.

The United States emerged from World War II with undamaged factories and the financial wealth to buy the goods these factories could produce. The United States had also accumulated $25 billion in gold by 1949 — some two-thirds of the world's monetary stockpile. The United States used some of its fortune in foreign aid programs to prop up the Bretton Woods monetary agreement by financing the balance-of-trade deficits of other nations. Two of the most notable programs were the Anglo-American Financial Agreement of 1945, which gave $3.75 billion to Britain, and the $12.5 billion Marshall Plan.

In 1970, the IMF expanded its reserve base even further by creating "paper gold," **Special Drawing Rights (SDRs)**, which are credited to members and can be used within the IMF to purchase hard currency. The SDR was initially valued at one U.S. dollar. Since 1974, the SDR's value relative to the dollar has been determined by a weighted average of the exchange rates of 16 countries relative to the dollar. The value of the SDR rose to $1.30 in 1980 (as the dollar weakened), fell to $0.96 in 1985 (as the dollar strengthened), and then rose to $1.38 in 1988.

SDRs are used by IMF members to purchase hard currency.

These SDRs have enlarged the IMF's pool of funds that can be lent to governments. They are also a tentative first step toward an international money, with the IMF as the international central bank. It has been proposed that the IMF raise funds by selling SDR-denominated securities and that SDRs be used by central banks as a multicurrency reserve. Although SDRs are not now traded privately, in 1980 Chemical Bank pioneered international securities with values indexed to SDRs. These are intended to reduce exchange-rate risks for international banks and businesses.

There are two other large international central banking institutions: the World Bank and the Bank for International Settlements (BIS). The World Bank was established at the same time as the IMF. It is legally owned by 135 governments and supported by contributions from these nations. The World Bank borrows in world financial markets and makes long-term loans to develop agriculture and industry in the world's poorest countries, many of whom cannot borrow from the IMF or private banks. Mixing metaphors, Alden Clausen, former World Bank president, says that World Bank loans are needed when "a country is really behind the goal posts and needs to borrow for a very long time at a marginal interest rate in order to keep the patient alive and effect the cure."[2]

The Bank for International Settlements was established after World War I to handle Germany's war-reparations payments. These payments ended in 1980, but the BIS had by then been transformed into a $50 billion bank for central banks — those government agencies, such as the Federal Reserve in the United States, that oversee a nation's money and banks. The BIS invests about 10 percent of the world's official central bank reserves, transfers funds from one central bank to another, and makes short-term loans to central banks.

The Fatal Weaknesses

As noted, the intention of the Bretton Woods agreement was to reestablish the stable exchange rates that everyone seemed to favor, without also accepting the booms and busts that accompanied the international gold standard. This separation was to be made possible by the central reserve fund, which would allow a nation time to choose the best way to strengthen its currency. It sounded plausible on paper, but there were two eventually fatal flaws:

1. Internationally mobile capital stalked weak currencies like vultures circling a wounded animal. When devaluation seemed possible, speculators would rush to sell that currency, thereby forcing a devaluation. From the speculators' viewpoint, it was a one-sided bet. The weak currency was surely not going to be revalued upwards. The worst that could happen then was that the exchange rate wouldn't change, with no loss to the speculator other than interest and transaction costs. If a devaluation was forced, then there would be a large gain on a brief investment.

The Bretton Woods agreement was undermined by currency speculation and chronic trade deficits.

To preserve the exchange rate, the beleaguered nation had to buy (at a high price) from the very speculators who were causing most of the trouble. When the nation's foreign currency reserves were exhausted and no more of the weak currency could be absorbed, devaluation gave large profits to these speculators and losses to the government. The rapid, aggressive international flow of funds meant that a nation did not, in fact, have much time to take the fundamental economic steps necessary to strengthen its currency.

2. Nations were too often unwilling to take these necessary steps. Consider again the law of one price, and assume that the domestic country's currency is overvalued at the existing exchange rate:

$$P_d > eP_f$$

The domestic country's products are overpriced, and this country will run persistent balance-of-trade deficits. If the existing exchange rate is to be preserved, then at least one of the following must occur:

1. The domestic country must accept a deflation.
2. Its foreign trading partners must accept an inflation.
3. Governments must continue to accumulate the domestic country's over-valued currency.

In practice, governments had little enthusiasm for any of these options. Stable exchange rates are possible only when nations pursue mutually consistent economic policies. In the absence of such international coordination and co-operation, fixed exchange rates cannot persist — a lesson painfully learned in the quarter century following the Bretton Woods agreement. We will review some of those instructive crises, and then look at the eventual retreat to flexible exchange rates.

The Fall of Bretton Woods

Under the Bretton Woods agreement, currency prices were specified in terms of gold, although the governments sold gold only to each other (and not to their citizens) at these official prices. These gold prices were used to set the implicit currency exchange rates. For example, the U.S. gold price was $35 an ounce and the initial English gold price was 8.75 British pounds per ounce, so that the fixed exchange rate was $4.00 per British pound:

$$\frac{35 \text{ dollars/ounce}}{8.75 \text{ pounds/ounce}} = 4 \frac{\text{dollars}}{\text{pounds}}$$

The specification of all currency prices in terms of another item, here gold, allows a nation confronted with a trade deficit to simultaneously devalue its currency against all other currencies. In 1949, the English gold price was raised to 12.5 British pounds per ounce, reducing the pound's exchange rate with respect to all fixed currencies by 30 percent. For example, the U.S.–English exchange rate fell 30 percent to $2.80 per British pound.

The United States played a crucial role in this arrangement because it had the strongest economy and owned three-fourths of the western world's monetary gold. United States dollars served as the world's money. Dollars were used for many transactions and held as reserves by most central banks. The U.S. dollar took its place alongside gold as an internationally accepted medium of exchange and as evidence that a central bank had something solid behind its currency.

One aspect of this special niche was that nations used dollars to support their exchange rates. If the British pound was weak, the Bank of England would use some of its U.S. dollar reserves to buy up British pounds and thereby support the price of the pound relative to other currencies. Whereas nations had before redeemed their paper currencies with gold, they now redeemed them with U.S. dollars. Thus the United States did not have to use foreign reserves to stabilize dollar exchange rates, because other nations stabilized their currencies relative to the dollar. The second aspect of the United States' special role was that all nations were keenly interested in the soundness of the U.S. dollar. Because they were holding dollars to serve like gold in backing up their currencies, central bankers wanted the dollar to be, in fact, as good as gold.

The Bretton Woods system worked tolerably well through the 1950s. The British pound and several other currencies had been initially overvalued but were devalued in 1949. Through the 1950s, Britain, Italy, and several smaller countries seemed to have chronic difficulties, but at least the system held together. However, in the 1960s people began to wonder aloud if the U.S. dollar really was as good as gold, at least at $35 an ounce.

The United States had been steadily supplying dollars to the world and exchanging gold for some of these dollars. By 1960, the foreign liquid short-term claims against the United States exceeded the value of the U.S. gold stock (at $35 an ounce). Because the United States no longer had enough gold to meet these foreign claims, many expected the U.S. dollar to be devalued against gold.

On the London and Zurich gold markets, the price of privately traded gold reached $40 an ounce. This was unnerving to many central bankers and tempting to a few who contemplated buying gold from the United States at $35 an ounce and reselling it privately for $40. To remove this anxiety and temptation, the United States and the leading Western European nations formed a "gold pool" syndicate to peg the free market price of gold at $35 an ounce by committing their resources to buy or sell gold at this price. To drive the price down from $40, they had to sell some of their gold. The gold pool managed to hold the market gold price at $35 an ounce until 1968, largely because the private gold market was very thin, with light trading, while governments held enormous gold reserves.

In 1968, the level of wholesale and consumer prices in the United States was about twice what it had been when the Bretton Woods agreement was signed and three times what it had been when Franklin Roosevelt set the price of gold at $35 an ounce in 1934. It would have been pretty surprising if the free-market price of gold hadn't also increased by 1968. In March 1968, U.S. inflation and the flow of dollars abroad to pay for the Vietnam War finally burst the $35 lid. In the preceding six months, the gold pool had been forced to sell $4 billion in gold; with a 60 percent share in the pool, $2.5 billion of that had come from the United States.

There seemed to be only three options: (1) the central banks could sell the rest of their gold, (2) the United States could have a domestic deflation, or (3) the market price of gold could be allowed to rise. They chose the third option. An emergency two-tier system was established. One tier was the private gold market; the second was the monetary gold market in which governments traded gold with each other at the official fixed price. The United States continued to sell gold for "legitimate monetary uses" at $35 an ounce and continued to lose gold reserves. Undoubtedly, many governments thought gold was a bargain at this price, and some may have sold gold in the forbidden private market.

The free-market price of gold unexpectedly fell below $35 an ounce in 1969 and then abruptly shot upward in the fall of 1971. The U.S. Treasury suspended gold sales to foreign governments in August 1971 and temporarily allowed the dollar to float in foreign-exchange markets. It was expected that the dollar would be devalued and that the Bretton Woods agreement could then be revived at new, more realistic exchange rates.

An emergency conference was held at the Smithsonian Institution in Washington, D.C., in December 1971, with President Richard Nixon hailing the resulting agreements as the greatest monetary reform in the history of mankind. This was somewhat of an overstatement. The official U.S. price of gold was raised to $38 an ounce, though the United States would continue not to sell gold. The official gold prices of other major currencies were also raised, the net effect being that the U.S. dollar was devalued about 12 percent relative to other currencies. Governments agreed to support these new currency exchange rates, allowing fluctuations within a 5 percent range.

In February 1973, the dollar had to be devalued again, this time raising the official price of gold to $42.22 an ounce and, in March 1973, fixed exchange rates were finally abandoned. Figure 2.1 in Chapter 2 shows that the market price of gold increased dramatically in the 1970s, reaching a high of $850 an ounce in January 1980, before falling back to the $300–$500 range where it traded during most of the 1980s.

Since 1973, the major exchange rates have floated.

Since 1973, the major exchange rates have been determined in the open market. (Most small countries have kept their currencies pegged to major currencies.) Because governments still intervene in exchange markets to stabilize their currency, to support its value, or to devalue it to encourage exports, this is called a "managed" or "dirty" float. We will now look briefly at how flexible exchange rates work.

FLEXIBLE EXCHANGE RATES

Under the gold standard, the trading of currencies was fairly uneventful — just a routine swapping of one currency for another using the fixed exchange rate. With flexible exchange rates, the currency market is the largest — and perhaps the most volatile — market in the world, with prices often changing by more than 5 percent in a single day.

The Foreign-Exchange Market

Unlike the trading of corporate stock on the New York Stock Exchange, the foreign-exchange market is not in a single physical location in which traders meet face to face; instead, traders are scattered throughout the world and trade currencies using telephones and computer terminals. Among the participants are importers who need foreign currency to pay for products, exporters who want to convert the foreign currency they receive into domestic currency, hedgers who

Currencies are traded using telephones and computers, usually through banks.

Highlight 3.4   Currency Traders

It does not require a college degree to be a trader. It does require an ability to think quickly and act decisively. Traders continually look for currencies that appear overvalued or undervalued by various criteria, including purchasing-power parity. When economic news is reported on a country's balance of trade, rate of inflation, or interest rates, traders are like gunslingers in a shootout, trying to trade within very short periods of time — perhaps only a few seconds — before other traders learn of the news.

In many other occupations, job interviewers look for people who are mature, responsible, and personable. However, interviews for trading jobs are often intense grillings, designed to test the applicant's ability to perform under pressure. One company routinely asks "What's the price of a $400 table that has been marked down 40 percent?" Anyone who takes more than a second to answer is disqualified. One company pays particular attention to how long it takes the job candidate to order lunch: those who ask if the fish is fresh or linger over the wine list are rejected. Another company leaves the candidate sitting in a secretary's office while the interviewer signs papers and talks on the phone, waiting to see how impatient the candidate becomes. Those who are soon disgusted and berate the interviewer's rudeness pass this test.

Many currency traders come to work before the sun comes up and leaves after it has gone down, spending 12–18 hours in between monitoring economic news and currency prices around the world and making trades. Some routinely make or lose more than a million dollars a day. Because of the physical and mental demands of the job, the average currency trader is less than thirty years old. After several years of intense pressure, traders are either promoted to management positions or leave the industry, professionally burned out.

do business internationally and want to protect themselves against unforeseen fluctuations in the prices of foreign goods and services, and speculators who want to bet on the movement of currency prices.

Most trades are made through banks. A 1986 Federal Reserve survey of one hundred large U.S. banks found that their foreign currency trades totaled about $60 billion a day. Worldwide, total currency trading exceeds $200 billion a day, more than twenty-five times the daily volume of exports of goods and services. The largest trading centers are London, New York, Tokyo, Frankfurt, and Singapore. The traded currencies are not carried from one country to another. Instead, bank accounts are debited and credited.

Suppose, for instance, that a U.S. importer owes 1,000,000 francs to a French exporter and that the current exchange rate is 0.15 dollars/franc, so that

Table 3.3 How Money Changes Hands

(U.S. importers do not mail dollars to French exporters; instead, a French bank receives dollar deposits in a U.S. bank and credits the exporter with a deposit of francs.)

U.S. Bank Deposits		French Bank Deposits	
U.S. importer	−$150,000	French exporter	+1,000,000 francs
French bank	+$150,000		

the cost of 1,000,000 francs is $150,000. The U.S. bank used by the importer buys 1,000,000 francs from the French bank used by the exporter. Table 3.3 shows that this $150,000 does not leave the United States; the U.S. bank simply debits $150,000 from the importer's account and credits it to the French bank, while the French bank credits 1,000,000 francs to the exporter's account. The French bank now has a $150,000 deposit in the U.S. bank that it can use to earn interest or to fulfill obligations from French importers. The two banks might even be international branches of the same bank.

If the French bank does not want to hold a deposit of U.S. dollars because it fears they will depreciate, it can sell these dollars for francs, or for another currency that it hopes will appreciate in value. This transaction will involve a debiting of its dollar account at the U.S. bank and a crediting to the account of the party that buys these dollars, at either this bank or another one. Major banks continually make these portfolio adjustments, reducing their holdings of some currencies and increasing their holdings of others. Fewer than 10 percent of their currency trades are for corporate accounts; 90 percent are trades among banks.

For simplicity, prices are almost always quoted in terms of the U.S. dollar — for example, 0.50 dollars per deutschemark or 2.00 deutschemarks per dollar — and trades generally involve dollars. A bank that wants to trade deutschemarks for yen sells marks for dollars and simultaneously buys yen with these dollars, because this is easier than trying to find someone who wants to trade yen for marks. Just as each nation's currency is a medium of exchange that avoids the inefficiencies of barter, so U.S. dollars are an international medium of exchange. The prices in many international contracts, such as European imports of oil from Saudi Arabia and Japanese imports of beef from Australia, are also specified in terms of U.S. dollars.

Spot prices for currency are for immediate delivery (within the next two days). **Forward prices** are prices agreed to today but not paid until a specified future delivery date, usually within a year; these might be used by an importer who has agreed to pay a certain amount of foreign currency for a product and wants to guarantee the cost in terms of domestic currency. A **swap** is an agreement to sell a currency at a stated price and then repurchase it at a stated

Spot prices are for immediate delivery, forward prices for future delivery.

price on a specified future date, with the difference between the sale and repurchase price called the **swap rate**. For instance, a New York bank might swap marks for dollars with a West German bank by agreeing to sell marks at a price of 0.50 dollars per mark on February 1 and to repurchase the deutschemarks at a price of 0.52 dollars per mark on March 1; thus the New York bank temporarily borrows some dollars and the German bank borrows marks.

The Effects of Exchange Rates on Economic Activity

The primary advantage of floating exchange rates is that they break the impasse created by inconsistent domestic economic policies. If there are differing rates of inflation in two countries, these can be offset by a simple devaluation of the currency of the nation with the more rapid inflation.

Recall again the purchasing-power-parity equation, which can be written

$$\frac{1}{e} = \frac{P_f}{P_d}$$

If we label the United States the domestic country, then movements in its exchange rate with another currency (measured in terms of the amount of foreign currency needed to purchase a dollar) depend on whether the second country's inflation is more rapid than that of the United States. If, for example, the second country is Germany and its prices increase faster than those in the United States, purchasing power parity can be maintained by an increase in $1/e$ — a devaluation of the German currency, in that it will take more marks to buy a dollar.

Figure 3.2 compares the changes in exchange rates and consumer prices for twenty western industrial nations from 1974 to 1988, using the United States as the benchmark domestic nation. The horizontal axis is the percentage change in P_f/P_d, with a positive value showing that there was a larger increase in consumer prices in this country than in the United States. The vertical axis is the percentage change in $1/e$, with a positive value showing a devaluation of this country's currency relative to the dollar. We shouldn't expect this comparison to be perfect, because it is impractical to trade many items included in the index of consumer prices and because central banks intervene in exchange markets. Nonetheless, the correlation is striking.

While purchasing power parity may be approximated in the long run, it does not hold in the short run. Exchange rates rise and fall daily, not to equate international commodity prices but because speculators think that one currency is a more attractive investment than another. In later chapters, we will look at the details of exchange-rate determination. For now, we observe that changes in exchange rates have real economic effects: the depreciation of a country's currency reduces the price of its exports and raises the price of its imports; currency appreciation has the opposite effects. Figure 3.1 earlier in the chapter showed that the value of the U.S. dollar rose relative to the Japanese yen and European

Purchasing power parity may be approximated in the long run, but not in the short run.

Figure 3.2   Inflation and Exchange Rates, Relative to the United States, 1974–88

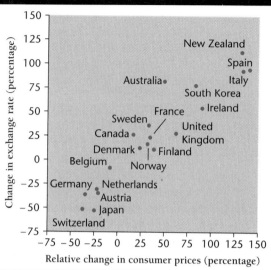

currencies by about 40 percent between 1980 and 1985, making U.S. products very expensive, and then fell by more than 30 percent between 1985 and 1987, making U.S. products inexpensive. Such swings buffet exporters, importers, and makers of competing products for reasons beyond their control.

Suppose that a Japanese automaker needs to sell a certain car for 2 million yen in order to cover its production costs. If, as in 1975, the exchange rate is 300 yen per dollar, it must price this car at

$$\frac{2,000,000 \text{ yen}}{300 \text{ yen/dollar}} = \$6,667$$

Fluctuating exchange rates have real economic effects.

to break even. If, on the other hand, the exchange rate is 200 yen per dollar (as in 1980), then the break-even price is

$$\frac{2,000,000 \text{ yen}}{200 \text{ yen/dollar}} = \$10,000$$

At a 250 yen per dollar exchange rate (as in 1982), the break-even price is $8,000; at 125 yen per dollar (as in 1988), it is $16,000. The Japanese automaker will make large, unexpected profits or losses — simply because of changes in the value of the yen relative to the U.S. dollar.

Similarly, when the value of the British pound fell from $2.45 in October 1980 to $1.12 in January 1985, Americans flocked to England looking for bargains. Harrods, a famous London department store, advertised its post-Christmas sale in the *New York Times* and reported a 21 percent increase in sales. One

American couple flew to London for a single whirlwind day of shopping, explaining that they saved more than enough to pay for their airplane tickets.[3]

A dirty float allows one nation's economic policies to affect those of other nations. For example, the German central bank might buy U.S. dollars and sell deutschemarks to reduce the price of marks in terms of U.S. dollars. This would encourage U.S. imports from Germany and discourage U.S. exports, in each case reducing the sales of U.S. producers. This might well provoke the U.S. monetary authorities to buy deutschemarks with dollars. A dirty float can become pretty vicious.

Nonetheless, flexible exchange rates have worked tolerably well during two decades of enormous financial upheaval with large trade imbalances and lightning capital mobility. Unprecedented increases in oil prices in 1973–74 and 1979–80 created hundreds of billions of dollars of balance-of-trade surpluses and deficits. The economies of many poorer nations might easily have been crushed by their inability to pay for oil and oil-related imports. The IMF, World Bank, and private banks have so far averted such national collapses by lending funds from trade-surplus nations to trade-deficit nations.

The IMF did this directly, borrowing heavily from Arab oil-exporting countries and lending to oil-importing nations. The OPEC nations also deposited large amounts in Western banks, and these banks simultaneously lent hundreds of billions of dollars to oil-importing nations. It remains to be seen whether these loans can be repaid. If they cannot, the potential financial default will surely rock the entire world.

The other lingering international-finance nightmare is that speculative bubbles or panics will develop, with adverse effects on real economic activity. Tens of trillions of dollars' worth of foreign exchange trades are now made annually, far more than needed to carry out international transactions. Most of these trades are for speculative purposes — buying currencies that are expected to appreciate and selling those expected to depreciate. Does international trade need to be protected from speculative bubbles and currency crashes?

SUMMARY

The exchange rate is the price of one currency in terms of another. Domestic prices, foreign prices, and exchange rates are roughly linked through purchasing power parity, an application of the law of one price. Although purchasing power parity does not hold exactly, at least in the short run, this concept is helpful in remembering the direction in which prices and exchange rates move.

The international gold standard pegged exchange rates. This system, and the modified Bretton Woods plan, broke down because nations were unwilling to sacrifice domestic economic stability in order to hold exchange rates constant. Since March 1973, the major exchange rates have been determined in the foreign-exchange market — a large, volatile international market in which currencies are traded, usually among banks, using telephones and computer terminals.

| Bargain Hunting for California Real Estate | Highlight 3.5 |

In 1987, the manager of McKinsey & Co.'s Tokyo office argued that changes in the dollar-yen exchange rate had made the United States a bargain basement for Japanese investors.* As an example, he related how a 1,500-square-foot apartment in Tokyo bought for $500,000 in 1982 was worth $8 million in 1987; using this property as collateral, the owner then borrowed $1 million and bought a five-bedroom waterfront house in Southern California.

The exchange rate was around 250 yen per dollar in 1982 and below 125 yen per dollar at the end of 1987. This Japanese apartment was worth one billion yen in 1987, which converts to $4 million at an exchange rate of 125 yen per dollar, but $8 million at the 1987 exchange rate of 250 yen per dollar.

The vast difference in home prices in Japan and the United States reflects the fact that the law of one price does not apply to real estate, because shelter is not a traded good. Even though the Japanese can purchase U.S. real estate and Americans can buy Japanese property, these are hardly perfect substitutes, because it is impractical for a Tokyo businessman to sell his cramped Tokyo apartment and commute to work from Southern California.

*Kenichi Ohmae, "Low Dollar Means U.S. Has Become Bargain Basement," *Wall Street Journal*, November 30, 1987.

Floating exchange rates help maintain the law of one price created when one country's prices increase faster than another's. But, because purchasing-power parity does not hold in the short run, changes in foreign-exchange prices have real economic effects. A currency depreciation reduces the price of a country's exports and raises the price of its imports; currency appreciation has the opposite effects. Flexible exchange rates have worked tolerably well since 1973, though there is some concern that fluctuating rates caused by speculative activity in the foreign-exchange market disrupt international trade and foreign investment.

IMPORTANT TERMS

bimetallic standard
Bretton Woods agreement
currency appreciation
currency depreciation

exchange rate
forward prices
gold standard
International Monetary Fund (IMF)

law of one price
London Interbank Offered Rate (LIBOR)
nontraded
purchasing power parity

Special Drawing Rights (SDRs)
spot prices
swap

EXERCISES

1. Use the data in Table 3.1 to determine these September 8, 1989, exchange rates:
   a. yen per mark
   b. francs per pound
   c. pounds per franc

2. Look in the most recent Friday edition of *The Wall Street Journal* and report the current exchange rates (U.S. dollars per currency) for the British pound, French franc, Japanese yen, and German mark. In comparison with the September 1989 prices that are shown in Table 3.1, which of these four currencies have appreciated relative to the U.S. dollar, and which have depreciated?

3. Look in the most recent Friday edition of *The Wall Street Journal* and report the current exchange rates (U.S. dollars per currency) for the Israeli shekel, South Korean won, and Swiss franc. What is the price of the shekel in terms of won (wons per shekel)? Of the franc in terms of shekels (shekels per franc)?

4. On October 20, 1989, the Canadian–U.S. and the Mexican–U.S. exchange rates were 0.8515 U.S. dollars per the Canadian dollar and 0.0003846 U.S. dollars per the Mexican peso. How many pesos did it take to buy a U.S. dollar? To buy a Canadian dollar?

5. Look in the most recent Friday edition of *The Wall Street Journal* and report the current exchange rates (U.S. dollars per currency) for the Canadian dollar and Mexican peso. In comparison with the October 20, 1989, prices given in Exercise 4, which of these three currencies have appreciated and which have depreciated relative to each of the others?

6. The Reagan administration tried to reduce the U.S. trade deficit by encouraging U.S. exports to Japan and discouraging U.S. imports from Japan. Did it try to raise or lower the value of the dollar relative to the yen?

7. How would you explain the observation that follows?[4]

   Today, almost anything made in France can be profitably sold in the United States. Four years ago, almost nothing made in France could be sold profitably in the United States.

8. A September 1986 survey by *The Economist* of the worldwide prices of Big Mac hamburgers found that the price was 1.60 dollars in the United States and 90 francs in Belgium.[5] At the time, the exchange rate was 0.0238 dollars per franc. What was the implied price of a Big Mac in the United States in Belgian francs and the price in Belgium in dollars? For purchasing power parity for Big Macs, should the dollar have appreciated or depreciated relative to the franc?

9. Use the 1986 local prices of Big Macs and the actual exchange rates (dollars per local currency) in Table 3.2 to calculate the dollar price of a Big Mac in each of the countries in the table. In which of these countries was the 1986 dollar price of a Big Mac more than the $1.60 U.S. price?

   Here are some comparable data from April 1988 (Brazilian data were unavailable):[6]

	Local Price, P_f	Exchange Rate (Dollars per Local Currency)
Australia (dollar)	1.95	1.36
Canada (dollar)	2.05	0.80

France (franc)	17.30	0.18
Hong Kong (dollar)	7.60	0.13
Japan (yen)	370	0.0081
Sweden (krona)	18.50	0.17
United States (dollar)	2.39	——
West Germany (mark)	4.10	0.60

In which of these countries was the 1988 dollar price of the Big Mac more than the $2.39 U.S. price? Were these the same countries as in 1986?

10. Between 1873 and 1896, wholesale prices fell by approximately 50 percent in the United States, the United Kingdom, Germany, and France — four countries on the gold standard. How would you explain the fact that prices in each of these four countries changed by roughly the same amount in this period? What do you predict would have happened if, instead, wholesale prices in the United States had been unchanged, while prices in the other three countries fell by 50 percent?

11. Here are some data comparing three nations' exchange rates in terms of the U.S. dollar in 1974 and 1988:

	1974	1988
Iceland (krona)	0.99	43.03
Taiwan (dollar)	38.0	28.5
Turkey (lira)	14	1419

If purchasing power parity held in 1974 and 1988, which of these countries had more rapid inflation than the United States between 1974 and 1988?

12. During the 10-year period 1976–85, the average rates of inflation were 13.0 percent in New Zealand, 4.7 percent in the Netherlands, and 7.3 percent in the United States. For purchasing-power parity to hold from 1976 to 1985, should the New Zealand dollar and the Netherlands guilder have appreciated or depreciated relative to the U.S. dollar during this period?

13. Table 3.1 shows an exchange rate of 147 Japanese yen for 1 U.S. dollar in September 1989. Were speculators who bought dollars and sold yen betting that this exchange rate would rise above 147 or fall below 147?

14. In 1985, many economists argued that the U.S. dollar was too strong, in that foreign goods were too cheap and U.S. goods too expensive. How could they have used foreign-exchange markets to bet this belief?

15. Between 1976 and 1988, consumer prices increased at an average annual rate of 8.60 percent in the United Kingdom and 6.28 percent in the United States. If purchasing-power parity held in 1976, should the U.S. dollar have strengthened or weakened relative to the British pound during this 12-year period? The exchange rate was virtually constant, at 1.80 dollars per pound in 1976 and 1.78 dollars per pound in 1988. Do these data suggest that the U.S. dollar was overvalued or undervalued relative to the British pound in 1988?

16. The Canadian consumer price index increased from 41.5 in 1974 to 113.1 in 1988; the United States consumer price index increased from 45.8 to 109.9 over this same period. According to the theory of purchasing power parity, what percentage change in the exchange rate (U.S. dollars per Canadian dollar) should have occurred between 1974 and 1988? In fact, the exchange rate was 1.0224 in 1974 and 0.8125 in 1988. If purchasing power parity held in 1974, do these data suggest that the Canadian dollar was overvalued or undervalued relative to the U.S. dollar in 1988? Should a speculator who wanted to act on the basis of these calculations have bought U.S. dollars and sold Canadian dollars, or the other way around?

17. Why do you suppose nations generally avoid barter transactions, such as directly trading American Coca-Cola for French wine?

18. Explain the logic behind this argument in a 1990 *Wall Street Journal* editorial:

The Japanese deserve credit for being canny enough to understand that a strong currency, allowing you to buy more, is better than a weak currency, allowing you to sell more.[7]

19. Comment on the following quotation:[8]

International currency stabilization will, however, only be possible when national economies are stable — when the industrial countries have succeeded in combining reasonably high employment with tolerably stable prices. Until then all talk of international currency reform will be in a vacuum and can safely be ignored except by those whose employment depends on the discussion.

20. Critically evaluate the following analysis:

Their leaders do not talk about it much, but a strong dollar carries some important benefits to the Europeans. While their imports cost more, their exports carry lower prices on foreign markets. That makes their goods more competitive around the world, and many economists believe Europe will gain in the end because increasing exports just as surely produces jobs as increasing domestic consumption.[9]

21. Fuji Bank's chief currency trader lost $48 million during four months in 1984 when he sold forward contracts agreeing to trade dollars for yen at a specified exchange rate on a given future date. Was he betting that the value of the dollar would rise or fall relative to the yen during this period?

22. After the United States suspended gold sales in 1971 and allowed the dollar to float, many nations bought U.S. dollars to keep the values of their currencies low. Why do you suppose they wanted their currency to be inexpensive?

23. During the three-year period that the following news story describes, did the value of the British pound rise or fall in relation to other currencies?[10]

British exporters find their products much more competitive in the international marketplace. . . . Three years ago . . . some companies . . . went out of business because they were unable to match foreign prices.

24. In March 1987, a real estate columnist wrote that[11]

Everybody in the business was struck by the prices the Japanese paid for some trophy properties last year — $610 million for the Exxon Building. . . . [F]ew have remembered the plunge of the dollar against the yen. That decline of 55 percent in value in 16 months has made U.S. property look especially cheap in Japanese eyes; applying that arithmetic to the prices paid means that Shuwa really laid out $274.5 million for the Exxon Building — less than what the seller would have gotten from an American institution.

Did the Japanese pay $610 million or $274.5 million for the Exxon building?

25. Explain how the following divergence is possible: "The dollar value of such imports [of Japanese goods into the U.S.] during February equaled $7.1 billion versus $6.1 billion a year ago and $5.1 billion two years ago. In yen terms, our imports from Japan are down 3.9 percent from a year ago and 17.3 percent from two years ago."[12]

BANK MONEY

AND

OTHER MONEYS

It is a singular and, indeed, a significant fact that, although money was the first economic subject to attract men's thoughtful attention, and has been the focal centre of economic investigation ever since, there is at the present day not even an approximate agreement as to what ought to be designated by the word. The business world makes use of the term in several senses, while among economists there are almost as many different conceptions as there are writers upon money.

A. P. Andrew

Most stores will sell you things even if you do not have a pocketful of coins and currency. You can use a traveler's check, a personal check, a credit card, or (if you are a familiar customer) a personal IOU. Which of these, and what else, should be labeled "money"?

As the epigraph (from 1899!) above indicates, there has long been disagreement about the proper definition of money. This debate is still unresolved, and data are currently collected on many different measures of a nation's money — called monetary aggregates. As financial markets have evolved, new aggregates have been constructed and old aggregates revised. In the 1950s, M1 and M2 were very popular. Then financial market innovations led observers to concoct M1+, M2', M3, M4, M5, and on and on. The list grew as the years went by. In some circles, double-digit Ms became popular.

In 1980, as the historic Depository Institutions Deregulation and Monetary Control Act neared completion, the Federal Reserve switched to a substantially revised set of aggregates: M1A, M1B, M2, M3, and L. Soon they added M1B–Shift Adjusted; then M1A dropped from view and M1B became M1. This bewildering plethora of monetary aggregates creates considerable difficulties for both serious and casual observers of monetary developments. As is the case with many popular songs, by the time you learn the words of the song, they are no longer popular.

One important lesson is that there is no firm, fixed definition of "money." There are temporary definitions of alternative monetary aggregates, because there is an evolving continuum of financial assets and no compelling reason to single out a specific aggregation of these assets as all-important. For any particular definition of money, there are other financial assets, near-moneys, that are not very different from those assets that are labeled "money." In addition, definitions of money have changed over the years, and they will undoubtedly continue to change in the future. Instead of restricting our attention to some artificially precise definition of money, we should look at several different types of financial assets.

BANK MONEY

Banks began as places to store precious metal.

Chapter 1 explained that commercial banks are financial intermediaries that accept deposits and make loans. Although banking existed as far back as Roman times, the first major public bank was established in Amsterdam in 1609. As a busy trading center, Amsterdam was flooded with foreign coins of widely varying quality. The Bank of Amsterdam was established to assay these coins and store the precious metals. There was no need for the metal to leave the bank and pass from hand to hand, because merchants could conduct business by simply instructing the bank to transfer funds among accounts. For many years, the bank stored deposits and kept accurate records. Eventually, the bank loaned some of its coins to the City of Amsterdam and to the prosperous Dutch East India Company. When prosperity faded and these loans were not repaid, anxious merchants tried to withdraw their coins, and the bank folded in 1819. The collapse of the bank and the evaporation of the merchants' presumed deposits depressed business and commerce.

This drama has been played out many times in many different places. Another notable episode occurred in eighteenth-century France. A Scotsman, John Law, had greatly impressed the Regent for the seven-year-old Louis XV with his gambling prowess. In 1716 he was permitted to establish what was to be known as the Banque Royale. The bank's primary function was to make loans to the hard-pressed government. The bank accepted deposits and printed notes that were declared legal tender and used as a medium of exchange. Law promised redemption in precious metal and declared that bankers with insufficient metal reserves deserved death.

With time, the bank's size and fame multiplied. It was given the tobacco monopoly, the right to coin money and collect the government's taxes, and exclusive trading privileges in China, India, and the South Seas. It planned to extract vast amounts of gold from Louisiana. Money poured into the bank from deposits and stock sales and flowed out as loans to private entrepreneurs and a rapacious government. Citizens owning deposits and stock counted these as wealth. When their deposits were recycled as bank notes borrowed and spent by the government, these were once again counted as wealth.

A thrifty citizen, Jean, might deposit 1,000 livres in the bank. This money would be promptly lent to the government and used to pay some of its tiresome expenses. Jeanne, who receives this payment from the government, can then redeposit the 1,000-livre note in the bank. Now two citizens, Jean and Jeanne, each have 1,000-livre deposits. As the note is loaned out, spent, and redeposited again and again, the citizens' money and wealth seem to expand indefinitely. Such imagined largess was good for spirit and for business. Law was proclaimed a financial genius and became the most respected person in France. He was appointed the Comptroller General of France and ennobled as the first, and only, Duc d'Arkansas.

Early banks that printed unbacked notes were usually profitable but often failed.

The problem was that the actual assets of the Banque were far smaller than the presumed value of the deposits and stock. The government had no hope of repaying its vast borrowings with precious metal, and gold had hardly been looked for, let alone discovered, in the Louisiana swamps. In 1720, suspicious, then worried, and ultimately panicky depositors tried to redeem their notes in hard money. On one frantic day 15 people were reported to have been killed in the crush of anxious note holders. The bank failed. Law fled to Venice, narrowly escaping the Paris mob. With so much apparent wealth evaporated, business and commerce sagged heavily.[1]

> *Of all the nations in the world the French are the most renowned for singing over their grievances . . . the streets resounded with songs . . . one . . . in particular counseled the application of . . . [the Banque's] notes to the most ignoble use to which paper can be applied.*

A Short History of U.S. Bank Money

At Alexander Hamilton's urging, the Bank of the United States was founded in 1791, with $2 million raised from the federal government and $8 million from private citizens. Modeled after the Bank of England, its eight branches stored private and government funds and made loans to citizens and to the government. It also issued bank notes that circulated as a medium of exchange and were exchangeable on demand for gold or silver. There were fewer than a hundred other banks in operation, all smaller and located on the east coast. From its favored position as holder and disburser of government funds, the Bank of the United States made loans to other banks caught short of funds. It also encouraged sound banking practices by refusing to honor bank notes that were not convertible to gold or silver on demand.

Less-privileged banks were envious of and sometimes hostile to the Bank of the United States. Agrarian interests were suspicious of all banks. Thomas Jefferson wrote in a letter to John Adams:[2]

> I have ever been the enemy of banks; not of those discounting for cash; but of those foisting their own paper into circulation, and thus banishing our cash. My zeal against those institutions was so warm and open at the establishment of the Bank of the U.S. that I was derided as a maniac by the tribe of bank-mongers, who were seeking to filch from the public their swindling, and barren gains. . . . Shall we build an altar to the old paper money of the revolution, which ruined individuals but saved the republic; and burn on that all the bank charters present and future, and their notes with them? For these are to ruin both republic and individuals.

The original and second Bank of the United States each lasted 20 years.

In 1810, by a narrow vote, Congress failed to renew the charter of the Bank of the United States, and it closed. In the succeeding ten years, state banks and bank notes of varying repute multiplied. One historian wrote that "corporations and tradesmen issued 'currency.' Even barbers and bartenders competed with banks in this respect . . . nearly every citizen regarded it as his constitutional right to issue money."[3] One successful midwestern banker related his start in the business: "Well, I didn't have much to do and so I rented an empty store and painted 'bank' on the window. The first day a man came in and deposited $100, and a couple of days later, another man deposited another $250 and so along about the fourth day I got confidence enough in the bank to put in $1.00 myself."[4]

Despite his belief that banks and paper money were immoral and that a federally chartered bank was unconstitutional, President James Madison proposed a national bank to rein in the reckless banks. In 1816, the Second Bank of the United States was chartered. It was larger than the first, but less interested in restraining fellow banks. It actively speculated, particularly in Western land, and its Baltimore branch made so many bad loans that it went bankrupt in 1818. In 1819, a new head of the Second Bank reduced its speculative activities by restricting new loans and by forcing some borrowers to pay off old ones, putting a discernible crimp in commerce. As one writer put it, "The Bank was saved and the people ruined."[5] The next president of the Second Bank, Nicholas Biddle, reinstituted the First Bank's policy of refusing to accept bank notes that were not redeemable in gold or silver.

The fight to renew the Bank's charter in 1832 was bitter. (Both Biddle's brother, the director of the St. Louis branch, and an antagonist were shot and killed in a duel — fought at a distance of only five feet because of Biddle's nearsightedness.) The populist president Andrew Jackson removed government deposits from the bank and vetoed a bill renewing its charter. Rechartered by the state of Pennsylvania, Biddle's bank was closed in 1839 after excessive speculation and questionable loans to bank officers.

After the restraining power of the Second Bank of the United States was lifted, there was a surge of new banks and of unbacked bank notes. The older, established banks in the East were typically managed conservatively, with substantial reserves of gold and silver, and a readiness to redeem their notes with precious metal. Banks in other parts of the country were more loosely managed and willing to loan unbacked paper to farmers and businessmen settling new territories. When the land was fertile and business good, the communities and their banks prospered; when crops and businesses failed, their banks failed with them.

Banks were regulated by the states in which they operated. In 1837 the Supreme Court ruled that the Constitutional ban against state-issued money did not prohibit the issuance of notes by state-owned banks. Such banks consequently spread across the country. In addition, thousands of private banks were established by financiers, blacksmiths, trading-post owners, and other banking entrepreneurs. State regulations regarding precious-metal reserves were unevenly enforced. A bank in conservative Massachusetts with $500,000 in notes outstanding was found to have $86.48 in reserves. In liberal Michigan, a common collection of reserves (including hidden lead, glass, and ten-penny nails) passed from bank to bank ahead of the state examiners.

Loosely regulated bank notes proliferated in the 1800s.

By the time of the Civil War, there were some 7,000 different types of bank notes in circulation, of which 5,000 were counterfeit issues. With the South and the Mississippi Valley not represented in Congress, legislation enacted in 1863 and 1864 created a system of nationally chartered and regulated banks. Congress levied a 1 percent, then a 2 percent, then in 1865 a 10 percent annual tax on state bank notes. State bank notes consequently declined, replaced by checking accounts. Banks that applied for and received national charters issued national bank notes, which were more uniformly printed and were backed by government bonds deposited with the Treasury. Federally chartered banks were required to hold 25 percent reserves against deposits.

In 1914, after a series of financial crises, Congress established the Federal Reserve System, which we will examine in detail in later chapters. Nationally chartered banks were required to join the system, and in 1935 their power to issue national bank notes was revoked. Banks today cannot print money, though they can create deposits that serve as money, thereby multiplying the money supply.

How Banks Multiply the Money Supply

Governments create fiat money simply by printing it and declaring that it is legal tender. Redemptions can be satisfied by printing more of the same — two $5 bills for every $10 bill. As long as nothing more is promised, governments need never fear a "run," with anxious citizens rushing to redeem their currency. Banks multiply the money supply a bit more mysteriously and much more dangerously. A run on the bank is the banker's nightmare.

The Bank of Amsterdam, as we have seen, began in the seventeenth century by assaying and storing funds, which then sat gathering dust. For such a bank, there is no danger of a bank run and bankruptcy, as long as there are sufficiently strong safes and personnel to guard the deposits. If all banks operated in this fashion — simply keeping records and guarding a safe full of safe-deposit boxes — depositors would be completely protected and banks would not multiply the money supply. This kind of system is said to have "100 percent reserves."

You could deposit $100 of government currency in such a bank and receive a bank note certifying that you have $100 stored safely. Your $100 bank receipt replaces $100 of currency and, if your bank receipt is accepted as a medium of exchange, there is no change in the total money supply. There is simply $100 of bank money instead of $100 of government money. If your $100 receipt is not accepted as a medium of exchange, then the bank deposit reduces by $100 the total amount of money in circulation outside banks — as if you had buried the $100 in your backyard.

A bank multiplies money (and risks) when it does not keep all of your $100 deposit in its safe but instead loans some of it. As the fictitious Mr. Dooley once said, a banker "takes care of your money by lending it out to friends." When only a fraction of deposits is kept on hand, this is called **fractional reserve banking**. The fractional reserve is the fraction, α, of your $100 that is kept in reserve at the bank; the remaining fraction, $1 - \alpha$, is lent out. Let's work through the consequences, initially assuming that 10 percent of each deposit is kept on reserve ($\alpha = 0.1$).

Fractional reserve banking multiplies deposits.

You deposit $100, and the bank keeps $10 and loans $90. The person who borrows the $90 undoubtedly has some worthwhile purpose in mind and will soon spend this $90. The seller who receives $90 from the borrower may well decide to deposit it in a bank (perhaps, by coincidence, the very same bank). She is credited with a $90 deposit, and the second bank now has $90 to loan.

If the second bank keeps 10 percent of this $90 and loans out the remaining $81, then this $81 can be spent and deposited in a third bank. A pattern is definitely appearing. In each round, 90 percent of the previous deposit is loaned and then redeposited in a bank. These deposits are $100, $90, $81, and so on. If we look far ahead and use a calculator to add up these deposits, the sum will be found to be $1,000. The sum of the reserves in bank vaults is $10 + 9 + 8.1 + \cdots = 100$. The banking system has multiplied $100 of government money into $1,000 of bank money. Is that magic? No, it's banking.

Banks do not print money. Their assets are the dollars they lend and hold as reserves. Their liabilities are the deposits, their debt to depositors. Their ledgers balance, because every dollar deposited is either loaned out or held as reserves. Table 4.1 demonstrates this formally by using **T-Accounts**, which show the changes in a balance sheet caused by some financial event.

T-Accounts show the changes in balance sheets.

The banks end up with $1,000 in deposits, $900 in loans, and $100 in reserves. As for the banks' customers, depositors have a total of $1,000 in assets, and borrowers have a total of $900 in debts. For the private economy as a whole, net financial wealth is $100, the initial amount of government money. What banks have done, as illustrated in Figure 4.1, is provide a way for some citizens to borrow $900 from other citizens. In this role as intermediary between borrowers and lenders, banks may well stimulate the economy. To the extent that

Table 4.1 Bank T-Accounts for a Sequence of Deposits and Loans

	Assets	Liabilities
First deposit and loan	$10 reserve $90 loan	$100 deposit
Second deposit and loan	$9 reserve $81 loan	$90 deposit
Third deposit and loan	$8.1 reserve $72.9 loan	$81 deposit
⋮	⋮	⋮
Total reserves, deposits, and loans	$100 reserves $900 loans	$1,000 deposits

bank deposits serve as money (for example, checking accounts), banking also facilitates trade.

If there were no banks or other financial intermediaries, borrowers and lenders would both have to agree to the repayment terms. Borrowers generally spend their borrowed money quickly and plan to pay it back in the future. Perhaps one uses the money to open a store and will use the profits from the store to repay the loan. Or a young couple may borrow money to buy a car, a house, or furniture, and repay the loan out of their future wage income. Typically, borrowers do not plan to repay the loan for some time. They prefer a fixed and inviolate repayment schedule or, even better, to decide themselves when to pay off the loan. Lenders have different preferences. They would like to be able to call in the loan and demand repayment whenever they need funds. With this fundamental conflict, there will be relatively few loans and those that are made will require one or both sides to settle for less than they prefer.

One advantage of financial intermediaries is that both borrowers and lenders can be accommodated. Those who borrow from banks receive loans with fixed repayment schedules that are convenient and consistent with their planned use of the funds. Lenders deposit their money in banks and are permitted to withdraw

Financial intermediaries accommodate the different preferences of borrowers and lenders.

Figure 4.1 **Financial Intermediaries Channel Funds from Depositors to Borrowers**

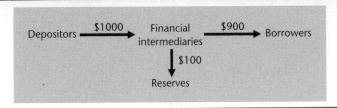

it whenever they please. Both sides are satisfied, and many more loans are made than would occur in the absence of banks. It is because they fulfill this valuable public service that banks throughout history have been so popular, pervasive, and profitable.

The darker side of the coin is that banks succeed only when all depositors do not in fact show up simultaneously to demand their deposits. With a large number of depositors and a reasonable store of reserves, a bank can easily satisfy the occasional depositor who needs funds. As long as depositors believe that their deposits can be claimed at any time, few will actually want to claim them. The danger is that they may lose faith. When depositors think that they may not be able to withdraw their deposits, they will all rush to try. Because the bank is unable to retrieve the loans it has made with their money, it collapses. This is the fundamental tension in banking that has permitted enormous social benefits and caused unforgettable panics. In later chapters, we will look closely at how modern banks — by and large successfully — cope with this tension.

> Bank runs occur when depositors fear that their money cannot be withdrawn.

Deposit Multipliers

We have seen how banks bring together borrowers and lenders and multiply the money supply. Let's look at the details again, this time considering the more general case in which the fractional reserve ratio α is not necessarily 0.1. Of each $1 of government money deposited in a bank, α is held as reserves and $1 - \alpha$ is loaned out. For each individual bank, reserves are a fraction α of deposits. The same is true of the banking system as a whole, so that total reserves are a fraction α of total deposits D. In the simplest deposit-multiplier, all government money B is held as bank reserves; none is held outside banks. The amount of government money B is consequently equal to the amount of bank reserves, αD,

$$B = \alpha D \tag{1}$$

If, as before, a fraction, $\alpha = 0.1$ of every deposit is held as reserves, then $1 in reserves can support $10 in deposits, $100 in reserves can support $1,000 in

Bank Runs in Ohio and Maryland

Deposits in U.S. banks are currently insured up to $100,000 by agencies of the federal government, but in 1985 there were ten states in which private companies insured deposits in some savings and loan associations (S&L's) and other thrift institutions. When a privately insured thrift fails, depositors may have to wait months to get their money or, worse, lose their money if the losses are so large that the insurance company itself fails. These risks understandably make depositors nervous when there are rumors of financial difficulties at a privately insured thrift.

E. S. M. Government Securities, a dealer in Treasury securities, was closed in March 1985 for fraudulent practices, with nine of its officers and an outside auditor eventually pleading guilty to or convicted of fraud charges. When E. S. M. was closed, it was soon revealed that Home State Savings Bank in Cincinnati had lost more than $140 million in loans to E. S. M. and that Home State was insured by a private firm, Ohio Deposit Guarantee Fund, which had only $136 million in reserves. Anxious depositors camped outside Home State Savings overnight and, when its doors opened in the morning, the line stretched around the block. As the news spread, depositors rushed to seventy other Ohio thrifts insured by the Ohio Deposit Guarantee Fund. Although most of these thrifts were financially sound, none had enough reserves on hand to satisfy nervous depositors. The governor of Ohio was forced to close these 70 thrifts for six days while it was determined which could qualify for federal deposit insurance.

Two months later, similar bank runs began in Maryland after the public learned that two savings-and-loan institutions had sustained losses that exceeded the reserves of the Maryland Savings–Share Insurance Corporation, a private company that insured 102 Maryland S&L's. The governor stopped the run by limiting withdrawals to $1,000 per month and creating a new state-operated insurance fund. A subsequent investigation concluded that some thrifts had been looted by their managers, who used depositor funds to pay for personal expenses and to finance speculative real estate investments by themselves and friends.*

---

*Steve Swartz, "Investigations Detail How Insiders Wrecked S&L's in Maryland," *Wall Street Journal,* March 12, 1986.

deposits, and $1 billion in reserves can support $10 billion in deposits. (We can think of Equation 1 as describing the supply of government money B and the banks' demand for government money to use as reserves as αD.)

Equation 1 can be rearranged to show that the banking system converts every dollar of government money into $1/\alpha$ dollars of deposits:

The deposit-multiplier model shows how fractional reserve banking multiplies deposits.

$$D = \frac{B}{\alpha} \tag{2}$$

The smaller α is, the less banks hold in reserves, the more they lend, and the more deposits are created. If only one penny out of every dollar is held as reserves ($\alpha = 0.01$), then bank deposits will be 100 times the initial deposit of government money, $D = 100B$. What if $\alpha = 0$? Then every dollar deposited is loaned out, and no reserves are held. If these loans are redeposited and re-lent over and over, there is no limit to the total deposits that can be created.

Early banks that printed their own bank notes could and did expand deposits even more aggressively since, when you are just printing paper, your loans can be larger than your deposits. A bank can have one million dollars in deposits, but print two, five, ten, or a hundred million dollars in notes to lend to optimistic entrepreneurs or a thankful government. As long as these notes just pass from hand to hand and borrowers never try to redeem them for hard coin, the bank can remain in the money-printing business. The danger is that depositors might try to claim their deposits and that borrowers might try to redeem their loans for precious metal. The wildest successes and most spectacular crashes in banking history accompanied such practices.

·Banks today cannot print money and cannot lend all of their deposits. Government **reserve requirements** compel banks to hold some fraction of their deposits as reserves, either cash in their vaults or deposits with the Federal Reserve that earn no interest. Any reserves held beyond those required are **excess reserves**, which allow banks to satisfy normal deposit withdrawals without falling below required reserves. The amount of excess reserves held by banks depends on their perception of withdrawal risks and the availability of attractive investments. Banks hold large excess reserves when withdrawal risks are great or when there are few tempting opportunities in which to invest these funds. In our deposit-multiplier model, the parameter α describes the fraction of deposits held as total bank reserves, required plus excess,

$$\text{Bank reserves} = \alpha D \tag{3}$$

Bank reserves are largely mandated by reserve requirements

In practice, banks today hold very few excess reserves, so that α is determined primarily by the reserve requirements set by government monetary authorities.

A second bit of realism, so far neglected, is that some of the money loaned by banks does not find its way back into banks. Citizens hold currency outside of banks for use as a medium of exchange. We will let the parameter β measure the ratio of currency outside banks to deposits:

$$\text{Currency outside banks} = \beta D \tag{4}$$

We're now ready to put the model together. A nation's **monetary base** B is the outstanding amount of government money that is held either as bank reserves or as currency outside of banks:

$$B = \text{bank reserves} + \text{currency outside banks} \qquad (5)$$

Substituting Equations 3 and 4 into Equation 5, we derive

$$B = (\alpha + \beta)D$$

We can solve this for D, the total level of deposits that is supported by the monetary base:

$$D = \left(\frac{1}{\alpha + \beta}\right) B \qquad (6)$$

The parenthetical term in Equation 6, $1/(\alpha + \beta)$, is the **deposit multiplier**, the ratio of bank deposits to the monetary base. Because the monetary base can support a much-larger quantity of bank deposits, economists often refer to the monetary base as **high-powered money**. Equation 6 is analogous to Equation 2, derived earlier for a simpler scenario in which there are no currency holdings outside banks ($\beta = 0$).

As of January 1990, the approximate values of α and β

$$\alpha = \frac{\text{reserves}}{\text{deposits}} = \frac{\$60 \text{ billion}}{\$3,000 \text{ billion}} = 0.02$$

$$\beta = \frac{\text{currency outside banks}}{\text{deposits}} = \frac{\$240 \text{ billion}}{\$3,000 \text{ billion}} = 0.08$$

The deposit multiplier was

$$\frac{1}{\alpha + \beta} = \frac{1}{0.02 + 0.08} = 10$$

so that deposits were 10 times the monetary base of $300 billion:

$$D = \left(\frac{1}{\alpha + \beta}\right) B$$

$$= (10)(\$300 \text{ billion})$$

$$= \$3,000 \text{ billion}$$

In 1990, every dollar of government money supported about 10 dollars in deposits. The value of the deposit multiplier changes if either of the parameters, α or β, changes. In particular, an increase in either of these parameters reduces the multiplier and reduces the amount of deposits supported by the monetary base. If the bank reserve-to-deposit ratio α is increased, perhaps by an increase in government reserve requirements, then a larger fraction of the money deposited in banks is held as reserves rather than loaned out. With less money recycled to be redeposited and re-lent, fewer bank deposits are created. If the currency-to-deposit ratio β increases, then a larger fraction of the money loaned by banks is held by the public rather than redeposited in banks. With less money returning to be re-lent and redeposited, fewer bank deposits are created.

Seemingly small changes in these parameters can have large effects on deposit creation. If α rose to 0.03 or if β rose to 0.09, the deposit multiplier would fall to 0.09 and deposits would contract by nearly 10 percent, to $2,727 billion. If α fell to 0.01 or β to 0.07, the multiplier would rise to 11.1 and deposits would expand by more than 10 percent, to $3,333 billion.

Checking Accounts Versus Savings Accounts

Now let's look at another, even more complicated, distinction. Some bank deposits are a medium of exchange; others are not. Funds in a checking account are payable on demand, so that for most (but admittedly not all) expenses, a check drawn on your checking account is as good as cash. Both government currency and checking account funds qualify as mediums of exchange. Most time and savings deposits do not qualify, because you cannot buy something from a store simply by displaying the passbook for your savings account. In practice, this distinction is more complicated and ambiguous, and we will return to it. But for now we can illustrate the general principle by drawing a sharp distinction between deposits D_1 in transaction accounts that are a medium of exchange and deposits D_2 that are not, with $D = D_1 + D_2$:

$$D_1 = \delta_1 D, \qquad D_2 = \delta_2 D, \qquad \delta_1 + \delta_2 = 1 \qquad (7)$$

As of January 1990, $\delta_1 = 0.18$ and $\delta_2 = 0.82$.

This distinction, in fact, underlay the pre-1980 monetary aggregates, which we will call Old $M1$ and Old $M2$:

Old $M1$ = currency outside banks plus commercial bank checking accounts
Old $M2$ = Old $M1$ plus commercial bank time and savings accounts

Banks are required to hold more reserves against transaction deposits than against other types of deposits. In 1990, transaction deposits had essentially a 12 percent reserve requirement (there was only a 3 percent reserve requirement on the first $41.5 million of transaction deposits, a threshold that increases each year), while most other deposits had no reserve requirements, with a few categories subject to a modest 3 percent requirement.

Banks may also choose to hold more precautionary excess reserves against transaction deposits, because these deposits, as a medium of exchange, are more likely to be withdrawn from a bank. The withdrawal of time and savings deposits may, at least formally, require either advance notice or the payment of a penalty. Our bank reserve Equation 4 should therefore be modified:

$$\text{Bank reserves} = \alpha_1 D_1 + \alpha_2 D_2 \qquad (8)$$

where α_1 and α_2 are the reserves held against deposits of type D_1 and D_2, respectively.

M1 originally included only currency and checking accounts.

M2 consisted of M1 and bank time and savings accounts.

If we substitute Equations 4, 7, and 8 into Equation 5, we find that

$$B = (\alpha_1\delta_1 + \alpha_2\delta_2 + \beta)D$$

Solving for total bank deposits, we derive the following:

$$D = \left(\frac{1}{\alpha_1\delta_1 + \alpha_2\delta_2 + \beta}\right) B \qquad (9)$$

This equation is an extension of our previous deposit-multiplier equation. The only difference between Equations 6 and 9 is that the latter recognizes that total bank reserves are the sum of reserves on Type 1 and Type 2 deposits, $\alpha = \alpha_1\delta_1 + \alpha_2\delta_2$.

The substantive difference is that in our expanded model we can track the creation of both types of deposits.

$$D_1 = \left[\frac{\delta_1}{\alpha_1\delta_1 + \alpha_2\delta_2 + \beta}\right] B$$

$$D_2 = \left[\frac{\delta_2}{\alpha_1\delta_1 + \alpha_2\delta_2 + \beta}\right] B$$

Letting C be currency outside banks, further manipulation yields the monetary aggregates

$$\text{Old } M1 = C + D_1 = \left[\frac{\delta_1 + \beta}{\alpha_1\delta_1 + \alpha_2(1-\delta_1) + \beta}\right] B$$

$$\text{Old } M2 = C + D = \left[\frac{1 + \beta}{\alpha_1\delta_1 + \alpha_2(1-\delta_1) + \beta}\right] B$$

These equations show how banks multiply government money into bank deposits and monetary aggregates. One pitfall to be avoided is the presumption that the various parameters are constant. Reserve requirements can change and *have* been changed by the government; currency, deposits, and excess reserves depend on the preferences of citizens and banks. Government monetary authorities may try to influence and estimate these parameters, but they cannot be taken for granted.

Both M1 and M2 are contracted by an increase in bank reserves, α_1 or α_2, caused either by an increase in reserve requirement or in excess reserves. An increase in δ_1 (the fraction of deposits that are a medium of exchange) expands M1 and contracts M2. An increase in β (holdings of currency relative to deposits) reduces M2 but has an uncertain effect on M1; holding more currency directly raises M1 but reduces the ability of banks to multiply deposits. Notice that the M1 and M2 monetary aggregates do not move in lockstep. M1 can increase substantially even while M2 is increasing only slightly, or even declining.

Sometimes, the changes in deposit multipliers are very large. During the banking panics of the Great Depression, many anxious depositors withdrew what

Changes in the preferences of citizens and banks cause M1 and M2 to fluctuate.

they could from banks. This caused β, the ratio of currency outside banks to bank deposits, to jump upward. Bank excess reserves also swelled enormously, because of fears of bank runs and a perceived absence of attractive loan opportunities. Excess reserves grew from $48 million in December 1929 to $6.6 billion in December 1940. These changes exerted an enormous contractionary effect on the deposit multiplier, which fell from more than 3 in 1929 to 2 in 1935 and to 1.5 in 1940.

Figure 4.2 shows the historical behavior of the Old M1 and Old M2 money multipliers. Here you can see the monetary collapse in the 1930s. You can also see that money multipliers wiggle around quite a bit in more normal times. Remember, a 10 percent change in a money multiplier corresponds to a 10 percent change in the monetary aggregate; such a change can be the difference between boom and recession. Notice also that, except for the banking collapse of the 1930s, the long-run trend in M2/B money multiplier was strongly upward, reflecting the relatively rapid long-run growth of banks and total bank deposits. In contrast, M1/B was relatively stagnant after World War II, because of the increased use of credit cards and other attractive alternatives to bank checking accounts.

The data in Figure 4.2 are annual averages, which smooth out the day-to-day fluctuations in the money multipliers. Figure 4.3 shows the monthly Old M1 money multiplier data for 1960–80. With the annual data in Figure 4.2, the 1960–80 period looks pretty sedate. The monthly data in Figure 4.3 give a sharply contrasting picture; weekly or daily money multipliers are even more erratic.

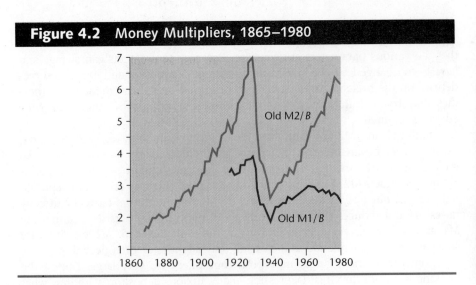

Figure 4.2   Money Multipliers, 1865–1980

Figure 4.3 Monthly Money Multiplier for Old M1

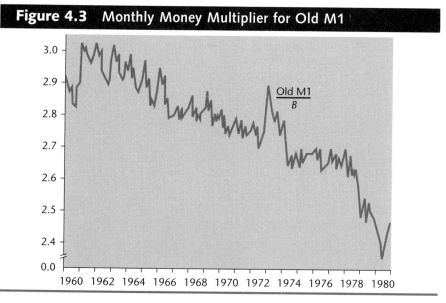

MONEY TODAY

The epigraph at the beginning of this chapter indicates that there has long been. disagreement about the definition of the word *money*. Some economists never accepted the idea that bank notes are money. H. Parker Willis of Columbia University, a leading monetary economist in his day, argued as late as 1925 that bank notes are not money, and as late as 1931 he (and many others) contended that Keynes should not have included checking accounts in his definition of money.[6] Today it is difficult to understand such debates. But changes are now occurring in the means of payment that are just as revolutionary as checking accounts were after the Civil War and that are creating just as much uncertainty about the meaning of money.

Money surely includes anything that is a medium of exchange which is commonly accepted as payment in economic transactions. Government currency and checking accounts clearly qualify, and this is why economists long studied M1. But even these funds are not universally accepted. Cash is often unsatisfactory for payments by mail or when proof of payment is desired. Many stores are reluctant to accept checks of uncertain reliability, and some buyers and sellers do not use or accept checks in order to avoid evidence of transactions that they want to keep secret — this is a popular explanation of why there are seven hundred million U.S. $100 bills in circulation.

Old *M1* did not include all mediums of exchange. Some of the more important and frivolous exclusions were traveler's checks, nonbank payment

Money includes cash, checking account balances, and other mediums of exchange.

accounts, food stamps, discount coupons, and subway tokens. Traveler's checks are "as good as cash," but were excluded from Old M1 simply because there were no reliable data on the quantity outstanding. Such data are now available, and traveler's checks are included in the current, revised definition of M1.

There are some philosophical problems, as well as data deficiencies, with food stamps and various coupons, passes, and discounts. These are a good substitute for cash, but only for certain restricted purchases, not as a generally accepted medium of exchange. However, food is a pretty big category, and in many grocery stores food stamps are accepted more readily than checks. Consider also this question: In some places, food stamps can be readily traded for nonfood items and for cash. Does that make food stamps as good as cash? Well, almost. There are some things, such as utility bills, for which food stamps won't be accepted as payment. And selling food stamps for cash is a little less convenient than having cash in the first place; moreover, food stamps must be sold for less than their face value.

It is uncertain whether money should include assets that are easily converted into a medium of exchange.

Is this extra step of having to convert an asset into cash sufficient reason to disqualify it as money? One view is that, no matter how fast and easy to accomplish, the additional step means that the asset is not yet money and should not be counted as money. Others argue that if the conversion is fast and easy, then the asset is so close to money that it ought to be called money. Of course, "fast" and "easy" are subjective assessments, and it is impossible to draw a sharp line that persuasively distinguishes fast from slow and easy from difficult. Food stamps may seem like a nuisance item, trivial enough to ignore. But there are many other assets, near-moneys, that are hard to overlook. Because these issues cannot be settled unambiguously, data are collected and reported on many monetary aggregates.

Checkable Deposits

The Banking Acts of 1933 and 1935 restricted checking accounts to commercial banks.

Old M1 neglected transaction deposits in financial institutions other than commercial banks. In popular usage, the term "banks" encompasses a wide variety of financial institutions: commercial banks, mutual savings banks, savings-and-loan associations, and credit unions. However, because of regulatory constraints, there have been important differences in the operations of these institutions.

In the aftermath of the 1929–1932 financial collapse in the United States, Congress acted to restrict speculative activities by financial institutions. Persuaded that competitive pressures to pay high interest rates on deposits had led banks to make high-interest, high-risk loans, the Banking Acts of 1933 and 1935 prohibited institutions other than commercial banks from offering checking accounts, prohibited the payment of interest on checking accounts, and, under **Regulation Q**, gave the Federal Reserve the power to set the maximum interest rates that banks could pay on other types of deposits.

Mutual savings banks, savings-and-loan associations, and credit unions were considered thrift institutions, designed for more permanent household savings accounts. As the years passed, these thrift institutions increasingly wanted to share in the lucrative checking-account business, which allows banks to borrow funds inexpensively from their depositors and then lend these funds at profitable interest rates. As interest rates rose to double-digit levels in the 1970s, many thrift institutions were eager to offer checking accounts, and many banks wanted to pay interest on their checking accounts in order to attract more deposits.

A favorable 1972 court decision in Massachusetts led to the proliferation of **negotiable order of withdrawal (NOW)** accounts — checking accounts paying $5\frac{1}{4}$ percent interest — throughout the six New England states, New York, and New Jersey. In 1974, credit unions began offering share drafts — checking accounts that pay interest on minimum account balances. A scattering of mutual savings banks and savings-and-loan associations set up noninterest-paying checking accounts. In November 1978, commercial banks were authorized to offer automatic-transfer-system (ATS) accounts, in which funds are automatically transferred from an individual's interest-paying savings account to a checking account, as needed. By 1980, the amount of money in these checking accounts with various names reached $20 billion, almost one-tenth the size of traditional commercial bank checking accounts.

Many of these and other similar developments had uncertain legal status. The landmark 1980 Depository Institutions Deregulation and Monetary Control Act clarified most of these ambiguities by explicitly authorizing the financial revolution that was occurring. Deposit institutions other than commercial banks were permitted to offer checking accounts, the prohibition of interest payments on checking accounts was removed, and all interest-rate ceilings on deposits were phased out.

Faced with the growing importance of nonbank checking accounts and increasing criticism of its Old M1 data, the Federal Reserve revised its definition of M1 to include all checkable deposits at both banks and thrifts, including NOW accounts, ATS accounts, and credit-union share drafts. Recognizing that some of the money in these versatile checkable accounts is there for saving rather than checking purposes, in 1981 the Fed introduced another aggregate, M1– shift adjusted, that subtracted from M1 an estimate of the funds that had been deposited in NOW accounts for saving rather than transaction purposes.

Much of the money in NOW accounts would otherwise be in checking accounts, but some would be in savings accounts. When the alternatives are a checking account paying no interest and a savings account paying $5\frac{1}{4}$ percent or $5\frac{1}{2}$ percent, depositors will make a serious effort to avoid leaving idle funds in their checking account. But when the alternatives are a checking account paying $5\frac{1}{4}$ percent and a savings account paying $5\frac{1}{4}$ percent or $5\frac{1}{2}$ percent, it costs little to leave extra money in a checking account, funds that can be used if needed for unanticipated expenses. This argument is supported by data on the annual deposit turnover rate, the ratio of total annual withdrawals (or debits) to average deposits. The annual turnover rate on ATS and NOW accounts is about 15, as compared to 3 for ordinary saving accounts and 40 for household checking accounts — suggesting that ATS and NOW accounts are a checking-and-saving hybrid.

1980 legislation authorized checking accounts at all deposit institutions and removed limits on deposit rates.

| **Highlight 4.2** | **Free Blankets, Toasters, and TVs** |

The Banking Act of 1933 prohibited the payment of interest on checking accounts and, through Regulation Q, empowered the Federal Reserve to determine the maximum interest rates that banks could pay on other deposits. On several occasions in the 1960s and 1970s, market interest rates on Treasury and corporate bonds rose far above the ceiling rates on bank deposits, persuading many depositors to withdraw their money from banks and invest elsewhere — a diversion of funds that is referred to as "disintermediation."

Banks tried to circumvent these rate ceilings by offering crockery, electrical appliances, and other baubles to depositors. One Colorado bank gave out hunting rifles. It would have been much more efficient to give depositors money (by paying them more interest) so that they could buy what they wanted, not necessarily a hunting rifle or another toaster oven.

The use of gifts to bypass rate ceilings reached the silly point where 25-inch color televisions were given to depositor "buddies." A *Wall Street Journal* employee wrote a memorable article telling of the difficulties he encountered when he deposited a large sum of money in a bank and discovered that he was entitled to a toaster for himself and a color television for a buddy.* A bank employee kindly explained that most people arrange for a buddy to accept delivery of the television and then give it to the depositor, perhaps in exchange for the toaster. The *Journal* writer dutifully left and returned to the bank with a buddy. His buddy was advised to use the depositor's social security number, so that he wouldn't have to pay taxes on the television, but told that he had to use his own address, which meant that the television would have to be carried across town to the depositor after delivery to the buddy. The *Journal* writer sent this buddy home and found a more convenient one — his babysitter, who could use her business address (his house). The bank officer objected that using the same address for the depositor and the buddy looked suspicious, but was persuaded to pretend that this was an apartment house, with the depositor having Apartment 1 and the buddy Apartment 2. The *Wall Street Journal* writer finally got his free color TV and a good story.

At the urging of consumer groups (who feel that deposit-rate wars are good for consumers) and of banks (who were losing depositors), the 1980 Depository Institutions Deregulation and Monetary Control Act phased out all deposit-rate ceilings.

---

*Jonathan Kwitny, "Finding a Buddy for My Free Color TV," *Wall Street Journal*, June 17, 1980.

Thus some of the funds the ATS and NOW accounts included in M1 are really savings rather than checking assets. These funds can be used to pay bills, but depositors don't plan to and usually won't use these funds for this purpose. Their inclusion in M1 forces us to ask this question: If "money" includes funds available for spending, what about other assets that are readily available for bill paying?

Other Accounts

Many of the funds in savings accounts at commercial banks, mutual savings banks, savings-and-loan associations, and credit unions can be easily used to pay bills. For instance, banks and savings-and-loan associations have provided automatic bill-paying services. Regular bills for utilities, rent, mortgage payments, and the like are sent directly to a bank or savings-and-loan association, where the appropriate amount is withdrawn from the depositor's savings account and credited to the recipient. (It is true that the funds in savings accounts that will be used to pay the mortgage cannot be used for discretionary purchases; however, the same is true of funds kept in checking accounts for paying the mortgage.)

Should money include easily transferred funds?

Since 1975, Federal Reserve member banks and federally chartered savings-and-loan associations have been permitted to accept telephone instructions to transfer funds from savings to checking accounts, allowing depositors to leave funds in high-interest-earning savings accounts until a check is written for some purchase. Because these savings account funds substitute for checking account funds, it is reasonable to argue that they, too, should be counted as money.

Ready Credit and Easily Liquidated Assets

Many checking accounts have liberal overdraft provisions, often called "ready credit" or "check credit" plans. If you have such an account, you can write a check for more than you have deposited, and the bank will honor the check. The bank uses its own funds to pay your bill and records this transaction as a loan to you. You may be able to repay the loan promptly with a slight service charge or to repay it later with interest. This overdraft privilege means that you have more funds available for spending than are contained in your checking account and than are recorded in M1. Overdraft provisions have been popular in Great Britain for a long time, and Keynes argued that these should be counted as money.[7]

This additional "money" consists of funds that you can spend, up to the overdraft limit set by your bank. In the near future, it will become commonplace for financial institutions to transfer funds automatically from savings to checking accounts whenever a checking account is overdrawn. This development will demolish the distinction between checking and savings accounts and put conventional M1 aggregates on extremely tenuous ground.

In an unforgettable scene in the 1967 movie, "The Graduate," Dustin Hoffman is advised that the future will be "plastic." We're living in 1967's future and, sure enough, it's plastic. Some 100 million Americans carry one or more credit cards. The average person owns seven credit cards and charges several hundred dollars a month. As a nation, we have a credit-card debt of nearly $100 billion. (A Californian is listed in the *Guinness Book of World Records* for the dubious achievement of having 1,159 different credit cards, giving him a theoretical ability to borrow $1.25 million.)

Credit cards are as widely accepted as checks, and they are used frequently enough to merit consideration as money. But how are we to measure the quantity of credit-card money? The average volume of purchases is not appropriate. Remember, checking-account money is measured by the amount of money in checking accounts at some point in time, not by the volume of checks written during the year.

Another possibility is the available credit limit specified by the credit-card companies. This is the maximum amount that can be charged, just as checking-account balances measure the maximum amount that can be purchased by check (neglecting overdrafts). Credit-card limits are unrealistic, because few households can prudently charge the credit limits on their seven credit cards, but this line of reasoning does suggest a sensible alternative.

It is uncertain how money measures should take into account the widespread use of credit cards.

The appropriate analog to the checking-account balance is the amount of funds households can easily obtain to pay their credit-card charges. Credit cards give shoppers access to easily liquidated assets, allowing them to make purchases with funds that are readily available. Therefore, effective credit-card money might be measured by the amount of readily available funds. This yardstick is imperfect because it neglects the frequently used possibility of paying back credit charges later out of future income; however, it seems better than completely neglecting credit cards or simply adding up maximum credit limits. The reality of credit cards suggests that "money" ought to be measured by broad monetary aggregates that include a variety of easily liquidated assets.

Series E and H government savings bonds are easily redeemable for specified amounts of money. Commercial paper and short-term Treasury bills can also be quickly sold for a relatively certain amount of money. Large negotiable **certificates of deposit (CDs)**, issued by banks in denominations of $100,000 or more, cannot be redeemed at the issuing bank before their fixed expiration date, but are easily sold in the short-term bond market.

Eurodollars, which are U.S. dollars deposited in foreign banks or foreign branches of U.S. banks, can often be quickly withdrawn for spending in the United States; for instance, overnight deposits in Caribbean branches of U.S. banks are available for spending the next business day. In a **repurchase agreement (repo)**, an investor buys securities and the seller agrees to repurchase them at an agreed-upon price and date, often the next day. For the seller (often a bank), this transaction is a one-day loan; for the buyer (often a corporation), it is a very liquid interest-bearing investment.

Many assets are easily liquidated to pay bills.

Money-market funds, mutual funds that invest in short-term securities such as bank CDs and Treasury bills, provide a very liquid investment for small investors. Shareholders can quickly and easily withdraw their money by giving written or telephoned instructions. Most funds allow shareholders to write checks payable to a third party, typically with a $500 minimum.

An Affinity for Credit Cards

Nearly half of all households pay their credit-card balances promptly each month to avoid finance charges; they use credit cards as a convenient way of making transactions and appreciate the delay between when the purchase is made and when the payment is due. Other households use credit cards as a credit line — a way of borrowing money without filling out loan applications or making a commitment to repay the loan according to a fixed schedule.

Credit-card issuers generally charge users a fixed annual fee of $25 to $75 plus an interest rate on unpaid balances that is several percentage points higher than interest rates on other types of loans. Merchants deposit a credit-card sales receipt in a bank just as they would a check and are given immediate credit for the value of the charge, less a fee typically set at 2–5 percent of the amount charged.

An affinity card is a credit card with a tie-in to a designated organization, which may receive part of the annual user fee, a fraction of a percent of the value of each transaction, and part of the monthly interest charges. Users of airline affinity cards are credited with frequent-flier mileage that can be redeemed for ticket upgrades or reduced prices. There are more than 3,000 groups with affinity cards in the United States, ranging from the Sierra Club to the Women's International Bowling Congress, the Society for the Preservation and Encouragement of Barber Shop Singing in America, and the Elvis card.

Money-market deposit accounts (MMDAs) were authorized in 1982 to allow deposit institutions to compete with money-market funds. Depositors can make an unlimited number of withdrawals in person or by mail and are allowed a maximum of three checks a month or a total of six monthly withdrawals by check, telephone, or automatic bill paying. These accounts have no reserve requirements and, unlike money-market funds, are federally insured.

What about stocks and long-term bonds? Many of these assets are easily sold in well-established markets. Anyone who owns Treasury bonds or IBM stock can sell these in minutes and will receive the proceeds within five business days. However, most economists frown on the counting of such assets as money, because the owner cannot be certain of the market value day to day. This argument applies with more force to less liquid assets such as land, houses, and rare paintings. There is a spectrum, and it is difficult to know where to draw the line.

Another ambiguous area is that most businesses and some households have preestablished lines of credit at banks, similar to the credit limits established by credit-card companies. The one difference is that the bank must be formally

| Highlight 4.4 | **AT&T's Universal Card** |

On March 26, 1990, American Telegraph & Telephone (AT&T) introduced its Universal credit card with a nationwide advertising campaign that included numerous full-page newspaper advertisements and a television commercial during that evening's Academy Awards show. AT&T received 75,000 telephone inquiries about its card between midnight and 5 A.M. that night and 250,000 calls during the first 24 hours. Over the next three months, AT&T received ten million inquiries and issued more than one million cards.

There were several lures. The Universal card can have either a Visa or Mastercard format, and hence can be used wherever these cards are accepted. While most banks that issue Visa and Mastercard charge an annual fee of $20 to $75, those who signed up for a Universal card in 1990 will never pay an annual fee, as long as the card is used at least once a year. The Universal card can also be used to charge long-distance telephone calls at a 10 percent discount. The one negative feature is that AT&T's interest rate on unpaid balances is a relatively high 18.9 percent.

In addition to its advertising blitz, AT&T recruited cardholders from its list of 70 million AT&T long-distance telephone users. The 46 million who use AT&T telephone calling cards are a natural audience, though perhaps not a very profitable one — because these people generally pay their bills on time and, with no annual fee on its Universal card, AT&T is hoping to profit from monthly finance charges.

AT&T's credit cards are issued and processed through contractual arrangements with Synovus Financial Corporation, a bank-holding company with headquarters in Columbus, Georgia. The cards are issued by a Synovus subsidiary, the Universal Bank of Columbus, a small Georgia bank with $3 million in capital. The receipts are handled by Total Systems Services, another Synovus subsidiary, which is the nation's second largest credit-card processor. AT&T puts its name and logo on the card, markets the card, and buys Universal Bank's credit-card receivables.

Citicorp, the nation's largest credit-card issuer, responded by transferring $30 million of its telecommunications business from AT&T to rival MCI and by offering users of Citicorp credit cards discounts on long-distance phone calls using MCI. Several banking companies, including Citicorp, BankAmerica, and Chase Manhattan, filed regulatory complaints. The Federal Reserve Board and the Federal Deposit Insurance Corporation were asked to investigate charges that AT&T violated federal laws prohibiting industrial and commercial companies from owning commercial banks. Legal briefs filed with the Federal Communications Commission also argued that the 10 percent discount on long-distance calls was unsanctioned "predatory pricing" against other telecommunications companies.

From the beginning, there was little doubt that AT&T's card is legal and that these complaints from banks were mere harassments, intended to slow AT&T's bold attempt to become one of the industry leaders. In 1990 Citicorp had nearly 30 million cards in the United States and 40 million worldwide. One industry analyst estimated that AT&T would have 35 million cardholders by 1995.* The advantage for all credit-card users is that AT&T's aggressive entry will force other issuers to make their cards more attractive.

_____

*John J. Keller and Robert Guenther, "As AT&T Credit Card Charges Ahead, Banks Fight Back," *Wall Street Journal*, May 18, 1990.

notified that some of the credit will be exercised so that funds can be transferred to the checking account. Credit lines are almost as good as cash, but it is unclear how they should be measured. The maximum credit limits are too large and the liquid assets are too small, since these loans will typically be repaid out of future income rather than current assets.

In practice, monetary aggregates are a conglomeration of various similar and dissimilar assets. Some of the underlying assets are mediums of exchange, and their owners plan to spend them. Other assets are mediums of exchange but will probably not be used for transactions. Still others are not mediums of exchange but can and will be quickly converted and spent. And yet others are not mediums of exchange, could be quickly converted, but probably won't. Which combination from this monetary smorgasbord best deserves to be called "money"? Because there is no clear answer to this fundamental question, the Federal Reserve collects and studies data on several monetary aggregates.

Monetary Aggregates in 1989

In recognition of the increasingly obvious ambiguities in its old monetary aggregates and the complete neglect of repurchase agreements, overnight Euro-dollars, and money-market funds, the Federal Reserve constructed new aggregates in 1980, and has since modified these series as financial markets have evolved. The composition of these aggregates in 1989 is shown in Table 4.2.

The table shows that the M1 aggregate attempts to measure money as a medium of exchange — funds that can be directly used for transactions. The M2, M3, and L (for "liquidity") series progressively expand to encompass funds that are stores of wealth that can easily be converted into a medium of exchange. This progression is far from perfect, though. For example, the small time-deposits included in M2 are generally less liquid than the large time-deposits included in M3 or the Treasury bills included in L.

In 1980, the Federal Reserve Board also began internally monitoring a variety of monetary indexes. These indexes are weighted averages of data on various

The Federal Reserve substantially revised its monetary aggregates in 1980.

financial assets, using weights that are estimates of the relative frequency with which the assets are turned over. Checking accounts, for instance, are given a heavier weight than savings accounts because money is deposited and withdrawn more frequently from the former.

Our financial markets are too complicated and dynamic for a single collection of assets to be clearly superior to other monetary aggregates. There are too many assets that are almost, but not quite, the same as others, and financial innovations are continually introducing new assets. Analysts of financial markets consequently watch many monetary aggregates.

Money multipliers fluctuate considerably from year to year.

Figure 4.4 graphs the annual money multipliers for the revised definitions of $M1$ and $M2$ back to 1970. As shown, $M2/B$ has generally increased while $M1/B$ is trendless, but there are substantial year-to-year fluctuations in each multiplier. Earlier in this chapter, the deposit-multiplier model was used to explain how deposit multipliers and money multipliers are affected by bank reserves relative to deposits, the public's holdings of currency relative to deposits, and the relative composition of deposits.

As a consequence, the historical correlation between changes in government money and changes in monetary aggregates is very tenuous. Two simple scatter graphs of the historical experience are given in Figures 4.5 and 4.6 — ink splotches with no apparent pattern. These figures use annual data; quarterly, monthly, or weekly data are no better. An increase in the monetary base does not cause an immediate, reliable increase in monetary aggregates, because the behavior of banks and the public causes the money multipliers to fluctuate.

Some monetary economists, following Milton Friedman, argue that a definition of money should be chosen not for its theoretical coherence but rather for its practical ability to explain fluctuations in gross national product (GNP) and other data of interest. The 1980 monetary aggregate revisions were at least partly motivated by a perceived deterioration in the empirical correlations between the old monetary aggregates and output, interest rates, and prices.[8]

The ratios of GNP to monetary aggregates sometimes fluctuate substantially.

For a time, some monetary economists believed that Old $M1$ was reasonably well correlated with GNP, though this assumption was disputed by other observers. Figure 4.7 shows the annual ratios of GNP to $M1$ and to $M2$ since 1970. The ratio of GNP to $M1$ has been increasing since the 1950s, because deposit innovations have diminished the attractiveness of checking accounts relative to savings accounts. However, this upward trend was broken by sharp, unexpected declines in GNP/$M1$ in 1982, 1983, 1985, and 1986. The ratio of GNP to $M2$ has been trendless since 1970, with annual fluctuations of 3 percent to 5 percent commonplace.

MONEY TOMORROW

Currency and paper checks are being replaced by plastic cards and electronic banking. **Debit cards** look like credit cards and are used in stores just like credit cards, but are really an electronic checking account in that funds are immediately

Table 4.2 Monetary Aggregates, Billions of Dollars, July 1989

Aggregate and Component[1]		Amount
M1		777.3
Currency	218.0	
Traveler's checks[2]	7.1	
Commercial bank checking accounts	279.0	
Other transaction accounts[3]	273.2	
M2		3,118.1
M1	777.3	
Overnight Eurodollars and repos	78.6	
Money-market deposit accounts	459.8	
Money-market mutual fund shares	274.6	
Savings deposits	401.5	
Small-time deposits[4]	1,126.3	
M3		4,000.6
M2	3,118.1	
Large time deposits	573.9	
Term Eurodollars	99.4	
Term repurchase agreements	111.0	
Institutional money-market funds	98.2	
L		4,770.8
M3	4,000.6	
Savings bonds	113.8	
Short-term Treasury securities	264.7	
Commercial paper	350.5	
Bankers' acceptances	41.2	

1. Components generally exclude amounts held by domestic depository institutions, foreign commercial banks, and official institutions, the U.S. government (including the Federal Reserve), and money-market mutual funds.
2. Dollar-denominated traveler's checks issued by nonbanks; those issued by deposit institutions are included in transaction accounts.
3. Includes NOW and ATS accounts, credit-union share-draft balances, and demand deposits at thrift institutions.
4. Time deposits issued in denominations of less than $100,000.

Figure 4.4 Money Multipliers, 1970–1988

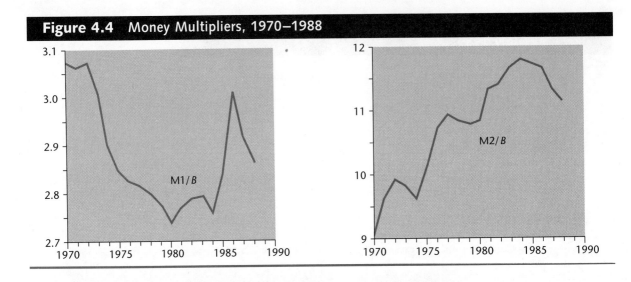

Figure 4.5 Annual Percentage Changes in M1 and B, 1970–1988

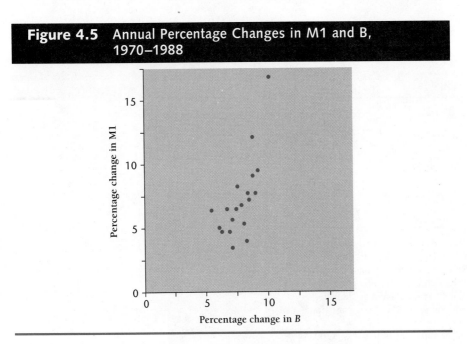

Figure 4.6   Annual Percentage Changes in M2 and B, 1970–1988

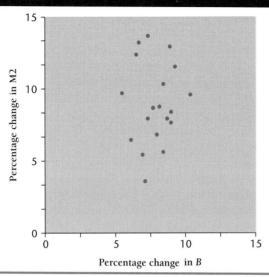

Figure 4.7   GNP Relative to Monetary Aggregates, 1970–1988

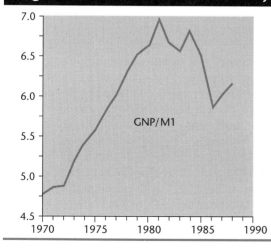

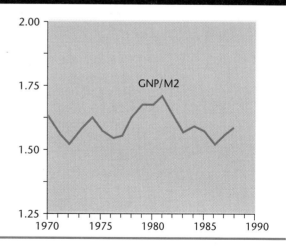

transferred from the customer's bank account to the merchant's account. Both merchants and banks like the fact that there is no paper to handle, no credit risk, and no delay in receiving payment. **Smart cards** are used like debit cards to make immediate payment for goods and services, but have embedded microprocessors that allow them to keep records of the user's transactions and financial situation.

Within the Federal Reserve System, $200 billion a day is electronically transferred among banks. The New York Clearing House International Payments System transfers a like amount through a computer network linking 80 banking offices. Both these systems are primarily used for large business transactions. The federal government uses the Federal Reserve Clearing House to make nearly 300 million transactions annually. These are mostly direct deposits for the wages of federal employees, Social Security payments, and government pension benefits. In 1987, the Treasury began paying its suppliers electronically through the Vendor Express system. These various government payments are electronically transmitted and deposited directly into the recipients' accounts. This saves time, paper, and postage, and eliminates stolen checks. The Treasury estimates that it saves about 25¢ per transaction.

In electronic home banking systems, households can pay their bills, transfer funds among accounts, buy and sell securities, and receive up-to-the-minute information using a personal computer and a modem to send instructions over the telephone wires. This is more convenient than mailing checks or standing in lines at banks, and allows households to delay payments until the last possible moment.

In an electronic funds transfer system, accounts are debited and credited electronically.

It is widely believed that these various developments are the initial stages of what may someday become a comprehensive electronic funds transfer system, in which a nationwide computer network will record transactions electronically and instantly transfer funds from the buyer's account to the seller's. Government offices and businesses will have computer terminals connected to this network. Wages, dividends, and interest payments will all be transferred directly between accounts. People with plastic identification cards will be able to pay for most purchases by inserting their cards in terminals located in retail stores. Transactions between individuals can be handled by public terminals or by home terminals. The complete elimination of cash will be resisted by participants in the underground economy made up of illegal and untaxed transactions. For the same reason, governments will try to reduce the use of cash.

Funds credited within the electronic network of accounts will earn interest, so that funds held in the system serve both as a medium of exchange and as savings, a store of value. It will not be necessary to have a positive balance in order to make transactions, because there will be liberal overdraft privileges with interest charged on debits.

In a pure currency system, every transaction requires a physical transfer of tangible currency. In this idealized accounting system of the future, there need not be any physical currency. Transactions will require only bookkeeping entries of debits and credits. What, then, will we call money? And will we call the system a bank? Both terms will be obsolete.

Most people will appreciate the ease of making transactions and the improved record keeping. The social advantages will be the saving in resources now spent reading and sorting currency and checks and shuffling paper throughout the country. There will probably be some loss of privacy. There will certainly be some uneasy years for economists trying to measure money and for public figures urging that we abolish fractional reserve banking and return to the gold standard. Most will conclude that these losses are well worth absorbing

---

Smart Cards   **Highlight 4.5**

Smart cards were introduced in France in 1974, are now used extensively there and in Japan. and seem poised to spread throughout the United States. With simple smart cards, the user pays in advance for 10 movie tickets, 100 pages of xeroxing, or 1,000 minutes of telephone usage. As the card is used, the outstanding credit is adjusted electronically until it is exhausted. The user can then pay to have it restored. In another variant, used on the Dallas North Tollway, commuters display a smart card while driving through the toll plaza; the identification number is read with a radio signal and each month's toll charge is billed to the driver's credit card.

More powerful smart cards can remember the owner's bank balance and keep detailed records of transactions much like an electronic checkbook. Point-of-sale transactions at participating stores are made by inserting the card into special terminals and punching in a secret identification number, which is verified by the card itself. Some terminals record the transactions on magnetic bands, which store owners periodically take to banks to credit their accounts and debit those of customers. Alternatively, stores can be electronically linked with banks to record transactions immediately. Smart cards can also provide information about customers that businesses may find helpful in understanding sales patterns and in targeting their advertising.

Super-smart cards have keypads and displays, enabling the user to store and retrieve information. Travelers using the Thomas Cook Group's services are given super-smart cards that allow them not only to obtain funds from any Thomas Cook travel agent, much like electronic traveler's checks, but also to record information about their trip's expenses, which can be fed into a personal computer and printed out after the trip is over.

.

SUMMARY

Banks multiply the money supply by holding fractional reserves against deposits. The amount of banking system deposits D that can be created is

$$D = \left(\frac{1}{\alpha + \beta}\right) B$$

where B is the monetary base

α is the fraction of each deposit held in reserve by banks

β is the ratio of currency outside banks to deposits

The more currency held outside banks and the more reserves held inside banks, the fewer deposits are created.

Banks serve as intermediaries between lenders and borrowers. Lenders are able to withdraw their deposits on demand, while each borrower is given a fixed repayment schedule for each loan. This process creates loans, money, and the risk of bank runs. In practice, banks hold little reserves beyond those mandated by government reserve requirements.

Analysts watch many monetary and liquidity aggregates, such as M1, M2, M3, and L. As the differences among various deposits and assets have become increasingly blurred, less importance can be attached to any one particular monetary aggregate.

IMPORTANT TERMS

certificates of deposit (CDs)
debit cards
deposit multiplier
Eurodollars
excess reserves
fractional-reserve banking
high-powered money
monetary base

money-market funds
money-market deposit accounts (MMDAs)
negotiable order of withdrawal (NOW) accounts
Regulation Q
reserve requirements
repurchase agreement (repo)
smart cards
T-Accounts

EXERCISES

1. Federally chartered banks were initially required to hold 25 percent reserves against deposits. If all banks hold 25 percent reserves against deposits and none of the monetary base is held outside of banks, how much in deposits and loans will be created by the banking system if the monetary base is $100 million? If the monetary base is $150 million?

2. In comparison with the preceding exercise, what happens to bank deposits and loans if the monetary base is $100 million and banks, fearful of bank runs, increase their reserves from 25 percent of deposits to 50 percent?

3. The monetary base is $60 billion and is held as bank reserves or as currency outside banks. What is the size of bank deposits and bank

loans if banks hold 10 percent reserves against deposits and the public's ratio of currency outside banks to deposits is 15 percent? What if the public increases the currency-to-deposit ratio from 15 percent to 20 percent? Explain why this shift in public preferences expands or contracts bank deposits and loans.

4. In the 1930s, Henry Simons, a University of Chicago economist, and Irving Fisher, a Yale University economist, argued that banks should hold 100 percent reserves against their deposits. How would this affect the banks' ability to multiply the money supply? How would it affect their ability to withstand bank runs?

5. What is the size of bank deposits and bank loans if the monetary base is $60 billion, banks hold 100 percent reserves against deposits, and the public's ratio of currency outside banks to deposits is 20 percent? What if the public increases the currency-to-deposit ratio from 20 percent to 25 percent? Explain why this shift in public preferences expands or contracts bank deposits and loans.

6. Look in the most recent issue of the *Federal Reserve Bulletin* and see if the definitions of M1, M2, M3, and L given in Table 4.1 are still used by the Federal Reserve. Report any changes. (These definitions are given in the notes to the *Bulletin's* Table 1.21, "Money Stock, Liquid Assets, and Debt Measures.")

7. Table 1.10 of the *Federal Reserve Bulletin* gives the seasonally adjusted annual rates of changes of the monetary base and of M1, M2, M3, and L during four recent quarters. Report these data from the most recent issue of the *Bulletin*. Did all five measures of the money supply increase by approximately the same percentage during each of these four quarters?

8. Give an example of an economic event that would cause M1 to increase even while the monetary base is constant.

9. Transaction deposits are about three times as large as currency holdings, but of the payments made by cash or check, more than 90 percent are made by check and less than 10 percent by cash. How is this possible? Use a simple example of a hypothetical economy in which there is $100 in currency and checking account balances are $300.

10. If depositors transfer funds from checking accounts, subject to a 12-percent reserve requirement, to new tax-free savings accounts, which are included in M2 and subject to no reserve requirements, what will be the effect on bank loans, M1 and M2?

11. "Banks monetize illiquid and poorly divisible assets." How do they do this and who pays them to do it?

12. Why are banks able to pay higher interest rates on deposits that are not subject to reserve requirements than on deposits that have reserve requirements, and still make a profit?

13. Here are the percentage changes in the monetary base, M1, M2, and GNP during 1984 and 1985:

	B	M1	M2	GNP
1984	7.3%	5.2%	8.4%	11.0%
1985	9.0%	11.6%	8.1%	5.8%

a. What happened to the money multipliers M1/B and M2/B during these two years?
b. What happened to the ratios of GNP to the monetary aggregates M1 and M2 during 1984 and 1985?
c. How can the rate of increase of M2 diminish while M1 is accelerating?

14. The Old M2 money multiplier tripled between 1950 and 1980. How could this have happened? Must the government's printing presses have run amok?

15. If there were no legal reserve requirements, would banks bother to keep reserves? Given total government money of $1 billion, what would be the maximum possible level of deposits?

16. "The latest available data show that M1, the basic money-supply measure, declined $500 million in the week ended December 19. The broader measure, M2, rose $700 million during the week."[9] What economic event could cause M1 to decline while M2 rose?

17. The ratio of currency to deposits doubled between 1929 and 1933. What effect do you think this increase had on M1?

18. In the 1930s, banks held enormous amounts of excess reserves. What effects, if any, would this have on M1? The government, aiming to eliminate these excess reserves, raised reserve requirements in August 1936, March 1937, and May 1937. However, banks continued to hold large excess reserves. What do you think happened to M1?

19. Should $100 bills buried in the backyard be counted as part of M1? Defend your position.

20. Money-market deposit accounts were introduced on December 14, 1982, followed by super-NOW accounts on January 5, 1983. Both types of accounts had no interest-rate ceilings, as long as the depositor maintained a minimum balance of $2,500. Super-NOW accounts allow unlimited checking, while money-market deposit accounts allow a maximum of three checks a month. Which do you suppose was included in M1 and which in M2? Explain your reasoning.

21. In 1983, the Federal Reserve removed Individual Retirement Accounts and Keogh accounts at depository institutions or in money-market funds from M2 and M3, because there is a substantial penalty for withdrawal of funds from these accounts before age 59½. What was their reasoning?

22. Some people almost always pay off the outstanding balance on their credit cards each month, while other people almost never do so. Which group would prefer a credit card with a low annual fee and high finance charges, and which would prefer a card with a high annual fee and low finance charges?

23. Banks make substantial profits from some credit-card users, but would prefer that others use debit cards instead of credit cards. What distinguishes these two groups?

24. Under the national banking system (1864–1914), out-of-town banks were allowed to count their interest-earning deposits in New York City banks as part of their required reserves. Did this provision increase or decrease the money multiplier? Twice a year, in the spring and fall, farmers drew funds out of their local banks, and these country banks withdrew deposits from New York City banks. What effects do you think this had on the nation's money supply?

25. Charles Ponzi, an enterprising Bostonian, is remembered for his chain-letter approach to investment management in the 1920s. For a while, he was able to pay investors a 50 percent return every 45 days by using the funds of new investors to pay off old investors. For example, John might invest $100. If George and Martha now invest $100 apiece, then John can be repaid $150, with the promoter keeping $50. Hearing of John's success, Bob, Carol, Ted, and Alice then rush to invest $100 each. This chain can be kept up until the pool of fish is exhausted. The net result is simply a transfer of wealth from the late entrants to the earlier investors and the promoter. Is banking a Ponzi scheme? Explain your reasoning.

Financial Markets

INTEREST RATES

The greatest of all gifts is the power to estimate things at their true worth.

La Rochefoucauld

A financial debt is a legally binding IOU from one person or institution to another. You issue debt when you take out a car loan, an education loan, or a home mortgage. You acquire the debts of others when you deposit money in a bank, buy Treasury bills, or invest in a money-market fund. One person's liability is, of course, another person's asset. Money deposited in a savings account is an asset for the depositor and a liability for the bank; a mortgage is an asset for the bank and a liability for the homeowner. In their role as financial intermediaries, banks borrow money by accepting deposits and selling bonds, and lend money by making loans and buying bonds.

The next three chapters describe the nature of debt and explain some of the factors that influence debt prices and interest rates. We will look at the general characteristics that differentiate debts and see why some debts have higher interest rates than others. This chapter focuses on prices and interest rates — how they are calculated and why they are interrelated. Chapter 6 considers default risk, and Chapter 7 analyzes interest-rate risk.

We begin this chapter by explaining how interest rates determine the future value of an investment and, as a consequence, affect the prices that investors are willing to pay for it. Then we will look at three types of bonds: zero-coupon bonds, bonds with coupons, and tax-exempt bonds. The last section of this chapter considers the effect of inflation on interest rates.

PRESENT VALUE AND REQUIRED RETURNS

The future value of an investment is its value after it has earned a specified rate of return for a given number of years.

The **future value** of an investment is its value after it has earned a specified rate of return for a given number of years. If, for example, you invest $1,000 and earn a 10 percent annual rate of return, at the end of one year you will have

$$\text{First year: principal} + \text{interest} = \$1,000 + 0.10(\$1,000)$$
$$= \$1,000(1+.010)$$
$$= \$1,100$$

If you reinvest this $1,100 for a second year at 10 percent, you earn interest not only on your original $1,000, but also on the $100 interest you earned the first year.

$$\text{Second year: principal} + \text{interest} = \$1,100 + 0.10(\$1,100)$$
$$= \$1,100(1.10)$$
$$= \$1,000(1.10)^2$$
$$= \$1,210$$

Compound interest is the earning of interest on interest.

This earning of interest on interest is called **compound interest**.

More generally, if you invest an amount P, earning an annual rate of return R for n years, your investment grows to

$$F = P(1 + R)^n \qquad (1)$$

If the rate of return varies year by year, say R_1 the first year, R_2 the second, and so on, then your investment grows to

$$F = P(1 + R_1)(1 + R_2) \ldots (1 + R_n) \qquad (2)$$

after n years. For instance, $1,000 invested for 3 years at 10 percent has a future value of

$$F = \$1,000(1.10)^3 = \$1,331$$

while $1,000 invested for 3 years at 10 percent, 11 percent, and then 12 percent has a future value of

$$F = \$1,000(1.10)(1.11)(1.12) = \$1,367.52$$

Present Value

A future-value calculation answers the question: If you invest P at a rate of return R, how much money will you have after n years? Often, we are interested in the reverse question: How much money do you have to invest now in order to have $100,000 after 10 years, perhaps to pay for a daughter's college education? This can be determined by solving Equation 1 for P, using $F = \$100,000$ and $n=10$:

$$P = \frac{F}{(1 + R)^n}$$

$$= \frac{\$100,000}{(1 + 0.10)^{10}}$$

$$= \$38,554.33$$

The future-value formula can also be used to answer another important but somewhat different question. Suppose that you have been offered an IOU for $100,000, to be paid 10 years from today. How much is this promise of a future payment worth to you *now*? The amount you are willing to pay for this IOU depends on the return you require on such an investment. If you are willing to pay $38,554.33 now for $100,000 in ten years, then you evidently require a 10 percent return on your investment, since $38,554.33 invested for ten years at 10 percent will grow to $100,000. If you require a 20 percent return on this investment, then the amount P that you are willing to pay is given by

$$P = \frac{\$100,000}{(1 + 0.20)^{10}} = \$16,150.56$$

An IOU for $100,000 ten years from now — even if issued by the U.S. Treasury — is not the same as $100,000 now, because $100,000 now can be invested for ten years. A payment of $100,000 ten years from now is worth much less than $100,000 now. The amount that you are willing to pay today to receive a specified future amount F after n years is called the **present value** of this future payment and can be calculated from a rearrangement of Equation 1:

> The present value is determined by discounting a cash flow by the investor's required return.

$$P = \frac{F}{(1 + R)^n} \tag{3}$$

The rate of return R that you use to determine this present value is called your **required rate of return**. If the required rate of return varies from year to year, a rearrangement of Equation 2 is appropriate:

$$P = \frac{F}{(1 + R_1)(1 + R_2) \cdots (1 + R_n)} \tag{4}$$

If there is more than one future payment, the present value of this **cash flow** is equal to the sum of the present values of the payments. Suppose, for instance, that an IOU promises to pay $1,000 a year from now and another $1,000 the year after that. At a required return R, the present value is

$$P = \frac{\$1,000}{(1 + R)} + \frac{\$1,000}{(1 + R)^2}$$

If R = 10 percent, then

$$P = \frac{\$1,000}{(1 + 0.10)} + \frac{\$1,000}{(1 + 0.10)^2}$$

$$= \$909.09 + \$826.45$$

$$= \$1,735.54$$

If, instead of a 10 percent return, you require $R = 20$ percent, then

$$P = \frac{\$1,000}{(1 + 0.20)} + \frac{\$1,000}{(1 + 0.20)^2}$$

$$= \$833.33 + \$694.44$$

$$= \$1,527.77$$

Highlight 5.1   Did Peter Minuit Pay Too Much for Manhattan?

In 1626, Peter Minuit purchased Manhattan Island from some Algonquian Indians for cloth, beads, and trinkets worth about $24 at the time, an apparent bargain compared to the price of Manhattan real estate today. But $24 in 1626 is not the same as $24 today, because $24 in 1626 could have earned nearly 400 years of interest. If it had been invested at 6 percent, then in 1991, 365 years later, it would have increased to

$$\$24(1.06)^{365} = \$41.4 \text{ billion}$$

The area of Manhattan is 31.2 square miles, so this is approximately $48 a square foot.

The so-called miracle of compound interest is that a seemingly modest rate of return, compounded over many years, turns a small investment into a fortune. The table below shows the corollary that slightly different rates of return compound to vastly different future values. While the difference between 6 percent and 7 percent interest may seem small, the farther ahead we look, the more the power of compounding separates the results. Thus, the answer to our question — did Peter Minuit pay too much for Manhattan? — depends critically on the rate of return that he and his heirs could have earned.

Annual Rate of Return	Future Value (1991)	Future Value per Square Foot
4%	$39.6 million	$0.05
5%	$1.3 billion	$1.50
6%	$41.4 billion	$47.58
7%	$1,274 billion	$1,465.10
8%	$38,009 billion	$43,697.80

> ## Creative Accounting by the Federal Home Loan Bank Board
>
>
> In 1988, Congress accused the Federal Home Loan Bank Board of making inconsistent and misleading estimates of the resources needed to clean up the savings-and-loan industry during the next ten years. In Congressional testimony that summer, Board Chairman M. Danny Wall estimated that the present value (in 1988) of closing or merging five hundred sick S&L's was $30.9 billion and that the Board expected to collect $42 billion in revenue during the ten years 1988–1998, giving it $12 billion more than it needed.* Congressional aides and industry analysts soon pointed out that by comparing a present value to a cash flow, the Board was, in the words of one senator, "comparing apples and oranges."
>
> The present value of a $42 billion cash flow spread over ten years may be substantially less than $30 billion. For instance, if the $42 billion cash flow is divided evenly, $4.2 billion a year for ten years, its present value at a 10 percent interest rate is only $25.8 billion — $5.1 billion less than the $30.9 billion present value of the expenses. If the $42 billion cash flow begins at $3.34 billion and grows by 5 percent a year, the present value is $24.9 billion — $6 billion less than the present value of the expenses.
>
> It is especially puzzling that a federal bank board would make such an obvious present-value mistake. After aides to the House Banking Committee uncovered this inconsistency in the way revenue and expenses were reported, the committee chairman said, "The miscalculations are serious. They are the result of either gross incompetence or deliberate attempts to mislead and minimize the problem to Congress and the public."
>
> _____
>
> *"Bank Board Accused of Misleading," *Washington Post,* October 3, 1988.

The Appropriate Required Return

The present value depends critically on your required return. Our calculations show that, for an IOU promising $1,000 for each of the next two years, you are willing to pay $1,735.54 if you require a 10 percent return, but only $1,527.77 if you require a 20 percent return: the higher the required return, the lower the present value of a given cash flow. Put somewhat differently, a reduction in the price paid for a given cash flow increases the prospective return. This important inverse relationship between required return and present value is shown in Figure 5.1.

What determines the required return and, implicitly, the amount that investors are willing to pay for future cash flows? One obvious influence is the rates

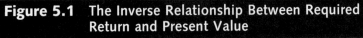

Figure 5.1   The Inverse Relationship Between Required
Return and Present Value

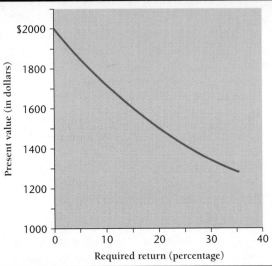

of return available on other investments. You won't settle for a 10 percent return on an IOU when bank deposits pay 15 percent, but you might when banks offer only 5 percent. Thus required returns rise and fall with the rates of return available on alternative investments.

Many commodities are very close substitutes: brown eggs and white eggs, butter by the pound or butter by the quarter-pound, California orange juice and Florida orange juice. The prices of such close substitutes are tightly linked. The price of brown eggs cannot double while the price of white eggs remains constant, because everyone would buy white eggs. Other commodities are weak substitutes: eggs and geraniums, butter and ketchup, orange juice and beer. The prices of poor substitutes are related only weakly.

The same is true of financial assets. If two investments are equally attractive, then they are **perfect substitutes** and will be priced using the same required return. Some assets are perfect substitutes (for example, checking accounts with different names); some assets are very close but imperfect substitutes (30-day and 60-day Treasury bills); and some assets are not good substitutes at all (a checking account and an apartment building). The more two assets are considered substitutes, the more their required returns move in unison.

If two assets are imperfect substitutes, the less-attractive investment has the higher required return. For instance, many people care about an investment's **risk** — how certain or uncertain the promised cash flow is. If you can invest your money safely in a bank at 10 percent and the IOU is just a shaky promise from a disreputable stranger, then you may well require a 20 percent, a 30 percent, or an even higher return. The less attractive the investment, the higher your required return and the lower its present value.

The required rate of return depends on an asset's riskiness and the returns available on alternative investments.

Think about this conclusion carefully, because it implies what many find counterintuitive — that the least-attractive investments have the highest potential returns. It is the requisite low prices and high potential returns that compensate for the otherwise undesirable features of these investments. This is why, as you will see in the next chapter, the "junk" bonds issued by shaky companies have lower prices and higher potential returns than the secure bonds issued by strong companies.

Constant Cash Flows

In many cases, the cash flow is the same, period after period; for example, constant monthly mortgage payments, constant semiannual income from a bond, and constant quarterly dividends from a stock. If so, the present value is

$$P = \frac{X}{1 + R} + \frac{X}{(1 + R)^2} + \cdots + \frac{X}{(1 + R)^n}$$

where

X = constant cash flow each period
R = required return per period
n = number of periods

The appendix shows that, in this special case, the present-value formula simplifies to

$$P = \frac{X}{R}\left(1 - \frac{1}{(1 + R)^n}\right) \tag{5}$$

This simplified formula can be used to determine the present value P of any investment that yields a constant cash flow. For example, a bond, stock, or machine that pays $1,000 a year for 10 years has, at a 10 percent required return, a present value of

$$P = \frac{\$1,000}{(1 + 0.10)} + \frac{\$1,000}{(1 + 0.10)^2} + \cdots + \frac{\$1,000}{(1 + 0.10)^{10}}$$

$$= \frac{\$1,000}{0.10}\left(1 - \frac{1}{(1 + 0.10)^{10}}\right)$$

$$= \$10,000 \, (1 - 0.386)$$

$$= \$6,140$$

Another application of Equation 5 is to a perpetual, never-ending cash flow, such as the bonds paying a constant annual amount forever that were issued by Great Britain in 1750 to consolidate its debts. Such bonds are generically labeled "perpetuities," and those issued by Great Britain are called "British consols." To value a perpetuity, observe that the term $1/(1+R)^n$ in Equation 5 approaches zero as n becomes infinitely large (as long as the required return is positive); therefore, the present value of a perpetuity is as follows:

Consols pay a constant amount forever.

$$P = \frac{X}{R}$$

If the cash flow is $100 a year forever and the required return is 10 percent, then the present value is

$$P = \frac{\$100}{0.10}$$

$$= \$1,000$$

This makes sense, in that a $100 annual return on a $1,000 investment does provide the requisite 10 percent return.

Compound Interest

The sale of Manhattan in 1626 is a dramatic example of the power of compound interest: earning interest on interest causes wealth to grow geometrically. In the 1960s, banks and other financial institutions began compounding interest more frequently than once a year in order to raise the effective rates of interest on their deposits above the ceiling rates set by Regulation Q.

Suppose that the quoted annual deposit rate is 6 percent. If there is no compounding during the year, then $1 grows to $1.06 by year's end. With semiannual compounding, the deposit is credited with 6%/2 = 3% interest halfway through the year, and then, during the next six months, with another 3 percent interest on both the initial deposit and the first six-month's interest, giving an effective rate of return for the year of 6.09 percent:

Frequent compounding increases the effective return.

$$\$1(1.03)^2 = \$1.0609$$

This is an effective rate of return in the sense that 6 percent compounded semiannually earns as much as 6.09 percent compounded annually.

With quarterly compounding, 6%/4 = 1.5% interest is credited every three months

$$\$1(1.015)^4 = \$1.0614$$

raising the effective rate to 6.14 percent. Monthly compounding, which pays 6%/12 = 0.5% each month, raises the effective return up to 6.17 percent. The general formula is that an amount P invested at an annual rate of return R, compounded m times a year, grows to $P(1 + R/m)^m$ after 1 year and to

$$F = P(1 + R/m)^{mn}$$

after n years.

The effective return is increased by more frequent compounding, up to the limit of continuous compounding, where the frequency of compounding is infinitely large and the time between compoundings is infinitesimally small.

The Value of a Lottery Jackpot

In May 1984, the headlines said, "Thousands Seek Millions as Jackpot Fever Grips New York," a fever that has broken out several times since.* The May 1984 story concerned a New York Lotto drawing with a $22.1 million jackpot that lured people into hour-long lines, beginning at 5 A.M., betting more than a million dollars an hour — a total of $24.1 million.

In the New York Lotto game, a machine randomly chooses 6 out of 44 Ping-Pong balls numbered 1 to 44. The jackpot is divided evenly among those who correctly predict all six numbers (not necessarily in order). The probability of doing so is about 1 in 7 million. The size of the jackpot depends on the amount wagered, with New York, like most states, keeping about 60 percent of the amount wagered and paying out 40 percent in prizes. For the May 12, 1984, drawing, there had been no winner for three straight games and the state accumulated the prize money, expanding the jackpot to $22.1 million.

There turned out to be four winning tickets, with each winner receiving $22,100,000/4 = $5,525,000 — not all at once, but in 21 annual installments of $5,525,000/21 = $263,095. What is the present value of these annual payments? That is, how much would someone pay for a winning ticket? Alternatively, how much would the State of New York have to deposit in a bank account in 1984 in order to pay a winner $263,095 a year for 21 years? The present value is

$$P = \$263,095 + \frac{\$263,095}{(1 + R)} + \frac{\$263,095}{(1 + R)^2} + \cdots + \frac{\$263,095}{(1 + R)^{20}}$$

which works out to $1.9 million with a 15 percent interest rate and $2.5 million at a 10 percent interest rate — only 35 percent to 45 percent of the reported value of $5.5 million! State lotteries not only keep 60 percent of the amount wagered, but they spread the jackpots out so that the present value of the payoff is less than half its reported value. No wonder governments like lotteries.

---

*John J. Goldman, "Thousands Seek Millions As Jackpot Fever Grips N.Y.," *Los Angeles Times,* May 12, 1984.

Mathematically,

$$F = \lim_{m \to \infty} (1 + R/m)^m = e^R$$

where $e = 2.718 \ldots$ is the base of the natural logarithms.

In practice, of course, banks don't continuously update their account balances. At some specified interval, perhaps quarterly or annually, they use this mathematical formula to determine the amount of interest each depositor has earned. In our example, with $R = 6$ percent, continuous compounding pushes the effective annual rate up to 6.18 percent, only a slight improvement over monthly compounding — even though advertisements proclaiming "continuous compounding" convey the feeling that the bank is doing something marvelous to our money.

ZERO-COUPON BONDS

Most bonds pay both periodic (usually semiannual) interest and a final maturation value when the bond matures. The interest payments are called **coupons** because, traditionally, they were literally part of the bond certificate, to be clipped with scissors and redeemed through a local bank or security dealer. The maturity value is also called the par value, or face value. Most corporate bonds have par values of $1,000 or $5,000; U.S. Treasury bonds range from $1,000 upward.

Zeros pay nothing before maturity.

Zero-coupon bonds (zeros) differ from ordinary bonds in that, as the name implies, they pay no coupons. Pepsico and J. C. Penney issued corporate zeros in 1981 and, a year later, a number of brokerage firms began marketing zeros created from coupon-paying Treasury bonds. Merrill Lynch introduced its version of zeros, called Treasury Investment Growth Receipts ("Tigers," for short) in 1982 by buying a pool of $500 million in long-term Treasury bonds. Merrill Lynch put these Treasury bonds in a trust and created a series of zeros maturing at six-month intervals by "stripping" away the coupons. For example, a 20-year bond paying $5,000 semiannual coupons and $100,000 at maturity can be separated into forty $5,000 zeros, with maturities ranging from 6 months to 20 years, and one 20-year $100,000 zero. These can be split into smaller denominations or combined with pieces of other bonds to give larger zeros. Salomon Brothers sells similar zeros, labeled Certificates of Accrual on Treasury Securities ("Cats"), and other firms use other labels. Encouraged by their success, the U.S. Treasury now strips its own bonds and sells zeros, too; their name is less colorful, but accurate: Separate Trading of Registered Interest and Principal of Securities (STRIPS).

The implicit annual rate of return on a zero that costs P and pays an amount F in n years is given by the compound interest formula

$$P(1 + R)^n = F$$

For instance, a $10,000 Tiger purchased in 1984 will pay $300,000 in 2014. The implicit interest rate is determined as follows. The future value equation is 12 percent:

$$\$10,000(1 + R)^{30} = \$300,000$$

Dividing both sides by $10,000 gives

$$(1 + R)^{30} = 30$$

Now, taking the 30th root,

$$1 + R = 30^{1/30} = 1.12$$
$$R = 0.12 \text{ (or } 12\%)$$

Many institutions appreciate the simplicity of zero-coupon bonds and the fact that they don't have to worry about reinvesting future coupons at uncertain interest rates. But, as we will see in the next two chapters, zero-coupon bonds are hardly worry-free.

Although zero-coupon bonds don't pay any interest until maturity, the investor pays taxes each year as if interest had been paid. For tax purposes, the value of the investment is assumed to increase each year at a rate R, and taxes are levied on this implicit increase. With this tax accounting, the implicit after-tax return is equal to $(1 - t)R$, where t is the investor's marginal tax rate. For example, in a 28 percent tax bracket, the implicit after-tax yield on a 12 percent zero is $(1 - 0.28)12$ percent = 8.64 percent.

Treasury Bills

Just as households borrow to buy cars and houses and businesses borrow to buy plants and equipment, so the government borrows to buy missiles and paper clips. When the federal government's expenditures exceed its tax revenues, the U.S. Treasury sells securities to raise cash. Treasury bonds have maturities of more than ten years; Treasury notes have maturities of 1 to 10 years; **Treasury bills (T-bills)** mature in less than a year.

Treasury bills are short-term zeros in that they mature within a year and pay no interest before maturity. The minimum face value is $10,000. Investors earn interest by buying T-bills at a discount from the face value received at maturity. For example, if you buy a one-year $10,000 T-bill for $9,400, you receive $10,000 after a year and the return on your investment is the $600 difference between the purchase price and redemption value of the bill. The IRS considers this $600 return interest, not a capital gain, and taxes it as such, the same as interest from a bank account.

T-bills are short-term treasury zeros.

Treasury bills are issued by the federal government at periodic auctions in which some 40 dealers submit bids, stating the quantity they want and the price they are willing to pay. These orders are filled, starting with the highest price, until the supply is exhausted. An individual investor can buy T-bills at the

Highlight 5.4   Prepaid Tuition Plans

In 1985, Duquesne University introduced a novel way to prepay college expenses, an idea that has since been imitated by dozens of other colleges and universities. By making a single $5,700 payment in 1985, parents could buy four years of tuition for a son or daughter, enrolling at Duquesne fourteen years later, in 1999.

Prepaid tuition is very similar to a zero-coupon bond, but the maturation value, Duquesne's tuition in 1999, is uncertain. In 1985, tuition was $5,850, and Duquesne officials assumed that it would increase by 6 percent a year, to

$$\$5,850(1.06^{14}) = \$13,226$$

in 1999. They multiplied by 4 to estimate the cost of four years of tuition:

$$4(\$13,226) = \$52,905$$

How much should they charge for this future value? Duquesne treated the $52,905 payoff as a zero-coupon bond with a 17.25 percent annual return and calculated the cost X from

$$X(1 + 0.1725)^{14} = \$52,905$$

implying

$$X = \$5,700$$

which is what they charged parents.

Duquesne invested each $5,700 payment in 11 percent zero-coupon bonds maturing in 1999 with a payoff of

$$\$5,700(1.11^{14}) = \$24,570$$

Thus Duquesne's future receipt was only about half of the school's own estimated future cost of tuition.

The parents were implicitly credited with a 17.25 percent annual return on their investment, although market interest rates were only 11 percent. The accompanying table shows how their implicit rate of return varies with the rate of growth of tuition.

Rate of Growth of Tuition	Total Four-Year Tuition in 1999	Implicit Return if Parent Pays $5,700 in 1985
4%	$40,521	15.04%
6%	52,905	17.25%
8%	68,730	19.46%
10%	88,861	21.68%

Another risk is whether the child, now three years old, will be accepted and want to attend Duquesne fourteen years later. Under Duquesne's plan, if the child does not attend, the parents get only their $5,700 investment back, with no interest at all. Thus the parents' alternatives are to invest $5,700 at 11 percent on their own, giving them $24,570 in cash to spend as they wish, or to invest $5,700 in Duquesne's prepayment plan, giving them $5,700 if the son or daughter does not attend or free tuition, worth some $40,000 to $90,000, if he or she does attend for four years.

The plan was initially marketed only to Duquesne alumni, and about five hundred signed up. During the subsequent three years, interest rates declined and Duquesne raised its estimated tuition growth rate to 8 percent. Together, these events boosted the parents' prepayment from $5,700 in 1984 to $25,300 in 1988, prompting the school to suspend the plan until the cost declined significantly.

average auction price by mailing a certified check for $10,000 and receiving a refund once the price is determined. Thirteen-week (91-day) and 26-week (182-day) T-bills are sold every Monday; 52-week (364-day) T-bills are sold every fourth Wednesday. After issuance, T-bills, like all government securities, are traded over the counter.

COUPON BONDS

To finance the federal deficit, the U.S. Treasury sells not only short-term T-bills, but also longer-term, coupon-bearing Treasury notes and bonds. **Corporate bond**s are fixed-income securities of various maturities issued by corporations to buy new plants and equipment, pay current bills, and finance the takeover of other companies. Specific corporate bonds have a number of ever-changing labels, often concocted for marketing purposes. These labels are less important than the general principles.

Yield to Maturity

The rate of return on a zero-coupon bond held to maturity depends on a relatively straightforward comparison of the purchase price with the maturation value. Coupon bonds are more complex because they involve a sequence of periodic payments. To illustrate the logic, we'll use the May 17, 1986, data in Table 5.1 for four corporate bonds, as reported in *The Wall Street Journal*.

These bonds were issued by AT&T, IBM, and Navistar. The first number after the company's name gives the **coupon rate**, the annual coupon as a percentage of the bond's maturation value. For a $1,000 AT&T bond, the annual

A bond's coupon rate is its annual coupon as a percentage of its maturation value.

Highlight 5.5 — Why Reported T-Bill Rates Are Misleading

Unlike virtually all other securities, the financial press traditionally calculates the returns on T-bill on a **discount basis**, relative to the face value rather than to the purchase price. If you buy a 52-week $10,000 T-bill for $9,400, this $600 discount is a 6 percent discount from the $10,000 face value and the T-bill rate is conventionally reported as 6 percent. But from the standpoint of the investor, this is a $600 return on an investment of $9,400, not $10,000, and the actual rate of return is $600/$9,400 = 0.0638 = 6.38%. Because T-bill rates are traditionally calculated on a discount basis (relative to the maturation value rather than to the purchase price), they understate the investor's actual rate of return.

The federal government does not allow banks to calculate consumer loan rates on a discount basis, but uses this misleading arithmetic for its own borrowings — thereby understating the interest rate it pays investors. Perhaps the calculation of T-bill rates on a discount basis made sense long ago when computations were done by hand and it was easier to divide by $10,000 than by $9,423.19, but today we have computers to do our arithmetic for us, and this anachronism either misleads investors or forces them to do the computations themselves.

coupon is $(3\frac{7}{8}\%)(\$1,000) = \$38.75$, paid in two semiannual installments of $38.75/2 = $19.38. Similarly, the $1,000 Navistar bond pays $45.00 every six months. The next number in the table is the year the bond matures, 1990 for AT&T, 2004 and 1995 for the two IBM bonds, and 2004 for the Navistar bond. You can consult a dealer or a bond fact book to find the exact payment dates for the coupons and maturation value. (The small s that sometimes appears between the coupon rate and the maturation date is just for style, to help separate the two numbers or because the natural pronunciation of the coupon rate includes an s.)

The closing price ("close") is the last price at which the bond traded that day, quoted as a percentage of the face value. (The buyer of a bond must also pay the seller a proportionate share of the next coupon payment; for example, if a bond is bought five months after the last coupon and one month before the next, the buyer must pay the seller an amount equal to $\frac{5}{6}$ of that next coupon.) The last trade in the AT&T bond was at 89, down $\frac{1}{4}$ from the closing price the day before, as the column headed "Net Change" shows. For an AT&T bond with a $1,000 face value, this translates to a price of $0.89(\$1,000) = \$890$, down from $892.50. The two IBM bonds also closed lower, while the Navistar bond closed at a higher price than it had the day before.

It is striking that the price of the Navistar bond was 20 percent less than the price of the first IBM bond, even though both mature in the same year and

Table 5.1	Prices and Yields of Four Bonds on May 17, 1986			
Bonds	Current Yield	Close	Net Change	Yield to Maturity
AT&T 3⅞s90	4.4	89	$-\frac{1}{4}$	7.1%
IBM 9¾ 04	9.1	102½	$-\frac{3}{8}$	9.1%
IBM 10¼ 95	9.3	110	-2	8.6%
Navstr 9s04	11.0	81⅞	$+\frac{7}{8}$	11.4%

pay virtually the same coupon. Similarly, we might wonder why the AT&T bond is relatively inexpensive and why one IBM bond sells for less than the other. We will answer these questions in the next two chapters.

The current yield shown in the table is the annual coupon as a percentage of the current price. Thus 3⅞ is 4.4 percent of 89,

$$(3\tfrac{7}{8})/89 = 0.044$$

The 4.4 percent current yield is not a very informative statistic. It is true that if you purchase a $1,000 AT&T bond for $890, the annual $38.75 coupon represents a 4.4 percent return on your $890 investment. But this calculation ignores the fact that you will make another $110 profit when the bond matures in 1990 and pays you $1,000. A calculation of your total return must take into account both coupons and maturation value.

Logically, the price that investors are willing to pay for a bond is the present value of the cash flow: the coupons and maturation value discounted by a required rate of return. The **yield to maturity** on a bond is the discount rate that makes the present value of the coupons and the maturation value equal to the price. If we use the following notation (and assume annual coupons for simplicity)

A bond's yield to maturity is the discount rate for which the present value of the coupons and maturation value is equal to the price.

P = bond price
C = annual coupon
n = number of years until maturity
M = maturation, or face value
y = annual yield to maturity

then the yield to maturity y is given by the solution of

$$P = \frac{C}{1+y} + \frac{C}{(1+y)^2} + \cdots + \frac{C}{(1+y)^n} + \frac{M}{(1+y)^n} \tag{6}$$

Because we know P, C, and M, we can solve Equation 6 for the yield to maturity y using a financial calculator or computer program that, by trial and error, tries different tentative values of y, until the present value is approximately equal to the price.

For the AT&T bond just discussed,

$$P = \$890$$
$$C = \$38.75$$
$$n = 4$$
$$M = \$1,000$$

and the appropriate present-value equation is

$$\$890 = \frac{\$38.75}{1+y} + \frac{\$38.75}{(1+y)^2} + \frac{\$38.75}{(1+y)^3} + \frac{\$38.75}{(1+y)^4} + \frac{\$1,000}{(1+y)^4}$$

The solution is $y = 0.071$, or 7.1 percent. Table 5.1 shows the yields to maturity for all four of the bonds just discussed. The puzzles to be explained in the next two chapters are why the Navistar bond is priced to have such a high yield to maturity and why there are variations among the other three bonds, two of which are issued by the same company.

Yield to Maturity Versus Price and Coupon Rate

When the financial press speaks of "interest rates," it is usually referring to bond yields to maturity, and we will use the same language. Because interest rates usually change by only a fraction of a percent each day, financial-market participants use the term **basis points** to describe hundredths of a percentage point. For example, if an interest rate rises from 5.80 percent to 5.87 percent, this is said to be an increase of 7 basis points.

Because the yield to maturity is the discount rate for which the present value of the coupons and the maturation value is equal to the price of the bond, bond prices fall when interest rates increase and rise when interest rates decline. Thus whenever the front page of the daily newspaper reports that interest rates have increased, the financial pages report a drop in bond prices.

Equation 6 shows mathematically the inherent inverse relationship between a bond's yield and its price. A bond has a fixed cash flow (that's why it's called a fixed-income security), and the higher the required return used to discount this cash flow, the lower the present value. Put somewhat differently, because the cash flow is fixed, the only way investors can get a higher return, if they require it, is if the price is lower.

Suppose, for instance, that you pay $1,000 for an IBM bond with 8 percent coupons ($80 a year). Interest rates now increase to 10 percent, so that for IBM to sell new bonds for $1,000, it must offer bonds with 10 percent coupons ($100 a year). Will investors pay $1,000 in the secondary market for your bond with $80 coupons if they can buy new bonds with $100 coupons for $1,000 in the primary market? No. No one will buy your bond unless the price falls enough to make the yield competitive.

People are sometimes puzzled by the fact that a drop in the price *raises* the yield. Don't investors *lose* money when the price falls? The explanation is that

Interest rate basis points are hundredths of a percentage point.

we must distinguish between the past rate of return on a bond and its current yield to maturity. The price falls so that, for those who buy at the new price, the future cash flow provides the requisite higher yield to maturity. Investors who bought before the price declined experience a capital loss — a negative rate of return that was no doubt unexpected, because they would have sold yesterday had they known the price would be lower today.

The inverse relationship between a bond's price and its yield to maturity has an important corollary. Notice that the first IBM bond in Table 5.1 has a price ($102\frac{1}{2}$) that is close to its face value (100) and a yield to maturity (9.1%) that is close to its coupon rate ($9\frac{3}{8}$). The second IBM bond, on the other hand, has a price above its face value and a yield to maturity below its coupon rate, while the AT&T and Navistar bonds have prices below face value and yields to maturity above their coupon rates. This is no accident. The Appendix shows that when a bond's yield to maturity is equal to its coupon rate, the price of the bond is equal to its face value. A bond sells for a premium above face value when the yield is below the coupon rate, and at a discount when the yield is above the coupon rate.

When a coupon-paying bond is first issued, the coupon rate is usually set close to the prevailing yield to maturity on similar bonds, so that the bond will sell for close to face value. If, after issuance, interest rates fall, the bond's price will rise above its face value, because its superior coupons make it more valuable. If interest rates rise, the bond's price will fall to a discount from face value, so that its coupons provide an adequate rate of return. For example, the AT&T bond in Table 5.1 was issued in 1956, when interest rates were about 4 percent, and sold for a discount in 1986 in order to provide a yield of 7 percent.

A bond's price is larger or smaller than its maturation value, as its yield to maturity is larger or smaller than its coupon rate.

Tax-exempt Bonds

The interest on bonds issued by state and local governments is generally exempt from federal income taxes; interest on U.S. Treasury securities, on the other hand, is not subject to state and local taxes. Because federal income taxes are the more substantial, state and local government bonds — often called "municipals" or "munis" — are said to be **tax-exempt bonds.**

Most states that have income taxes do not tax interest on their own bonds, making these bonds double tax-exempt; for example, Californians who buy bonds issued by the state of California do not have to pay either state or federal income taxes on the interest. New York City levies a city income tax, making its bonds triple tax-exempt for residents.

The interest on most state and local government bonds is exempt from federal income taxes.

There are two primary types of state and local securities. General-obligation bonds are backed by the full faith and credit of the issuer and, more importantly, by its ability to levy taxes. A revenue bond, in contrast, is issued to finance a specific project, such as a road, sports facility, or water project, and will be repaid with the income from the completed project. Usually, the agency that issues a revenue bond has no taxing authority and the bond is not an obligation of the state or local government.

About half of the state and local bonds issued in 1985 were private-purpose revenue bonds for such projects as hotels, stores, irrigation projects, and industrial parks.[1] Concerned about apparent abuses, Congress put restrictions in the Tax Reform Act of 1986 on the amount and type of munis used to finance essentially private projects. Bonds falling outside of these restrictions are not exempt from federal taxes, creating a new class of bond — taxable munis. For instance, municipal bonds used to finance sports stadiums or convention facilities owned by private interests are no longer exempt from federal taxes. Congress did include a "grandfather" clause, allowing an exemption for existing bonds and even for some private projects that had been planned, but not yet financed, before the Reform Act.

Because of the tax advantages, investors in high tax brackets buy state and local bonds even when the before-tax yields to maturity are substantially below those on equally safe, but taxable, corporate bonds. In recent years, as Figure 5.2 shows, the interest rates on highly rated state and local bonds generally have been roughly 1–2 percent below the interest rates on similarly rated corporate bonds. For instance, in January 1986, yields to maturity averaged around 10 percent on highly rated corporate bonds and about 8 percent on comparable state and local bonds. College endowments and other investors who don't pay taxes prefer 10 percent corporates, whereas those in high tax brackets prefer 8 percent tax-exempts. What is the break-even tax rate that would make an investor indifferent between the two bonds? If t is the tax rate, the after-tax yields are $(1 - t)10\%$ and 8%, and these are equal

$$(1 - t)10\% = 8\%$$

for

$$t = 0.20$$

Taxable corporate bonds paying 10 percent appeal to those with tax rates below 20 percent, while tax-exempt munis pay 8 percent are preferred by those in higher tax brackets.

TAKING ACCOUNT OF INFLATION IN PRESENT-VALUE CALCULATIONS

Many people make the mistake of thinking that present-value logic — that a dollar today is worth more than a dollar tomorrow — hinges on inflation: "A dollar today is worth more than a dollar tomorrow, because prices tomorrow will be higher than they are today." It is true that dollars lose purchasing power as prices rise, but present-value logic hinges on something else — that a dollar today can be *invested* to grow to more than a dollar tomorrow.

Imagine a not-so-hypothetical experiment. It is 1982 and safe Treasury bills yield a 14.9 percent rate of return, while the rate of inflation is 3.9 percent; or, to make the conclusion even more obvious, let's assume that the rate of inflation is zero. In such a situation, how much would you pay today for a guaranteed

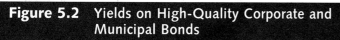

Figure 5.2 Yields on High-Quality Corporate and Municipal Bonds

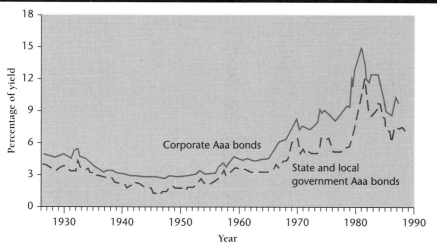

source: Federal Reserve *1987 Historical Chart Book*

Figure 5.3 Interest Rates and Inflation, 1926–87

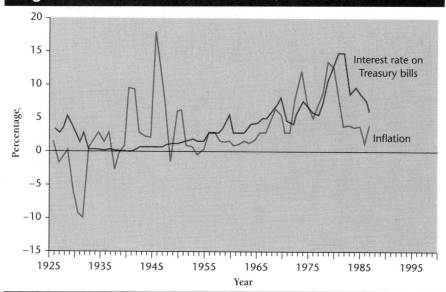

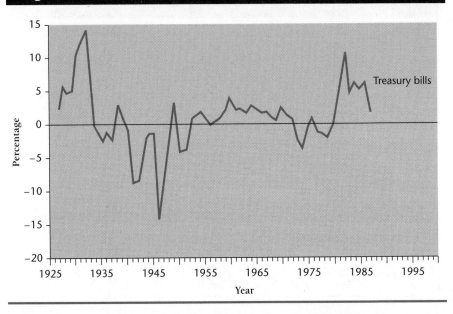

Figure 5.4 **Real Interest Rates, 1926–87**

$1,000 a year from now? Would you pay $1,000 because there is no inflation? Or would you pay $1,000/1.149 = $870 because you could otherwise invest $870 in Treasury bills for a year and have it grow to $1,000? It is rates of return that make current dollars valuable, and it is rates of return, not inflation, that should be used to discount future cash flows.

> Interest rates, not inflation, make current dollars valuable.

A more subtle question is whether nominal or real required returns should be used in present-value calculations. The answer is that either will do, as long as we are consistent with the way the cash flows are measured. If we use nominal cash flows, then we should discount by nominal required rates of return; if we use real cash flows, then real rates of return are appropriate.

The Effect of Inflation Expectations on Nominal Interest Rates

We saw in Chapter 1 that the real rate of return r on an investment is equal to the nominal rate of return R minus the rate of inflation π,

$$r = R - \pi$$

Even if the nominal rate of return is known in advance, the rate of inflation and the real rate of return are not. The expected real return r^* depends on the expected rate of inflation π^*:

$$r^* = R - \pi^*$$

Suppose that the nominal return is 5 percent and the inflation rate is expected to be 2 percent. The anticipated real rate of return is 5% − 2% = 3%. If the rate of inflation rises to 12 percent, people won't be enthusiastic about investing at a 5 percent nominal return, because their anticipated real return will be a disheartening −7 percent. Instead, they may try to stockpile some of the commodities whose prices are rising by 12 percent a year. Neglecting storage and other expenses, stockpiling will give a 12 percent nominal return, for a 0 percent real return — not much, but better than −7 percent. For bonds to be competitive with commodities when a 12 percent inflation is expected, they must offer more than a 5 percent nominal return.

Real interest rates are not invariably positive. Throughout the 1970s, many people kept funds in savings accounts paying about 5 percent interest while consumer prices relentlessly increased by more than 5 percent a year. They accepted negative real returns because they believed that these savings accounts were the best of their alternatives. Stocks, bonds, and other assets that might have earned higher yields were too risky or had high brokerage fees for small investors. Some assets had stiff minimum-investment requirements. It took $10,000 to buy a Treasury bill. It takes millions to buy a shopping center. And it is not possible to guarantee a zero real rate of return by investing in the Consumer Price Index. Some people may have stocked up on wine and soup. But it is difficult to stockpile flammable gasoline, perishable food, fashionable clothing, advanced computers, medical services, haircuts, sales taxes, and other components of the CPI.

Investor reluctance to hold securities whose anticipated returns are less than the expected rate of inflation does tend to increase interest rates during inflationary periods. However, an increase in the expected rate of inflation does not automatically raise nominal interest rates by an equal amount, leaving real interest rates constant.

Anticipated inflation tends to increase nominal interest rates; however, real interest rates are not constant.

Before-tax real interest rates were relatively stable and generally positive in the 1950s and 1960s in the United States, lending credence to the idea that real interest rates are approximately constant and always positive. But these assumptions were treated roughly in the 1970s and 1980s, when real interest rates turned first persistently negative and then substantially positive, as shown in Figures 5.3 and 5.4. A look in the other direction reveals that real interest rates were not very stable before the 1950s, either.

A very specific example of volatile real interest rates occurred in 1985. In January, the average inflation forecast of 462 financial professionals was 5.2 percent inflation over the next decade, and the yield on 10-year Treasury bonds was 11.4 percent. A year later, in February 1986, the consensus inflation forecast was still above 5 percent, and the 10-year yield had dropped nearly 3 percentage points, to 8.7 percent.[2]

Careful empirical studies seem to confirm these informal observations. A study of the real returns on corporate bonds all the way back to 1791 found that real interest rates tend to fall during inflation (averaging −7 percent during 17 years when prices rose by 7.5 percent or more) and to rise during deflation (averaging more than 12 percent during eleven years when prices fell by 6 percent or more).[3] A more mathematical study, by Lawrence Summers, found that during the years 1860–1940 there was "no tendency for interest rates to increase with movements in expected inflation."[4] In the years since World War II, he found a slight positive relationship, but he also found that "In almost every case the data reject quite decisively the hypothesis" that real interest rates are constant.

SUMMARY

The future value of an investment is the value it will grow to at a stated date if it earns a specified rate of return. The present value of a cash flow is the amount you are willing to pay for it, and is determined by discounting the cash flow by your required rate of return. The higher the required return, the lower the present value. This required rate of return depends on the returns available on alternative investments and other characteristics, such as the riskiness of the cash flow, that make this investment relatively attractive or unattractive. An investment that is risky, or otherwise undesirable, has a low present value; risk-averse investors will not acquire risky investments unless the price is low and the potential return high.

Compound interest describes the earning of interest on interest, a powerful mathematical concept that causes seemingly slight differences in annual returns to grow to large differences in wealth after many years. Over short horizons, compound interest — crediting interest monthly, daily, or even continuously — can be used to boost the effective return on a bank deposit or other investment.

Treasury bills mature within a year and pay a single lump sum at maturity. Interest rates on T-bills are often quoted on a discount basis, relative to face value rather than current price, and therefore understate the actual rate of return. The yield to maturity on a bond, coupon-paying or not, is the interest rate for which the present value of the cash flow, coupons and maturation value, is equal to its current price.

Bond prices and interest rates (that is, yields to maturity) are inversely related. When interest rates rise, bond prices fall; when interest rates decline, bond prices increase. A bond's yield to maturity is equal to its coupon rate (the ratio of its annual coupon to face value) if the bond's price is equal to its face value. Because the price and the yield to maturity are inversely related, a bond sells at a discount from face value when its yield is larger than its coupon rate and at a premium when the yield is below the coupon rate.

Bonds issued by state and local governments are called municipal bonds, munis, or tax-exempts, because most are exempt from federal income taxes. If a corporate bond yields 10 percent and a comparably risky tax-exempt bond yields 8 percent, investors with marginal income-tax rates larger than 20 percent can earn a higher after-tax return from the tax-exempt bond, whereas the reverse is true of those in lower tax brackets.

The nominal return from an investment compares the dollars received with the dollars invested. The real return, measuring the percentage increase in purchasing power, is equal to the nominal return minus the rate of inflation. Present-value logic, that a dollar today is worth more than a dollar tomorrow, is based not on the observation that inflation reduces the purchasing power of dollars but on the fact that money invested today will earn additional dollars. Thus the required return used to discount nominal cash flows depends on the rates of return available on alternative investments, not the rate of inflation. Nominal interest rates do tend to increase during inflations but not invariably by an amount equal to the rate of inflation, and thus real interest rates do vary from year to year.

IMPORTANT TERMS

basis points
cash flow
compound interest
corporate bonds
coupon rate
coupons
discount basis
future value

perfect substitutes
present value
required rate of return
risk
tax-exempt bonds
Treasury bills (T-bills)
yield to maturity
zero-coupon bonds (zeros)

EXERCISES

1. Which grows to a larger future value, $1,000 invested for two years at
   a. 10 percent each year?
   b. 5 percent the first year and 15 percent the second year?
   c. 15 percent the first year and 5 percent the second year?

2. Which grows to a larger future value,
   a. $2,000 invested for 20 years at 10 percent?
   b. $1,000 invested for 20 years at 20 percent?

3. A 1987 advertisement in *The New Yorker* solicited offers on a 1967 Mercury Cougar XR7 (*Motor Trend*'s 1967 car of the year) that had been stored undriven, in a climate-controlled environment for 20 years.[5] If the original owner paid $4,000 for this car in 1967, what price would he have to receive in 1987 to obtain a 10 percent annual return on his investment?

4. Vincent van Gogh sold only one painting during his lifetime, for about $30. A sunflower still life he painted in 1888 sold for $39.85 million in 1987, more than three times the highest price paid previously for any work of art. If this sunflower painting had been purchased for $30 in 1888 and sold in 1987 for $39.85 million, what would have been the annual rate of return?

5. In 1987, a small company estimated that someone who invested $6,600 in the company might have $106,500 after $5\frac{1}{3}$ years, a "total percentage return" of 1,614 percent and a 303 percent "average percentage return." Show the errors in these percentage-return calculations.

6. In 1940 your grandmother put $1,000 into a special trust to be paid to a future grandchild (you) 60 years later, in the year 2000. How much will this trust be worth then if it has been earning 8 percent a year?

7. "The United States made the Louisiana Purchase in 1808 for $15 million — a bargain at only $2\frac{1}{2}$ cents an acre." What is the future value of $2\frac{1}{2}$ cents invested for 182 years, until 1990, at 4 percent a year? At 6 percent? At 8 percent?

8. What interest rate was used to determine the following settlement?[6]

The [British] Treasury, after 775 years, has settled a debt for death and damage caused by Oxford people in 1209.

    The Government has been paying £3.08 a year compensation to Oxford University after people in the city hanged two students for helping a student to murder his mistress. Now the University has accepted a [once-and-for-all] payment of £33.08 in settlement.

9. A college is considering establishing a publishing house. It can borrow at 10 percent or use endowment funds currently invested in bonds earning an average return of 12 percent. One trustee says that the appropriate required return is 10 percent, while another says it is 12 percent. What do you say?

10. An "annualized" return is calculated by ignoring compounding; for example, the annualized interest rate for a credit-card company that charges 1.5 percent a month on unpaid balances is 12(1.5%) = 18%. What is the effective interest rate, taking monthly compounding into account?

11. A million-dollar state lottery pays $25,000 a year for 40 years. At a 10 percent required return, what is the present value of this payoff?

12. Explain why you either agree or disagree with this argument:

Your great-grandfather has just died and left you $120,000, which you will invest in a small winery; because this inheritance cost you nothing, your required rate of return is 0 percent.

13. In 1987, the College Savings Bank introduced the CollegeSure CD, which its president called "the single most important financial product of the century, and that's an understatement."[7] By paying $14,570 in 1987, the parent of a 5-year-old buys one year of private college education thirteen years later — when its esti-mated cost will be $28,580. If the cost does turn out to be $28,580, what is the implicit rate of return on such an investment? If the cost of a comparable year of college education was $11,500 in 1987, what annual rate of increase of college prices is assumed in the $28,500 estimated future cost?

14. One financial observer wrote that a U.S. Treasury bond is "backed by the full faith and credit of the national government. To put it more directly, government paper is backed by the federal government's power to tax."[8] If a balanced-budget amendment or other law restricted the federal government's ability to increase taxes, would there be serious doubts about the U.S. government's ability to pay the interest due on its debt?

15. Listed below are four bonds and their yields to maturity on November 8, 1988. Which bonds were selling for a premium over face value and which at a discount?
   a. Texaco 13s 91, yield to maturity = 11.9 percent.
   b. Texaco $13\frac{5}{8}$ 94, yield to maturity = 11.5 percent.
   c. Texaco $5\frac{3}{4}$ 97, yield to maturity = 10.0 percent.
   d. Texaco $7\frac{3}{4}$ 01, yield to maturity = 10.3 percent.

16. Explain why these two 1984 statements by the same author are either consistent or inconsistent:[9]

Daily price fluctuations of government securities are minimal. [p. 44]

Since the late seventies, interest rates have fluctuated widely and wildly, with significant changes occurring not only week to week, but even daily. [p. 45]

17. Critically evaluate this statement:[10]

Investors flee from bonds when interest rates rise — or when they think they're going to rise — because bond prices move in the opposite direction from interest rates. Thus bonds — which are interest-bearing debt securities issued by governments and corporations to raise money — are a good investment during periods of low interest rates.

18. A bond paying a 10 percent annual coupon for 20 years is selling for its maturation value, $1,000. What is the annual yield to maturity?

19. A firm that markets time-share condominiums offers prizes to those who endure a tour and sales talk. One prize is a savings account paying $1,000 after 45 years, in return for a $55 fee for "handling, processing, and insurance."[11] What is the implicit annual rate of return to someone who accepts this prize?

20. A home-seller was offered $290,000: $140,000 cash plus zero-coupon bonds paying $150,000 after 20 years.[12] If the annual interest rate on these bonds is 10 percent, what is the buyer's actual cost for the property?

21. In 1986, Duquesne University offered these prepaid tuition options:

Number of Years Until Enrollment	Cost If Prepaid Today	Estimated Cost at Enrollment
10	$13,061	$54,675
15	$ 8,837	76,685

What are the implicit rates of return if we consider each of these plans to be a zero-coupon bond paying the estimated enrollment cost in a single lump sum at enrollment?

22. Here is a 1987 analysis of municipal bond prices:[13]

Demand for the bonds of states, cities, and public authorities, which offer tax-exempt interest payments, has been tremendous. So many have rushed to buy what bond houses advertise as the last tax shelter of the middle class that customary price differentials between tax-exempt and taxable bonds have narrowed. Crowd psychology rather than economics is at work.

Consider equally risky tax-exempt and taxable bonds with equal coupons. Which will have the higher price? If the demand for tax-exempts surges, will the price differential narrow?

23. Historically, the yields on tax-free municipal bonds have averaged about 70 percent of the yields on comparable, taxable corporate bonds; for instance, municipals might yield 7 percent whereas corporates yield 10 percent. If so, investors in which tax brackets receive a higher after-tax return from municipals?

24. A *Wall Street Journal* article began, "Pay $1,200 or more for a municipal bond that will return only $1,000 [at] maturity? That strikes most investors as a stupid idea."[14] Would it ever be a good idea?

25. The 1986 Tax Reform Act imposed restrictions on municipal bonds used to finance private projects. Why did projects financed by municipal bonds have an "unfair advantage" over projects financed by corporate bonds?

26. Historically, banks have been major purchasers of municipal bonds, but the Tax Reform Act of 1986 changed the tax code so that when banks and other financial institutions calculate their taxable income, they can no longer deduct the interest paid for deposits and other money borrowed to finance the purchase of munis. Can you think of any reason for this change? How do you think it affected bank demand for municipal bonds?

27. In 1979, Treasury bills yielded a 10.7 percent return (correctly calculated) and the inflation rate was 13.3 percent. In 1982, Treasury bills yielded 14.9 percent and the inflation rate was 3.9 percent. What were the real after-tax returns during these two years for someone in a 30 percent tax bracket?

28. An entrepreneur is considering building a facility for recreational indoor soccer. Because she anticipates 4 percent inflation over the next few years, she argues that the projected

cash flows should be discounted by a 4 percent required return. A financial adviser says that she should use a 10 percent required rate of return because she can earn 10 percent by investing in U.S. Treasury bonds. What do you advise?

29. It has been argued that nominal interest rates move up and down with inflation so as to hold real interest rates constant at, say, 2 percent. If a 5 percent *fall* in prices is anticipated, what nominal rate of return will give a 2 percent real return? (Ignore taxes.) How much does a

$100 investment have to pay a year from now to give this nominal return? Why won't people willingly make such an investment?

30. In 1984 a Harvard Business School professor observed that during the period 1926–76 the average real rate of return on long-term Treasury bonds was 1.1 percent and reasoned that, "With long-term Treasury bonds yielding a nominal return of 11 percent [in 1984], this suggests that investors harbor long-term inflation expectations close to 10 percent."[15] What is the implicit assumption?

Chapter 5 APPENDIX

THE PRESENT VALUE OF A CONSTANT CASH FLOW

The present value of a constant cash flow is

$$P = \frac{X}{1+R} + \frac{X}{(1+R)^2} + \cdots + \frac{X}{(1+R)^n}$$

If we factor out $X/(1+R)$ and set $b = 1/(1+R)$, then

$$P = \frac{X}{(1+R)}(1 + b + b^2 \cdots + b^{n-1})$$

It can be shown that the series $1 + b + b^2 + \cdots + b^{n-1} = (1 - b^n)/(1 - b)$. Applying this formula to the present-value equation, we obtain

$$P = \frac{X}{1+R}\left(\frac{1 - b^n}{1 - b}\right)$$

Now, substituting $1/(1+R)$ back in for b,

$$P = \frac{X}{(1+R)}\left[\frac{1 - \frac{1}{(1+R)^n}}{1 - \frac{1}{(1+R)}}\right]$$

Bringing $1 + R$ inside the brackets,

$$P = X\left[\frac{1 - \frac{1}{(1+R)^n}}{(1+R) - 1}\right]$$

$$= \frac{X}{R}\left[1 - \frac{1}{(1+R)^n}\right]$$

which is Equation 5 in the text.

The application of this simplification to Equation 6 gives

$$P = \frac{C}{y}\left[1 - \frac{1}{(1+y)^n}\right] + \frac{M}{(1+y)^n}$$

Dividing by M,

$$\frac{P}{M} = \frac{C/M}{y}\left[1 - \frac{1}{(1+y)^n}\right] + \frac{1}{(1+y)^n}$$

Rearranging,

$$\frac{P}{M} - 1 = \left[\frac{C/M}{y} - 1\right]\left[1 - \frac{1}{(1+y)^n}\right]$$

This equation confirms the assertion in the text that a bond's price P is larger or smaller than its maturation value M, depending on whether its coupon rate C/M is larger or smaller than its yield to maturity y.

6

DEFAULT RISK

If a bank lends you $1,000, the bank controls you. If a bank lends you $1,000,000, you control the bank.

Anonymous

Why did investors hold IBM bonds in May 1986 with a 9.1 percent yield when they could have purchased Navistar bonds with an 11.4 percent yield? These 9.1 percent and 11.4 percent yield calculations assume that the coupons and principal will be paid as scheduled. In 1986, investors were more confident of IBM's promises than they were of Navistar's.

Those who borrow money are not always able to repay their loans. Individual borrowers may lose jobs, firms may lose customers, and state and local governments may lose their tax base. Only the U.S. Treasury is absolutely certain of always having enough money to repay its debts — because the federal government can literally print money.

In this chapter we will look at how banks and other lenders evaluate the credit-worthiness of potential borrowers and at how market prices and interest rates reflect this assessment. You will see how bonds are rated and why bonds with low ratings have high yields to maturity. An extreme example is junk bonds — bonds that have the lowest ratings or aren't rated at all.

We will apply these same principles to bank loans and investigate how banks evaluate loan applicants and determine loan rates. We will consider not only household and business loans but also loans to foreign countries. For a time, international loans provided large profits to banks; however, potential international defaults have threatened the solvency of some of the largest banks.

BONDS

Borrowers **default** when they don't pay what was promised at the time they promised to pay it. Holders of defaulted debt may sympathize with the ill fortune of the issuer, but they feel their own personal loss even more keenly, because they may get back nothing or only a few cents of each dollar they invested. A default is not necessarily a complete loss, in that it may represent merely a temporary suspension of payments or a prelude to a partial payment; in the first month after default, a bond typically trades at about 40 percent of its face value.[1] The price doesn't fall all the way to zero as long as there is still some hope of a resumption of at least partial payments.

Historically, bond defaults have been relatively infrequent, because likely defaulters haven't been able to borrow much. The ideal borrower has profitable plans for the borrowed money but doesn't need cash to stay afloat. In recent years, investors have shown an increasing willingness to buy high-risk bonds — junk debt — issued by businesses and state and local government agencies with acknowledged financial problems.

Even apparently safe loans can be jeopardized by unexpected events. A financially sound firm that issues a 20-year bond may run into unexpected difficulties 10 years later — perhaps the loss of key executives, technological advances by competitors, changes in public tastes, or the imposition of onerous government regulations. Penn Central, Chrysler, Lockheed, New York City, and Texaco were all safe investments until the unexpected happened.

Bond Ratings

To evaluate the creditworthiness of debt issuers, a considerable amount of information must be gathered, processed, and analyzed carefully. Some large institutional investors have their own internal staffs that specialize in evaluating the merits of bond issuers. Small purchasers usually find it more economical to rely on the evaluations of professional rating agencies such as Moody's and Standard & Poor's. These private organizations provide impartial and up-to-date assessments of thousands of corporate and government bonds using the quality categories summarized in Table 6.1. Finer gradations are made within the categories Aa (or AA) to B, Moody's using the numbers 1, 2, and 3, and Standard & Poor's + or −.

U.S. Treasury securities are not rated, because the chances of default are negligible. Corporate and state and local government bonds, as many investors have learned painfully, can and occasionally do default. Unfortunately, many municipalities do not provide enough information to gauge their financial condition accurately. In 1980, the SEC concluded that "the market for municipal securities provides investors with only limited protection compared with corporate, [federal] government or other issuers."[2] A Harvard Business School professor wrote in 1985 that "Within wide limits, government accounting rules permit accountants to play games that lead to whatever bottom line the mayor

Borrowers default when they don't pay their debts on time.

Many bonds are rated by Moody's and Standard & Poor's.

Table 6.1   Bond-Rating Categories

Moody's		Standard & Poor's	
Rating	Assessment	Rating	Assessment
Aaa	Best quality	AAA	Highest rating
Aa	High quality	AA	Very strong
A	Upper medium grade	A	Strong
Baa	Medium grade	BBB	Adequate
Ba	Speculative elements	BB	Somewhat speculative
B	Lack characteristics of a desirable investment	B	Speculative
Caa	Poor standing; may be in default	CCC–CC	Highly speculative
Ca	Speculative in a high degree; may be in default	C	Income bonds with no interest being paid
C	Lowest rated class; extremely poor prospects	D	In default

source: *Moody's Bond Record*, October 1988; *Standard & Poor's Bond Guide*, October 1988. Reprinted by permission.

or governor wants," usually a small surplus so that voters will neither be upset by a deficit nor demand lower taxes.[3]

Standard & Poor's estimated that about half of the state and local governments issuing bonds in 1980 didn't comply with generally accepted accounting principles. Most report only current expenditures and revenues and ignore anticipated revenues and spending commitments. Many habitually omit important information, and most do not submit to independent audits. Standard & Poor's has even threatened to stop rating the bonds of municipalities that ignore sound accounting practices.

Corporate borrowers provide better information and are rated more confidently by Standard & Poor's and Moody's. Bonds put in the first four categories (AAA to BBB or Aaa to Baa) are considered investment grade. Historically, about 90 percent of all rated corporate issues have been placed in the first three categories. This doesn't mean that 90 percent of all corporations are this financially sound, only that less-secure companies don't issue many bonds. Table 6.2 shows some examples of corporate ratings in 1989. (Bonds from the same issuer are sometimes put in different ratings classes because some bonds have "senior" status, with first claim on the issuer's funds; in the event of financial distress, "junior" issues do not receive any funds until more senior debt is completely

Table 6.2 Selected Corporate Bond Ratings, 1989	
Rating	Company
AAA	Exxon, General Electric, IBM
AA	AT&T, Citicorp, Sears
A	Teledyne, Merrill Lynch, Xerox
BBB	Chrysler, Manufacturers Hanover, Texas Power & Light
B	Continental Airlines, Embassy Suites, Viacom

source: *Standard & Poor's Bond Guide*, April 1989.

repaid.) Bonds rated outside of the first four categories are somewhat speculative and considered imprudent by many institutional investors.

Financial Ratios and Bond Ratings

How do Moody's and Standard & Poor's determine the appropriate rating for a company's bonds? They conduct a quantitative evaluation of its current and past financial condition and make a subjective assessment of the firm's future. The relevant question is "Will this firm have enough profits (and, in particular, enough cash flow) to meet the mandated payments on its debts?" Among the data examined are the four financial ratios in Table 6.3, with the numbers showing average values for seven Standard & Poor's rating categories.

The pre-tax fixed-charge coverage ratio is the ratio of profits (before taxes and interest payments) to bond payments, lease payments, and other nondiscretionary expenses. Pre-tax profits are used because interest payments are tax deductible; if a firm has $1 million of pre-tax profits and $1 million of interest to pay, it can do so, because it will then owe no taxes. If this pre-tax fixed-charge ratio is less than 1:1, the firm is having trouble making ends meet. For the most highly rated firms, profits are many times more than enough to cover mandated expenses.

Financial ratios are used to help rate bonds.

Of course, the profit calculations of creative accountants do not always ensure that sufficient dollars really are on hand to meet expenses. Cash flow measures the money actually coming into the firm, and the ratio of cash flow to debt (or, more relevantly, a comparison of this ratio with the interest rate on this debt) gauges its adequacy. The most highly rated firms have both high profits and a generous cash flow relative to interest expenses and other fixed charges.

The pre-tax return on long-term capital is a measure of the firm's basic profitability; a firm that doesn't make money is not economically healthy. Long-term debt-to-capitalization is the ratio of the firm's long-term debt to the sum of its short-term debt, long-term debt, and stock — essentially the total value of the firm, because those who own its debt and stock receive all of the money (interest and dividends) paid out by the firm. If the value of these debt and

Table 6.3 Average Values of Four Financial Ratios Used to Judge Financial Condition

Rating Category	Pre-Tax Fixed-Charge Coverage	Cash Flow to Total Debt	Pre-Tax Return on Long-Term Capital (percent)	Long-Term Debt to Capitalization
AAA	6.05	0.48	23.8	0.12
AA	4.68	0.32	21.9	0.19
A	2.97	0.13	17.9	0.28
BBB	2.32	0.07	12.4	0.34
BB	1.74	−0.01	11.5	0.48
B	1.45	−0.06	10.6	0.57
CCC	0.12	−0.02	−2.2	0.73

source: *Standard & Poor's CreditWeek,* September 5, 1988.

stock claims is approximately equal to the value of the firm's assets, then the liquidation of an AAA-rated firm with a 0.16 ratio would yield six times the amount of money needed to retire its long-term debt.

Risk and Promised Return

Calculated yields to maturity use market prices of bonds and promised cash flow — promises that may or may not be kept. The larger the probability that a firm will default, the lower is the market price of its bonds and the higher the computed yield to maturity. This is why bonds from IBM and Navistar with very similar coupons and maturation dates sold for very different prices in May 1986.

IBM bonds had Standard & Poor's highest rating (AAA), whereas Navistar bonds were rated a speculative B. Under its former name, International Harvester, Navistar lost staggering amounts of money for five straight years, from 1980 through 1985, and by the end of 1985 had a total long-term debt of $888 million as compared to a slender net worth of $42 million (after subtracting its debts from its assets). Its long-term debt-to-capitalization ratio was nearly 1.0, and one more bad year would have pushed its net worth into the red.

Nervous investors paid only 81⅞ for Navistar's bonds in May 1986, as opposed to 102½ for similar promises from IBM, giving Navistar's bonds a 11.4 percent calculated yield to maturity and IBM's 9.1 percent. These two yields are consistent with the May 1986 average yields to maturity by rating category shown in Table 6.4.

Figure 6.1 shows the historical differences between the yields on U.S. government bonds and corporate Baa and Aaa bonds. In recent years, Baa bonds have been priced to yield about 1 percent per year more than Aaa bonds. Bond

Relatively risky bonds have high promised yields to maturity.

Table 6.4 Yield to Maturity by Rating Category, May 1986	
Rating Category	**Yield to Maturity**
AAA	9.19%
AA	9.51%
A	9.75%
BBB	10.32%

source: *Standard & Poor's Bond Guide*, January 1987.

buyers and sellers price these bonds so that the yields generally move up and down together, keeping the yield spread remarkably stable. If risky bonds were priced to yield only slightly more than safe bonds, many investors would switch from risky bonds to safe ones. If risky bonds yielded substantially more than safe bonds, investors would move in the other direction. To persuade investors to hold both types of bonds, the yields tend to move together.

When a bond's rating changes, so do its price and promised yield to maturity. For instance, as a company's financial difficulties mount and its chances of bankruptcy grow, Moody's and Standard & Poor's downgrade the bond as its price slips in financial markets. There is some evidence that investors see changes in the financial condition of firms before the rating agencies do. One study found that bond prices reflect changing default conditions a full 6–18 months before subsequent rating changes, and that the rating changes themselves (being so late) have no perceptible effect on bond prices.[4]

Junk Bonds

Junk bonds is the generic label for low-quality debt — unrated bonds or low-rated bonds issued by companies that are either not well known or known to be risky. Some of these bonds are new junk, sold to finance risky ventures, and some are fallen angels — bonds issued by companies that were once financially secure and now are not. Before the 1980s, most investors wouldn't touch junk; this was particularly true of mutual funds, pension funds, and other institutional investors who feared lawsuits if they breached their fiduciary duties with imprudent investments.

Then, according to popular legend, Michael Milken, a student at the University of Pennsylvania, decided that this aversion to junk bonds was excessive. Most companies whose bonds were low rated or unrated were not on the verge of default. Some were experiencing temporary financial difficulty; many were just unknown or didn't have a lot of tangible assets. According to Milken's calculations, the occasional default was more than offset by the fact that the bonds' prices were very low and the promised returns high. Milken joined a

Junk bonds are low-rated or unrated debt.

| Highlight 6.1 | **The Whoops Default** |

Municipal-bond defaults have been infrequent, and usually involve a post-ponement of payments because the project financed by the bond takes longer than expected to earn sufficient revenue. For instance, some West Virginia Turnpike bonds issued in 1952 were in default for 20 years before enough toll revenue finally accumulated to pay off the bonds.*

In 1975, the municipal-bond market was rocked by New York City's financial troubles. With a weak economy and shrinking tax base, the city declared a moratorium on some $2.4 billion in short-term notes. After the courts ruled this action unconstitutional, the city found ways to pay its bondholders, though the principal payments were delayed for up to two years and only 6 percent interest was credited during this delay.

In 1983, it was the Washington Public Power Supply System (WPPSS), widely known by the ironic label Whoops, that disappointed investors. A consortium of nearly one hundred public utilities in the Pacific Northwest established WPPSS to sell $8.4 billion in municipal bonds to finance the construction of five nuclear power plants. These public power agencies backed the bonds by signing "take-or-pay" (also known as "come hell or high water") contracts, agreeing to pay for specified amounts of electricity at set prices whether or not the power was actually delivered.

Construction costs turned out to be much higher than had been anticipated, and the Northwest's demand for electricity much lower. Two of the plants (#4 and #5) were canceled in January 1982 after almost all of the $2.25 billion raised by bond sales had been spent to finance their construction. Projects #1 and #3 were later suspended semipermanently, leaving only #2 producing any electricity. WPPSS stopped making payments on its #4 and #5 bonds in January 1983 and formally defaulted on them later that year, after the Washington State Supreme Court ruled that the public utilities had no authority to sign take-or-pay contracts and, therefore, had no obligation to fulfill them. Coupons and principal continue to be paid on the bonds for projects #1, #2, and #3 which (unlike #4 and #5) are backed by the Bonneville Power Administration, a federal agency that distributes electricity to public utilities in the Northwest.

WPPSS was the nation's largest issuer of municipal bonds, and the $2.25 billion default on its #4 and #5 bonds was, by far, the largest ever. Moody's gave the #4 and #5 bonds an A1 rating until June 1981 and Standard & Poor's rated them A until January 1982. Investors were shocked and then enraged that these seemingly safe investments were made a shambles by a court-backed default. A collection of lawsuits alleging fraud

*Lynn Asinof, "Possible Effects of a WPPSS Bond Failure Are Visible in Past U.S. Municipal Bond Defaults," *Wall Street Journal,* July 13, 1983.

by WPPSS, the Wall Street firms that marketed the bonds, and other convenient targets (91 defendants in all) is now working its way through the courts.

Despite dire warnings in 1983 of shock waves from this precedent, the municipal bond market recovered quickly, leading some to call WPPSS a "no-fault default." To reassure nervous investors (and reduce interest costs), many local governments and agencies now buy special insurance that guarantees the payment of principal and interest on their bonds. Standard & Poor's automatically gives an AAA rating to bonds that are backed by either of the two major insurers, the Municipal Bond Insurance Association and the American Bond Assurance Corporation. Nonetheless, these insured bonds have been priced to yield up to ½ percent more than noninsured AAAs, because the latter are judged AAA on the strength of the issuing municipality, and there is apparently some fear that a wave of defaults would bankrupt the insurers.

small securities firm, Drexel Burnham, and made his argument over and over to anyone who would listen, marketing junk bonds to those he persuaded.

Once Milken found junk buyers, more sellers appeared. A takeover wave hit the United States in the 1980s, and corporate raiders acquired companies that appeared to have grown large and lazy and then resold them, often in parts, to those who thought they were better managers. Sometimes a company's managers borrowed money to buy up the shareholder's stock, converting the firm from a public corporation to a private business. Raiders, external or internal, need financing, and many financed their takeovers by issuing junk bonds, implicitly using the assets of the target company as collateral.

With willing buyers and sellers, there was now a junk-bond market, with Drexel Burnham the middleman. Those who wanted to issue junk came to Drexel, which had established a long list of buyers; those who wanted high potential returns knew that Drexel was the place to buy junk bonds. But there was more to it than that. Drexel didn't just know the names of buyers and sellers; it had their confidence. With traditional investment-grade bonds, the ratings by Moody's and other services give a stamp of approval that facilitates trading. The seller of a triple-A bond knows that there are plenty of buyers; the buyers know from the independent ratings that they are buying quality securities. Not so with junk bonds. By definition, these haven't been certified as safe investments by independent rating services. Junk buyers relied on the knowledge and reputation of Drexel (or whoever the middleman might be) that this is an investment well worth making. Issuers count on the middleman's reputation, too, to ensure that all of their bonds will be sold quickly, and at less-than-exorbitant interest rates.

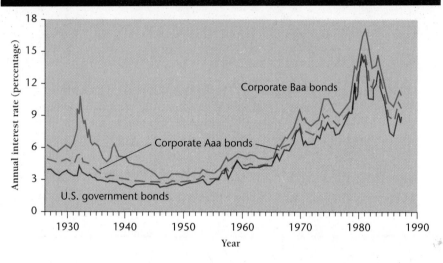

Figure 6.1 Yields on Moody's Aaa and Baa Corporate Bonds and on U.S. Government Bonds

source: Federal Reserve Board, *Historical Chart Book*.

By 1988 there were $160 billion in actively traded junk bonds, more than half of it through Drexel. Milken was at the core of this market, with first-hand knowledge of most of the buyers and sellers and a reputed ability to recite the terms of every junk bond in the country. Under him were some 150 traders working 12-to-15-hour days, beginning at 4:30 A.M. Junk turned Drexel into a major securities firm and provided it with $2 billion a year in revenue.

Milken was reportedly paid $550 million in 1987 and became a billionaire in 1988, at age 42. However, in 1988 Drexel was accused of a variety of securities-fraud charges and agreed to plead guilty to six felonies, pay $650 million in penalties, and accept Milken's resignation. Milken was separately indicted for 98 counts, including insider trading, stock manipulation, "parking" of securities with associates to avoid ownership disclosure, the maintenance of false and misleading records, and false disclosures to the Securities and Exchange Commission. Milken vowed not to plea bargain, but eventually pleaded guilty to a handful of charges. Without Milken's stabilizing skills and with its reputation tarnished, Drexel Burnham was forced into bankruptcy in February 1990.

Junk bonds are generally priced to yield 4 to 6 percentage points more than less-speculative securities and so far, on average, some 2 percent of all junk bonds have defaulted each year. Table 6.5 compares the average promised yields to maturity and actual realized returns (coupons plus capital gains) from junk bonds and long-term government securities during the years 1978–86. However, these calculated default rates are somewhat misleading. Few defaults occur during the first few years after issuance and, because of the rapid growth of the junk-

Table 6.5	Junk Bonds and U.S. Treasury Securities, 1978–86	
	Promised Yield	**Actual Return**
Treasury bonds	10.80%	12.25%
Low-rated junk	14.54%	13.24%

— price of Treas. went up

(Int. rates fell)

source: Edward I. Altman, "The Anatomy of the High-Yield Bond Market," *Financial Analysts' Journal,* July/August 1987, pp. 12–25.

bond market, the overwhelming majority of junk bonds have been issued relatively recently. Perhaps only 2 percent of the bonds defaulted this year because 98 percent were issued during the last six months. A 1988 study by Paul Asquith, David Mullins, and Eric Wolf calculated cumulative default rates for junk bonds of various ages.[5] They found that 34 percent of the junk bonds issued in 1977–78 and 23 percent of those issued during the period 1979–83 had defaulted by 1988.

The years 1982–88 were recession-free. Many observers worry that junk has been used to finance increasingly dubious ventures, gambles that will collapse when a recession does come. In October 1988, a senior partner of a prominent investment firm that had acquired several corporations without using junk wrote, "Surely, when the history books are written, the reason so many investors bought these bonds will be the financial riddle of our age."[6]

Realized Returns

W. B. Hickman did an exhaustive study of the corporate bonds issued during the period 1900–43 and, as shown in Table 6.6, found a striking correlation between a bond's initial quality rating and its chance of eventual default.[7] Only 6 percent of the bonds in the top two rating categories eventually defaulted. Bonds that were lower-rated did, in fact, default more often. Of those few issues outside of the first four categories, a stunning 42 percent defaulted. These default fractions are fairly high because so many firms were bankrupted by the Great Depression in the 1930s. No investment-grade bonds defaulted in the 1950s and 1960s.[8] However, several did in the 1970s and 1980s, including Braniff Airlines, W. T. Grant, and Penn Central. Between 1970 and 1984, on average, approximately 0.1 percent of all outstanding corporate bonds and 2.5 percent of the low-rated corporate bonds defaulted each year.[9]

Notice in Table 6.6 that the promised yields to maturity (assuming coupon and maturation value will be paid as promised) are higher the lower the bond's rating. The fourth column shows the actual yields, taking into account that defaulting companies did not pay all that they had promised. The realized yields

Highlight 6.2   RJR Becomes Junk

Chapter 1 explained that debt provides a tax shield for firms because, unlike dividends, the interest on debt can be deducted from taxable income. This tax advantage encourages management (or outside raiders) to increase a firm's indebtedness — in the extreme, to the point where its income is exhausted by interest payments and the company pays no taxes at all. The danger is that income may drop below the firm's interest obligations, forcing it to default on its debts. As firms increased their indebtedness in the 1980s, the ratings of their bonds deteriorated: the median rating of industrial bonds fell from A in 1981 to BB in 1988, leading the managing director for industrial and utility ratings at Standard & Poor's to comment that "Most companies are junk today."[*]

When a firm increases its indebtedness substantially, those who already own bonds issued by the firm are hurt financially, because their bonds are downgraded as the firm's chances of bankruptcy increase. For example, after the 1988 debt-financed buyout of RJR Nabisco was announced, existing RJR bonds were downgraded from A to junk and their prices fell by 20 percent. In addition to this immediate loss, the prices of RJR bonds began fluctuating with the prices of other speculative junk. In 1989 and 1990, investors grew increasingly nervous about the junk-bond market; during an especially unsettling two-day period in January 1990, the prices of some RJR bonds fell by more than 20 percent.

Investors who bought RJR bonds when the company was financially strong were understandably upset when their conservative investment became junk. Some pension funds and insurance companies began pushing for takeover-proof bonds that can be redeemed at face value if there is a large increase in a firm's indebtedness. Other investors refused to buy anything but U.S. Treasury bonds, which are presumably safe from a leveraged buyout.

[*]Bill Sing, "Mega-Mergers Leave Bondholders Counting Their Losses," *Los Angeles Times,* November 9, 1988.

are virtually identical for the first three rating categories and rise somewhat for the last two. One complication with these data is that the substantial drop in interest rates in the 1930s made it profitable for many firms to exercise the call provisions in their bonds, by paying bondholders a premium over more the bond's face value (but a discount to the current market price). Hickman's data include these call payments, which push the actual yields above the promised yields for the first four rating categories. Two other researchers redid Hickman's

Table 6.6 Corporate Defaults by Rating Category, 1900–43			
Initial Rating (Composite of Rating Agencies)	Promised Yield to Maturity	Fraction Defaulted (Percent of Par Value)	Actual Yield to Maturity
1 (highest)	4.5	5.9	5.1
2	4.6	6.0	5.0
3	4.9	13.4	5.0
4	5.4	19.1	5.7
5–9 (lowest)	9.5	42.4	8.6

source: W. Braddock Hickman, *Corporate Bond Quality and Investor Experience* (New York: National Bureau of Economic Research, 1958). Reprinted by permission.

calculations for the first four rating categories, this time assuming that no bonds were called, so as to focus solely on how defaults affected yields. They found that the actual yields, taking into account defaults, were the same, 4.3 percent, in each category, the higher promised yields just offsetting the higher chances of default.[10]

Matters have turned out differently since World War II. There have been so few defaults that lower-rated, higher-yielding bonds have generally outperformed more highly rated bonds. This does not mean that, at present, AA bonds are a better investment than AAA bonds and that junk bonds are better still, only that risky bonds are priced to take into account their susceptibility to default during bad times, and times have, as it turns out, been relatively good since World War II.

LOANS

Large, well-known companies either issue bonds or borrow from banks. Small- and medium-size firms, in contrast, find it difficult and expensive to issue bonds. Without access to the bond market, they rely on local banks and other financial institutions for loans. Individuals, too, have little alternative to borrowing from a bank or other financial intermediary in order to finance the purchase of houses, automobiles, and vacations.

We can divide loans into three categories: mortgages, commercial loans, and consumer loans. Table 6.7 shows that the largest category is mortgages and that most mortgages are made by savings-and-loan associations and other thrift

Households and most businesses rely on local banks for loans.

Table 6.7 Assets of Deposit Institutions, December 1988 (in billions of dollars)

	Commercial Banks	Thrift Institutions	Total
Mortgages	$ 669	$ 938	$1,607
Commercial loans	606	33	639
Consumer loans	361	62	423
Investment securities	533	168	701
Cash and deposits	244	19	263
Other	623	131	754
Total	$3,036	$1,351	$4,387

source: *Federal Reserve Bulletin*, September 1989.

institutions. Mortgages comprise 70 percent of the assets of thrift institutions; commercial banks are more diversified and are the primary source of consumer and business loans.

Some commercial loans are long term and are used to buy machinery, land, and structures. Many business loans are short term, providing the working capital needed to plug gaps between income and expenses by financing the purchase of labor, materials, and unfinished goods used in production. There are time lags between employing inputs and producing output, between production and sales, and between sales and receipt of payment. Loans help businesses bridge these gaps. Some delays are almost continual, some are seasonal, and some vary with the business cycle. In economic slumps, firms accumulate unsold products. In credit crunches, they accumulate unpaid bills. In both cases — slumps and crunches — firms need extra cash.

Individual businesses can get cash by accelerating receipts and delaying payments — an ongoing tug-of-war between customers, retailers, wholesalers, and manufacturers that gets a bit rougher when business is slow and interest rates are high. Buyers put off payments, while persistent sellers remind, threaten, and plead for payment. A *Wall Street Journal* article written during the credit crunch in the winter of 1980 quoted a New York apparel maker's observation that "as interest rates go higher, the payments get slower."[11] Another manufacturer said that its phone calls to tardy customers were 50 percent more frequent than they had been a year earlier. A retailer noted the other side of the struggle: "Vendors are trying to accelerate payment terms and are ignoring terms on purchase orders." Some suppliers were billing first and shipping later.

A firm usually keeps a cash reservoir by establishing a working relationship with a bank. The bank provides a line of credit, which allows the firm to borrow funds as needed; the firm pays its bills through the bank, keeping a substantial amount of funds deposited there. The firm may be expected, or even required, to maintain a **compensating balance** deposited in the bank, equal to 10–20 percent of the size of its loan. Banks profit from compensating balances, particularly funds kept in low-interest or no-interest checking accounts, because these deposits allow banks to borrow money from businesses at lower interest rates than the firms are paying on their loans. In recent years, many banks have eliminated compensating balances, allowing businesses to choose separately how much to borrow and how much to deposit.

Banks sometimes require borrowers to deposit compensating balances.

Loan Evaluation

Personal and business loans are initiated with an application and an interview with a loan officer, who is sometimes given a more congenial title, such as "relationship manager." The loan officer's responsibility is to acquire information about the customer, the purpose of the loan, and the likelihood of its repayment. Those who have a long-standing relationship with the bank — involving deposits, previous loans, and other services — naturally expect to have their loans approved more readily than applications from strangers. Presumably, a continuing close relationship with a customer gives a bank information about the borrower that is not easily available to others. The cost of obtaining and verifying such information makes it impractical for little-known firms to make public security offerings and makes it economical to maintain ongoing relationships with banks.

Local banks use customer relationships and scoring systems to judge loan applicants.

The evaluation of a personal loan involves an investigation of the applicant's employment and credit history. The loan officer looks for a record of stable employment at a wage adequate to repay the loan and meet other financial obligations, and for evidence of the repayment of earlier credit obligations, including a home mortgage, car and education loans, and credit-card purchases. Some banks quantify an individual's credit-worthiness using a **credit scoring** system based on the economic and demographic characteristics and default frequencies of past borrowers. People who change jobs frequently often default on loans, so loan applicants are given points for job stability. Single people default more often than married couples, so those who are married get points. In theory, a credit-scoring system uses past experience to predict the probability of default. In practice, such systems have been challenged as discriminatory for judging individuals based on the behavior of groups.

For a commercial loan, the loan officer tries to become familiar not only with individual executives but also with the business itself and the industry in which it operates. Sometimes a bank is satisfied with a subjective appraisal. More often, the bank examines the same sort of financial ratios used by Moody's and Standard & Poor's to quantify a firm's financial strength. However, many of the companies that borrow from banks do so because they are too small or young to qualify for the issuance of investment-grade bonds. Banks know that a firm's potential for future profits is more important than its current or past financial ratios, and try to assess this potential as best they can.

| Highlight 6.3 | Handshake Loans from Local Banks |

Banks are in an advantageous position for judging the creditworthiness of local businesses and households, particularly those that have maintained a long-standing customer relationship. In comparison with Moody's and the other agencies that rate securities issued by nationally known firms, a local bank may be intimately familiar with a person's competency and integrity, and with unique circumstances that affect that person's ability to repay a loan.

With familiar customers, some local banks don't bother with a loan application and a credit check: a handshake and a promise are enough when you're dealing with family. Local bankers often feel that their banks are an integral part of the community, donating money for civic improvements and lending money during hard times to residents who don't satisfy conventional credit standards.

First National Bank of Midland, Texas used to be this way, supporting the local community and lending money easily: a superior's signature was required if a loan request was rejected; no signature was required to approve a loan. But First National collapsed in 1983, along with Texas oil and real estate, and it was taken over by another Texas bank, RepublicBank Corporation, which merged with InterFirst Corporation to become First RepublicBank Corporation. In 1988 First RepublicBank was acquired by a regional giant, NCNB Corporation of North Carolina.

Some Midland residents were flabbergasted to find that NCNB insisted on loan applications and credit checks. Many were disappointed at NCNB's reluctance to lend money to those in financial difficulty, and claim that most of their deposits are being channeled to loans outside of Texas. One local business executive said "The only way you can get a loan is by putting up an arm or a leg or maybe both." Some Midland residents dubbed NCNB "Nobody Cares, Nobody Bothers" or "No Credit for No Body."*

---

*Michael Allen, "Out-of-State Bankers Tight with a Dollar Rile Old-Style Texans," *Wall Street Journal*, August 10, 1989.

Increasingly, computerized simulation models of the company's financial statements are used to project cash flow under a variety of plausible scenarios, to assure the bank that the firm's ability to repay its loan is not critically dependent on one particular set of perhaps overly optimistic assumptions. These simulations can also alert the bank to important factors that might imperil the loan.

No matter how conscientious the loan-evaluation process is, there is always the possibility that unexpected developments — the illness of a key person, an earthquake, unfavorable legislation — will undermine the financial viability of a company or a household. When substantial sums are involved, the bank may try to identify the most important risks and take measures to protect its loan. It may insist on adequate insurance against natural disasters and on the development of strategic plans to respond to changes in consumer tastes, to congressional legislation, or to competition from other companies. If the business depends on a single supplier, purchaser, or product, the bank may encourage it to diversify. If the company's business is vulnerable to technological change, the bank may insist that more effort be spent on research and development.

Once the loan has been approved, the bank monitors its timely repayment. For personal loans of modest size, this monitoring simply involves an alert if a scheduled loan payment is missed. For large commercial loans, the loan officer receives regular financial statements, meets with management occasionally, and visits the company personally to confirm construction progress, business production, or other tangible evidence that the company is using the loan for its intended purpose and will generate a cash flow adequate to ensure its repayment. The loan officer also stays informed about economic developments in the industry or the nation that might endanger the loan. For very large loans, bank officers become virtual partners in the business, advising the company's management about significant decisions that might affect its financial stability.

> Banks monitor large loans carefully.

Loan Rates

The major determinants of loan rates are the bank's cost of funds, the interest rates the bank can earn on other investments, and the risk of default. Banks cannot afford to pay their depositors 7 percent and lend out money at 5 percent. They generally require an average spread between their deposit rates and loan rates of 1 to 3 percentage points — for example, borrowing at 7 percent and lending at 8 percent to 10 percent — in order to cover their administrative expenses. Bank loan rates also depend on the interest rates available on Treasury securities and other potential investments, because banks won't lend money at 8 percent when they can buy Treasury bonds paying 9 percent.

> Loan rates depend on other interest rates and default risk.

The lower the risk of default, the more attractive the loan and the lower the interest rate charged. The **prime rate** has traditionally been the interest rate charged on six-month commercial loans to customers (usually businesses) believed to have the lowest risk of default. Other customers are charged a little above prime or a lot above prime, or have their loan requests denied entirely. Loans are less risky when they are secured by collateral — legal claims in the event of default to such assets as bonds, stock, real estate, or consumer durables.

> Traditionally, the interest rate on the safest loans has been called the prime rate.

In the past, loan rates changed infrequently. A drop in bond rates had little effect on loan rates because households and many businesses could not issue bonds. Banks chose to use this power over loan applicants to encourage semipermanent customer relations. Loan-rate competition was seen as unprofessional and unhealthy for the industry. If one bank cut its loan rate and others followed, all banks suffered. On the other hand, blatant rate gouging hurts the industry's reputation and, if enough people become upset, unfavorable political repercussions are possible.

Banks instead competed for deposits by promising preferential treatment of loan applications from customers who use the bank for deposits and other banking services. To secure stable deposits, banks implicitly agreed to make funds available, when needed, at a stable rate of interest. The primary means of rationing available bank funds was to scale down loan requests or to downgrade some customers' creditworthiness, thereby putting them in higher loan-rate categories.

The prime rate charged by major banks did not change — at all! — between 1933 and 1947 (it was then 1½ percent). Between 1947 and 1966, it was changed only 19 times, less than once a year. Figure 6.2 compares the prime rate at major banks with the interest rate on prime **commercial paper**, short-term bonds issued by low-risk companies. Prior to the mid-1960s, these rates often drifted far apart. Notice particularly that banks several times adjusted the prime rate to stay above the commercial paper rate, but resisted matching its declines. During this period, banks refrained from rate wars.

Figure 6.2   **Prime Loan Rate and Rate on Prime Commercial Paper**

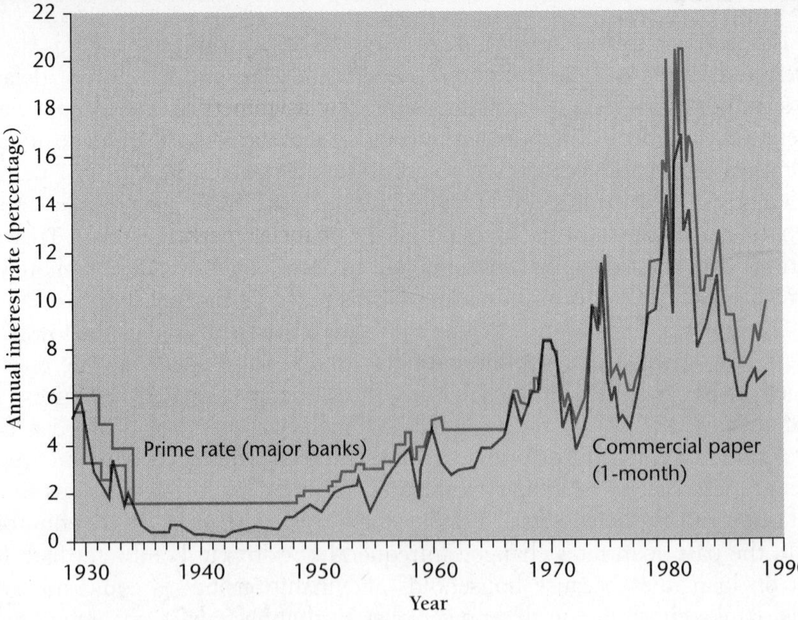

source: Federal Reserve Board, *Historical Chart Book.*

Beginning in the late 1960s, high interest rates and the volatility of financial markets eroded this civilized behavior. In 1971, Citibank announced that it would adjust its prime rate weekly, keeping it ½ percent above the prime commercial paper rate. Other large banks followed suit, using various "floating formula prime rates" based on averages of weekly money-market rates. In 1973, banks were forced to suspend such formulas (and roll back the prime rate) under pressure from the federal government's short-lived price-control program. Since then, banks have resumed frequent adjustments, though most say that they now use judgment rather than mechanical formulas.

Banks tend to have very similar prime rates, which they hold constant until a leading bank decides that financial-market conditions warrant a change. After it announces its new prime lending rate, other banks follow suit. For instance, virtually every major U.S. bank adopted a 10.5 percent prime rate on July 31, 1989, or shortly thereafter. Five months later, on Monday, January 8, 1990, First National Bank of Chicago reduced its prime rate to 10 percent, and most other major banks — including Citibank, Morgan Guaranty, and Bank of America — reduced their prime rate that same day.

Figure 6.2 indicates that there is a strong correlation between the prime rate and the commercial-paper rate. On the other hand, former Federal Reserve Board chairman Paul Volcker has observed that "the prime rate is sometimes a little more jumpy on the up side than it is on the down side."[12] There is probably still some lingering distaste for mutually destructive rate wars. Interest rates on loans to households, which have little bargaining power, have been particularly sticky.

Large banks have, by-and-large, switched from fixed-rate to variable-rate business loans. With wildly volatile interest rates in the 1970s and 1980s, bankers came to view fixed-rate loans as a dangerously asymmetrical gamble. If interest rates go up, the bank loses money on the loan. If interest rates go down, the corporation takes out a new loan, from another bank if necessary, at the lower interest rate. Banks decided that renegotiation could work in both directions. If firms can demand revised loan rates when financial markets ease, then banks can require revised loan rates when markets tighten. Most loans now carry an interest rate equal to a benchmark rate (such as the prime rate) plus some fixed percentage and call for adjustment of this loan rate every 30, 60, 90, or 120 days, or every time the benchmark rate changes.

Large businesses are generally reluctant to tie their lending rate to the prime rate, which is set unilaterally by banks. Instead, they insist on a benchmark rate that is determined in competitive financial markets. One common benchmark is the **London Interbank Offered Rate (LIBOR)**, a measure of what international banks charge each other for large Eurodollar loans — loans denominated in U.S. dollars. Another popular benchmark is the interest rate on 30-day certificates of deposit (CDs). Both of these benchmarks measure not what banks say they charge on loans, but what banks pay to obtain funds for lending.

By 1990, almost all large companies — and many medium-size firms, too — had loan rates that adjusted with market interest rates, rather than with the

Loan rates have become more flexible.

Today, the prime rate is seldom used for loans to large businesses.

Highlight 6.4	False Prime Rates?

The prime rate is supposed to be the interest rate that banks charge on loans to their most creditworthy customers. However, business customers are often offered below-prime-rate loans. Between early April and May 1980, for example, most short-term interest rates dropped by close to 10 percentage points, although the prime rate fell by only 6 percentage points, from 20 percent to 14 percent, making the prime rate uncompetitive. Some large banks offered business loans for up to seven years at 3–6 percentage points below the stated prime rate. A May 1980 survey of the 48 largest U.S. banks found that 59 percent of their short-term business loans were made at least 4 percentage points below the prime rate — irking other banks and angering some customers who weren't offered these unadvertised specials.*

These false prime rates were especially annoying to borrowers who had outstanding variable-rate loans tied to the posted prime rate. Some of the aggrieved, including Jackie Kleiner, a lawyer and business professor at Georgia Tech, got so angry that they sued their banks for violating federal truth-in-lending laws. Kleiner had borrowed some $400,000 at an interest rate pegged 1 percentage point above the rate on loans to the bank's "best commercial borrowers." When the prime rate rose to 20 percent in the spring of 1980, Kleiner's loan rate jumped to 21 percent. This new rate was expensive and also annoying, because some customers were paying less than the prime rate. Kleiner indignantly complained that "the banks artificially created the prime to make higher profits and then artificially discounted it. They aren't pillars of society — they're white-collar criminals in three-piece suits."** Such lawsuits had mixed success.

---

*Wall Street Journal, November 7, 1980; Wall Street Journal, May 29, 1980.
**Wall Street Journal, November 7, 1980.

stated prime rate. Household loans, ranging from credit-card loans to home-equity loans, are increasingly using the prime rate as a benchmark. No doubt, many households erroneously believe that their loan rate is tied to the interest rate charged prominent corporations, when, in fact, most large corporate loans no longer use the stated prime rate.

International Loans

In the 1970s, the largest U.S. banks dramatically expanded their loans to foreign businesses and governments. One impetus was that unprecedented increases in oil prices created enormous balance-of-trade deficits for oil-importing countries and surpluses for oil exporters. The economies of many poorer countries might have been crumpled by an inability to pay for oil and oil-related products. The IMF, the World Bank, and private banks averted such national collapses by channeling funds from trade-surplus countries to trade-deficit nations.

The IMF did this directly, borrowing from oil exporters and lending to importers. The recycling of petrodollars by private banks was less direct, because bank funds often pass through several hands. The OPEC nations purchased bonds and made deposits in banks in Europe and the United States, while banks looking for profitable investments increased their lending to foreign countries. Some of these foreign loans were to less developed countries (LDCs) with balance-of-trade deficits; others were to oil-exporters like Mexico that had aggressive development plans and intended to pay for this development out of future oil revenue. In 1986, Latin American loans from foreign banks and governments were 2½ times larger than loans from their domestic banks.[13]

Foreign loans offer banks new opportunities, but also new challenges, because it is difficult to evaluate the creditworthiness of distant and unfamiliar borrowers. In addition, banks cannot force a foreign government into bankruptcy and seize its assets. The only real power banks have over a foreign government is to refuse to lend it additional funds.

During the 1970s, large U.S. banks loaned almost $200 billion to Latin American countries — chiefly Argentina, Brazil, and Mexico — and by the late 1970s, nearly half of the total profits of the ten largest U.S. banks came from foreign loans. But the worldwide recession in 1980–82, high interest rates, and unfavorable movements in export prices and exchange rates crippled the ability of many less developed countries to repay their loans. Squeezed by declining oil prices, Mexico restructured $30 billion of foreign debt in 1982, adjusting the interest rate and the payment schedule. In 1983, *Fortune* estimated that interest payments on the foreign debts of 21 major borrowers had reached nearly 80 percent of their export earnings.[14] In February 1987, Brazil declared a unilateral moratorium on all $70 billion of its commercial loans and, in 1988, forced a refinancing agreement on its debt, by then swollen to $82 billion. Other countries — including Costa Rica, Mexico, the Philippines, and Venezuela — also renegotiated their loans, reducing and postponing the payment of interest and principal. By 1989, large U.S. banks had set aside reserves equal to 25 percent of their third-world debt to cover losses on these loans.

Table 6.8 shows the burden that debt payments had become to developing countries and indicates that banks responded to this increasingly precarious situation by curtailing their lending, reluctant to throw good money after bad. Between 1981 and 1987, the slow growth of developing countries and their increasing inability to repay their loans nearly doubled their external debts, both in absolute amounts and relative to their gross national products (GNPs). New long-term lending declined substantially, especially from private banks, causing an even more dramatic decline in net lending, the difference between new loans granted and the repayment of principal on old loans. In 1981, banks were repaid $39 billion and lent $92 billion, a net increase in lending of $53 billion; in

Foreign loans were profitable for many large U.S. banks in the 1970s, but caused a debt crisis in the 1980s.

| Highlight 6.5 | The Market for LDC Debt |

A bank that has lent money to a foreign country can hold onto its loan note and hope that the loan is repaid or sell the note to someone else who is willing, for the right price, to take this gamble. The prices at which LDC loan notes are traded reflect the participants' views about the probability that the loans will be repaid and about the timing of these payments. Loans that are likely to be repaid in full sell for close to face value, whereas those that will probably be repaid in part or not at all sell for a steep discount.

The accompanying table shows the average prices of foreign loans for eight selected countries in 1989.* On March 1 of that year, only Chile's loans sold for more than 50 percent of face value. Argentine debt was the most heavily discounted, trading at 18¢ per dollar of face value. The prices of many of these loans rose sharply on March 10, 1989, after the U.S. government announced that it would provide LDCs with some $30 billion to help them repay their loans.

Average Price of Foreign Debt per Dollar of Face Value		
	March 1, 1989	July 17, 1989
Argentina	$0.18	$0.19
Brazil	0.28	0.32
Chile	0.56	0.65
Mexico	0.34	0.44
Philippines	0.38	0.54
Poland	0.32	0.39
Venezuela	0.27	0.40
Yugoslavia	0.44	0.54

*These data were provided by Salomon Brothers to Peter Truell, "Banks' Credits Buoyed by U.S. Debt Strategy," *Wall Street Journal,* July 19, 1989.

1987, banks were repaid $51 billion and lent $49 billion, a net *decrease* in lending of $2 billion. The net flow of funds shown in Table 6.8 is the amount of new loans minus the payment of both principal and interest on existing loans — measuring whether there is an inflow of funds or an outflow. In 1981, developing countries were receiving funds; in 1987, their inability to repay existing loans and the reluctance of banks to lend yet more money resulted in a net transfer of funds out of these countries.

Table 6.8 Loans to Developing Countries, 1981 and 1987

	All Developing Countries		Latin America and Caribbean		Middle East, Europe, and North Africa		Asia		Sub-Saharan Africa	
	1981	1987	1981	1987	1981	1987	1981	1987	1981	1987
Outstanding Debt										
Total (billions)	$503	$996	$209	$384	$134	$260	$110	$244	$50	$109
Relative to GNP	23%	42%	27%	52%	30%	47%	12%	21%	26%	85%
Gross Long-Term Lending										
Total (billions)	$124	$87	$61	$20	$28	$27	$25	$32	$11	$9
Private (billions)	$92	$49	$53	$10	$17	$18	$15	$18	$6	$3
Net Lending										
Total (billions)	$77	$16	$39	$5	$14	$3	$16	$2	$8	$5
Private (billions)	$53	−$2	$34	$1	$7	$0	$9	−$4	$4	$1
Net Flow of Funds										
Total (billions)	$35	−$38	$16	−$19	4	−$12	$10	−$11	$6	$2

source: Adapted from *World Development Report 1989* by The World Bank. Copyright © 1989 by The International Bank for Reconstruction and Development/The World Bank. Reprinted by permission of Oxford University Press, Inc.

Most proposed solutions to this debt crises involve little more than lending or giving LDCs enough money to pay the interest owed on previous loans. An agreement between borrowers and banks to reschedule loans by postponing the payment of principal and interest reduces the burden of these loans to the borrowers and, correspondingly, reduces the value of the loans to the banks. During 1988 and 1989, bank and government officials formally acknowledged that debt relief had to be given to the poorest and most heavily indebted countries. Agreements by the U.S. government and international lending institutions, such as the World Bank or IMF, to lend LDCs enough money to make their interest payments are, in effect, a subsidy to the banks that made bad loans.

SUMMARY

Bond issuers with assets, profits, and cash flow that are relatively small in comparison with their debts are given low-quality ratings by Standard & Poor's, Moody's, and other professional rating agencies. Their bonds must have low prices and high (promised) yields to maturity to compensate investors for the risk of default. Low-rated and unrated issues are called junk bonds. Some junk bonds are issued by small, little-known companies; others are fallen angels, once-safe bonds issued by once-strong companies; some are issued to finance take-overs.

Thrift institutions have historically focused on mortgage lending and have been the primary source of mortgage loans. Most business and consumer loans have been from commercial banks. A bank's prime rate has traditionally been the loan rate that it charges those borrowers who are thought to have the least risk of default; higher rates are charged on riskier loans. The prime rate used to be fixed for years at a time, but is now adjusted by banks when there are significant changes in short-term interest rates. Most business loans today have variable loan rates, equal to the current value of a benchmark rate — such as the prime rate, LIBOR, or 90-day CDs — plus a specified number of percentage points.

Many large U.S. and European banks loaned hundreds of billions of dollars to less developed countries in the 1970s. In the 1980s, their inability to repay these loans caused an LDC debt crisis — involving loan defaults, restructurings, and additional loans from the U.S. government, the World Bank, and the IMF to help these debtor nations and the banks that lent them money.

IMPORTANT TERMS

commercial paper
compensating balance
credit scoring
default

junk bonds
London Interbank Offered Rate (LIBOR)
prime rate

EXERCISES

1. Go to a library and use the most recent issue of *Standard & Poor's Bond Guide* to see if there have been any changes in the ratings of the corporate bonds in Table 6.2.

2. Use a recent publication by Moody's and one from Standard & Poor's to determine if the rating of Navistar bonds has changed from the speculative B assigned in May 1986. Look in a recent issue of *The Wall Street Journal* and find the prices of the Navistar 9s04 and the IBM 9⅜ 04 bonds discussed in this chapter and the previous one. Does the Navistar bond still sell for 20 percent less than the IBM bond?

3. Explain this observation by Andrew Tobias:[15]

   Even without checking the ratings, you can tell the quality of a bond just by looking at how its yield compares with the yield of other bonds. . . . If anything, you should shy away from bonds that pay exceptional interest: there is a reason they pay so well.

4. In explaining its criteria for rating municipal bonds, Standard & Poor's states, "It is important for an area to offer economic diversity . . . in employment and income."[16] Why?

5. Standard & Poor's states, "An S&P rating is not a recommendation to purchase, sell, or hold a security."[17] Why not? What else should an investor consider?

6. Other things being equal, which would you expect to have the higher yield to maturity,
   a. corporate or Treasury bonds?
   b. corporate or municipal bonds?
   c. AA or A corporate bonds?

7. A delayed bond payment reduces the "investors' actual return. For a simple example, consider a bond selling for $1,000 that has only one payment left, a $50 coupon and the $1,000 maturation value, scheduled to be paid six months from now. What is your (annual) rate of return if the company
   a. makes the payment on time?
   b. delays it six months?
   c. delays it four years?

8. John Kenneth Galbraith wrote that "anyone who buys a junk bond known as a junk bond deserves on the whole to lose."[18] Why would any rational investor buy a junk bond when it is clearly labeled a junk bond?

9. Traditionally, an asset-based loan, in which some of a company's assets are used as collateral for the loan, has been viewed as risky, because the pledging of assets was considered a sign of financial distress. Why might a bank consider an asset-based loan relatively safe?

10. Most credit-scoring systems look at whether the applicant is a renter or homeowner and how long the applicant has lived at the current address. Why might the probability of the applicant defaulting on a loan be related to these variables?

11. Many credit-scoring systems take into account the age of the loan applicant. Why might default rates be related to age?

12. Do you think that the probability of default on a commercial loan is higher for a one-year or a ten-year loan? Why?

13. Why might a bank rationally charge a higher interest rate on a vacation loan than on an auto loan?

14. A certain bank has offered to sell for $400 million a collection of commercial loans which, if paid off immediately, would realize $500 million. Why might other banks be unwilling to pay $500 million for these loans? Why, under different circumstances, might they be willing to pay *more* than $500 million?

15. In November 1988, commercial bank loan rates averaged 11.22 percent for the purchase of a car, 15.06 percent for a personal loan, 13.61 percent for the purchase of a mobile home, and 17.77 percent for credit-card borrowing.[19] How would you explain these differences?

16. There is a 2–3 percentage-point difference between the interest rate on a loan to buy a new car and the rate on a loan to buy a used car. Which loan do you suppose has the higher rate? Why?

17. In March 1983, the Federal Reserve Board estimated that the average interest rate on short-term commercial and on industrial loans (weighted by the size of the loan) was nearly one percentage point lower than the posted prime rate.[20] Are large or small businesses more likely to borrow below prime? Why? Why might a bank find it profitable to post a prime rate higher than the loan rates that it charges many of its customers?

18. Junk bonds are also called "high-yield bonds." In what sense do these bonds have high yields? Why do you suppose that Drexel Burnham preferred the "high-yield" label?

19. In July 1989, rumors circulated that an agreement had been reached at a Paris meeting on the LDC debt crisis to give Mexico the option of repaying its bank loans at 65 percent of their face value or exchanging its debt for new

loans with a 6.25 percent interest rate. Why would banks agree to accept 65 percent of the face value of their loans? Why would Mexico consider exchanging its debts for new loans, instead of paying 65 percent of their face value?

20. In January 1990, Mexico agreed to buy 30-year zero-coupon bonds from the U.S. Treasury to use as collateral for a restructuring of its bank loans. The Treasury priced these zeros using an interest rate of 7.925 percent, ⅛ of a percentage point below the average market interest rate on 30-year Treasury bonds at that time. Did this extra ⅛ of a point benefit Mexico or the U.S. Treasury?

INTEREST-RATE

RISK

The adviser's strategy was long and wrong.

Wall Street trader

Investors who bought 20-year 4-percent bonds in the 1960s lost money when interest rates rose to 9 percent in 1970. Corporations that sold 30-year bonds in 1982 at 15 percent were dismayed when rates fell below 10 percent in 1986. Banks that bought Treasury bills yielding 8 percent in 1985 were frustrated when they had to reinvest their money at 6 percent in 1986. Many savings-and-loan institutions that borrowed short term and lent long term in the 1960s and 1970s went bankrupt in the 1980s.

These are examples of interest-rate risk, gambles on the future course of interest rates. The cases cited are all gambles lost; there are an equal number of gambles won. This chapter will help you understand the interest-rate wagers implicit in all investment and borrowing decisions.

First, we will look at why bonds and loans of different maturities usually have different interest rates — why long-term interest rates are often higher than the rates on short-term bonds, and why the reverse is sometimes true. Then we will compare the risks borne by those who buy long-term assets with the risks inherent in buying short-term securities. Finally, we will look at some tools that have been developed to measure interest-rate risk and, if possible, reduce it.

THE TERM STRUCTURE OF INTEREST RATES

In May 1985, the interest rates on short-term Treasury bills were below 8 percent, but long-term Treasury bonds yielded more than 11 percent. Neither had any default risk, yet some investors willingly settled for an 8 percent interest rate on one Treasury security when another offered 11 percent. Was this an overlooked bargain, or is there some rational explanation?

Figure 7.1 shows the yields on several zero-coupon Treasury bonds in May 1985, with maturities ranging from one to twenty years. There is a whole spectrum of interest rates in this figure, with yields that are relatively low for short-term bonds but that rise for bonds that take longer to mature. This is an example of the **term structure of interest rates**, describing the yields to maturity on zero-coupon bonds that have different maturities but are otherwise identical. All of the securities considered in a term structure have the same default risk; if we compare the yields on a short-term Treasury bond and a long-term BB corporate bond, we don't know if the difference in yields reflects the term structure or default risk.

Notice also that the term structure compares the yields on zero-coupon bonds which, for reasons that will be explained shortly, are not necessarily equal to the yields on coupon-paying bonds. It is easiest to work with zero-coupon bonds because then each interest rated is associated with a single future payment. A comparison of the yields to maturity on coupon-paying bonds with different maturities is called a **yield curve**.

The term structure compares the yields on zero-coupon bonds with different maturities.

THE EXPECTATIONS HYPOTHESIS

Figure 7.1 shows that the term structure in May 1985 was upward sloping, with long-term bonds yielding more than bonds with shorter maturities. Sometimes the term structure is flat, with short-term and long-term bonds having the same yields, and sometimes it is inverted, with short-term bonds having the highest yields.

The Influence of Interest-Rate Expectations

The most important explanation for these variations in the term structure is interest-rate expectations. Consider a choice between two default-free, zero-coupon securities, the first maturing in one year and paying an annual return R_1, the second maturing in two years with an annual rate of return R_2.

A prospective purchaser of the two-year zero should consider the alternative of "rolling over" one-year zeros by purchasing a one-year zero and, when it matures, purchasing a new one-year zero. Every dollar invested in a two-year zero will grow to $(1 + R_2)^2$ whereas every dollar invested in a sequence of one-

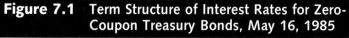

Figure 7.1 Term Structure of Interest Rates for Zero-Coupon Treasury Bonds, May 16, 1985

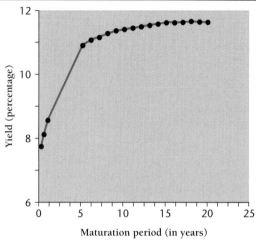

year zeros grows to $(1 + R_1)(1 + R_1^{+1})$, where R_1^{+1} is the interest rate on one-year zeros a year from now. The **Expectations Hypothesis** says that such securities must be priced so that both strategies do equally well:

$$(1 + R_2)^2 = (1 + R_1)(1 + R_1^{+1}) \qquad (1)$$

Otherwise, investors will shun the inferior bond, reducing its price and raising its return until it is competitive.

Similar logic applied to longer-term securities gives the following extrapolation of Equation 1:

$$(1 + R_n)^n = (1 + R_1)(1 + R_1^{+1})(1 + R_1^{+2}) \cdots (1 + R_1^{+n-1}) \qquad (2)$$

The expectations hypothesis uses interest-rate expectations to explain the term structure.

where R_n is the annual yield on an n-year, zero-coupon security and the returns on the right-hand side are the one-year rates over the next n years. For doing calculations mentally, rather than on a computer, we can use the approximation

$$R_n = \frac{R_1 + R_1^{+1} + R_1^{+2} \cdots + R_1^{+n-1}}{n} \qquad (3)$$

Equation 2, sometimes called the **Hicks equation,** in recognition of the work of John Hicks, a Nobel Prize–winning British economist, is the fundamental equation of the Expectations Hypothesis: according to the Expectations Hypothesis, the relationship between short-term and long-term interest rates reflects the anticipated future course of interest rates.

If, for example, the one-year rate is 10 percent now and will be 10 percent next year, then two-year zeros must yield 10 percent, too, to be competitive:

$$(1 + R_2)^2 = (1 + R_1)(1 + R_1^{+1})$$
$$= (1 + 0.10)(1 + 0.10)$$
$$= 1.21$$

implies

$$1 + R_2 = \sqrt{1.21}$$
$$R_2 = 0.10, \text{ or } 10\%$$

If, on the other hand, the one-year rate is 10 percent now and will be 12 percent next year, then comparable two-year assets must yield approximately 11 percent a year:

$$(1 + R_2)^2 = (1 + R_1)(1 + R_1^{+1})$$
$$= (1 + 0.10)(1 + 0.12)$$
$$= 1.232$$

This implies that

$$1 + R_2 = \sqrt{1.2232}$$
$$R_2 = 0.10995, \text{ or } 10.995\%$$

According to the expectations hypothesis, whether long-term interest rates are above or below short rates depends on whether interest rates are expected to increase or decline.

If, instead, the one-year rate is expected to decline from 10 percent this year to 8 percent next year, then two-year assets must yield about 9 percent a year:

$$(1 + R_2)^2 = (1 + R_1)(1 + R_1^{+1})$$
$$= (1 + 0.10)(1 + 0.08)$$
$$= 1.188$$

This implies that

$$1 + R_2 = \sqrt{1.188}$$
$$R_2 = 0.08995, \text{ or } 8.995\%$$

The general rule is short and easy: the two-year rate will be above or below the one-year rate depending upon whether the one-year rate is expected to rise or fall.

Extending the lesson to longer-term assets, we conclude that if no change in one-year rates is anticipated, comparable assets of differing maturities will be priced to have the same yield. Longer-term rates will be above the current one-year rate if rates are expected to rise, and below it if rates are expected to decline.

Three simple term structures are shown in Figure 7.2. More complex interest-rate expectations (for example, rates expected to rise for a few years and then decline) imply more complicated term structures.

The Yields on Coupon Bonds

The pure term structure of interest rates reflected in the Hicks equation applies to zero-coupon bonds, but most bonds pay semiannual coupons. A yield curve showing the yields to maturity for coupon-paying bonds of differing maturities is not identical to the term structure of returns on zero-coupon bonds,

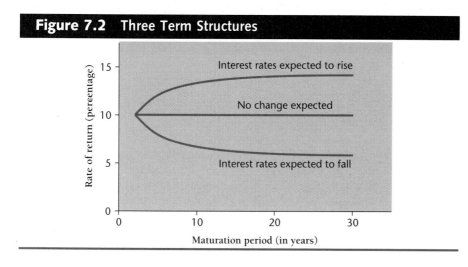

Figure 7.2   Three Term Structures

(Rate of return (percentage) on vertical axis, Maturation period (in years) on horizontal axis)

Interest rates expected to rise

No change expected

Interest rates expected to fall

except in the special case of a flat term structure. To illustrate this point, we assume annual coupons for simplicity. The present value P of an n-year bond, with annual coupons C and maturation value M, is obtained by summing the present values of the annual payments, using the appropriate required returns:

$$P = \frac{C}{(1 + R_1)} + \frac{C}{(1 + R_2)^2} + \cdots + \frac{C}{(1 + R_n)^n} + \frac{M}{(1 + R_n)^n}$$

The yield to maturity y is the constant required return that solves the present-value equation

$$P = \frac{C}{(1 + y)} + \frac{C}{(1 + y)^2} + \cdots + \frac{C}{(1 + y)^n} + \frac{M}{(1 + y)^n}$$

If the term structure is flat ($R_1 = R_2 = \ldots = R_n$), then the calculated yield to maturity y equals R_n, and the yield curve and term structure agree. If, on the other hand, the term structure is upward sloping, then the yield to maturity y is an average of the n values of R_t and will be somewhat less than R_n, depending on the size of the coupons. For a zero-coupon bond, y equals R_n; Figure 7.3 shows that, as the coupon rate increases, the calculated yield to maturity falls below the return on a zero-coupon bond. Similarly, when the term structure is downward sloping, the yield to maturity is above R_n; the larger the coupon, the greater the difference.

The most important implication is that the term structure provides a logical explanation for why bonds from the very same issuer with the same maturity may have different yields to maturity. If you look in the newspaper now, you might find two ten-year U.S. Treasury bonds — one with, say, an 8 percent yield to maturity and the other at 8.5 percent. The latter is not necessarily an overlooked bargain. Perhaps the term structure is upward sloping and the second bond has coupons lower than those of the first.

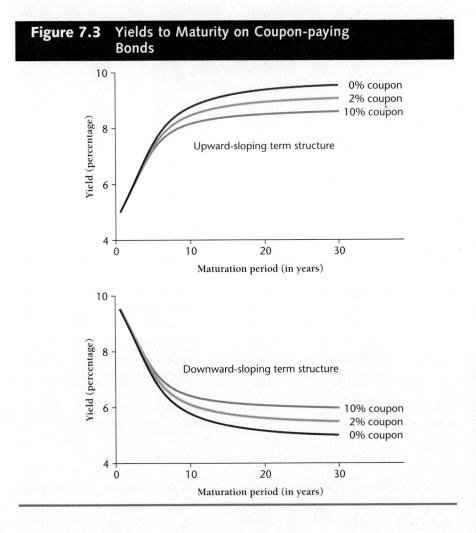

Figure 7.3 Yields to Maturity on Coupon-paying Bonds

Is the Term Structure Always/Ever Right?

The Expectations Hypothesis is a straightforward yet elegant theory. Because rolling over short-term assets ("shorts") is an alternative to holding long-term assets ("longs"), the yields on short- and long-term assets are linked together by interest-rate expectations. Anticipated movements in short-term rates determine whether long rates will be above or below short rates and, conversely, we can use the observed relationship between short and long rates to infer the interest-rate expectations of financial experts. For instance, the Expectations Hypothesis interpretation of Figure 7.1, in which long rates are above short rates, is that in May 1985 investors expected interest rates to increase.

Mexico Profits from the Term Structure

Highlight 7.1

In January 1990, the Mexican government bought 30-year zero-coupon U.S. Treasury bonds paying $33 billion in 2020 to collateralize a debt-refinancing agreement with foreign banks. To price these 30-year zeros, the U.S. Treasury agreed to use the interest rate on 30-year Treasury coupon bonds rather than the interest rate on 30-year Treasury zeros. Because the term structure was downward sloping at the time, the interest rate on coupon bonds was somewhat higher than the rate on zeros, causing the Treasury to use an interest rate of 7.925 percent instead of 7.625 percent.

How much difference did this make in the price Mexico paid for the zero? Nearly $300 million:

$$\frac{\$33 \text{ billion}}{1.07625^{30}} - \frac{\$33 \text{ billion}}{1.07925^{30}} = \$3.640 \text{ billion} - \$3.349 \text{ billion} = \$291 \text{ million}$$

Mexico saved nearly $300 million because the term structure was downward sloping and the U.S. Treasury agreed to use the wrong interest rate.

Figure 7.4 shows that interest rates actually fell by several percentage points during the next 12 months, causing investors, in retrospect, to regret that they had not bought long-term securities in May 1985 and locked in high rates of return. Those who passed up long-term bonds yielding more than 11 percent in the spring of 1985 and bought one-year Treasury bills yielding less than 8 percent, counting on a rise in interest rates, ended up rolling over their money in the spring of 1986 at lower interest rates.

This was not the first time that the interest-rate forecasts implicit in the term structure turned out to be wrong. Interest rates are notoriously difficult to forecast, and investors have made many costly errors. In 1982 and 1983, as in 1985, long-term Treasury bond rates were some two percentage points above the yields on short-term Treasury bonds, indicating (according to the Expectations Hypothesis) that interest rates were expected to increase sharply, yet interest rates tumbled. In 1979 and 1980, long rates were below short rates, but interest rates rose.

The interest rate expectations implied by the term structure are often wrong.

Empirical studies suggest that the term structure mispredicts the direction of interest rates as often as not.[1] The safest conclusion is that the term structure may well reflect investors' best guesses about the future course of interest rates, but these guesses are far from guarantees.

The Expectations Hypothesis was derived by assuming that future interest rates are known with certainty. When the future is certain, short-term and long-term bonds are priced so that all strategies are guaranteed to do equally well. In reality, the future course of interest rates is unknown and investors gamble,

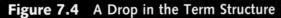

Figure 7.4 A Drop in the Term Structure

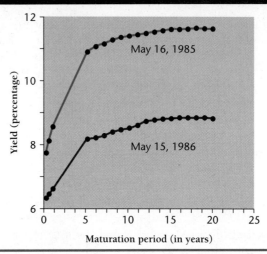

whichever strategy they follow. If they roll over shorts, they can be hurt by an unexpected drop in interest rates; if they buy longs, an unexpected increase in interest rates is their downfall. Let's now look at how investors can choose a strategy that reflects their opinions about the future course of interest rates.

Betting Against the Term Structure

For any given term structure, we can infer the future interest-rate values for which the strategies of buying longs and of rolling over shorts do equally well. If we disagree with these projections, we have a reason for choosing between shorts and longs. Suppose, for example, that one-year bonds are priced to yield 8 percent and two-year bonds 9 percent a year; that is, $R_1 = 0.08$ and $R_2 = 0.09$. The Hicks equation (either Equation 1 or 2 given earlier) implies that shorts and longs will, in retrospect, do equally well if the one-year rate a year from now, R_1^{+1}, turns out to be about 10 percent:

$$(1 + R_2)^2 = (1 + R_1)(1 + R_1^{+1})$$
$$(1.09)^2 = (1.08)(1 + R_1^{+1})$$

This implies that

$$1 + R_1^{+1} = \frac{(1.09)^2}{1.08} = 1.1000925$$

$$R_1^{+1} = 0.1000925, \text{ or } 10.00925\%$$

The logic is as follows: the two-year bond pays 9 percent a year. To do as well buying a one-year bond at 8 percent, the investor has to be able to reinvest the second year at 10 percent. The implicit future rates of return, here 10

Expert Forecasts Aren't Reliable

In December 1986, *The Wall Street Journal* asked 35 top forecasters to predict the interest rates on 3-month Treasury bills and 30-year Treasury bonds six months later, in June 1987. In June 1987, it asked for predictions for December 1987. The results are shown in the accompanying table. In December 1986, the average prediction for the T-bill rate in June 1987 was 4.98 percent, with the individual forecasts ranging from as low as 4.1 percent to as high as 6 percent, a span of nearly two percentage points. The actual value turned out to be 5.73 percent, 75 basis points above the average prediction. The June 1987 30-year bond rate was 8.5 percent, a full 1.5 percent above the average prediction and, indeed, outside the range spanned by the predictions. Not one of these 35 experts was within 50 basis points of the actual value. There was even more disagreement in the predictions for December 1987, with the average T-bill forecast turning out to be slightly too high and the long-term bond forecast much too low.

Nine of these forecasters had been surveyed by *The Wall Street Journal* over all ten of the preceding six-month periods (from December 1981 through June 1986). On six of these ten occasions, the actual Treasury-bill rate was outside the range of the nine forecasts made six months earlier. Of the 90 individual forecasts of the T-bill rate, there were 38 correct and 52 incorrect predictions of the direction of change of the T-bill rate. The average error was 1.6 percentage points.*

Interest Rate Forecasts by Thirty-five Experts

	December 1986 Predictions of June 1987 Interest Rates		June 1987 Predictions of December 1987 Interest Rates	
	3-Month T-bill	30-Year Bond	3-Month T-bill	30-Year Bond
Average	4.98%	7.05%	5.91%	6.19%
Range	4.10%–6.00%	6.10%–8.00%	4.25%–6.63%	5.88%–9.40%
Actual	5.73%	8.50%	5.77%	9.12%

source: Tom Herman and Mathew Winkler, "Economic Expansion Will Keep Going for at Least Another Year and Interest Rates Won't Change Much, Say Analysts in Survey," *The Wall Street Journal*, July 6, 1987. Reprinted by permission of *The Wall Street Journal*, © 1987 Dow Jones & Company, Inc. All Rights Reserved Worldwide.

The problem is not that these forecasters are uninformed, but that interest rates are notoriously difficult to forecast. Interest rates fluctuate considerably, causing large changes in bond prices and substantial capital gains and losses for bond traders. Each gain or loss is largely unexpected. If it was clear that bond prices were about to fall, there would be no buyers at current prices. If a sharp increase were certain, there would then be no sellers.

Instead, there is always, at the current price, a balance between buyers expecting prices to rise and sellers expecting prices to fall.

*Michael T. Belongia, "Predicting Interest Rates: A Comparison of Professional and Market-Based Forecasts," Federal Reserve Bank of St. Louis *Review*, March 1987, pp. 9–15.

The term structure implies forward rates such that all strategies do equally well.

percent, that is embedded in the term structure are called **forward rates**. The relevant question is whether or not the investor expects the one-year rate next year to be above or below the 10 percent forward rate which is implicit in the term structure.

If you also predict a 10 percent rate next year (or have no basis for making an informed prediction), then you have no reason to believe that shorts will do better or worse than longs. If, however, you disagree with the term structure's 10 percent forward rate, then you have a reason to bet against the term structure. You prefer the two-year bond if you don't think the one-year rate will reach 10 percent; you favor the one-year bond if you believe that the rate will go above 10 percent.

Those who expect interest rates to be higher than the term structure's implicit forward rates can buy short-term bonds; those who expect lower rates can buy long-term bonds.

Notice that a belief in rising interest rates is not sufficient reason for buying short-term bonds. If you think interest rates will rise from 8 percent to 9 percent, a two-year bond at 9 percent still does better. You must believe that interest rates will rise above the 10 percent forward rate already embedded in the term structure.

Whether or not your decision is an informed bet, there is risk in whichever strategy you choose. If you buy a two-year bond yielding 9 percent when one-year bonds yield 8 percent, you are betting implicitly that next year's rate will be below 10 percent. If it is, you earn more than you would have by rolling over shorts. If it isn't, you are long and wrong, as was the financial adviser mentioned in the quotation prefacing this chapter.

Either way you go, buying shorts or longs, there is the possibility of disappointment — with longs, if interest rates rise unexpectedly; with shorts, if rates drop unexpectedly. Economists label the first danger capital risk and the second income risk, concepts that we will now examine.

CAPITAL RISK

The short-term purchase of a long-term asset creates the **capital risk** that an unexpected change in interest rates will cause an unanticipated change in the asset's price. To illustrate, consider an investor with $10,000 when interest rates on default-free Treasury bills are 10 percent and are widely expected to stay at 10 percent for the foreseeable future. In accord with the Expectations Hypothesis, one-year, two-year, and thirty-year zero-coupon Treasury bonds are all priced to yield 10 percent a year, as shown in the second column of Table 7.1. The future values of these three assets have been set so that the present value of each at a 10 percent required return is $10,000. The next column in the table shows that if interest rates stay at 10 percent, as anticipated, the present value of each asset a year from now will be $11,000 — providing the requisite 10 percent return.

Unexpected changes in interest rates cause unexpected capital gains and losses — capital risk.

But what if interest rates rise unexpectedly to 20 percent? The fourth column of Table 7.1 shows that the one-year asset will be worth $11,000 in a year, because it matures then, but that the present value of the two-year asset will be $917 less than expected. This asset now has one year left until maturity and investors will not pay $11,000 to get $12,100 a year later, a mere 10 percent return, when interest rates on other one-year assets have risen to 20 percent. They will pay only an amount such that $12,100 provides the requisite 20 percent return, and that amount is $12,100/1.20 = $10,083. An increase in the required return reduces the present value of a given future cash flow, and this price variability is labeled capital risk. Capital risk is two-sided, of course; just as an unexpected rise in interest rates reduces the present value, so an unexpected drop in interest rates raises the present value.

The drop in the value of the two-year asset here is disappointing, but not nearly as crushing as the collapse of the value of the 30-year asset if interest rates rise to 20 percent. One year later, there are still 29 years until maturity and the present value at a 20 percent required return is $882, some 92 percent less than the $11,000 that had been anticipated.

The startling magnitude of this price decline is a dramatic example of a general principle that we will explore in more depth later in this chapter: the longer the term of the asset, the more sensitive its price to interest-rate fluctuations and the larger the capital risk.

Long-term assets have substantial capital risk.

INCOME RISK

Should nervous investors forgo long-term assets to avoid the terrors of capital risk? Not necessarily, because rolling over short-term assets is risky, too. If you invest in a perfectly safe one-year Treasury bill, then you are guaranteed $10,000 when the bill matures a year hence (and the price won't stray far from $10,000

Table 7.1 **Three Strategies**

Strategy	Current Price	Price Next Year	
		If Rates Stay at 10%	If Rates Rise to 20%
buy 1-year asset	$\dfrac{\$11,000}{1.10} = \$10,000$	$\$11,000$	$\$11,000$
buy 2-year asset	$\dfrac{\$12,100}{1.10^2} = \$10,000$	$\dfrac{\$12,100}{1.10} = \$11,000$	$\dfrac{\$12,100}{1.20} \doteq \$10,083$
buy 30-year asset	$\dfrac{\$174,494}{1.10^{30}} = \$10,000$	$\dfrac{\$174,494}{1.10^{29}} = \$11,000$	$\dfrac{\$174,494}{1.20^{29}} = \$882$

in the meantime). But what rate of return will you earn when you reinvest your $10,000 a year from now, and the year after that? This uncertainty about the rates of return prevailing when you reinvest your money is called **income risk** (or "reinvestment risk"). Income risk refers to the fact that the future value of an investment depends on the rates of return prevailing when the cash flow is reinvested.

Income risk describes the uncertain returns on reinvested money.

Consider the three assets in Table 7.1 again. If the 30-year Treasury zero is purchased, the investor is assured of $174,494 30 years from now, representing a 10 percent annual rate of return. If, instead of locking in this 10 percent return, the investor rolls over one-year assets year after year, $11,000 is assured at the end of the first year, but there are no guarantees beyond that. If, as is currently anticipated, interest rates stay at 10 percent, the investor's wealth will grow to

$$\$10,000(1.10^{30}) = \$174,494$$

just as with the 30-year asset. But if interest rates drop unexpectedly to 5 percent and stay there, the future value will be only

$$\$10,000(1.10)(1.05^{29}) = \$45,277$$

some 75 percent less than with the thirty-year asset.

The purchase of a 30-year zero guarantees a specified payment in 30 years, when the asset matures, but not its present value in the intervening years. Rolling over one-year assets guarantees a payment next year, but not beyond that. With capital risk, you may experience a sudden large loss; with income risk, you may suffer slowly.

Taking into account opportunity losses, no strategy is safe. You could always do better if you had an accurate crystal ball. Lacking one, remember this general principle: The purchase of long-term assets is profitable if interest rates fall unexpectedly; rolling over short-term assets does well if interest rates rise unexpectedly. For borrowers, the reverse is true. Borrowing long term at a fixed interest rate will turn out to be profitable if interest rates rise unexpectedly; rolling over a sequence of short-term loans turns out well if interest rates decline unexpectedly.

INFLATION RISK

Although a 30-year asset locks in a fixed dollar amount at the end of 30 years, there is still **inflation risk**, in that the purchasing power of these dollars depends on what happens to prices during the intervening 30 years. Let's set the price level today at $1. If, miraculously, there is no inflation for the next 30 years, the price level will still be $1, and $174,494 will buy as much then as it does now. If instead there is 5 percent inflation each year, the price level will more than quadruple:

> A fixed dollar payment has inflation risk because of uncertainty about future prices of goods and services.

$$\$1(1.05^{30}) = \$4.322$$

and $174,494 will buy then only what $40,374 buys now,

$$\$174,494/4.322 = \$40,374$$

Inflation at 10 percent, year after year, will just offset the 10 percent nominal return, giving a 0 percent real return. Your wealth goes up by a factor of 17, but so do prices, so that the real value of the investment stays at $10,000. And for a final scare, if prices rise by 20 percent a year, the investor with $10,000 who locks in a guaranteed 10 percent annual nominal return winds up with only enough money to buy what $735 buys today.

A long-term asset with a guaranteed nominal payoff does not protect investors from unanticipated inflation. An unexpected increase in the rate of inflation erodes the purchasing power of fixed nominal cash flows; an unexpected decrease swells it. We saw in Chapter 5 that, although inflation and interest rates do not move in lockstep, an increase in the rate of inflation does tend to increase nominal interest rates. If that is so, a strategy of rolling over short-term bonds offers some protection against unexpected inflation. Remember, however, that it is only unanticipated changes in inflation that are risky. Anticipated inflation is presumably already built into interest-rate expectations and, hence, the term structure.

> Long-term bonds may have substantial inflation risk.

RISK AND THE SHAPE OF THE TERM STRUCTURE

The Expectations Hypothesis must be modified to account for risk preferences. The Expectations Hypothesis predicts that short-term and long-term securities will all be priced to have the same anticipated return, taking into account investor expectations of future interest rates. But uncertainty regarding interest rates creates income and capital risk, causing risk-averse investors to prefer shorts to longs, or vice versa. If so, the expected returns need not be equal: the inferior asset will have to offer a higher expected return — a risk premium — to attract investors.

> The liquidity-premium hypothesis states that investor concerns about capital risk cause the term structure to be typically upward sloping.

The **liquidity-premium hypothesis** holds that investors are more concerned with capital risk than with income risk because of the ever-present possibility that they will need to sell their bonds to raise cash. They consequently have a natural preference for short-term assets and require relatively high returns on long-term bonds — higher than predicted by the Expectation Hypothesis. According to this theory, the term structure is normally upward sloping, as illustrated in Figure 7.5. In this figure, interest rates are equally likely to rise or to fall and therefore the term structure predicted by the expectations hypothesis is flat. But those investors who are concerned with capital risk will not buy long-term bonds paying 10 percent in this situation if they can invest in short-term bonds paying 10 percent. In order to persuade them to hold long-term bonds with substantial capital risk, such bonds must be priced to yield somewhat more than 10 percent.

> The market-segmentation hypothesis says that diverse investors specialize in different maturities.

The **market-segmentation hypothesis**, in contrast, holds that investors have diverse preferences and specialize in different maturities. Some investors, such as life insurance companies and pension funds, have long horizons. To the extent that such institutions have promised to pay relatively fixed nominal amounts many years from now, based on assumed rates of return, there is considerable danger for them in a strategy of rolling over short-term investments. Insurance companies and pension funds are, in fact, the largest holders of long-term bonds. Other investors, particularly those most concerned with real rates of return, consider long-term bonds very risky and prefer to roll over short-term investments.

If the market is sharply segmented, then the interest rates on different maturities might depend solely on demand and supply within that segment of the market — allowing very different interest rates on bonds with only slightly different maturities. Although some investors do have preferred habitats, the evidence is that there are no discontinuities in the term structure; maturities are linked by the willingness of many investors to seek out the highest returns.

On balance, capital risk seems to be the predominant concern of investors; rigorous studies indicate that long-term interest rates have, on average, been somewhat higher (roughly half a percentage point) than short-term interest rates, evidence that investors need some extra return — a liquidity premium — to overcome their aversion to capital risk and to persuade them to hold long-term bonds.[2] Similarly, comparisons of the term structure with actual surveys of rate expectations indicate that the interest rates on longer-term securities are slightly higher than implied by the Expectations Hypothesis, again evidence in support of the liquidity-premium hypothesis.[3]

Figure 7.5 Interest Rates Expected to Stay at 10 Percent

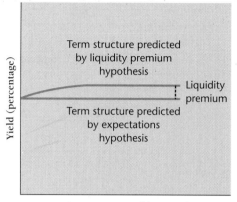

Maturation period (in years)

Interest-rate expectations are the primary determinant of the shape of the term structure and exert a decisive influence on shifts in the term structure. But, in addition, investor distaste for capital risk requires long-term bonds to be priced to yield somewhat more than would be projected by the Expectations Hypothesis.

EXCHANGE-RATE RISK

A key determinant of investor demand for a currency, such as U.S. dollars, German marks, or Japanese yen, is the anticipated rate of return on deposits and other investments denominated in that currency, taking into account not only the interest rate on the investment, but also the anticipated appreciation or depreciation of the currency.

Consider, for instance, a hypothetical case in which the interest rate on a one-year U.S. Treasury security is 8 percent and the interest rate on a comparable one-year French security is 5 percent. The dollar rate of return on a security denominated in a foreign currency, here the franc, is equal to the interest rate on the foreign security minus the rate of depreciation of its currency relative to the dollar. Suppose that the anticipated exchange rate in one year is $e^* = 0.05$ dollars per franc. If the current exchange rate is also 0.05 dollars per francs, then the French security is less attractive than the U.S. one because its return — measured in either francs or dollars — is 5 percent, whereas U.S. securities earn 8 percent. For the French security paying 5 percent to be as attractive as the U.S. security paying 8 percent, the current value of the franc must be 3 percent lower than its anticipated value a year from now — that is, the current exchange rate must be (1-0.03)(0.05) = 0.0485 dollars per franc — so that investors in the French bond earn not only 5 percent interest but also a 3 percent appreciation in the value of the franc relative to the dollar.

In general, let R_d be the nominal rate of return on a domestic asset (denominated in our example in dollars) and let R_f be the nominal rate of return on a foreign asset (denominated here in francs):

$$1 + R_d = \frac{\text{Dollars earned}}{\text{Dollars invested}}$$

$$1 + R_f = \frac{\text{Francs earned}}{\text{Francs invested}}$$

To make these returns comparable, a common currency (either dollars or francs) must be used. Let e be the exchange rate (dollars for francs) at the time of the investment, and let $e + \Delta e$ be the exchange rate at the end of the investment period. The earnings in dollars divided by the cost in dollars for the French investment are

$$\frac{\text{Dollars earned}}{\text{Dollars invested}} = \frac{(\text{Francs earned})(e + \Delta e)}{(\text{Francs invested})(e)}$$

$$= \left(\frac{\text{Francs earned}}{\text{Francs invested}}\right)\left(\frac{e + \Delta e}{e}\right)$$

$$= (1 + R_f)\left(1 + \frac{\Delta e}{e}\right)$$

The dollar rate of return on a foreign investment is equal to the foreign rate of return plus the appreciation of the foreign currency relative to the dollar.

This dollar rate of return on the French investment equals the return on the U.S. investment if the following equation is satisfied:

$$1 + R_d = (1 + R_f)\left(1 + \frac{\Delta e}{e}\right)$$

or, approximately,

$$R_d = R_f + \frac{\Delta e}{e} \tag{4}$$

Assets that are close substitutes — with comparable risk, liquidity, and so forth — should be priced to yield similar percentage rates of return. For this to be true of U.S. and French bonds, U.S. interest rates must equal French interest rates (on comparable securities) plus or minus the anticipated percentage change in the exchange rate (dollars per franc).

If, when French bonds yield 10 percent, the exchange rate is expected to be stable, then comparable U.S. bonds must yield 10 percent, too, or funds will be invested only in the bond with the higher anticipated return. If U.S. bonds have higher yields, funds will flow out of the French bond market into the U.S.

bond market, thereby driving French bond prices down and U.S. bond prices up until parity is restored.

If the U.S. dollar is expected to depreciate against the franc, U.S. investments will be unattractive unless they offer relatively high interest rates. If, for example, the dollar-to-franc exchange rate is expected to rise 5 percent over the next year, then U.S. one-year interest rates must be 5 percent higher than French one-year interest rates. Analogous comparisons can naturally be drawn for exchange-rate appreciation and for interest rates in other countries.

U.S. interest rates are high relative to foreign interest rates when the dollar is expected to depreciate.

Equation 4 implies that changes in interest rates in one country should cause corresponding changes in interest rates in other countries, or changes in exchange rates. Suppose again that U.S. interest rates are 8 percent, French interest rates are 5 percent, and a 3 percent appreciation of the franc relative to the dollar is anticipated. If economic events in the United States cause interest rates to rise from 8 percent to 10 percent, then interest rates must rise in France, too, or currency traders will dump francs and buy dollars, reducing the current value of the franc sufficiently so that the anticipated future appreciation of the franc relative to the dollar is 5 percent rather than 3 percent.

Every day, *The Wall Street Journal* reports the yields to maturity on selected international government bonds. Table 7.2 shows some of their data for September 8, 1989. Assuming that these bonds are comparable, the fact that U.S. interest rates were higher than Japanese interest rates and lower than British interest rates indicates that investors anticipated a depreciation of the dollar relative to the yen and appreciation of the dollar relative to the pound over the next 10 years.

Exchange-rate risk (or currency risk) exists because there is uncertainty about the future course of exchange rates. Banks and other investors who hold currencies suffer capital losses when these currencies depreciate unexpectedly. Even if a bank deals only in dollars and holds only dollars, it still suffers an opportunity loss if it could have earned a larger return on its assets had it invested in securities denominated in other currencies.

Uncertainty about future exchange rates creates exchange-rate risk.

Table 7.2	Yields to Maturity on Selected International Government Bonds			
Country	**Maturity**	**Coupon**	**Price**	**Yield**
Japan	September 2009	5.00%	97.740	5.18%
United Kingdom	October 2008	9.00%	96.313	9.41%
United States	November 2008	8.75%	104.13	8.22%

source: *The Wall Street Journal*, September 11, 1989.

DURATION

So far, we have focused on zero-coupon securities, which pay a lump sum at maturity. Most investments provide a regular cash flow: the monthly payments from an amortized loan, the semiannual coupons from a bond, and the quarterly dividends from corporate stock. Table 7.1 showed that a 30-year zero-coupon bond has much more capital risk than a 2-year zero. But what about a 10-year bond with large coupons versus a 5-year bond with no coupons? You have to wait longer to receive the face value of the 10-year bond, but you also receive some coupons before the 5-year bond matures. On balance, which bond has more capital risk? An asset's **duration** is a measure of the sensitivity of its present value to changes in its required return, taking into account all of the cash flow. We will see first how duration is measured and then how it can be used to gauge capital risk.

The Duration Formula

The present value P of an n-year investment with cash flow X_t in year t and a constant required return R is

$$P = \frac{X_1}{(1+R)} + \frac{X_2}{(1+R)^2} + \cdots + \frac{X_n}{(1+R)^n} \qquad (5)$$

The value of an asset's duration is given by this equation:

$$D = (1)\left[\frac{X_1/(1+R)}{P}\right] + (2)\left[\frac{X_2/(1+R)^2}{P}\right] + \cdots + (n)\left[\frac{X_n/(1+R)^n}{P}\right] \qquad (6)$$

An understanding of this formula may be helped by analogy to a course grade that depends on the scores on two midterms and a final examination, with 50 percent of the grade determined by the final-exam score and 25 percent by each midterm. A student who gets 82 on the first midterm, 75 on the second midterm, and 93 on the final has a course score of

$$X = 84(0.25) + 78(0.25) + 93(0.50) = 87$$

The course score is a weighted average in that the individual scores are multiplied by weights of 0.25, 0.25, and 0.50 to reflect the relative importance of each.

Duration is also a weighted average. In Equation 6, the numbers 1, 2, . . . , n, are the number of years the investor must wait to receive the cash flow; X_1 is received after one year, X_2 after two years, and so on. An asset's duration is a weighted average of these years, using weights that reflect the fraction of the total present value received at that time; for example, $[X_2/(1+R)^2]/P$ is the fraction of the present value received in the second year.

To illustrate the calculation of duration, consider a two-year asset paying $100 one year from today and $100 the year after. At a 10 percent required return, the present value is

An asset's duration is the present-value-weighted average number of years until the cash flow is received.

$$P = \frac{X_1}{(1 + R)} + \frac{X_2}{(1 + R)^2}$$

$$= \frac{\$100}{(1.10)} + \frac{\$100}{(1.10)^2}$$

$$= \$90.91 + \$82.64$$

$$= \$173.55$$

The second $100 payment has a lower present value than the first because it comes a year later. Of the total $173.55 present value, the first $100 payment represents $90.91/$173.55 = 0.524, slightly more than 52 percent, and the second $82.64/$173.55 = 0.476, the remaining 48 percent. The duration is

$$D = (1)\left[\frac{X_1/(1 + R)}{P}\right] + (2)\left[\frac{X_2/(1 + R)^2}{P}\right]$$

$$= (1)\left[\frac{\$100/(1.10)}{\$173.55}\right] + (2)\left[\frac{\$100/(1.10)^2}{\$173.55}\right]$$

$$= (1)(0.524) + (2)(0.476)$$

$$= 1.476$$

or slightly less than 1½ years. Thus the average wait until receiving this asset's present value is 1½ years.

Using Duration to Gauge Capital Risk

Duration is useful because it gauges the sensitivity of present value to changes in the required return. In particular, the application of calculus to Equation 5 shows that the percentage change in an asset's present value, written as %P, resulting from a small change ΔR in the percentage required return is given by

$$\%P = -\frac{D}{1 + R}\Delta R \tag{7}$$

or, approximately,

$$\%P = -D\ \Delta R \tag{8}$$

In the preceding example, the two-year asset has a duration of 1.5 years, and Equation 8 says that a 1-percentage-point increase in the required return ($\Delta R = 1$) will reduce the present value by about 1.5 percent. Let's see if this is correct. If R rises by 1 percentage point, to 11 percent,

The percentage change in an asset's present value resulting from a 1-percentage-point change in the required return is approximately equal to the asset's duration.

$$P = \frac{X_1}{(1 + R)} + \frac{X_2}{(1 + R)^2}$$

$$= \frac{\$100}{(1.11)} + \frac{\$100}{(1.11)^2}$$

$$= \$90.09 + \$81.16$$

$$= \$171.25$$

about a 1½ percent decline: ($171.25-$173.55)/$173.55 = −0.013. Thus an asset's duration, the present-value-weighted average number of years until the cash flow is received, is approximately equal to the percentage change in the asset's present value resulting from a 1-percentage-point change in the required return.

For a zero-coupon bond with a maturity of n years, all of the present value is received in year n and, therefore, duration is simply equal to n, the number of years until maturity. It immediately follows that long-term zero-coupon bonds have a great deal of capital risk. The duration of a 30-year zero is 30 years, implying that a 1-percentage-point rise in interest rates reduces its present value by roughly 30 percent. The other side of this coin is that a 1-percentage-point drop in interest rates *raises* its present value by about 30 percent.

Empirical confirmation of the usefulness of duration for gauging risk is provided by the data in Table 7.3, which show the annual standard deviations of the prices of zero-coupon Treasury bonds during the years 1984–87. Because the duration of a zero is equal to its maturity, we might expect 10-year, 15-year, and 20-year zeros to have, respectively, about 2, 3, and 4 times as much capital risk as a 5-year zero. During this period, judging by the relative standard deviations, they did.[4]

A bond with coupons has a duration that is less than its maturity and is shorter the larger the coupons are. For instance, a 20-year bond with a 10 percent coupon and 10 percent yield to maturity has a duration of 9.01 years, less than half that of a 20-year zero-coupon bond. It follows that the price of a longer-term bond with high coupons is less affected by interest rates than is the price of shorter-term bonds with low coupons — for instance, the 20-year bond with 10 percent coupons just mentioned has a duration of 9.01 years, less than that of a 10-year zero. A bond's maturity is an inaccurate measure of capital risk; its duration is the appropriate gauge.

Assets with long durations have substantial capital risk.

ASSET DURATION AND LIABILITY DURATION

So far, we have focused on the risks borne by investors who buy assets. Those who issue bonds also gamble on interest rates. If you take out a 30-year fixed-rate mortgage, you will congratulate yourself if interest rates rise and regret your choice if interest rates decline. If you take out a loan with an adjustable interest rate, you will pay more if interest rates go up and less if they go down.

The effect of interest rate changes on net worth depends on both asset and liability duration.

Individuals and businesses have both assets and liabilities, each with associated future cash flows. Households take out mortgages and buy bonds; businesses sell bonds and buy plants and equipment. Each side of a balance sheet has some interest-rate risk and, to the extent that the durations of the assets and

Table 7.3	Annual Standard Deviations of Treasury Zeros, 1984–1987
Maturity (years)	**Standard Deviation**
5	10.8%
10	20.7%
15	28.8%
20	38.1%

source: Gary Smith, "Coping with the Term Structure," in *Essays in Honor of James Tobin*, William C. Brainard, ed. (Cambridge, Mass.: MIT Press, 1990). Reprinted by permission.

liabilities are not matched, there is an implicit wager on the future course of interest rates. Anxiety over such wagers during interest-rate turbulence in the late 1970s and early 1980s led to the creation of financial-futures contracts and other hedging instruments that we will discuss in later chapters.

Banks, savings-and-loan associations (S&L's), and other financial intermediaries provide an especially interesting example in that by borrowing from some to lend to others, they maintain a clear and controllable link between their financial assets and liabilities. In Britain, the actuaries who certify the financial soundness of an insurance company or pension fund are required to compare the maturities of assets and liabilities. There is no such requirement in the United States, and the interest-rate gambles that savings-and-loan institutions have won and lost have not only shaken the S&L's, but have scared depositors and policymakers, too.

SUMMARY

The term structure of interest rates describes the relationship between interest rates on zero-coupon bonds (with similar default risk) of varying maturities; the yield curve describes a similar relationship for coupon bonds. The Expectations Hypothesis says that the shape of the term structure depends on interest-rate expectations, with long rates above, equal to, or below short rates, depending on whether interest rates are expected to rise, stay the same, or decline. Therefore, we can infer from the shape of the current term structure the direction that investors expect interest rates to move.

Interest rates are very difficult to predict. Those who buy long-term bonds, locking in a rate of return, are betting that future interest rates will be lower than the forward rates implied by the term structure. Those who roll over short-term bonds implicitly wager that future interest rates will be higher than the

Highlight 7.3	**Borrowing Short and Lending Long**

In the 1970s, the balance sheets of a small, traditional savings-and-loan institution might have looked like this:

Assets (millions of dollars)		Liabilities (millions of dollars)	
Cash reserves	5	Deposits	96
Loans	95	Net worth	4
	100		100

Let's assume that the interest rates paid on the deposits change daily, giving deposits a duration of virtually zero, and that the loans are conventional 30-year mortgages. At a 10 percent interest rate, the duration of a 30-year mortgage works out to be 8.5 years. In practice, not all of the S&L's mortgages were made today, so let's assume that the average duration of the loan portfolio is roughly four years. If so, an unanticipated 1-percentage-point increase in interest rates will reduce the present value of this portfolio by 4 percent (about $4 million), enough to wipe out the S&L's net worth:

Assets (millions of dollars)		Liabilities (millions of dollars)	
Cash reserves	5	Deposits	96
Loans	91	Net worth	0
	96		96

(The present values of the deposits and cash reserves do not change, because these have a duration of zero.)

Duration provides a dramatic way of understanding how the traditional S&L strategy of borrowing short and lending long is a very dangerous bet on the future course of interest rates. In the simplified example given here, an unexpected 1-percentage-point reduction in interest rates doubles net worth, but a 1-percentage-point increase reduces the S&L's net worth to zero, so that if it were to sell its loans, it would barely have enough cash to pay off its depositors.

As interest rates rose during 1979–82 (and, to make matters worse, there were significant defaults on farm, oil-industry, and foreign loans), financial institutions with balance sheets comparable to those shown here were devastated. So widespread and severe was the damage that one influential analyst, Edward Yardeni of Prudential-Bache, based his 1984 and 1985 predictions of lower interest rates largely on his belief that the Federal

Reserve would have to lower interest rates to bail out financial intermediaries that had borrowed short and lent long.

Duration also helps us understand why banks that have substantial amounts of short-term consumer and commercial loans are less susceptible to interest-rate fluctuations than thrifts, which rely on long-term mortgages; we also see how a thrift can adjust its portfolio to stabilize its net worth. A move to shorter-term loans (consumer loans and 15-year mortgages in place of 30-year mortgages) reduces asset duration. Even more effective are adjustable-rate mortgages, which can have durations of one year or less, depending on the adjustment provisions of the contract. On the liability side, longer-term deposits "with substantial penalties for premature withdrawal" can push duration upward. If these steps roughly match the duration of the assets to the duration of the liabilities, then the net worth of the financial intermediary is insulated from unanticipated interest-rate fluctuations. If the asset duration exceeds its liability duration, then the institution is implicitly betting that interest rates will fall. A liability duration in excess of asset duration is a wager that interest rates will rise.

term structure's forward rates. Short-term bonds have income risk, because the interest rates at which the funds can be reinvested is uncertain. Long-term bonds have capital risk, because changes in interest rates affect their market value. Fixed-income securities, especially long-term ones, also have inflation risk, because the purchasing power of the cash flow depends on uncertain rates of inflation. Exchange-rate risk arises from unexpected fluctuations in the relative values of currencies.

The liquidity-premium hypothesis holds that investors fearful of capital risk prefer short-term securities, and therefore long-term securities must have relatively high expected returns (higher than predicted by the expectations hypothesis) to compensate for their capital risk. The market-segmentation hypothesis says that some investors have short horizons and prefer short-term securities, but others, such as pension funds and life insurance companies, have long horizons and a natural preference for long-term bonds.

An asset's duration is the present-value-weighted average length of time until its cash flow is received. The percentage change in an asset's present value resulting from a 1-percentage-point change in the required return is approximately equal to its duration. A complete picture of exposure to interest-rate risk must consider both assets and liabilities. A savings-and-loan association, for example, that borrows short and lends long has an asset duration that significantly exceeds the duration of its liabilities: its net worth will be increased by an unexpected decline in interest rates and reduced by an unanticipated increase in interest rates.

IMPORTANT TERMS

capital risk
duration
exchange-rate risk
Expectations Hypothesis
forward rates
Hicks equation

income risk
inflation risk
liquidity-premium hypothesis
market-segmentation hypothesis
term structure of interest rates
yield curve

EXERCISES

1. If the future is certain and the Hicks equation holds, which of the following strategies will be more profitable: buying a 7-year note followed by a 3-year note, or buying a 6-year note followed by a 4-year note?

2. The rate of return on 1-year zero-coupon bonds is now 10 percent and is expected to be 15 percent next year and for at least 2 years after that. According to the Expectations Hypothesis, what should be the current annual yields on 2-year, 3-year, and 4-year zero-coupon bonds?

3. The annual rates of return on 1-year, 2-year, and 3-year zero-coupon bonds are 8 percent, 10 percent, and 12 percent, respectively. According to the Expectations Hypothesis, what is the expected return on a 1-year zero issued a year from now? Two years from now?

4. Look in the most recent Monday issue of *The Wall Street Journal* for the bond prices and yields reported in the section "Treasury Bonds, Notes & Bills." Find the subsection titled "Stripped Treasuries" and report the maturity dates and the yields for Treasury zeros that mature in approximately 1, 5, 10, and 20 years. Does the Expectations Hypothesis interpretation of these data imply that investors expect interest rates to rise or fall in the coming years?

5. Look up the prices and yields of "Stripped Treasuries" in the "Treasury Bonds, Notes & Bills" section of the most recent Monday issue of *The Wall Street Journal*. Report the maturity dates and the yields for Treasury zeros that mature in approximately 1, 2, and 3 years. Calculate the anticipated yields implied by the Expectations Hypothesis on 1-year Treasury zeros issued one and two years from now.

6. Will Rogers once said, "I am not so much concerned with the return on my money as with the return of my money." Would you say that he was more concerned with income or capital risk?

7. Here is some advice offered in *Woman's Day* to bond investors.[5]

   Many conservative investors are attracted to "income funds" — mutual funds invested mostly in [long-term] bonds — but they are not always as safe as they sound. Bond funds do well when long-term interest rates fall. . . . But bond funds do poorly when long-term interest rates rise. . . .

   Michael Lipper of Lipper Analytical Services, which specializes in mutual-fund analysis, urges investors to think of bond funds as speculative securities: investments to buy and sell according to market conditions, rather than to hold for the long term. . . . if rates rise again, he says, it will pay to sell income funds and switch to the greater security of short-term money-market mutual funds.

   a. Why do bond funds do well when long-term rates fall and poorly when they rise?

   b. What does the Expectations Hypothesis imply about the profitability of shifting to short-term securities after interest rates rise?

c. In what sense do short-term money-market funds offer greater security than do long-term income funds?

8. In November 1988, 2-year Treasury notes had 8½ percent yields to maturity and 30-year Treasury bonds had 9 percent yields. An article in *The Wall Street Journal* began.[6]

    Why would anyone buy 30-year Treasury bonds right now when they can earn nearly the same returns on short-term issues that aren't as susceptible to price decline?

    Investors are confronting that dilemma because of an unusual development in the bond market — a "flat yield curve."

    a. Why are long-term bonds more susceptible to price decline?
    b. Why is a flat yield curve unusual? What is the usual shape?
    c. Why would anyone (and someone must) buy 30-year bonds when the yield curve is flat?

9. In a May 1985 *New York Times* interview, John T. Haggerty, National Director of Personal Financial Planning for Prudential-Bache Securities, advised[7]

    I wouldn't buy any bond, except maybe a Treasury, that was 30 years in maturity. I don't know if the world is going to be around 30 years from now. . . . If I had to buy, or if I wanted to buy, I'd probably be looking at discount bonds. There you have the maturities working in your favor. You know the bond's going to be going up in price, because it's getting closer to maturity with the passage of time.

    a. Why is the existence of the world 30 years from now of little relevance to an investor's choice between short-term and long-term bonds?
    b. Evaluate Haggerty's apparent claim that the returns from bonds selling at a discount are inherently more certain than the returns from bonds selling at par or for a premium.
    c. Interest rates dropped substantially in 1985. Why, in retrospect, would Haggerty

have made especially large profits from the purchase of 30-year bonds early in 1985?

10. A vice-president at E. F. Hutton says of zero-coupon bonds backed by U.S. Treasury notes: "The beauty of it is that the investor knows exactly how many dollars go in, and how many dollars will come out"; a Merrill Lynch vice-president says: "This suits the little old lady in tennis shoes who's watching her nickels, and it's ideal for your kids."[8] Can you think of any reason why little old ladies and kids might be nervous about zeros? Is there any risk in such an investment?

11. In 1985, Ed Yardeni, Prudential-Bache's chief economist, forecast "lower-than-expected interest rates."[9] Why was he careful to say "lower-than-expected interest rates" rather than just "lower interest rates"? Should those who agreed with Yardeni have
    a. bought Treasury bills, or long-term bonds?
    b. borrowed at a fixed or a variable interest rate?
    c. sold 15-year or 30-year bonds?

12. An investment textbook states that "bond investors will prefer to buy short-term bonds whenever they expect interest rates to rise."[10] What is the logic behind this assertion? Why is it incorrect?

13. In 1990, the Resolution Funding Corporation, a U.S. government agency established to finance the bailout of the thrift industry, sold 40-year zero-coupon bonds. A *Wall Street Journal* article asked[11]

    So who would want a 40-year bond? One group of buyers is expected to be pension funds and insurance companies who need bonds with extra-long maturities . . . Another likely group of buyers is professional traders eager for yet another vehicle to bet on swings in interest rates.

    Explain why pension funds and insurance companies "need bonds with extra-long maturities" and why 40-year zeros are especially attractive for traders who want to bet on interest rates.

14. Critically explain and evaluate these excerpts from a *Wall Street Journal* article.[12]

    With inflation abated and interest rates down sharply on money-market funds and bank accounts, consumers are turning to bond products for higher yields. Many investors have shifted dollars out of money funds paying around 7% and into [long-term] Treasury securities paying more than 10%. . . .

    A California real estate attorney admits that he was "dumbfounded" to find that $192,000 in Treasury zeros he bought in January 1984 were valued at $156,000 when he went to sell them four months later. . . .

    Nelson Chase, a West Blomfield, Mich., attorney is representing a group of zero-coupon bond investors that is suing New York–based Merrill, Lynch & Co. "All the literature talks about how safe these investments are," he says. "Unless you can be absolutely sure you will hold to maturity, these aren't safe investments."

    In particular, explain
    a. what circumstances, if any, would dissuade you from shifting out of a bank paying 7 percent into Treasury securities paying 10 percent.
    b. how Treasury zeros could lose nearly 20 percent of their value in four months.
    c. why zeros held to maturity may not be safe.

15. Using the data in Table 7.2, does Equation 4 imply that in September 1989, financial-market participants anticipated the pound to appreciate or depreciate relative to the yen over the coming ten years?

16. As of January 1, 1990, the Federal Reserve authorized U.S. banks to offer customers federally insured deposits denominated in foreign currencies. On March 1, 1990, Citibank $100,000 3-month certificates of deposit (CDs) paid the following annualized returns (in foreign currency):

British pound	14.41%
German mark	7.69%
Japanese yen	6.63%

The annualized returns in U.S. dollars turned out to be 20.7% for the British pound CDs, 16.7% for the mark CDs, and 1.9% for the yen CDs.[13] Which of these three currencies appreciated relative to the dollar, and which depreciated?

17. Many lending institutions have been pushing 15-year mortgages in place of the traditional 30-year mortgages. Why do they prefer the 15-year mortgages?

18. In the spring of 1986, David Marks, Senior Vice-President of Cigna Investments, explained how he used duration to implement his fixed-income strategy.[14]

    To look at maturity alone, you are generally not taking into account interest income and reinvestment income. . . . If you're bullish, expecting interest rates to go down and prices up, then your duration should be slightly longer than the [Shearson Lehman bond] index. If you're bearish, your duration should be slightly shorter or the same.

    Explain the advantages of a long-duration portfolio when you are bullish and of a short-duration portfolio when you're not. Are there any circumstances in which, confident that interest rates will fall, you would nonetheless choose a short-duration portfolio?

19. Frederick Macaulay's pioneering studies of duration were instigated by his observation that investors seem to prefer high-coupon bonds to otherwise identical bonds with low coupons.[15] Does this preference suggest that investors are more concerned with income or capital risk? Explain your reasoning.

20. In 1986, *The Wall Street Journal* reported that[16]

    Falling interest rates prompt corporations to refinance short-term, high-cost debt with bonds with lower rates and longer maturities, reducing costs and making them less vulnerable to interest-rate moves. . . . Still, many corporations delay refinancing, expecting interest rates to drop further.

Why might long-term debt have lower interest rates than short-term debt? In what way are those who borrow long-term still vulnerable to interest-rate moves?

21. In April 1987, long-term interest rates on Japanese bonds were below 4 percent, whereas the rates on comparable U.S. bonds were close to 9 percent. What anticipated annual rate of appreciation or depreciation of the U.S. dollar relative to the Japanese yen would make these alternative investments equally attractive?

22. During October 1987, the average (dollar) return, coupon plus capital gain, on U.S. Treasury bonds was 2.605 percent and the average (pound) return on comparable British bonds was 1.165 percent. During this same time period, the pound depreciated by 2.291 percent against the dollar. Taking into account this depreciation, did U.S. or British bonds give U.S. investors a higher rate of return? What about British investors?

23. Explain why you agree or disagree with this advice: "In an inflationary era, when depreciation of the currency is the order of the day, a fixed, long-term obligation is not the thing to own."[17]

24. Evaluate this argument by a prominent economics professor.[18]

We should curb the political influence that the banking community has achieved through its formal alliance with the Fed. It is not surprising, of course, that creditors are more interested in relatively tight money and high interest rates than debtors and consumers.

25. A commonplace bank procedure to control for interest rate risk is "gap management," where gap = (rate-sensitive assets − rate-sensitive liabilities)/total assets.[19]

Interest-sensitive assets are those that mature, or are repriced, within a designated time-frame. For example, a loan may have a stated maturity of one year, but can be subject to rate changes tied to the prime rate and is, therefore, immediately sensitive to interest rate changes. Similarly, rates paid on money market accounts generally can change daily and are, therefore, immediately sensitive to interest rate movements.

. . . When the gap is zero, net interest income is fully insulated from interest rate risk because the maturity of rate-sensitive assets and liabilities should cause them to offset each other and to leave the net interest margin unchanged.

For example, if 10 percent of assets and 12 percent of liabilities have rates that change with market rates, then the gap is −2 percent.

a. If a bank has a negative gap, will its net interest income rise or fall if interest rates increase?

b. If a bank wanted to bet that interest rates were headed downward, should it have a positive or negative gap?

c. Explain how a bank with a gap of zero could nonetheless find itself bankrupted (that is, with its market value driven to zero) by an unexpected decline in interest rates.

26. Here are some excerpts from a 1986 *New York Times* article:[20]

"In my view, making long-term fixed-rate mortgages is simply not a viable strategy any longer," said Dennis Jacobe, director of research at the United States League of Savings Associations.

The widespread issuance of fixed-rate mortgages in the 1970's led to the collapse or merger of nearly a quarter of the nation's 4,000 savings associations then existing. . . . Of those that survived, some remain in extremely poor shape. . . .

Adjustable-rate mortgages reached their height of popularity in late 1984, when 70 percent of the mortgages issued by savings and loan associations were adjustable-rate, according to the savings league.

. . . Fixed-rate loans, [however], were the only type Washington Federal [a Seattle S&L] was making. . . .

"You can't be reckless, but right now we're in a deflationary cycle . . . ," Mr. Knutson [the company's president and chief executive] said. Referring to 1981, he added that "you can't operate based on one devastating period; otherwise you leave too much profitability on the table."

a. What economic event caused trouble for S&L's with fixed-rate mortgages? How do adjustable-rate mortgages provide protection?

b. Some S&L's have moved to shorter-term mortgages and longer-term deposits. If the duration of their liabilities is greater than the duration of their assets, are they protected from interest-rate fluctuations?

c. Why do you suppose many S&L's now wish they had issued fixed-rate mortgages during 1981–84?

27. The Student Loan Marketing Association (Sallie Mae) is a private corporation that uses borrowed money to buy government-guaranteed student loans from banks. The interest rates on all of its assets and liabilities adjust up or down with changes in T-bill rates. What is the duration of its assets? Of its liabilities? How is its net worth affected by interest rates?

28. Explain the logic behind this assertion and then explain why it is misleading.[21]

The essential difference between fixed- and adjustable-rate mortgages is the party at risk. In fixed mortgages, the lender takes all the risk, profiting or suffering from changes in the interest rate. . . . With an ARM, the borrower, not the lender, is at the mercy of fluctuating interest rates.

29. In contrast to producers, retailers have traditionally used mostly short-term debt to finance their inventories and consumer credit. But volatile financial markets have persuaded some retailers to use long-term debt. For instance, J. C. Penney converted almost all of its debt from short-term to long-term in 1980. *The Wall Street Journal* reported that this strategy "reduces the danger of a potential cash shortage, should the nation's financial markets run into a crisis. . . . A company with a large amount of short-term debt must constantly refinance its borrowings as they come due. . . . For some companies, in the worst possible case, failure to refinance their debt could force them into bankruptcy court."[22] What risk is inherent in a strategy of financing inventories with long-term debt?

30. A money manager recommends buying long-term bonds when the yield on long-term bonds is more than 3.0 percentage points higher than the yield on three-month Treasury bills, and buying Treasury bills when this yield differential is less than 1.5 percentage points.[23] Why is this yield differential normally positive? What logical explanation is there (other than mispriced bonds) for a differential of more than 3.0 points? Of less than 1.5 points?

8

Optional Chapter

FINANCIAL FUTURES

AND

OPTIONS

If you bet on a horse, that's gambling. If you bet you can make three spades, that's entertainment. If you bet cotton will go up three points, that's business. See the difference?

Blackie Sherrod

The previous chapter explained how changes in interest rates affect the market prices of bonds, mortgages, and other financial assets. You saw how the net worth of a financial intermediary is vulnerable to unanticipated interest-rate fluctuations if the duration of its assets does not match the duration of its liabilities. Many savings-and-loan associations learned this lesson the hard way: with long-term assets and short-term liabilities, their net worth disappeared when interest rates increased unexpectedly in 1979–82.

Financial intermediaries have tried to protect themselves from interest-rate fluctuations by using shorter-term or adjustable-rate loans to reduce the duration of their assets and by using longer-term, fixed-rate deposits to lengthen the duration of their liabilities. But many customers resist such changes; they prefer long-term loans and short-term deposits. One way out of this impasse is provided by financial futures and options — the subject of this chapter — which allow financial intermediaries and others to cope with interest-rate risk by compensating for mismatched durations of their assets and liabilities.

This chapter explains the general nature of futures and options contracts, emphasizing the financial contracts used by banks and other financial intermediaries. You will see how these contracts can be used for hedging, speculation, and arbitrage and learn what factors influence their prices. We will also look at stock-index futures, which have been blamed by some for the October 19, 1987, crash, in which stock prices fell by more than 20 percent in a single day. We begin by explaining the difference between futures and options.

FUTURES VERSUS OPTIONS

Futures and forward contracts specify a future delivery at a specified price paid at delivery.

Futures and **forward contracts** are agreements to deliver items on a specified future date at a price agreed to today, but not paid until delivery; for example, a mill might agree to pay a farmer $3 a bushel for 100,000 bushels of wheat delivered six months from now. This futures contract insulates both from fluctuations in the market price, or **spot price**, of wheat for immediate delivery, thus eliminating the mill's uncertainty about the cost of wheat and the farmer's uncertainty about revenue. Futures are standardized contracts traded on organized exchanges, while forward contracts are private agreements with no organized secondary market.

Option contracts give the right to buy or sell at a specified price.

An **option contract** is an agreement conveying the right, but not the obligation, to buy or sell an item in the future at a price specified now. A mill might pay a farmer $20,000 for an option giving it the right to buy 100,000 bushels of wheat six months from now at $3 a bushel. If the market price of wheat drops below $3, then the mill will not exercise its option.

THE DEVELOPMENT OF FUTURES AND OPTIONS TRADING

One of the earliest references to such agreements is in the Old Testament, where Laban agreed to let Jacob marry his youngest daughter, Rachel, in return for seven years of labor. It is not clear whether Jacob could change his mind (whether this was an option or a futures contract) but, in any case, after Jacob had worked for seven years, Laban broke the contract and gave Jacob his older daughter, Leah. Jacob persisted, working another seven years so that he could marry Rachel, too.

Another early reference is in Aristotle's *Politics,* which recounts how Thales became wealthy through an astute use of options. Based on his study of the stars, Thales believed that the next olive crop would be enormous and, for a small fee, bought options from the local olive-press owners. When the crop did turn out to be large, Thales exercised his options and leased the olive presses at a considerable profit.

Options and futures began trading in the United States shortly after the Revolutionary War and were widely used for both commodities and stock during and after the Civil War. Then, as now, the overwhelming majority of trades were made not by millers, farmers, or other business people seeking to guarantee the price of a future business transaction, but rather by speculators hoping to profit from short-term fluctuations in the value of these contracts. In the late 1800s, the progressive movement succeeded in having commodity options classified as gambling, rather than an investment, making them illegal under anti-gambling statutes. Stock options continued to flourish, particularly in the 1920s, and in the aftermath of the Great Crash attracted the attention of Congress, which considered but did not pass a bill outlawing stock options entirely.

Futures and options have long been considered speculative gambles.

Contributing to the speculative and somewhat unsavory reputation of stock options was the fact that they were not traded on organized exchanges. A loose collection of dealers brought together buyers and sellers through newspaper advertisements, mimeographed sheets, and telephone calls. Each option was virtually unique in its terms — the number of shares, the exercise price, and the date of expiration. Without standardization, there could be no organized secondary market and little basis for comparing prices.

In 1969, an abundance of agricultural crops brought commodity trading to an almost complete stop, and the Chicago Board of Trade decided to experiment with stock-options trading. After considerable planning, the Board received SEC approval and in 1973 opened the Chicago Board Options Exchange. (One of the five SEC Commissioners voted against approval, arguing that this "was essentially a gambling operation. There are enough of those in Las Vegas.")

The organized trading of stock options proved to be very popular and has since been augmented by the trading of a variety of financial options and futures contracts traded on several exchanges. Options and futures are used not only by speculators looking for easy riches but also by arbitragers trying to exploit price differentials among similar securities for a virtually risk-free profit and by institutions trying to insure their portfolios against losses.

FUTURES

Futures contracts are traded on several exchanges, with the largest the Chicago Board of Trade and the Chicago Mercantile Exchange. Table 8.1 shows the types of futures contracts traded on all exchanges in 1987 and Table 8.2 shows the most actively traded contracts. Although agricultural products are still important, they have been joined in recent years by a wide variety of other real and financial assets. The daily pages of *The Wall Street Journal* and other major newspapers list the specific items and the current prices. There is also extensive trading of currency forward contracts among banks, and these can be analyzed using the same principles that we will apply to futures contracts.

The Advantages of Standardized Contracts

Organized exchanges standardize the terms of futures contracts and enforce their terms. For example, the corn futures contracts traded on the Chicago Board of Trade specify the delivery of 5,000 bushels of No. 2 yellow corn to an approved

Standardized futures contracts are now traded on several organized exchanges.

Table 8.1	**Contracts Traded on Futures Markets in 1987**	
Group	Contracts (millions)	Percent of Total
Bonds	88.0	41.2%
Agricultural	39.6	18.6%
Stock indexes	26.3	12.0%
Energy	20.3	9.5%
Currencies	19.9	9.3%
Metals	19.4	9.1%
Total	213.5	100.0%

source: Paula A. Tosini, "Stock Index Futures and Stock Market Activity in October 1987," *Financial Analysts' Journal*, January/February 1988, pp. 28–38.

warehouse on a specified date. The processor who takes delivery receives a receipt from the warehouse certifying that sufficient quantity of the appropriate corn has been stored there. An International Monetary Market futures contract for German marks calls for the delivery of 125,000 deutschemarks on a specified date; a Chicago Board of Trade Treasury-bond futures contract calls for the delivery of $100,000 face value U.S. Treasury bonds with at least 15 years until maturity.

The trading of standardized contracts on organized exchanges allows traders to cancel contracts before the delivery date. A bank that sells Treasury-bond futures but does not own a sufficient number of Treasury bonds as the delivery date approaches can repurchase futures contracts; a pension fund that buys Treasury-bond futures and later decides that it wants fewer Treasury bonds can sell some of its futures contracts.

Futures contracts can be used to hedge positions.

Participants can also use the futures market to protect themselves — to "hedge" — against fluctuations in the prices of securities that are similar, but not identical, to those specified in the futures contracts; for example, a bank may own mortgages rather than Treasury bonds, or a pension fund may want to buy AA corporate bonds rather than Treasury bonds.

Suppose that a pension fund intends to buy $10,000,000 worth of corporate bonds six months from now, and wants protection against a decline in interest rates and an increase in bond prices. This pension fund can buy 100 Treasury-bond futures contracts on the Chicago Board of Trade. If interest rates decline and the prices of Treasury and corporate bonds rise by comparable amounts, the pension fund can use the profits on its Treasury-bond futures to cover the increase in the cost of the corporate bonds.

Table 8.2 Most Actively Traded Futures Contracts in 1987		
Contract	Contracts Traded (millions)	Exchange
U.S. Treasury bonds	61.1	Chicago Board of Trade (CBT)
S&P 500 stock index	19.9	Chicago Mercantile Exchange (CME)
Eurodollars	17.8	Chicago Mercantile Exchange (CME)
Crude oil	12.8	New York Mercantile Exchange (NYMEX)
Gold	9.8	Commodities Exchange, Inc. (COMEX)
Corn	7.2	Chicago Board of Trade (CBT)

source: Paula A. Tosini, "Stock Index Futures and Stock Market Activity in October 1987," *Financial Analysts' Journal*, January/February 1988, pp. 28–38.

With a futures market, the pension fund can also make day-to-day adjustments, buying more contracts to lock in the price of additional anticipated bond purchases or, at times, becoming a net seller to protect the value of a large bond inventory. Pension funds, banks, and other investors can also speculate, buying or selling futures contracts to bet on movements in interest rates.

Futures Trading

Futures are bought and sold through traders who own seats on the exchange. Each item has a trading pit — an oval area with steps leading down to a central floor — where traders buy and sell, either for their own accounts or on behalf of orders from outside the exchange. All offers to buy or sell are by "open outcry" so that, in theory, every trader in the pit has an opportunity to accept the offer. In practice, the pits are often crowded with people pushing and shoving as they use arcane hand signals and loud shouts to try to communicate with each other. At particularly anxious moments, fights break out and someone on the steps will fall, toppling everyone in front.

Futures are created by the willingness of people to sell contracts. Those who own contracts are said to be "long" while those who have sold contracts are "short"; the **open interest**, or the number of outstanding contracts, fluctuates daily. Some data from *The Wall Street Journal*'s report on futures trading on Wednesday, November 15, 1989, are shown in Table 8.3.

Longs buy contracts issued by shorts.

The first line identifies the item, the exchange, the size of a contract, and the units in which prices are quoted — thus the reported December $241\frac{1}{2}$ price for corn is $2.415 per bushel. The December Treasury-bond price of 99–18 is $99\frac{18}{32}$ percent of face value: $99,562.50 for Treasury bonds with $100,000 face value.

Table 8.3 Selected Futures Prices, Wednesday, November 15, 1989

CORN (CBT) 5,000 bushels; cents per bushel

	Open	High	Low	Settle	Change	Lifetime High	Lifetime Low	Open Interest
Dec	$241\frac{1}{2}$	$241\frac{3}{4}$	239	$239\frac{3}{4}$	$-\frac{1}{4}$	295	$218\frac{1}{2}$	97,577
Mr90	$244\frac{1}{4}$	$244\frac{3}{4}$	$242\frac{1}{4}$	$243\frac{1}{4}$	$+\frac{3}{4}$	$286\frac{1}{2}$	226	63,292
May	$247\frac{1}{4}$	$248\frac{1}{4}$	$246\frac{1}{4}$	$246\frac{3}{4}$	$+\frac{3}{4}$	$289\frac{1}{2}$	230	16,157
July	250	$251\frac{1}{4}$	$249\frac{3}{4}$	$250\frac{1}{4}$	$+1\frac{1}{4}$	285	231	15,934
Sept	244	$244\frac{1}{4}$	$243\frac{1}{2}$	$243\frac{3}{4}$	$+1\frac{3}{4}$	271	229	973
Dec	$239\frac{1}{2}$	241	$239\frac{1}{2}$	$240\frac{1}{2}$	$+2$	$263\frac{1}{2}$	222	5,358
Mr91	247	$247\frac{1}{4}$	$246\frac{3}{4}$	$247\frac{1}{4}$	$+2$	255	241	112

Estimated volume 38,000; volume Tues 41,702; open interest 199,403, −49

TREASURY BONDS (CBT) $100,000; points 32nds of 100%

	Open	High	Low	Settle	Change	Yield Settle	Yield Change	Open Interest
Dec	99-18	100-03	99-17	99-26	+ 10	8.019	− .032	273,885
Mr90	99-16	100-02	99-16	99-24	+ 9	8.025	− .029	69,557
June	99-12	99-25	99-10	99-16	+ 7	8.051	− .022	13,696
Sept	99-06	99-13	99-05	99-06	+ 6	8.083	− .019	5,836
Dec	98-26	99-02	98-26	98-28	+ 4	8.115	− .013	2,536
Mr91	98-20	98-24	98-19	98-19	+ 3	8.144	− .009	936
June	98-11	98-13	98-11	98-11	+ 2	8.169	− .007	522
Sept				98-03	+ 1	8.195	− .004	161

Estimated volume 310,000; volume Tues 488,647; open interest 367,197, +2,096

GERMAN MARK (IMM) — 125,000 marks; $ per mark

	Open	High	Low	Settle	Change	Lifetime High	Lifetime Low	Open Interest
Dec	.5433	.5448	.5421	.5441	− .0014	.5895	.4925	78,894
Mr90	.5429	.5446	.5421	.5440	− .0013	.5487	.5000	3,658
June	.5424	.5437	.5423	.5436	− .0013	.5455	.5057	1,138

Estimated volume 31,875; volume Tues 46,729; open interest 83,696, +8,339

The left-hand column identifies the delivery dates of the available contracts, and the next three columns show the opening price and the high and low prices for trades made that day. The settlement price ("settle") is like a closing price and will be discussed shortly. The next column shows the change in the settlement price from the day before. (For Treasury bonds, these changes are in 32nds, ranging here from $\frac{1}{32}$ to $\frac{10}{32}$.) The lifetime highs and lows in the corn-futures section are the highest and lowest prices at which the contract has traded. In place of lifetime high and low prices, the Treasury-bond data show the yield to maturity corresponding to the settlement price and the change in this yield.

The exchanges try to control short-run price fluctuations by imposing **daily limits** on the price changes of many futures contracts. For instance, the daily settlement price cannot rise or fall by more than $0.10 ($500 per contract) for corn, 3 points ($3,000 per contract) for Treasury bonds, or $0.01 ($1,250 per contract) for deutschemarks.

The last column shows the open interest, the number of outstanding contracts. As Figure 8.1 illustrates, the open interest is zero when a contract is first introduced, rises as trading increases, typically reaches a peak a few months before expiration, and then declines to zero on the delivery date. The bottom row for each item in Table 8.3 shows the total trading that day and the day before, the total open interest, and the net change in the open interest.

Covering Positions

The buyer of a futures contract agrees to pay the seller an agreed price F when the item is delivered. In about 97 percent of the cases, however, there turns out to be no delivery, because the shorts repurchase contracts from the longs before the delivery date. On the delivery date, the price of a futures contract equals the spot price P, because both now call for immediate delivery. Suppose that a trader has purchased corn futures at $F = 240$ cents per bushel, and the spot price on the delivery date is $P = 250$ cents per bushel. By taking delivery, the trader can buy for 240 and sell for 250, a profit of 10 cents per bushel (neglecting various transaction costs). This gain can be realized without an actual delivery, because the futures price on the delivery date is equal to the spot price. In what is called **covering** or **reversing** a position, the holder of a futures contract sells it for the current price of 250, realizing a 10-cents per bushel profit, while the contract writer purchases a contract for 250, taking a loss of 10 cents per bushel.

Almost all futures positions are covered before delivery.

Virtually all futures traders are either speculators, who have no intention of making or taking delivery, or producers and users, who (like the pension fund planning to buy corporate bonds) trade through accustomed channels in the spot market and use the futures market to hedge their position. Any tales of tons of sugar dropped on someone's front lawn are amusing but untrue. The worst that can happen is that the commodity will be put in a warehouse and the buyer will be billed for the cost of the commodity plus storage charges.

| Highlight 8.1 | The Chicago Sting |

In January 1989, the federal government revealed a two-year undercover investigation of trading at the Chicago Mercantile Exchange and the Chicago Board of Trade (using the code names Operation Hedgeclipper and Operation Sour Mash). With the cooperation of some colleges and businesses, the Justice Department manufactured phony academic and professional records for several undercover FBI agents (moles). Archer-Daniels-Midland, the world's largest soybean processor, trained the agents in commodities trading. The federal government spent over a million dollars buying seats on the exchanges; it spent thousands more for offices, high-rent apartments, luxury automobiles, health-club memberships, and other accessories to create an illusion of success for its agents; and it spent hundreds of thousands of dollars covering their trading losses.*

Some of the moles' conversations, on and off the trading floors, were recorded with hidden video cameras or microphones. In addition, at least one trader was persuaded to join the government investigation and wear a hidden microphone. Several alleged misdeeds were uncovered. Some traders "front ran" large orders, buying or selling for their own accounts before executing large customer orders. Some executed customer orders by making reciprocal trades with each other at noncompetitive prices. Some skimmed money by trading at one price and reporting a different price to their customers, somewhat higher for a buy order and lower for a sell order. One of the government moles told other traders that a private company he owned had large tax losses that could be used to shelter profitable trades. These traders were reportedly persuaded to give some of their profitable trades to the government informant, in return for cash passed in plain envelopes. Despite the widespread negative publicity generated by this sting operation, the exchanges have so far resisted reform proposals, including a ban on dual trading — the practice of trading both for the trader's own account and for customer accounts.

*Scott McMurray and John Koten, "Probe of 2 Exchanges Shows Wild Fraternity of Traders in Yen Pit," *Wall Street Journal*, January 26, 1989.

Figure 8.1 Daily Open Interest, September 1988 Wheat Futures

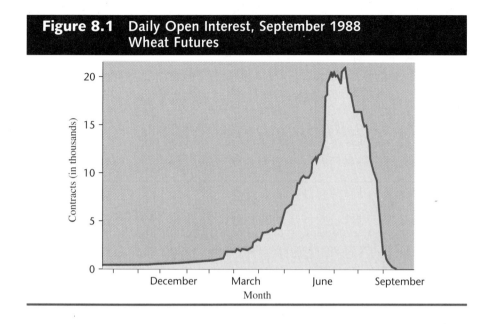

Because the reckoning of profits and losses does not depend on an actual delivery, futures contracts can be written on intangible things, which cannot be delivered, such as the S&P 500 index of stock prices. All that is needed is a rule for determining the spot price P on the delivery date, so that the profit, $P - F$, can be calculated. For the S&P 500, P is the value of this index on the delivery date; a futures contract at a price of, say, $F = 250$ is a wager on whether the value of the index will turn out to be above or below 250.

Marking to Market

To ensure the financial integrity of the market, exchange clearinghouses require a daily settlement of all unrealized profits and losses using, for each contract, a **settlement price** set by the exchange at the end of each trading day. For actively traded contracts, the settlement price is the closing price, the price of the last transaction. For inactive contracts, the exchange estimates what the price would have been had there been transactions at the close. These settlement prices are used to calculate the change in the value of each trader's position; traders with losses that day must make cash payments to the brokerage accounts of those with profits before the beginning of the next trading day. This daily transfer of funds from losers to winners is called a **daily settlement** or **marking to market**.

Suppose that you buy two June Treasury-bond futures contracts this coming Monday for 99. Because each contract is for bonds with $100,000 face value, the total value of your position is $198,000. We'll assume that the Monday

Futures profits and losses are settled daily, using the settlement price.

Table 8.4	Four Days in the Treasury-Bond Futures Market			
Day	Settlement Price	Value of 2 Contracts	Daily Profit	Cumulative Profit
Monday	99	$198,000		
Tuesday	$97\frac{16}{32}$	$195,000	− $3,000	− $3,000
Wednesday	98	$196,000	$1,000	− $2,000
Thursday	97	$194,000	− $2,000	− $4,000

settlement price is $99 and that your broker requires a $10,000 deposit, called a **margin**, to ensure your ability to cover your possible losses. Table 8.4 shows what might happen to your account during the next three days.

On Tuesday, the settlement price drops to $97\frac{16}{32}$ and your two contracts are worth $195,000 — a $3,000 loss for the day. This $3,000 is deducted from your account and credited to the account of someone who is short Treasury bonds (has sold Treasury-bond futures); your broker will most likely now demand that you either put up an additional margin deposit or sell your contracts. The price rises to 98 on Wednesday, and you receive $1,000 from those who are short Treasury bonds. On Thursday, the price dips to 97 and you pay $2,000.

If you sell on Thursday at 97, your position is closed, with a cumulative loss of $4,000. Unlike other stocks and bonds, where you don't realize your capital gains and losses until you actually sell the securities, the daily settlement of futures contracts gives you a profit or loss each day. These daily settlements make it very clear that, except for brokerage costs, futures contracts are a zero-sum game — any profits for some must be losses for others.

Speculation

Futures have a well-deserved reputation for being speculative gambles, a way to make or lose a lot of money in a hurry. David Dreman, a portfolio manager and *Forbes* columnist, wrote that "futures have no place in the portfolio of a conservative investor and should be looked at only by masochists or the wildest of dice players."[1] Highlight 8.2 tells how one family wagered billions of dollars on silver futures.

Futures are risky for several reasons. There are no dividends, interest, or other cash flow. A futures contract is just a bet on the price of the underlying item. The prices of futures contracts are volatile, and margin requirements are very low, 15 percent or less, and can typically be met by leaving interest-earning Treasury bills with the broker. In the hypothetical example in Table 8.4, 40 percent of the initial $10,000 margin was lost in four days.

People are sometimes lured into the futures market by firms that make phone calls peddling hot tips ("Our computer says that silver is going to double

Futures can be used for speculation.

The Hunt Brothers Buy Silver

The great East Texas oil fields made H. L. Hunt one of the richest men in America, what a reporter for the *London Sunday Times* called "the archetype of a Texas oil billionaire — arrogant, prejudiced, mean, eccentric, and secretive."* Two of his sons, Bunker and Herbert, stayed in the oil business, and Bunker found oil in Libya in the 1960s, enough to give him control over more oil than any single individual in the world. When Colonel Qaddafi nationalized his Libyan fields in 1973, Bunker Hunt lost $15 billion in oil reserves.

Bunker and Herbert turned to the silver market in late 1973, acquiring futures contracts for 35 million ounces of silver and creating suspicion that they were trying to corner the market. Normally, almost all futures contracts are liquidated before expiration. But what if the Hunts, or others, decide not to liquidate a large block of futures contracts? The shorts, betting against a rise in the price of silver are squeezed, or cornered, in that if they can't find millions of ounces of silver on short notice, they will be forced to buy the Hunts' futures contracts at whatever price the Hunts demand.

The growing fear of a silver squeeze pushed the price of March 1974 futures from $2.90 in December 1973 to $4 in January and $6.60 in late February. At this point, the Bank of Mexico sold 50 million ounces of silver that it had acquired at less than $2 per ounce, thereby providing the spot market with more than enough silver to meet the Hunts' futures contracts. Even though the Hunts ended up buying much of this silver themselves (billionaires can do that), the squeeze fizzled and futures prices fell back to $4 per ounce.

The Hunts continued to roll over a sequence of futures contracts and by the end of 1976, had accumulated 100 million ounces of silver and some anticipated an eventual attempt to squeeze the market. In January 1980, the price of March silver futures hit $37.10, with the Hunts and associates controlling nearly 300 million ounces of silver and silver futures, 80 percent of the total amount mined worldwide in 1979. Some 20–50 million ounces of silver came onto the market, melted down from coins, jewelry, teapots, and so on; but this was not nearly enough to satisfy the Hunts' buying power.

On January 9, 1980, the Commodity Futures Trading Commission (CFTC) abruptly increased the margin requirements for silver futures to $75,000 per contract ($15 per ounce) during the delivery month. Still, on January 14 the price of March futures reached an unprecedented $42.50. At this point, the Hunts made a private deal with Engelhard, the world's

---

*Stephen Fay, *Beyond Greed* (New York: Viking Press, 1982). Much of this example is based on his book.

largest bullion dealer, agreeing to buy 19 million ounces of silver at $35 per ounce on March 31, 1980 (the day the March futures would expire), thereby canceling 3,800 of Hunt's long and Engelhard's short contracts and relieving the margin pressure on both. Two days later, they agreed to cancel another 2,200 contracts by trading 11 million ounces on July 1; as collateral, the Hunts put up 8.5 million ounces of silver. The Hunts bought time in that margin calls were replaced with a two-month deadline for finding a billion dollars in cash. It was a billion-dollar gamble that the price of silver would stay above $35 per ounce.

Bunker still held 8,580 March contracts (42.9 million ounces) and his associates held more, enough to squeeze the remaining shorts who, unlike Engelhard, didn't own any silver. On January 18, the price of silver topped $50, giving a total market value for the 300 million ounces of silver and silver futures contracts held by the Hunt group of almost $15 billion — ironically the same amount Bunker Hunt had lost to Colonel Qaddafi.

On January 21, the COMEX board changed the rules again, raising margin requirements once more and, in an unprecedented move, henceforth allowing trades only for liquidation — the longs could sell to the shorts but could not buy any more contracts. The price of March futures promptly dropped to $44, and it dropped another $10 the next day, after the Chicago Board of Trade adopted similar rules. Now it was the Hunts who were squeezed. As their profits evaporated, their brokers made urgent margin calls. Every dollar drop in the futures price cost Bunker $42.9 million in equity; the two-day $16 decline cost a staggering $686 million. In all, during January and February, the Hunts had to borrow $1 billion and an associated company had to put up another $500 million, secured by land, oil leases, and 70 million ounces of silver.

On March 14, the rules changed once again on the Hunts. As part of the Fed's anti-inflation policies, Federal Reserve Chairman Volcker announced a special credit-restraint program, telling banks to stop lending money to finance speculation in commodities and precious metals. Bunker Hunt hurried to Europe and then Saudi Arabia to borrow money, without success. The Hunts were due to pay Engelhard $665 million on March 31, and the margin calls provoked by sagging silver prices were increasingly difficult to meet. On March 25, the price of silver fell to $20.20 and the Bache brokerage firm, which had lent the Hunts $233 million, informed the brothers that it would begin selling silver, silver futures, and other stocks in their accounts to meet margin calls. On March 26, March futures slumped to $15.80, and not only the Hunts were worried.

At 8:00 A.M. on March 27, Herbert Hunt told the CFTC that the Hunts would not sell any of their uncollateralized silver to repay their borrowings and advised the CFTC to close the market and settle all contracts at the previous day's price of $15.80. The CFTC let the exchange open. Fear of the unknown and Bache's liquidation of the Hunts' futures contracts knocked the price as low as $10.40 that day, dubbed Silver Thursday. Friday, the price rallied to $12 and Bache sold the remaining March futures.

The Hunts' outstanding loans still topped a billion dollars. With Fed Chairman Volcker's blessing, a consortium of 13 banks agreed to make a ten-year, $1.1-billion loan (at the prime rate plus 1 percent) to the Placid Oil Company, a Hunt family trust, which Placid then lent the Hunts so that they could pay off their short-term loans. Among the conditions was a requirement that the Hunts not speculate in commodities or futures markets for ten years, until 1990.

Unfortunately, a worldwide drop in oil prices reduced the market value of Placid Oil's assets, and in 1986 it filed for bankruptcy to protect itself from increasingly worried bankers. It has been estimated that the Hunts lost $1.5 billion in the silver market and that, overall, the total market value of their assets had fallen from $8 billion in 1980 to zero (plus or minus a billion dollars) in 1987. In 1988, in the first of several civil suits, a federal jury ruled that the Hunt brothers had conspired to corner the silver market and awarded $130 million to a Peruvian company that had shorted silver in 1979. Personal bankruptcy proceedings for the Hunt brothers began in September 1988. One of the more unusual twists in this unique story was a lawsuit filed by the Hunts, charging that the banks had engaged in fraudulent practices by lending $1.1 billion to such poor credit risks.

within a month") or that advertise exaggerated claims in newspapers and magazines — "Spectacular new system. $374,566.47 profit in two days!" These are the same kind of people who auction oriental rugs in motels, push disreputable multilevel distribution plans, and sell books on how to profit from the end of the world. A financial reporter for *Barron's* told how she was bombarded by high-pressure phone calls: "Most of my clients have doubled their money in gold options in the last six or eight weeks, and that's just the beginning. I want to get your $5,000 up to $10,000. I feel the worst we should do is 100 percent in a year . . . but the timing is critical. We really have to make a move by Friday."[2] A 1981 survey found that 40 percent of the readers of *The Wall Street Journal* had similar experiences.[3]

Even if there were no brokerage commissions, futures trading would be, at best, a zero-sum game. The only way one person can make a dollar is if another loses a dollar. The commissions make trading considerably worse than a zero-sum game — much like a high-stakes poker game in which the house confiscates part of every pot. Very few people can play cocoa prices against Hershey, orange juice prices against Sunkist, Treasury-bond prices against Salomon Brothers and go home a winner.

Futures Prices

Some futures prices reflect the anticipated price on the delivery date.

The most obvious interpretation of a futures price F is as a bet on the price P of the item on the delivery date. Speculators can buy futures contracts if they believe that P will be larger than F and sell futures if they believe the opposite will be true. The market price is a consensus on the anticipated price, in the sense that there is a balance between buyers, who expect P to be higher than F, and sellers, who expect P to be lower than F.

By this interpretation, the corn-futures prices in Table 8.3 imply that in November 1989 traders anticipated that corn prices would increase until July 1990, decline in September and December, and then begin rising again — a seasonal pattern that is consistent with the spring planting and fall harvest of corn. Even nonparticipants consequently find it useful to look to futures markets for expert opinion on the course of prices. Farmers who do not buy futures nonetheless look at corn, wheat, and soybean futures prices before making their crop plans. Building contractors look at lumber futures before submitting bids, and cattle breeders follow cattle futures.

The Cost of Carry

For some contracts, the futures price is determined not by the anticipated price of the item in the future, but by the cost of buying the item now and holding it until the delivery date. The cost of buying the commodity now and holding it until the futures' delivery date is called the **cost of carry**, and includes the cost of storage, spoilage, insurance, and forgone interest, minus any cash flow from the item while it is being held. The forgone interest arises because buying the item now ties up your money, money that could have been earning interest if you instead bought a futures contract and agreed to pay for the item later.

Some futures prices reflect the current spot price and the cost of carry.

Because buying now (for the spot price plus the cost of carry) and buying later (for the futures price) are alternative ways of acquiring the same commodity, the net cost should be the same:

$$\text{Futures price} = \text{Spot price} + \text{Cost of carry} \tag{1}$$

Equation 1 has the very strong and perhaps counterintuitive implication that the price of a futures contract depends on the current spot price, not the anticipated futures spot price.

Equation 1 can be rewritten to show that the difference between the futures and spot price (what is called the **basis**) should equal the cost of carry:

$$\text{Futures price} - \text{Spot price} = \text{Cost of carry} \tag{2}$$

If the cost of carry is positive and increases as time passes, the futures price will exceed the spot price and increase with the length of the contract. If the cost of carry is negative, the futures price will be less than the spot price. No matter which is the case, the cost of carry declines as the time horizon shrinks until, on the delivery date itself, the cost of carry is zero and the futures price equals the spot price.

| **Baseball Futures** | **Highlight 8.3** |

There is an unofficial, unsanctioned market in baseball futures involving some two hundred investment professionals who otherwise spend their time trading futures in wheat, silver, and the S&P 500.* Like other intangible futures, there is no actual commodity to be delivered. Instead, the value of the contract at expiration (the end of the baseball season) is determined by the number of games that the specified team wins.

For example, at the start of the 1988 season, the price of New York Yankees futures was 93. If the Yankees had ended up winning 103 games that season, those who bought contracts at 93 would have received an amount equal to $103 - 93 = 10$ times the agreed value of a game, anywhere from $5 to $500. At $100 a game, there would have been a $1,000 payment from those who were short Yankees to those who were long. If the Yankees had won fewer than 93 games, the longs would have paid the shorts.

As with other futures contracts, there is daily trading at prices reflecting current market conditions. Dedicated participants are short dozens of teams and long dozens of others, making hundreds of trades during the course of the season. One reportedly lost $60,000 in 1987. Yankee futures dipped into the low 80s in September 1988 and finished at 85 because the Yankees had won 85 games. The Los Angeles Dodgers, in contrast, opened the season at 81 and finished at 94. Those who were long Dodgers and short Yankees made money in 1988.

---

*John Crudele, "Baseball Futures Latest Way to Score on the Street," *Los Angeles Times,* September 18, 1988.

Arbitrage Between the Spot and Futures Markets

Someone who believes futures are mispriced according to Equations 1 and 2 — that the cost of carry differs significantly from the basis — can **arbitrage**, trying to profit from this mispricing by buying the item and selling a futures contract, or vice versa. Consider, for instance, a one-year futures contract on a generic commodity with a current spot price of $10. At a 10 percent interest rate, the forgone interest from buying the commodity rather than a futures contract is $10\%(\$10) = \$1$. If the annual cost of storage, insurance and so on is $0.50, then the total cost of carry is $1.50, and the price of a futures contract should be $11.50:

Arbitrageurs can sometimes profit when the basis is not equal to the cost of carry.

$$\text{Futures price} = \text{Spot price} + \text{Cost of carry}$$
$$= \$10.00 + \$1.50$$
$$= \$11.50$$

If the futures price exceeds this — at, say, $12 — then an arbitrageur can buy the item for $10 and sell a futures contract for $12. On the delivery date, the arbitrageur delivers the item for a profit of $2 which, by assumption, exceeds the $1.50 cost of carrying the item.

If the futures price is too low — at, say, $11 — then an arbitrageur who already owns the item can sell it for $10, thereby avoiding the $1.50 carrying costs, and buy a futures contract for $11 so as to recover the item in a year's time with a $0.50 profit. An arbitrageur who does not own the item may be able to borrow it and sell it short for $10, hedging the position with an $11 futures contract; if the $10 proceeds can be invested to earn $1 interest and the person who lent the item can be persuaded to pay for the storage costs that would otherwise be incurred, then a $0.50 profit can be realized.

Many commodities, such as butter, potatoes, hogs, and live cattle, are expensive to store and difficult to sell short. The practical impossibility of arbitrage undermines Equation 1, and the futures price is not determined by the current spot price and the cost of carry but instead largely reflects the anticipated spot price on the delivery date.

Other items, particularly financial assets, are relatively easy to store and sell short or, even more simply, sold by investors who already have these assets in their portfolios. Thus the price of financial futures is determined not by the expected future spot price but by the cost of carry. For financial assets, insurance, storage, and spoilage are negligible, making lost interest the biggest expense of buying now. This lost interest may be offset to some extent by the fact that many financial assets also yield a cash flow: stocks pay dividends, and bonds pay interest. Thus for financial assets,

$$\frac{\text{Cost of}}{\text{carry}} = \frac{\text{Lost interest}}{\text{from buying now}} - \frac{\text{Dividends or interest}}{\text{from holding the asset}} \tag{3}$$

We will now apply this logic to three specific futures contracts: foreign currency, Treasury bonds, and stock indexes.

Foreign Currencies

The previous chapter discussed how banks and others can be hurt by unanticipated changes in currency prices. This exchange-rate risk can be reduced now that there are futures markets in several foreign currencies, including the British pound, German mark, Japanese yen, and Swiss franc. (There are also, as noted earlier, very similar forward currency agreements among banks.) Because foreign currency can be invested to earn the interest rate prevailing in that country, the cost of carry is (approximately) equal to the difference between domestic and foreign interest rates.

The difference between the futures and spot price of foreign currency depends on the difference in interest rates.

$$\frac{\text{Cost of}}{\text{carry}} = \frac{\text{United States}}{\text{interest rate}} - \frac{\text{Foreign}}{\text{interest rate}}$$

and thus, according to Equation 1,

$$\text{Future price of}\atop\text{foreign currency} \;-\; \text{Spot price of}\atop\text{foreign currency} \;=\; \text{U.S.}\atop\text{interest rate} \;-\; \text{Foreign}\atop\text{interest rate} \quad (4)$$

The exact relationship, called the **interest-rate parity equation**, is

$$\frac{F}{1 + R_{US}} = \frac{P}{1 + R_{for}}$$

where F is the futures price,
     P the spot price,
     R_{US} the U.S. interest rate,
     and R_{for} the foreign rate.

Each side of this equation is the cost of obtaining one unit of the foreign currency on the delivery date. This equation can be written as

$$\frac{F}{P} = \frac{(1 + R_{US})}{(1 + R_{for})}$$

with Equation 4 an approximation.

For example, on August 16, 1988, the West German deutschemark cost $0.530 U.S. dollars; U.S. Treasury-bill rates were about 8 percent; German risk-free rates were about 5 percent; and the price of six-month mark futures was $0.538. It cost more dollars to buy mark futures than to buy current deutschemarks, because those who bought marks earned low West German interest rates, whereas those who bought mark futures could temporarily invest their dollars at high U.S. interest rates. Specifically, consider someone who wanted 1,000 deutschemarks in six months. Because these marks could be invested for six months to earn 5 percent/2=2.5 percent interest, that investor needed to buy only 1,000/1.025 = 975.6 marks, at a cost of 975.6($0.53) = $517. Alternatively, the investor could buy a futures contract for 1,000 marks at a cost of 1,000($0.538) = $538 after six months. The amount of dollars needed today to provide $538 in six months is $538/1.04 = $517 — the same cost as the first method. Thus, in August 1988, six-month deutschemark futures were 1.5 percent above the current spot price for marks, because German six-month interest rates were about 1.5 percent lower than U.S. interest rates. Futures for the British pound, in contrast, were below the current exchange rate because British short-term interest rates were around 10 percent, 2 percent higher than U.S. rates; carrying costs were negative because dollars invested while waiting for a pound futures delivery earned less than British pounds earned.

Foreign-currency futures can be used for arbitrage if Equation 4 is not satisfied or for speculation by those wanting low-money-down bets on the direction of exchange rates (definitely not a recommended gamble). Currency futures can also be used by importers, exporters, and their banks to hedge against exchange-rate fluctuations.

Suppose, for instance, that it is November 15, 1989, so that the prices in Table 8.3 apply, and a U.S. bank expects to receive 125 million German marks in March 1990. It can protect itself against a decline in the value of those marks relative to the dollar by selling 1,000 March 1990 futures contracts at $0.5440. The possession of these contracts guarantees that the bank will be able to sell the marks when it receives them in March 1990 at a fixed dollar price of $0.5440. Equivalently, a decline in the value of the mark will be offset by a profit on the futures contracts that the bank has sold.

Similarly, suppose that in November 1989 a U.S. bank anticipated making a payment of 250 million deutschemarks in March 1990. The bank can protect itself, hedging its exposure to exchange-rate risk, by buying 2,000 March 1990 futures contracts at $0.5440, thereby ensuring that it will be able to buy marks in March 1990 at this fixed dollar price.

Treasury Securities

Futures contracts are traded for a number of Treasury securities. The cost of carry is the difference between the interest lost by purchasing the bonds now rather than later, minus the coupons that can be earned by owning the bonds now. The cost of carry is close to zero if the term structure is flat and the Treasury bond coupon rates are approximately equal to current interest rates. (For Treasury bills, which have no coupons, the cost of carry is simply equal to the lost interest between the futures purchase and the delivery.) An upward-sloping term structure, with short-term rates lower than long-term rates, reduces the cost of carry and pulls futures prices down relative to spot prices; futures prices have to be low because those who buy bonds earn more interest than those who hold Treasury bills and wait.

As with currency futures, bond futures are used by arbitrageurs (who try to wring profits out of mispriced futures), speculators (who want to bet on interest-rate movements), and individuals or institutions that want to hedge interest-rate risk. When interest rates rise, bond prices decline and so do the prices of bond futures, which call for the delivery of now-less-valuable bonds. Those who buy bond futures are wagering that interest rates will fall (relative to the expectations already embedded in the term structure), whereas those who sell futures are implicitly betting on rising interest rates.

Bond futures can be used to hedge against unexpected interest-rate movements.

Banks and other risk-averse investors can use bond futures to offset implicit interest-rate wagers elsewhere in their portfolios. For instance, a corporation that has borrowed a large amount at a long-term fixed interest rate can hedge against a fall in interest rates by buying bond futures. If interest rates fall, making its long-term loan more burdensome, its loss is offset by the profits it makes on its bond futures contracts, because the prices of bond futures increase as interest rates decline and bond prices rise.

Similarly, consider a savings-and-loan association holding long-term, fixed-interest mortgages. These fixed-interest mortgages are an implicit wager that interest rates will decline, making its mortgages more valuable. The risk is that interest rates will rise unexpectedly, reducing the value of these mortgages. This risk of rising interest rates can be hedged by selling bond futures. If interest

Stock-Index Arbitrage

When stock-market index futures were introduced in 1982, the annual dividend yield on the S&P 500 stock index was about 6 percent and the annual rate of return on Treasury bills was 10 percent, leading many to predict that the price of an S&P futures contract should be larger than the value of the S&P index. Specifically, the no-arbitrage pricing relationship in Equation 5 implies that the futures price should have been about 4 percent higher than the value of the stock index:

$$F = P(1 + R - d)$$
$$= P(1 + 0.10 - 0.06)$$
$$= P(1.04)$$

Futures prices in 1982 were, in fact, typically below the value of the S&P 500, and arbitrageurs exploited this difference by buying index futures and selling the stocks in the S&P 500.

Suppose, for simplicity, that the value of the S&P 500 is $P = 100$ and that a one-year futures contract sells at a 1 percent discount below the S&P 500, $F = 99$. A pension fund holding the stocks in the S&P 500 valued at 100 is anticipating a dividend of 6 and capital gains of $P^* - 100$, where P^* is the value of the S&P 500 index on the delivery date. Its total percentage return is $6 + (P^* - 100)$. This pension fund can increase its return by 5 percentage points by selling its stocks for 100, investing the proceeds in Treasury bills paying 10 percent, and buying S&P futures at 99. The value of the futures contracts on the delivery date will be P^*, and the pension fund's percentage return is now $10 + (P^* - 99)$, a risk-free 5-percentage-point increase:

Percentage profit on T-bills and futures	$10 + (P^* - 99)$
Percentage profit on stock portfolio	$6 + (P^* - 100)$
Increase in percentage profit	5

Early index arbitrageurs made large profits with little effort. Their growing numbers subsequently eliminated such obvious mispricing. Today, arbitrageurs have to work hard to make small profits.

rates increase, bond prices will decline and so will the value of bond futures. A savings-and-loan institution that has sold bond futures at a price F reaps a profit $F - P$ as bond prices slump. If an appropriate quantity of futures is sold, any losses on the mortgage portfolio as interest rates rise will be offset by profits on the futures.

This S&L, with long-term assets and short-term liabilities can use bond futures to insulate its net worth from interest-rate fluctuations, just as if it had short-term assets and short-term liabilities. Bond futures can, in essence, be used to transform fixed-rate mortgages into synthetic adjustable-rate loans. In this way, customers can have the long-term fixed-rate loans they want, and the financial intermediary gets the desired protection from interest-rate risk.

Stock Indexes

Stock-index futures are heavily traded.

Many institutional investors use stock-index futures as a fast and inexpensive way of adjusting their portfolios' exposure to the stock market. In 1987, the daily volume of trading in futures contracts for the S&P 500 stock index routinely topped 100,000 contracts, with an aggregate market value of $15 billion — more than the total value of all the stock traded daily on the New York Stock Exchange.

The S&P 500 can be acquired by buying the 500 stocks included in the index, and sold by an institution that holds a large, diversified portfolio of stocks. Because it is easy to arbitrage S&P futures, their price is determined not by the expected performance of the stock market but by the cost of carry — the lost interest, net of dividends from the stocks. Investors can either buy the stocks in the S&P 500 today for P or buy them later for F, the futures price agreed to today. The advantage of the first strategy is that the buyer receives dividends D between now and delivery; the second strategy earns interest RP by postponing payment. For both strategies to be equally attractive,

$$\begin{aligned} F &= P + RP - D \\ &= P(1 + R - d) \end{aligned} \tag{5}$$

where $d = D/P$ is the dividend yield on the S&P 500 stocks.

Program Trading

Stock-index futures are used for a variety of purposes. **Program trading** is a loosely used term that originally meant buying or selling a diversified portfolio of stocks. Although program trading existed before stock-index futures were introduced in 1982, it has been associated with futures ever since because these are the easiest way to trade baskets of stocks. It is helpful to distinguish two very different kinds of program trading — index arbitrage and portfolio insurance — and we will do so.

Portfolio insurers buy futures when stock prices rise and sell when prices fall.

An institutional investor holding a diversified portfolio of stocks practices **portfolio insurance** by automatically selling stock futures contracts whenever stock prices fall, an action equivalent to selling stock but with lower transaction costs. If stock prices continue to fall, even more futures are sold, until at some preset floor (say 10 percent losses), the portfolio is fully hedged in that the value of the outstanding futures is equal to the value of the portfolio.

Index arbitrage is a very different type of program trading, with the objective of earning risk-free profits whenever the spread between the index-futures price and the index itself differs from the no-arbitrage equilibrium in Equation 5 by more than the transaction costs that arbitrage entails. Arbitrageurs buy stocks and sell futures if the futures price is too high and do the reverse if it is too low.

Index arbitrageurs try to profit from gaps between index futures and the value of the index.

The price differences are so slight and the transactions costs on small trades so large that a portfolio of at least $25 million is needed for index arbitrage to be profitable. The practice is dominated by a few dozen brokers and institutional investors, who try to earn a few cents per share that will add up to thousands of dollars when millions of shares are traded. A risk-free extra 1–2 percent annual return gives them around $150 million in annual profits.

Index arbitrageurs do not inherently push stock prices up or down. They buy in one market and sell in another, so as to keep the price of index futures close to the index itself. Buying or selling pressure that shows up in one market but not the other will be transmitted to the second market by arbitrageurs. For example, when the stock market rises, portfolio insurers need less protection and consequently buy futures. If futures prices subsequently rise more than stock prices, index arbitrageurs sell futures and buy stock until equilibrium is reestablished. But it is not the arbitrageurs who push up stock prices; it is the portfolio insurers who buy stocks indirectly, through futures — a buying power that arbitrageurs transmit to the stock market itself. If there were no futures market, or if futures prices were allowed to rise significantly above stock prices, portfolio insurers would presumably buy stocks instead of futures and have the very same effect on stock prices. Arbitrageurs are just the messengers who bring the news to the stock market that portfolio insurers are buying.

The same logic applies to the more worrisome case, in which portfolio insurers react to a drop in stock prices by selling index futures. If futures prices drop more than stock prices, arbitrageurs buy futures and sell stock, transmitting the portfolio insurers' sales to the stock market. Again, the cause of the pressure on stock prices is not the arbitrageurs but the portfolio insurers who follow the seemingly destabilizing rule of buying stock after prices rise and selling after they fall.

The Brady Commission, a presidential task force, concluded that portfolio insurance was the catalyst for the collapse of stock prices on October 19, 1987, when the Dow Industrial Average fell by 508 points (22 percent) and the S&P 500 index dropped 57.6 points (21 percent). The Commodity Futures Trading Commission estimated that portfolio insurers accounted for between 12 percent and 24 percent of the trading in S&P 500 index futures on October 19 and that about 9 percent of the NYSE trading that day was associated with index arbitrage. The rest of the year, index arbitrage accounted for as little as 1 percent and as much as 19 percent of NYSE trading.

Portfolio insurance has been accused of contributing to stock-market crises.

Portfolio insurance assumes that index futures can be sold continuously at the equilibrium values given by Equation 5. In the market collapse of October 19, the sellers of index futures far outnumbered the buyers, and any trades that did take place were at prices at least 10 percent below the no-arbitrage equilibrium price. An astonishing 608 million shares of stock were traded on the New York Stock Exchange. Yet, many sales could not be completed because buyers could not be found. Trading stopped in many stocks, and the reporting of prices lagged far behind recent trades, let alone the prices at which new trades could be made. Even though futures prices were much too low, arbitrageurs couldn't make risk-free profits because they did not know current stock prices and couldn't execute offsetting orders simultaneously. Portfolio insurers were reluctant to sell at these sharp discounts, and those who tried to sell had difficulty finding buyers.[4] Portfolio insurance is supposed to provide protection during a market collapse, but, ironically, this is when it is least effective.

Many clients became disenchanted with portfolio insurance, and some institutions reacted to the public distrust of all program trading by voluntarily stopping their index arbitrage. As a result, trading in S&P futures fell by half after the October crash.

OPTIONS

An option contract conveys the right, but not the obligation, to buy or sell something in the future at a price that is specified now. The reporting of daily stock-option trading takes up a full page in *The Wall Street Journal* and other newspapers. Options for commodities, currencies, bonds, and other financial instruments are scattered throughout the financial pages. We'll use Treasury bonds in most of our examples, because these are appealing contracts for financial institutions.

Because the option seller makes a commitment that may be exercised at the buyer's discretion, the seller is said to have "written" the option. Before 1973, each option agreement was between two specific parties, and the buyer who exercised an option went to the option writer for fulfillment of its terms. With the trading of standardized contracts on the Chicago Board and other exchanges, there is no need to associate a particular writer with a specific contract, or to hold a contract until expiration. When a buyer exercises an option, payment is made to the exchange, which then collects the promised bonds, shares of stock, or other items from the option writers without ever identifying a particular option writer with a particular option holder.

In practice, options are seldom exercised. Instead, on the expiration date, any outstanding options are sold back to the option writers, thereby extinguishing the contract, at a price reflecting the value the contract would have if it had been exercised. Option writers can also close out (or "cover") their position by repurchasing options before expiration. The number of outstanding options (called, as with futures, the open interest) fluctuates daily, as some write new options and others close their positions.

There are two types of option contracts, puts and calls, which can be combined to create a variety of leveraged and hedged portfolios. We'll look first at calls, then at puts, and then at a few portfolio strategies.

Call Options

A **call option** gives the holder of the option the right, but not the obligation, to buy an asset at a fixed price on or before a specified date. For instance, a call option could give the purchaser the right to buy a Treasury bond with an 8 percent coupon maturing in the year 2010 at a price of 100 (100 percent of its face value) any time within the next three months. The standard Treasury-bond option contract traded on the Chicago Board Options Exchange is for $100,000 of face value; a quoted price of 100 signifies $100,000; a price of 99 means $99,000. The fixed price of 100 that is specified in the option contract is called the **exercise price** or the **striking price**, and the date on which the contract expires is called the **exercise date.**

The value of a call option depends on the exercise price and the value of the underlying asset. The right to buy Treasury bonds for 100 is worth little if they are selling for 80 (80 percent of face value), but is worth a lot if they are trading at 130. The minimum value of a call option is its **exercise value**, the amount you could save if you purchased the bond by exercising the option. If the bond is selling for 100 or less, an option to buy at 100 saves you nothing; if the bond is selling for 130, the option saves you 30. Thus the exercise value is equal to the difference between the market value of the bond P and the option's exercise price E, if the bond's price is higher than the exercise price:

$$\text{Exercise value} = P - E \quad \text{if } P > E \atop = \quad 0 \quad \text{if } P \leq E \tag{6}$$

This relationship is graphed in Figure 8.2. The value of an option is never negative, because you are not compelled to exercise it. An option that has a positive exercise value is said to be "in the money"; one with no exercise value is "out of the money."

If we neglect transaction costs, an option should always sell for at least its exercise value, because it is worth at least this much to investors who want to buy the bond. If an option sells for less than its exercise value, arbitrageurs can buy the option, exercise it, and sell the bond for an immediate easy profit. Suppose, for instance, that the Treasury bond is selling for 108 and an option to buy at 100 is selling for only 2. An arbitrageur can pay 2 for the option, exercise it by paying another 100, and then sell the bond for 108 — making a quick profit of 6 ($6,000 per $100,000 of face value). The eagerness of arbitrageurs to exploit such opportunities keeps option prices from falling below their exercise value.

On the expiration date, the value of an option is equal to its exercise value because then it must be exercised or discarded. Before expiration, option prices are invariably above their exercise value, because those who buy options do so in the hope that the price of the underlying asset will rise and make their option

A call option conveys the right to buy an asset at the specified exercise price.

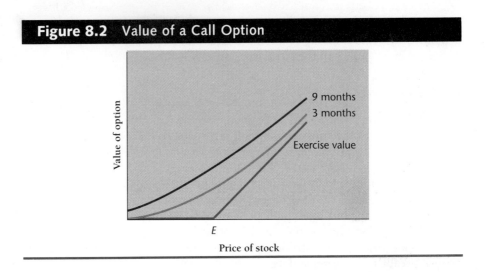

Figure 8.2 Value of a Call Option

more valuable. As Figure 8.2 shows, options are more valuable when there is more time until expiration.

The Lure of Leveraged Profits

Options provide leverage in that for the price of the option, you earn profits on an asset worth much more than the option. Consider again a three-month call option on a Treasury bond with a 100 exercise price, and suppose that the price of the option is 1, whereas the price of the bond is 100. Table 8.5 shows the percentage profits for someone who buys the bond and for someone who instead purchases an option to buy the bond.

If you buy the bond for 100 and its market value rises to 101 after 3 months, you make a 1 percent profit. If you instead buy a call option on the bond, its value at expiration is its exercise value of 1, just what you paid for it, and your profit is 0 percent. Not very attractive so far! But consider what happens if the price of the bond rises to 102, giving a 2 percent profit to the person who bought the bond. The person who bought the option finds its value rising from 1 to 2, a 100 percent profit. If the price of the bond rises to 103, the option will be worth 3, a 200 percent profit. Because the bond is initially worth 100 times as much as the option, there is 100/1 leverage, in that each 1-percentage-point increase in the value of the stock brings a 100-percentage-point increase in the value of the option. It is this chance for enormous leveraged profits that has historically lured investors to options. This leverage is not symmetrical, because the value of the option cannot be negative. As the option advisory services say, "The most you can lose is the cost of your option" — a peculiarly cheerful way of noting that if the price of the bond doesn't go up, your option will be worthless and you will have a 100 percent loss.

Options can be used for speculation.

Table 8.5 Options Provide Leverage			
Price at Expiration		Percentage Gain	
Bond	Option	Bond	Option
98	0	− 2%	−100%
99	0	− 1%	−100%
100	0	0%	−100%
101	1	1%	0%
102	2	2%	100%
103	3	3%	200%

Put Options

A **put option** is similar to a call except that the owner has the right to *sell* an asset at a fixed price on or before a specified date. For instance, a put option could give the owner the right to sell an 8 percent coupon Treasury bond maturing in 2010 for 100 at any time within the next three months. If the price of the bond declines, this put option becomes increasingly valuable. Specifically, the exercise value of a put is equal to

A put option gives the right to sell an asset at the specified exercise price.

$$\text{Exercise value} = E - P \quad \text{if } P < E \\ = \quad 0 \quad \text{if } P \geq E \tag{7}$$

Figure 8.3 graphs this relationship.

As with a call, the exercise value of a put is the minimum value that it can sell for without attracting profitable arbitrage. On the exercise date, the market price of a put is equal to its exercise value; before this date, the price is somewhat higher, as bearish investors buy puts in anticipation of profiting from a drop in the price of the underlying asset.

Option Strategies

A put is a bet that the price of the underlying asset will fall; a call is a bet that it will rise. Because interest rates and bond prices are inversely related, a call option on Treasury bonds is a bet that interest rates will fall (raising bond prices), and a put is a wager that interest rates will increase. Bond puts and calls need not be purchased in isolation, as all-out bets on the direction of interest rates. A variety of positions can be created by buying or selling various combinations of put, calls, and bonds.

A bank may, for example, have a portfolio of long-term bonds, mortgages, and other assets whose value is very sensitive to interest rates. The bank can purchase protection against a rise in interest rates and a corresponding decline

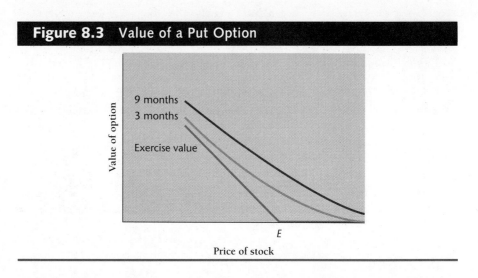

Figure 8.3 Value of a Put Option

in the value of these assets by purchasing Treasury-bond put options. Suppose, for instance, that it has $500 million in Treasury bonds that it wishes to ensure. If it buys 5,000 Treasury-bond puts, then it has the right to sell $500 million in Treasury bonds at a fixed price, ensuring that the value of its portfolio won't drop below this fixed price. The price of this insurance is the cost of the put options.

What if the traded option contracts are for 20-year Treasury bonds with 8 percent coupons and the bank owns bonds and mortgages of various maturities? By comparing the duration of its portfolio with the duration of the 20-year Treasury bonds, it can estimate the relative sensitivity to interest rates. If, for instance, it estimates that a 2-percentage-point decline in the market value of Treasury bonds will typically be accompanied by a 1-percentage-point decline in the market value of its $500 million portfolio, it can buy 2,500 Treasury-bond puts, anticipating that any losses on the portfolio will be offset by profits on the put contracts.

A bank might also consider writing call options against its bond portfolio. These "covered calls" are a fairly conservative strategy, suitable for those who expect modest increases in bond prices. If bond prices hold steady or decline, the proceeds from selling now-worthless call options provide extra income; the cost is that the bonds will be called away if prices increase, putting a ceiling on profits. The writer of covered calls trades away the chance for large profits in return for extra income. Many college endowments and pension funds follow this conservative strategy for a portion of their stock and, to a lesser extent, their bond portfolios.

Index Options

In addition to the Treasury-bond options used in these examples, financial institutions can trade options on futures contracts for a variety of securities and

Options can be used to hedge positions.

Betting on Interest-Rate Volatility

A straddle on, say, Treasury bonds is the simultaneous purchase of a Treasury-bond call option (a bet that the bond's price will rise) and a put option (a bet that bond prices will fall). Someone who creates a straddle makes money if Treasury-bond prices either rise or fall — it doesn't matter which — above or below the exercise price by an amount equal to the price of the call plus the price of the put. Thus a Treasury-bond straddle is an implicit bet that there will be a large change in interest rates.

Someone who writes a Treasury-bond straddle, simultaneously selling a call and a put, is betting that interest rates will not change much, in either direction, during the life of the options. One investor who routinely wrote stock straddles, betting that stock prices wouldn't change much, built his account up to $120,000 in October 1987. Then the market fell by more than 20 percent on October 19, 1987, and he had to repurchase his puts for far more than he received when he sold them. He lost $450,000 in a single day, leaving his account $330,000 in the hole.*

*Tim Metz and James A. White, "A Year after Its Peak, Stock Market Battles a Pervasive Malaise," *Wall Street Journal,* August 25, 1988.

for currency. As with futures, because a delivery is not needed to realize profits, options can be written on intangible items that cannot be delivered. An **index option** is an option contract based on the value of an index of asset prices such as the S&P 500 index of stock prices, an index of the prices of oil stocks, or an index of the prices of municipal bonds.

Options can be written on stock and bond indexes.

In each case, we can use the same principles that we applied to Treasury-bond options. For instance, consider options on the S&P 500 stock index. Those who don't wish to select individual stocks but think they can predict the overall direction of the stock market, can buy stock-index calls if they are bullish and puts if they are bearish. A pension fund that is willing to trade a chance at large profits for some extra income can write covered calls by buying a diversified portfolio of stocks and writing stock-index calls. A fund that wants to protect itself against a market collapse can buy insurance in the form of stock-index puts. An arbitrageur who thinks that index options are mispriced can create hedges.

Option Valuation

Option values depend on the price of the underlying asset relative to the option's exercise price, the length of time until expiration, the volatility of the price of the underlying asset, and interest rates. The first two factors are straightforward. The third reflects the asymmetrical nature of an option: if the price of the asset rises, the price of a call option rises, too, without bound, but if the asset's price falls below the exercise price, a call option has no exercise value, no matter how low the asset's price. Similarly, put options become increasingly valuable the lower the asset's price sinks, but the exercise value can never be less than zero. Thus an asset whose price will go up or down a lot is attractive to both put and call option holders.

The fourth factor, high interest rates, is also subtle. Consider a one-year call option that is likely to be exercised. You can either buy the asset now for its current price or buy an option and then pay the exercise price in one year. If interest rates are high, the advantage of paying for the asset later makes the call option more valuable.

To the extent that option and asset prices are related, riskless hedges can, in theory, be constructed by continuously maintaining an appropriate hedge ratio between assets and options. The observation that the return on a riskless hedge should equal the return on safe Treasury bills led Fischer Black and Myron Scholes, using some strong assumptions and advanced mathematics, to derive what is now called the Black–Scholes option-pricing formula, a complex equation that is beyond the scope of this book.[5] Many investors now use these theoretical formulas to look for mispriced options, an arbitrage activity that eliminates significant mispricing.

SUMMARY

A futures contracts is an agreement to deliver an item on a specified date at a price agreed to today but not paid until delivery. Futures can be used to hedge a position (a farmer selling corn futures), to speculate (a wager on the value of the deutschemark), or to engage in arbitrage (between bonds and bond futures). Except for transaction costs, futures contracts are a zero-sum game, and contracts are marked to market each trading day by transferring funds between shorts and longs, depending on whether futures prices went up or down.

Shorts and longs can cover their positions before the delivery date, and almost all do. On the delivery date, the futures price is approximately equal to the spot price. Before the delivery date, the futures price may be influenced by investor expectations of the spot price on the delivery date. For precious metals, financial assets, and other items that can be stored and sold short, the spread between the futures price and the current spot price is determined by the cost of carry — the cost, including forgone interest, of buying the item now and holding it until the delivery date. If the cost of carry is positive, futures prices will be above spot prices and will increase with the time until delivery.

A call option gives a person the right, but not the obligation, to buy an asset at a fixed price on or before a specified date. A put option gives the holder the right (but no obligation) to sell at a specified price. Option agreements are between private parties and, except for transaction costs, are a zero-sum game in that one's gain is the other's loss.

Options are seldom exercised. Instead, on the expiration date, any outstanding options are sold back to the option writers at a price approximately equal to the option's exercise value — the amount an option holder could save by exercising the option instead of buying or selling the underlying asset at its market price.

Traditionally, many have been lured to options and futures contracts for speculation — high-stakes wagers on whether asset prices will rise or fall. However, the combination of futures, puts, calls, and the underlying asset offers banks and other financial intermediaries a wide variety of hedging strategies — for instance, insuring a mortgage portfolio by selling Treasury-bond futures or buying Treasury-bond puts.

IMPORTANT TERMS

arbitrage
basis
call option
cost of carry
covering
daily limits
daily settlement
exercise date
exercise price
exercise value
forward contracts
futures
index arbitrage

index option
interest-rate parity equation
margin
marking to market
open interest
option contract
portfolio insurance
program trading
put option
reversing
settlement price
spot price
striking price

EXERCISES

1. Use the data on December 1990 Treasury-bond contracts in Table 8.3 to answer the following questions:
   a. What was the opening price on November 15?
   b. How many contracts were in existence?
   c. If a bank bought 1,000 contracts at the November 15 settlement price and took delivery, how much would it have to pay at delivery? (Ignore transaction costs.)
   d. What was the change between the opening and settlement prices on November 15?
   e. What was the change between the settlement price on November 14 and the settlement price on November 15?

2. Find Chicago Board of Trade corn futures in the most recent Monday issue of *The Wall Street Journal*. Report the settlement prices and compare these current prices with those in Table 8.3, both in their level and in the existence of a seasonal pattern.

3. Look up COMEX silver futures in the most recent Monday issue of *The Wall Street Journal*. How does the current level of silver-futures prices compare with silver prices when the Hunt brothers had billions of dollars invested in silver? Does the pattern of silver-futures settlement prices for different delivery dates suggest that silver-futures prices are deter-

mined by anticipated prices on the delivery dates or by the current spot price and cost of carry?

4. Why might a wheat farmer sell wheat-futures contracts even though he doesn't plan on selling his wheat until two weeks after the delivery date?

5. Why might a wheat farmer buy a wheat-futures contracts even if he doesn't plan on buying wheat on the delivery date?

6. The text explains how a U.S. bank that expects to receive 125 million German marks in March 1990 can, on November 15, 1989, sell 1,000 March 1990 futures contracts at $0.5440 to protect itself from exchange-rate fluctuations. The dollar price of deutschemarks on the March 1990 delivery date turned out to be $0.5952. Did this hypothetical bank make or lose money on its futures contracts?

7. Highlight 8.3 tells of a baseball futures market. When the Yankees opened the 1988 season at 93, did this price reflect expectations or the cost of carry?

8. Rebut this argument by a Kansas congressman in 1890:[6]

   Those who deal in "options" and "futures" contracts, which is mere gambling, no matter by what less offensive name such transactions be designated, neither add to the supply nor increase the demand for consumption, nor do they accomplish any useful purpose by their calling; on the contrary, they speculate in fictitious products [which are never actually delivered]. The wheat they buy and sell is known as "wind wheat" and doubtless for the reason that it is invisible, intangible, and felt or realized only in the terrible force it exerts in destroying the farming industry of the country.

9. The cost of storing platinum is $2 per 50 troy ounces per month. If the interest rate is 6 percent, what pattern would you expect to find in three-month, six-month, and nine-month platinum-futures prices?

10. Carefully explain why someone who expects the price of gold to rise from $400 an ounce now to $450 an ounce a year from now would prefer paying $420 an ounce for a one-year gold futures contract to paying $400 an ounce for gold today.

11. On November 15, 1989, the spot price of the German deutschemark was 0.5437 dollars. Do the prices of deutschemark futures in Table 8.3 suggest that German interest rates were higher, lower, or about the same as U.S. interest rates?

12. On August 16, 1988, the exchange rate for Japanese yen was $0.007488 and the prices of yen futures contracts were $0.007589 for December delivery, $0.007660 for March 1989 delivery, and $0.007741 for June 1989 delivery. Were Japanese interest rates higher or lower than U.S. interest rates? Explain your reasoning.

13. Investment bankers hold inventories of bonds that they have purchased from some clients and intend to sell to others. To hedge their exposure to interest-rate risk, should they buy or sell bond futures? Explain.

14. A bank has made a commitment to lend a real estate developer $10 million at a 10 percent interest rate three months from now. Will this bank suffer a financial loss on this commitment if interest rates move up or move down during the next three months? To hedge this risk, should it buy or sell Treasury-bond futures?

15. Many savings-and-loan associations have short-term deposits and long-term mortgages. Will they lose money if interest rates go up or go down? Explain which of the following actions are appropriate to protect themselves and which are inappropriate:
    a. Lengthening the maturity of their assets.
    b. Issuing more variable-rate mortgages.
    c. Buying 30-year zero-coupon bonds.
    d. Buying Treasury-bond futures.
    e. Buying call options on Treasury bonds.
    f. Buying put options on Treasury bonds.

16. In 1987, many pension funds grew increasingly nervous about their stock portfolios as price-to-earnings ratios approached all-time highs. Indicate which of the following they could have bought and which they could have sold to protect themselves from a collapse in stock prices:
    a. Stock-index call options.
    b. Stock-index put options.
    c. Stock-index futures.

17. The Chicago Board of Trade requires that the purchaser of a U.S.-Treasury-bond futures contract put up an initial margin of $5,000 per contract and at all times maintain a margin of at least $4,000 per contract. What criteria do you suppose they used to choose these particular numbers?

18. In November 1984, Professor Stephen Figlewski was quoted in the *New York Times* as saying that stock-index futures are so new and complex that the market is not yet dominated by arbitrageurs and other professionals, and is consequently not yet efficient.[7]

    According to Professor Figlewski, a simple formula tells what the stock index future's price should be, if the market were efficient. Take whatever the index is, say 100, and add the interest rate that an investor would make on his money if it were invested in a money market fund or Treasury bills, say 10 percent. Then subtract the dividend rate, for example 4 percent. In this case the answer is 106, so if index futures were selling above or below that, then clearly the market is inefficient, Professor Figlewski said.

    Clearly explain the logic behind the professor's formula. If, in the above example, the index future were selling for less than 106, how could you make a safe profit larger than that available on Treasury bills?

19. The interest rates on Eurodollars are typically a percentage point above Treasury-bill rates. An investment advisory service recommends a TED Spread under certain circumstances, buying Treasury bill futures and selling Eurodollar futures.[8] For this to be profitable, are they counting on the interest-rate differential between Eurodollars and T-bills to widen or narrow? Explain.

20. An investment advisory service wrote:[9]

    The relationship between the price of gold and the price of silver has changed considerably since the days when Menes I [an Egyptian Pharaoh of around 2850 B.C.] could trade three ounces of silver for one ounce of gold. In 1932, for example, in the midst of The Great Depression, it took 20 ounces of silver to buy one ounce of gold. By 1960, the Ratio was 16-to-1. In recent years, however, it has stabilized in the range of 34 to 38 ounces of silver for every ounce of gold . . .

    The Ratio has fluctuated widely just in the past seven or eight years, dipping as low as 19-to-1 in 1980 and soaring as high as 52-to-1 in 1982 and 55-to-1 in 1985.

    But, as you can also clearly see, it has always — ALWAYS — returned to the range between 34-to-1 and 38-to-1.

    The advisory service recommends acting when the Ratio is above 45-to-1 or below 15-to-1. In which case should you buy gold futures and sell silver futures, and in which case do the reverse? Is there any risk in this strategy?

21. Investors who had been following a stock-options strategy touted by brokers as a sure thing lost hundreds of millions of dollars when the Dow dropped 508 points on October 19, 1987. Were they buying calls, selling calls, buying puts, or selling puts? Explain your reasoning.

22. A financial columnist offered several tips to stockholders who want protection from a decline in stock prices, while "allowing yourself room to make money if the bull is still alive."[10] One of his tips was to buy put options. Explain how this action accomplishes the stated objective — and the drawback (if any).

23. On October 6, 1989, March 1990 Treasury-bill call options with an exercise price of 92.75 traded for 0.86 and March 1990 Treasury-bill put options with an exercise price of 92.75 traded for 0.41. All of these prices are as a percentage of the $1,000,000 face value of a contract; thus the price of one call option is $8,600. Graph the dollar gain from each of the following strategies as a function of the price of Treasury bills on the exercise date: (a) buy one call option; (b) buy one put option. Which strategy is a bet that interest rates will rise?

24. Using the data in Exercise 23, graph the dollar gain from a strategy of buying both one call option and one put option as a function of the price of Treasury bills on the exercise date.

25. Here are some selected prices from November 15, 1989, for options for Japanese yen futures, to be delivered in December 1989, January 1990, and March 1990:

Exercise Price	Call Options			Put Options		
	Dec.	Jan.	Mar.	Dec.	Jan.	Mar.
69	1.07	1.55	2.04	0.40	0.63	1.13
70	0.51	0.98	1.50	0.83	1.06	1.58
71	0.21	0.58	1.09	1.52	1.66	2.14

All of these prices are in U.S. cents per 100 yen; at the time, the spot price was 69.56 cents for 100 yen.
  a. Why do these call prices decline as the striking price increases, although the put prices increase?
  b. Why are the March calls worth more than the December calls and March puts worth more than the December puts?

26. Use the data in Exercise 25 to graph the dollar gain from each of the following strategies as a function of the price of Japanese yen futures on the exercise date: (a) buy one call option; (b) buy one put option. Should a speculator

who believes that the value of the dollar will rise relative to the yen buy yen put or call options? Why might a bank that is not interested in speculating on the value of the yen nonetheless buy yen put options?

27. When Professor Smith came to Pomona College, he encountered the Economics Club's annual investment contest. Each contestant is given $10,000 in play money to manage over a three-month period; the winner is given a real cash prize. Smith managed the portfolios of two contestants, his secretary, and a student. All of the secretary's money was invested in a put option for a certain company's stock; all of the student's money was invested in a call option for the same stock. At the end of three months, the student's portfolio had grown to nearly $50,000 — easily winning the contest. Explain Smith's strategy. What do you think happened to the secretary's portfolio?

28. E. G. Capital Management, an investment-management company, buys high-dividend stocks and writes call options against them. The *New York Times* says that this fund has done very well in sluggish markets, but "in surging markets . . . will almost always underperform market indexes."[11] Explain why this is so.

29. A *New York Times* financial reporter wrote, "Professional stock market traders like [dealing in options] because it affords them an opportunity to lose money profitably."[12] Give a specific example of how a trader might lose money in options while making an overall profit.

30. Most corporate bonds have call positions that allow the firm to repurchase the bond at a set price before maturity. Interpret the position of the firm and the bondholders using the language of puts and calls; for example, "the bondholders have implicitly bought a bond and sold a put."

LOANS

I'm going to do you a favor. . . .

Anonymous car dealer

People borrow money to finance the purchase of homes, cars, and household appliances. Businesses borrow to finance the construction of new plants and equipment and the takeover of existing companies. Financial intermediaries borrow from some to lend to others. For each borrower, a loan is a debt, an obligation to repay the borrowed money plus interest. For each lender, a loan is an investment comparable to bonds, stocks, or other assets. This chapter explains how debt creates leverage, multiplying profits and losses from an investment. You will see how loan payments are determined and how the total-payments criterion often used to compare loans is flawed. We will look at fixed-rate, variable-rate, and graduated-payment loans and consider the interest-rate gambles implicit in these loans for both borrowers and lenders. The principles that will be explained in this chapter apply to all loans, but we will focus on home loans — mortgages — to make the discussion more concrete.

THE POWER OF LEVERAGE

We have all seen reports of people, perhaps even relatives or neighbors, who lost their home, farm, or business because they could not repay a loan. This is one reason why many people consider debt to be one of those four-letter words that decent people avoid: if you can't pay cash, then you can't afford it. Yet,

Highlight 9.1   The Downfall of the No-Money-Down Gurus

Many have made fortunes using borrowed money to invest in rapidly appreciating real estate; others have grown wealthy selling this secret to people with dreams of getting rich quickly. Look at Table 9.1 again, and this time label the investment "real estate" and dream along with this sales pitch. If you borrow $90,000 at 10 percent and buy a $100,000 property that appreciates by 30 percent in a year's time, your $10,000 will increase by 210 percent, to $31,000. Now sell this property and use your $31,000 as a 10 percent down payment on a $310,000 property. If you borrow the remaining 90 percent at a 10 percent interest rate and this property appreciates by 30 percent, then — presto! — your personal wealth is up to $96,100. Two more years of trading up and, dare to believe it, you are a virtual millionaire with $923,521 in personal wealth. It sure beats waiting on tables or pumping gas. You don't have the $10,000 to get started? No problem. You can begin with no money down — just attend a $495 seminar, listen to an inspirational pep talk, and buy a $19.95 book and a $79.95 tape.

Two of the best-known enthusiasts, Albert J. Lowry (*How You Can Become Financially Independent by Investing in Real Estate*) and Robert Allen (*Nothing Down*), had books on the *New York Times* best-seller list in 1980. Inspired by their success, dozens of imitators bought television time, gave hotel seminars, and wrote books preaching the no-money-down gospel, using such alluring titles as "Millionaire Maker," "Million Dollar Secrets," "Two Years to Financial Freedom," and "How to Wake Up the Financial Genius Inside You." At its peak, it has been estimated that the promoters took in $150 million a year. As it turned out, most of the eager buyers were not latent financial geniuses after all; it isn't all that easy to buy property with no money down, and it became very difficult to make money borrowing at double-digit mortgage rates when the rate of growth of real estate prices slowed to the single digits. By 1987, many of the gurus were bankrupt and most had moved on to other schemes.*

One of the ironies of the business is explained by a cassette supplier: "We laugh about it. They talk about buying stuff with no money down, but when we deal with them we demand our money up front. That's what you learn after you get burned enough times."† Similarly, a cable-TV distributor observed, "In broadcasting, the preachers, the politicians, the car transmission shops and the get-rich-quick guys are all money up front." If you reflect on it, there is a fundamental reason for skepticism about any get-rich-quick advice. As the ex-president of one of Lowry's seminar companies said of the no-money-down gurus

I've known most of them and I don't know of one who made a fortune investing in real estate, at least prior to the time they amassed some wealth

*Robert Guenther, "'Nothing-Down' Gurus Wane; Critics Say Concept Is Flawed," *Wall Street Journal,* January 14, 1987; James Bates, "'Get Rich' Story Ends at Chapter 7," *Los Angeles Times,* June 3, 1987.

†James Bates, "Promoters of Easy Street Seen on Bankruptcy Lane," *Los Angeles Times,* April 6, 1987.

putting on seminars. If you know how to make a fortune in real estate, you would spend your time doing it, rather than conducting seminars.†

others swear by, not at, debt. Borrowing allows you to invest other people's money, and many a fortune has been built with other people's money.

Debt has these two faces, like the proverbial two-edged sword, because it creates **leverage**, in that a relatively small investment reaps the benefits or losses from a much larger investment. Suppose that you have $10,000 of your own money and borrow $90,000 of other people's money, giving you $100,000 to invest. We'll look a year into the future and assume that the $90,000 is a simple one-year loan at 10 percent interest, so you must pay $99,000 at the end of the year. Your net financial gain depends on the rate of return R you earn on your $100,000 investment, with Table 9.1 showing some possible outcomes.

Debt creates leverage, magnifying profits and losses.

Look first at $R = 10$ percent. A 10 percent return on $100,000 is $10,000, enough to pay the $9,000 interest due on the $90,000 loan with $1,000 left over — a 10 percent return on the $10,000 that is your own money. This illustrates the general principle that if you borrow at 10 percent in order to invest at 10 percent, then the borrowing is neither an advantage nor a disadvantage. If the rate of return on the total investment is equal to the rate of interest owed on other people's money, this will also be the rate of return on your money.

What if the rate of return on the total investment turns out to be 20 percent? Twenty percent of $100,000 is $20,000, minus $9,000 interest leaves an $11,000 gain on your $10,000 — a 110 percent return. You more than double your wealth in a year by borrowing $90,000 at 10 percent and investing at 20 percent!

Because the total $100,000 investment is ten times the size of your own

Table 9.1   Potential Returns with 10-to-1 Leverage

Return on $100,000 (Percentage)	(Dollars)	Interest on $90,000 (Dollars)	Return on $10,000 (Dollars)	(Percentage)
0%	$ 0	$9,000	−$9,000	−90%
10%	10,000	9,000	1,000	10%
20%	20,000	9,000	11,000	110%
30%	30,000	9,000	21,000	210%

$10,000, you have 10-to-1 leverage. The consequence is that every percentage point by which the investment return exceeds the loan rate is multiplied by 10 in determining the return on your own money. A total return of $R = 20$ percent is a 10 percent excess over the 10 percent loan rate, so that multiplication by 10 pushes the excess return up to 110 percent.

To formalize this logic, a few mathematical symbols are helpful. If a fraction x of an investment is your own money, then your degree of leverage is $1/x$. If you pay a rate B on the borrowed money and earn a rate of return R on the total investment, then the rate of return on your own money is

$$B + \frac{1}{x}(R - B)$$

Let's apply this rule to our numerical example with $B = 10$ percent and $R = 30$ percent. If R were 10 percent, the borrowing would have no net effect and you would have a 10 percent return on your own money. Because $R = 30$ percent is 20 percentage points above $B = 10$ percent and you have 10-to-1 leverage, the return on your own money is $10\% + 10(20\%) = 210\%$. The step-by-step calculations in Table 9.1 confirm that this is correct.

The two-edged sword comes into play because leverage works on the down side too, multiplying shortfalls. If your $100,000 investment just breaks even ($R = 0$ percent), this is 10 percentage points less than the loan rate and multiplication by the 10-to-1 leverage gives you a return of $10\% + 10(-10\%) = -90\%$. You have $100,000 at the end of the year and, after paying your $99,000 debt, are left with $1,000 — a $9,000 loss on a $10,000 investment. Notice that your investment doesn't have to lose money for leverage to be a disaster; what hurts is that the investment's rate of return is less than the rate you are paying on the borrowed money. You lose money borrowing at 10 percent to invest at 5 percent, and the more you borrow the more you lose.

CALCULATING LOAN PAYMENTS

When a bank lends money, the borrower signs an agreement promising to pay back the amount borrowed plus interest. Before the Great Depression of the 1930s, most home mortgages were three- to five-year **balloon loans**, in which interest is paid on the loan until maturity, at which time a balloon payment equal to the size of the original principal is due. For instance, on a $100,000 4-year balloon loan with annual 10 percent interest payments, the homeowner pays $10,000 a year for four years and then repays the $100,000 loan or, more likely, refinances it. In the 1920s, balloon loans were routinely renewed at maturity. But the 1930s were not routine, and many banks and other lending institutions were unable or unwilling to renew loans. Homeowners who were out of work or earning reduced wages had trouble paying interest, let alone a balloon, and by 1935, more than 20 percent of the assets of savings-and-loan associations was real estate, mostly foreclosed properties.

Today, most mortgages are **amortized loans**; the periodic payments include principal as well as interest so that the loan is paid off gradually rather than being paid off with a balloon payment at the end. The most common amortized loan involves constant monthly payments over the life of the loan.

> The periodic payments on an amortized loan include both principal and interest.

No matter how the payments are structured, the general rule for all loans is very simple: The present value of the loan payments, discounted at the stated loan rate, is equal to the amount borrowed. For a conventional amortized loan, we can use this notation:

> The present value of loan payments is equal to the amount borrowed.

$$P = \text{Amount borrowed}$$
$$X = \text{Monthly payments}$$
$$R = \text{Monthly loan rate (annual percentage rate/12)}$$
$$n = \text{Number of monthly payments}$$

The size of the monthly payment is the value of X that solves the present-value equation

$$P = \frac{X}{(1 + R)} + \frac{X}{(1 + R)^2} + \cdots + \frac{X}{(1 + R)^n} \qquad (1)$$

The solution is given by a rearrangement of Equation 5 from Chapter 5:

$$X = \frac{RP}{1 - \dfrac{1}{(1 + R)^n}} \qquad (2)$$

For instance, if we borrow $4,000 for a year at 12 percent,

$$P = \$4,000$$
$$R = 0.12/12 = 0.01$$
$$n = 12$$

which implies

$$X = \frac{0.01(\$4,000)}{1 - \dfrac{1}{(1.01)^{12}}}$$

$$= \$355.40$$

Twelve monthly payments of $355.40, discounted at a 12 percent annual rate, have a present value of $4,000.

The Unpaid Balance

The present-value logic can be confirmed by dividing each monthly payment into interest and principal. Continuing with the example of a 12-month, $4,000 loan at 12 percent, after one month the borrower owes one month's interest on $4,000. At a 12 percent annual rate, the monthly interest rate is 12%/12 = 1%; the interest due is 0.01($4,000) = $40. The $355.40 monthly payment covers this $40 in interest and also the extra $355.40 − $40.00 = $315.40 reduces

Table 9.2 A 12-Month $4,000 Loan at 12 Percent

Payment Number	Total Payment	Interest Payment	Principal Payment	Unpaid Balance
1	$355.40	$40.00	$315.40	$3,684.60
2	355.40	36.85	318.55	3,366.06
3	355.40	33.66	321.73	3,044.32
4	355.40	30.44	324.95	2,719.37
5	355.40	27.19	328.20	2,391.17
6	355.40	23.91	331.48	2,059.68
7	355.40	20.60	334.80	1,724.89
8	355.40	17.25	338.15	1,386.74
9	355.40	13.87	341.53	1,045.21
10	355.40	10.45	344.94	700.27
11	355.40	7.00	348.39	351.88
12	355.40	3.52	351.88	0.00
Total	4,264.80	264.80	4,000.00	

the principal (or unpaid balance) to $4,000 − $315.40 = $3,684.60.

For the second month, the amount borrowed is $3,684.60; the interest due at the end of the month is 0.01($3,684.60) = $36.85. The monthly $355.40 payment includes this interest and $355.40 − $36.85 = $318.55 repayment of principal, reducing the unpaid balance to $3,684.60 − $318.55 = $3,366.05.

Table 9.2 gives the month-by-month details. After eleven months, the principal is down to $351.88, and the final $355.40 monthly payment covers this amount plus interest, so that the loan is fully repaid after twelve months. Thus, the present-value calculation of the appropriate level of monthly payments is logically consistent. Loan payments whose present value is equal to the amount borrowed will, period by period, pay the interest due on the unpaid balance and reduce the principal until, after the last payment, the unpaid balance is zero.

Notice in Table 9.2 that the total interest payments on this one-year loan add up to $264.80, although 12 percent interest on a $4,000 loan is apparently almost twice this amount: 0.12($4,000) = $480. The answer to this seeming paradox is that $480 in interest would be due if you borrowed the $4,000 for a full year, but the unpaid balance on an amortized loan shrinks month by month. Here, $4,000 is borrowed for the first month, then $3,684.60 for the second month, $3,366.06 for the third month, and so on until the last month, when only $351.88 is borrowed. The average amount borrowed is only about half of $4,000, and thus the interest is only about half of what would be due if $4,000 were borrowed for the entire year. Table 9.2 also shows that, as time passes and the unpaid balance declines, the monthly payments increasingly contain less interest and more repayment of principal. This inherent shift from interest to principal is pronounced for a long-term loan, such as a 30-year mortgage.

The periodic payments on an amortized loan reduce the unpaid balance to zero.

Table 9.3   A 30-Year $100,000 Loan at 12 Percent

Payment Number	Total Payment	Interest Payment	Principal Payment	Unpaid Balance
1	$1,028.61	$1,000.00	$28.61	$99,971.39
2	1,028.61	999.71	28.90	99,942.49
3	1,028.61	999.42	29.19	99,913.30
⋮				
12	1,028.61	996.69	31.92	99,637.12
⋮				
24	1,028.61	992.64	35.97	99,228.22
⋮				
60	1,028.61	977.15	51.47	97,663.22
⋮				
120	1,028.61	935.11	93.50	93,418.00
⋮				
240	1,028.61	720.03	308.58	71,694.83
⋮				
293	1,028.61	505.74	522.88	50,050.82
⋮				
300	1,028.61	468.02	560.59	46,241.32
⋮				
358	1,028.61	30.25	998.36	2,026.77
359	1,028.61	20.27	1,008.34	1,018.42
360	1,028.61	10.18	1,018.43	0.00
Total	370,299.60	270,299.60	100,000.00	

Table 9.3 shows some details for a 30-year loan of $100,000 at 12 percent. The initial monthly payments are almost entirely interest, so that after the first year's payments of more than $12,000, the principal has declined by less than $400. After two years, the unpaid balance is only down to $99,228.22, and after five years to $97,663.22. The loan is not half repaid until the twenty-fourth year. In the twenty-fourth year, the monthly payments finally become mostly principal, and the unpaid balance shrinks rapidly during the last five years of the loan.

People who buy a house and then move, paying off their mortgage after only a few years, are often surprised to find that the money they have paid each month has made barely a dent in the principal. They have not been cheated. Each month, they paid the interest due on their loan, fairly calculated, and every dollar beyond that reduced the principal. What they don't realize is that an amortized loan does not reduce the principal equally each month (because more interest is due when the loan is large and less when it is small).

Effective Loan Rates

Another often-overlooked fact is that just as monthly compounding increases the interest earned on a savings account, so monthly compounding increases the effective interest rate paid on a loan. If an annual percentage rate *APR* is applied monthly to the unpaid balance, the effective interest rate *R* is given by

$$1 + R = \left(1 + \frac{APR}{12}\right)^{12}$$

If, for example, the *APR* is 12 percent, the effective rate is

$$1 + R = \left(1 + \frac{0.12}{12}\right)^{12}$$

$$= 1.1268$$

an effective yield of 12.68 percent.

When banks pay depositors or charge borrowers an annual percentage rate divided by 12 each month, this monthly compounding increases the effective interest rate in each case. Bank reporting, however, is asymmetrical in that eye-catching advertisements inform us that the effective rates paid on deposits are higher than the annual percentage rates, but similar information about loan rates is nowhere to be found.

EVALUATING LOANS: TOTAL PAYMENTS VERSUS PRESENT VALUE

Loans should be evaluated by present values, not total payments.

Truth-in-Lending laws require lenders to reveal not only the annual percentage rate, but also the total amount (principal plus interest) that will be paid over the life of the loan. Unfortunately, the prominent display of this information encourages borrowers to make the mistake of judging loans by the total payments, as illustrated in the accompanying Highlight about *Consumer Reports*. Why is this a mistake? Because it doesn't take into account *when* the payments are made, and a dollar paid today is more burdensome than a dollar paid thirty years from now.

A simple-minded comparison of total payments says that a one-year loan at a 100 percent interest rate is better than a 150-year loan at a 1 percent interest rate, a conclusion that present-value logic says is nonsense. A total-payments analysis also implies that, for any given loan rate, you are always better off borrowing less money and repaying the loan as soon as possible, because this reduces your total payments. The ultimate strategy, according to a total-payments analysis, is never to borrow any money at all — no matter what the loan rate! Present-value analysis reaches a different conclusion: if the loan rate is favorable (for instance, a below-market loan from the government or your employer), you want to borrow as much as you can for as long as you can.

The Total-Payments Error	**Highlight 9.2**

It is not only unwary borrowers who fall into the total-payments trap; so do otherwise sensible financial advisers. For example, in 1972, *Consumer Reports* compared the purchase of appliances from a builder for $450, repaid over 27 years at 7.75 percent, with the purchase of the same goods from an appliance store for $675, repaid over 2 years at 15 percent, and came to the conclusion that "the appliances would cost $290 more from the builder."* With the builder, the buyer pays $3.32 a month for 12(27) = 324 months, a total of 324($3.32) = $1,075, of which $625 is interest. With the store, the buyer pays $32.71 a month for 24 months, a total of 24($32.71) = $785, of which $110 is interest. The difference is indeed $1,075 − $785 = $290, yet intuition signals that something is amiss. If the builder charges a third less for the appliances and half the interest rate, how can the store's deal be better?

It isn't. *Consumer Reports*' error is that it simply compared the total payments, $1,075 versus $785, ignoring the fact that the payments to the store are made during the next two years, while the payments to the builder are spread over 27 years. In the eyes of *Consumer Reports*, time isn't money; a dollar paid two years from now is the same as a dollar paid 25 years later.

If we accept the argument that time is money, then we want to compare the present values of these two cash flows,

$$\text{Store: } P_S = \frac{\$32.71}{(1 + R)} + \frac{\$32.71}{(1 + R)^2} + \cdots + \frac{\$32.71}{(1 + R)^{24}}$$

$$\text{Builder: } P_B = \frac{\$3.32}{(1 + R)} + \frac{\$3.32}{(1 + R)^2} + \cdots + \frac{\$3.32}{(1 + R)^{324}}$$

Consumer Reports implicitly used $R = 0$ when it just added up the undiscounted monthly payments. It makes more sense to use a required rate of return that reflects the reality that a dollar today is worth more than a dollar tomorrow. Instead of buying from the store and paying $32.71 a month for 24 months, the appliance buyer can pay the builder $3.32 a month and deposit the difference, $32.71 − $3.32 = $29.39, in a bank earning a modest 5 percent return. If so, we can use 5 percent as the annual required return (and $R = 0.05/12$ as the corresponding monthly return) in the above present-value formulas, and the answers work out to be

$$\text{Store: } P_S = \$745.59$$
$$\text{Builder: } P_B = \$589.66$$

---

*"Notes to Home Buyers on Financing Future Schlock," *Consumer Reports*, April 1972, pp. 258–59.

Instead of charging $290 more, the builder actually saves us, in present-value terms, $745.59 − $589.66 = $155.93.

Of course, 5 percent is not the only possible value for the required return. For some values (such as 0 percent), the store's deal is more attractive; for others (such as 5 percent) the builder's looks better. In general, the higher the interest rate, the more attractive the builder's deal is, because those distant payments are less and less burdensome in present-value terms. The accompanying graph compares the present values of the cash flows for a variety of interest rates. For any required return above 2.7 percent, the builder's deal is the better option.

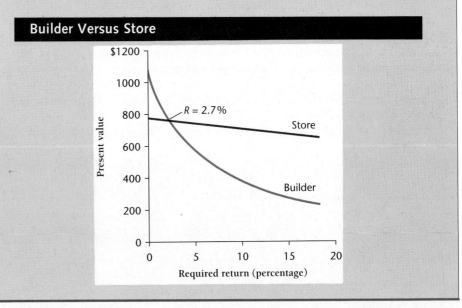

Builder Versus Store

CREATIVE FINANCING

The typical home buyer finances most of the purchase with a mortgage from a bank, savings-and-loan association (S&L), or other lending institution. If the house costs $100,000, the buyer might make a down payment of $20,000 and borrow $80,000 from an S&L, to be repaid over 30 years. At the closing, when the deal is completed, the buyer's $20,000 plus the S&L's $80,000 are given to the seller. Some of it may be used to pay the unpaid balance on the mortgage that financed the seller's original purchase years earlier. The seller is thus paid in full, as is the seller's mortgage institution, and the new homeowner now makes monthly payments to the institution that holds the new mortgage.

In the 1970s and early 1980s, the lethal combination of inflation and the Federal Reserve's efforts to wring inflation out of the economy drove nominal

Buying a House with Creative Financing   **Highlight 9.3**

The following is a fairly typical real-estate transaction made in 1980 on Cape Cod, Massachusetts. At the time, Cape mortgage institutions were charging a minimum of 18 percent and rejecting most loan applications. The seller of this home was eager to move, and agreed to sell for $66,000 with the buyer putting $30,000 down and borrowing $36,000 from the seller at 10.5 percent "amortized over ten years, with a balloon after five." This language means that the buyer makes monthly payments as if it were a ten-year amortized loan, but makes a balloon payment to cover the unpaid balance after five years.

Equation 2 with

$$P = \$36,000$$
$$R = 0.105/12$$
$$n = 120$$

gives the appropriate monthly payment as $485.78. Calculations such as those in Table 9.3 show the unpaid balance after 5 years to be $22,599.08.

What is the value to the buyer of this below-market loan? The seller's 10.5 percent rate is substantially below the 18 percent–plus charged by lending institutions, but it is only a five-year loan. Is this deal worth hundreds, or thousands? To answer this question, we can calculate the present value of the payments, using an 18 percent annual interest rate.

$$P = \frac{\$485.78}{(1 + 0.18/12)} + \frac{\$485.78}{(1 + 0.18/12)^2} + \cdots + \frac{\$485.78}{(1 + 0.18/12)^{60}}$$

$$+ \frac{\$22,599.08}{(1 + 0.18/12)^{60}} = \$28,379.86$$

which is about $7,600 less than the $36,000 borrowed. The buyer is indifferent between this creative financing deal and borrowing from the bank at 18 percent with the seller reducing the price by $7,600.

interest rates skyward. Meanwhile, banks, S&L's, and other deposit intermediaries were restricted by Regulation Q in the rates they could pay depositors. They tried monthly, daily, and then continuous compounding. They gave away dishes, toasters, and even color television sets. But still they could not compete with market interest rates, and they lost depositors.

These credit crunches battered the housing market. In the midst of the 1980 crunch, Federal Reserve chairman Paul Volcker was quoted as saying that he wouldn't be satisfied "until the last buzz saw is silenced."[1] When he was asked if the Fed's tight monetary policies would bring a recession, he responded "Yes, and the sooner the better."[2] Lending institutions raised mortgage rates to un-precedented levels and, even then, rejected loan applications because they had no money to lend. The president of a major savings-and-loan association noted that its mortgage rate was 16⅜ percent, but "we're not making any loans" and he didn't know anyone who was.[3] Home buyers were dissuaded by high mortgage rates and rejected loan applications; sellers were discouraged by the lack of buyers.

Creative financing usually involves a loan from the seller.

In this environment, buyers and sellers turned to **creative financing** — novel ways of financing real-estate deals, usually involving a loan from the seller. In 1980 and 1981, roughly half of all sales of existing homes involved some sort of creative financing. If possible, instead of the buyer turning over enough money to pay the unpaid balance on the seller's mortgage, the buyer assumes the mortgage by taking over the monthly payments. If the old mortgage is at, say 8 percent, assumption is clearly better than borrowing money at 18 percent to pay off the old mortgage. Creative financing also typically involves some owner financing, with the buyer borrowing money from the seller at, say, 12 percent rather than borrowing from an S&L at 18 percent. The buyer appreciates the lower interest rate, and the seller is relieved to have sold the house. Many owner-financing deals have balloon payments due after 3–5 years, with borrowers hoping that loan rates will fall by then, so that they can refinance inexpensively through a conventional lending institution. Observers called the balloons launched in 1980 and 1981 "the ticking time bomb" in the residential real-estate market. Fortunately, mortgage rates finally did drop in 1986, a bit late for some, but just in time for others.

POINTS

During the 1960s and most of the 1970s, mortgage rates averaged some 1½ to 2 percentage points above the interest rates on long-term U.S. government bonds. But government bond rates jumped to 10.8 percent in 1980 and then to 12.9 percent in 1981, whereas many lending institutions were prohibited by state usury laws from charging more than 10 percent on mortgage loans. Unable to charge mortgage rates comparable to the rates of return they could earn on bonds and other investments not subject to usury ceilings, some lending institutions stopped writing mortgage loans. Others discovered that they could circumvent usury ceilings, which restrict stated rather than effective interest rates, by charging **points** (sometimes called an "origination fee" or "buy down"), a fee equal to a specified percentage of the loan paid at the time the loan is made. For example, if you borrow $100,000 via a conventional 30-year mortgage at "12 percent plus 5 points," you receive only $95,000 ($100,000 less the 5 percent points charge), but pay 12 percent interest on the full $100,000 loan.

The Impact of Points on the Effective Loan Rate

Because you pay 12-percent interest on $100,000, the implicit interest rate on the $95,000 you actually receive is somewhat more than 12 percent, the exact value depending on the length of the loan and whether it is repaid early. With a 30-year amortized mortgage, Equation 2 shows that the requisite monthly payments on a $100,000 loan at a 12-percent annual percentage rate (a 1-percent monthly rate) are $1,028.61. The effective interest rate can be determined from Equation 1, setting the present value of these monthly payments equal to the amount actually borrowed,

Points increase the effective loan rate.

$$\$95{,}000 = \frac{\$1{,}028.61}{(1+R)} + \frac{\$1{,}028.61}{(1+R)^2} + \cdots + \frac{\$1{,}028.61}{(1+R)^{360}}$$

and then solving, by trial and error, for the effective monthly interest rate. (Financial calculators can do this very quickly.) The solution turns out to be $R = 0.010583$, implying an annual percentage rate of $12(0.010583) = 0.1270$, or 12.70 percent. Thus the monthly payments are the same on a 30-year 12-percent mortgage with 5 points and a 12.7-percent mortgage with no points.

The average U.S. family moves every six years. What if our borrower changes jobs, marries, divorces, has children, or for some other reason decides to pay off the mortgage before 30 years pass? This effectively shortens the loan and raises the implicit interest rate. Suppose that the loan is paid off after 10 years. The unpaid balance at this point is shown in Table 9.3 to be $93,418. Setting the present value of the borrower's payments equal to the $95,000 actually received,

$$\$95{,}000 = \frac{\$1{,}028.61}{(1+R)} + \frac{\$1{,}028.61}{(1+R)^2} + \cdots + \frac{\$1{,}028.61}{(1+R)^{120}} + \frac{\$93{,}418}{(1+R)^{120}}$$

and solving by trial and error gives a monthly interest rate of $R = 0.0107583$. The annual percentage rate is $12(0.0107583) = 0.1291$, or 12.91 percent, somewhat higher than when the mortgage is kept until the very end. If the mortgage is paid off before 10 years passes, the implicit interest rate rises very quickly, as shown in Table 9.4.

THE PLIGHT OF S&L'S

Interest rates have fallen from their 1981 peaks, and most usury ceilings have been abolished, but points continue to be added to mortgage loans. Many savings-and-loan associations now routinely resell mortgages to the Federal National Mortgage Association ("Fannie Mae"), Government National Mortgage Association ("Ginnie Mae"), Federal Home Loan Mortgage Corporation ("Freddie Mac"), and other nationwide mortgage pools. These pools raise money to purchase mortgages, either by selling bonds or by selling shares to investors, who then receive

Table 9.4 A 30-Year Mortgage at 12 Percent Plus 5 Points

Years to Repayment	Effective Interest Rate
1	17.5%
2	14.9%
5	13.4%
10	12.9%
20	12.7%
30	12.7%

the monthly payments that are forwarded from the original lender. The points charged the home buyer provide an immediate, safe profit to the S&L.

One reason that S&L's now resell so many of their mortgages is their memory of past problems. In the 1960s and early 1970s, S&L's paid their depositors interest rates ranging from 2 percent to 5 percent and lent the money out in mortgages at 4 percent to 8 percent, enough to pay depositors, cover expenses, and make a profit, too. Mortgage rates topped 8 percent in 1971 and hit an unprecedented 10 percent in 1978. Most observers thought that interest rates would soon fall to more normal levels. They were wrong. Interest rates went higher still, to 18 percent plus in 1981, and those who borrowed at 8 percent to 10 percent were lucky to have what, in retrospect, were low-interest loans. The S&L's they had borrowed from were not so lucky.

Having lent virtually all of their depositors' money out in long-term mortgages, S&L's literally could not afford substantial withdrawals. While compelled to raise deposit rates to double-digit levels to hold onto depositors who would otherwise invest their money elsewhere, these S&L's were receiving fixed, single-digit interest rates on mortgages written in the 1960s and 1970s. In 1982, the U.S. League of Savings Associations estimated that the average cost of funds (mainly deposit rates) for S&L's was 11½ percent and that a mortgage would have to yield 13 to 13½ percent to cover these costs and other expenses. Yet 87 percent of the outstanding mortgages at that time had rates below 13 percent, and 58 percent had rates below 10 percent.[4] This is why the aggregate net worth of S&L's fell from $23 billion at the end of 1977 to a frightening −$44 billion at the end of 1981,[5] and why nearly a quarter of the S&L's operating in the 1970s collapsed or merged in the early 1980s.[6] Collecting single-digit rates on their mortgages while paying double-digit rates to depositors, they suffered alarming losses, simply because interest rates had risen unexpectedly.

And what if interest rates had instead fallen unexpectedly? S&L's would have made enormous profits if they could have reduced the rates paid depositors down to 1 percent while still collecting 4 percent–8 percent on mortgages. But, in reality, they would not have been able to keep these high-interest mortgages,

Rising interest rates hurt S&L's who made long-term fixed-rate mortgages.

because borrowers would have refinanced at the new, low interest rates. S&L's made a very asymmetrical bet in the 1950s, 1960s, and early 1970s. Depositors could refinance if rates fell, but S&L's could not renegotiate if rates rose. Heads, depositors win; tails, S&L's lose.

When S&L's realized how expensive this asymmetrical bet could be, they changed the rules of the game by revising their standard mortgage contracts in two important ways:

S&L's now commonly require due-on-sale clauses and prepayment penalties.

1. They inserted "due-on-sale" clauses to make mortgages nonassumable: if the borrower sells the house, the old, possibly low-interest mortgage must be repaid and cannot be passed on to the buyer.
2. To discourage or at least penalize borrowers who refinance when interest rates go down, they inserted **prepayment penalties,** additional charges that the borrower must pay the S&L if the loan is repaid early. Borrowers are, of course, not thrilled with prepayment penalties, and fourteen state legislatures have outlawed them. Points can, however, serve as a rough substitute, because 5 points on a new loan is about as discouraging as a 5 percent prepayment penalty on the old.

ADJUSTABLE-RATE LOANS

Imposing prepayment penalties and passing mortgages on to mortgage pools were two S&L responses to the losses sustained in the early 1980s. Another was a shift from fixed-rate mortgages to **adjustable-rate loans,** in which the loan rate rises and falls with market interest rates. If the problem is that the interest rates on old mortgages are fixed while deposit rates increase, then the solution is either to fix deposit rates or to adjust mortgage rates. S&L's tried both — encouraging time deposits with rates that are fixed for 2, 5, or even 10 years, and encouraging mortgages with interest that varies with market interest rates. Most bank loans to businesses today also have variable rates — for example, the current prime rate, or another benchmark rate, plus 2 percent.

In an adjustable-rate loan, the loan rate changes with market interest rates.

These flexible-rate loans go by a variety of names: adjustable-rate, variable-rate, renegotiable-rate, rollover, and so on. In each case, the lender adjusts the interest rate to reflect current financial conditions. Often there is a formula that ties the loan rate to current market rates — approximating the rates paid depositors, with some additional percentage points tacked on to cover expenses. Many S&L's use the yield on 1-year Treasury bills; others use explicit industry estimates of the average cost of funds. Many variable-rate mortgages have caps limiting the rate adjustment to, say, 2 percent in any given year and 5 percent during the life of the mortgage. The widespread use of variable-rate mortgages was first permitted in April 1981, and during 1982–85 roughly half of all new mortgages had variable rates.

There are a number of ways to adjust the payment stream as the loan rate varies. The essential rule is that the present value of the payments equals the amount borrowed or, equivalently, that the amount by which the monthly payment exceeds the interest due on the unpaid balance reduces the unpaid balance each month, until it hits zero.

Variable Payments

A benchmark payment structure is provided by amortizing the loan at a specified interest rate to obtain a planned constant stream of payments; for instance, a 30-year $100,000 mortgage at 12 percent implies monthly payments of $1,028.61, some of which is interest on the unpaid balance and the remainder of which reduces that balance. As interest rates fluctuate, each month's payment can rise or fall with changes in the interest charged on the unpaid balance, keeping the planned reduction of principal on course. The borrower pays somewhat more than $1,028.61 if the interest rate rises above 12 percent and somewhat less if it falls below.

As an example, look again at Table 9.3. As shown, after the first month's payment, the unpaid balance declines to $99,971.39. If the interest rate charged in the second month rises to 12.2 percent, then the interest owed increases by $16.67, to $(0.122/12)\$99,971.39 = \$1,016.38$, and the monthly payment must also increase by $16.67 in order to reduce the unpaid balance by $28.90 as planned:

Planned		Actual	
Interest	$999.71	Interest	$1,016.38
Principal	28.90	Principal	28.90
Total payment	$1,028.61	Total payment	$1,045.28

By adjusting the monthly payment, the unpaid balance declines as scheduled and reaches zero after 30 years.

Negative Amortization

Another possibility is to hold the monthly payments constant (at least temporarily) by varying the division of the monthly payment between interest and principal. Instead of increasing the monthly payment by $16.67 to cover the extra interest due, the repayment of principal can be reduced by $16.67:

Planned		Actual	
Interest	$999.71	Interest	$1,016.38
Principal	28.90	Principal	12.23
Total payment	$1,028.61	Total payment	$1,028.61

If the interest rate rises so much that the fixed $1,028.61 monthly payment is insufficient to cover the interest charge, there is **negative amortization**, in that the unpaid balance actually increases.

Negative amortization occurs when the loan payment doesn't cover the interest charge.

If the monthly payments are held constant and the interest rate stays above 12 percent, the unpaid balance will continue to decline more slowly than originally planned and will not hit zero after 30 years. A balloon payment can be made at that time, or the loan can be lengthened. If, on the other hand, the interest rate averages less than the planned 12 percent, the loan will be paid off before the end of 30 years.

One variation is a temporarily fixed payment. Here the borrower selects a period of time, usually one to five years, during which the monthly payments are constant even while the interest rate being charged varies. After the specified period of fixed monthly payments is over, a new payment schedule is reestablished to get the unpaid balance back on schedule.

In many business and personal loans (for example, lines of credit from a bank, loans from a stockbroker, or credit-card balances), there is no set repayment schedule. Each month, interest is charged at a fixed or variable rate on the unpaid balance, and the borrower chooses how much to repay. The unpaid balance grows if the payment does not cover the interest charge, and declines if it does.

GRADUATED-PAYMENT LOANS (Optional)

A conventional amortized loan sets a constant-dollar payment for the length of the loan. During inflationary periods, the real value of these monthly payments declines steadily. For instance, if prices rise by 10 percent a year, the price level will nearly double every seven years and, at the end of a 30-year mortgage, be some 17½ times higher than when the loan began:

$$1.10^{30} = 17.45$$

As a consequence, the real value of the constant monthly payment at the beginning of the mortgage is some 17½ times the real value at the end, and so is the sacrifice needed to make these payments. Even with a 5 percent inflation rate, the price level doubles in 14 years and at the end of 30 years is some 4.3 times the initial level.

In place of constant nominal monthly payments, it is more reasonable to have monthly payments that are constant in real terms. Imagine, for example, that you are just beginning a career and expect your salary to grow at the same rate as prices in general. If you have a mortgage with constant nominal payments, the fraction of your income spent on housing is highest when you are young and then declines steadily. Isn't it more sensible to have mortgage payments grow with your income, keeping the ratio of housing expenses to income roughly constant?

| Highlight 9.4 | **A Great Investment** |

The best investment that many consumers can possibly make is to pay off their credit-card debt. The interest rate that banks charge on credit-card balances is typically around 18 percent and often much higher. And, as of 1991, none of this interest is tax deductible. This means that paying off $100 of credit-card debt saves $18 in interest charges, which is like investing $100 and receiving an $18 profit after taxes. In the 33 percent tax bracket, this is equivalent to earning an unheard of 27 percent return before taxes!

Some who don't have spare cash to pay off their credit-card borrowings may be able to take out home-equity loans, which usually have much lower interest rates and are generally tax deductible. Borrowing at a tax-deductible 12 percent to pay off a nondeductible 18 percent loan is extremely profitable. Even better, if you can manage it, is never to use a credit card to borrow money. Credit cards are a wonderful convenience if you pay the monthly balance immediately but extremely expensive if you don't.

Unaffordable Housing

As a practical matter, constant mortgage payments may be such a large fraction of income in the early years that a young household cannot qualify for a mortgage even though it will have plenty of income later. Fannie Mae requires a 20 percent down payment and advises that housing expenses (including mortgage-loan payments, homeowner's insurance, and taxes) not exceed 28 percent of household income. (For many years, the rule at lending institutions was a more conservative 25 percent of income.) In July 1989, the average price of a new home was $174,500 and the average conventional mortgage was for $125,300 for 28.6 years at a 10.06 percent interest rate, plus 2.42 points. The average new buyer put $49,200 down (plus $3,000 in points) and accepted a mortgage with monthly payments of $1,114, which, by Fannie Mae's guidelines and ignoring insurance and taxes, required an annual income of about $48,000. Needless to say, few young households had $52,200 in cash and an annual income of $48,000.

Mortgage Payments That Increase With Income

To ease the financial burden on young households who expect nominal income to grow steadily (as is particularly likely during inflationary periods), there are **graduated-payment mortgages (GPM)** in which the monthly payments are initially low and then grow with income. Consider a couple whose monthly income is now $2,000 and is expected to grow by about 5 percent a year, and

In a graduated-payment loan, the monthly payment increases over time.

who want to borrow $100,000 for 30 years at the prevailing 10 percent mortgage rate. With a conventional loan, the requisite monthly payment is $877.57, 44 percent of the household's current income — a fact that would probably cause the loan application to be rejected — but only 10 percent of the household's projected $8,935 monthly income 30 years from now.

We can create an alternative, graduated-payment plan with mortgage payments growing by 5 percent a year. (The exact formula is not important here.) The first monthly payment works out to be $537.79 and the last to be $2,402.69, each 27 percent of monthly income. A graduated-payment mortgage attempts to keep housing expenses at a relatively constant share of household income, making mortgages more accessible for people who expect their income to rise as time passes.

In practice, the monthly payments in a typical GPM contract begin low, rise gradually for 5–10 years, and then level off. If the early payments are not enough to cover the interest due on the loan, then there is negative amortization for a while. This is true of our example, in that the first month's $537.79 payment does not cover the interest of (0.10/12)$100,000 = $833.33. The unpaid balance grows for several years until the rising monthly payments overtake the monthly interest. Franco Modigliani, a Nobel Prize–winning economist and enthusiastic advocate of GPMs, attributes their lukewarm acceptance by lenders and borrowers to an irrational distaste for negative amortization.[7] Even some otherwise informed observers are put off by this characteristic. In a 1983 article on mortgage alternatives, *Business Week* treats negative amortization as a drawback and goes on to state that[8]

> *In the long run it's more expensive than other mortgages. In fact, a $67,000 GPM at a fixed 15% rate would start out with monthly payments that are $120 cheaper than the conventional mortgage but would end up costing about $16,000 more over 30 years.*

The total-payments error again! The borrower pays more total interest with a GPM because the unpaid balance grows at first instead of declining, and you pay more interest whenever you borrow more money for a longer period of time. Here your monthly payments are lower at the beginning and higher at the end, and *Business Week* obtains its $16,000 difference by simply adding up the total payments, regardless of when they are made. Discounted at the mortgage rate, the present values of a GPM and a conventional mortgage are exactly the same — the amount borrowed.

SUMMARY

Borrowed money is often used to finance the purchase of real and financial assets. This use of other people's money creates leverage, in that the return on your relatively small investment depends on the profitability of a much-larger investment. If the total investment earns a rate of return larger than the interest rate paid on the borrowed money, this differential is multiplied by the degree of leverage. Leverage is a double-edged sword, in that any shortfall between the investment's return and the loan rate is magnified, too.

Loan payments are calculated so that the present value of the payments, discounted at the quoted loan rate, is equal to the amount borrowed. In a conventional amortized mortgage, the constant monthly payments cover the interest due and also reduce the principal — slowly at first, rapidly at the end — so that the last payment reduces the unpaid balance to zero. In a balloon loan, the periodic payments do not reduce the principal sufficiently (often not at all), and a large balloon payment must be made at maturity to cover the still-substantial unpaid balance.

Loans are often evaluated and compared on the basis of the total (undiscounted) payments made during the life of the loan — a flawed procedure that favors borrowing as little as possible for as brief a period as possible. A present-value analysis is more appropriate, discounting the loan payments by a required rate of return that depends on market-interest rates.

Points, a percentage fee paid when a loan is made, raise the effective interest rate on the loan — especially if it is a short-term loan or a loan that is repaid early. On an adjustable-rate loan, the interest rate is periodically adjusted to reflect current market rates or the lender's cost of funds. These adjustments must alter either the size of the payments or the amount of time it takes to repay the loan. When the loan rate increases and monthly payments don't, there can be negative amortization, so that the loan payments don't cover the interest due and the unpaid balance increases.

In a conventional constant-payment mortgage, the fraction of household income devoted to mortgage payments is high when the household is young and declines as its income grows over time. Graduated-payment mortgages were developed so that monthly payments would rise with income and thus be a relatively constant fraction of household income. In either case, the present value of the payments, at the quoted loan rate, is equal to the amount borrowed.

IMPORTANT TERMS

adjustable-rate loans
amortized loan
balloon loans
creative financing
graduated-payment mortgages (GPM)

leverage
points
prepayment penalties
negative amortization

EXERCISES

1. You want to invest $80,000 for one year but have only $20,000. You borrow an additional $60,000 at 10 percent, and owe $66,000 one year from now. What is the percentage return on your $20,000 if the rate of return earned on the entire $80,000 is 10 percent? 50 percent? −10 percent?

2. You have inherited $50,000 and hope to multiply your new wealth by buying undeveloped

land in a resort area. You are considering borrowing $50,000 and buying a $100,000 parcel, or else borrowing $450,000 and buying a $500,000 property. Assume that either way you will have to pay back your loan plus 12 percent interest after a year and that each property will appreciate equally. If, for instance, property in this area appreciates by 20 percent, you will either make $20,000 − $6,000 = $14,000 or $100,000 − $54,000 = $46,000, depending on which property you buy. Fill in the rest of the table below, showing the net gain on your $50,000 wealth. For what rate of property appreciation do these two strategies do equally well? How much leverage do you have with each strategy?

Property Appreciation	Borrow $50,000		Borrow $450,000	
	Dollars	Percent	Dollars	Percent
−10%				
0%				
10%				
20%	$14,000	28%	$46,000	92%
30%				
40%				

3. Banks make profits with other people's money, investing what they have borrowed from their depositors. Consider a bank for which, out of every $100 that it invests, $95 is borrowed and $5 is net worth. The rate of return that it pays its depositors is generally specified ahead of time, whereas the rate it earns on its investments depends on loan defaults and other economic conditions. What is the annual rate of return on the bank's net worth if it borrows at 7 percent and invests at 7 percent? If it borrows at 7 percent and invests at 9 percent? If it borrows at 7 percent, what rate of return on its investments will bankrupt the bank in one year (a −100 percent return on net worth)?

4. You are going to borrow $10,000 for 10 years at a 10 percent interest rate. What is the size of your payments if you make constant
   a. annual payments?
   b. monthly payments?

   Why are the annual payments less than 12 times the monthly payments?

5. In 1980, Chrysler announced that interest rates (then about 20 percent on car loans) were "7 percent too high" and that it was consequently giving a 7 percent rebate on new cars financed by car loans. Consider a new car costing $10,000 for which you will put $2,000 down and pay the remainder over 5 years with a conventional, amortized monthly car loan. Would you rather have the price reduced 7 percent to $9,300 or have the loan rate reduced to 13 percent?

6. Before the 1969 Truth-in-Lending law, a finance company using the "add-on" method could lend you $1,000, charge you $100 interest (with $1,100/12 = $91.67 due each month for 12 months), and say that the interest rate was only 10 percent. What is the true annual percentage rate on such a loan?

7. At age 82, Fred Benson won a $50,000 state lottery prize paying $100 a month for 500 months. He sold his claim to a local bank for $13,500 and threw the biggest party in the history of Block Island. What is the bank's implicit rate of return on its investment? (*Hint:* if this were a $13,500 mortgage to be repaid in 500 monthly $100 installments, what would the implicit mortgage rate be?)

8. Rent-A-Center rents televisions and other appliances by the week without a credit check, allowing them to apply the rental payments toward eventual purchase; for example, for a 19-inch portable TV that can be purchased from a discount store for $229, Rent-A-Center charges $9.95 a week for 78 weeks.[9] If a customer does buy the set by paying $9.95 a week for 78 weeks, what is the implicit annual interest rate on this $229 TV?

9. On August 28, 1986, General Motors announced "The Big One," a 2.9 percent interest rate on 36-month loans for its 1986 models; Ford and Chrysler followed with similar deals. If you are buying a $12,000 car and have $2,000 for a down payment, would you rather borrow the difference at 2.9 percent or have the price reduced by $1,000 and borrow from a credit union at 10 percent?

10. A 1986 *Newsweek* article said of the 2.9 percent loan rate offered by GM and the 0 percent rate from American Motors,[10]

    Don't think this is a never-again opportunity. The American auto market is going to be flooded with new cars in the years ahead . . . there seems no way to avoid a market where there will be too many cars chasing too few passengers. So what will come next — a pitch featuring negative interest rates?

    How would a negative interest rate work? In particular, would the total of the monthly payments on a $10,000 loan with a negative interest rate amount to more or less than $10,000?

11. A consumer-finance book advises that[11]

    A second method of reducing costs is to make the largest down payment possible and repay in the shortest period of time.

    How does this strategy reduce costs? Would you recommend this strategy, no matter what the loan rate?

12. The owner of a Washington, D.C., real-estate firm says that an equation basic to real estate is[12]

    Principal × Interest Rate per Period
        × Interest Periods (time)
        = Total Interest Paid

    Explain why the total interest paid on a $100,000 conventional 30-year mortgage at 12 percent is *not* $100,000 × 12%/year × 30 years = $360,000.

13. Mr. I. M. Gone moved to Houston in 1978 and had to sell his home in Philadelphia. He asked $100,000, but mortgage rates were a staggering 18 percent, and many banks weren't approving any new mortgage loans. Mr. Gone finally agreed to owner-financing by lending the buyer $80,000 for thirty years at 12 percent. The buyer came up with the remaining $20,000. From the buyer's standpoint, how large a price cut was this owner-financing equivalent to?

14. Ms. Yup must sell her Houston home in order to take a job in California. She has two offers on her house. The first is $160,000 cash. The second is $180,000, of which $30,000 is cash and the remaining $150,000 is an owner-financed, 30-year mortgage at 8 percent. Which offer is the more financially attractive?

15. In 1985, a Los Angeles mortgage company was charging 15 percent plus 10 points on second mortgages. What is their implicit annual percentage rate of interest on a 20-year $100,000 loan that is not repaid early?

16. On May 1, 1986, Imperial Savings in California offered conventional 15-year fixed-rate mortgages for either 9.875 percent with 1 point or 9 percent with 4.5 points. Explain, without doing the necessary calculations, how you, the home buyer, would choose between these two alternatives.

17. In 1985, the *Los Angeles Times* described the "sudden, almost explosive, acceptance of the 15-year fixed rate mortgage," in place of a traditional 30-year mortgage, citing a Mortgage Bankers Association estimate that from "minimal acceptance" just a year ago, the 15-year loans now account for $1/7$ of all new mortgages.[13] In explanation, the *Times* cites "common sense economics":

    At the end of 30 years, that $100,000 mortgage [at 13 percent, with $1,106.20 monthly payments] has cost the home buyer a grand total of $398,232 — a mind boggling $298,232 in interest. . . . *by cutting the same mortgage down to 15 from 30 years (and raising the monthly payments from $1,106.20 to $1,265.25), the total cost to the home buyer is $227,745 for a net saving in interest of $170,487.*

While you certainly can't quarrel with the arithmetic of the 15-year mortgage — and the sudden popularity of it . . . there are limits on how far the trend can go," according to Fred E. Case of UCLA's Graduate School of Management. *"Not everyone who sees the sense of the 15-year mortgage is in a position to qualify for one."*

The *Times* also quotes an anonymous "cynical" midwestern lender:

I'd like to think that home buyers have suddenly gotten smart — that they've looked at those figures and realized how much interest they're paying over 30 years. God knows they've been dumb about it long enough.

Why, by their reckoning, is a 30-year mortgage so expensive? Is there any interest rate at which you would choose a 30-year rather than a 15-year mortgage at the same interest rate?

18. Find the error in the following financial analysis of three auto deals (Chrysler (no rebate), Ford (5 percent rebate), and GM (12.8 percent financing).[14]

Assume, for instance, that you are going to buy a car with a $10,000 sticker price. It would normally be financed for 48 months at 16.5% interest . . . after a 20% or $2,000 down payment. If the manufacturer doesn't provide any assistance in the purchase of the car, the total cost at the end of the four-year financing period would be $12,979.04 according to Detroit Bank & Trust. Monthly payments would amount to $228.73. That is what a buyer would pay under Chrysler's incentive plan, which offers no help on the purchase price.

If you bought that same car from Ford, the purchase price plus financing interest would amount to $12,479.04, reflecting a 5% or $500

rebate paid to you by Ford and used as part of your $2,000 down payment. Again monthly payments would be $228.73. You could lower the total cost and the monthly payments slightly if you used the rebate to increase the down payment to $2,500.

The same $10,000 car purchased from a GM dealer under the 12.8% financing program, which expires May 31, would cost $12,263.68. Monthly payments would drop to $213.83. Thus, it appears that the GM financing plan saves the customer the most money in the direct purchase of the car, all other things being equal.

19. A real-estate broker argued that Mike, after buying a $100 raffle ticket, might walk away from the prize, a $150,000 house, because (a) he will have to pay the IRS $75,000 (in a 50 percent tax bracket then prevailing); (b) "Mike does not have $75,000 in cash to pay the tax; he hardly had the $100 for the raffle ticket"; and (c) if he borrows this $75,000 from a bank at 18 percent for 20 years, he will have to pay $1,157 a month × 12 months per year × 20 years = $333,120 total mortgage payments on the house.[15] Would you walk away from this prize?

20. *Consumer Reports* gave the following advice about auto loans.[16]

The nice thing about auto loans is that you can locate the lemons before you sign on the dotted line. Just keep your eye on the APR — the Annual Percentage Rate. . . . Obviously, the lower the APR, the better. Another point to keep in mind: the shorter the loan the better . . . a one-year loan is much cheaper than a four-year loan. Say you borrow $4,000 at 11%. For a one-year loan, the total interest would be $242. The total interest for a four-year loan would be $963 — about four times as much. Of course, the monthly payments for the longer loan would be smaller, but remember that you pay heavily for that convenience.

a. Why is the $242 total interest on a one-year loan far less than 11 percent of $4,000?
b. Why is the total interest on a four-year loan more than on a one-year loan?
c. Why are the monthly payments smaller on the four-year loan?
d. What is the present value of each stream of monthly payments, discounted at an 11 percent required return?
e. Assuming the same interest rate on each loan, are there any circumstances in which "the shorter the loan, the better" is not true?

21. Critically evaluate this advice.[17]

Want to build equity in your home fast, slash 60 percent off the total interest you pay on a mortgage held to maturity, retire the major debt of your lifetime — your home loan — before the kids' college bills come steamrolling in?

The 15-year-fixed- or adjustable-rate mortgage (ARM) can help you accomplish all that for a relatively low price. For $105 more per month, a 15-year, fixed-rate mortgage saves you $115,000 in interest charges (compared to a 30-year fixed-rate mortgage) over the life of the mortgage. A 15-year ARM saves you $95,400 in interest charges (compared to a 30-year fixed-rate mortgage) in this example [$75,000 borrowed for 30 years at 12% or for 15 years at 9.25% the first year and 15% thereafter] provided by Carteret Savings and Loan Association of Morristown, New Jersey. Even though monthly ARM payments may increase each year (if interest rates rise), you come out ahead, thanks to a maximum 15 percent interest-rate ceiling built into this loan agreement. . . .

If you can afford modestly higher monthly payments and meet stricter borrowing requirements, there's no denying the advantages of a 15-year versus a 30-year mortgage.

22. "Insurance companies tend to be leveraged at between 10 and 20 to 1 for life companies and 4 or 5 to 1 for casualty companies."[18] If you were assigned to estimate the leverage ratio for a company, which of these data would you use, and how: sales, before-tax profits, after-tax profits, assets, liabilities, net worth, or stock price?

23. In a biweekly mortgage, monthly payments are calculated as if the mortgage were a conventional 30-year amortized monthly mortgage, but then half this calculated monthly amount is paid every other week. The result is that[19]

at 9.25% interest, a biweekly $100,000 mortgage pays off in slightly more than 21 years, instead of 30, and saves $63,819 in interest.

"And," as G. Randall Kinst, director of secondary marketing for Mortgage Loans America, a large wholesale mortgage banking firm located in Campbell, Calif., says, "a 30-year conventional loan would need an unheard of 6.7% interest rate to achieve the same savings realized on a biweekly."

How do biweekly payments reduce the interest paid and the length of the mortgage? Would you choose a 9.25 percent biweekly or a 6.7 percent monthly mortgage?

24. One California mortgage banker set up a "simulated" biweekly plan:[20]

It simply sets itself up as a trust, collects biweekly mortgage payments from its clients and then turns around and pays their lender the regular monthly payment. . . . What it amounts to is simply one extra payment a year being made on the mortgage, so it's slower — by about seven months — in paying off the mortgage.

Why would a mortgage banker do this for its clients?

25. In July 1986 an elderly couple received a letter from their savings bank that began[21]

We are very pleased to offer you the opportunity to save a minimum of $1,370.91 in future interest on your mortgage loan. Yes, you can save $1,370.91 in future interest by increasing your monthly payment by only $25.00 per month beginning in August. This extra $25.00 per month *will also pay off your mortgage 3 years and 7 months early.*

An enclosed analysis showed that this couple had an unpaid balance of $8,479.53 on a 7.25 percent loan, with 11 years and 11 months of $89.00 monthly payments remaining, and that

With your present monthly payment of $89.00, your future interest paid over the next 11 years 11 months will be $4,185.04

By increasing your monthly payment by $25.00 per month, your future

interest over the next 8 years 4 months will be   <u>2,814.13</u>

Interest savings (will also pay off your mortgage 3 years 7 months early) $ 1,370.91

a. If we look at the total payments, principal plus interest, how much does the couple save?
b. Why does an extra $25 a month reduce the length of the mortgage?
c. Why do you think the bank offered this opportunity?

Optional Chapter

THE

STOCK MARKET

If you don't know who you are, the stock market is an expensive place to find out.

George Goodman

Loans, bonds, and other fixed-income securities are legally binding agreements to pay specified amounts of money. Corporate stock, in contrast, represents equity — ownership of a company — and the return, dividends plus capital gains, depend on the profitability of the company. This chapter examines the nature of corporate stock and the markets in which it is traded. We will see why firms choose to incorporate and how stock is traded, after issuance, on the stock exchanges and in the over-the-counter market. We will discuss why the value of a stock depends on its cash flow and on interest rates. We will also see some examples of the madness of crowds, instances in which investors as a group pushed stock prices to levels that, in retrospect, were unjustified. Finally, we will consider the important and provocative assertion that, because financial markets are efficient, changes in stock prices are unpredictable.

STOCK ISSUANCE AND TRADING

A corporation's legal owners are its common shareholders.

The owners of a corporation's **common stock** are the legal owners of the firm, the name indicating that the shareholders own the firm "in common." Although they do not normally make production, pricing, and personnel decisions, shareholders elect (normally with one vote per share) a board of directors that hires the top executives and supervises their management of the firm. Some firms have two or more classes of common stock; for example, Ford Motor Company's Class B common stock, owned by the Ford family and related trusts, is not publicly traded and has 40 percent of the total stockholder vote though it makes up only 15 percent of the total outstanding shares.

Debt and Equity

The loans, bonds, and other fixed-income securities issued by a corporation are legal debts; common stock is equity, a claim to the residual value of the firm after its debts have been paid. An extremely condensed balance sheet of a hypothetical firm is shown in Table 10.1. This firm has $100 million in assets, mostly plant, equipment, and other real assets. Because it has $40 million in debts outstanding, shareholders' equity (what would be left if the firm were liquidated and the debts repaid) comes to $60 million. If there are 5 million shares outstanding, this works out to $12 a share. This estimate of the firm's value per share is called the **book value** of the firm's stock, because it is derived from the firm's books — the accountants' balance sheets.

> A firm's book value is tabulated by its accountants, using historical cost data, and need not equal the firm's market value.

The market price of a firm's stock may be above or below the book value, because investors don't value a firm in the same way that accountants do. Assets are generally carried on the accountants' books at original cost and, in the case of buildings and equipment, depreciated over time to indicate wear and tear. However, if land prices and construction costs increase, the replacement cost of a firm's real assets may be far larger than their original cost, let alone their depreciated cost. If so, the firm's stock may be worth far more than its book value, here $12 a share. On the other hand, a firm may have very expensive assets that are not profitable, and investors won't pay $12 a share for a company that won't make money and can't afford to pay dividends. A banana plantation on Mount Everest may cost millions to construct, but not be worth a dime.

Bondholders hold legally binding promissory notes. If the firm does not earn enough money to pay these debts in full, then it may be forced into bankruptcy, so that its assets are sold and the proceeds paid to the bondholders and other creditors. The stockholders get nothing but their worthless stock certificates and, we are told, an expensive lesson. On the other hand, if the firm grows and prospers, the bondholders receive only the fixed income they have been promised, nothing more, whereas the stockholders, as owners of the firm, share these growing profits. The firm's directors, acting on behalf of the shareholders, decide how much of these profits to distribute as dividends and how much to retain for buying more plants and equipment to expand the firm.

Limited Liability

The legal concept of a corporation in the modern sense began in England in the early stages of the industrial revolution with the intention of dividing ownership among many investors and protecting them if the firm is mismanaged. Most investors are "outside" shareholders in the sense that they have nothing to

Table 10.1   A Small Firm (values in millions)

Assets		Liabilities	
Real	$ 90	Debt	$ 40
Financial	10	Equity	60
	$100		$100

do with the day-to-day operations of the company, leaving that to the firm's management. While stockholders are the legal owners of a corporation, they have **limited liability** in that they are not personally responsible for its debts. Their potential loss is limited to the amount of money they have invested in the firm's stock. Limited liability is the reason many British and Canadian firms have "Limited" or the abbreviation "Ltd." as part of the company's name.

A corporation's shareholders have limited liability.

If a corporation cannot pay its debts, then its bankruptcy leaves the shareholders with worthless stock certificates — a disappointing outcome, but still better than having to come up with additional money to satisfy the firm's creditors. Presumably, this limited liability encourages people to invest in stock, becoming part owners of large businesses.

Corporate shareholders are subject to double taxation.

There are disadvantages to being a public corporation; perhaps the most important being the double taxation of earnings. Suppose that a company earns $10 a share and wants to distribute this to the owners. If the company is not a corporation, each owner receives $10 and pays perhaps a 28 percent personal income tax, keeping $7.20. If the business is a corporation, though, then it must pay a 34 percent corporate income tax, leaving $6.60 to be distributed as dividends, on which shareholders then pay a 28 percent tax — leaving each only 0.72($6.60) = $4.75. The double taxation amounts to an effective 52.5 percent tax rate!

Investment Banking

Businesses typically begin as small, privately held companies. Imagine that you have an idea for the proverbial better mousetrap and want to produce and market these wonders. After exhausting your own savings, you may be able to borrow some additional funds at, say, a 10 percent interest rate from relatives, a bank, or sympathetic investors. But their enthusiasm is dampened by your inexperience and lack of tangible assets. If sales happen to be disappointing, as they usually are with new businesses, you won't be able to repay your debts and their hoped-for 10 percent interest will turn into a 100 percent loss.

If you can't find willing lenders, you may have to settle for partners, investors willing to bankroll your expansion in return for a share of the profits. Although the possibility of a 100 percent loss is still there, they now have the chance of large profits, too. You can form a partnership or, instead, a corporation to obtain limited liability. Businesses can incorporate without selling shares to the public: an individual can form a sole-owner corporation and a small group (35 or fewer investors) can form a privately held corporation. But if your small business proves successful, there may come a point at which your ambitious plans for expansion require a great deal of money and you decide to sell shares to the public at large.

The public offering will have to meet the disclosure requirements of the Securities and Exchange Commission (SEC). An investment banker (such as Morgan Stanley, Salomon Brothers, or Goldman Sachs) will prepare a prospectus for potential investors, revealing relevant data about your past performance, laying out your plans, and giving boldface warnings: "These shares are very risky." An advertisement may appear in *The Wall Street Journal* announcing the planned incorporation and stating that "This announcement is neither an offer to sell nor a solicitation of offers to buy any of these securities. The offering is made only by the Prospectus." Listed will be several underwriters, including your investment banker and others that have agreed to distribute the shares. This syndicate of investment bankers has regular customers — including insurance companies, pension funds, and individual investors — who can be persuaded to buy shares. The underwriters may also agree to buy for their own accounts any shares they cannot sell to the public.

You and your investment banker will agree on the price at which the shares are offered. Experienced financial analysts will scrutinize your books and come up with an estimate of what the company is worth — how much you could sell it for. Suppose that the number they come up with is $20 million. (If we're dreaming, let's make it a good one.) Now, you don't intend to sell your company and walk away. You want funds to expand and, in return, are willing to share your company with others. If you were to raise, say, another $20 million, then you would have $40 million in assets — your company, which is worth $20 million by itself, plus $20 million in cash. In addition, this cash will not sit idle, but rather be used to enlarge your business. With this new money and your patented mousetrap, you can make enough profit so that the company will be worth at least $50 million.

Armed with these conservative estimates, you issue 10 million shares of stock, priced at $5 a share. Six million you keep for yourself and your original partners, and your investment banker pledges to sell four million at $5 a share to raise the intended $20 million. The buyers are getting, with each share, one ten-millionth of a $50 million company. You and your initial partners get shares worth $30 million — $20 million for the company as it is today, plus $10 million for the profit you can make with this new money. If things work out as planned, everyone will be happy.

Notice that incorporation apparently creates instant millionaires. You were plugging along, building mousetrap after mousetrap, working long hours and plowing every penny back into the firm. You lived a frugal, workaholic lifestyle and didn't look at all like the rich and famous folk seen on television. Then comes incorporation and, all of a sudden, you (and your initial partners, if any)

Investment bankers help businesses issue securities.

have stock worth $30 million. George Goodman calls these instant riches "supermoney" and wrote a book with that title. What might be overlooked is that, as owner of a profitable firm, you were really a millionaire all along. Your mousetrap business was worth millions, and incorporation disclosed this fact by transforming your illiquid business into liquid securities.

The Stock Exchanges

After issuance, stock is traded on organized exchanges or over the counter.

Once issued, shares of stock trade in the secondary market, either on an organized exchange or by other means. The most important stock exchange is the New York Stock Exchange (NYSE), followed by the American Stock Exchange (AMEX) and various regional exchanges (Boston, Philadelphia, Pacific, and so on). Securities that aren't listed on organized exchanges are said to be traded **over the counter (OTC).** The prices of many, but by no means all, OTC securities are reported on the National Association of Securities Dealers (NASDAQ) system.

The exchanges are closed on weekends and some holidays. On a typical trading day on the NYSE, about 110 million shares are traded with an aggregate market value of around $4 billion. Table 10.2 compares the NYSE, AMEX, and NASDAQ at the end of 1989. (The regional exchanges, added together, are roughly comparable to the AMEX.) The average NYSE company had a market value of $1.3 billion, 11 times the size of the average AMEX firm and 18 times that of the average NASDAQ company. The NYSE is called the "big board," not only because of the number of listed companies and the volume of trading, but also because the NYSE companies are mostly the biggest and the best.

To be listed on the NYSE, a corporation must have $18 million in tangible assets, before-tax profits of $2.5 million, at least 1.1 million publicly held shares with an aggregate market value of at least $18 million, and at least 2,000 stockholders owning 100 shares or more. Some large companies have chosen not to be listed; for example, Apple Computer is not, and (to avoid the NYSE's disclosure requirements) many financial institutions are not. But most companies believe that being listed on the NYSE makes their stock more attractive to investors; about half of all investors own only NYSE stocks.

The NYSE and other organized exchanges are physical locations, trading floors, where securities are bought and sold by exchange members, who have seats on the exchange (a terminology dating back to when members had armchairs to rest in). There are 1,366 seats on the New York Stock Exchange, which are bought, sold, or leased at negotiated prices reflecting supply and demand. The price of a seat began at $1,000 in 1850, reached $625,000 in 1929, before the stock market crash, and has fluctuated considerably since, trading for $250,000 in 1965, $40,000 in 1976, and $1 million in 1987.

Each stock traded on the NYSE is assigned to a **specialist** who acts as both a broker (an agent trading for others) and a dealer (trading for himself or herself). As a broker, the specialist collects orders from other members of the exchange and executes a transaction when someone is willing to buy at a price at which

The Reporting of Stock Trading

Daily newspapers record summaries of stock trading on the previous business day. Here is an example of the trading in one stock on November 8, 1989, as reported in *The Wall Street Journal* on November 9 of that year:

52 Weeks Hi	Lo	Stock	Sym	Div	Yld %	PE	Vol 100s	Hi	Lo	Close	Net Chg
$70\frac{3}{8}$	$42\frac{7}{8}$	FstInterste	I	3.00	5.4	8	1061	$56\frac{3}{8}$	$55\frac{1}{2}$	56	$+\frac{5}{8}$

Many company names are abbreviated to save space. Here, "FstInterste" is an abbreviation of First Interstate, one of the nation's largest banks; the symbol I is used by the exchange for recording transactions. After finding the company in the financial pages, investors invariably look first at the last two columns on the right, showing the closing price and the change in closing price from the day before. The last trade of First Interstate stock on November 8 was at a price of $56 a share, up $\frac{5}{8}$ of a dollar from the closing price the day before. Moving leftward, we see the high and low prices for the day and the volume of trading (in hundreds of shares). On this day, 106,100 shares of First Interstate were traded at various prices ranging from $55.50 per share to $56.375 per share.

Right after the company's name and symbol is the latest declared annual dividend, here $3 a share. The "Yld %" is the dividend yield, calculated by dividing the dividend by the closing price of the stock ($3/$56 = 0.054, or 5.4 percent). A 5.4 percent dividend yield may seem like a modest return, but shareholders were undoubtedly expecting dividends to increase in the future and to earn capital gains, too.

The reported PE (price-earnings ratio) is the ratio of the firm's closing price to the most recently reported annual earnings; growth stocks tend to have relatively high price-earnings ratios because investors are willing to pay more for a firm whose future profits are expected to be much higher than current earnings. For comparison, in November 1989, Apple Computer traded at 13 times earnings and Genentech, a biotechnology company, traded at 139 times earnings. On the far left, *The Wall Street Journal* provides some historical perspective by showing the highest and lowest prices during the previous 52 weeks.

U.S. stock exchanges quote prices in $\frac{1}{2}$, $\frac{1}{4}$, $\frac{1}{8}$, $\frac{1}{16}$, and even $\frac{1}{32}$ of a dollar, apparently an anachronistic remnant of earlier days when arithmetic was done by hand. The calculations are done by computers now, and most foreign exchanges quote prices in decimals, a logical practice still resisted by U.S. exchanges.

Table 10.2   Stock Trading, 1989

	NYSE	AMEX	NASDAQ
Companies listed	1,720	859	4,293
Shares of listed companies (billions)	83	10	39
Volume of shares traded (billions)	42	3	34
Value of shares listed (billions)	$3,030	$133	$386
Value of shares traded (billions)	$1,556	$ 44	$431

source: National Association of Securities Dealers, *1990 Fact Book*. Reprinted by permission.

another member is willing to sell. Specialists have an obligation to maintain a fair and orderly market and, in this capacity, act as dealers by buying or selling, as needed, for their own accounts. At any moment, a specialist will quote a "bid" price at which he will buy and an "ask" price at which he will sell. The bid price is, of course, somewhat lower than the ask price.

When an investor places an order with a brokerage firm, it contacts a broker on the floor of the exchange who forwards the order to the appropriate specialist for execution. When the trade is completed, the brokerage firm charges the customer a commission, and the customer then generally has five working days to settle the trade by paying for purchased securities or delivering securities that were sold.

All of the organized exchanges restrict members from trading listed stocks outside the exchanges. Because most major brokerage firms are exchange members, these restrictions hamper the trading of listed stocks outside of the exchanges. Critics have long accused the exchanges of operating monopolies that enrich specialists. Prodded by perceived abuses, Congress passed the Securities Acts Amendments of 1975, instructing the SEC to develop a national market system that would be more competitive and efficient than the exchanges. Many economists envision a national auction market, linked by computers, with the specialist nowhere to be seen. But, by and large, the NYSE has resisted this vision successfully.

Trading is very different off the exchanges, in the over-the-counter market. Dealers voluntarily maintain a market in a security by quoting bid and ask prices at which they are willing to buy or sell securities. Market makers must register with the Securities and Exchange Commission, but there is no limit to their number or their geographic location. At present, the average OTC stock has about eight active market makers. All of the market makers' bid and ask prices are public knowledge, to each other and to interested investors. When you place an order to buy an OTC stock, your broker uses a computer to survey current bid-ask prices and determine the most advantageous offer and then make a transaction with that market maker, via either the computer or a phone call.

OTC trades are made through competing market makers.

London's Big Bang

On October 1, 1986, London's financial markets were transformed by extensive deregulation, changes so significant that they were labeled the "Big Bang." Previously, the London Stock Exchange had been much like a private club, where well-bred gentlemen in bowler hats showed up at 10 A.M. and went home at 4 P.M., with a leisurely two-hour lunch in between. In this relaxed, noncompetitive atmosphere, the brokers made a fixed 1.65 percent commission on each trade, and all trades passed through "jobbers" on the floor who, like the New York Stock Exchange's specialists, quoted bid and ask prices and made their profits on the spread.

Foreign banks and securities firms were allowed to join the London Stock Exchange in 1986 and, within a year, one-third of the members were foreign. Fixed commissions were abolished, as was the distinction between brokers and jobbers. In its place, authorized members act as market makers, quoting prices at which they are willing to buy or sell securities. To keep track of competing prices, the exchange spent millions of dollars on a massive computer system and, once computerized prices defined the market, there was no real need for the floor of the exchange at all. Now, transactions are made from securities houses by traders watching computer screens.

The gentlemen in bowler hats have been replaced by American-style whiz kids driving Porsches, who show up at 7 A.M. and work until the New York Stock Exchange closes at 10 P.M. London time. Their wide-ranging trades for worldwide clients make London the International Stock Exchange, the center of trading in currencies, Eurobonds (dollar-denominated bonds issued by non–U.S. institutions), and some commodities such as gold, tin, and rubber. In addition, hundreds of U.S. stocks are traded on the London Exchange, as are the stocks of a dozen other countries. In 1987, some 15 percent of the trading in French stocks took place on the London Exchange; for some Dutch companies, the figure was closer to 40 percent.

Stock-Market Indexes

More than 100 million shares of more than 1,500 different stocks are traded daily on the New York Stock Exchange alone, providing a mountain of statistical data, more than anyone could absorb or appreciate. Stock-market indexes are statistical averages intended to summarize changes in stock prices as time passes.

The most widely reported index is the **Dow Jones Industrial Average**, an average of the prices of the 30 prominent companies shown in Table 10.3, calculated by adding up these 30 prices and dividing by the divisor k, which was equal to 0.586 in November 1989.

Table 10.3 The Stocks of the Dow Jones Industrial Average, May 1, 1989

Stock	Price per Share	Number of Shares (millions)	Total Market Value (billions)
Alcoa	$62\frac{3}{4}$	88.3	5.5
Allied Signal	$33\frac{1}{2}$	148.7	5.0
American Express	$32\frac{1}{2}$	417.1	13.6
AT&T	$34\frac{1}{2}$	1,073.7	37.0
Bethlehem Steel	$22\frac{1}{2}$	74.5	1.7
Boeing	$77\frac{1}{8}$	153.2	11.8
Chevron	$53\frac{5}{8}$	342.1	18.3
Coca Cola	$54\frac{3}{4}$	359.0	19.7
DuPont	$109\frac{1}{4}$	239.4	26.2
Eastman Kodak	$47\frac{1}{8}$	324.2	15.3
Exxon	$42\frac{7}{8}$	1,289.0	55.3
General Electric	$48\frac{3}{4}$	900.5	43.9
General Motors	$41\frac{1}{4}$	612.9	25.3
Goodyear	$52\frac{1}{4}$	57.3	3.0
IBM	$113\frac{3}{8}$	591.4	67.0
International Paper	$49\frac{1}{8}$	111.1	5.5
McDonald's	$55\frac{3}{8}$	188.0	10.4
Merck	$67\frac{3}{8}$	396.5	26.7
MMM	$71\frac{1}{2}$	226.8	16.2
Navistar	$5\frac{3}{8}$	252.8	1.4
Philip Morris	$126\frac{3}{8}$	231.0	29.2
Primerica	$21\frac{1}{8}$	96.0	2.0
Procter & Gamble	$97\frac{5}{8}$	169.4	16.5
Sears Roebuck	$45\frac{3}{4}$	380.0	17.4
Texaco	$54\frac{1}{4}$	244.3	13.3
Union Carbide	$31\frac{5}{8}$	135.6	4.3
United Technologies	$51\frac{3}{8}$	130.7	6.7
USX	$34\frac{1}{2}$	260.8	9.0
Westinghouse	$57\frac{1}{2}$	144.0	8.3
Woolworth	$52\frac{1}{4}$	63.9	3.4

$$DJ = \frac{P_1 + P_2 + \cdots + P_{30}}{k}$$

In order to avoid discontinuities in the index, the divisor k is changed when a stock is split — for example, doubling the number of shares and halving the price of each share — or when one of the 30 stocks in the index is replaced with another stock. The current value of the divisor is printed each day in *The Wall Street Journal*.

The Dow Jones Industrial Average is an average of the stock prices of 30 prominent corporations.

Unlike the Dow average, most other stock indexes multiply the per-share prices by the number of shares outstanding, giving an index of the total market value of the stocks monitored. The Standard & Poor's 500 (S&P 500) contains 500 NYSE stocks, representing about three-fourths of the market value of all NYSE stocks, and the NYSE Composite Index includes all NYSE stocks. The AMEX index covers the American Stock Exchange; the NASDAQ index includes over-the-counter stocks; and the Wilshire 5000 has 5,000 stocks from all of these sources. Because these indexes represent a broader selection of stocks and reflect the market value of the stocks in the index, they are a more accurate gauge of what is really happening to the value of investor portfolios. But the Dow has its long tradition and an entrenched spot in the newspaper headlines. When the Dow is up 50 points, people can interpret that statistic readily as very good news about the stock market, simply because they remember that the Dow seldom goes up as much as 50 points in a single day. If they were to read that the NYSE composite was up 5 points, they wouldn't know what to make of that statistic, even though it is describing the same events and probably describing them more accurately.

STOCK VALUATION

What is the value of a share of First Interstate or another stock? According to what is called **fundamental analysis**, the **intrinsic value** of a stock is the present value of its prospective cash flow, discounted by the shareholders' required return, taking into account the returns available on alternative investments, its risk, and other salient considerations.[1] True investors consider stocks a long-run investment with a cash flow consisting of an endless stream of dividends. A used postage stamp has no intrinsic value; neither does a stock that will never pay dividends. John Burr Williams, a Harvard economics professor temporarily turned poet, wrote[2]

The intrinsic value of a stock is the present value of its dividends.

> A cow for her milk
> A hen for her eggs
> And a stock, by heck
> For her dividends.
>
> An orchard for fruit
> Bees, for their honey
> And stock, besides
> For their dividends.

Speculators buy an asset, not
for its cash flow, but to sell a
short while later for a profit.
In contrast to investors who are willing to hold an asset for keeps, **specu-lators** buy not for the long-run cash flow, but to sell a short while later for a profit. To speculators, a stock (or used postage stamp) is worth what someone else will pay for it, and the game is to guess what others will pay tomorrow for what you buy today. John Maynard Keynes, an economist and successful spec-ulator, put it this way.[3]

> It is not sensible to pay 25 for an investment of which you believe the prospective
> [cash flow] to justify a value of 30, if you also believe that the market will value
> it at 20 three months hence.

Those who believe in fundamental analysis consider such guessing games the Greater Fool Theory: you buy shares at an inflated price, hoping to find an even bigger fool who will buy these shares from you at a still higher price.

Fundamental analysts readily admit that many who buy and sell stock are speculators, hoping for quick profits, and that speculative binges can cause prices to depart from intrinsic values. Speculators are like the wind that blows a boat about its anchor — present value. Fundamental analysis can be used to provide a rational explanation of stock prices.

Present Value Again

If D_t is the dividend t periods from now and R is the shareholder's required return, then the present value of this cash flow is

$$P = \frac{D_1}{(1 + R)} + \frac{D_2}{(1 + R)^2} + \frac{D_3}{(1 + R)^3} + \cdots \tag{1}$$

(Companies usually pay dividends quarterly, and hence a quarterly required return is in order; but, for simplicity, we use annual dividends and annual required rates of return.)

The constant-dividend-growth model can be used to show how a stock's value depends on a firm's divi-dends and the shareholders' required return.
A special case is the **constant-dividend-growth model**, in which the divi-dend grows at a steady rate g each period: $D_{t+1} = (1 + g)D_t$. If $g < R$, then the present value given by Equation 1 simplifies to

$$P = \frac{D_1}{R - g} \tag{2}$$

Equation 2 gives the present value of a stock whose dividends grow at a constant rate g. Dividends *never* grow at an absolutely constant rate. The appeal of Equation 2 is that it is a reasonable and manageable approximation that has some very logical implications.

Notice, particularly, how important the growth rate is to the value of a stock. At a 10 percent required return, a stock paying a $5 dividend is worth $P = \$5/(0.10 - 0.00) = \$50$ if no growth is expected, and worth twice as much if the dividend is expected to grow by 5 percent a year: $P = \$5/(0.10 - 0.05) = \$100$. The present values for other growth rates are shown in Table 10.4.

Growth makes a big difference because of the power of compounding. The difference between 0 percent and 5 percent growth may not sound like much

Table 10.4	Present Value of a $5 Dividend, R = 10 Percent
Growth Rate g	**Present Value P**
0%	$ 50.00
2%	62.50
4%	83.33
6%	125.00
8%	250.00

(and it really isn't for the first few years), but 50 years down the road, the first company will still be paying a $5 dividend while the second pays $5(1.05^{50}) = $57.34. A present-value calculation whittles down the difference somewhat, but still, when all is said and done, taking into account the small difference in near dividends and the big difference in distant dividends, the second stock is worth twice as much as the first.

The Stock Market and the Economy

The National Bureau of Economic Research has long considered stock prices one of the best leading indicators of changes in economic activity. Stock prices usually decline shortly (on average, 4½ months) before a recession begins and rise shortly before a recession ends. Figure 10.1 compares the U.S. unemployment rate and the S&P 500, with the colored time periods identifying economic recessions. Each of the eight recessions since 1948 has, in fact, been preceded by a noticeable decline in stock prices. However, stock prices also fell sharply in 1962, 1966, 1977, and 1984 without a recession. To paraphrase Paul Samuelson, the stock market has predicted twelve of the last eight recessions.

Changes in stock prices often precede changes in the economy.

Nonetheless, there does seem to be a striking correlation between the stock market and the economy. Why? Three possible explanations are consistent with fundamental analysis: the stock market may influence the economy, the economy may influence the stock market, or some third factor may influence both. Most likely, all three explanations are correct. As is so often true in economics, everything *does* depend on everything else, though in varying degrees.

Let's look first at how the stock market influences the economy. When stock prices are high, those who own stock feel richer (with good reason; they *are* richer). They tend to spend more and live in a manner befitting their new wealth. When stock prices decline, households are likely to retrench, increasing their saving and trying to rebuild their lost wealth. One of the Federal Reserve Board's economic models estimates that each $1 change in the market value of stocks tends to change consumer spending by about 5 cents. With the substantial fluctuations in stock prices in recent years, those nickels add up. In 1973–74, the aggregate market value of stocks dropped by about $500 billion, implying a

Figure 10.1 **Stock Prices and the Economy**

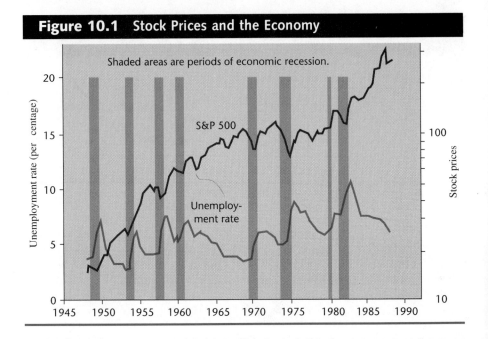

$25 billion depressant for consumer spending that helps explain the 1974–75 recession. The 1985–86 bull market increased stock values by nearly a trillion dollars, and the implied $50 billion spending stimulus helps explain why household spending as a fraction of income reached record levels. The $500-billion crash on October 19, 1987, made many, including the Federal Reserve, fearful of recession; the Fed immediately responded by increasing the nation's money supply to support financial markets and the economy.

The economy, in turn, undoubtedly affects the stock market. Stock prices are influenced by anticipated dividends, and when the economy is strong, profits surge and dividends follow close behind. When recession hits, profits slump and dividends grow slowly, or even decline. Why does the market go up or down 4½ months *before* the economy does likewise? Perhaps stock analysts can see booms and recessions coming in advance of their actual arrival (at least, in twelve out of eight cases).

Another explanation for the observed correlation is that some third factor influences both the stock market and the economy. The possibilities are endless, ranging from skirt lengths to the water levels in the Great Lakes. A more plausible factor is interest rates. As Andrew Tobias, a popular financial writer, put it, "The key to everything financial, and to nearly everything economic, is interest rates."[4]

The Stock Market and Interest Rates

When investors' required rate of return increases, there is a decline in the present value of any given cash flow. Earlier chapters discussed this inverse price-yield relationship for bonds; the very same logic applies to stocks. For a given dividend stream, a high rate of return requires a low price, whereas a low required rate of return necessitates a high price.

Because so much of their cash flow is in the distant future, stocks, especially growth stocks, are similar to very-long-term bonds in that they have long durations and substantial capital risk. A 20-year bond with a 10 percent coupon and a 10 percent yield has a duration of 9 years; a stock with a 12 percent required return and a 5 percent anticipated growth rate has a duration of 16 years.

To illustrate the effect of required return on present value, consider again the example of a stock with a current $5 dividend and a variety of possible growth rates, this time comparing 11 percent with 10 percent required returns, as in Table 10.5. Notice, first, that stock prices are very sensitive to required returns and, second, that this is especially true of growth stocks. Because a large part of their present value consists of distant dividends, stocks are long-term assets with substantial capital risk.

It is often thought, wrongly, that the only reason high interest rates depress the stock market is that higher interest rates may mean increased costs for businesses or a weaker economy and depressed sales. Even if costs are constant and the economy stable, higher interest rates depress stock prices for the same reason they depress bond prices. Assets are, to varying degrees, substitutes in investors' eyes, and the required rates of return that investors use to discount the cash flow from assets depend on the yields available on alternative investments. When the returns available on Treasury securities rise, so do the required returns on corporate bonds and stocks, pushing these asset prices downward. Otherwise, investors would forsake corporate stocks and bonds for the higher yields available on Treasury securities.

An increase in interest rates reduces the present value of a stock's dividends.

To the extent that financial markets are competitive and efficient, these ripples are felt almost immediately. Because of the dissatisfaction that would otherwise occur, prices fall across a broad spectrum of assets virtually simultaneously. Stock-market analysts pay close attention to other financial markets and to news of government financial policies. Stock prices jump right after (and sometimes before) the Fed announces an easing of monetary policy or Citibank announces a drop in its prime lending rate. Daily reports on the stock market routinely refer to interest-rate developments and to perceived changes in financial policies. To cite just one example, a *New York Times* story begins, "Stock prices tumbled yesterday, with the Dow Jones Industrial Average dropping more than 11 points, following apparent confirmation that the Federal Reserve was permitting short-term interest rates to move higher."[5] More dramatically, the 1973–74 stock-market crash ended just when interest rates peaked, and the 1985–86 surge coincided with a 3-percentage-point drop in long-term bond rates. The October 1987 crash began after interest rates rose, and the market recovered when the Federal Reserve pushed interest rates back down.

The fact that low interest rates increase both bond and stock prices (and higher interest rates reduce both) does not mean that bond and stock prices always move in the same direction. Although bonds have a fixed cash flow (except in defaults), stocks have a variable cash flow with dividends that go up

Bond prices depend on interest rates; stock prices depend on interest rates and the economy.

Table 10.5   The Effect of the Required Return on a Stock's Present Value

Growth Rate g	Present Value		Percentage Change
	R = 10%	R = 11%	
0%	$50.00	$45.45	− 9.1%
2%	62.50	55.55	−11.1%
4%	83.33	71.43	−14.3%
6%	125.00	100.00	−20.0%
8%	250.00	166.67	−33.3%

and down with the economy. Because the economy and interest rates can move in the same or opposite directions, sometimes bond and stock prices move together and, at other times, they diverge.

If the economic outlook is unchanged while interest rates fluctuate, stock and bond prices will move together. If the economic outlook changes, then the relative movements of bond and stock prices depend on whether the economy and interest rates move in the same or opposite directions. When interest rates rise, bad economic news reinforces the drop in stock prices but good economic news cushions the drop, perhaps even propelling stock prices upward at the same time that bond prices are falling. When interest rates decline, good economic news reinforces rising stock prices, whereas a weak economy restrains stock prices.

Tobin's q

A strong economy encourages businesses to expand and increases stock prices. Low interest rates also encourage business expansion and raise stock prices. James Tobin of Yale University argues that the net effect of the current state of the economy and of interest rates on business investment can be gauged by the level of stock prices, specifically by the value of **Tobin's q**, the ratio of the value placed on a firm by financial markets to the replacement cost of its assets:

Tobin's q is the ratio of a firm's market value to the replacement cost of its assets.

$$q = \frac{\text{Market value of firm}}{\text{Replacement cost of firm's assets}} \tag{3}$$

If a corporation has bonds and other debts, these can be added to the market value in Equation 3 or subtracted from the replacement cost of its assets.

The logic behind Tobin's q can be illustrated by a simple example: Consider a restaurant chain that is considering building another restaurant that will cost $1 million to construct and is expected to earn a constant $200,000 annual profit (a 20 percent return on its cost), which will be paid out each year to the chain's shareholders. The value that financial markets place on this restaurant depends not on its $1 million cost of construction, but on the value of its $200,000 annual cash flow.

If Treasury bonds yield 5 percent, then perhaps stock in a risky restaurant is priced to yield 10 percent. If so, then Equation 2 with a zero growth rate gives a market value of

$$P = \frac{\$200,000}{0.10 - 0.00} = \frac{\$200,000}{0.10} = \$2,000,000$$

Valued at $2 million, the $200,000 cash flow gives shareholders their requisite 10 percent return. The market value of this restaurant is twice its cost of construction

$$q = \frac{\text{Market value of firm}}{\text{Replacement cost of firm's assets}} = \frac{\$2,000,000}{\$1,000,000} = 2$$

The value of Tobin's q is larger than 1 because the restaurant's 20 percent profit rate is larger than the shareholders' 10 percent required return.

If, on the other hand, Treasury bonds pay 20 percent and restaurant shareholders price their stock to give a 25 percent return, then the value of a $200,000 annual cash flow is only $800,000.

Tobin's q depends on a firm's profitability relative to shareholder required returns.

$$P = \frac{\$200,000}{0.25 - 0.00} = \frac{\$200,000}{0.25} = \$800,000$$

Because the restaurant's 20 percent profit rate is less than shareholders' 25 percent required return, the value of Tobin's q is less than 1:

$$q = \frac{\text{Market value of firm}}{\text{Replacement cost of firm's assets}} = \frac{\$800,000}{\$1,000,000} = 0.8$$

Table 10.6 shows some estimates of Tobin's q using market-value and book-value data for the 20 largest firms in the computer and office-equipment industry. The ratio of market value to book value is a crude estimate of Tobin's q because book values reflect historical cost, which may be very different from current replacement cost. Nonetheless, as shown in this table and in Figure 10.2, firms with high profit rates tend to have high values of Tobin's q, whereas firms with low profit rates have low qs.

The link between Tobin's q and investment is provided by the observation that business expansion benefits shareholders only if the rate of return that the firm can earn on its investments is larger than shareholders' required rate of return — as when the restaurant can earn a 20 percent return and the shareholders require only 10 percent. This is one of the primary ways in which financial markets affect real economic activity. When interest rates are low, so are shareholders' required returns, making it more likely that prospective investments are sufficiently profitable to justify making them on behalf of shareholders. If, as in the second case, shareholders require a 25 percent return, construction of the restaurant does not benefit shareholders; they would be better off if the firm paid out the $1 million as a dividend and let shareholders invest it themselves.

Equivalently, the firm can ask whether, if it were to sell shares in its new restaurant venture, it could raise enough money to cover the cost of constructing the restaurant. It can if the value of Tobin's q is larger than 1, but not otherwise. Thus Tobin's q provides a barometer of the financial incentives for business expansion, and we will use it for this purpose in later chapters.

MASS PSYCHOLOGY

Investment decisions are more than arithmetic calculations and mechanical rules. Our information is usually incomplete and often contradictory, and there is always considerable uncertainty about the future. Inevitably, we make subjective decisions influenced by our all-too-human emotions. It is natural to hope that a clever investment will yield quick and easy wealth. This hope sometimes turns into a greed that blurs our vision and dulls common sense.

From time to time, investors are gripped by what, in retrospect, seems to have been mass hysteria. A **speculative bubble** occurs when the price of some commodity or security climbs higher and higher, beyond all reason, and nothing justifies the rise in price except the hope that it will go higher still. Then, suddenly, the bubble pops and the price collapses. With hindsight, it is hard to see how people could have been so foolish and bought at such crazy prices. Yet, paradoxically, at the time of the bubble, it seems foolish to sit on the sidelines while others become rich.

A speculative bubble is a self-fulfilling prophecy of rising asset prices.

Speculative bubbles generally begin with important events of real economic significance, such as the building of railroads, the discovery of gold, or the outbreak of war.[6] Seeing the profits made by some, others rush to participate, pushing prices higher. Soon, greed displaces common sense and swindlers emerge to fleece the gullible. The upward rush of prices becomes a speculative bubble in the sense that most of the participants are buying not for the cash flow that their investment might produce but in anticipation that prices will keep rising — a self-fulfilling prophecy as long as there are more buyers than sellers.

When everyone has been convinced that something is a good investment, there is no one left to buy and push the price still higher. The bubble bursts when buyers no longer outnumber sellers. There is a selling stampede and prices collapse. In the frantic rush for the exit, very few make it through the door.

There have been several dramatic historical episodes when the stock market was seized by a collective euphoria, as investors seemed to put aside common sense and, instead, were willing to believe whatever was necessary to justify ever-higher stock prices. The subsequent, terrifying collapse of prices not only evaporated fortunes, but persuaded many never again to buy stock. We'll look first at the stock market crash that accompanied the Great Depression, and then at a more recent one-day crash of unprecedented magnitude.

Table 10.6 The Twenty Largest Firms in the Computer and Office Equipment Industry, 1989

Company	Market Value (millions)	Book Value (millions)	Tobin's q	Profit Rate
IBM	$94,644	$66,299	1.43	14.7%
Xerox	20,122	18,787	1.07	11.2
Hewlett-Packard	14,865	6,335	2.35	18.0
Digital Equipment	14,853	10,553	1.41	17.4
Unisys	11,394	12,203	0.93	9.0
Apple	6,692	1,764	3.79	39.9
Pitney-Bowes	6,016	3,925	1.53	18.7
Tandy	5,521	3,211	1.72	19.7
NCR	5,412	3,204	1.69	19.6
Automatic Data Processing	3,687	1,868	1.97	17.3
Compaq	3,453	1,248	2.77	30.5
Wang Laboratories	3,410	3,769	0.90	5.8
Control Data	2,633	2,872	0.93	3.5
Amdahl	2,397	1,388	1.73	21.2
Prime Computer	2,293	1,892	1.21	10.2
Tandem Computers	2,256	1,466	1.54	11.7
Sun	1,907	912	2.09	18.0
Cray Research	1,756	906	1.94	23.1
Intergraph	1,133	925	1.22	12.5
Seagate Technology	1,053	798	1.32	17.7

source: *Value Line Investment Survey*, May 5, 1989, pp. 1076–1118. Copyright © 1990 by Value Line Publishing, Inc.

The Great Crash

The 1920s were an exciting and turbulent decade — for the economy, for social mores, and for the stock market.[7] In 1924, the Dow Jones Industrial Average hit 100. In December 1927, it roared past 200, hitting 250 in October 1928 and 300 in December. Nine months later, in September 1929, it reached a peak of 386. It seemed that investors could make money effortlessly by buying stock in rock-solid companies. Between March 1928 and September 1929, American Can went from 77 to $181\frac{7}{8}$, American Telephone from $179\frac{1}{2}$ to $335\frac{5}{8}$, General Electric from $128\frac{3}{4}$ to $396\frac{1}{4}$, and U.S. Steel from $138\frac{1}{8}$ to $279\frac{1}{8}$.

Predicting the future is always treacherous, and history is full of well-informed people making what, with hindsight, are foolish statements. At breakfast before Waterloo, Napoleon remarked, "Wellington is a bad general, the English

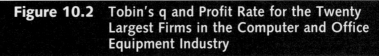

Figure 10.2 Tobin's q and Profit Rate for the Twenty Largest Firms in the Computer and Office Equipment Industry

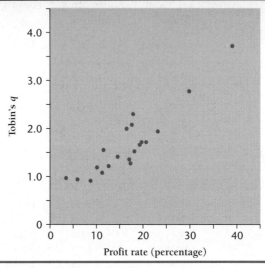

are bad soldiers; we will settle the matter by lunch time." In 1899, the Director of the U.S. Patent Office said, "Everything that can be invented has been invented." Thomas Edison believed that "the phonograph is not of any commercial value," and President Hayes said of the telephone, "That's an amazing invention, but who would ever want to use one?" Lord Kelvin, a scientist and president of Britain's Royal Society proclaimed, "Heavier-than-air flying machines are impossible," and "Radio has no future." Harry Warner, the president of Warner Brothers said, "Who the hell wants to hear actors talk?" and Thomas Watson, the CEO of IBM, said, "I think there is a world market for about five computers."

The stock market and the economy are never easy to predict, and the Crash and Great Depression were no exception. In his final message to Congress, on December 4, 1928, Calvin Coolidge boasted that "No Congress of the United States ever assembled, on surveying the state of the Union, has met with a more pleasing prospect than that which appears at the present time." Herbert Hoover took office and in July 1929 predicted that "The outlook of the world today is for the greatest era of commercial expansion in history." On October 17, 1929, Irving Fisher, the greatest American economist of his day, asserted that stocks had reached "what looks like a permanently high plateau."

However, the five-year bull market was over. After a number of bad days, panic selling hit the market on Thursday, October 24. Terrified investors tried to sell at any price and market prices plunged, with the panic heightened by the fact that the ticker tape reporting transactions ran hours late, so that investors had no information about current prices. The market finally steadied in the

Widespread euphoria preceded the 1929 stock market crash.

The South Sea Bubble   Highlight 10.3

In 1720, the South Sea Company took over the British government's debt in exchange for exclusive trading privileges with Spain's American colonies. Encouraged by the company's inventive bookkeeping, English citizens rushed to invest in this exotic venture. As the price of the South Sea Company's stock soared from £120 on January 28 to £400 on May 19, £800 on June 4, and £1,000 on June 22, some became rich and thousands rushed to join their ranks. Soon other entrepreneurs were offering stock in ever more grandiose schemes and were deluged by frantic investors not wanting to be left out. It scarcely mattered what the scheme was. One company promised to build a perpetual-motion device. Another was formed "for carrying on an undertaking of great advantage, but nobody is to know what it is." These shares were priced at £100 each, with a promised annual return of £100; after selling all of the stock within five hours, the promoter immediately left England and never returned. Yet another stock offer was for the "nitvender," or selling of nothing.* When the bubble burst, most of the stock became worthless and fortunes and dreams were lost.

As with all speculative bubbles, there were many believers in the Greater Fool Theory. Although some suspected that prices were unreasonable, the market was dominated by people who believed that prices would continue to rise, at least until they could sell to the next fool in line. In the spring of 1720, Sir Isaac Newton said, "I can calculate the motions of the heavenly bodies, but not the madness of people," and sold his South Sea shares for a £7,000 profit. But later that year, he bought shares again, just before the bubble burst, and lost £20,000. Similarly, when a banker invested £500 in the third offer of South Sea stock (in August 1720), he explained that "When the rest of the world are mad, we must imitate them in some measure."† After James Milner, a member of the British Parliament, was bankrupted by the South Sea Bubble, he explained that "I said indeed that ruin must some day come upon us but I owe it came two months earlier than I expected."‡

---

*John Carswell, *The South Sea Bubble* (London: Cresset Press, 1960), p. 142.
†Carswell, p. 161.
‡Virginia Cowles, *South Sea: The Greatest Swindle* (London: Crowley, 1960).

Highlight 10.4	Ponzi Schemes

In 1920, Charles Ponzi promised to pay Massachusetts investors 50 percent interest every 45 days — compounded eight times a year, $1 would grow to $1.50^8 = 25.63, an effective annual rate of return of 2,463 percent! His stated plan was to arbitrage the difference between the official and open-market price of Spanish pesos: he would buy Spanish pesos cheap in the open market, use these pesos to buy International Postage Union coupons, and then trade these coupons for U.S. postage stamps at the higher official exchange rate.* If everything worked as planned, he could buy 10 cents' worth of U.S. postage stamps for a penny, though it was unclear how he would convert these stamps back into cash. In practice, he received $15 million from investors and appears to have bought only $61 in stamps.

If he didn't invest the money he received, how could he possibly afford to pay a 50 percent return every 45 days? He couldn't. But he could create a temporary illusion of doing so. Suppose that one person invests $100, which Ponzi promptly spends on himself. If Ponzi now finds another two people to invest $100 apiece, then he can pay the first person $150 and keep another $50 for himself. Now, he has 45 days to find four more people willing to invest $100, so that he can pay each of the previous two investors $150 and spend $100 on himself. These four investors can be paid off with the money from eight new ones, and these eight from sixteen more.

In a **Ponzi scheme**, money from new investors is used to pay off earlier ones, and it works as long as there are enough new investors. The problem is that the pool of fish is exhausted surprisingly soon. The twenty-first round requires a million new people and the thirtieth round requires a billion more. At some point, the scheme runs out of new people and those in the last round (most of the investors) are left with nothing. A Ponzi scheme merely transfers wealth from late entrants to early entrants.

Ponzi's scam collapsed after eight months when a Boston newspaper discovered that, during the time Ponzi had supposedly bought $15 million in postage coupons, the total amount sold worldwide came to only $1 million. Despite his protestations that he could pay off his investors by incorporating and selling shares of stock to other investors, the state of Massachusetts froze his accounts and sent Ponzi to jail for ten years.

---

*A fictionalized account is given in Donald H. Dunn, *Ponzi: The Boston Swindler* (New York: McGraw-Hill, 1975).

afternoon, when six prominent New York bankers put up $40 million apiece to buy stocks. But the market dropped again the following Monday and was hit by panic selling the next day, Black Tuesday, October 29. Again there was an avalanche of sell orders, more than the brokers and ticker tape could process, and, more important, dwarfing the scattered buy orders. White Sewing Machine had recently traded for 48; on Monday it closed at $11\frac{1}{8}$. On Black Tuesday, in the complete absence of buy orders, a messenger boy bought shares for $1.[8]

With fits and starts, the market decline continued. By November 13, the Dow had fallen an incredible 48 percent as the prices of America's premier companies collapsed: American Can was down 53 percent, American Telephone 41 percent, General Electric 58 percent, and U.S. Steel 46 percent. The Dow recovered to nearly 300 in the spring of 1930, but then began a long, tortuous slide, punctuated by brief but inadequate rallies, before finally touching bottom at 42.84 in June of 1932 — down 89 percent from September 1929. It wasn't until 1956, 27 years later, that the stock market regained its 1929 peak.

The Great Depression was more than a stock-market crash. Between 1929 and 1933, output fell a third, while the unemployment rate rose from 3 percent to 25 percent. More than a third of the nation's banks failed, and household net worth dropped by 30 percent. Behind these aggregate numbers were millions of private tragedies. One hundred thousand businesses failed and twelve million people lost their jobs and, with them, their income and, in many cases, their self-respect. Many lost their life savings in the stock-market crash and the tidal wave of bank failures. Without income or savings, people could not buy food, clothing, or proper medical care. Those who could not pay their rents lost their shelter, those who couldn't make mortgage payments lost their homes. Farm income fell by two-thirds, and many farms were lost to foreclosure. Desperate people moved into shanty settlements (called Hoovervilles), slept under newspapers (Hoover blankets), and scavenged for food where they could. Edmund Wilson reported that[9]

> There is not a garbage-dump in Chicago which is not haunted by the hungry. Last summer in the hot weather when the smell was sickening and the flies were thick, there were a hundred people a day coming to one of the dumps.

There was severe economic hardship during the Great Depression.

The unemployment rate averaged 19 percent during the 1930s and never fell below 14 percent. The Great Depression didn't end until the federal government began spending nearly $100 billion a year during World War II.

October 19, 1987

On October 19, 1987, there was a stock-market crash that exceeded any single day's decline during the Great Depression. Fortunately, the 1987 collapse was temporary and there were no long-lasting effects on the economy — though the same cannot be said for investors who experienced it first hand. We'll look at the events leading up to October 19 and then at the collapse.

The **Federal Reserve Board (Fed)** controls monetary policy in the United States. Alarmed by inflation, in late 1979 the Fed began a tight-money policy

The 1982–87 bull market was fueled by declining interest rates and an expanding economy.

that pushed interest rates up and discouraged spending, particularly for houses, factories, and other investment projects. By 1982, the economy had been brought to its knees with long-term Treasury bond rates above 12 percent and the unemployment rate above 10 percent for the first time since the Great Depression. Satisfied that inflation had been brought under control — down to a livable 3.9 percent — and fearing the complete collapse of the economy, the Fed gradually eased up. The subsequent decline in unemployment and interest rates fueled a five-year bull market in stocks.

In August 1982, the Dow Jones Industrial Average was at 777. Five years later, it had more than tripled, to 2,722. Of course, no one bought at exactly 777 and sold at exactly 2,722. But along the way, a lot of people noticed the run-up in stock prices and wanted to hop on for at least part of the ride.

Stocks were widely perceived to be overvalued in 1987.

When the Dow surged past 2,000 in January 1987, stocks were widely perceived to be overvalued by conventional criteria; yet players stayed in the market, hoping for more profits and believing that they could get out before the bubble burst. *The Wall Street Journal* ran a front-page story titled "Stock Market's Surge Is Puzzling Investors; When Will It End?"[10] The story began with the exclamation "Wheee!" and went on to say that "the market madness is as puzzling as it is exhilarating." For a typical view, the story quoted Steven Leuthold, the head of a financial advisory service: "You have to realize we're in Looney Tunes land and you should stay fairly close to the exits. . . . [But] it's a lot of fun, and you could make a lot of money here."

When the Dow topped 2,700 in August, stocks were selling for 23 times earnings and dividend yields were a mere 2.2 percent, compared to the 10 percent interest rates on Treasury bonds. Fundamental-analysis models showed intrinsic values to be some 20 percent to 40 percent below market prices.[11] But buyers weren't planning on holding for keeps. There was a lot of wishful thinking, including wildly optimistic forecasts of future earnings and interest rates, and a big dose of the Greater Fool Theory, with hopes that the Japanese were the ultimate bigger fools, with unlimited cash and an eagerness to pay twenty times earnings for U.S. stocks because Japanese stocks were selling for sixty times earnings. *The Wall Street Journal* used this story to illustrate the market's predisposition to believe.[12]

> On June 23, an obscure investment advisor, P. David Herrlinger, announced a $6.8 billion offer for Dayton Hudson Corp. Mr. Herrlinger appeared on his front lawn to tell the Dow Jones News Service that he didn't know whether his bid was a hoax. "It's no more of a hoax than anything else," he said. Later, he was taken to a hospital.
>
> Yet the news sent the giant retailer's stock soaring, with 5.5 million shares changing hands in frantic trading.

After topping 2,700 in late August, the Dow Industrial Average slipped back to 2,500 in October. Then the Dow fell by a record 95 points on Wednesday, October 14, dropped by another 58 points on Thursday, and fell an unprecedented 108 points on Friday, to close at 2,246.74. The volume of trading on Friday was also the highest ever, with 338 million shares traded, and falling prices outnumbering gainers by a staggering 17 to 1.

Monday's "Abreast of the Market" column in *The Wall Street Journal* suggested that Friday's bloodletting might have been the "selling climax" that many technical analysts believe precedes a bull market. One said that "the peak of intensity of selling pressure has exhausted itself" and another said that "if we haven't seen the bottom, we're probably very close."[13]

The very day this article appeared was Black Monday, a frightening market convulsion that participants will never forget. When the market opened, the excess of sell orders was so large that trading was suspended for an hour in eight of the 30 Dow Industrial stocks. For the day, an astounding 604 million shares were traded and the Dow dropped 508 points (23 percent). Losers outnumbered gainers by 40 to 1 and the aggregate market value of stocks fell by roughly $500 billion.

The stock market crashed on October 19, 1987, and almost disintegrated the next day.

On the next day, Terrible Tuesday, markets came close to a total collapse. At the opening, many specialists and other market makers quoted prices far above Monday's close and sold heavily. The Dow opened with an extraordinary 200-point gain, but by noon had fallen back below Monday's close. During the day, trading was temporarily suspended in many of the best-known stocks, including IBM for two hours and Merck for four hours. Several major financial institutions were rumored to be bankrupt, and some banks cut off credit to securities firms. Several specialists had difficulty raising cash to buy securities, and some of the largest securities firms urged the NYSE to shut down completely.

The day was saved when the Federal Reserve promised to supply much-needed cash, and pressured banks to lend money. In addition, with vigorous encouragement from investment bankers, several major corporations announced plans to repurchase their stock, and the system held together — if just barely. (For the week, the ten largest New York banks ended up lending an extra $5.5 billion to securities firms.) One market participant said that "Tuesday was the most dangerous day we had in 50 years. I think we came within an hour [of the disintegration of the stock market]."[14] The Dow closed Tuesday up 102 points and rose another 187 points the next day, ending the short-run crisis.

Tidbits of bad economic news preceded the October 19 crash — Congressional discussion of restrictions on corporate takeovers, a larger-than-expected trade deficit, and slightly higher interest rates — but nothing that seems substantial enough to explain the magnitude of the crash. A mail survey of individual and institutional investors found little reason for the collapse in prices other than a widespread belief that prices had been too high and that, once prices started declining, people (including the program traders discussed in Chapter 8) tried to sell all at once, swamping the will and financial ability of specialists to maintain orderly markets.[15] Recalling the January advice in *The Wall Street Journal* that "we're in Looney Tunes land and you should stay fairly close to the exits," it appears that on October 19 too many people tried to squeeze through the exit door at the same time.

THE EFFICIENT-MARKET HYPOTHESIS

In an efficient market, there are no obviously mispriced securities.

In an **efficient market**, there are no obviously mispriced securities and, therefore, no transactions that can be counted on to make abnormally large profits. An efficient stock market, however, does not assume zero profit. Stockholders receive dividends and, as time passes, can expect stock prices to increase along with corporate assets, profits, and dividends. Because safe bank accounts and Treasury securities pay positive returns, stocks are priced to have positive anticipated returns, too — indeed, relatively high returns to the extent that stocks are risky. The efficient-market hypothesis says that, in comparison with other investments, and taking into account the risk and other characteristics thought relevant by investors, stocks will not be priced to give a return that is clearly inadequate or excessive.

The stock market would be inefficient if some investors could take advantage of others' ignorance — for example, if some investors, knowing that a company had discovered an extremely profitable cure for baldness, could buy stock in this company at an unreasonably low price from other investors unaware of this discovery. If information is disseminated quickly, so that many investors have the same information, then market prices are efficient in that there is no advantage to "trading on information": buying or selling on the basis of information about a company or the market as a whole. An efficient market is a fair game in the sense that no investor can beat the market (except by luck) because no investor has an information advantage over other investors.

The efficient-market hypothesis implies an important distinction between events that have been anticipated in advance and those that haven't. For instance, if a toy store's sales increase before Christmas, will the price of its stock rise, too? When the stock trades in June, the price that buyers are willing to pay and sellers accept reflects the common knowledge that toy sales increase during the holiday season. Based on the information available in June, buyers and sellers can estimate these sales and value the stock accordingly. If the actual increase in sales turns out to be equal to these forecasts, there is no cause for a revision in the value of the stock. The price will change, however, if sales are unexpectedly brisk or disappointing. Future events anticipated by investors are already embedded in today's stock prices. Unexpected returns are caused by unexpected events.

In an efficient market anticipated events are already embedded in stock prices.

It is not enough to know that IBM will make more profits next year than Sears, that ice cream sales increase in the summer, or that auto sales increase when the economy gets stronger. The benchmark to gauge your investment ideas is not "How will tomorrow differ from today?" but "How does my perception of tomorrow differ from what others believe?" Do you really know something that the experts don't know? If you do, then you may be guilty of using inside information that is illegal for reasons discussed later in this chapter. If you don't, then your information is already embedded in market prices.

Investment decisions are influenced by many different bits and pieces of information, such as recent price movements, measures of investor sentiment,

The Super Bowl System

On Super Bowl Sunday in January 1983, both the business and sports sections of the *Los Angeles Times* carried articles on the "Super Bowl Stock Market Predictor."* The theory is that the stock market goes up if the National Football Conference (or a pre-merger NFL team now in the American Football Conference) wins the Super Bowl. The market goes down if a former AFL team wins. This theory had proven correct for 15 out of 16 Super Bowls — the one exception was 1970, when Kansas City beat Minnesota and the market went up 0.1 percent. In 1983, an NFC team, the Washington Redskins, won, the market went up, and the Super Bowl system was back in the newspapers the next year, stronger than ever. From its birth through 1989, the Super Bowl system has been right five out of seven times.

The accuracy of the Super Bowl system is obviously just an amusing coincidence, because the stock market has nothing to do with the outcome of a football game. Over these 22 years, the stock market has generally gone up and the NFL has usually won the Super Bowl. The correlation is made more startling by the gimmick of including the Pittsburgh Steelers, an AFC team, in with the NFL. The excuse is that Pittsburgh was in the NFL before the leagues merged; the real reason is that Pittsburgh won the Super Bowl four times in the years when the market went up.

Inspired by the success of the Super Bowl indicator, a *Los Angeles Times* staff writer uncovered several other entertaining but worthless co-incidences.† The "Yo, Adrian Theory" holds that if a Rocky or Rambo movie is released, the stock market will go up that year. On average, the Dow increased by 173 points in the four years when a Rocky movie appeared and 245 points in the years when a Rambo movie was released. The Geraldo Rivera indicator notes that the Dow has fallen an average of 13 points on the day after seven major Geraldo Rivera TV specials. The George Steinbrenner indicator monitors his firing of Yankee managers. On the five occasions that he fired Billy Martin, the Dow rose an average of 5 points the following day; for the eight times Steinbrenner fired someone else, the Dow fell an average of 3 points the next day.

---

*Sue Avery, "Market Investors Will Be High on Redskins Today" and "Morning Briefing: Wall Street 'Skinish on Big Game,'" *Los Angeles Times*, January 30, 1983.

†James Bates, "Reality Wears Loser's Jersey in Super Bowl Stock Theory," *Los Angeles Times*, January 22, 1989.

unemployment forecasts, perceptions of Federal Reserve policy, and takeover rumors. It is useful to group such disparate information into three general categories: past prices, other public data, and private information. The corresponding efficient-market hypotheses have been labeled weak, semi-strong, and strong, and we will discuss each in turn.

The Weak Form

The weak form of the efficient-market hypothesis says that price changes cannot be predicted from past prices.

The **weak form of the efficient-market hypothesis** holds that past data on stock prices are of no use in predicting future price changes. Past price data are widely available, and there is no logical reason for investors to revise their opinions of a stock based on old data. The immediate implication is that technical analysts who scrutinize historical charts of stock prices are wasting their time. This is often called the "random walk hypothesis" in that it says that each change in a stock's price is unrelated to previous changes, much as each flip of a coin is unrelated to previous tosses and each step by a drunkard is unrelated to previous steps. Academics overwhelmingly believe that technical analysis is worthless, and that whatever patterns are discovered in historical data are coincidences that cannot be counted on to persist in the future.[16]

The Semi-Strong Form

The semi-strong form of the efficient-market hypothesis says that abnormal returns cannot be earned consistently, using public information.

The **semi-strong form of the efficient-market hypothesis** says that abnormal returns cannot be consistently earned using any publicly available information — not only past prices but also such data as interest rates, inflation, and corporate earnings. For instance, most of the data printed in a company's annual report may be known months in advance by analysts who follow the company, and they are certainly known by investors in general once the report appears. It is hard to see how one could consistently beat the market by trading on the basis of the information in annual reports and, no surprise, academic studies indicate that such information is already embedded in market prices in the sense that it is of little use in predicting prices *after* the report appears.[17]

One way of testing the efficient-market hypothesis is to identify an event, such as the publication of a company's annual report, and then see if there is any evidence of a later effect on prices. Another approach is to look at significant price changes themselves. For instance, every day *The Wall Street Journal* lists the stocks that experienced the largest percentage price change on the preceding trading day. Two researchers randomly selected 36 days in 1977, and then examined the behavior of the five stocks that experienced the largest percentage price increases on each of these days.[18] Their intent was to see if these price increases, apparently the consequence of a change in the companies' fortunes, were either preceded or followed by similar price increases. If so, this would indicate that information spreads gradually through financial markets. If not, this would indicate that whatever event triggered the price increase was truly a surprise, whose full price effect was felt on a single trading day. Figure 10.3 summarizes their results. The price changes were small and seemingly random,

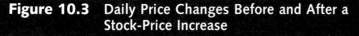

Figure 10.3   Daily Price Changes Before and After a
Stock-Price Increase

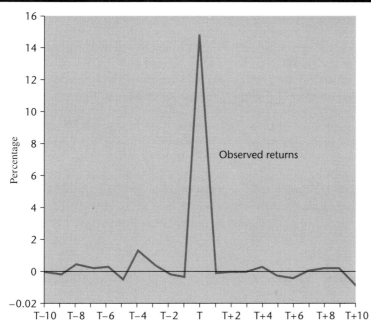

source: Avner Arbel and Bikki Jaggi, "Market Information
Assimilation Related to Extreme Daily Price Jumps,"
Financial Analysts' Journal, November/December
1982, p. 62. Reprinted by permission.

both before and after the large increase, indicating that, without warning, some event caused a sudden jump in prices, followed by random fluctuations.

Another way of testing the semi-strong form of the efficient-market hypothesis is to look at the records of professional investors, who presumably base their decisions on publicly available information. If they consistently beat the market, then public information is apparently of some value.

The record of professional investors as a group has been mediocre, at best. A compilation of 52 surveys of the stocks or stock portfolios recommended by professional investors during the years 1929–80 found that 77 percent of the professional recommendations underperformed the market.[19] Similarly, a tracking of 44 prominent investment advisory services from 1980–85 found that only 14 outperformed the S&P 500, while 30 underperformed it.[20]

In addition, there is little or no consistency in which particular investors do relatively well and which do poorly. There is no correlation between a mutual fund's performance one year and its performance the next year; those funds in

Professional investors have been, on average, mediocre and individually inconsistent.

the top 10 percent this year and those in the bottom 10 percent are equally likely to be in the bottom 10 percent next year.[21] A study of 200 institutional stock portfolios found that, of those which ranked in the top 25 percent in the period 1972–77, 26 percent ranked in the top 25 percent during 1977–82, 48 percent ranked in the middle 50 percent, and 26 percent were in the bottom 25 percent.[22] A similar scrutiny of 32 bond managers found no correlation at all between the performance rankings for 1972–76 and 1976–81.[23]

Many institutions have themselves been persuaded by such evidence and switched at least part of their portfolio to indexing — trying merely to replicate the market, rather than outperform it — reasoning that matching a stock-market index will beat most of their competitors. The three largest stock managers — Wells Fargo Investment Advisors, Bankers Trust, and the College Retirement Equities Fund — are all index enthusiasts.

It is tempting to think that, as in any profession, good training, hard work, and a skilled mind will yield superior results. And it is especially tempting to think that you possess these very characteristics. The market is not all luck, but it is more luck than nervous investors want to hear or successful investors want to admit.

The Strong Form

The strong form of the efficient-market hypothesis is contradicted by evidence that some insiders have made large profits.

The **strong form of the efficient-market hypothesis** holds that there is no information, public or private, that allows some investors to beat the market consistently. This hypothesis is contradicted by evidence that a few do profit by using information not available to other investors — often in violation of federal laws.

Historically, these market-beaters have often been corporate insiders who bought or sold stock in the company they worked for, based on advance knowledge of new products, sales data, and so on. More recently, the feverish takeover activity in the 1980s provided valuable privileged information to accountants, lawyers, and investment bankers — a few of whom profited by purchasing stock in advance of the public announcement of the takeover bid.

Indirect evidence of the value of inside information is provided by the behavior of market prices shortly before important announcements, such as that of a takeover offer. According to an SEC study released in 1987, trading volume usually increases noticeably 10 days before a takeover announcement. On average, trading volume is three times normal three days before the announcement, five times normal the following day, and twenty times normal on the day of the announcement. The stock's price increases, on average, by 38.5 percent before the takeover attempt is formally announced. Much of this trading is an educated guess based on public information (both fact and rumor) that is widely reported in newspapers and on the Dow Jones ticker service — for instance, the filing of Form 13D with the SEC when a raider has accumulated 5 percent of a company's stock. Other investors are lured into purchases by the scent of a rising price and surging volume. Some purchases are less innocent.

Section 10(b)5 of the 1934 Securities and Exchange Act makes it *unlawful for any person to employ any device, scheme or artifice to defraud or to engage in any act, practice or course of business which operates as a fraud or deceit upon any person.*

Insider information is not even mentioned, let alone defined in this law, but over the years, the SEC has successfully applied this law to insider-trading cases. The SEC is empowered to seek a penalty equal to three times illegal profits and has also sought prison terms, not only for securities violations, but also for mail or wire fraud, obstructing justice, and income-tax evasion.

The SEC interprets illegal insider trading as trading based on material information not yet made public if the information was obtained wrongfully (such as by theft or bribery) or if the person has a fiduciary responsibility to keep the information confidential. Nor can investors trade on the basis of information that they know or have reason to know was obtained wrongfully. For example, the SEC charged that W. Paul Thayer violated Section 10(b)5 when, as chairman of LTV, he tipped his stockbroker about two takeover bids. Both were eventually convicted of obstructing justice and sentenced to four years in prison. The SEC is unlikely to press charges if it is convinced that a leak of confidential information was inadvertent; for example, a conversation overheard on an airplane. Many stock purchases and sales are made on the basis of tips and rumors, from unknown sources and of questionable accuracy. The courts are still shaping the boundaries of insider trading.

Illegal insider trading uses confidential information that was wrongfully obtained or violated a fiduciary duty.

The SEC has frequently taken the position that any trading in securities by anyone in possession of material nonpublic information is illegal. By this definition, the SEC is trying to enforce a level playing field on which all traders have access to the same information — the economists' definition of an efficient market. The SEC worries that insider traders, playing with marked cards, will undermine the integrity of financial markets and drive away honest players.

The SEC has also won cases based on a different principle — that insider trading is robbery, the theft of information. A recent example involved *The Wall Street Journal*'s daily column "Heard on the Street," which reports financial rumors and gossip. In 1983, R. Foster Winans was $18,000 in debt and earning $28,000 a year writing this column when a leading broker at Kidder, Peabody convinced Winans to give him the columns a day in advance of their publication, on the presumption that a stock's price is influenced by the appearance of a favorable or unfavorable story.[24] Some of the trades worked and some didn't; the SEC claims that the profits came to $690,000, of which Winans received $31,000.

Computers at the SEC and the stock exchanges monitor trading continuously, looking for unusually heavy volume and sudden price changes (announcing any unusual patterns with a computer-generated voice or whistle). Investigators then ask the company about impending announcements and look at brokerage records for suspicious connections. Even if there is no computer alert, after important news is released about a company, employees of the SEC and the exchanges both go back and look at the numbers again for suspicious prior trading activity. Considerable detective work may be needed to penetrate covers created by trades through friends, dummy corporations, and foreign banks. This

Highlight 10.6   The King of the Arbitrageurs

Ivan Boesky was a high-profile trader who bet millions of dollars on takeover candidates, usually in advance of any public offer, often winning big and occasionally losing big. In 1985, he had a very hot hand, consistently buying target stocks shortly before a takeover was publicly announced. He boasted of his success and attributed it to superior judgment and sleeping only three hours a night.*

> We get up earlier and tend to go to bed later at night. Like all disciplines, when you apply a great deal of energy and work effort and careful judgment, then you have a greater chance of success.

Another time, he claimed†

> What I am is the best odds-maker in the world. . . . I calculate risk better than anybody else, and that is why our firm has had the success it has. I take pride in that.

As it turned out, there was little or no risk because Boesky was cheating, playing poker with marked cards.

In 1986, the SEC accused Dennis Levine, the 33-year-old co-director of Drexel Burnham's mergers-and-acquisitions department, of trading on the basis of inside information as far back as 1980, while holding jobs at a variety of firms, and, later, of supplying Ivan Boesky with advance notice of mergers and takeovers. In return, Boesky was to have paid Levine $2.4 million shortly before Levine's arrest.

Levine agreed to pay the SEC $11.6 million in civil penalties and pleaded guilty to four felony charges, for which he was fined $362,000 and sentenced to two years in prison. He also revealed a network of investment bankers and lawyers who supplied him with inside information. More than a dozen men, almost all under the age of 40, pleaded guilty to felony charges and, perhaps worse, had their reputations and careers ruined.

The SEC accused Boesky of making at least $50 million in illegal profits based on inside information obtained from Levine, about seven major takeovers from April 1985 to April 1986. Boesky agreed to pay an astonishing $100 million — $50 million in illegal profits to reimburse investors who sold their shares to Boesky, plus a $50 million fine to the U.S. Treasury. (Shortly before his arrest, *Fortune* estimated Boesky's wealth at about $200 million.)

Boesky also pleaded guilty to a felony (for which he was sentenced to three years in prison), agreed to withdraw permanently from the U.S. securities industry (except as an individual investor), and cooperated with the authorities such as by secretly recording all of his conversations for more than a month, until this eavesdropping was discovered.

*Quoted in Michael A. Hiltzik, "Ivan Boesky: Prominence Led to Scrutiny, Charges," *Los Angeles Times,* November 16, 1986.
†Quoted in James Srodes, "We Have All Been Robbed by Deceit of 3 'Geniuses,'" *Los Angeles Times,* March 1, 1987.

search is aided by a computerized data bank that lists the personal and professional associations of half a million corporate executives and people involved in the securities industry.

In the Winans case, the stock exchanges were alerted almost immediately by an unusually heavy volume of trading and noticed that the stocks were subsequently mentioned in the "Heard on the Street" column. Soon the SEC learned that the broker was the common denominator in the trades and established his ties to Winans, who admitted his actions. Winans was immediately fired by the *Journal* and was eventually fined and sentenced to federal prison for 18 months. The broker pleaded guilty to two counts of fraud and testified against Winans.

Winans's lawyers appealed the case to the Supreme Court, arguing that Winans had no inside information and was merely passing along gossip. His information was literally heard on the street. Interestingly, the Securities Industry Association, which represents stockbrokers, was worried that stockbrokers might be prosecuted for doing the same thing, and filed a brief in support of the appeal. The SEC argued that Winans had violated a fiduciary duty, not to the companies he wrote about, but to his employer, *The Wall Street Journal,* by misappropriating confidential information about the content and timing of columns that the *Journal* planned to publish. The Supreme Court accepted the SEC's arguments and upheld Winans's conviction.

SUMMARY

Common stock is equity, representing ownership of the company, and stockholders' dividends depend on the company's profitability. Shareholders have limited liability in that they are not personally responsible for the firm's debts. Because dividends are not a tax-deductible expense for the corporation, these are taxed twice, once as corporate profits and again as shareholder income.

Stock is initially offered through investment bankers and then traded on a stock exchange or over the counter. The largest and most prominent U.S. companies are generally listed on the New York Stock Exchange. Here, representatives of brokerage firms bring investor orders to a specialist who keeps a book of orders, executing trades when possible or buying or selling for his own account, if this is necessary to fulfill an obligation to maintain a fair and orderly market. Off the exchanges, trades are made by consulting the bid and ask prices

quoted by competing market makers. The Dow Jones Industrial Index is calculated by adding up the per-share prices of 30 large, established companies and
dividing by the current value of the divisor. The S&P 500, NYSE composite,
and most other stock indexes are market-value indexes, in which each stock's
price is multiplied by the number of shares outstanding, thereby reflecting what
is happening to the market value of investor portfolios.

Fundamental analysis advises investors to compare a stock's market price
with its intrinsic value, the present value of the prospective dividends, or other
cash flow, using a required return that depends on the returns available on other
investments and on the relative riskiness of these investments. The intrinsic-
value model can be used to explain why stock prices are buoyed by a strong
economy and low interest rates. Stock prices tend to change direction a few
months before the economy, suggesting that investors anticipate economic developments before these are reflected in unemployment and GNP data, or that
changes in the stock market influence the economy. Because stocks are long-
duration assets with substantial capital risk, stock prices, like the prices of long-
term bonds are very sensitive to interest rates.

A firm should expand if the rate of return it can earn on its investments is
larger than its shareholders' required rate of return. When interest rates are low,
so are shareholder required returns, making it likely that prospective investments
are sufficiently profitable to justify making them on behalf of shareholders. The
value of Tobin's q, the ratio of the market value of a firm to the replacement
cost of its assets, provides a barometer of incentives for business expansion.

A Ponzi scheme is a zero-sum game that transfers wealth from late entrants
to early ones. The promoters, pretending to be financial wizards, send investors
fraudulent financial statements and spend most of the money raised on themselves. At times, investors are overcome by what, in retrospect, seems a collective
euphoria. In a speculative bubble, asset prices lose touch with intrinsic values
as people hope to profit not from the asset's cash flow, but from selling the asset
at ever-higher prices. When buyers cannot be found, the bubble collapses and
prices fall precipitously.

The efficient-market hypothesis says there are no clearly mispriced securities,
whose purchase or sale will yield an abnormally large return, because there are a
sufficient number of well-financed investors to eliminate obvious mispricings. One
implication is that, to the extent anticipated future events are already embedded in today's stock prices, price revisions are surprises caused by the occurrence
of unexpected events. The weak, semi-strong, and strong forms of the efficient-
market hypothesis say abnormal profits cannot be made using information about
past stock prices, all public information, and all information, respectively.

IMPORTANT TERMS

book value	efficient market
common stock	Federal Reserve Board (Fed)
constant-dividend-growth model	fundamental analysis
Dow Jones Industrial Average	intrinsic value

limited liability
over the counter (OTC)
Ponzi scheme
semi-strong form of efficient-market hypothesis
specialist

speculative bubble
speculators
strong form of efficient-market hypothesis
Tobin's q
weak form of efficient-market hypothesis

EXERCISES

1. Before the 1986 Tax Reform Act, the corporate tax rate was 46 percent and the top individual tax rate was 50 percent. Taking into account the double taxation of dividends, what was the effective tax rate on a dollar of corporate profits paid out as dividends to someone in a 50 percent tax bracket?

2. *The Wall Street Journal* awarded its tongue-in-cheek 1986 "Charity Begins at Home Award"[25]

   To Merrill Lynch Capital Markets, for its underwriting of Home Shopping Network. Merrill priced the stock at $18 a share. The day it began trading, the stock more than doubled to $42.625. . . . By June the stock had more than doubled again to $100.

   Why is the price given to three decimal places ($42.625)? The creators of Home Shopping Network sold 2 million shares to the public and kept 10 million shares for themselves. What was the total market value of the company at a price of $18? At $42.625? At $100? at $5, the price one year later? Did it really make any difference to anyone whether the two million shares were initially sold at $18 or $42 a share?

3. The investment banking firm of Morgan Stanley went public on March 21, 1986, by selling 4,500,000 shares at $56\frac{1}{2}$. In the secondary market, the stock closed at $71\frac{1}{4}$ that day on the NYSE. Who gained and lost from this mispricing?

4. Look in the most recent Friday newspaper to see what happened to IBM on the NYSE the previous day.
   a. What is IBM's current annual dividend?
   b. How many shares were traded on Thursday?
   c. What was the price of the last trade on Thursday?
   d. What was the closing price on Wednesday?

5. Look in the most recent Friday newspaper to see what happened to Apple Computer in the OTC market the previous day.
   a. What is Apple's current annual dividend?
   b. How many shares were traded on Thursday?
   c. What was the price of the last trade on Thursday?
   d. What was the closing price on Wednesday?

6. Below are the closing prices on Friday, October 16, 1987, and on Monday, October 19, 1987. Do these data indicate that stock prices fell more on this "Black Monday" for large established companies or for smaller, more speculative firms?

	Friday	**Monday**
Dow Industrials	2246.74	1738.74
NYSE Composite	159.13	128.62
AMEX Composite	323.55	282.50
NASDAQ	406.33	360.21

7. The Dow Jones Industrial Average closed at 144.13 on December 31, 1935, and at 1,546.67 on December 31, 1985. The Standard & Poor's 500 closed on these same dates at 10.60 and 211.28. Which index increased more, in percentage terms? How would you explain this difference?

8. In 1981, a New York retailer paid $24,000 for the first case of wine produced in a joint venture by Robert Mondavi and Baron Philippe de Rothschild from Cabernet Sauvignon and Cabernet Franc grapes. A commentator wrote: "With such a beginning, one wonders if any bottles of the 1979 will ever be enjoyed at a meal. Would you drink up part of your investment portfolio?"[26] Would a fundamental analyst classify the purchaser of this wine as an investor or a speculator?

9. You have decided to endow an economics chair (named, coincidentally, in your honor) at your college. Assuming that salaries are paid once a year, at the end of each year, and that the college can earn 10 percent per year on your gift, how much must you donate in order to provide $100,000 a year forever? A trustee points out that salaries may rise each year. If so, how large an endowment is needed to provide $100,000 at the end of the first year and 5 percent more each succeeding year, forever?

10. A certain stock is expected to pay an end-of-year dividend of $10 a share. What is its present value if
    a. the dividend is not expected to increase, and the shareholders' required return is 10 percent?
    b. the dividend is expected to grow by 5 percent per year, and the shareholders' required return is 10 percent?
    c. the dividend is expected to grow by 10 percent per year, and the shareholders' required return is 15 percent?

11. A famous stock adviser once suggested that a conspiracy between stock specialists and bankers is suggested by the fact that[27]

    when you're having a decline in stock prices you can always anticipate an increase in interest rates.

    The idea is apparently that when specialists lower stock prices so that insiders can accumulate stocks cheaply, banks raise interest rates so that the public cannot borrow money to purchase stocks at these bargain prices. Is there any nonconspiratorial explanation for the observation that a drop in stock prices is often accompanied by an increase in interest rates?

12. On July 19, 1984, Chrysler sold all of the stocks in its pension fund and bought bonds with the proceeds. In January 1987, rumors that Chrysler was going back into stocks[28]

    prompted some guffaws on Wall Street because, on the surface, it might appear that Chrysler has missed an enormous stock rally and now wants to get back in at the top.

    But it isn't quite that simple, because the bond market did nearly as well as the stock market in the 2½ years between July 1984 and December 1986.

    In that period . . . the S&P 500-stock index returned 25% annually, counting dividends [while] the Shearson Lehman aggregate bond index returned 22.4 percent annually. . . . In fact, the bonds held by Chrysler equaled the stock market's performance because they were slightly longer in maturity than the Shearson index.

    What economic event would explain simultaneous bond- and stock-market rallies? What does maturity have to do with performance?

13. An article in the *American Banker's Association Journal* discusses the estimation of commercial damages when one company's violation of a contract forces another to go out of business.[29] Instead of trying to estimate the liquidation value, the author argues that a company with current net earnings of $50,000 growing at 5 percent a year would, at a 25 percent discount rate, have a "capitalization rate" of 5, giving it a value of 5($50,000) = $250,000. Where did the value 5 for the capitalization rate come from?

14. In 1986 Michael Sherman, head of Shearson Lehman's investment-policy committee, recommended a portfolio of 70 percent stocks,

30 percent long-term bonds, and no short-term bonds. "If you have cash [short-term bonds] in your account, it means you don't trust what you're doing. . . . More stocks than bonds generally indicates a positive outlook both in Treasury rates and the economy."[30] (The opposite occurred in early 1982, when more bonds than stocks in portfolios said that investors liked interest rates but not the economy.) Explain why forecasts of interest rates and the economy should influence the portfolio allocation between stocks and bonds. Are there any circumstances in which you would recommend holding a substantial amount of "cash"?

15. Peter L. Bernstein found that stock and bond prices generally moved in *opposite* directions during most of the 1960s, but in the *same* direction in the 1970s.[31] Is there any logical explanation?

16. Here are excerpts from a 1986 newspaper article.[32]

The underlying U.S. economy today is not strong enough to support the market's enthusiasm, and it is not gaining. The force driving stock prices up is declining interest rates (and oil prices). Well, interest rates decline when lenders have lots of money but borrowers don't have lots of need for it; that is, when business is slow. Like now.

Every new statistic — retail sales off a bit, unemployment up a bit — indicates that the economy is only so-so. Which wouldn't be so bad if the outlook for the economy were better. But it's not.

Despite lower interest rates, business doesn't seem in a hurry to invest in new plant and equipment. . . .

What does it all mean? Only that the economy will putter along — no disaster but no great glory either — and the stock market will probably take a sharp decline.

Is there any rational explanation for why the stock market might be strong, even while the economy is not?

17. In 1948, a distinguished economist proclaimed that "Never in the lifetime of anyone in this room will government two-and-a-halves [2½ percent coupon bonds] sell below par."[33] Was he right?

18. The International Bank of Roseau made this offer: for $300, you can receive a short course on international banking and earn the right to sign others up for this course. If you sign up six people, you receive a $1,000 "loan" from the bank that does not have to be repaid. Suppose that you sign up six people, and each of these sign up six people, and so on eight more times. How many people will have taken this course? How much money will the bank have taken in and paid out? Why do you think the attorney general of Florida shut down this bank?

19. In late 1983, the J. David investment company sent a memo to a bank stating that J. David's cash-flow problems were temporary because its investor requests for withdrawals could soon be satisfied by the arrival of funds from new investors. Why might such a memo suggest fraud? Why might a legitimate business do the same thing, with no fraud whatsoever? If you were a bank officer, how would you tell the difference?

20. A newspaper columnist wrote that[34]

More than $500 billion was wiped off stock prices on Oct. 19. . . . Yet there is hope, even a growing belief, that somehow that $500-billion loss doesn't touch the real American economy.

Unfortunately, the hope is false — as you'll see if you think about it. The $500 billion was real enough when it increased corporate cash flow; real enough when investors paid it out for stocks at high prices. Stocks do not rise on air, but on somebody paying real money to buy them.

Where is that real money now? It is gone. It is as if that $500 billion had built 10,000 factories and office buildings and homes and shopping centers and they had all burned down in a single day.

a. Do investors buying stock increase a corporation's cash flow?

b. If the market value of a company's stock rises by $1 million, must investors have purchased $1 million worth of stock?

c. Where does the money that investors spend on stock go?

d. If you were the President of the United States, would you rather have the stock market fall by $500 billion or have $500 billion worth of factories destroyed by fire?

21. The fifth edition of Graham and Dodd's classic *Security Analysis* was published in late 1987, updated by three long-time associates.[35] In it, they use the following economic projections from financial institutions to estimate the fundamental value of the S&P 400 Industrial Stock Index:

Dividend   = $9.00
Growth rate   = 7.5 percent
Required return = 11.25 percent (8.5 percent Aaa industrial bond rate + 2.75 percent risk premium)

What was their estimate of the fundamental value of the S&P 400 Index? (On October 13, 1987 the actual value was 364.)

22. Explain why this advice is not very helpful.[36]

Since we know stocks are going to fall as well as rise, we might as well get a little traffic out of them. A man who buys a stock at 10 and sells it at 20 makes 100 per cent. But a man who buys it at 10, sells it at 14½, buys it back at 12 and sells it at 18, buys it back at 15 and sells it at 20, makes 188 per cent.

23. A man gives inspirational lectures on how to make a fortune in real estate by buying "bargain properties"; for example, "if you buy a $100,000 house for $80,000 you've got a $20,000 profit right off the bat." If so, is the real-estate market efficient? If the real-estate market is reasonably efficient, what is the flaw in his advice?

24. Briefly explain why the following allegations, if true, either would or would not provide evidence against the efficient-market hypothesis.

a. A well-known investment strategy consistently earns a return greater than zero.

b. When the stock market goes down in January, it usually goes down during the next 11 months.

c. The stock market almost always goes up at least 20 percent in the 9 months preceding a presidential election and goes down 20 percent during the 12 months following elections.

d. Corporate bonds consistently give higher returns than municipal bonds.

25. Explain why you won't get rich following this advice in *Consumer Digest's Get Rich Investment Guide*.[37]

The ability to track interest rates as they pertain to bonds is made easier by following the path of the Prime Rate (the rate of interest charged by banks to their top clients). If the consensus shown in top business journals indicates that rates are going up, this means that bonds will go down in price. Therefore, when it seems that rates are moving up, an investor should wait until some "peaking" of rates is foreseen.

26. An advertisement for a penny stock report was headlined "5,500 percent profit" and explained[38]

EXAMPLE: On Sept. 1983 if you had purchased 25,000 shares of MAX AXAM at .25 a share ($6250), you could have sold on Feb. 1986 at $14.00 per share and pocketed $350,000. Imagine a gain of 5500%!

Why is this example unpersuasive?

27. In November 1985, Edward Yardeni of Prudential-Bache said, "We still like stocks not so much because we foresee better-than-expected profits, but because we foresee lower-than-expected interest rates."[39] Why do stock prices

depend on profits and interest rates? Why was Yardeni careful to say "higher-than-expected" and "lower-than-expected"?

28. In 1987, a brokerage firm observed that "since 1965, the Dow Jones Industrial Average declined 16 out of 21 times during the month of May. As of this writing, it appears as if another down May is in the offing. We offer no rational explanation for this 'May phenomenon.' We only observe that it often sets up attractive trading opportunities."[40] Does this evidence persuade you to buy lots of stock next April? Why or why not?

29. R. Foster Winans, who leaked stories that were going to be published in *The Wall Street Journal,* wrote that "The only reason to invest in the market is because you think you know something others don't."[41] Is there any other reason to buy stock? If everyone had exactly the same information, would anyone buy stock?

30. In 1983, the SEC enforcement chief said that "Anyone who engages in insider trading is clearly a thief."[42] Explain what the following insiders are stealing and from whom they are stealing it.

    a. A chemist discovers a cure for baldness and buys stock in the company he works for before revealing his discovery.

    b. A company's chief executive officer sells half of his stock in the company before releasing a disappointing earnings report.

    c. A merger-and-acquisitions lawyer working for a corporate raider buys stock in the target company before a tender offer is announced.

The Management of Financial Intermediaries

RISK

AND

RETURN

The safest way to double your money is to fold it over once and put it in your pocket.

Frank McKinney Hubbard

Our lives are filled with uncertainties, ranging from tomorrow's weather to the success of a marriage to war and peace. Should you invite someone to a movie? Should you accept a job offer? Should you buy a house or rent an apartment? Banks, too, must confront the unknown.

What interest rate should they offer on deposits?
Should they open new branches?
Should they buy short-term or long-term bonds?
Should they emphasize adjustable-rate or fixed-rate loans?

Uncertainty, with all its attendant excitement and frustration, is unavoidable. But, in both our personal and business decisions, we can use probabilities to make rational choices. There will still be surprises, pleasant and unpleasant, but we can anticipate faring better, on average, if we think about our alternatives and their likely consequences before we act.

A number of techniques have been developed to help people make rational decisions in an uncertain world, and these tools can be applied to a wide variety of choices. In this chapter we will see how uncertainty can often be quantified by specifying probabilities and calculating two statistical measures — the mean and the standard deviation. We will see that these two measures are useful for describing opportunities, but that our choices ultimately depend on our attitude toward risk. We begin by looking at how probabilities can be used to gauge uncertainty.

USING PROBABILITIES

Probabilities can be used to quantify uncertainty.

Whenever there is uncertainty, a variety of outcomes is possible. **Probabilities** can quantify these uncertainties by describing which outcomes are likely and which are unlikely. When a coin is fairly flipped, the two possible outcomes, heads and tails, are equally likely, so we assign a probability of ½ to each outcome. What about an investment with two possible outcomes, a $100 loss and a $200 gain? If a financial analyst considers these outcomes equally likely, then each has a probability of ½. If the $100 loss is twice as likely as the $200 gain, then there is a ⅔ probability of a $100 loss and a ⅓ probability of a $200 gain.

Subjective Probabilities

With coins, dice, and cards, we may be able to reason out the probabilities by counting the number of equally likely outcomes. In other situations, where the outcomes are not equally likely, historical data may be useful: the 0.51 probability that a baby will be born male and the 0.53 probability that a twenty-year-old woman will live to be eighty can be estimated from the observed frequencies with which babies are born male and women live to be eighty. In most personal and business decisions, subjective probabilities must be used to assess the likelihood of various outcomes.

Many probabilities are subjective, and vary from person to person.

Consider, for instance, the probability that the next President of the United States will be a Republican. Unlike a coin flip, the chances are not necessarily 50 percent. In 1946, the "Wizard of Odds" used historical data.[1]

Miss Deanne Skinner of Monrovia, California, asks: Can the Wizard tell me what the odds are of the next President of the United States being a Democrat? . . . Without considering the candidates, the odds would be 2 to 1 in favor of a Republican because since 1861 when that party was founded, there have been 12 Republican Presidents and only 7 Democrats.

The probability that the next president will be Republican need not equal the historical frequency with which presidents have been Republican. The electorate, the parties, the candidates, and the nation all evolve as time passes, making the outcome of an election 100 years ago of little relevance today.

In 1936, Franklin Roosevelt ran for reelection against Alf Landon. Should the forecasters have assumed that Landon had a 70 percent chance of winning because Republicans had won 70 percent of the previous contests? Or should they have taken into account that Roosevelt was a popular president running for reelection against the unexciting Governor of Kansas, the standard-bearer of the

| **Probabilities Clarify Our Views** | **Highlight 11.1** |

In some situations, such as a severe sunburn or a broken bone, the doctor is certain about the patient's medical condition. Other conditions, such as heart disease, are uncertain, and a diagnosis may be clarified with probabilities. Consider a patient who takes an electrocardiographic stress test and shows some inconclusive symptoms of coronary heart disease. When the patient asks, "Do I have heart disease?" a definite answer of "yes" or "no" is unwarranted, because the test is imperfect. The patient should be told that the results suggest disease, but words alone can be misunderstood.

When sixteen doctors were asked to assign a numerical probability to the diagnosis "cannot be excluded," the answers ranged from 5 percent probability to 95 percent, with an average of 47 percent.* When they were asked to interpret "likely," the probabilities ranged from 20 percent to 95 percent, with an average of 75 percent. Even the phrase "low probability" elicited answers ranging from 0 percent to 80 percent, with an average of 18 percent. If one doctor means an 80 percent chance by "low probability" and another means no chance at all, then it is better to state the probability that one has in mind than to risk an unfortunate misinterpretation of ambiguous words.

The same lesson applies to a bank's diagnosis of economic conditions. Instead of saying that the possibility of higher interest rates "cannot be excluded" or that a recession "is likely," strategists should use probabilities to clarify their forecasts and ensure that their views are understood.

---

*George A. Diamond and James S. Forrester, "Metadiagnosis," *American Journal of Medicine*, July 1983, pp. 129–137.

party that many voters blamed for the Great Depression? Were the odds the same in 1972, when Richard Nixon ran against the liberal George McGovern, as in 1964, when conservative Barry Goldwater battled the incumbent Lyndon Johnson? Were George Bush's chances in 1988 identical to Landon's in 1936? The odds change from election to election, along with the candidates and the state of the nation.

So it is with many situations. If you buy a certain computer program, what is the probability that, six months from now, you will regret having done so? It is certainly not a 50-50 coin flip, and you surely shouldn't estimate the probability simply by calculating the historical frequency with which people regret their purchases. Your chances of being dissatisfied depend on your needs and on the details of this particular program.

A bank's decision to buy short-term or long-term bonds also depends on subjective probabilities. The bank has some information on past interest-rate fluctuations, but the present situation is always unique. An assessment of the chances of interest rates rising or falling must be a subjective blending of information about such matters as the state of the economy, government monetary policy, and the volatility of bond prices.

The best alternative to a shrug of the shoulders and a sheepish "Who knows?" is to list the possible outcomes and use whatever information is at our disposal to assign probabilities as best we can. Unlike a coin flip, estimates of economic probabilities no doubt vary from person to person, leading some to believe that one investment is very attractive while others think the opposite. This disagreement is one reason there are financial markets, so that the bulls can buy from the pessimists.

Probability Distributions

A probability distribution shows the probabilities for ranges of outcomes.

Outcomes are seldom as simple as the heads-or-tails possibilities for a coin flip. The infinite variety of possible returns precludes an exhaustive enumeration, so, instead, we specify a **probability distribution**, giving the probabilities for ranges of outcomes. Table 11.1 shows an example for a hypothetical investment. There is a 0.10 probability that the return will turn out to be between 20 percent and 30 percent, a 0.30 probability that it will be between 10 percent and 20 percent, and so on. Figure 11.1 is a graphic representation of this probability distribution, using the area of each block to show the probability for that range of outcomes. With a graph, we can tell at a glance which outcomes are considered likely and which are thought unlikely. Highlight 11.2 tells how one bank uses probability distributions to help make its investment decisions.

EXPECTED RETURN

Now we will look at how probabilities can be used to make informed decisions. Probability theory was originally developed in the 1600s by Blaise Pascal, Pierre de Fermat, and other mathematicians interested in games of chance. One of the questions that Pascal sought to answer was posed by a French nobleman, the Chevalier de Mere. The nobleman asked why, on average, he made money betting that he could roll at least one 6 in four throws of a single die, but lost money betting that he could roll at least one double-6 in twenty-four throws of a pair of dice. Pascal showed that de Mere, in fact, had a 0.518 probability of winning the first bet but only a 0.491 probability of winning the second. With these probabilities, Pascal could calculate de Mere's expected profits.

Calculation of the Expected Value

The expected value is a probability-weighted average of the possible outcomes.

The **expected value**, usually denoted by the Greek symbol μ (pronounced "mew"), is a weighted average of the possible returns, using probabilities as weights to reflect the likelihood of each outcome. Suppose, for instance, that there are two outcomes, winning or losing $100, and each is equally likely.

Table 11.1	**A Probability Distribution for an Investment Return**

Return	Probability
20% to 30%	0.10
10% to 20%	0.30
0% to 10%	0.30
−10% to 0%	0.20
−20% to −10%	0.10
	1.00

Return x_i	Probability $P[x_i]$
+$100	0.5
−$100	0.5

The expected value uses the probabilities to average these two possibilities.

$$\mu = (+\$100)(0.5) + (-\$100)(0.5) = 0$$

The general formula for the expected value is

$$\mu = x_1 P[x_1] + x_2 P[x_2] + \cdots + x_n P[x_n] \qquad (1)$$

The expected value is a statistical average, not (as in everyday English) the outcome that we expect or consider most likely. Indeed, in the example, there is no chance that you will win \$0 — you will either win \$100 or lose \$100.

Figure 11.1	**Return Probabilities**

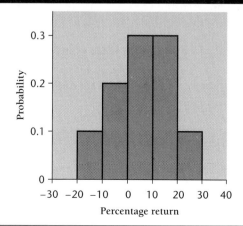

The expected value is the long-run average return if the frequency with which each outcome occurs is equal to its probability. If you do win $100 half the time and lose $100 the other half, your average winnings will be zero.

The expected value can be used to measure the amount, on average, that de Mere could expect to win or lose in his gambles. If he bet the equivalent of $100 that he could roll one 6 in four throws of a single die, then his expected value is

$$(+\$100)(0.518) + (-\$100)(0.482) = \$3.60$$

On a single wager, he will win or lose $100. But, in the long run if, as expected, he wins 51.8 percent of these bets, he will win an average of $3.60 per wager. On his second game, betting that he could roll at least one double-6 in twenty-four throws of a pair of dice, the 0.491 chance of winning gives an expected value of

$$(+\$100)(0.491) + (-\$100)(0.509) = -\$1.80$$

showing that he could expect his losses to average $1.80 per wager.

Should You Maximize Expected Value?

It is not necessarily optimal to maximize expected return.

Pascal and other early probability theorists used probabilities to calculate the expected value of various games of chance and to determine which were the most profitable. They assumed that a rational person should choose the course of action with the highest expected value. This expected-value criterion is appealing for gambles that are repeated over and over. It makes good sense to look at the long-run average when there is a long run to average over. Casinos, state lotteries, and insurance companies are very interested in the expected returns on the repetitive gambles they offer, since anything with a negative expected return will almost certainly be unprofitable in the long run.

However, an expected-return criterion is often inappropriate. State lotteries have a positive expected return for the state and, because their gain is your loss, a negative expected return for people who buy lottery tickets. Those who buy lottery tickets are not maximizing expected return. Insurance policies give insurance companies a positive expected return and insurance buyers a negative expected return. People who buy insurance are not maximizing expected return, either. Diversified investments provide yet another example. An expected-return maximizer should invest everything in the single asset with the highest expected return. Individuals, banks, and businesses that hold dozens or thousands of assets must not be maximizing expected return.

We can also construct hypothetical situations to show that expected-return maximization is not always appealing. Suppose that a messenger from a rich recluse were to burst into class and announce that you have been chosen to receive a gift of $1 million. He opens a briefcase filled with $100 bills to show you that he is serious; but, as you reach for them, he closes his briefcase and asks if you would like something a bit more sporting. You can either take the

Interest Rate Uncertainty at Morgan Guaranty   Highlight 11.2

The success of asset/liability decisions made by financial institutions depends critically on future interest rates. When interest rates rise unexpectedly, those who invested long-term at a fixed interest rate and those who borrowed short-term at a variable interest rate find that they made an expensive mistake. An unexpected drop in interest rates is costly for those who invested short-term or borrowed long-term. Yet interest rates are notoriously difficult to forecast.

Up until 1971, the top managers at Morgan Guaranty Trust met regularly to determine the interest-rate forecasts to use in all asset/liability decisions. For each interest-rate prediction, they would come up with a single number, such as "our best estimate of the Treasury-bill (T-bill) rate three months from now is 6 percent." Yet, as the senior operations research officer explained*

> *Considerable discussion normally preceded the managers' arrival at the single-valued expectation, but there was no formal procedure for quantifying the collective expectations of the participants, and the uncertainty surrounding these expectations.*

How confident were they in their 6 percent forecast? Did they mean 5¾ percent to 6¼ percent, or 4 percent to 8 percent? If the T-bill rate isn't 6 percent, is it more likely to be somewhat higher or a bit lower? The answers to such questions require probabilities, so, in 1971, they began reporting probabilities in place of a single interest-rate forecast.

Twice a month, specialists write down interest-rate probabilities individually and then meet as a group to compare notes. Instead of thinking of the most likely value for the interest rate, perhaps 6 percent, each member thinks of the possible values — 5 percent, 5½ percent, 6 percent, and so on — and assigns probabilities to each possibility.

The probability distribution in Panel (a) of the accompanying figure reflects a committee member who is pretty confident that the T-bill rate will be 6 percent; the distribution in Panel (b) shows considerable uncertainty. In Panels (c) and (d), 6 percent is the most likely value; but in one case the person feels that there is a good chance that the T-bill rate will be less than 6 percent, and in the other the opposite is true. None of these subtleties is revealed in a 6 percent forecast unaccompanied by probabilities. With probabilities, we can see not only the most likely value but also the likely range, and we can see whether the forecaster believes that the rate is more likely to be above or below 6 percent.

The senior research officer describes how valuable these probability graphs were at a November 13, 1972, group meeting.

it was useful to know why both Griffin and Riefler felt the rate would stay essentially the same, whereas the others felt it would rise; and to find out why Engle felt that there was no chance the rate would drop below 5⅛% and felt so strongly that it would rise over 5⅝%, when nobody else in the group felt that way.

After such discussion, the committee constructs a consensus probability distribution, which is then presented to top management.

Four Interest-Rate Forecasts

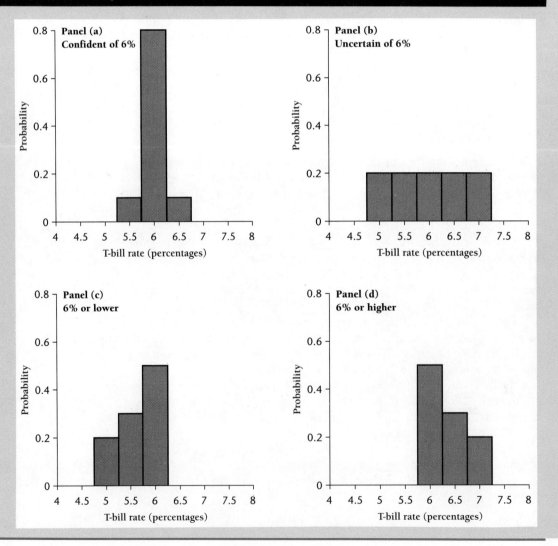

The probabilities used by Morgan Guaranty are necessarily subjective, but they accomplish their task of describing the beliefs of committee members.

the only "incorrect" [distribution] is one which does not correctly reflect its creators' expectations. While there is no guarantee that [probability distributions] will give an accurate picture of the future, they will give an accurate picture of an individual's view of the future.

*This and following quotations and the accompanying discussion are based on Irwin Kabus, "You Can Bank on Uncertainty," *Harvard Business Review*, May–June 1976, pp. 95–105.

$1 million or flip a coin five times. If you get heads on every flip, you get $40 million; any tails and you get nothing but a good story. Think about it. If, like most people, you would take the sure million, then you are not maximizing expected return.

Risk Aversion

The primary inadequacy of expected-return maximization is that it neglects risk — how certain or uncertain a situation is. An expected-return maximizer considers a sure $1 million, a 50 percent chance at $2 million, and a 1 percent chance at $100 million all equally attractive, because each has an expected value of $1 million. If these alternatives were offered over and over, there would be little difference in the long run because the payoffs from each would almost certainly average close to $1 million per play. But if you get only one chance at the game, the possible payoffs are very different, a difference ignored by an expected-value calculation. In an expected-return computation, it doesn't matter that in the first option there is a 100 percent chance of receiving $1 million and in the third option there is a 99 percent chance of receiving nothing. But this difference does matter to many people.

Much of the uncertainty we face is unique, not repetitive, and it does matter that the actual outcome may differ from its expected value. This possible divergence is called risk; how people react reflects their risk preferences.

Risk preferences can be gauged by whether a person prefers to take a gamble or, instead, to receive the expected value of the gamble. Consider, for example, a gamble with a 50 percent chance of receiving $100 and a 50 percent chance of receiving nothing. Would you rather take this gamble or, instead, receive $50, which is the gamble's expected value? There is no right or wrong answer, but how you answer reveals your attitude toward risk.

There are three broad categories of risk preference.

A person who is **risk neutral** chooses the alternative with the highest expected return and thus is indifferent between a safe $50 and a 50 percent chance at $100.

A person who is **risk seeking** would rather take the gamble than receive its expected value.

A person who is **risk averse** prefers the expected value to the gamble and takes the $50.

Risk-averse people accept lower expected returns in order to avoid risk.

While the risk-neutral person maximizes expected return, a risk-seeker is willing to give up some expected return to get more risk and a risk-averse person is willing to give up expected return to avoid risk. A risk-neutral person does not like insurance or lottery tickets because both have negative expected returns. A risk seeker may buy lottery tickets even if the expected return is negative. A risk-averse person may purchase insurance with a negative expected return.

Risk Bearing

This acknowledged variety in risk preferences explains why some people accept gambles that others shun, and why some buy insurance that others avoid. A person's response to risk may also depend on the size of gamble. It is not unreasonable to be risk neutral about a wager involving a few dollars, but risk averse about a gamble involving all of one's wealth. You might flip a coin to see who buys coffee — and still buy fire insurance.

One implication of this argument is that wealthy citizens may take gambles that others shun because these gambles have relatively small effects on their wealth. People who own little more than the house they live in buy fire and life insurance, even though the expected return is negative, to avoid the possibility of a catastrophic loss. For the very wealthy, the loss of a house or wages has little effect on family wealth, and a decision not to purchase insurance is a relatively small gamble with a positive expected return.

In fact, a wealthy person might be willing to sell insurance to a person of more modest means. Consider Joe, who owns a $50,000 house and little else. This house is near an earthquake fault, and Joe is afraid that he will lose his house in a quake. Jane, on the other hand, is very rich, and winning or losing $50,000 is, for her, no scarier than it is for Joe to flip a coin to see who pays for beer. If both believe that the probability that the house will be destroyed by an earthquake is 0.001 and Jane is risk neutral about a $50,000 gamble, she may offer to insure Joe against an earthquake for a $100 fee. The expected value of the insurance payoff is

$$0.001(\$50,000) + 0.999(\$0) = \$50$$

only half the $100 cost of the policy. A risk-neutral person, like Jane, is willing to take this gamble, selling for $100 something with an expected value of $50. Joe, on the other hand, may be sufficiently risk averse that he pays $100 to avoid a gamble with an expected loss of $50. If so, there is room for a deal, in that he is willing to buy what she is willing to sell.

An earthquake is a real physical danger, a natural risk that has to be borne by someone. Those who are the least risk averse are the most willing to bear such risks. Those who are more risk averse can, for a price, use financial contracts to pass such risks on to others. In the same way, stocks and bonds reflect real economic risks — including the chances of recession or high interest rates — and their prices are set so that, considering the risk and the expected return, some investors are willing to hold such assets. Banks and other financial intermediaries offer a variety of financial contracts to depositors, borrowers, and other customers that help the risk averse shift risks to others.

Financial contracts can be used to shift real economic risks.

The Standard Deviation as a Measure of Risk

Drawing on their statistical backgrounds, in the 1950s Harry Markowitz and James Tobin proposed measuring risk by the standard deviation of the probability distribution — a procedure that is widely used today by financial analysts.[2] If the possible returns are denoted by x and the expected value of x by μ, then the **variance** σ^2 of a probability distribution is the expected value of $(x - \mu)^2$; that is, the probability-weighted, average squared deviation of the possible outcomes about their mean:

$$\sigma^2 = (x_1 - \mu)^2 P[x_1] + (x_2 - \mu)^2 P[x_2] + \cdots + (x_n - \mu)^2 P[x_n] \qquad (2)$$

The square root of the variance is the **standard deviation** σ (pronounced "sigma").

The standard deviation is a widely used measure of risk.

For each possible outcome x_i, we calculate how far x_i is from the expected value μ, and then square this deviation. By squaring, we do two things. First, we eliminate the distinction between positive and negative deviations. What matters to a variance calculation is how far the outcome is from μ, not whether it is above or below μ. Second, squaring gives primary importance to large deviations. One deviation of 10, squared, will increase the variance as much as four deviations of five, squared.

After calculating the squared deviations for each possible outcome, we calculate the average squared deviation using the outcome probabilities as weights. This weighted average of the squared deviations from μ is the variance, and its square root is the standard deviation. Either can be used, but the standard deviation is usually easier to interpret because it has the same units (% or $) as x and μ, while the units for the variance are dollars-squared or percent-squared.

The standard deviation measures uncertainty by considering the probability of returns far from the expected value. Table 11.2 illustrates this principle by showing the means, variances, and standard deviations of the returns after one year for three alternative investments that a bank might make. The bank's estimates of the returns assume, unrealistically, that there are only two possible outcomes: interest rates will rise or fall by 1 percentage point.

The return on one-year Treasury bills has an expected value of 8 percent and a standard deviation of 0 percent, since the return is certain. For the

Table 11.2   Gauging Three Investments

Investment	Mean	Variance	Standard Deviation
1-year Treasury bills $P[8\%] = 1$	8%	0	0%
10-year Treasury zeros $P[18\%] = 0.5$ $P[-2\%] = 0.5$	8%	100	10%
20-year Treasury zeros $P[30\%] = 0.5$ $P[-10\%] = 0.5$	10%	400	20%

10-year Treasury zeros, the return will be either 18 percent or −2 percent. The mean (or expected value) is

$$\mu = (18\%)(0.5) + (-2\%)(0.5) = 8\%$$

and the variance

$$\sigma^2 = (18\% - 8\%)^2(0.5) + (-2\% - 8\%)^2(0.5) = 100$$

implies a standard deviation of

$$\sigma = \sqrt{100} = 10\%$$

For the 20-year Treasury zeros, the return will be either 30 percent or −10 percent. The mean, variance, and standard deviation are

$$\mu = (30\%)(0.5) + (-10\%)(0.5) = 10\%$$
$$\sigma^2 = (30\% - 10\%)^2(0.5) + (-10\% - 10\%)^2(0.5) = 400$$
$$\sigma = \sqrt{400} = 20\%$$

Treasury bills have a 0 percent standard deviation, because the return is certain to be 8 percent. The Treasury bills and 10-year Treasury zeros each have an 8 percent expected return, but different degrees of uncertainty or risk. The 10-year Treasury zeros have a large standard deviation and the 20-year Treasury zeros have an even larger one, because there is a substantial chance that the return will be far from its expected value.

If the standard deviation is an appropriate measure of risk, then a risk-averse bank prefers Treasury bills to these 10-year zeros and, depending on the degree of risk aversion, may also prefer them to the 20-year zeros. A risk-neutral or risk-seeking bank prefers the 20-year zeros.

The Normal Distribution

Often it is useful to assume that we can approximate the possible returns in an uncertain situation by a standard probability distribution, such as the bell-shaped Gaussian or **normal distribution** shown in Figure 11.2.

Figure 11.2   The Normal Distribution

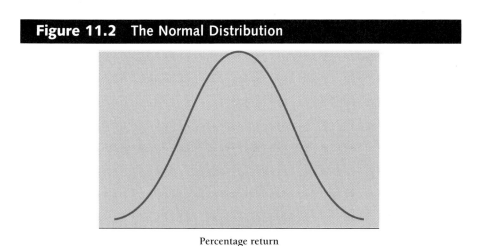

Percentage return

Many outcomes are the cumulative consequences of large numbers of random events. The central limit theorem, the most important discovery in the long history of probability and statistics, says that outcomes that are the cumulation of independent, identically distributed random events are described (approximately) by the normal distribution. In nature, the number of ridges on scallop shells, the number of kernels on ears of corn, the number of leaves on trees, the number of hairs on dogs, the breadths of human skulls, heights, weights, IQ scores, and the position of molecules and planets all conform to an approximate normal distribution.

The normal distribution is often used to describe uncertain situations.

In financial markets, the efficient-market hypothesis implies that asset returns are the cumulative consequence of independent random events and thus may be approximated by the normal distribution. For example, Figure 11.3 shows that the actual distribution of the daily rates of return from IBM stock in 1983 is roughly normal, with a mean of 0.12 percent and a standard deviation of 1.28 percent. The actual distribution is not *exactly* normal, but it is close enough so that the normal distribution can be used as a simplifying approximation.

Two convenient rules of thumb can help us interpret the standard deviation of a normally distributed random variable. There is about a ⅔ probability (more precisely, 0.683) that the value of a normally distributed variable will be within one standard deviation of its mean and a 0.95 probability that it will be within two standard deviations.

For the IBM data in Figure 11.3, the one-standard-deviation rule of thumb tells us that approximately 68 percent of the daily returns should be in the interval 0.12 percent ± 1.28 percent; that is, −1.16 percent to 1.40 percent. In fact, 69 percent fall in this range. With a normal distribution, there is a 95 percent probability of being within two standard deviations of the mean; 96 percent of the IBM daily returns are in this range.

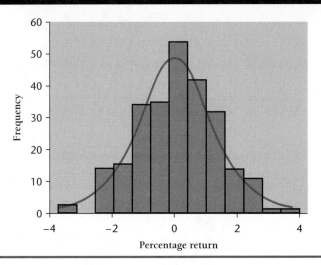

Figure 11.3 Daily Percentage Returns, IBM, 1983

If a bank estimates that the return on its bond portfolio during the next 12 months is normally distributed with an expected value of 10 percent and a standard deviation of 5 percent, there is a 0.95 probability that the return will be between 9 percent and 20 percent. There is a 0.025 probability that the return will be less than 0 percent and a 0.025 probability that the return will be larger than 20 percent.

Long Shots and Skewness

The standard deviation is a satisfactory measure of risk if the returns are, like the daily IBM returns, approximated by the normal distribution. Some asset returns, however, are very asymmetrical, and the standard deviation is not an adequate explanation of why investors find these assets appealing or unattractive. For example, why do otherwise risk-averse people, who buy insurance and own diversified portfolios, buy lottery tickets — risky long shots with negative expected returns? Similarly, the relatively low average return and high standard deviation cannot explain why risk-averse people invest in young, unproven companies, hoping to catch the start of an eventual spectacular success such as IBM or McDonald's.

Because the squaring of deviations about the mean treats gains and losses symmetrically, the standard deviation cannot distinguish between the two investments in Table 11.3. These investments have the same expected value and the same standard deviation, yet many people prefer the first asset to the second. These investments have very asymmetrical, skewed returns, quite unlike the normal distribution. The first is a positively skewed long shot, with a small chance of a large gain; the second is a negatively skewed long shot with a small

Some people are attracted to positively skewed long shots.

Table 11.3   **Two Asymmetrical Investments**

Investment	Expected Return	Standard Deviation
1. $P[-\$100] = 0.999$ $P[\$99,900] = 0.001$	$0	$3,160.70
2. $P[-\$99,900] = 0.001$ $P[\$100] = 0.999$	$0	$3,160.70

chance of a large loss. Figure 11.4 shows continuous probability distributions with similar positive and negative skewness.

The purchase of a lottery ticket is a positively skewed gamble like the first investment in Table 11.3, but with a negative expected return. A decision not to purchase fire insurance is a negatively skewed gamble, similar to the second example in Table 11.3, but with a positive expected return. The use of the standard deviation to measure risk explains why a risk-averse person might buy insurance and spurn lottery tickets, while a risk seeker does the opposite. But the standard deviation offers no easy explanation for the simultaneous purchase of both lottery tickets and insurance.

Perhaps some otherwise risk-averse people enjoy the mild suspense provided by lottery tickets and consider the purchase inexpensive, if brief, entertainment. Or they may have a very mistaken assessment of their chances of winning (what Adam Smith called "absurd presumptions in their own good fortune"[3]). Another possibility is that people care not only about the uncertainty, as gauged by the standard deviation, but also about the skewness. Long shots offer them the slim chance of changing their lives completely, or, as one Pennsylvania woman put it, "My chances of winning a million are better than my chances of earning a million."[4]

The popularity of lottery tickets suggests that people like positively skewed returns, a conclusion that is supported by the overbetting on long shots at horse races and by a number of empirical studies.[5] We should consequently be cautious in using the standard deviation alone to gauge risk if the probability distribution for the returns is highly skewed, as with lottery tickets and stock in new companies. In other situations, where the probability distribution is reasonably symmetrical (or, even better, approximately normal), the standard deviation is a very simple and powerful way to measure risk.

THE GAINS FROM DIVERSIFICATION

We will now conclude this chapter by applying probabilities and risk preferences to an investment decision faced by banks. A risk-neutral investor maximizes expected return by investing all funds in the single asset with the highest expected

Figure 11.4 Skewed Probability Distributions

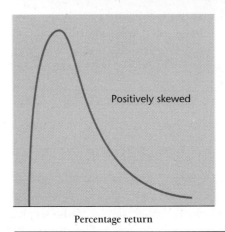

Positively skewed

Percentage return

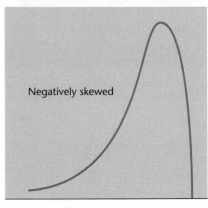

Negatively skewed

Percentage return

Diversified portfolios can be used to reduce risk.

return. A risk-averse person, in contrast, builds a **diversified portfolio** by investing in several dissimilar assets. The prevalence of diversified portfolios suggests that most investors, including banks, are risk averse.

Diversification reduces the chances of an extreme outcome, either good or bad. If you invest all of your money in one stock, then your return hinges entirely on the performance of that stock: if the company goes bankrupt, you will, too. Similarly, a bank that lends all of its money to a single borrower is literally betting the bank on the ability of that borrower to repay the loan. If the bank instead spreads its loans among hundreds or thousands of borrowers, it will take an incredible string of bad luck for it to lose everything. With thousands of loans, it is unlikely that no one will default, but it is extremely unlikely that everyone will.

Asset Correlations

The degree of risk reduction provided by diversification depends on the correlations among the returns on the individual assets. A large number of independent investments provides very effective diversification. If you flip a coin 10,000 times, you don't know which flips will be heads and which tails, but you can be confident of the average result — roughly half heads and half tails. (There is only a 0.02 probability of more than 51 percent heads in 10,000 coin flips and a 0.0003 probability of more than 52 percent heads.) In the same way, a bank doesn't know which loans will default but, if it has estimated the default probability accurately, can be confident of the average default rate for 10,000 independent loans.

The gains from diversification depend on whether the correlations among asset returns are zero, positive, or negative.

If the outcomes are not independent, then they may be either positively or negatively correlated. If the returns from two assets are negatively correlated,

Figure 11.5   The Effect of a Portfolio's Size on Its Standard Deviation

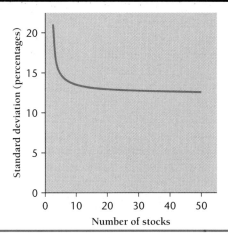

then when one does poorly, the other is likely to do well. Because the losses tend to be offset by gains, and the gains offset by losses, a portfolio of negatively correlated assets has little risk of large losses or gains. The extreme case consists of returns that are perfectly negatively correlated, so that the outcome from one investment is certain to be the opposite of the other. In gambling, bookmakers strive for a perfectly hedged portfolio, with an equal volume of wagers on each side of a bet, so that they are guaranteed a profit no matter which team wins. Among loans, bonds, and stocks, there are few negatively correlated returns, because most are affected similarly (though to varying degrees) by interest rates and the economy. However, banks can hedge their portfolios by using financial options and futures.

If asset returns are positively correlated, there is less potential for risk reduction through diversification. The extreme case is perfect positive correlation, where, if one investment does poorly, it is certain that all will. If so, banks cannot benefit from the primary advantage of diversification — the balancing out of gains and losses. Fortunately, although most asset returns are positively correlated, this correlation is far from perfect and diversification can reduce risk substantially.

Figure 11.5 illustrates this point using data for randomly selected stock portfolios of different sizes.[6] Risk, as measured by the standard deviation, is substantially reduced by diversifying among 15 to 30 stocks. Of course, banks and other investors need not, as in this figure, diversify randomly. A randomly selected stock portfolio might, by the luck of the draw, contain a dozen savings-and-loan associations, with highly correlated returns; a randomly selected loan portfolio might accidentally consist entirely of loans to soybean farmers. Such a portfolio would be fine for a mutual fund that wants to bet on the health of the

Highlight 11.3	Continental Illinois Bets the Bank on Oil Prices

In 1981 it was estimated that Continental Illinois Bank had $4 billion (more than 15 percent of its loan portfolio) in energy loans, mostly to independent oil and gas companies. The bank was confident that these energy loans would be profitable, the senior vice president responsible for oil and gas lending explaining that the 1981 drop in oil prices was "just a little blip."* Even though it consisted of a large number of loans to independent producers, this $4 billion energy-loan portfolio was not well-diversified because the ability to repay the loans depended critically on oil and gas prices. When the 1981 blip in prices turned into a long-term collapse, Continental Illinois had serious financial problems.

In 1983, the federal government bailed out Continental Illinois with a $4.5 billion subsidy and became an 80 percent owner of the bank. The bank's top management was removed in 1984. Continental Illinois had a number of problems, and an undiversified portfolio of energy loans was one of its biggest.

*Laurel Sorenson, "In the High Flying Field of Energy Finance, Continental Bank Is Striking It Rich," *Wall Street Journal,* September 18, 1981.

S&L industry or a bank that wants to gamble on soybeans, but it would be inappropriate for risk-averse investors seeking diversified portfolios. A diversified portfolio should be deliberately chosen from a wide range of diverse industries: farms, automobiles, computers, chemical, forestry, entertainment, medical, and so on.

Asset returns are necessarily uncertain, because no one can infallibly predict the future course of the economy, as well as interest rates, tax laws, and the fortunes of individual households and businesses. Banks can confront this uncertainty rationally by estimating the expected returns from various assets and by using standard deviations to gauge uncertainty. While a single asset may, in isolation, be very risky, risk-averse banks can invest in several imperfectly correlated (or, even better, negatively correlated) assets, using this diversification to reduce risk.

SUMMARY

The uncertainty of asset returns can be quantified by specifying probabilities, describing the relative likelihood of the possible outcomes. These probabilities are influenced by historical data but are necessarily subjective. The expected value is the long-run average return if the frequency with which each outcome occurs is equal to its probability. The variance is the average squared deviation

Global Diversification

Much of the early empirical work on diversified portfolios focused on U.S. stocks. These academic studies demonstrated the advantages to risk-averse investors of selecting a wide variety of dissimilar stocks. Many banks and other institutional investors have also traditionally restricted their attention to U.S. securities, perhaps reasoning that this is their area of expertise.

However, several studies suggest that the risk-return opportunities available to investors can be made more attractive by including foreign securities.* One investment firm that stresses the benefits of international diversification is Huntington Advisers.† This firm argues that there are several persuasive reasons why it is advantageous to supplement a portfolio of New York Stock Exchange stocks with other securities, such as these:

Small U.S. stocks:	Large and small stocks may be affected differently by the economy and interest rates.
Long-term bonds:	Stocks are affected by the economy and interest rates, bonds just by interest rates.
Treasury bills:	The shape of the term structure changes, so that short-term and long-term interest rates are not perfectly correlated.
Foreign bonds:	U.S. and foreign interest rates are imperfectly correlated and, more importantly, exchange-rate movements cause divergences in the dollar value of foreign and domestic securities.
Foreign stocks:	U.S. and foreign economic conditions are not perfectly correlated.

The portfolio managers at Huntington Advisers have made a number of empirical studies buttressing their arguments. Using quarterly data from 1972 through 1987, they managed hypothetical portfolios using, each quarter, data from the preceding five years to estimate the means, standard deviations, and correlations among the real rates of returns on the assets described above. While the S&P 500 stock index had an average real return of 2.6 percent with a standard deviation of 60.1 percent, this internationally diversified portfolio had an average real return of 11.4 percent with a standard deviation of 43.5 percent — a higher expected return with less risk. Persuaded by this evidence, Huntington Advisers now uses global diversification in the portfolios that it advises and manages.

---

*For example, J. Madura, "International Portfolio Construction," *Journal of Business Research,* 1985, pp. 87–95, and Haim Levy and Zvi Lerman, "The Benefits of International Diversification in Bonds," *Financial Analysts Journal,* September–October 1988, pp. 56–64.
†Edward Franks and Donald Gould, Huntington Advisers, personal correspondence, 1989.

of the possible returns about the expected value; the standard deviation is the square root of the variance. The standard deviation (or the variance) gauges risk by measuring how certain we are that the return will be close to its expected value.

For many assets, the normal distribution is a reasonable approximation useful for describing our uncertainty about the return. Two convenient rules of thumb are that there is about a ⅔ probability that a normally distributed variable will be within one standard deviation of its mean and about a 95 percent probability that it will be within two standard deviations. Some asset returns are very asymmetrical and cannot be approximated by a normal distribution — for instance, lottery tickets, stock in new companies, and other long shots. Investors who like positive skewness buy such assets, even though the expected returns are low and the standard deviations high.

A risk-neutral person chooses the alternative with the highest expected return, leading to the placement of all eggs in one basket. A risk-seeker accepts fair bets and will even sacrifice expected return to increase risk. A risk-averter sacrifices expected return to reduce risk and selects a diversified portfolio, containing dissimilar assets. Diversification reduces risk most effectively if the asset returns are uncorrelated or, even better, negatively correlated.

IMPORTANT TERMS

diversified portfolio	risk averse
expected value	risk neutral
normal distribution	risk seeking
probabilities	standard deviation
probability distribution	variance

EXERCISES

1. A bank thinks that the average annual rate of inflation during the next four years is twice as likely to be below 5 percent as to be 5 percent or higher. What is the bank's subjective probability that the rate of inflation will be below 5 percent?

2. A bank is considering investing $1,000,000 in either Treasury bills, with a guaranteed 5 percent return, or in Raider junk bonds, which have a high prospective return if there is no default:

Raider Return

No default	+20%
Partial default	−10%
Total default	−100%

Historical data for bonds issued by similar companies suggest that 5 percent have a total default and another 20 percent a partial default. If the bank applies these probabilities to the Raider bond, does the expected value of its return exceed that of Treasury bills? If the bank buys the Raider bonds, what can we conclude about its risk preferences?

3. A bank's economists have assigned the probabilities below to three economic scenarios over the next two years. They have also estimated the fraction of their loans that will default and the return on their loan portfolio in each scenario.

Economy	Probability	Loan Defaults	Return
Boom	0.30	1%	12%
Muddle	0.40	3%	10%
Recession	0.30	8%	5%

Calculate the expected values of the percentage of loans that will default and the portfolio return.

4. A bank estimates that during the coming year a Treasury bond has a 0.5 probability of yielding a 15 percent return and a 0.5 probability of yielding a 5 percent return, while a Brazilian bond has a 0.9 probability of yielding a 20 percent return and a 0.1 probability of yielding −60 percent. Calculate the expected return and standard deviation for each bond. Which is riskier? Which bond is preferred by a risk-neutral investor? By a risk seeker? By a risk-averse investor? Are the returns from these bonds positively skewed, negatively skewed, or symmetrical?

5. The following table shows a firm's anticipated revenues in each of four inflation-unemployment scenarios and the probabilities it assigns to these scenarios. What is the expected value of revenue? Is the expected value also the most likely value?

Scenario	Inflation	Unemployment	Probability	Revenue (in millions)
1	high	high	0.16	$2.0
2	high	low	0.24	4.0
3	low	high	0.36	1.0
4	low	low	0.24	3.0

6. Major League baseball players can file for salary arbitration. In arbitration, the player submits a contract, the owner submits a contract, and a three-person panel chooses one of these two contracts. Neither side knows the details of the other side's contract until both contracts have been submitted. In February 1990, California Angels pitcher Chuck Finley filed for arbitration, asking for a one-year contract for $810,000; the Angels filed a one-year contract for $600,000. After learning of each other's contract, Finley and the Angels canceled the arbitration hearing by agreeing to a one-year contract for $725,000. If P is the probability that the arbitration panel would have chosen Finley's $810,000 contract, for what value of P is the expected value of the arbitration ruling equal to the agreed-upon $725,000 contract?

7. The text tells of a hypothetical choice between a sure $1 million and a chance to win $40 million by having five coin flips turn out to be all heads. What is the probability of five heads in five flips? What is the expected value of this $40 million gamble? Would you take the sure $1 million or go for $40 million?

8. In 1987, with gold selling for $460 an ounce, a mining company offered investors a chance to buy gold at $250 an ounce — but they would have to pay the money immediately and not receive their gold for 15 months. The company would purportedly use the investors' money to obtain the gold from a mine with uncertain reserves.[7] Suppose that there is a probability P that you will get the gold and a probability 1 − P that you won't. If you are risk neutral and determined to buy gold (and to hold it for at least 15 months), what is the lowest value of P that persuades you to accept this company's offer?

9. Limited Liability is considering insuring Howard Hardsell's voice for $1,000,000. The firm figures that there is only a 0.001 probability that it will have to pay off. If it charges $2,000 for this policy, will it have a positive expected value for them? What is the expected value of

the policy to Howard? If Howard's expected value is negative, why would he consider buying such a policy?

10. *Donoghue's Moneyletter* developed a test to differentiate speculators from the risk averse.[8] One of the questions is

   You are on a TV game show and can choose one of the following. Which would you take?
   a. *$1,000 cash.*
   b. *A 50 percent chance at winning $4,000.*
   c. *A 20 percent chance at winning $10,000.*
   d. *A 5% chance at winning $100,000.*

   Which answer indicates risk-averse behavior? Risk-neutral? Risk-seeking?

11. Which would you prefer: (a) $200,000 or (b) a lottery with a 20 percent chance of winning $1,200,000 and an 80 percent chance of losing $50,000? How would you characterize a person who prefers (a) to (b)? Prefers (b) to (a)? Is indifferent between (a) and (b)?

12. A computer company must decide whether its new computer, Granny Smith, will have a closed architecture or an open one, allowing users to add enhancements. The estimated profits, in millions of dollars, depend on whether potential customers prefer an open or closed architecture, events considered to be equally likely:

Customer Preferences

Design	Open	Closed
Open	500	300
Closed	100	900

(For example, if the company uses an open design, there is a 0.5 probability that their profits will be $500 million and a 0.5 probability that profits will be $300 million.) Which action maximizes expected return? If the company chooses a closed architecture, how would you characterize the risk preferences of that choice?

13. You have been offered $2 for a raffle ticket with a 1 percent chance of winning $100. What can we say about your risk references if you decline this offer?

14. A bank estimates that the return from a portfolio of Mexican bonds has an expected value of 18 percent and a standard deviation of 20 percent, and that the return from a portfolio of U.S. corporate bonds has an expected return of 8 percent and a standard deviation of 10 percent. A senior officer argues that, because the bank is risk averse, it should invest in both. Is this argument more persuasive if the returns on the U.S. and Mexican bonds are positively correlated or negatively correlated? Why?

15. Jill owns stock in company NEW, which may be taken over by company GLOM. If so, her stock will be worth $40 a share; if not, it will be worth $20. She considers the two possible outcomes to be equally likely.
   a. What is the expected value of her stock?
   b. If she accepts $27 a share for her stock, is she acting in a risk-averse or risk-seeking manner?
   c. Would anyone pay her more than $30 a share for her stock?

16. Four thousand years ago, Chinese shipowners, worried about pirates and natural disasters, put part of their cargoes on each other's ships. How would you explain this behavior?

17. A stock analyst has found the following probability distribution "to be very useful"[9]

Stock Price Change During Next Six Months	Probability
+40%	0.1
+20%	0.2
0%	0.4
−20%	0.2
−40%	0.1

What are the expected value and the standard deviation?

18. A bank is going to construct either a 20-story or a 30-story office complex. The market value of the completed building will depend on the strength of the rental market when construction is finished. The bank's Chief Executive Office (CEO) has assigned the subjective probabilities shown below for the net profit with each option. Use the mean and standard deviation to compare these two alternatives.

| Rental | | Profit (millions) | |
Market	Probability	20-story	30-story
Strong	0.2	$100	$150
Medium	0.5	50	50
Weak	0.3	−50	−100

19. Program traders, as we saw in Chapter 8, simultaneously buy and sell stocks, stock options, and stock futures. When the options or futures expire, these traders unwind their position by liquidating their stock holdings. One study looked at the volume of trading on the New York Stock Exchange during the last hour on Friday afternoon, comparing those days when stock market index options and futures both expired with days when neither expired.[10]

	Expiration Day	No Expiration
Mean Volume	31,156	15,959
Standard deviation	11,612	5,011

Based on these data, write a brief paragraph comparing the last hour of trading on expiration and nonexpiration Fridays.

20. A certified financial planner wrote[11]

Allow me one of Cohen's Laws: It is far better to be very aggressive with your investments and hedge them by diversification than to be conservative and put all your eggs in one supposedly safe basket. You're going to do much better if you buy six or seven aggressive stocks than if you buy one conservative stock. How do you limit your risk? By buying different kinds of stocks, say a mix of electronics, drugs, retailing, computers.

How can a basket of aggressive stocks be safer than a conservative stock? Why would you want to mix a variety of stocks? Isn't it better to find a very profitable investment and stock with it?

21. Identify each of these probability distributions as positively skewed, negatively skewed, or symmetrical.
    a. The normal distribution.
    b. A Superfecta bet, where correctly picking the first four finishers in a horse race wins a large amount of money.
    c. The purchase of a junk bond.

22. Why might an insurance company limit the number of homes it would insure against loss by fire or flood in a given area, while remaining willing to write such policies in different areas?

23. Figure 11.3 shows that the daily returns on IBM stock were distributed in an approximately normal manner with a mean of 0.12 percent and a standard deviation of 1.28 percent. According to the normal distribution rules of thumb, what range encompasses about 95 percent of the returns?

24. An examination of the annual return on stocks and corporate bonds for 1926–1978 yielded these estimates.[12]

	Stocks	Bonds
Average return	11.2%	3.4%
Standard deviation	22.2%	5.7%

Assuming these numbers to be the expected return and standard deviation for the coming year, would a risk-neutral investor prefer stocks to bonds, or vice versa? Why might a risk-averse investor prefer to hold both bonds and stocks?

25. A unit bond trust pools money from thousands of investors and buys a package of bonds. Which of these two opinions do you agree with?[13]

   Many trust sponsors argue that because a trust is diversified, investors can accept the higher risk — and higher income — of lower-rated bonds. "A trust is stronger than any of its parts in the same way that a bundle of pencils is stronger than one pencil," insists Norman Schvey, a Merrill Lynch Vice President. "Not so," says Diana Munder, a New York CPA whose clients often ask her for advice about their investments. "If you would not feel comfortable buying individual issues of obscure revenue bonds or lower-grade utilities," she believes, "there is no reason why you should feel more comfortable buying a whole package of them."

THE

BENEFITS AND PITFALLS

OF

BANKING

THE FAIRLY INTELLIGENT FLY

A large spider in an old house built a beautiful web in which to catch flies. Every time a fly landed on the web and was entangled in it the spider devoured him, so that when another fly came along he would think the web was a safe and quiet place in which to rest. One day a fairly intelligent fly buzzed around above the web so long without lighting that the spider appeared and said, "Come on down." But the fly was too clever for him and said, "I never light where I don't see other flies and I don't see any other flies in your house." So he flew away until he came to a place where there were a great many other flies. He was about to settle down among them when a bee buzzed up and said, "Hold it, stupid, that's flypaper. All those flies are trapped." "Don't be silly," said the fly, "they're dancing." So he settled down and became stuck to the flypaper with all the other flies.

MORAL: There is no safety in numbers, or in anything else.

James Thurber

Banks and other financial intermediaries borrow funds from some economic agents and lend funds to others. We call these institutions "intermediaries" because that is just what they are. Instead of John lending directly to Mary, John lends to a bank, which then lends to Mary. Why does this happen? Why do John and Mary, and you and I, use financial intermediaries?

This chapter examines some of the economic advantages of using financial intermediaries that have made them such a crucial part of modern industrial economies. However, some banking practices that banks consider sound can exacerbate economic booms and recessions and do not protect banks from runs. We will see in this chapter that the economic importance of banks and their historical vulnerability to financial crises — particularly the financial collapse in the 1930s — has led to substantial legal constraints on their operations. Chapters 13 and 14 then discuss the current regulatory environment and the management of modern financial intermediaries.

INTERMEDIATION

The real resource costs to society of financial intermediation are the labor, equipment, buildings, and land used by financial institutions. These costs are shouldered by borrowers and lenders in the gap between what borrowers pay and what lenders receive. Instead of John lending to Mary at a 10 percent interest rate, he lends to an intermediary at 9 percent, which then lends to her at 11 percent. The 2 percent differential pays for the resources used by the intermediary. Why do we pay higher rates when we borrow and receive lower rates when we lend? What social benefits justify the real resources consumed by intermediaries?

Financial intermediaries have economies of scale.

The benefits — both private and social — of intermediaries generally derive from their size. Instead of individuals buying securities directly from issuers, there are advantages to having an intermediary collect and invest the savings of a large number of people and businesses. These advantages are called "economies of scale" and fall into two broad categories: risk-pooling and specialization.

RISK-POOLING

Risk-pooling is a fundamental characteristic of financial intermediaries. Funds are taken from many different sources and invested in many different assets. This diversification of funds reduces risk for the intermediary and for the people who have lent it funds. Chapter 11 introduced the idea of risk-pooling by explaining the appeal of diversified portfolios to risk-averse investors. The practice of risk-pooling can be found in many forms in the operation of various financial intermediaries. Let's look at some of these practices.

Safety in Numbers

Risk-pooling is based on the Law of Large Numbers.

Risk-pooling is based on a statistical principle called the Law of Large Numbers, which states that the average outcome is more certain when the number of outcomes is large. There is considerable uncertainty about the results of a few flips of a coin, a few dice rolls, or a few spins of a roulette wheel. But with a large number of occurrences, the expected statistical regularities appear. In a million flips of a fair coin, you can be very confident that the proportion of heads will be extremely close to 0.5. (Statistically, it is 95 percent certain that the fraction that are heads will be between 0.499 and 0.501.) Similarly, you can be very confident that in a million rolls of a single die the number 4 will come up close to one-sixth of the time and that in a million roulette spins each number will occur almost equally often. This fundamental statistical principle is what gambling casinos bank on and what banks gamble on.

To make the concept concrete, consider a bank that is concerned about the amount of money that depositors might withdraw on a given day. Withdrawal probabilities vary with the day of the week, of the month, and of the year and with business cycles, credit crunches, and other economic events. Perhaps on this particular day, the bank estimates that each dollar that has been deposited with it has a 0.1 probability of being withdrawn. If the bank has only one dollar in deposits, the probability is 0.1 that it will be withdrawn and 0.9 that it won't. If the bank wants to be confident of meeting withdrawal demand, then it doesn't dare lend out that dollar. There is too great a chance that the depositor will show up.

What if there are two dollars in deposits? Both dollars will be withdrawn, or only one dollar, or none. The probabilities are

Dollars Withdrawn	Fraction of Deposits	Probability
0	0.0	0.81
1	0.5	0.18
2	1.0	0.01

Since the probability of both dollars being claimed is only $(0.1)(0.1) = 0.01$, the bank may be willing to lend out a dollar.

With \$10 deposited, the probabilities are

Dollars Withdrawn	Fraction of Deposits	Probability
0	0.0	0.3486784401
1	0.1	0.3874204890
2	0.2	0.1937102445
3	0.3	0.0573956280
4	0.4	0.0111602610
5	0.5	0.0014880348
6	0.6	0.0001377810
7	0.7	0.0000087480
8	0.8	0.0000003645
9	0.9	0.0000000090
10	1.0	0.0000000001

The odds of all deposits being withdrawn at once are now minuscule, at 1 chance in 10 billion. Surely some funds can be safely loaned out. Even if half the deposits are loaned out and half kept on reserve, there is only about a one-in-ten-thousand chance of withdrawals exceeding reserves.

The most likely outcome is that one-tenth of the deposits will be withdrawn. As the quantity of deposits increases, it becomes more and more certain that withdrawals will be extremely close to a tenth of deposits. With $10,000 deposited, the chances are only one in a thousand that more than 11 percent of deposits will be withdrawn. With $1 million deposited, the chances are only one in a thousand that more than 10.09 percent will be withdrawn; almost 90 percent can now be safely lent.

This is a simple, stylized example of the general principle of reducing risk through diversification. In a large number of draws, independent risks are diversified away. There will be some bad luck and some good — here some individuals will withdraw money and some won't — but the good and bad luck will roughly balance each other out. This is the same idea we encountered in Chapter 11 in the discussion of risk reduction through the selection of a diversified portfolio. With financial intermediaries, this principle applies to a variety of risks on both the asset and liability sides of the balance sheet.

Diversification can reduce risk.

Withdrawal Risk

A fundamental characteristic of deposit intermediaries is the simultaneous accommodation of the preference of borrowers for illiquid debts and the preference of lenders for liquid assets. Borrowers seek funds to finance the acquisition of real assets (cars, houses, factories, and equipment) that will yield profits or services over a substantial period of time and generally prefer to repay the loan over a similar period of time. Most households and businesses that borrow money are in no position to repay their loans at a moment's notice. If they had such surplus funds lying about, they would not have borrowed in the first place. Instead, borrowers typically have illiquid real assets that cannot be quickly converted into cash.

Lenders like liquid assets; borrowers prefer illiquid debts.

Those who borrow money to pay for their education would be hard-pressed if repayment were immediately demanded. Those who borrow money to pay for furniture, a car, or a house, usually do so because they do not have the funds available to pay cash. If they were suddenly forced to repay their loans, they would have to sell their furniture, car, or house at distress prices. The same is true of businesses. When a firm borrows to pay for labor, materials, equipment, or the construction of a factory, it is normally in no position to pay off its debt at a moment's notice. If that were a provision of the loan, the firm would be reluctant to borrow, and so would you and I.

While borrowers prefer long-term, illiquid loans, lenders prefer short-term and very liquid loans. Unexpected needs always arise, and it is reassuring to know that a loan can be quickly and inexpensively converted into cash. Thus there is a considerable gap between the preferences of borrowers and the preferences of lenders. In the absence of financial intermediaries, both would compromise and fewer loans would be made.

A primary benefit of deposit intermediaries is that they accommodate the conflicting liquidity preferences of borrowers and lenders by, in essence, manufacturing (and selling) liquidity. Depositors rightfully consider their deposits to be very liquid — redeemable at any time. Simultaneously, the deposit institution has used most of the funds deposited with it to make illiquid loans that it cannot redeem and cannot sell quickly, except at a substantial loss. It can get away with this sleight of hand because withdrawal risks have been pooled. With a large number of depositors, the institution can confidently estimate a prudent level of reserves.

Banks manufacture liquidity by diversifying withdrawal risks.

Individual **microrisk**, or **idiosyncratic risk**, is diversified away, and only **macrorisk**, or **systematic risk**, remains. In the numerical example, individual withdrawals were assumed to be independent: whether or not someone made a withdrawal had no effect on the likelihood of others making withdrawals. This is the individual microrisk that can be diversified away. It concerns withdrawals that are made for private, idiosyncratic reasons that do not matter to others: the purchase of a new television, wedding expenses, a sudden illness.

Idiosyncratic risk can be diversified away, macrorisk cannot.

Systematic risk, or macrorisk, concerns the danger of events that may cause many people to withdraw money at once. Some of these events, like Christmas spending in December and tax payments in April, are easily anticipated. To the extent that they can be predicted, these variations are not risky. The deposit intermediary simply adjusts its estimates of withdrawal probabilities and needed reserves. Other macroeconomic events may be more difficult to predict: recessions, credit crunches, and regulatory changes that allow other institutions to lure away depositors. Macroeconomic risks may be international (a worldwide recession), national (a tight-money policy of the Federal Reserve), or purely local (a drought, a hurricane, or the closing of a factory). The most dangerous and unpredictable macrorisk is a panicky run on the bank. If depositors fear that they may not be able to withdraw their deposits, they are all sure to try.

Because such macroeconomic risks affect most depositors, they cannot be diversified away simply by having a large number of depositors. An intermediary's only protection is to keep funds near at hand that can be mobilized in an emergency. This is a key decision that a deposit intermediary must make: how much should be kept in precautionary liquid assets and how much can be safely used for illiquid loans.

The pooling withdrawal risks occurs in other forms besides deposits. Banks commonly extend lines of credit, enabling businesses to borrow money as needed to cover lags between expenses and receipts. Individuals may also have lines of credit — for instance, overdraft provisions with their checking accounts — that enable them to borrow money from the bank at a moment's notice. From the bank's standpoint, credit lines and overdraft privileges are withdrawal risks, a chance that customers will remove funds from the bank; the danger is that a great many of them may do so at the same time.

Credit lines are another form of withdrawal risk.

Again, much of this risk can be diversified away. With a large number of credit lines, a bank can generally count on those borrowing unusually large amounts to be offset by those borrowing unusually small amounts or repaying earlier loans. In essence, banks are a conduit through which those with excess funds lend to others with temporary deficits. The private and social benefits are that agents can obtain the financing to carry out productive activities.

The provision of credit lines requires banks to keep liquid funds near at hand. But these funds are small relative to the amount of outstanding loans and credit lines, because of the pooling of idiosyncratic withdrawal risks. There remain undiversifiable macroeconomic risks. An economic boom or credit crunch may cause many to want to borrow money at the same time, and a bank must be concerned about the danger that it will not be able to fulfill its promises and honor these loan requests.

Another illustration of pooling withdrawal risks is the actuarial risks borne by insurance intermediaries. Insurance companies use the funds of policyholders to acquire financial and real assets. The securities issued to policyholders are special in that the payouts are based on the occurrence of natural events. These institutions are nonetheless financial intermediaries, selling financial obligations to some people and buying securities from others. The withdrawal risk is that the specified natural events will occur, causing the insurance benefit to be paid and funds to be withdrawn from the intermediary.

Again, to the extent that these natural events are independent, the withdrawal risk can be diversified away. If the probability of a certain person dying at age 72 is P, then, out of a large group of such people, the fraction that die at age 72 will be very close to P. There remain macrorisks that cannot be eliminated by the insurance of a large number of people: a cancer cure that increases life expectancy, national speed limits that reduce automobile accidents, a revolution that destroys life and property. As with other intermediaries, some macroevents are pleasant financial news to insurance companies, while others are expensive surprises.

Portfolio Risk

In addition to withdrawal risks, banks are concerned with portfolio risk. In Chapter 11, you saw how risk-averse investors can use diversified portfolios to reduce risk, or uncertainty, about the return on investments. The return on a diversified portfolio is more certain than the return on the individual assets in the portfolio because investments that do poorly will be partly balanced by investments that do well.

Transaction expenses and indivisibilities make it impractical for many people to construct well-diversified portfolios on their own. A few thousand dollars cannot be economically divided among dozens of securities. Many poorly divisible assets such as real estate, corporate loans, and $100,000 CDs are inaccessible to a small investor.

Financial intermediaries can reduce portfolio risks with diversification.

A large financial intermediary, in contrast, can easily acquire thousands of assets, including the most poorly divisible, effectively diversifying away idiosyncratic risks. (There remain such macrorisks as uncertainty about the future course of interest rates and the economy.) By reducing the risk borne by investors, intermediaries increase the funds available to borrowers.

Diversification of portfolio risk is the basic concept underlying mutual funds. An individual investor who does not want to put all of his or her savings into a single bond, stock, or other asset feels more secure, and correctly so, in pooling funds with other investors to buy a package of assets. The historical record indicates that mutual funds are no wiser than other investors or even than dart-throwing chimpanzees. But they do provide plain and simple risk-pooling.

Although the organization of other financial intermediaries is more complex, diversified portfolios remain important. Consider commercial-bank loans. Uncertainty about the return on any single loan is due mainly to the risk that the borrower will default. Most loans are too large for an individual to construct a diversified portfolio, but a bank with many depositors can effortlessly make even multimillion dollar loans and still diversify away independent default risk; there of course remains macroeconomic risk such as a stiff recession that causes many borrowers to default. The same principles apply to savings-and-loan associations making mortgages, credit unions making consumer loans, pension funds buying bonds, and insurance companies acquiring real estate.

SPECIALIZATION

In addition to pooling risks, financial intermediaries provide specialized services that are impractical for small savers and borrowers to perform on their own. Modern industrial economies rely on specialization: each person does a few tasks very well and trades the product of this specialized labor with other people. The efficient use of large, very productive machinery requires specialized tasks within large firms. Specialization enhances farming, automobile production, and financial intermediation.

Financial intermediaries provide a variety of specialized services. In each case, it is more economical to pay the institution for the service than to provide it on your own. Some of these payments are explicit, such as management fees and checking-account service charges. Others are implicit in the gap between the interest rates charged on loans and the rates paid on deposits.

Financial intermediaries supply many specialized services.

One of these services is deposit and loan brokerage — the bringing together of buyers and sellers of loans. It is expensive for individuals to identify attractive investments or to locate someone who will lend them money at fair terms. Financial intermediaries provide easily located, convenient locations for borrowing and lending. Deposit intermediaries provide facilities — including buildings, telephones, clerks, and automated tellers — for the "loan market" and the "deposit market" that make it easy for borrowers to secure and repay loans and for depositors to invest and withdraw funds.

Intermediaries also provide detailed, accurate records of transactions, safe storage of these records, and written evidence of financial assets and debts. All of these services are provided by intermediaries because there are substantial economies of scale in assembling structures, equipment, and skilled employees.

Banking institutions offer a valuable bill-paying service. If you had to pay for all your purchases with cash, in person or by mail, it would be time-consuming, expensive, and risky. Instead, you can pay by check. When the recipient gives the check to his or her bank, your account is debited and the recipient's account is credited — quickly, safely, and efficiently. Banks use a considerable amount of labor and equipment to provide this service, but it is far less expensive than making cash payments.

Intermediaries also reduce the transaction expenses involved in buying and selling assets because it is proportionately less expensive to trade large assets. For example, brokerage fees are typically a fixed minimum amount ($25, $35, or more) plus a declining percentage based on the size of the transaction. Thus brokerage fees are proportionately smaller for large institutions making large transactions.

Large intermediaries also find it economical to acquire expertise that an individual household or nonfinancial business would find prohibitively expensive. Considerable knowledge and experience are required to understand financial dealings. Some of this expertise is mechanical and mundane: how to calculate interest rates, where to call to get a good price, what are the tax implications, what is the appropriate legal wording. Some expertise is very subjective and challenging: which stocks to buy, whether or not to approve a loan, what interest rate to pay or charge. There are considerable economies of scale in acquiring both kinds of expertise.

For example, an accurate estimate of default risk is needed for an informed decision about whether or not to approve a loan and, if the loan is approved, to determine its terms. It would be very inefficient if every household had to evaluate the creditworthiness of loan applicants; instead, specialists collect, process, and assess information relevant to loan requests. More generally, a rational evaluation of any security requires a careful assessment of a great many facts. It is most efficient to have specialized experts and high-speed computers collecting and weighing up-to-date information. Individuals benefit from these economies of scale by lending through intermediaries.

Some of the financial expertise and computer facilities accumulated within financial institutions are also useful for decisions made by households and firms. As a consequence, intermediaries advise customers on such matters as financial strategies, tax laws, and estate planning. This advice is usually part of an overall customer relationship and is paid for implicitly through the relatively high rates charged on loans and the low rates received on deposits. In recent years, some intermediaries have moved to unbundle these services by levying explicit charges. In this way, those who don't use services don't have to pay for them.

Large financial intermediaries profit from risk-pooling and specialization.

All of the economies of scale discussed here under the headings of risk-pooling and specialization argue for intermediaries — large institutions through which households and firms can lend and borrow. These economies of scale explain why John lends to an intermediary at 9 percent, which then lends to Mary at 11 percent. The intermediary is worth even more than the 2 percent it keeps.

Many of these advantages are interrelated. A large intermediary can simultaneously pool several types of risk. Structures, machinery, and skilled employees can accomplish several purposes. Thus it usually is most sensible to have multi-faceted intermediaries that simultaneously exploit several economies of scale and scope. In the past, however, many intermediaries in the United States were specialized, borrowing and lending only for certain restricted purposes — a specialization due more to regulatory constraints than economic principles. Economic pressures have been eroding these constraints, allowing intermediaries to become financial supermarkets.

Now that we have considered their compelling social benefits, in the remainder of this chapter we will examine some of the pitfalls that intermediaries have fallen into in the past and how these stumblings created a legacy of regulatory constraints. We will look at present regulations in the next chapter and at the management of modern full-service financial intermediaries in the chapter after that.

PITFALLS IN COMMERCIAL BANKING

The largest, and in many ways the most important, financial intermediaries are those that issue liquid deposits, including commercial banks, savings-and-loan associations, mutual savings banks, and credit unions. Deposit intermediaries monetize illiquid and poorly divisible assets. If you lend money to a friend or a small business, you have an illiquid asset. You cannot use the IOU to buy anything, and you would have a tough time trying to sell it to raise cash. If you instead deposit your money in a bank, and the bank lends out this money, then you have a very liquid asset. The intermediary monetizes your loan by transforming your illiquid asset into a liquid one.

In the discussion in Chapter 4 of how banks create money, you saw that this alchemy is profitable, socially useful, and risky. Now we will look more closely at how banks have tried to cope with these opportunities and dangers in the past, and how their failures led to a web of government regulations. Although we focus on commercial banks, the historical morals are applicable to other deposit intermediaries as well.

Commercial Banks and the Invisible Hand

The early history of U.S. commercial banks was briefly sketched in Chapter 4. Throughout this history, the banking system did not seem particularly adept at providing a stable supply of money to the economy or at avoiding financial panics and bank runs. Part of the problem was that the private self-interests of individual banks did not ensure aggregate welfare. The invisible hand of market forces was a bit clumsy.

When speculative fever was high and it seemed easy to make money, banks tried to increase profits by issuing more bank notes, which exacerbated the speculative excesses. When the economy was in recession and the outlook gloomy, banks reined in loans and bank notes, intensifying the crisis. When it was in the interest of all to reduce speculation by restraining the money supply, individual banks were imprudent. When it was in the interest of all to be generous, each was frugal. Attempts to maximize private profits do not always serve the public interest.

It is not easy to recognize excessive speculation or gloom. Profits seem certain and easy just before a speculative bubble bursts; in crises, it is difficult to be optimistic when everyone else is so worried. These human emotions affect all participants in these high dramas, but are particularly important for banks, given their power to create and destroy money. A speculative bubble is fueled far less by an individual buying land instead of milk than by a bank issuing money to buy the land.

This dangerous power wielded by banks is an argument for a public-spirited central monetary authority that is concerned with more than profit maximization. However, a monetary authority's success may be hindered by the difficulty of perceiving whether prudence or aggressiveness is appropriate. This blurred vision is a continuing criticism of monetary authorities, which we will look at in some detail in Chapter 16.

Another noteworthy aspect of the banking system's problems in the nineteenth century was the undisciplined behavior of small country banks. Opening a bank and issuing bank notes seemed like a pretty easy way literally to make money. It was an occupation that attracted not only the most reputable and public-spirited people but also the lowest and most down-and-out scoundrels. Many banks helped the country to prosper, and many other banks simply redistributed the country's wealth.

In the early crises and panics, it often seemed that bank failures were a fitting end for poorly managed banks. Banks that made questionable loans and kept little reserves got what they deserved. Nor were many tears shed for their depositors, who (by some unexplained means) should have exercised better judgment in selecting a bank. As long as the failed banks were small, run by somewhat suspect characters, and outside the Eastern banking establishment, there was little effort to regulate banking. With time, the economy grew increasingly interdependent, and the waves of crisis became wider, toppling even scrupulous Eastern banks. With these widespread crises came regulation and reform.

It is now apparent that even "sound" banking practices exacerbate business cycles and that, with a fractional reserve system, no bank is immune to bank runs. For both reasons, there is a legitimate role for a central monetary authority. In practice, you will see that monetary authorities have been more successful in averting bank runs than in eliminating business cycles.

Sound Banking Practices

Throughout the nineteenth century, sound banking practices rested on two precepts:

1. A bank's note issues should be limited by its reserves of precious metals.

A Vietnamese Pyramid

In 1987, Vietnam implemented economic reforms that were intended to replace central planning with market forces. One reform was the encouragement of private entrepreneurs, another the introduction of a banking system comprised of government-owned banks that were supposed to lure deposits (encouraging saving) and make loans (financing entrepreneurs). However, these official banks didn't attract many deposits and were reluctant to loan money to small businesses. In their place, small, privately run, credit cooperatives sprang up that aggressively sought depositors and borrowers. These cooperatives were unregulated and unsupervised — according to one official, "No legislation, no rules, no nothing."*

The government-owned banks paid depositors 8 percent interest each month; the private cooperatives paid 10 percent, then 12 percent, and then 15 percent monthly. One of the most prominent was Thanh Huong, a combination bank and perfume factory, run by 32-year-old Nguyen Van Muoi Hai. Muoi Hai appeared in newspaper advertisements and television commercials, accompanied by his glamorous wife, hawking Thanh Huong's deposits and perfumes. Sirens blaring, a convoy of limousines and motorcycles carried Muoi Hai about. At each destination, helmeted bodyguards formed two lines for Muoi Hai to walk through, with an aide bowing and announcing "Welcome, General Director. You have arrived." Vietnamese lined up by the thousands, waiting hours for a chance to invest their life savings in Thanh Huong and share in Muoi Hai's success. When the bank distributed numbered slips to mark people's places in line, a black market developed for these slips, as people paid for the right to go to the front of the line and guarantee themselves an opportunity to make a deposit.

In 1988, Vietnamese newspapers began questioning Thanh Huong's success, noting that its perfume didn't seem popular and Muoi Hai lived very well. Suspicions increased when Muoi Hai refused to allow reporters to inspect his books or factory. In spring 1990, Muoi Hai was arrested and Thanh Huong exposed as a Ponzi, or pyramid, scheme, that used money from new depositors to pay interest to old depositors. Government officials found that 140,000 people had invested a total of $27 million in Thanh Huong, but that its only remaining assets were $7 million in cars, houses, and jewelry. Even the perfume factory was phony. Thanh Huong imported and diluted cheap perfume, and attached labels to make it look like an expensive Western perfume, such as "Charlie." The unraveling of this swindle set off a financial crisis in Vietnam as anxious depositors attempted to withdraw their money from other credit cooperatives.

*This quotation and many of the details in this example are from Barry Wain, "Big Swindle Throws Vietnam's Experiment in Banking into Chaos," Wall Street Journal, May 14, 1990.

2. Banks should make "commercial" loans, which are short-term and self-liquidating.

The first rule put the nation's money supply at the mercy of mining discoveries and foreign trade. Foreign trade had a particularly pronounced roller-coaster effect on a nation's economy. We'll use the United States as a concrete example.

When foreign demand for U.S. goods increased, output increased. In addition, as gold flowed into the United States to pay for these exports, U.S. banks had greater precious-metal reserves, and so issued more bank notes, as called for by Rule 1. As banks increased the money supply, an already stimulated economy was heated further. In theory, the boom would end when U.S. prices had increased sufficiently to choke off foreign demand.

In the opposite case, when there was weak foreign demand for U.S. goods, output declined. As gold left the United States and bank metal reserves declined, banks curtailed their loans and note issuance, thereby magnifying the economic recession until prices fell far enough to restore foreign demand for U.S. goods.

A precious-metal standard for bank notes was intended to stabilize the balance of trade, but magnified the amplitude of economic booms and busts. These painful roller-coaster episodes eventually led to the worldwide abandonment of the principle that a nation's money supply should be rigidly linked to its gold reserves. The first sound banking principle was not a stabilizing influence. Neither was the second.

The second principle is known both as the **commercial loan theory of banking** and the **Real Bills doctrine**: bank loans should be short-term, self-liquidating, and productive. A classic example is a loan to a business to pay for labor and raw materials, with the revenue from the sale of the finished goods used to repay the loan. Also acceptable are loans to farmers to enable them to plant and harvest crops. Business loans for more than a few months, consumer loans, mortgages, and loans to buy securities were all considered inappropriate for a bank. Some proponents were willing to permit a small amount of these forbidden loans if they were financed out of the bank's capital (the funds invested by the bank's owners) instead of deposits.

In England, where the concept originated, the Real Bills doctrine was long considered sound banking practice. Early U.S. banks tried to follow suit, granting only nonrenewable loans for no longer than 30 or, with some banks, 60 days; they soon found that their customers wanted longer-term loans. Up until the 1930s, the Real Bills doctrine was accepted by academics, politicians, and regulatory agencies; but, in practice, U.S. banks were directly, or through automatic renewals, making significant long-term loans to buy land, structures, machinery, and securities. Only consumer loans were neglected. By the start of the twentieth century, probably less than half of bank assets were pure commercial loans.[1]

Advocates believed that adherence to the Real Bills principle assured bank liquidity. There is merit in the argument that short-term deposit liabilities call for a strategy of holding short-term assets. However, a bank's liquidity is not fully guaranteed unless its loans are entirely safe and liquid. In practice, they are

A precious-metal standard for bank notes tends to stabilize trade balances, but to amplify business cycles.

The Real Bills doctrine says that bank loans should be short-term, self-liquidating, and productive.

Short-term loans enhance, but do not ensure, bank liquidity.

neither. If, for example, a bank makes only 60-day loans, then each day, on average, ⅟₆₀ of the loans are being repaid. These repayments provide some liquidity, but hardly enough to stave off a bank run.

Commercial loans are not liquid unless the bank can demand repayment at any time. And they are not safe unless it is certain that the financed goods will, in fact, be sold. In a recession, when depositors may want to withdraw their deposits for safety or for food, businesses that are accumulating unsold goods may find it difficult to repay their loans. Self-liquidating loans are then no longer self-liquidating.

It was also believed that the Real Bills doctrine ensured that a nation's money supply was well behaved. In 1839, a proponent, Condy Raguet, explained the prevailing view.[2]

> [A bank's] loans should not only be for short periods, but should be confined solely to the discounting of what is called "business paper," that is, promissory notes and acceptances received by the holders for merchandise and property sold. If none others were discounted, the expansion of the paper system would only be in proportion to the expansion of business. When this was extended, so as to call for more currency, as at particular seasons of the year, more currency would be created; and when business was diminished as at other seasons, so as to require less currency, the excess would be absorbed by the payments made back to the banks. In these operations, the level of the currency would not be disturbed to produce a depreciation [inflation], for although at times there would be a greater quantity of bank notes in existence than at other times, yet this quantity would be in exact proportion to the increased demand, arising from an increase in transactions.

Real Bills enthusiasts believed that their banking strategy ensured that, as business transactions expanded and contracted, the money supply would change proportionately, thereby holding the price level stable. Their analysis was, first of all, incomplete. They considered bank-issued money, but ignored fluctuations in the amount of government money available to the public and to banks. For example, nineteenth-century farmers preferred to be paid in cash rather than by check, creating a seasonal withdrawal of government money from banks that restricted the banks' ability to make loans and reduced the nation's total money supply even as transactions increased. Similarly, Real Bills proponents did not take into account transactions that are not financed by bank loans. A Real Bills banking strategy does not ensure that an increase in aggregate transactions is matched by a proportionate increase in the aggregate money supply, because such a strategy encompasses neither aggregate transactions nor the aggregate money supply.

A second flaw is that the nominal value of loans requested depends on nominal rather than real transactions. A rise in prices increases the amount of financing desired by firms and, if the Real Bills doctrine is followed, banks will meet this demand by issuing more money. Thus a rise in prices will increase the money supply, and this increased money supply may increase prices even more,

The Real Bills doctrine causes the money supply to increase during booms and fall during recessions.

causing businesses to ask for more loans and banks to print more money. Under the Real Bills doctrine, the money supply and price level may rise (or fall) together indefinitely.

In practice, there will not be an unlimited inflation or deflation because there is more to the money supply than bank money and more to transactions than bank-financed loans. But there remains the essential problem that an increase in real economic activity or in prices leads banks to issue more money — an action that further increases economic activity and prices. The Real Bills doctrine gives a nation a procyclical monetary policy, automatically expanding during booms and contracting during slumps.

Overall, the Real Bills idea does contain two important insights.

1. Liquidity crises are less likely when banks hold short-term liquid assets.
2. It is advantageous for a nation's money supply to adapt to seasonal, cyclical, and long-run changes in economic activity.

But the Real Bills principle is not sufficient to avoid liquidity crises or to assure a well-behaved aggregate money supply. In addition, it prohibits what many view as the principal accomplishment of financial intermediaries: allowing small investors to finance much of a nation's physical capital. Under the Real Bills theory, banks should provide only short-term financing of production and trade. In practice, banks have successfully financed long-lived plant and equipment.

Liquidity Crises and the Creation of the Federal Reserve System

The inadequacy of "sound banking practices" was exposed in a succession of U.S. financial crises that led to the creation of the Federal Reserve System. The end of the nineteenth and the beginning of the twentieth centuries were, for the most part, golden times for the U.S. economy. Adventurous and energetic people had spread throughout the country, and many cities were now linked by railroads. Agriculture and industry flourished. Banks gave individuals a place to save and farmers and businesspeople a place to borrow. At the time of the Civil War, there had been about 1,500 commercial banks, with aggregate assets of a billion dollars. By the turn of the century, there were 12,000 banks with assets of $4 billion. At the start of World War I, there were 27,000 banks with $12 billion in assets.

Banks failures and financial panics led eventually to reform and regulation.

Banks seemed to be everywhere — eight separate banks opened in 1886 and 1887 in Meade, Kansas, a town with a population of 457.[3] Bank failures were also plentiful throughout the nineteenth century and into the twentieth. By 1860, two-thirds of the banks that had been chartered up until that time had failed. Between the Civil War and 1890, bank failures averaged thirty per year. There were 1,200 bank failures between 1904 and 1920, 5,000 between 1921 and 1929, and 9,000 between 1930 and 1933. These failures were not a steady, though disagreeable, by-product of banking. Rather, like the economy, banks rode a roller coaster of booms and busts, with financial panics in 1819, 1837, 1857, 1873, 1884, 1893, 1907, 1921, and, most dramatically, 1929.

Postal Savings

After the banking panic of 1907, many frightened people started putting their money in cookie jars, under their mattresses, and beneath their floorboards — anywhere but in banks. In 1910, Congress created the Postal Savings System, hoping to lure some of this cash out of people's houses. For every $1 deposit, a saver had to go to a local post office, purchase a 10-cent card and nine 10-cent stamps, and paste the stamps on the card. At a time when bank accounts paid 5 percent to 7 percent annual interest, postal savings accounts paid only 2 percent. But, for many, the inconvenience and modest interest were outweighed by the security of having a deposit with the federal government. Postal savings deposits grew to $1.2 billion in 1933 and, even after the introduction in 1933 of federal insurance for bank deposits, to $3.4 billion in 1947. Eventually, as deposit rates increased in the 1960s, even the most skeptical overcame their distrust of private banks, and, in 1966, the Post Office stopped accepting postal savings deposits.

In the 1893 panic, 496 banks closed. In the 1907 panic, 246 failed. These painful experiences convinced the public and their elected officials that something had to be done. The 1907 crisis was particularly persuasive because it shook respected New York City banks. In its aftermath, Congress set up commissions, studies, and hearings, and in due course (1913) established the Federal Reserve System. There were many sides to this political tug-of-war: country banks versus city banks, states rights versus a central bank, easy money versus hard, and academics versus bankers versus politicians. The result was a compromise.

1. Twelve regional Federal Reserve Banks were established, to be guided by a Federal Reserve Board in Washington, D.C.
2. Reserve Banks could issue Federal Reserve notes backed 100% by commercial paper or 40 percent by gold or gold certificates.
3. Nationally chartered banks were required to enter the system; state-chartered banks could join if they wished.
4. Member banks were required to hold reserves against checking and time deposits: 18 percent for banks in reserve cities, 15 percent for banks in other cities, and 12 percent for country banks.
5. Reserve Banks could buy and sell government securities as directed by the Federal Reserve Board.
6. Member banks could borrow from Reserve Banks, using commercial paper as collateral.
7. Reserve Banks were to operate a check-clearing system that was open to all banks.

Even as a compromise, the system was greeted with very mixed reviews, ranging from the American Bankers Association's complaint that "For those who do not believe in socialism, it is very hard to accept," to the Comptroller of the Currency's argument that it made financial panics "mathematically impossible."[4] It was neither socialism nor foolproof.

Banks borrow from the Fed through the discount window.

The most important innovation was thought to be Number 6 on the previous page, the so-called **discount window**, which allows member banks to borrow money in times of distress. The **discount rate** is the interest rate charged on these loans. (For many years these were commonly called the "rediscount window" and "rediscount rate," a reference to the Real Bills idea that banks discount business IOUs when a commercial loan is made, and then rediscount these IOUs when they are used as collateral for loans from the Federal Reserve.)

The discount window was designed to defuse bank runs by making Federal Reserve Banks reliable lenders of last resort, a source of emergency cash for banks. There was no intent to have the Federal Reserve banks use monetary policy to stabilize aggregate output and prices, because the architects were too closely wedded to the gold standard and the Real Bills doctrine to believe that stabilization policy was necessary.

Early Federal Reserve Policy

As the Federal Reserve System was being set up, World War I began, and with it both the established order and the gold standard began crumbling. England, France, and other combatants sent $1.5 billion in gold to the United States to pay for food and weapons. As their gold supplies dwindled, the belligerent governments abandoned the gold standard. Private holdings of gold were called in and replaced with paper notes. Citizens were no longer allowed to redeem these paper notes for gold, nor were they permitted to take gold out of their country.

The classical gold-standard scenario would have been for each of these nations to reduce its money supply drastically, thereby reducing domestic prices. As European prices fell, U.S. citizens would buy more European goods, and the balance of trade would balance. Europeans would pay for U.S. wheat and weapons with sweaters and wine instead of gold. In practice, only the British government was willing to inflict deflation and depression upon its people, and even the ringing oratory of Winston Churchill, then Chancellor of the Exchequer, was insufficient to persuade the people of the rightness of this course.

During and after World War I, gold flowed to the U.S., and its money supply increased substantially.

In the United States, the World War I export boom, the gold inflow, and domestic war spending greatly stimulated the economy and increased prices. Commercial banks and the new Federal Reserve System played a key role in this inflation. Spending by the federal government increased from $0.7 billion in 1916 to $18.5 billion in 1919, mostly financed by the banking system, as the Federal Reserve Banks made low-interest loans to member banks, which then either bought Treasury securities themselves or lent the money to customers who bought Treasury obligations. This was a considerably different use of the discount window than had been intended by the architects of the Federal Reserve System. During World War I, this usage was patriotic and helpful. But after the war and through the 1930s, Federal Reserve loans through the discount window continued to be misused, with regrettable consequences.

When the war ended, the Federal Reserve kept a low discount rate on loans to member banks, primarily to accommodate the Treasury, which desired low interest rates on its borrowings and, in addition, did not want to see bond prices fall, causing capital losses to those patriotic citizens who had bought low-interest Liberty Bonds. But a low discount rate also encouraged member banks to borrow freely from the Reserve Banks so they could lend more money to an already strong economy. Much of this money fueled speculation in land, commodities, and securities.

In the spring of 1920, a slackening of exports and government spending began to weaken the U.S. economy. The Federal Reserve Banks had by now issued almost as many Federal Reserve notes as permitted by the war influx of gold and, eager to maintain the convertibility of the nation's money into gold, decided to reduce member-bank borrowings by raising the discount rates to an unprecedented 6 percent and then 7 percent. The Federal Reserve also hoped that a diminished use of the discount window would force member banks to sell their government securities and return to the commercial loans acceptable under the Real Bills doctrine.

Member bank borrowings did fall sharply, and the economy collapsed. Millions lost jobs, and farm prices fell by 50 percent. The Federal Reserve had helped fuel the speculation and then worsened the recession. Nor did they do anything to cushion the economic collapse, although it was the sharpest yet experienced by the nation. Not until April 1921 — a full year after the recession began — did the Reserve Banks lower the discount rate (or do anything else to ease the credit crisis). It was not an auspicious beginning for the Federal Reserve System.

Fed policies contributed to the 1920–21 recession and financial panic.

The Reserve Banks also did little to eliminate bank failures. In 1921, 505 banks failed. And this number turned out to be a below-average failure rate for the 1920s! The Reserve Banks provided little supervision of banks and few loans of last resort. They seemed wedded to the view that a bank's failure reflected its poor management and was of little concern to the System: "Each year the Board reported the melancholy figures . . . and confined itself to noting that suspensions were in disproportionate number of nonmember rather than member banks, of banks in small communities . . . of banks in agricultural rather than industrial areas."[5] Two-thirds of the nation's banks, holding one-third of all bank assets, remained outside the system. These nonmember banks were usually managed less conservatively, and they failed disproportionately. But member banks — many of them large member banks — failed, too. Each year throughout the 1920s, from 30 percent to 50 percent of the deposits in failed banks were in failed member banks.

The Fed did little to reduce bank failures in the 1920s.

The Roaring Twenties

The 1920s was an exciting and turbulent decade, both for the economy and for commercial banks. Banks moved into investment banking, acting as brokers for firms selling securities to the public. They added trust departments, managed individual portfolios, and even started a few mutual funds. Banks bought speculative securities and lent money to their customers to do the same. It was a competitive, rough-and-tumble decade. Twenty percent of the banks in existence in 1920 had failed by 1929. There were also almost 4,000 bank mergers, and nearly 4,000 bank branches opened.

Consistent with the belief of presidents Harding and Coolidge that government should not interfere with business, the Federal Reserve paid little attention to supervising bank loans. Instead, by and large, the Federal Reserve System financed the aggressive activities of banks by keeping a low discount rate and purchasing large amounts of government securities.

By 1922, the Federal Reserve Banks had discovered that purchases and sales of securities were powerful monetary actions. When the Federal Reserve printed Federal Reserve notes and purchased government securities from banks, bond prices went up (and interest rates down), while the money supply and bank loans increased.

The Fed's easy-money policies contributed to speculation in the 1920s.

One reason for the Federal Reserve's easy-money policies during the 1920s was the Real Bills doctrine — the belief that banks should make commercial loans rather than hold government securities. Buying government bonds from banks was one way to encourage this, but it also increased the money supply and stimulated the economy.

A second reason was a desire to help the world return to the prewar gold standard. The appropriate consequence of the flow of gold to the United States, which now held nearly half of the world's monetary gold, was a large increase in the money supply and the price level in the United States. If U.S. prices rose sufficiently, Europeans would stop buying U.S. wheat, U.S. citizens would buy lots of French wine and English sweaters, and gold would flow from the United States back to Europe. The European governments repeatedly urged the Federal Reserve to follow easy money policies, and this advice from more experienced and respected central bankers was followed. As the speculative boom developed in the 1920s, a final argument for monetary ease was a desire to avoid precipitating a financial collapse.

In December 1927, the Dow Jones Industrial Average of stock prices topped 200, double its level three years earlier. The index reached 250 in October 1928 and 300 two months later. Some people borrowed heavily to buy stocks, and made enviable gains. Many of the envious decided to buy stocks, too, and the Dow index reached 386 in September 1929.

Many historians have criticized the people running the Federal Reserve during this period.[6] For most of the 1920s, the Chairman of the Federal Reserve Board was a Warren G. Harding appointee, whose chief qualification seems to have been that he was a friend and neighbor of Harding. President Herbert

Hoover described other members of the Board as "mediocrities." One exception was Benjamin Strong, who had considerable influence as President of the New York Reserve Bank and has received generally favorable reviews from historians. Some see his untimely death in 1928 as a major factor in bringing on the Great Depression.[7]

The Crash and the Great Depression

In 1928, the Federal Reserve decided that the time had come when something had to be done to discourage stock market speculation. The new president of the New York Reserve Bank, George L. Harrison, argued for a "sharp, incisive" increase in discount rates. The New York Reserve discount rate was raised from 4 percent in February 1928 to 5 percent in July, and then to 6 percent in August 1929. The Federal Reserve also sold a half-billion dollars in government securities from the end of 1927 through the summer of 1929, thereby removing that much currency from circulation. The interest rate on loans to stockbrokers fluctuated wildly, reaching 12, 16, and 20 percent.

In October 1929, the stock market crashed. After a number of bad days, there was panic selling on Thursday, October 24, and then again on Tuesday, October 29. It was like a drunk stumbling down stairs — a bit of unsteady calm, perhaps a step upward, and then a tumble down a few more steps. When the Dow index finally hit the floor, in July 1932, it was at 41, a fall of nearly 90 percent from its 1929 peak.

The stock market crashed in 1929.

It is a matter of continuing debate how much the stock market crash contributed to the economic depression in the 1930s and how much it was simply a barometer of the economy's collapse. Assuredly, it was both to some degree. The low levels of output, profits, and dividends called for low stock prices. And the collapse of stock prices surely depressed the spending of those who owned stocks — a group that was relatively small in numbers but large in discretionary spending. The market crash also dealt a stunning blow to the nation's self-confidence.

As financial markets reeled and sordid tales of financial chicanery spread, anxious depositors converged on banks. Many banks lost money in the stock market crash, both by their own speculation and by their now-worthless loans to others. They were in no shape to meet the anxious demands of depositors. Bank failures became an epidemic as each failure sent depositors rushing to neighboring banks to withdraw their funds before they, too, collapsed. All told, 1,350 banks failed in 1930, 2,290 in 1931, 1,460 in 1932, and 4,000 more in 1933. In desperation, states began declaring banking holidays in late 1932, closing the banks to protect them from their depositors. Looking for an excuse for a bank holiday, the governor of Louisiana, Huey Long, considered honoring Jean Laffite, a pirate; he decided instead to celebrate the breaking of diplomatic relations with Germany in 1916.[8]

Thousands of banks failed during 1929–33.

By Franklin Roosevelt's inauguration in the spring of 1933, only banks in the Northeast remained open. He soon declared a nationwide holiday and closed all banks. Federal regulatory authorities divided banks into three groups: the good, the bad, and the ugly but salvageable. The good reopened within the next week or so, and the bad were permanently closed. Those in the middle group were opened later after being given temporary deposit insurance and loans from the newly created Reconstruction Finance Association.

The withdrawal of deposits from banks, the proclivity of frightened banks to hoard funds rather than make loans, and the closing of banks all contracted the nation's money supply and the availability of credit, surely exacerbating the Great Depression. The Federal Reserve System did not perform well in this, its greatest test. Part of the difficulty was the stubborn belief that only the wicked would be bankrupted.[9]

> *The purgative conception of economic policy . . . held that the boom built damaging, though often unspecified, distortions into the economic system.*
>
> *Recovery could only come as these were eliminated. Deflation and bankruptcy were the natural correctives. Joseph Schumpeter, his country's Finance Minister during much of the Austrian inflation, was now emerging as a major figure on the American economic scene. He argued that the economic system had, through depression, to expel its own poisons. Looking at the history of business cycles, he concluded that no recovery was ever permanent until this happened and that any public intervention to speed recovery merely postponed the therapy and therewith the recovery. Lionel Robbins . . . offered essentially the same advice. . . . "Nobody wishes for bankruptcies. Nobody likes liquidation as such. . . . [But] when the extent of malinvestment and over indebtedness [sic] has passed a certain limit, measures which postpone liquidation only tend to make matters worse." A rather cruder formulation came from Secretary of the Treasury Andrew Mellon. To promote recovery, he advised, the country needed to "liquidate labor, liquidate stocks, liquidate the farmers, liquidate real estate."*

Few recognized the interdependent nature of modern economies. When workers lose jobs, businesses lose sales. When businesses reduce production, employees are let go. When depositors withdraw funds from banks, loans are reduced and both spending and production contract. When households, businesses, and banks are liquidated, their neighbors recoil, thereby making matters worse — not better. Reducing spending, withdrawing deposits, cutting production, and curtailing loans are all understandable reactions, designed to protect the individual but destined to harm the nation.

Despite disapproval and censure by the Federal Reserve Board, the Federal Reserve Bank of New York lowered its discount rate in stages down to 1.5 percent in mid-1931, and the other Reserve Banks eventually followed suit. But the Treasury bill rate had by then dropped below 1 percent. In addition, member banks could borrow only by putting up short-term commercial paper as collateral, which was by then in short supply, a requirement that reflected the influence of Real Bills doctrine. It was not until the Emergency Act of 1933 that banks were allowed to use U.S. government securities as collateral. Member bank borrowings from the Fed actually declined significantly in 1930 and 1931.

| The Failure of the Bank of the United States | Highlight 12.3 |

Chapter 4 discusses two early United States experiments with central banking: the Bank of the United States (1791–1810) and the Second Bank of the United States (1816–1835). Each was modeled after the Bank of England and given a 20-year charter; in each case, Congress voted not to renew its charter.

In the 1920s, a private New York bank with the name Bank of the United States grew to become the twenty-third largest bank in the country. Because of its size and name, many people — both in the United States and abroad — apparently believed that it was part of the federal government. In the aftermath of the 1929 stock market crash, the Bank of the United States, like many other banks, was in danger of collapse; yet many government officials were unsympathetic to the plight of these banks and their customers. An officer of the Philadelphia Fed stated that

> the correction must come about through reduced production, reduced inventories, the gradual reduction of consumer credit, the liquidation of consumer loans and the accumulation of savings through the exercise of thrift. . . . [T]here is no shortcut or panacea for the rectification of existing conditions.*

Andrew Mellon, the Secretary of the Treasury, argued that bankruptcies "will purge the rottenness out of the system. People will work harder, live a more moral life. Values will be adjusted and enterprising people will pick up the wreck from less-competent people."†

The New York Federal Reserve Bank made a modest effort to persuade some large New York banks to lend money to the Bank of the United States. However, there was some feeling in the banking establishment that this bank had been less than ideally managed and that it was tied too closely to the garment industry, which some thought not worth saving, because of prejudice against its mainly Jewish owners.‡ The bank of the United States was allowed to fail in December 1930. With more than $200 million in deposits, this was, at that time, the largest bank failure in U.S. history and the shock waves were felt across the nation and even overseas.

---

*William Greider, *Secrets of the Temple* (New York: Simon & Schuster, 1987), p. 300.
†Greider, p. 300.
‡John K. Galbraith, *Money* (Boston: Houghton Mifflin, 1975), p. 191.

The Federal Reserve did undertake some modest open-market purchases of government securities. It bought $100 million in 1930 and then, worried that a speculative inflation might be around the corner, sold back $40 million in the first half of 1931. It bought $175 million in the second half of 1931 and, convinced that more than a speculative fever had been broken, bought another $1.1 billion in 1932.

Some economists have been very critical of this lackluster performance, arguing that the Federal Reserve should have flooded the country with currency in an all-out effort to end the economic depression. Others, including Keynes, were skeptical of the monetary authority's ability to turn the tide. Interest rates fell to very low levels, and it is hard to see how they could have gone much lower. Even at these extremely low interest rates, households were reluctant to borrow because they feared unemployment. Borrowing to invest in physical capital seemed mad when so much of the nation's capital was already idle. Afraid of the future, households, banks, and businesses all hoarded cash. The ratio of currency outside banks to checking accounts rose from ⅙ in 1929 to ⅓ in 1933. Member banks' excess reserves rose from $48 million in 1929 to $766 million in 1933 to $6.6 billion in 1940. If more cash had been pumped into the economy, it, too, might have been hoarded.

The Fed did little to support the economy or stop bank runs in the 1930s.

Some argue that in an extreme slump there are limits to the effectiveness of monetary policy. The monetary authorities can stop a boom by tightening credit, but cannot ensure recovery by easing credit — it is a lot easier to squeeze the toothpaste out than to put it back into the tube. The only sure way to end an economic collapse is an increase in government spending and employment. Critics of the Federal Reserve's inaction admit that aggressively expansionary monetary policies might not have worked, but argue that at least they should have been tried.

The most stinging indictment is that the Reserve Banks did not find a way to accomplish what they had been created for, to stop panicky bank runs. Bank runs involve a very delicate but obvious element of mass psychology. When depositors believe that their money can be safely withdrawn, they have no desire to withdraw it. No bank, unless it operates as a mere safe-deposit box with 100 percent reserves, can really stand ready to satisfy all depositors at a moment's notice. But it will not be in jeopardy as long as it maintains confidence by meeting modest tests of its ability to pay depositors. The banks that survived in the 1930s were those that were able to acquire funds promptly to cut short any sign of panic.

Often banks were saved by short-term loans from neighboring banks that realized the contagious nature of bank runs. Too often the Federal Reserve Banks would not make similar loans. The Reserve Banks were run by the most reputable bankers, who had an ingrained aversion to risky loans. To get a loan from a Federal Reserve Bank, a member bank seemingly had to prove that it didn't need it. This attitude may have enhanced the profits of the Reserve Banks, but it was hardly a strategy for ending bank runs.

Breaking a Bank Run   Highlight 12.4

Banks normally don't need to keep much currency in their vaults, because daily withdrawals are generally offset by daily deposits. As long as depositors believe that they can withdraw their money when they need it, they are content to leave their money in the bank, earning interest.

A run on the bank is an abnormal event, instigated by depositors' anxiety about the safety of their money. If depositors fear that they may not be able to withdraw their money, they will try to withdraw it. Banks consequently try to stave off bank runs by demonstrating to their depositors' satisfaction that their money is safe. With fractional reserve banking, no bank has enough cash on hand to satisfy all its depositors. So, historically, banks have used a variety of ploys to show that what cash they can muster is sufficient.

In September 1720, for instance, there was a run on the Bank of England after it failed to honor its promise to buy South Sea Company bonds at a price of £400. The Bank successfully defended itself against this run by arranging for allies to be in the front of the line of anxious depositors. These friends were paid slowly in sixpences, which the bank then retrieved and recycled, paying the same money over and over to its allies. The long line melted as depositors grew tired of waiting for their money and became convinced that the bank had the means to pay everyone.*

A similar strategy was employed by Marriner Eccles, who was to become the first Chairman of the Federal Reserve Board. As manager of a prominent Utah bank during the Great Depression, he received word early one morning that a neighboring bank was not going to allow depositors to withdraw their money. Correctly anticipating that this action would cause a run on his own bank, he telephoned the Federal Reserve Bank in Salt Lake City and requested an urgent delivery of currency by armored car.

Before opening his bank, he instructed his bank tellers to smile, talk about the weather, verify all customer signatures very carefully, and double count their money slowly, paying all withdrawals in small bills. Sure enough, when the bank's doors opened, a crowd of anxious depositors surged inside. As instructed, the tellers made small talk and pretended that nothing unusual was happening, while stalling as long as possible.

The armored car from Salt Lake City arrived in time. As the guards brought in sacks of cash, Eccles climbed on top of a table and announced that

> instead of closing at the usual hour of three o'clock, we have decided to stay open just as long as there is anyone who desires to withdraw his deposit or make one. . . . As all of you have seen, we have just brought up from Salt Lake City a large amount of currency that will take care of all your requirements. There is plenty more where that came from.

Later, in his autobiography, he added "This was true enough — but I didn't say that we could get it."†

---

*A. Andreades, *History of the Bank of England* (London: P.S. King, 1909), p. 137, citing McLeod, *The Theory and Practice of Banking* (London: Longmans, Green and Co., 1875), p. 428.

†Marriner S. Eccles, *Beckoning Frontiers* (New York: Alfred A. Knopf, 1951), p. 60.

Reform and a Legacy of Regulation

The financial debacle led to the Banking Act of 1935, which gave the 7-person Federal Reserve Board of Governors in Washington, D.C., the dominant role in setting monetary policy. The Board of Governors was given the authority to approve the Presidents and First Vice-Presidents of the 12 district Reserve Banks, to set reserve requirements within limits fixed by Congress, and to determine Reserve Bank discount rates. The Board occupies 7 of the 12 seats on the Open Market Committee, which eases and tightens financial markets by buying and selling Treasury securities. Among the other provisions in this legislation,

Legislation in the 1930s increased the power and responsibilities of the Fed's Board of Governors.

1. Member banks were allowed to use securities other than commercial paper as collateral for Federal Reserve loans. However, in continued deference to the Real Bills doctrine, loans backed by government securities could not exceed 15 days, and those backed by other securities were assessed a penalty discount rate. (These restrictions have since been removed.)

2. Member banks were severely restricted from acting as investment bankers (underwriting or trading securities) and from investing in stock.

3. Banks were prohibited from paying interest on checking accounts, and the Board of Governors of the Federal Reserve was given the power (Regulation Q) to limit the interest rates that banks pay on time deposits. (It was thought that fierce deposit-rate competition in the 1920s had pushed banks into making high-yielding but speculative investments.)

4. The Federal Reserve Board of Governors was allowed to establish margin requirements, limiting the use of borrowed money to buy stock. With a 25 percent margin requirement, for example, an investor buying $1,000 worth of stock must put up at least $250 and can borrow only $750 from a brokerage firm or other institution. Margin requirements give the Fed a scalpel for cooling stock speculation without precipitating a general credit crunch. When stock prices increased sharply in 1958, the Fed raised margin requirements from 50 percent to 70 percent, and then to 90 percent, to wring out what it perceived as excessive speculation.

5. The Federal Deposit Insurance Corporation (FDIC) was established to insure bank deposits.

This is the legacy of early bank management, early Federal Reserve policies, the excesses of the 1920s, the ensuing financial collapse, and the 1930s reforms. There are several lessons from these historical experiences.

Early banking was a useful but risky business. Banks exerted a strong influence on the economy and were strongly influenced by the economy. What appeared as sound banking practices for an individual bank often exacerbated both the nation's economic fluctuations and bank failures. Early Federal Reserve Banks were ineffectual or worse, because they, too, tried to follow sound banking practices: automatically adjusting Federal Reserve notes as their gold reserves fluctuated and denying loans to member banks that were not creditworthy.

The legislation of the 1930s strongly constrained and shaped the activities of financial intermediaries for the next half-century. In the next two chapters we will look at the recent evolution of these institutions. The legislation of the 1930s also laid the basis for the transformation of the Federal Reserve into a powerful, activist, central monetary authority. In later chapters, we will look at the present Federal Reserve's powers and their implementation.

SUMMARY

Financial intermediaries pool funds to provide safe financial investments to small investors, while lending large amounts to those who want to purchase productive commodities. Borrowers prefer long-term, illiquid loans; lenders prefer short-term, liquid loans. Deposit intermediaries bridge this gap by monetizing illiquid and poorly divisible assets.

Intermediaries can diversify away much idiosyncratic withdrawal and portfolio risk. They must worry about such macrorisks as credit crunches, regulatory changes, droughts, and revolutions. There are also important economies of scale in the provision of structures, machinery, and skilled employees for such purposes as bringing together borrowers and lenders, paying bills, maintaining records of transactions, and evaluating loans and other investments.

It was long thought bank liquidity would be assured and the supply of money appropriately regulated if banks made only short-term, self-liquidating loans. In practice, this strategy helps liquidity but does not guarantee it, and causes the money supply to exaggerate rather than restrain business cycles. The excesses of the 1920s and the Great Depression led to regulations and restrictions that shaped financial intermediaries and the Federal Reserve for decades.

IMPORTANT TERMS

commercial loan theory of banking
discount rate
discount window
idiosyncratic risk

macrorisk
microrisk
Real Bills doctrine
systematic risk

EXERCISES

1. Write a rebuttal to this argument made by the Locofoco Party in the 1830s.[10]

   [Bankers are] the greatest knaves, impostors, and paupers of the age who swear they have promised to pay their depositors 30 or 35 millions of dollars on demand, at the same time that they have only 3 or 4 million to do it with. We are opposed to all bank charters because we believe them at war with good morals.

2. Financial intermediaries earn profits essentially by borrowing at low interest rates and lending out the proceeds at higher rates. Why don't savers simply lend directly to borrowers and earn these higher interest rates themselves?

3. Why do you suppose bigger banks tend to be more profitable than smaller banks?

4. In the 1930s, president Franklin Roosevelt said, "All we have to fear is fear itself." How does this reasoning apply to bank runs?

5. Explain this observation.[11]

   The key function of a financial system is to offer people opportunities to invest without saving and to save without investing.

6. In 1920, the Federal Reserve Banks raised their discount rates, hoping to compel member banks to raise cash by selling some of their government securities. Did this action weaken or strengthen the shaky economy?

7. The last banking panic in England occurred in 1866, when the Bank of England refused to assist a major English bank that had lost a considerable amount of money. The bank declared its insolvency on the afternoon of May 10, and "The next day, there were runs on all banks. People scrambled for cash because no bank was trusted."[12] On the evening of May 11, the Bank of England announced that it would provide whatever funds were needed to satisfy all depositors of all banks, and the panic ended abruptly. Why did this action end the banking panic of 1866 and make future panics less likely? Did the Federal Reserve Board act similarly in the 1930s in the United States?

8. "Deposit Intermediaries monetize illiquid assets." How do they do this and who pays them to do it?

9. The single-index model of stock prices assumes that the return on a company's stock depends on both macro (systematic) factors and micro (idiosyncratic) factors. Which of these risks can investors diversify away by holding a large diversified portfolio of stocks? Which of the following risks would you classify as macro, and which as idiosyncratic?
   a. A company loses an important patent-infringement lawsuit.
   b. A new person is elected president of the United States.
   c. A new person is chosen as the company's Chief Executive Officer.
   d. The value of the dollar declines in foreign-exchange markets.
   e. An oil embargo causes an economic recession.

10. A bank's assets consist mostly of bonds and loans. Give two examples of macro (systematic) risk and two examples of micro (idiosyncratic) risk.

11. A life-insurance company cannot predict with certainty when its policyholders will die. Give two examples of macro (systematic) risk and two examples of micro (idiosyncratic) risk. Which type of risk can be diversified away by writing a large number of policies?

12. Identify which of the following loan purposes were acceptable under the Real Bills doctrine, and briefly explain why.
    a. To pay for seed and fertilizer.
    b. To pay workers' wages.
    c. To pay for a house.
    d. To restock grocer's shelves.

13. Use the distinction between macro and idiosyncratic risk to explain why the following observation is misleading.[13]

A widely diversified portfolio is not supposed to break downward in value very fast because all its "eggs" won't go bad at once. . . . But this safety mechanism doesn't seem to work particularly well. When steel and motors take a dreadful fall, almost the entire diversified list of securities takes it right along with them.

14. Irving Fisher, a prominent U.S. economist, compared the 1929 stock market crash to a run on a bank that did not have enough gold in its vaults to redeem all of the bank notes that it had issued.[14] In his analogy, U.S. industry was a bank, its stock was the paper money it had issued, and the bank's real assets were the nation's factories and machines. Explain why this is not an apt analogy.

15. In the spring of 1920, with the economy weakening, the Federal Reserve increased discount rates to record levels in order to maintain the convertibility of the nation's currency into gold. Why would an increase in the discount rate affect convertibility? Did this action strengthen or weaken the economy?

16. "By 1922, the Federal Reserve Banks had discovered that purchases and sales of securities were powerful monetary actions." When the Federal Reserve purchased government securities from banks, what happened to bond prices, interest rates, the money supply, and bank loans?

17. By the 1920s, the United States had accumulated nearly half the world's monetary gold. Under the gold standard, what should have happened to the U.S. money supply? How would this required change in the money supply affect U.S. prices, U.S. demand for foreign products, and foreign demand for U.S. products?

18. Between 1924 and 1929, the Dow Jones Industrial Average of stock prices rose from 100 to a peak of 386. What was the annual percentage increase in stock prices during these five years?

19. Member bank borrowings from the Fed fell significantly in 1930 and 1931. If the Federal Reserve had wanted to offset the effect of this diminished borrowing on the amount of currency in circulation, should the Fed have purchased government securities or sold them?

20. Interest rates fell to very low levels during the Great Depression, and there was very little borrowing or lending. One imaginative proposal to encourage lending was to tax money holdings: for a dollar to remain legal tender, small stamps would have to be purchased periodically and affixed to it. If this proposal had been enacted, what would have happened to the rate of return on currency?

13

GOVERNMENT REGULATION

OF BANKS

[Governments] should be as tough as they can about policing financial markets for fraud, and as relaxed as they can about companies going bust if they borrow or lend stupidly.

The Economist, 1990

You have seen some of the motivation for government regulation of financial intermediaries — that banking is too important and crises too frequent for society to rely solely on the self-interest of individual banks. What is good for one bank may not be good for all banks. In addition, there have been too many unscrupulous bankers and mismanaged banks, and it is difficult for depositors, by themselves, to identify these villains until it is too late. Finally, even honest, well-managed banks are vulnerable to bank runs. These concerns have created a web of regulation designed to protect depositors and banks.

Policymakers need to understand the powerful tools at their disposal and the consequences of ways they use those tools. As private citizens, we need to anticipate how the government's financial policies will affect us; as voters, we judge the wisdom with which these tools are employed.

In this chapter, we will look at various ways in which government agencies regulate financial intermediaries — trying to ensure that they are solvent and well-managed by inspecting their books, insuring their deposits, and restricting their activities. In Chapter 14, we will explore the management of intermediaries in this regulatory environment. We begin by identifying the regulators.

THE DUAL BANKING SYSTEM

The United States has a diverse and complex governmental structure with origins in the American Revolution and the formation of the Union. As the states banded together, they were quite wary of a centralized, authoritarian government. The founders divided power among three branches of the federal government — executive, legislative, and judicial — and reserved substantial powers for the individual state governments. It was hoped that this complex system of checks and balances would keep any single branch of government from becoming excessively powerful. This philosophy has strongly shaped the development and present regulation of U.S. financial institutions.

Early U.S. money and banking history has been described in Chapters 2 and 4. To recap briefly, the U.S. Constitution seemingly prohibited the issuance of paper money by the federal government or by state governments. Early banks were state-chartered and issued paper money. At the time of the Civil War, a new system was established, which allowed banks to obtain national charters and issue national bank notes, which were liabilities of the private banks that issued them. Bank notes issued by state-chartered banks were taxed out of existence. Private national-bank notes were prohibited in 1935 and replaced by Federal Reserve Notes.

Early attempts at a Central Bank were bitterly opposed and short-lived. The First and Second Banks of the United States each lasted only twenty years (1791–1811 and 1816–1836, respectively), and nearly a century then passed before the Federal Reserve System was established and operated like a central bank. The Federal Reserve was conceived as a decentralized organization that would pay due respect to states' rights. State-chartered banks are not required to join the System, and 90 percent choose not to belong. Power within the System initially resided with the 12 regional Federal Reserve Banks, but after the Great Crash, considerable authority was given to the Federal Reserve Board in Washington, D.C. Yet, banks and other intermediaries are still governed by a complex web of state and federal regulations.

The U.S. did not have a permanent central bank until 1913.

Overlapping Authority

One aspect of this dispersion of authority is a **dual banking system** in which a bank can be chartered (and supervised) by either the federal or a state government. Currently, about one-third of all banks are federally chartered. These banks tend to be larger banks, and they hold nearly 60 percent of all deposits. Nationally chartered banks are supervised by the Comptroller of the Currency, an executive of the U.S. Treasury. State-chartered banks are regulated by individual state agencies.

In the U.S. dual banking system, banks can have state or federal charters.

National banks and state banks that have joined the Federal Reserve System are also regulated by the Federal Reserve. The Federal Deposit Insurance Corporation (FDIC) is yet another regulatory layer. All Federal Reserve member

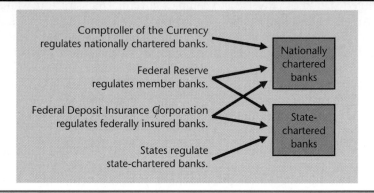

Figure 13.1 **Overlapping Regulatory Authority in the United States**

banks are required to join the FDIC, and almost all nonmember banks have chosen to join. The FDIC has its own set of regulations and bank examiners. Thus a nationally chartered bank is supervised by three separate entities: the Comptroller of the Currency, the Federal Reserve, and the FDIC. A state-chartered bank is typically regulated by the FDIC and its state agency, and it may also be supervised by the Federal Reserve. Figure 13.1 depicts this system of overlapping authority.

Coordination and Conflict

In practice, some duplication is avoided. The Federal Reserve and FDIC accept the Comptroller of the Currency's examinations of national banks, and the FDIC accepts Federal Reserve examinations of state-chartered member banks. However, neither accepts the reports of state bank examiners. A state bank that belongs to either the Federal Reserve or FDIC is examined by one or the other, in addition to the state authorities.

In 1978, the Comptroller of the Currency, the Federal Reserve, and the FDIC adopted a common framework and guidelines for assessing a bank's soundness. The Comptroller's Office examines the balance sheet of each national bank four times each year. Two of these examinations occur regularly in June and December, and two are unannounced calls. Bank examiners determine a so-called CAMEL rating of five bank characteristics —

Government bank examiners assign CAMEL ratings.

Capital adequacy
Asset quality
Management ability
Earnings level and quality
Liquidity

— giving each characteristic a rating of 1 (strong) to 5 (unsatisfactory). The bank is also given an overall composite rating of 1 (sound in almost every respect) to 5 (requires immediate aid and corrective action). This common framework is intended to provide uniform supervision of individual banks.

There may be conflicts in the regulation of banks as a group. In the mid-1960s, the Comptroller of the Currency fought with the Federal Reserve over which types of bank liabilities should be subject to reserve requirements, and over the expansion of bank subsidiaries into nonbank activities. Similarly, in 1974, the Comptroller of the Currency ruled that remote electronic tellers are not branches of a bank and therefore are not subject to state restrictions on the operation of bank branches. This decision was sharply criticized by other regulatory authorities, and the Comptroller amended his ruling to exclude terminals that were more than 50 miles from a bank. A number of state courts subsequently ruled that remote terminals are indeed branches, and the Supreme Court has let these rulings stand. Since then, about a third of the state legislatures have passed laws stating that remote terminals are branches, and another third have passed laws saying that they are not.

Bank regulators sometimes disagree among themselves.

In the 1980s, several states allowed state-chartered banks to engage in activities that are prohibited for national banks. Some states, including California, permitted banks to invest in real estate. Some allowed securities underwriting and travel-agency services. South Dakota openly invited banks to move to South Dakota, from which they had permission to sell insurance in all 50 states.

Critics argue that this duplication and triplication of authority is chaotic and wasteful. Despite the recommendations of various study groups, Congress has resisted consolidating power in a single agency. A natural candidate would be the Federal Reserve, but some feel that bank supervision and regulation should be divorced from the conduct of monetary policy. In addition, those who now have power are understandably reluctant to give it up.

There is also a continuing sentiment for the checks and balances provided by diffused power. Proponents of the existing system argue that competing regulatory authorities provide more flexibility and opportunity for innovation: when one agency is moribund, another can authorize imaginative changes. Unsatisfied banks can even change regulators by switching from a national to state charter, or vice versa. However, some fear that regulations are dangerously weakened by the banks' opportunity to pit one regulator against another. Arthur Burns, a former Federal Reserve Chairman, has stated that[1]

> *The present regulatory system fosters what has sometimes been called "competition in laxity." Even viewed in the most favorable light, the present system is conducive to subtle competition among regulatory authorities, sometimes to relax constraints, sometimes to delay constructive measures. I need not explain to bankers the well-understood fact that regulatory agencies are sometimes played off against one another.*

A not so subtle example of this occurred in 1975 when the FDIC reversed its earlier rejection of a proposed bank merger. The FDIC Chairman, Frank Wille, dissented from this reversal and wrote[2]

I suppose it is indelicate to suggest that the real reason for the Board's reversal has something to do with the explicitness of Mr. _____'s reminder that he can recast the proposal so that the resulting bank would be a national bank, thus permitting the Comptroller of the Currency alone to approve the desired transaction under the Bank Merger Act.

THE FEDERAL RESERVE SYSTEM

From the beginning, there has been debate about whether all banks should be compelled to join the Federal Reserve System. This is a question of the virtues of central control, of focused versus dispersed power. The compromise adopted permits state-chartered banks to choose and, as noted, 90 percent have chosen not to join the Federal Reserve System.

Historically, member banks could use the Fed's discount window, but they were subject to relatively high reserve requirements.

Historically, only member banks had access to the Federal Reserve's discount window, a privilege offset by the fact they were subject to relatively high reserve requirements that could not be met by holding liquid, interest-earning assets, as the reserve requirements of many states could. In addition, many state regulatory agencies have been more lenient than the Federal Reserve on such issues as permissible banking activities and asset holdings, loans to bank officers, required disclosures, and interlocking organizations. For instance, federally chartered banks are prohibited from investing in bonds rated below investment grade, but many state-chartered banks are allowed to invest in low-rated and unrated securities.

In the late 1960s and through much of the 1970s, high interest rates made it increasingly expensive to hold idle reserves. A substantial number of state banks dropped their Federal Reserve membership and some national banks converted to state charters and left the Federal Reserve System. The Federal Reserve was disturbed because these defections lessened its control and even its knowledge of the banking system and the money supply. There were renewed calls for compelling all banks to join the System or giving the Federal Reserve the power to regulate all banks, whether they join or not. The historic 1980 Depository Institutions Deregulation and Monetary Control Act included the following provisions:

1. It authorized interest-bearing checking accounts and phased out all deposit-rate ceilings.
2. It set aside state usury ceilings, though these can be reimposed by individual states.
3. It broadened lending opportunities for thrift institutions — for example, allowing federally chartered savings-and-loan associations to offer consumer and commercial loans, credit lines, and credit cards.
4. It authorized the Federal Reserve to set reserve requirements on checking-account balances and on nonpersonal time deposits in all depository institutions.

5. It gave all depository institutions offering checkable deposits access to the Federal Reserve's discount window.
6. It instructed the Federal Reserve to charge for various services, including check clearing and collection, wire transfer, and securities safekeeping.

The first three provisions were important steps to deregulate deposit intermediaries. In the fourth and fifth provisions, the Federal Reserve Board was given the authority to set reserve requirements at all financial institutions offering checkable deposits. In return, nonmember institutions are now entitled to use the Federal Reserve discount window and other services. The 1980 Monetary Control Act was a landmark centralization of authority, leading the *Financier* to editorialize, "Now, suddenly, the truce is over after all these years. The centralizers have won."[3]

The initial conception of the Federal Reserve System placed considerable power in the 12 district Federal Reserve Banks shown in Figure 13.2. Each Reserve Bank is privately owned by the member banks in its district, though the member banks cannot be paid more than a 6 percent annual return on their compulsory investment in the Reserve Banks. Part of the extra revenue generated by the Reserve Banks is used to pay for the operations of the Washington Federal Reserve Board; the remainder is turned over to the U.S. Treasury.

The perceived failure of the Reserve Banks in the Great Crash led to the centralization of power in Washington, D.C. Today, the 12 Reserve Banks have been reduced to little more than centers for clearing checks and carrying out the financial transactions of the government.

The Board of Governors

The Federal Reserve Board (the Fed) is an independent branch of government — what some have called the Supreme Court of Finance. It is not quite this, but there are definite similarities between the Fed and the Supreme Court, in that both consist of a small number of unelected members who may serve very long terms and decide matters of great importance.

The seven Governors of the Federal Reserve Board are appointed to overlapping 14-year terms, one term ending in January of each even-numbered year. Thus, during four years in office, the President of the United States normally appoints two of the seven members. Deaths or resignations may create additional openings. Governors cannot be appointed to two full terms, but can serve part of an unexpired term and one full term. In continuing deference to the dispersion of power, no two Board members can come from the same Federal Reserve district.

In the past, Governors have often been successful private businessmen, with backgrounds in business or finance. In recent years, many have been professional economists, including Alan Greenspan, the current chair. The Board employs a large staff of professional economists who, at the request of Board members, prepare reports on policy issues. Although Board members usually have well-formed opinions on most monetary issues, the staff studies and discussions do

Now, all deposit intermediaries have uniform reserve requirements and access to the Fed's discount window.

The seven Fed Governors are appointed to overlapping 14-year terms.

Figure 13.2   Federal Reserve Banks and Districts

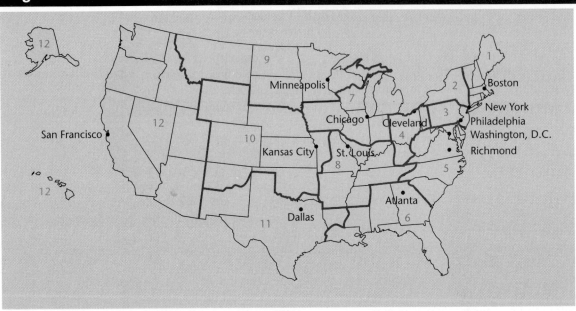

source: Federal Reserve *Bulletin*.

reshape some of these views. The collaboration between the Board and its staff has been enhanced by the fact that several recent Governors had worked on the staff before their appointment to the Board.

Chairman of the Board

The Chairman of the Board of Governors is appointed by the president of the United States to a four-year term, which is not coincident with the president's term. The Chairman's term can be renewed (and often is). As with the Supreme Court, a new Chairman is normally appointed to the Board and made Chairman simultaneously. And traditionally, as with the Supreme Court, the Chairman is the dominant figure on the Board. Like the Warren Court and the Burger Court, we speak of the Burns Federal Reserve Board, the Volcker Board, and now the Greenspan Board.

Marriner S. Eccles, the first Fed Chairman, was the principal architect of the 1930s banking legislation that consolidated power in Washington under Eccles' Board. Eccles was an early and successful advocate of the use of monetary, spending, and taxation policies to stabilize the economy. During the Great Depression, he was convinced that monetary policy was ineffectual (you can give people money, but you can't make them spend it), and argued for increased

The Fed chair often has a strong personality.

government spending. Eccles was chairman for 15 years, from 1934 to 1948, and continued to serve on the Board until 1951.

Thomas McCabe was appointed Chairman by President Truman in 1948, and served through three stormy years in which the Board tangled with both the U.S. Treasury and Truman (the details are in Chapter 18). When McCabe resigned, in 1951, he was replaced by William McChesney Martin, who served for 20 years, from 1951 to 1970. After Martin, Arthur Burns was Chairman from 1970 to 1978. G. William Miller served briefly, resigned under pressure, and was replaced in August 1979 by Paul Volcker, who almost immediately began a tight-money policy that, during the next three years, slowed inflation from double-digit rates to under 4 percent. Volcker stepped down in 1987 and was replaced by Greenspan.

The chairmen are purposely chosen for their dynamic leadership and the respect that they command in the financial community. In addition, the chair has various duties and powers that can be subtly employed to sway the other Governors. Eccles, Martin, Burns, and Volcker all fit the mold of a strong, forceful leader who can direct a Supreme Court of Finance. Indeed, the primary criticism of Miller was that he did not dominate the Federal Reserve Board. The financial community was aghast when it learned that Miller had been outvoted by the other members of the Board. In contrast, there are no calls for impeachment when the Supreme Court Chief Justice is outvoted.

Open Market Committee

The **Federal Open Market Committee (FOMC)** meets approximately every four weeks to discuss and decide policy matters. Its twelve members are the seven Board Governors, the President of The New York Federal Reserve Bank, and four of the other eleven Reserve Bank Presidents. All of the Reserve Bank Presidents usually attend the monthly FOMC meetings and participate in the discussion.

The FOMC makes monetary policy decisions at its monthly meetings.

The permanent seat for the New York Reserve Bank reflects New York's traditional role as the nation's financial capital. The New York Reserve Bank holds nearly a quarter of the aggregate assets of the 12 Reserve Banks and the salary of its President is nearly double that of the Chairman of the Federal Reserve Board. In addition, the FOMC's open-market operations are executed by the New York Reserve Bank.

The Open Market Committee discusses the state of the economy and financial markets and makes monetary policy decisions. With 7 of 12 votes, the Board of Governors dominates these meetings. In addition, the Board itself has the final say on policy matters. Thus, in essence, the monthly FOMC meetings are where monetary policy is discussed, recommendations are offered by the Reserve Bank Presidents, and decisions are made by the Board of Governors, normally in accordance with the wishes of the Board Chairman.

The dynamics of decision making are, of course, more subtle and complex than this caricature. Although the Chairman and the Governors have authority and want that authority to be clearly understood, there is always a risk that arrogance will sufficiently alienate others so that they seek to undermine that power. The Board tries to avoid offending the Reserve Banks, and the Chairman of the Board does not bully the other Governors. When others feel strongly about an issue, the Chairman is likely to be flexible. When opinion is divided, the Chairman molds a consensus, giving considerable weight to the Chair's own views. This is surely a delicate business, but Board Chairmen are chosen and respected because they are good at it.

Open Market Committee meetings are held in secrecy. Before 1967, the FOMC wouldn't even announce when it was meeting, let alone what was decided. Since the passage of the 1967 freedom-of-information laws, the FOMC has been compelled to report its deliberations. Currently, a summary of FOMC discussion and policy actions is released about a month after each meeting and subsequently published in the *Federal Reserve Bulletin*. In addition, since 1975, the Chairman of the Board of Governors has met quarterly with Congress to discuss the Board's objectives for the coming year, including target rates of growth of key monetary aggregates. The Chairman also meets regularly with White House economists to discuss the state of the economy and monetary policy.

THE FEDERAL HOME LOAN BANK SYSTEM

The FHLB system was established to supervise and assist savings-and-loan associations.

The **Federal Home Loan Bank (FHLB) system** was created in the 1930s to supervise and assist savings-and-loan associations. Its structure is similar to that of the Federal Reserve System. All federally chartered savings-and-loan associations must join the FHLB system. Qualified state-chartered savings-and-loan associations may join if they wish. Mutual savings banks may apply for membership in either the Federal Reserve or the FHLB system. Currently, a sixth belong to the FHLB and only a few have joined the Federal Reserve.

There are 12 district Federal Home Loan Banks which, since 1951, have been privately owned by the member institutions. The Federal Home Loan Bank Board supervised the FHLB system until 1989, when it was replaced by two new organizations:

1. The Office of Thrift Supervision, which now charters, regulates, and supervises S&L's.
2. The Federal Housing Finance Board, which now oversees the 12 Federal Home Loan Banks.

The FHLB banks can loan funds to member institutions, a service analogous to the Federal Reserve's discount window. These loans have been particularly helpful to savings-and-loan associations during credit crunches in 1966, 1969–1970, 1973–1974, and 1978–1980. Figure 13.3 summarizes FHLB loans since World War II. The important difference between the FHLB banks and Federal Reserve is that the FHLB banks cannot issue currency. The Federal Reserve can

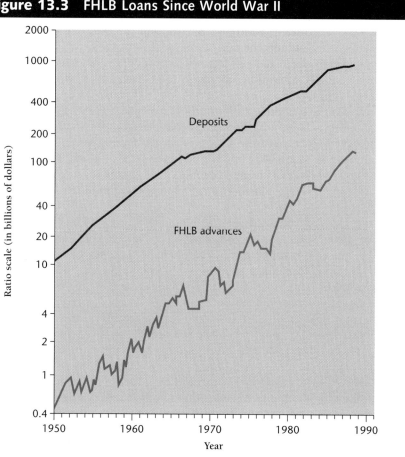

Figure 13.3   **FHLB Loans Since World War II**

source: Federal Reserve *Historical Chart Book,* 1990.

print Federal Reserve notes and lend them to member banks or use them to buy bonds in the open market. In contrast, the FHLB banks must raise funds from its members or by selling bonds. Because it does not have a printing press, the FHLB system is not an utterly reliable lender of last resort. The 1980 Deregulation Act filled this gap by permitting all deposit intermediaries to use the Federal Reserve discount window.

MORTGAGE LOANS AND POOLS

The federal government uses a variety of loans and loan guarantees to subsidize housing. For instance, many home mortgages are insured by the Federal Housing

Fannie Mae, Ginnie Mae, and Freddie Mac buy mortgages and issue mortgage-backed securities.

Authority (FHA) or guaranteed by the Veterans Administration (VA). In addition, three major federally established agencies buy mortgages.

The **Federal National Mortgage Association (FNMA, or Fannie Mae)** was established in 1938 to funnel funds to mortgage borrowers. In 1968, it was split into two separate organizations: a private corporation that retained the name Fannie Mae and a government corporation, the **Government National Mortgage Association (Ginnie Mae)**.

Fannie Mae sells short- and medium-term bonds, using the proceeds to buy mortgages from mortgage bankers and other mortgage originators. Fannie Mae was relatively inactive until the 1960s, when its debt issues jumped from $2.5 billion in 1960 to $15 billion in 1970 and then to $65 billion by 1980. During the 1966 and 1969–1970 credit crunches, thrift institutions sold mortgages to Fannie Mae in order to obtain cash to satisfy withdrawals and to make new mortgage loans.

In the 1968 separation, Fannie Mae became a privately owned corporation, subject to government supervision. Five of the fifteen board directors are appointed by the President, and the Department of Housing and Urban Development (HUD) must formally approve all of Fannie Mae's borrowing. In addition, HUD sets the rate of return paid to stockholders and requires Fannie Mae to channel some mortgage money to low-income buyers. In return, Fannie Mae borrows some money directly from the federal government and can borrow privately at relatively low rates because it is a quasi-governmental agency. Since 1968 Fannie has mostly bought mortgages from private mortgage bankers.

Wall Street was enthusiastic about Fannie Mae. By borrowing short and lending long, with some government protection, Fannie Mae offers another way to bet on the course of interest rates — an unanticipated decline in interest rates is good for Fannie Mae; an increase is bad. Fannie Mae is allowed to have a debt-equity ratio of 25 to 1, creating enormous leverage. When Fannie Mae stock was first sold, it was exempt from all SEC regulations and initially subject to only a 25 percent margin requirement, while all other stocks required 65 percent margin. On the fourth day after issuance, Fannie Mae was the most actively traded stock on the New York Stock Exchange. The price of FNMA stock went from $5 a share in 1968 to $15 in 1969, $8 in 1970, and $27 in 1972.

The Government National Mortgage Association (Ginnie Mae), part of the Department of Housing and Urban Development, was created in 1968 to administer government mortgage-subsidy programs that had previously been handled by Fannie Mae — for example, using Treasury money to make HUD-subsidized housing mortgages. In 1970, Ginnie Mae created the revolutionary idea of selling Ginnie Mae certificates to finance the purchase of FHA and VA mortgages from private institutions. The issuing institutions send the mortgage interest and principal payments to GNMA, which passes them through to those who own Ginnie Mae certificates, hence the label **pass-through securities**. GNMA guarantees the payment of interest and principal and, in return, levies a fee on each mortgage pool it creates. The minimum Ginnie Mae denomination is $25,000, but several brokerage houses have GNMA investment trusts with units priced at around $1,000.

In 1970, the Federal Home Loan Board established the **Federal Home Loan Mortgage Corporation (Freddie Mac)**, which is owned by the twelve federal home loan banks and individual thrift institutions. Freddie Mac is similar to both Fannie Mae and Ginnie Mae in that it puts together pools of mortgages, financing its purchases by the sale of pass-through mortgage Participation Certificates and bond-like instruments called Guaranteed Mortgage Certificates (GMCs) and **Collateralized Mortgage Obligations (CMOs)**. CMOs have fixed interest rates and are typically divided into four classes. The first three classes receive regular, usually semiannual, interest with all mortgage principal payments and prepayments initially given to the class-one CMOs. After the class-one CMOs are retired, all mortgages payments and prepayments go to the class-two CMOs, until these are retired, and then to the class-three CMOs. The last securities, called the accrual class or Z class, receive no interest or principal until the prior three classes are repaid.

The total value of mortgage-backed securities issued by Fannie Mae, Ginnie Mae, and Freddie Mac was more than $700 billion in 1988. There are also a number of private firms that provide a secondary market in mortgages, including MGIC Mortgage Corporation (Maggie Mae), a subsidiary of MGIC Investment Corporation ("MAGIC"), which insures private mortgages.

These institutions with the funny names have revolutionized deposit intermediaries and the mortgage market. More than half of all residential mortgages are now resold in the secondary mortgage market — a process called **securitization** in that illiquid mortgages are converted into marketable mortgage-backed securities. The securitization of mortgages means that you no longer have to be a mortgage banker or a savings-and-loan association to invest in mortgages.

Some deposit institutions sell their mortgages to GNMA and then purchase Ginnie Mae securities, which are federally insured against default, more geographically diversified, and can be sold quickly if cash is needed. Other deposit institutions use the secondary market to avoid holding mortgages. Burned too often by borrowing short and lending long, they convert most of their mortgages into cash or other short-term securities.

Conversely, those who buy into mortgage pools assume some of the risks that worry thrift institutions. An increase in interest rates reduces the present value of the cash flow from fixed-rate mortgages, giving capital losses to mortgage holders. A drop in interest rates can also be bad news. Suppose that pass-through certificates are issued for a pool of 30-year mortgages with 10 percent interest rates. If interest rates drop, borrowers may repay their mortgages ahead of schedule in order to refinance at lower interest rates. The pass-through owners receive these prepayments and now must reinvest their money at lower interest rates. Because interest rates and the prepayment of mortgage loans are uncertain, it is difficult to estimate the rate of return on mortgage pools. The GNMA yields typically reported in the financial press assume that the average mortgage in the pool will be paid off after 12 years, which is the approximate historical average. But the future is unlikely to replicate the past.

In the early 1980s, when interest rates were very high, GNMA certificates issued during the 1970s sold at substantial discounts from their initial issuing

Mortgage-backed securities have revolutionized deposit intermediaries and the mortgage market.

| Highlight 13.1 | Farmer Mac |

Farm income is much more volatile than nonfarm wage income, and the private securitization of farm mortgages has been inhibited by a relatively high and volatile default rate on farm mortgages. Throughout the 1980s, the default rate on nonfarm mortgages held by life insurance companies was consistently less than 1 percent; the default rate on farm mortgages was 1 percent in 1980; 3 percent in 1983; 8 percent in 1986; and 6 percent in 1987.* In addition, unlike conventional home mortgages, farm mortgages commonly include a revolving credit line that allows farmers to vary the amount borrowed with seasonal needs — which makes it difficult to estimate the lender's cash flow and to value farm-mortgage securities.

The Agricultural Credit Act of 1987 created the Federal Agricultural Mortgage Corporation (Farmer Mac) to encourage the securitization of farm mortgages. Farmer Mac is a private corporation that guarantees the repayment of principal and interest on privately issued securities that are backed by farm mortgages. To obtain Farmer Mac's guarantee, the institution that issues the farm mortgage must pay initial and annual fees and cover at least 10 percent of any losses due to defaults.

Farmer Mac's solvency is guaranteed by the U.S. government. There is little reason to think that Farmer Mac will be able to estimate default rates and the timing of payments with great accuracy. Because of its size, Farmer Mac may be able to diversify away some idiosyncratic default risk, but it is still vulnerable to interest rates, farm prices, and other macroeconomic risks.

---

*James R. Booth, "Farmer Mac and the Secondary Market," *Federal Reserve Bank of San Francisco Weekly Letter,* January 5, 1990, pp. 1–3.

price because high interest rates had reduced the present value of the low-interest mortgages in the pool. At these low market prices, and assuming that the mortgages in the pool would be repaid 12 years after their issuance, these Ginnie Mae certificates were calculated to have very high yields. But homeowners fortunate enough to have old low-interest mortgages were understandably reluctant to prepay. The longer they held on to their mortgages, the lower the actual return to Ginnie Mae investors.

The development of a secondary mortgage market weakens the separation between mortgages and other securities, making more money available for mortgages from such nontraditional sources as individuals and pension funds. Mortgages now compete with Treasury bonds, IBM securities, and junk bonds. Mortgage availability and housing construction now depend on the overall level of interest rates and national saving, not merely on how much money can be attracted to deposits in thrift institutions.

DEPOSIT INSURANCE

The New York Safety Fund was created in 1829 to protect the creditors of New York-chartered banks. This central emergency fund was financed by bank contributions equal to 3 percent of their capital, paid over six years, and protected both depositors and holders of bank notes. In 1842, coverage was restricted to noteholders. A few other states set up similar plans, but charter expirations and bank failures largely exhausted these scattered safety funds.

In 1933, with the banking system a shambles, Congress created a nationwide **Federal Deposit Insurance Corporation (FDIC)** to insure deposits in commercial and mutual savings banks. The companion **Federal Savings and Loan Insurance Corporation (FSLIC)** was established at the same time to insure deposits in savings-and-loan associations. Because of the rapid growth of credit unions since World War II, the **National Credit Union Administration** was established, and it initiated nationwide credit-union deposit insurance in 1970.

Deposit insurance was opposed by the American Bankers Association, which called the FDIC "inherently fallacious . . . one of those plausible, but deceptive, human plans that in actual application only serve to render worse the very evils they seek to cure."[4] On another occasion, the ABA called it "unsound, unscientific, unjust, and dangerous."[5] President Roosevelt threatened to veto the Banking Act of 1933 if it contained deposit insurance. In retrospect, the FDIC succeeded in eliminating contagious bank runs, benefiting depositors, the nation, and even the reluctant bankers.

Federal deposit insurance has virtually eliminated bank runs.

The initial money for the FDIC, some $289 million, came from the Treasury and the Federal Reserve Banks. Member banks pay an annual fee, now equal to 15¢ for every $100 of insured deposits. The FDIC long ago repaid the initial $289 million grant and, at the end of 1989, had accumulated more than $18 billion for assisting troubled banks.

Initially, FDIC deposit insurance was limited to $2,500 per depositor per bank. With the growth of the economy and deposits, this limit has been steadily raised and, in March 1980, was increased to its current limit of $100,000 — which just covers a single $100,000 negotiable CD. Because larger deposits are at risk, rumors of insolvency can precipitate a liquidity crisis at a bank with a substantial number of large deposits; for example, the Franklin National Bank collapsed when it lost a half billion dollars in unrenewed CDs during five anxious months in 1974.

Why Does It Work?

Overall, nearly a trillion dollars in deposits are covered by FDIC insurance, an amount that dwarfs the FDIC's reserves. On the whole, banks have the assets to back up their deposits because the FDIC supervises its insured banks closely and withholds insurance from any that are poorly managed. One of the subtle virtues of the FDIC is that it brought almost all state-chartered banks under the supervision of a hard-nosed federal agency. Both the FDIC and the Federal Reserve Board have the power to remove officers or directors of member banks who have taken reckless actions that threaten a bank's solvency. The typical risk is not that banks have insufficient assets to support their deposits, but that much of their assets are illiquid and cannot be mobilized in a hurry — they are illiquid, not insolvent. Temporary loans from the FDIC stave off bank runs and, if necessary, allow a gradual liquidation of the bank's assets.

The second reason the FDIC's assets are adequate is that it has the complete support of the President, Congress, and the Federal Reserve. If a panic began to develop, these sources would provide as much cash as necessary to abort the panic. When Franklin National, then the nation's twentieth largest bank, was squeezed in 1974, the Federal Reserve made $1.7 billion in emergency credit available to keep it afloat until it could be permanently salvaged.

The third reason the FDIC works is that when depositors are confident that their funds are safe, there is no need for the funds to be available. The runs on the Ohio and Maryland savings-and-loan associations described in Chapter 4 occurred because they did not have federal insurance. By being a completely reliable lender of last resort and by promptly helping troubled banks, the FDIC reassures depositors and eliminates contagious bank panics. This is the primary reason why bank runs have virtually disappeared.

In practice, the FDIC seldom closes large banks. The standard operating procedure is to stabilize an endangered bank until a shotgun wedding with a strong bank can be arranged. Even troubled banks have substantial, though illiquid, assets, and a suitor can be found, especially if the FDIC pays a generous price for some of the bank's questionable assets. In such a merger, no depositor (even those with deposits beyond the insurance limit) loses a penny, though the stockholders of the disappearing bank can lose plenty.

The FDIC seldom closes large banks.

For example, Franklin National lost a great deal of money in 1974 in foreign-exchange transactions and what turned out to be bad loans. Nevertheless, it had plenty of attractive assets and was quickly taken over by the European-American Bank and Trust Company, a New York bank owned by six large European banks. Another prominent example occurred in 1980 when First Pennsylvania, then the nation's twenty-third largest bank, was bailed out by the FDIC. First Pennsylvania held billions of dollars in long-term bonds and mortgages and sustained large losses when interest rates rose sharply in 1979 and 1980. As fears for its solvency spread, it lost $1.6 billion in deposits — mostly very large CDs. The FDIC and 22 private banks put together a $1.5 billion loan package to avert a liquidity crisis. As part of the bailout plan, First Pennsylvania sold a half billion dollars' worth of government bonds, sold its mortgage banking and consumer finance subsidiaries to Manufacturers Hanover, and liquidated a bond-trading subsidiary. In all, 25 percent of its assets were liquidated, but it continued in business as a slimmed-down, more conservative bank.

| An FDIC Barbecue | Highlight 13.2 |

In 1985, a *Los Angeles Times* reporter was allowed to accompany FDIC officials when they seized an insolvent San Diego bank.* Because the target bank was state chartered, the California banking commissioner issued the formal closure order and appointed the FDIC to act as receiver. Fifty FDIC employees were summoned to a secret four-day meeting at a hotel near the bank to scrutinize the bank's records and make a realistic estimate of its net worth. To avoid frightening depositors, the officials registered as employees of a fictitious company, Mission Bay Ltd., and referred to the takeover as a "barbecue." Only a handful of FDIC employees knew which bank was to be closed before they were sequestered at the hotel.

Two days before the scheduled closure, seven San Diego banks were invited to examine the records and submit bids for the troubled bank. On Friday, the day of the seizure, the head of the operation reminded everyone to be polite, say as little as possible, and accept no money from any bank employee. That evening, minutes before the bank's regular six o'clock closing time, two FDIC officials walked into the bank president's office, while two state banking officials locked the bank's doors. After the closure notice was delivered to the bank president, the head of the FDIC team addressed the bank's employees: "I'd like to welcome you aboard. You are all now employees of the FDIC." He explained the situation and asked each employee to stay late that night and work through the weekend, helping the FDIC organize and examine all of the bank's records. Each bank employee would be paid time and a half. As the bank no longer existed, the phone should be answered "FDIC." Dozens of FDIC employees then entered; a locksmith changed all of the bank's locks, while armed guards stood outside.

On Saturday morning, the FDIC accepted a bid from another bank; that afternoon, the new owners arrived and invited the employees to continue working at the bank. Sunday, the signs were changed and plans were made to serve customers coffee and doughnuts Monday morning. Large depositors were telephoned and reassured that their money was safe. When the bank's doors opened Monday at 8 A.M., there were two customers waiting. Both had come to deposit money.

---

*Bruce Horovitz, "Behind the Scenes of a Bank Turnover by FDIC," *Los Angeles Times,* January 5, 1986.

The FDIC does close smaller banks with severe problems, paying each depositor up to the limit allowed. After the failed bank is liquidated, the proceeds are divided among the FDIC, the depositors not entirely covered by insurance, and other creditors. Although it may take several years, these claimants — including the FDIC — usually get back almost all of their money.

The S&L Crisis

During the last 6 months of 1981, 85 percent of all thrifts insured by the Federal Savings and Loan Insurance Corporation (FSLIC) lost money. During the two-year period 1981–1982, the industry lost $8.9 billion and 813 thrift institutions disappeared — mostly through absorption by stronger institutions. The FSLIC provided financial assistance to 92 thrifts and liquidated 2 others. In the Federal Home Loan Bank Board's own words, "so intense was the search for healthy merger partners" that it authorized the FSLIC to arrange interstate mergers.[6]

In response to losses at federally insured thrifts, the 1982 Garn-St Germain Act deregulated banks and thrifts.

In response to this crisis, the **Garn-St Germain Depository Institutions Act** of 1982 hastened the deregulation of the banking industry in several ways. Some of the most important provisions were these:

1. Banks and thrifts were authorized to offer money-market deposit accounts, with no interest-rate ceiling and no reserve requirement, so that they could compete with money-market funds.
2. Federal thrifts were allowed to diversify their assets away from home mortgages by making business loans and by increasing their consumer loans and loans secured by nonresidential real estate.
3. The Act affirmed the power of the FDIC and FSLIC to arrange interstate mergers if necessary and to allow banks to make interstate acquisitions of closed banks or thrifts with assets of at least $500 million.

Interest rates declined in the second half of 1982, and the losses stopped at many thrifts. However, a third of the FSLIC-insured thrifts continued to lose money in 1983 and, even using generous accounting procedures, the ratio of net worth to assets was below the mandated 3 percent level at one-fourth of all FSLIC-insured institutions.[7] Interest rates continued to fall in 1984 and 1985, but losses at the weaker institutions continued to increase. The problem was no longer an interest-rate squeeze, but mounting loan defaults — caused too often by excessive risk-taking or outright fraud that ultimately reflects inadequate supervision by state regulators and the FSLIC.

Some thrifts used deregulation to take excessive risks or to commit fraud.

Gambling and Fraud

Most problem loans — to wildcat oil drillers, farmers, real estate developers, and developing countries — can be attributed to unforeseen economic developments and, in retrospect, excessive optimism. Some losses were less innocent: depositor money squandered on palace offices, private planes, classic automobiles, large yachts, beach houses, trips to Europe, and lavish bonuses.

The Worst of the Worst?	**Highlight 13.3**

In 1984, American Continental Corporation of Phoenix, a real estate development company controlled by the family of Charles H. Keating, Jr.,
acquired Lincoln Savings & Loan of Irvine, California. When it was seized
by federal regulators five years later, it was estimated that Lincoln had lost
$2 billion in federally insured deposits plus an additional $200 million
raised from the sale of bonds to 22,000 investors, of whom some 15,000
were elderly Southern Californians who purchased the bonds at Lincoln
branch offices, many incorrectly believing the bonds were federally insured
CDs.

    Under Keating, Lincoln virtually abandoned traditional single-family
mortgages in favor of junk bonds, corporate stock, currency futures, and
real estate development. Officials of the California Office of Thrift Supervision, a state regulatory agency, later told Congress that "A thrift was a
perfect cash cow for a real estate developer."* According to this congressional testimony, a typical Lincoln acquisition, construction, and development (ADC) loan involved no down payment and included funds not only
for the property and construction, but also for architectural fees, developer
fees, points and other loan fees, and the first few years' interest on the
loan. No principal payments were required for the first 2 to 5 years of the
loan. Lincoln recorded the loan fees and interest as income, though it
received no cash from the developer for at least two years. According to
the regulator, "hundreds of such loans were made with no loan application,
no credit checks, with no appraisal or feasibility study." After the Federal
Home Loan Board (FHLB) imposed restrictions on direct investments,
Lincoln allegedly made loans to straw companies that never intended to
repay the loans, leaving Lincoln with ownership of the foreclosed property.

    If a thrift is growing fast enough, losses on defaulted loans can be
covered by recording ever larger loan fees and interest on new loans, income
that isn't received by the thrift, but merely loaned to the developer. To
disguise the lack of cash flow, some troubled thrifts swapped loans, paying
each other more than the book value of the loans. No money changed
hands, but each recorded a profit based on the sham sale. According to
the California regulator, a common expression was, "I'll trade you my dead
cow for your dead horse."

    In 1986, FHLB regulators in the San Francisco regional office began a
year-long audit that concluded that federal government should take over
Lincoln Savings & Loan and that the Federal Bureau of Investigation should
look into possible crimes by Lincoln officials. M. Danny Wall, then head

*William J. Eaton, "Lincoln Exemplifies How S&Ls Collapse, Official Says," *Los Angeles
Times,* October 28, 1989.

of the FHLB, overruled their recommendation and, a year later, transferred the responsibility for supervising Lincoln from San Francisco to the Washington offices of the FHLB.

The Washington examiners eventually confirmed the San Francisco investigation and, in addition, suggested that Lincoln had improperly channeled $94 million to its parent company, American Continental, under the guise of a nonexistent tax liability. An accounting firm hired by the FHLB concluded that "Seldom in our experience have we encountered a more egregious example of the misapplication of generally accepted accounting principles. . . . Lincoln was manufacturing profits by giving money away."†

Federal authorities seized Lincoln in April 1989; many wondered if the seizure had been delayed, allowing losses to reach unprecedented levels, because of Keating's political connections — including five U.S. senators who spoke with FHLB officials on Keating's behalf and accepted $1.4 million in contributions from Keating, his family, and business associates. In December 1989, Wall was forced to resign as head of the FHLB and an investigation was begun into possible improprieties by those senators.

†Brooks Jackson, "How Regulatory Error Led to the Disaster at Lincoln Savings," *Wall Street Journal,* November 20, 1989.

Some states, including California and Texas, allowed state-chartered thrifts to invest in almost anything, including restaurants, health clubs, and wind farms. The biggest lure was commercial real estate. In many cases, real estate developers bought S&L's so that they could, in effect, lend themselves money to finance speculative real estate projects, sometimes paying themselves large fees for finding such attractive borrowers — themselves! One developer acquired an $11 million savings bank in California and increased its deposits to $1 billion in 2½ years, using half of the deposits to finance the developer's real estate deals. After the FSLIC forced the developer out, claiming that too much had been invested in overvalued real estate, he defended his actions: "Who would you rather lend to, yourself or to a stranger?"[8]

Some lost money, particularly in Texas, when real estate prices collapsed. Some lost money on dubious developments. If they lost money, too often they tried to recoup their losses by investing more money in even riskier ventures. Once the S&L's net worth vanished, there was little personal risk in taking more chances. They were literally throwing good money after bad, but it wasn't their money — it was their depositors' money and, because it was federally insured, ultimately the taxpayers' money. If they couldn't get enough money from local depositors, they turned to deposit brokers who channel deposits from investors looking for high rates of return. The ailing S&L has to pay an extra 1 percent or so for brokered deposits, but this is little deterrent to a thrift desperate for one more roll of the dice.

In the infamous I-30 case, the chief executive officer of Empire Savings and Loan in Texas was accused of defrauding the thrift of $142 million through speculative loans for condominiums along Interstate 30 in Dallas. The FSLIC paid $300 million to Empire's depositors, and 83 people were eventually convicted of a variety of charges, including perjury, tax fraud, and racketeering. In 1984, Empire's chief executive officer agreed to pay a $100-million civil penalty to the FSLIC. While the FSLIC did not expect to receive $100 million from the CEO, it intended this penalty to result in the forfeiture of virtually all of his assets.

Some frauds escaped detection from the regulators; many were uncovered but ignored because of political pressure from sympathetic congressmen, their sympathy seemingly encouraged by large campaign contributions. Vernon Savings and Loan of Texas kept a 112-foot yacht in Washington, D.C., that was frequently used by the Democratic Congressional Campaign Committee. When Vernon was taken over by the FSLIC in 1987, it was reported that 96 percent of its loans were delinquent and that millions had been spent on Vernon's president, including $2 million for a beach house in California, plus $200,000 for furnishings and $36,780 for one month's flowers.[9] Eight Vernon officials were convicted of a variety of federal charges including fraud, conspiracy, and the use of bank funds to make political contributions and pay prostitutes.

The Bailout

In the summer of 1989, it was widely estimated that the federally insured deposits at insolvent S&L's exceeded the assets of these institutions by at least $100 billion. The FSLIC didn't have enough money to pay off depositors or to subsidize acquisitions by stronger institutions. The insolvent S&L's that couldn't be buried became known as zombies. The zombies paid high deposit rates to persuade their depositors not to leave, thereby forcing healthy thrifts to lose deposits or pay high deposit rates too — either way, squeezing the industry's profits.

In August 1989, President George Bush signed the **Financial Institutions Reform, Recovery and Enforcement Act** (with the catchy acronym FIRREA). Among its provisions:

> The 1989 FIRREA was intended to close insolvent thrifts and prevent a future crisis.

1. The insolvent FSLIC was replaced with a new deposit insurance fund for thrifts, the Savings Association Insurance Fund (SAIF), administered by the FDIC. The annual FDIC deposit insurance premiums paid by banks increased from 8¢ to 15¢ on every $100 of insured deposits; annual thrift premiums to SAIF are 23¢ per $100 of deposits, and can be increased to 32.5¢.
2. Thrifts must have capital equal to at least 3 percent of assets by 1994, and can no longer count "goodwill" as capital. In addition, capital requirements for depository institutions now depend on the riskiness of their assets — for instance, no requirements on Ginnie Mae securities, 1.6 percent on Fannie Mae and Freddy Mac securities, 4 percent on nonsecuritized mortgages, and 8 percent on commercial loans and other assets.

3. The Office of Thrift Supervision (OTS) was established, with the power to charter, regulate, and supervise all thrifts, whether state or federally chartered. OTS can prohibit the use of brokered deposits and restrict what it considers excessively rapid growth. No thrifts are permitted to invest in securities rated below investment grade.

4. Qualified Thrift Lenders must hold 70 percent of their assets in residential mortgage-related assets, and are allowed to borrow at low interest rates from Federal Home Loan Banks. Insured thrifts that do not meet this 70 percent minimum must convert to bank charters; those that do convert to bank charters continue to pay thrift deposit insurance premiums for at least five years.

5. Because insolvent thrifts have nothing more to lose and are tempted to plunge into increasingly speculative gambles, FIRREA authorized the FDIC to terminate deposit insurance with as little as six months' notice and to close or take over the operations of any insured bank or thrift, no matter whether it is state or federally chartered.

6. The Resolution Trust Corporation, a division of the FDIC, will use $50 billion raised through bond sales to terminate insolvent thrifts by subsidizing acquisitions or paying off depositors. In addition, $1.8 billion in retained earnings held by the Federal Home Loan Banks and most of the $1.2 billion annual dividend paid to member thrifts was turned over to the FDIC.

7. Commercial banks are authorized to acquire healthy thrifts.

The stricter capital requirements required by FIRREA have several objectives: One is to weed out small, financially tenuous thrifts. Those that do not meet the capital requirements must raise more money (perhaps by the sale of stock), reduce their assets to a scale consistent with their capital, or merge with stronger institutions. In December 1989, Richard Pratt, a former chairman of the Federal Home Loan Bank Board, predicted a "financial meltdown" in which 70 percent of the existing thrifts might be forced out of business by their inability to meet FIRREA's capital requirements.[10]

A second objective of FIRREA's strict capital requirements is to protect the deposit insurance fund. A bank's capital absorbs its profits and losses; the more capital it has, the more losses it can endure before it becomes insolvent and forces the deposit insurance system to cover its losses. A third objective is that, with more of the deposit institution's money at stake, the managers will be more cautious. Fourth, the risk-based capital requirements strongly encourage investment in liquid, marketable securities.

In the past, regulatory authorities were often reluctant to close insolvent thrifts because of the costs of arranging a merger or paying depositors. But allowing the thrift to continue its operations, paying high rates for deposits and making speculative gambles, is even more expensive. FIRREA gives the FDIC and OTS the authority, a mandate, and some money to enforce capital requirements strictly and to move quickly to contain the financial damage that zombie thrifts impose on themselves and on healthy institutions.

The $50 billion liquidation fund will no doubt prove inadequate, as it is based on incredibly optimistic assumptions:

There will be virtually no inflation between 1989 and 1994.
Treasury-bill rates will fall to 4.4 percent in 1994.
S&L deposits will grow by 7 percent a year.
There will be no economic recession between 1989 and 1999.

The lowest credible private estimate in 1989 of the cost of liquidating insolvent thrifts was $100 billion. Some government officials were candid about the inadequacy; an assistant Treasury secretary argued that "It's a good start. You shouldn't give anyone more than $50 billion to play with at one time."[11]

Are Banks Overprotected?

There is a **moral-hazard** problem when one of the parties to a contract alters his or her behavior so as to profit from the contract at the other party's expense. For example, a homeowner who has fire insurance may become less careful about avoiding a fire; a person with medical insurance may be less frugal about medical expenses. The primary criticism of deposit insurance is that there is a moral-hazard problem in that it encourages reckless banking practices. Because the owners of the deposit intermediary keep the profits if their speculation turns out to be profitable, and the federal government absorbs the losses if the speculation fails, there is an incentive for excessive risk-taking. And, perversely, if the intermediary loses money, the incentive for risk-taking becomes even larger.

Critics of the FDIC often speak as if there were no penalty for failure. The stockholders of a failed bank do lose a lot, and so do the bank's officers, who are likely to become unemployed if the bank flounders. The problem is that these penalties do not increase with the size of the risks taken.

Some observers consequently argue that deposit-insurance premiums should vary with the riskiness of the bank.[12] In this way, reckless bank management can be discouraged. There is merit in this argument, but riskiness is difficult to quantify. How are government regulators to measure the riskiness of loans to finance a New York apartment building, oil exploration in the Gulf of Mexico, or a shoe manufacturer in Brazil? Not only are such loans difficult to gauge individually, but we saw in Chapter 11 that, to judge the overall riskiness of a bank's portfolio, we need to separate the systematic risk from the idiosyncratic risk that can be diversified away.

Even if government regulators could quantify the riskiness of a bank's loan portfolio, much of the excessive risk-taking occurs when a deposit institution is insolvent, or nearly so, and has nothing more to lose. These one-sided bets won't be discouraged by modest increases in deposit-insurance premiums. The only sure cure for a zombie thrift is burial.

The FDIC does closely supervise bank practices and, if there is a danger of insolvency, it can close the bank or, what is virtually the same thing, terminate

Deposit insurance creates a moral-hazard problem by encouraging excessive risk-taking.

| Highlight 13.4 | Buying Junk with Insured Deposits |

Junk bonds are risky and, because most investors dislike risk, priced to offer relatively high expected returns. Those who buy junk bonds are less risk averse than others or more optimistic about the junk firm's chances of paying its debts. Some savings-and-loan associations bought junk because they were using other people's money — their federal insured deposits.

These S&L junk purchases are a clear example of the moral hazard problem. S&L's were willing to borrow from their depositors at 5 percent to 10 percent interest to invest in junk bonds promising 15 percent to 20 percent returns, because any profits would go to the S&L and most of the losses would be paid by federal deposit insurance. Heads, the S&L wins. Tails, the FSLIC loses.

As it turned out, up until the end of 1989, junk bonds were, on average, relatively profitable investments for thrifts. A 1989 General Accounting Office Report found that junk had not contributed to the S&L crisis to that point and that, after credit cards, junk bonds had in fact been the S&L industry's second most profitable category of investments.*

However, the years surveyed in this report had been recession free. Concerned about potential future defaults and recognizing the moral hazard problem, the 1989 Financial Institutions Reform, Recovery and Enforcement Act (FIRREA) prohibited thrifts from buying additional junk bonds and gave them five years to sell their current holdings. As FIRREA neared completion, some thrifts made substantial last-minute junk purchases. One industry analyst said that these thrifts "realized this was their last window of opportunity, so they jumped in. It was a case of speeding up at the yellow light."† During the last forty days before FIRREA was enacted, ten of these hot-rod thrifts bought a total of more than $1 billion in junk bonds, increasing their holdings by 19 percent.

In retrospect, their timing couldn't have been worse. With further purchases prohibited and sales mandated, FIRREA created an excess supply of junk. Coupled with Drexel-Burnham's bankruptcy, the junk bond market collapsed, as prices fell some 10-to-15 percent in the first three months after FIRREA's prohibition went into effect. The industry analyst quoted above continued the analogy: "After they got the [yellow] light, the market went over the cliff."

---

*Glenn Emory, "Reading Between the Lines of High Risk and Reward," *Insight,* September 4, 1989.

†Roger Lowenstein, "Junk Buying Thrifts Made Problems Worse with Purchases Made before Market Plunge," *Wall Street Journal,* January 15, 1990.

its deposit insurance. The real danger to the FDIC is that it will mis-estimate the risks that the bank is taking and not recognize the insolvency until it is too late. The risk is not that the bank will take chances and lose money, but that the FDIC will not notice that this is happening. How is the FDIC to price this elusive monitoring risk? The higher capital requirements mandated by FIRREA for assets that are not securitized is one rough way of penalizing risks that are difficult to detect.

The $100,000 limit on deposit insurance encourages the largest (and probably best informed) depositors to scrutinize a bank's financial strength carefully. When Penn Square Bank became insolvent in 1982, the FDIC decided not to arrange an acquisition by another bank, which would have protected all depositors. Instead, the FDIC closed the bank and paid each depositor up to the $100,000 limit, no more, hoping to encourage large depositors to monitor the condition of other banks.[13] Because a loss of large deposits and the accompanying damage to the bank's reputation is costly, such monitoring exerts market pressure for prudent behavior by bank management.[14] However, since 1982, whenever there have been rumors of trouble at any of the nation's biggest banks, the FDIC has given assurances of full repayment of all deposits, no matter how large. Apparently, the FDIC believes that market discipline is less important than preventing a bank run by large depositors.

England did not adopt deposit insurance until 1979, but has had no major banking panics since one in 1866, which the Bank of England ended in a day by announcing that it would be a reliable lender of last resort, providing cash to any bank that needed funds to satisfy depositors. In the United States, FDIC funds would surely have to be supplemented with Federal Reserve loans in a national banking panic. Nonetheless, U.S. depositors may have become psychologically accustomed to the idea that the liquidity of their deposits is dependent on federal insurance, not on the willingness of the Fed to supply cash in an emergency.

The 1985 Ohio and Maryland bank runs recounted in Chapter 4 are instructive. There were no runs on federally insured institutions. Moreover, Federal Reserve loans to the privately insured institutions did not stop the panic. The panic ended when the governor of each state required privately insured institutions to either obtain federal deposit insurance or close.

Throughout the 1980s, the public was well aware of the enormous financial losses of the S&L industry and knew that depository institutions were failing in numbers not seen since the Great Depression. Yet there were no runs on federally insured institutions. In theory, the public's confidence could have been maintained by a widely recognized and well-established commitment of the Federal Reserve to supply cash in an emergency. In practice, it was the public's faith in deposit insurance that held the fragile system together.

Market-Value Accounting

When interest rates change, so do the market values of all assets with fixed cash flows: a given cash flow is worth more at low interest rates and less at high

| Highlight 13.5 | **The Tobin Plan** |

Nobel Prize winner James Tobin of Yale University argues that deposit insurance encourages banks and thrifts to gamble with taxpayers' money, but that checking-account deposits must be insured, because the nation's means of payment is too important to be allowed to collapse, as happened in the 1930s. His proposed solution is to make a sharp distinction between checking accounts, which should be fully insured, and other deposits, which should have no insurance.* To protect taxpayers, financial intermediaries can be required to hold 100 percent reserves against insured checking accounts. The reserves must be free of default risk and have very little market-value risk: cash, balances at Federal Reserve banks, and short-term U.S. securities. These reserves would be segregated from other bank assets, to ensure that they are always available to cover checking-account deposits and never used for any other purpose.

Intermediaries could offer other deposits that cannot be used for checking, but, like money-market funds, are backed by the intermediary's investment in Treasury bills, commercial paper, and other short-term liquid assets. Yet other segregated categories of deposits could be invested in commercial loans, mortgages, junk bonds, or stock, with the depositor fully aware of how the funds will be invested. The federal government would not implicitly or explicitly guarantee any deposits other than checking accounts. The uninsured deposits would be much like mutual funds are today, to be evaluated by depositors with no federal guarantee of their market value.

*James Tobin, "Financial Innovation and Deregulation in Perspective," *Bank of Japan Monetary and Economic Studies,* September 1985, pp. 19–29.

interest rates. However, the balance sheets of banks and thrift institutions do not show the effects of interest-rate changes on the value of their assets. The accounting value of a bond is its cost plus any accrued interest; the accounting value of a loan is its unpaid balance. Changes in market values are recorded only if the institution realizes the profit or loss by selling the bond or loan to someone else.

In 1986, for example, almost all of troubled Bank of America's reported profit came from the $80 million sale of some Tokyo property it had acquired in 1946 for $50,000. The property had long been worth millions and would have been worth $80 million in 1986 whether or not Bank of America decided to sell it. But to the accountants, it wasn't worth a penny more than $50,000 until the bank did sell it.

These misleading accounting conventions lead some institutions to take actions that are superficially beneficial, but actually undesirable. Many banks do not sell assets that have declined in value, because this will force them to show losses on their balance sheets, even though they might have a better use for the funds and could receive a tax break by using realized losses to offset operating profits. Others sell appreciated assets in order to disclose publicly the profits that they have made, even though this disclosure forces them to pay taxes on their profits. A sound investment rule is to realize your losses and hold onto your gains,[15] but book-value accounting induces many financial institutions to do just the opposite.

The capital requirements in FIRREA are based on book rather than market values. A bank could be book-value solvent, but market-value bankrupt, in that the FDIC could not sell its assets for enough to cover the institution's deposits. A bank that realizes that it is market-value bankrupt, even though book-value solvent, may be tempted to take the same kinds of risks that plagued the S&L industry before FIRREA.

Several people have recommended that banks and thrifts change to market-value accounting,[16] and FIRREA requires studies, due in 1991 on market-value accounting and risk-based deposit insurance. One reason for hesitation is that assets and liabilities not traded in organized markets may be difficult to value. Market-value accounting requires an estimate of loan defaults and early repayments, which can be subject to legitimate debate and intentional fraud.

Market-value accounting might provide a more accurate measure of a bank's solvency.

If financial intermediaries switch to market-value accounting, they will either be extremely vulnerable to insolvency, or else have to hedge away most of their exposure to interest-rate risk. In 1979, for instance, a sudden increase in interest rates gave the ten largest mutual savings banks in New York $2 billion in unrealized losses on their bond holdings alone, an amount equal to 93 percent of their net worth. Had they been using market-value accounting for their bonds and loans, all would have been bankrupt.[17]

Market-value accounting would give financial intermediaries a compelling reason to match the duration of their assets and liabilities, eliminating interest rate risk. The social cost is that savers who prefer short-term assets and borrowers who prefer long-term assets will have to compromise and settle for less than they would like. (Banks and thrifts can use pass-through contracts and bond futures, discussed in Chapter 8, to shift these risks onto others, but, ultimately, if borrowers issue long-term debts, someone must hold these contracts and bear the associated interest-rate risk.)

INTEREST-RATE CEILINGS

The Banking Acts of 1933 and 1935 prohibited the payment of interest on checking accounts and, through Regulation Q, gave the Federal Reserve Board the power to set maximum allowable interest rates on the time and savings deposits offered by member institutions. Beginning in the mid-1960s, the Federal

Home Loan Bank (FHLB) system and Federal Deposit Insurance Corporation (FDIC) imposed analogous ceiling rates on their member institutions. Deposit rate ceilings ended in 1986, but deserve a brief eulogy,

Safety by Collusion

Deposit-rate ceilings were intended to protect bank solvency.

The original rationale for deposit-rate ceilings was to protect bank solvency by stifling deposit-rate competition. It was thought that excessive competition for depositors in the 1920s had seduced banks into making risky, high-yielding investments in order to pay high deposit rates. H. Parker Willis, a prominent monetary economist, expressed this common view in a 1933 book.[18]

> *There is no doubt that payment of higher interest rates [on deposits] has been the cause for the making of speculative loans and the purchase of doubtful securities which have, in turn, contributed so largely to bank failures during the past decade of this century.*

Banks in the 1930s generally endorsed rate ceilings because these kept costs low and profits high.

An across-the-board 3 percent rate ceiling was imposed on commercial-bank savings and time deposits in 1933. This ceiling was reduced to 2½ percent in 1935, adjusted slightly in 1936, and then held constant for the next 20 years. During this long period, ceiling rates were generally above market interest rates and above the deposit rates paid by commercial banks and consequently of little practical importance. There were two notable exceptions. One was the prohibition of interest payments on checking accounts. The second was that businesses and government units were not allowed to open passbook savings accounts, and the ceiling rates on permissible deposits were often below market interest rates on Treasury bills and the like.

As market rates rose above 2½ percent in the 1950s, pressure built for a relaxation of ceiling rates. In January 1957, the Federal Reserve raised ceiling rates a half percentage point and publicly expressed its skepticism of using ceiling rates to control bank-lending practices.[19] Through the 1960s and 1970s, the Board raised ceiling rates repeatedly and permitted banks to offer an increasing variety of deposits. Banks competed aggressively, keeping deposit rates at the maximum allowable limits and offering innovative instruments, including large CDs without ceiling rates and money-market certificates tied to Treasury-bill rates.

However, throughout this period, the belief lingered that ceiling rates should be used to protect the profits of otherwise uncompetitive (often small) intermediaries from competition by more efficient institutions. Most economists do not think much of wage, price, or interest-rate controls that distort the verdict of the marketplace: if some intermediaries are less efficient, they shouldn't be in business. (It is said that economists are the social scientists with keen minds, but no hearts.)

Disintermediation

Interest-rate controls, like wage and price controls, eventually prove futile as people find ways to circumvent them. Institutions paid implicit interest by distributing gifts, reducing loan rates to depositors, and opening convenient branches. Money-market mutual funds were created to surmount the barriers placed between savers and high market interest rates. Such evasions forced the monetary authorities to relax deposit-rate ceilings.

Figure 13.4 compares the Treasury-bill rate with the ceiling rate on commercial-bank savings deposits. There are, of course, other institutions and other types of deposits, but Figure 13.4 gives an adequate picture of the relevant history. The four periods 1966, 1969–1970, 1973–1974, and 1978–1980 are noteworthy in that the monetary authorities kept deposit-rate ceilings significantly below market rates. During each of these periods there was financial **disintermediation** — instead of depositing money in financial intermediaries, savers withdrew money and purchased Treasury bills and other market securities. During periods of disintermediation, when deposits shrink, intermediaries must look elsewhere for funds and cut back on their lending.

Savings-and-loan associations and mutual savings banks were squeezed the hardest during these credit crunches. Their long-term mortgages made them especially vulnerable to unexpected increases in interest rates, and they had much less flexibility than banks in seeking alternative sources of funds. Deposit-rate ceilings seemed necessary to keep them afloat, but caused them to lose depositors.

The regulatory authorities tried compromise policies with, as might be expected, mixed success. The minimum Treasury-bill purchase was raised to $10,000. Temporary reserve requirements were imposed on money-market funds. The FHLB and other organizations pumped money into savings-and-loan associations and mutual savings banks. Thrifts were allowed to offer special deposits to try to hold on to mobile funds without increasing the cost of immobile deposits. Deposit-rate ceilings were used to protect them from commercial banks — in the 1966 crunch, the Fed tried to help beleaguered savings-and-loan associations by *lowering* the maximum rate that commercial banks could pay on small time deposits.

Profits were hurt, but not destroyed; depositors left, but not all of them. During the four credit crunches illustrated in Figure 13.4, mortgage rates increased and mortgage loans contracted; many S&L's stopped even taking mortgage applications. When mortgage loans dry up, home purchases and housing construction are never far behind, as documented in Figure 13.5. The four crunches (1966, 1969–1970, 1973–1974, and 1978–1980) were all difficult times for housing construction. Comparing Figures 13.4 and 13.5, we see that the less-publicized periods 1951–1953, 1956–1957, and 1959 also fit the pattern. When market rates rose above ceiling rates, mortgages sagged and housing construction slumped.

Disintermediation occurs when deposit rates are kept artificially low.

Housing construction slumps during credit crunches.

Figure 13.4   Three-month Treasury-bill Rate and Ceiling Rate on Commercial Bank Savings Deposits

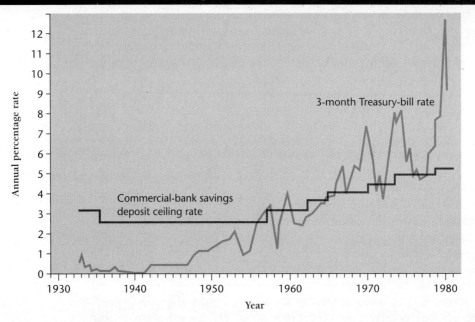

source: Federal Reserve *Bulletins* and *Historical Chart Book*, 1985.

The Fed deliberately threw these body blows at housing. To cool the economy and thereby restrain inflation, the Fed periodically combined tight monetary policies with deposit-rate ceilings to knock out home building. In the midst of the spring-1980 crunch, Fed chairman Volcker reportedly said that he wouldn't be satisfied "until the last buzz saw is silenced."[20]

There is another side to disintermediation — the small savers left behind. Deposit-rate ceilings cost them billions of dollars in interest payments. James Tobin has eloquently condemned this inequity.[21]

> *One of the least attractive features of recent policy has been discrimination against the small saver. . . . The small saver cannot easily go into the open market in search of higher yields. He is impeded by the significant minimum denominations and lot sizes of market instruments, by brokerage fees, by his own unfamiliarity and ignorance. Of course, the policy makers were counting on precisely this segmentation of the market; without it the ceiling rate policy could not work at all. But from a larger perspective, the reason that financial intermediaries exist and receive government support is to overcome just this kind of segmentation, to make markets more perfect rather than to exploit their imperfections.*

Figure 13.5 **New Private Housing Starts**

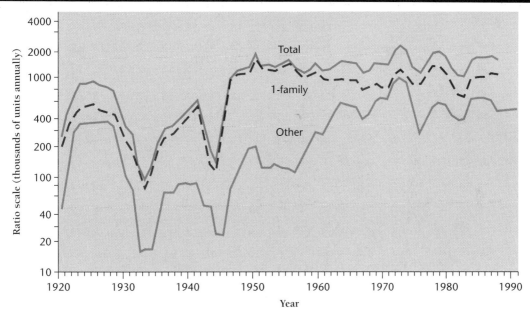

source: Federal Reserve *Historical Chart Book*, 1990.

Because of ceiling rates and the structure of deposit institutions, tight-money policies were felt most strongly by thrift institutions, small savers, and the housing industry. This uneven pressure is illogical and inequitable. One of the motivations for deregulation in the 1980s was to remove these distortions by eliminating ceiling rates and permitting deposit institutions to become more balanced intermediaries.

BRANCH BANKING

Many surveys have shown that depositors and borrowers are attracted to banks that are convenient, both in location (near one's home or business) and in banking hours. Knowing this, banks compete with one another by offering attractive locations and hours. Figure 13.6 shows that, although there has been little change in the total number of banks, the number of branches has increased dramatically since World War II. (These data do not include foreign branches of U.S. banks, which have also increased greatly.) The increase in bank branches reflects the provision of convenient locations within large cities, expansion into suburbia to compete with savings-and-loan associations, and the acquisition of

Branching restrictions protect small banks.

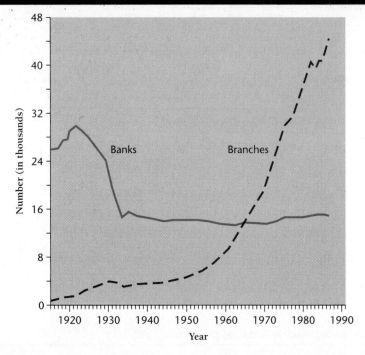

Figure 13.6   Number of U.S. Banks

source: Federal Reserve *Historical Chart Book*, 1985.

small banks in order to take advantage of some of the economies of scale discussed in Chapter 12.

Branching has, however, long been constrained by state and federal laws designed to protect small banks from competition from the branches of large banks. The United States is unique in having nearly 30,000 deposit intermediaries (roughly half commercial banks and half thrifts), of which 85 percent have assets of less than $100 million and 97 percent less than $500 million. In contrast, Canada has 11 banks, Great Britain 35, Japan 86, France 206, and West Germany 243.

The U.S. has far more banks than do other nations.

The **McFadden Act** of 1927, which was largely motivated by a fear that the Bank of America would span the nation, prohibits interstate branching and allows branching within a state to be regulated by each individual state. In 1975, there were still 15 states (mostly in the Midwest) that prohibited branching entirely; their **unit banking** laws permit a bank to have only one geographic location. By 1987, 11 of these 15 states had passed laws allowing branch banks. In 1987, 14 states (mostly in the East) allowed limited branching, usually within one county, and 32 states (and the District of Columbia) allowed unlimited statewide branching.

Some banks have evaded restrictions on branching and other activities by setting up **holding companies**, which can control a variety of banking and nonbanking subsidiaries. Some holding companies are established to administer several banks; others are conglomerates like C.I.T. Corporation and Hershey Foods, which control a variety of nonfinancial businesses as well as banks. The holding company may be able to engage in nonbanking activities (such as investment banking) or issue commercial paper or corporate bonds, although the bank cannot. Branching barriers may also be breached by a holding company; in a unit-banking state, for instance, a holding company may be able to acquire a large number of individual banks — although customers still cannot use the facilities of one bank to make deposits or withdrawals in another bank.

Holding companies circumvent some banking regulations.

In 1960, there were only 47 bank holding companies, and they controlled less than 10 percent of aggregate bank assets; in 1987, there were more than 6,000 bank holding companies, encompassing more than 90 percent of all bank assets. All bank holding companies are regulated by the Federal Reserve.

In many states, electronic banking has, in effect, multiplied bank branches through **automated teller machines (ATMs)**, which allow one to make deposits and withdrawals and to receive account information without entering a traditional "brick-and-mortar" bank branch. The first ATMs were installed in the outside walls of banks, to allow for after-hours' transactions. Much of the subsequent growth has been off-premises, to provide convenient banking locations. Half of all off-premises ATMs are in shopping malls and supermarkets; many others are in office and apartment buildings. ATMs at universities are among the most heavily used, averaging more than 300 transactions a day.[22]

ATMs effectively multiply bank branches.

Interstate Banking

The Douglas Amendment to the McFadden Act prohibits holding companies from crossing state lines unless specifically authorized by state authorities. Banks have nonetheless breached state borders in several ways. For example, the 1919 **Edge Act** allows bank holding companies to establish interstate subsidiaries (known as Edge Act corporations) for accepting deposits and making loans related to international business transactions; the Bank of America has a dozen such subsidiaries which, if combined as a separate bank, would be one of the nation's largest banks.

Interstate banking is still restricted.

The **Bank Holding Company Act** of 1956, amended in 1970, defines a bank as an institution that accepts deposits that can be withdrawn on demand and also makes commercial loans. A financial institution that did one of these activities, but not both, was technically not a bank — what some call a **nonbank bank** — and hence was not regulated by the Federal Reserve. For example, J. C. Penney's federally chartered J. C. Penney National Bank accepts deposits but is not considered a bank, because it does not make commercial loans. The Bank-Americorp and Citicorp holding companies have hundreds of interstate subsidiaries that don't accept deposits but that do arrange business and personal loans and engage in mortgage banking, leasing, and pension-fund management. The

Competitive Banking Equality Act of 1987 closed the nonbank-bank loophole by defining a bank as any FDIC-insured institution, but it exempted nonbank banks established before March 5, 1986.

Bank holding companies also cross state lines when they offer nonbank services such as credit cards. Interstate automated teller machines allow customers to withdraw cash and transfer funds among accounts, but not to make interstate deposits. Because these systems are not owned by banks, but paid for on a per-transaction basis, they are not considered bank branches. The Federal Home Loan Bank Board allowed all S&L's to install ATMs nationwide. Three of the largest shared-banking ATM networks are the New York Cash Exchange, the PLUS SYSTEM, and CIRRUS.

By 1986, 39 state legislatures had approved some form of interstate banking. Three states allow any out-of-state bank to acquire a bank within the state. Three other states require a reciprocal arrangement: banks from State B can operate in State A if banks from A are allowed in B. Twenty-seven other states have approved regional interstate zones that are intended to allow the development of large regional banks protected from the nation's giant banks. Regional banking zones were challenged in court by some of the giant banks, but upheld in a unanimous 1985 Supreme Court decision.

As noted earlier in this chapter, banks and thrifts have been allowed to cross state lines to acquire financially troubled institutions. The first major acquisition occurred in 1982, when New York's Citicorp acquired Fidelity S&L of Oakland, California. Fidelity S&L was renamed Citicorp Savings and now operates nearly 100 branches in 66 California cities as a subsidiary of the Citicorp holding company.

Citibank lobbied for years for a reciprocal banking bill that would allow New York and California banks to open branches in each other's state. Such bills were repeatedly defeated in the California legislature because California banks felt that they were getting the short end of the stick. One California banker said, "I wouldn't trade two blocks of Fresno for the entire city of New York."[23] Nonetheless, large California banks did want to spread eastward, one observing that "Someday an earthquake might make California an island. We want to have operations on the mainland."[24] In 1986, the California legislature finally approved a bill allowing reciprocal interstate banking, initially within a nine-state western region, but nationwide after January 1, 1990.

Is it better for a nation to have a handful of giant banks spanning the nation, or thousands of local banks? Regulation Q, higher reserve requirements on large banks, and antibranching restrictions were at least in part intended to protect small banks. In recent years, the trend has been in the opposite direction — to remove barriers to the formation of giant banks. The hope is that the branches of these giants will be as competitive, as small, local banks, or more so.

Barriers to interstate banking will eventually disappear. Such restrictions are an obvious nuisance for households and businesses that cross state lines. These restrictions are outmoded and discriminatory at a time when credit cards, money market funds, security brokers, and other financial institutions span the nation. In an electronic age, you don't need bricks and mortar to operate a bank.

INVESTMENT BANKING

The **Glass-Steagall Act** of 1933 prohibits U.S. commercial banks from engaging in investment-banking activities — helping businesses and state and local governments raise money through the sale of securities. To comply with the law, the most prominent bank of the day, J. P. Morgan, was split into an investment bank (Morgan Stanley) and a commercial bank (J. P. Morgan). Other banks were forced to separate, too, or to specialize in either commercial or investment banking. (Foreign banks can operate as both commercial and investment banks in the United States, unconstrained by Glass-Steagall.)

The Glass-Steagall Act separates commercial banks from investment banks.

In the 1970s and 1980s, investment banks increasingly encroached on commercial-bank turf, persuading many large corporations to issue securities instead of taking loans from commercial banks. Commercial banks, in turn, lobbied for the right to underwrite securities and looked for loopholes in the Glass-Steagall Act. Large commercial banks now handle private placements, quietly finding purchasers of corporate IOUs, and help plan, finance, and execute business mergers and acquisitions — activities long restricted to investment bankers. Many large U.S. banks use foreign branches to underwrite and deal in securities outside of the United States.

In 1987, the Federal Reserve Board gave commercial banks approval to underwrite and deal in municipal revenue bonds, commercial paper, and securities backed by either mortgages or consumer receivables. In June 1989, J. P. Morgan & Co., the commercial bank created in the 1930s, received approval from the Federal Reserve Board to underwrite and deal in corporate bonds in the United States. Several other major banks soon received similar authorization. In 1990 Morgan received approval for corporate stock. These various activities must be carried out within a holding company in which the investment banking subsidiary is independent of the commercial banking subsidiary. This structure technically conforms to the Glass-Steagall Act and insulates the FDIC from responsibility for investment-banking losses.

Commercial and investment banks are increasingly overlapping.

Another important change in investment banking is Rule 415, adopted by the Securities and Exchange Commission (SEC) in 1982, allowing shelf registration of securities. Traditionally, businesses issued bonds or stock infrequently and in large amounts, using a familiar investment bank that had been relied on for decades. This trusted investment bank might have a seat on the company's board of directors and would advise the company on its financing options, price new issues, and form a syndicate of investment banks to market the securities at the designated time.

Under Rule 415, corporations can file a single statement with the SEC describing the company's total potential stock and bond issues during the following two years. They need not rely on a syndicate to market a large issue in a timely fashion. Once the company has the securities on the shelf, it can invite competitive bids and issue securities in moderate sizes. It might negotiate to sell the securities to a single investment bank, for the bank to resell, or it can bypass investment banks and sell the securities itself to pension funds, to insurance

Highlight 13.6   The Fall of Banking's Berlin Wall

Much as the Berlin Wall divided Germany into East and West, the Glass-Steagall Act of 1933 forcibly divided banking into two separate activities: commercial banking and investment banking. Thus the banking power-house J. P. Morgan was separated into a commercial bank (Morgan Guaranty) and an investment bank (Morgan Stanley). This financial Berlin Wall was intended to protect depositors (and the deposit-insurance system) from losses that might be incurred by security underwriting, trading, and brokerage. Morgan Guaranty, Citibank, and other commercial banks were allowed to accept insured deposits and make loans, but could not deal in securities. Morgan Stanley, Merrill Lynch and other investment banks were permitted to deal in securities, but could not offer insured deposits.

This legal separation is clearly artificial. Many commercial and investment banking activities overlap, and these activities can be done more economically by sharing buildings, equipment, and information. Much of the financial expertise that is crucial to successful commercial banking is also essential to profitable investment banking. For example, a commercial bank's evaluation and pricing of a business loan is not very different from an investment bank's evaluation and pricing of a security issue.

For nearly 60 years, Congress resisted banking industry appeals to overturn the Glass-Steagall Act. Commercial banks suffered as homes and businesses transferred deposits to money-market funds and other securities firms. The banks' most credit-worthy corporate borrowers took out fewer loans and increasingly issued securities through investment banks.

In January 1989, the Federal Reserve gave J. P. Morgan and three other commercial banks permission to underwrite corporate debt. J. P. Morgan is the holding company for Morgan Guaranty, the giant New York commercial bank created after passage of the Glass-Steagall Act. In September 1990, the Fed put another large crack in the wall separating commercial and investment banking by giving J. P. Morgan permission to underwrite, trade, and sell corporate stock, a clear sign that commercial and investment banks will soon compete head to head. The Securities Industry Association, which had lobbied long and hard against an expansion of commercial bank activities, called the Fed's momentous decision "astonishing."

The Fed's approval requires that J. P. Morgan's investment banking activities be handled by a subsidiary, J. P. Morgan Securities, with its own capital and management, to ensure that Morgan Guaranty's assets are protected from any losses incurred by Morgan's investment banking activities. Banking's Berlin Wall is not expected to crumble overnight, as Fed permission will be given only to the very strongest banks. It is fitting that the Fed's initial approval went to J. P. Morgan. Will the House of Morgan, like East and West Germany, someday be reunited?

companies, and to other investors. As investment banks lose their privileged relationships with businesses, others, including commercial banks and thrift institutions, are competing on a more equal footing.

SECURITY BROKERAGE

In 1982, banks began setting up independent divisions to offer discount brokerage services, arguing that technically they weren't violating the Glass-Steagall prohibition against security dealing, because they weren't buying or selling securities, merely handling their customers' orders. At such discount brokerages, orders to buy and sell securities are placed over the telephone and handled by whichever clerk happens to answer the phone. Unlike Merrill Lynch and other full-service brokerage firms, there are no designated account executives to advise clients, no research reports on securities, and no branch offices where the customer can drop in to read financial reports and chat with brokers. With most bank discount brokerages, customers can pick up and deliver securities through a local bank branch and can use their checking account to settle transactions.

Some banks now offer discount brokerage services.

SUMMARY

Bank runs and insolvencies have inspired a web of regulation designed to protect depositors and banks. The U.S. has a dual banking system in which banks can be chartered (and supervised) by either the federal or state government, sometimes leading to conflicts among state regulatory officials, the Comptroller of the Currency (which charters national banks), the FDIC (which insures bank deposits), and the Federal Reserve (which controls the nation's monetary policies).

The Federal Reserve Board is a largely independent branch of government, with the Board's seven Governors appointed to overlapping 14-year terms. The Federal Open Market Committee (FOMC), consisting of the Board's seven Governors and five Reserve Bank presidents, meets approximately every four weeks to discuss the state of the economy and of the financial markets and to make monetary policy decisions.

Fannie Mae, Ginnie Mae, and Freddie Mac have revolutionized deposit intermediaries and the mortgage market by creating mortgage-backed securities readily traded in secondary markets. Federal deposit insurance has virtually eliminated contagious bank runs, but also encouraged insured institutions to take excessive risks, especially if they are close to or actually insolvent. Unexpected increases in interest rates, plunges into speculative real estate, and fraud caused the S&L crisis in the 1980s, as hundreds of S&L's went bankrupt and cost the federal deposit insurance system more than $100 billion.

The Financial Institutions Reform, Recovery and Enforcement Act (FIRREA) imposes higher, asset-based capital requirements, which are to be strictly enforced, with insolvent institutions promptly closed. An insured deposit intermediary must either be chartered as a bank or be a Qualified Thrift Lender with 70 percent of its assets in residential mortgage–related assets.

Deposit-rate ceilings were created during the New Deal and phased out in the 1980s. These ceilings stifled competition and protected small banks; in the 1960s and 1970s, they repeatedly caused disintermediation. Small banks have also been historically protected by restrictions on bank branches within a state and between states. As these barriers disappear, it is expected that the United States will evolve to a banking system similar to those of other countries, dominated by a small number of giant banks with nationwide branches.

IMPORTANT TERMS

automated teller machines (ATMs)
Bank Holding Company Act
Collateralized Mortgage Obligations (CMOs)
disintermediation
dual banking system
Edge Act
Federal Deposit Insurance Corporation (FDIC)
Federal Home Loan Bank (FHLB) system
Federal Home Loan Mortgage Corporation (Freddie Mac)
Federal National Mortgage Association (FNMA, or Fannie Mae)
Federal Open Market Committee (FOMC)
Federal Savings and Loan Insurance Corporation (FSLIC)

Financial Institutions Reform, Recovery and Enforcement Act (FIRREA)
Garn-St Germain Depository Institutions Act
Glass-Steagall Act
Government National Mortgage Association (GNMA, or Ginnie Mae)
holding companies
McFadden Act
moral-hazard
National Credit Union Administration
nonbank bank
pass-through securities
securitization
unit banking

EXERCISES

1. Historically, banks that belonged to the Federal Reserve System had higher reserve requirements than nonmember banks. Why are high reserve requirements expensive, and how does this expense vary with the condition of the economy?

2. In 1986, Herbert Stein wrote[25]

   On Monday, March 17, the Evans and Novak column broke the news that the Board of Governors had voted 4-3 against Chairman Paul Volcker and in favor of cutting the discount rate. Wow!

   Why was this narrow vote to cut the discount rate so interesting?

3. The FDIC gives banks a rating of 1 to 5, but it is illegal to divulge these ratings to the public. Why do you suppose this information is kept confidential?

4. Between 1982 and 1985, interest rates fell, yet there were 289 bank failures in the United States, of which 70 percent were in just ten states: Illinois, Iowa, Kansas, Missouri, Nebraska, Oregon, Oklahoma, and Texas. How would you explain this concentration of bank failures?

5. Explain this *Wall Street Journal* editorial: "Regulation Q, which has been part of the banking laws for years, has done a fine job of . . . limiting the interest income small savers can earn."[26]

6. Comment on the following quotation.[27]

This discriminatory policy [deposit rate ceilings] will gradually be eroded by the arbitrage which makes it possible. The gaps between market lending rates and the ceiling rates on small savings will encourage new ways of bringing together small lenders and large borrowers. What mutual funds have done in equities can be done in other markets; the growing popularity of mortgage trusts is indicative. Here again the authorities, by stimulating some irreversible creation of institutions outside their control, may have bought future trouble in return for present expediency.

7. Why is it that when the Fed steps on the monetary brakes, it is housing construction that comes to a stop?

8. Why did Fannie Mae stock tumble in 1969–1970 when interest rates rose?

9. A Texas Congressman who frequently criticized the Federal Reserve Board once called it "a wholly owned subsidiary of the ABA [American Bankers Association]."[28] For each of the following actions, explain how the Federal Reserve Board either helps or hurts banks as a whole.
   a. Engineers a credit crunch that increases all interest rates.
   b. Lowers the discount rate.
   c. Imposes tight interest-rate ceiling on deposits.
   d. Imposes reserve requirement on money-market mutual funds

10. In the 1800s, Walter Bagehot argued that a central bank should plainly and clearly announce that it is a lender of last resort, always willing to lend at high interest rates to any bank in need of cash. Why is it important that a central bank announce this policy to the public? Why do you think Bagehot specified high interest rates?

11. In every major U.S. banking panic during the 1800s, the banks in large cities stopped withdrawals by collectively declaring a moratorium on cash payments. Depositors and noteholders were not allowed to redeem their claims against the banks for gold and silver coins or, after 1860, for national-bank notes. They could continue to write checks and make payments to other depositors within the banking system, with the banks making bookkeeping entries of the transfer of funds among accounts. After several months, when the panic ended, the banks permitted withdrawals again. In comparison with unrestricted withdrawals during a banking panic, how did a moratorium affect the total amount of gold and silver coins in circulation? The total amount of bank deposits?

12. The Federal Home Loan Bank Board estimated that during the second half of 1981, thrift institutions had an average return of 10.02 percent on their mortgage portfolios and paid an average of 11.53 percent on their deposits. Yet withdrawals from FSLIC-insured institutions exceeded deposits by $32 billion in 1981–1982.[29] How do you explain the gap between the return on their mortgages and the cost of deposits? Won't they always set their mortgage rates above their deposit rates? How do you explain the large withdrawals when their deposit rates seem so generous?

13. What aspect of deregulation is responsible for the following observation?[30]

Deregulation has, for example, clearly diminished the tendency for savings deposits to drain out of banks and savings institutions whenever interest rates rise elsewhere . . . a situation long deemed unfair to depositors and dangerous to the institutions and to the housing industry.

14. The Federal Home Loan Bank System says that one of the advantages of Freddie Mac to thrift institutions is[31]

higher yields. When interest rates are rising, lenders can sell off their older, low-interest loans and reinvest in mortgages at higher interest rates.

What is the implicit assumption?

15. Does the following 1984 statement sound as if it were made by the president of a bank, or a brokerage firm?[32]

I am sure that the Congress that repeals the Glass-Steagall Act will go down in history for reshaping financial institutions by breaking down the shackles of the past, facing reality, following a path that makes sense and acting when action was necessary.

16. In 1979, Gibraltar Savings & Loan of California made $1.2 billion in new fixed-rate mortgages at an average interest rate of 11.3 percent, increasing its loan portfolio by 29 percent, to $3.69 billion. These new loans were financed by $1.2 billion in short-term money-market certificates and $100,000-plus CDs. In 1980, a financial analyst concluded that "Gibraltar gambled and lost."[33] What was Gibraltar gambling on and how did it lose?

17. An employee of a California bank that had been seized by the FDIC said afterwards, "It was almost a relief when they finally closed us. We could stop looking out the window every Friday to see if they were coming up the walk."[34] Why do you suppose they expected the regulators to come on a Friday?

18. In April 1986, Center National Bank, a one-branch California bank, was declared insolvent. Independence Bank, a large local bank, paid the FDIC $322,000 for the right to absorb Center National's $36.7 million in deposits and $19.7 million of its assets. In addition, the FDIC paid Independence $16.9 million for the remaining $18.7 million in Center assets.[35] Why do you suppose Independence agreed not only to sell $18.7 million in Center assets to the FDIC for $16.9 million, but to pay an additional $322,000?

19. Explain this observation regarding pass-through mortgage securities: "These securities pose minimal credit risk; however, they still expose investors to interest-rate and early repayment risk."[36]

20. A California S&L used a question-and-answer format to explain the 1989 Financial Institutions Reform, Recovery and Enforcement Act to its customers. Explain why the following answer is misleading.[37]

Q. Why does the taxpayer have to pay to bail out the S&L's?

The taxpayer is not paying to bail out the S&L's or anyone else in the industry. Taxpayer funds will be used solely to help uphold the Government's promise to protect insured depositors' money. Consumers will pay nothing directly; the legislation does not directly increase taxes at all.

21. Why were financially sound S&L's eager to see the 1989 Financial Institutions Reform, Recovery and Enforcement Act passed, so that insolvent S&L's could be closed down?

22. In 1989, a *New York Times* writer observed that, "Because price changes in the securities are reported only when the notes and bonds are sold, analysts say, many banks and other firms tend to sit on paper losses and sell only those issues that show a profit."[38] Ignoring accounting conventions, do such actions increase or decrease the total value of the firm's assets? That is, would an outside firm pay more for a bank that has realized gains and held on to losses, or one that has held on to both gains and losses?

23. In 1989, the American Institute of Certified Public Accountants proposed that banks, thrifts, and other financial institutions report the value of their bond holdings at cost or market value, whichever is lower, unless they have the ability and intention to hold the securities until maturity. In what ways is this proposed accounting convention potentially misleading, as compared to reporting all assets at market value?

24. The Financial Accounting Standards Board issued Financial Accounting Standard #33 in 1979, requiring large, publicly held firms to include supplementary information in their annual reports showing how inflation has affected the firm's balance sheets. Why, for a bank, is this not the same as market-value accounting?

25. Shortly after the passage of Financial Institutions Reform, Recovery and Enforcement Act, a *Wall Street Journal* article was titled "High

Yields for Deposits Fall, Thanks to Thrift Rescue."[39] How could this act, which closed some insolvent thrifts and lent money to others, affect deposit rates at healthy thrifts?

26. In the 1980s, some prominent banks increased the net worth shown on their balance sheets by selling their corporate headquarters and then renting the building back. If the price they receive for the building is its fair market value, why would this sale cause a large sudden increase in the bank's net worth?

27. When the Banking Acts of 1933 and 1935 were passed, some members of Congress argued that Regulation Q was needed to help banks pay their annual FDIC premiums. Explain how banks might find Regulation Q helpful in this way.

28. "State law in Texas prohibits full-scale branch banking but, paradoxically, allows financial institutions (including the state's 1,400 commercial banks) to place ATMs in supermarkets, airports, and shopping centers."[40] What are ATMs, and why could this state law be considered paradoxical?

29. For decades, Canada has had unlimited branching, interest-bearing checking accounts, and no deposit-rate ceilings. Explain what, if any, relationship there is between these regulations and the fact that Canada has only 11 banks.

30. Critically evaluate the following quotation.[41]

California is already so competitive, what would more competition do for the public? The smaller banks in the West have strong misgivings about such basic changes [interstate banking]. . . . It wouldn't be the smaller banks that would gain.

THE

PRACTICE

OF BANKING

Banking is the art of lending money and getting it back.

Anonymous

Historically, the differences among banks, savings-and-loan associations, credit unions, and other financial intermediaries were due primarily to legal restrictions on their operations. They were all financial intermediaries, but they differed in what was permitted and not permitted for each — for instance, only banks could offer checking accounts. High interest rates and new technology made many of these restrictions impractical and unenforceable, and banking is now emerging from the regulatory web erected in the 1930s in response to earlier banking debacles. It is hoped that the changes now occurring will enable financial institutions to serve their customers better, strengthen the institutions by broadening and diversifying their operations, and promote competition among intermediaries.

In this chapter, we will examine some important fundamentals of modern-day banking, with the conviction that these banking principles are more important than temporary, rapidly disappearing, distinctions between intermediaries. As the differences fade, the management issues confronting banks, savings-and-loan associations, mutual savings banks, and credit unions will become increasingly similar.

We already know much about the usefulness, pitfalls, and history of banking. Here we will learn more about the operations of modern banks and how they manage their assets and liabilities to cope with opportunities, risks, and regulatory constraints. We will see that banking is a very intense and innovative business. Bankers face tremendous pressures, as well as exciting opportunities, and have responded in flexible and innovative ways. We begin by looking at their over-riding goals.

PROFITS, SAFETY, AND LIQUIDITY

Banks have several, sometimes conflicting, objectives — including profits, safety, and liquidity. A bank's rate of return — its percentage profit — can be calculated in a variety of ways; two of the most common measures are return on assets and return on equity. Suppose that a bank with $500 million in assets earns an annual profit of $5 million. Its return on assets is ($5 million)/($500 million) = 0.01, or 1 percent. If this bank's equity, or net worth, is $30 million (equal to 6 percent of its assets), then its return on equity is ($5 million)/($30 million) = 0.167, or 16.7 percent. As will be explained later in this chapter, bank leverage turns a seemingly modest return on assets into an impressive return on equity.

Bank profits are often measured by return on assets and return on equity.

Profitability is clearly crucial to a bank, but it is also very difficult to predict and control. Will borrowers default on loans? Will households prepay their mortgages? Will businesses exercise lines of credit? Will interest rates rise, or fall? Will the Federal Reserve raise reserve requirements? Management decisions made today affect a bank's profits for years to come and depend on future events that cannot be confidently foreseen.

A revolutionary and still evolving aspect of banking is the use of formal computer models to help manage bank assets and liabilities. An important part of this quantification of banking is "management by objectives," in which bank officers establish numerical goals and are judged by whether or not they meet them. A second part is the use of computer-simulation models to project the consequences of various bank decisions.

It is now commonplace in large banks to periodically review sophisticated projections of anticipated inflows and outflows of funds. Some of these projections are very mechanical, though technical, such as interest payments on deposits, loans, and mortgages. Others rely on a blending of computer models and informed assumptions about economic activity and the state of financial markets which affect loan defaults, deposit withdrawals, the use of credit lines, and the market value of the bank's portfolio.

Computer models are used to help banks manage assets and liabilities.

These computer models tell bank management how much cash will soon be available to invest, or, if the bank is in deficit, how much cash it must raise. Subject to this budget constraint and taking into account a modest margin for error, the bank decides how much to invest in (or borrow by means of) various specific financial instruments. This is a portfolio allocation problem — the use of discretionary funds made available by the projected cash flow.

Computer-simulation models can also be used to trace out the consequences of investment and borrowing decisions. How will profits be affected if the economy weakens and interest rates decline? How will profits be affected by stagflation, a slowdown in the economy with rising inflation and rising interest rates? If the bank's senior managers assign probabilities to the various possible scenarios, they can calculate the expected value of profits, as we saw in Chapter 11. They can also assess risk, either by calculating the standard deviation of profits using these scenarios or by estimating the probability that profits will fall below some minimum threshold, perhaps a loss that might jeopardize the bank's ability to meet minimum regulatory capital requirements.

In addition to return and risk, banks must maintain an effective balance between illiquid assets and **liquid assets** — either cash, or assets that can be readily converted into cash — which are needed to accommodate withdrawal risks, both through deposits and loans. Banks must always have enough funds to meet depositor withdrawals; an inability to do so would destroy depositor confidence and precipitate a run on the bank.

Banks try to maintain a profitable balance between liquid and illiquid assets.

Borrowers also need to be accommodated. Many of a bank's customers have established banking relationships over the years by depositing money, repaying loans in a timely fashion, and compensating the bank for other services. They expect, in return, that they will be able to borrow money when they need it. If the bank cannot accommodate their loan requests, then it destroys the incentive for establishing a banking relationship.

Liquidity can be maintained with **primary reserves** — cash, deposits with the Fed, and deposits in other banks — and with **secondary reserves**: Treasury bills and other very safe, short-term assets that can be converted into cash almost immediately. A prudent bank needs enough liquidity to satisfy depositors and borrowers, but it would be foolish to hold 100 percent liquid assets. Some funds can surely be safely invested in illiquid assets, which usually yield more than liquid ones. The danger is that the bank may become too illiquid. If it exhausts its liquid funds, it will be forced to resort to emergency borrowing or to distress sales of illiquid assets — or, in the worst possible case, be unable to accommodate withdrawals.

Bank liabilities also influence liquidity; for example, transaction accounts are more volatile than passbook savings accounts, and certificates of deposit are more mobile than long-term bonds. Within the regulatory boundaries, how hard should a bank compete for deposits of differing volatility? Much of the withdrawal risk in individual accounts can be diversified away. But there remain macro risks. A general increase in interest rates will lure hot money out of a bank, unless it raises its deposit rates. A slowdown in the economy will squeeze household income and corporate profits, and may cause a net outflow from banks. Again, computer-simulation models may help a bank identify the possible effects of today's decisions on future liquidity. Estimates can be made of a deposit floor (the minimum level to which deposits might drop) and a loan ceiling (the maximum level of loans), so that the bank can maintain sufficient liquidity to deal with these extremes.

A bank's liquidity needs vary with the economy.

Banks use quantitative models and careful monitoring to better understand the difficult choices that they must make. The large New York City banks have been playing this technologically sophisticated game for years. Now it is spreading to the hinterlands. Seat-of-the-pants judgments are giving way to numbers-oriented and, it is hoped, scientific management. One of this new breed, Gerald Fronterhouse, president and chief executive officer of the giant First Republicbank of Texas, made a clever analogy in 1980: "We've begun to fly by instruments rather than by sight."[1] Unfortunately First Republicbank crashed and burned in 1988 when the Texas economy fell farther than Fronterhouse, or almost anyone, anticipated. Fronterhouse resigned in April 1988 and NCNB took over First Republicbank four months later, aided by $4 billion from the federal government. Even flight instruments sometimes fail.

Quantitative models can help a bank make informed decisions by tracing out the complex consequences of various actions under a variety of economic scenarios. But a model is ultimately no better than its assumptions. If the assumptions are wrong, seemingly reasonable management decisions may have disastrous consequences. The real virtue of model-building is that it helps management formulate the right questions. A successful strategy still depends on whether the managers, not the computers, have the right answers.

LEVERAGE

Chapter 9 discussed the concept of leverage — how it is created and what its consequences are. Someone who borrows and invests other people's money, so that the total amount invested is larger than his or her own personal investment, creates **leverage**, which magnifies gains and losses because the personal return depends on the return on a much larger investment.

Leverage magnifies gains and losses.

For a business, we can restate these principles in terms of the firm's total assets and net worth. A hypothetical balance sheet is shown in Table 14.1. The total amount invested is given by the firm's total assets. These assets are financed in part by the firm's debts (loans plus bonds) and in part by the firm's own money, its net worth. The firm's leverage is

$$\text{Leverage} = \frac{\text{Total assets}}{\text{Net worth}} \tag{1}$$

The return on its net worth depends on the gap between the gross return on its assets (before interest payments) and the interest rate it pays on its debts.

$$\begin{pmatrix} \text{Return on} \\ \text{net worth} \end{pmatrix} = \begin{pmatrix} \text{Interest rate} \\ \text{on debt} \end{pmatrix} + (\text{Leverage}) \left[\begin{pmatrix} \text{Gross return on} \\ \text{total assets} \end{pmatrix} \right.$$
$$\left. - \begin{pmatrix} \text{Interest rate} \\ \text{on debt} \end{pmatrix} \right] \tag{2}$$

The firm shown in Table 14.1 has 2-to-1 leverage

$$\text{Leverage} = \frac{\text{Total assets}}{\text{Net worth}} = \frac{100}{50} = 2$$

| Highlight 14.1 | **The Citi Never Sleeps** |

New York's Citibank is by far the nation's largest bank, a position achieved under the aggressively innovative leadership of the legendary Walter Wriston, president and chief executive officer of Citicorp (Citibank's holding company) from 1967 until 1984. Citicorp has aggressively pushed for deregulation and, when legislators dawdled, found loopholes through which it could expand anyway.

Citibank tries to span the financial world, offering virtually all financial services to everyone, everywhere. While other banks turn away small depositors, Citibank seeks to be everyone's banker. Under Wriston, Citicorp spent hundreds of millions of dollars on technology, pioneering 24-hour automated teller machines and banking by interactive home computers (prompting the advertising campaign, "The Citi never sleeps"). Citibank has nearly 300 New York City branches and thousands of ATMs — ATMs that can be used only by its 2 million Citibank cardholders. As early as 1980, two-thirds of Citibank's cash withdrawals in New York city were handled by ATMs. In 1990, Citibank introduced an Enhanced Telephone (E.T.) that, for a $49.95 installation charge and a $9.95 monthly leasing fee, works as a sophisticated telephone and can also be used, like a home computer, to obtain bank account information, to transfer funds, and to pay bills.

Citibank's approach to consumer banking has two sides. One is the sleek easy-to-use ATMs that are to be used by small depositors and for routine transactions. The second side is relationship banking: personal service and financial incentives for depositors with substantial accounts, especially those who do all of their banking with Citibank.

Citicorp is the largest issuer of bank cards, with nearly 30 million Citibank Mastercard and Visa cardholders in the United States, most recruited through nationwide mailings, and another 10 million cardholders outside the United States. In 1979, when New York usury laws prevented Citicorp from charging more than 12 percent on its credit-card balances, Wriston persuaded South Dakota to abolish its usury ceiling and, in return, purchased a bank in Sioux Falls, South Dakota, and moved all of Citicorp's card-processing operations there. In 1989, Citicorp began selling small investors "plastic bonds" — four-year $1,000 bonds backed by its credit card loans.

In 1986, Citicorp introduced its MortgagePower program, a nationwide network of 3,000 real estate brokers, lawyers, and mortgage bankers who are connected by computer to Citicorp and can get a home buyer's no-hassle mortgage application approved or rejected within 15 business days. In 1981, Citicorp wasn't among the top 100 companies in the mortgage business; in 1988, it wrote $15 billion in mortgages and was by far the largest mortgage lender in the nation.

Acting as a holding company, Citicorp opened nonbank banks throughout the country. For example, in several states it established "industrial banks" which accept time and savings deposits (but not checking accounts) and make consumer and mortgage loans. Citicorp also acquired footholds in California, Florida, and other states by taking over insolvent S&L's. In 1989, Citicorp had 600 U.S. subsidiaries and was planning to triple this number. Ultimately, when all barriers to interstate banking are removed, most of these subsidiaries will operate as branches of Citibank. In 1990, it was allowed to change the names of all of its S&L's to Citibank FSB and to offer Citibank credit cards to these customers.

Even now, Citicorp's offices worldwide are linked by satellite and computer. As part of its investment in technology, Citicorp installed its own underground fiber-optic cables at its New York headquarters and produced its own internal telephone system. Robots walk the halls delivering mail.

Citicorp has also been very aggressive in lending to developing companies and establishing foreign subsidiaries, aiming to make Citibank branches and credit cards familiar symbols worldwide, what *The Wall Street Journal* called the "McDonald's and Coke of Consumer Banking."* In 1989, Citibank had 8 million household customers in 40 countries outside of the United States and hoped to double that by 1994. Its foreign branches are run almost entirely by local citizens and emphasize customer service. As one Citicorp executive observed, "There's enough anxiety associated with financial services that people will pay a premium for comfort and peace of mind. This is a people business, not a money business."† In Spain, Citibank employees seated at desks replaced tellers behind elevated counters; customers who formerly had to wait two months to have their mortgage applications considered now are told "yes" or "no" within 48 hours. Computerized equipment allows automobile buyers in Spain to contact Citibank from automobile showrooms and have financing approved in a few minutes. In Germany, Citibank executives make evening house calls to their busy customers.

Citicorp was widely criticized when it lost millions of dollars in the 1970s trying to expand its consumer banking business, but in the 1980s, its consumer banking became highly profitable. In 1988, Citicorp earned $1.9 billion, of which $500 million came from U.S. consumer banking and $170 million from international consumer banking. In 1990, Citicorp forecast $5 billion in annual profits by the mid-to-late 1990s, of which 65 percent would come from its worldwide consumer business.

---

*Robert Guenther, "CitiCorp Strives to Be McDonald's and Coke of Consumer Banking," *Wall Street Journal,* August 9, 1989.

†Guenther.

Highlight 14.2   Morgan Guaranty

Citicorp is the world's most prominent retail banker, aiming to provide all banking services to everyone, everywhere and at any time. A very different approach has been followed by Morgan Guaranty and its holding company, J. P. Morgan. Morgan Guaranty is at the pinnacle of wholesale banking, providing high-quality financial expertise and personal attention to those who need (and can afford) the very best.

While Citicorp strives to be everyone's banker, Morgan deals exclusively with governments, large corporations, and a small number of wealthy individuals (with a minimum of $5 million in investable assets). While Citibank has three hundred Manhattan branches, Morgan has six. Citibank has thousands of ATMs; Morgan has none. Citibank advertises in buses and subway stations; Morgan Guaranty's Wall Street location is identified only by a small, gold "23" on the door.

While Citibank has succeeded in becoming the nation's biggest bank, Morgan Guaranty has consistently had a higher rate of return on equity. Value Line, a private investment advisory service, predicted in 1990 that J. P. Morgan's return on equity over the next five years would average 18 percent, while Citicorp's would average 15 percent.* There is a difference between growth for the sake of growth and growth for the sake of profits, as emphasized in J. P. Morgan's stiffly worded 1985 annual report.†

> We continue to find growth opportunities in serving corporations, institutions, governments, and a select private clientele around the world, but growth of assets has no attraction if the additions cannot meet our expectations for return on equity and our standards of credit quality. We are also cautious about embarking on new activities. . . . We seek to provide financial services that our clients value highly and that command a price reflective of that value. . . . We believe that the best course for us . . . is to stay with the kind of client we have always served.

*The Value Line Investment Survey, March 6, 1990, pp. 2013, 2034.
†J. P. Morgan & Co., Annual Report, 1985, p. 3.

Table 14.1 A Firm's Balance Sheets (millions of dollars)

Assets		Liabilities	
Plant	70	Bank loans	20
Equipment	20	Bonds	30
Financial	10	Net worth	50
	100		100

Table 14.2 A Leveraged Firm's Return on Net Worth

Gross return on assets (before interest), 10.2%($100,000,000)	$10,200,000
Interest, 9.2%($50,000,000)	4,600,000
Return on net worth, 11.2%($50,000,000)	$ 5,600,000

which doubles the difference between the gross return on its assets and the interest rate on its debts.

A firm's interest rate on its debts is a weighted average of the interest rates on its various loans and bonds. The firm in Table 14.1 has $50 million in debts, of which $20/50 = 0.40$ is loans and $30/50 = 0.60$ is bonds. If R_L is the interest rate on its loans and R_B the interest rates on its bonds, then the weighted average interest rate on its debt is given by

$$R = 0.40R_L + 0.60R_B$$

If, for example, the interest rate on its loans is 8 percent and the interest rate on its bonds is 10 percent, then the average interest rate on its debt is

$$R = 0.40(8\%) + 0.60(10\%)$$
$$= 9.2\%$$

Whether the return on its net worth turns out to be larger or smaller than 9.2 percent depends on whether the gross return on its assets is larger or smaller than 9.2 percent.

Suppose that the gross return on the firm's assets is 10.2 percent. Equation 2 tells us that the return on net worth is

$$\left(\begin{array}{c}\text{Return on}\\ \text{net worth}\end{array}\right) = 9.2\% + 2(10.2\% - 9.2\%) = 9.2\% + 2\% = 11.2\%$$

Table 14.2 confirms this formula with a detailed calculation.

Finding a Niche Among the Financial Giants

Many manufacturers use rebates to persuade bargain-hunters to buy their products. To get a rebate, usually for a few dollars, the shopper must mail in a sales receipt and a rebate coupon by a specified date. The manufacturer could instead reduce the product's price, but then everyone would pay less. Rebates allow the cost-conscious to get a discount, while others pay full price — many people don't bother to request a rebate, and some of those who plan to do so misplace their sales receipt or forget to mail it in.

Commercial processors called fulfillment houses process the rebate requests by verifying the sales receipt and rebate coupon and then mailing rebate checks. Seventy percent of these rebate checks are drawn on accounts in a small, otherwise obscure bank, First State Bank of Lake Lillian — a Minnesota town with 350 residents, some of whom ride to the bank on their tractors.* First State got into the rebate business in 1976 when the bank's president heard from a relative who worked at a fulfillment house that large banks charged 6 cents a check to process rebate checks. First State offered to do it for 2 cents; thirteen years later, in 1989, it still charged only 2.2 cents a check.

Bargain-hunting manufacturers gave their rebate business to First State, which now processes as many as a million rebate checks a day, providing a nice income (and some hectic days) for a bank with only $18 million in assets. One East Coast manufacturer did become nervous when it couldn't find Lake Lillian on a Minnesota map. Suspecting a hoax, executives were dispatched by corporate jet and then rental car to determine the truth. They found Lake Lillian, and First State got their business.

*Bill Richards, "The Hero in All This Is the Person who Balances First State's Books," *Wall Street Journal,* June 7, 1989.

Bank Leverage

Nonfinancial businesses are considered highly levered if their net worth is only half the size of their assets — a leverage factor of 2 to 1. Financial intermediaries have much less net worth and much more leverage. Table 14.3 shows the balance sheets of a representative bank. Its assets are financed 94 percent by borrowing (some from depositors, some from bond sales) and 6 percent by net worth, giving it a degree of leverage of $1/0.06 = 16.67$.

Banks have tremendous leverage.

A commercial bank generally has a net worth between 6 percent and 10 percent of its total assets. Before the passage of the 1989 Financial Institutions Reform, Regulation and Enforcement Act, most thrifts were allowed to have as little as 3 percent, and those that were nearly insolvent had virtually 0 percent.

Table 14.3 **A Bank's Balance Sheets (millions of dollars)**

Assets		Liabilities	
Cash	5	Deposits	74
Loans	70	Bonds	20
Securities	25	Net worth	6
	100		100

Table 14.4 **Bank Leverage Depends on the Ratio of Net Worth to Total Assets**

$\dfrac{\text{Net Worth}}{\text{Total Assets}}$	$\text{Leverage} = \dfrac{\text{Total Assets}}{\text{Net Worth}}$
0.10	10.0
0.08	12.5
0.06	16.7
0.04	25.0
0.02	50.0

In 1989, the average ratio of net worth to total assets was 7 percent for commercial banks and 4 percent for thrift institutions. These thrift data counted intangible "goodwill" as an asset and valued many assets and liabilities at historical cost; the use of market-value data would no doubt have reduced the ratio of net worth to assets.

Table 14.4 shows the implied leverage factors for selected ratios of net worth to total assets. This enormous leverage explains why a thin margin between an intermediary's cost of funds and its return on assets give a substantial return on net worth, and why a seemingly small change in its cost of funds or return on assets can turn a large profit into a large loss, or vice versa.

Suppose that a bank has a leverage factor of 16.67 and that the average interest rate on its deposits and bonds is 10 percent. If its gross return on assets is 11 percent (a slight 1 percent margin), its return on net worth will be a very satisfactory

$$\left(\begin{matrix}\text{Return on}\\ \text{net worth}\end{matrix}\right) = 10\% + 16.67(11\% - 10\%) = 10\% + 16.67\% = 26.67\%$$

If the bank can earn a 2 percent spread between its gross return on assets and its cost of borrowing, the bank's return on net worth will then increase to

Table 14.5 A Bank's Return on Net Worth	
Gross return on assets (before interest),	
7%($100,000,000)	$7,000,000
Interest, 10%($94,000,000)	9,400,000
Return on net worth, −40%($6,000,000)	−$2,400,000

Table 14.6 Commercial Bank Assets and Liabilities, July 1989 (billions of dollars)			
Assets		**Liabilities**	
Cash	190.1	Transaction deposits	570.2
Loans	1,918.1	Savings deposits	511.3
Securities	514.2	Time deposits	989.9
Other assets	148.2	Other borrowing	498.0
		Net worth	201.2
	2,770.6		2,770.6

$$\left(\begin{array}{c}\text{Return on}\\\text{net worth}\end{array}\right) = 10\% + 16.67(12\% - 10\%) = 10\% + 33.34\% = 43.34\%$$

Of course, leverage works both ways. If a financial intermediary borrows at 10 percent and invests at 7 percent, it will lose 40 percent of its net worth if its leverage is 16.67 and 65 percent of its net worth if its leverage is 25. Table 14.5 confirms these calculations for the bank in Table 14.3 with 16.67 leverage.

Because of their enormous leverage, it is crucial that banks choose a profitable combination of assets and liabilities. Table 14.6 shows the aggregate balance sheets for commercial banks in July 1989. We will look first at bank liabilities (their sources of funds), then at asset opportunities (how they use these funds), and then at the matching of assets and liabilities.

LIABILITY MANAGEMENT

The banking Acts of 1933 and 1935 prohibited the payment of interest on checking accounts and, through Regulation Q, constrained rates on other deposits. Throughout the 1930s and 1940s and into the 1950s, interest rates were low, and there was little competition for depositors. As interest rates rose, the competition heated up, opportunities for depositors increased, and, eventually, deposit-rate ceilings were abolished.

The Beginning of Deposit-Rate Competition

In the 1950s, checking accounts were a large and profitable source of funds for commercial banks. Interest payments were prohibited and other intermediaries couldn't offer checking accounts at all. Banks seemed reluctant to compete for time deposits and sometimes even discouraged them, particularly for corporate customers, because it was felt that any expansion of time deposits would be largely at the expense of more profitable checking accounts. Banks hoped that special customer relationships, including preferential loan treatment and financial advice, would ensure the maintenance of substantial checking accounts. This strategy was not successful.

The primary source of funds for banks used to be deposits subject to interest-rate ceilings.

Throughout the 1950s, time-deposit rates at commercial banks averaged a full percentage point less than at mutual savings banks and 1½ percentage points less than at savings-and-loan associations. The spreads were narrower in large cities, but in the suburbs and small cities the rate spreads were even wider, and commercial banks grew slowly while their competitors thrived. The high rates on time deposits offered by other institutions were doubly harmful to banks in that money was lured not only out of bank time deposits, but checking accounts too. Households and businesses used credit cards and transferred funds among accounts as needed to economize on holding cash and checking account balances that earned no interest. National income doubled while checking account balances did not increase at all.

In the 1960s, commercial banks decided to play some financial hardball by offering new deposit accounts and competitive deposit rates to lure households away from thrifts and to win back business customers who increasingly had been making direct short-term investments in such money-market instruments as Treasury bills and commercial paper.

With a variety of minimum-deposit requirements, expiration dates, and other features, banks tried to attract the mobile "hot" money without making expensive across-the-board rate increases. Over the years, other deposit institutions retaliated by introducing competitive accounts and by encroaching on the banks' traditional checking-account territory.

Liability Hunting

This flexibility in seeking funds is now a way of life for banks, particularly large banks. In the three decades from the Great Depression through the 1950s, banks focused on asset management — the allocation of available funds. Checking-account rates were fixed by regulation, and time-deposit rates were very sticky. For the most part, banks accepted whatever funds depositors made available and then decided how to invest those funds. The classic conflict was between investing in high-yield illiquid assets or in liquid assets that can accommodate deposit fluctuations. Deposit variations were taken to be a regrettable but uncontrollable fact of nature.

Since the early 1960s, deposit rates have become increasingly variable, and banks have increasingly come to view the garnering of funds as just as important

Banks now aggressively seek funds from many sources.

as their allocation. This aggressive search for attractive funds is called **liability management.** Banks have become more symmetrical intermediaries, voluntarily borrowing from some in order to lend to others. Table 14.6 earlier in this section shows aggregate commercial bank assets and liabilities.

Figure 14.1 shows that, at the conclusion of World War II, nearly 70 percent of all bank funds came from depositor checking accounts. Now 20 percent do. At large commercial banks, the figure is 15 percent. The declining importance of checking accounts is due partly to the growing importance of small time and savings accounts, for the reasons given earlier. The rest of the story is the dramatic increase in bank money-market borrowing, which is the cornerstone of liability management. Short-term notes are now nearly as important as checking accounts; at most of the very large banks, short-term notes are actually more important than checking accounts.

Certificates of Deposit

One of the most important innovations was large, negotiable **certificates of deposit (CDs).** Corporate time deposits in banks had been stuck at $1 billion throughout the 1950s. Then, in 1961, Citibank and other large New York City banks began promoting CDs and, in a few years, corporate CD investment swelled to $20 billion. Large CDs have become a prominent form of liability management, and in 1989 more than $400 billion in large CDs were outstanding.

Large CDs are an important source of bank funds.

Initially, these were used by aggressive banks to circumvent Regulation Q deposit-rate ceilings. Large CDs remain popular today because administrative expenses are relatively small, and CDs can be readily used to pay competitive interest rates to attract funds when needed. Businesses and wealthy individuals find large CDs an attractive, liquid, short-term investment. In the late 1970s, these big spenders were joined by money-market funds, which, in essence, recycle dollars flowing out of small deposit accounts back into large CDs. The large banks gain funds, while small institutions lose deposits.

Eurodollars

In the late 1960s, severe Regulation Q ceilings were temporarily imposed on bank CDs, which temporarily dried up this source of funds, and banks hunted elsewhere for funds. One source was **Eurodollars** — deposits of U.S. dollars in foreign banks or foreign branches of U.S. banks. More generally, the term *Eurocurrency* has come to encompass any deposit denominated in a foreign currency. These foreign banks need not be in Europe. London has long been the center of the Eurodollar market because of its financial expertise and attractive regulatory climate. There has also been a thriving Eurodollar business in Caribbean branches of large U.S. banks. These branches give regulatory and tax advantages to their parents and are in the same time zone as New York.

Eurodollars are dollar-denominated deposits in foreign banks or in foreign branches of U.S. banks.

The first significant Eurodollar deposits were made by the Soviet Union in 1960. During World War II, Soviet deposits in the United States had been impounded. Remembering this and yet still wanting to earn interest on dollar

Figure 14.1   Commercial Bank Liabilities

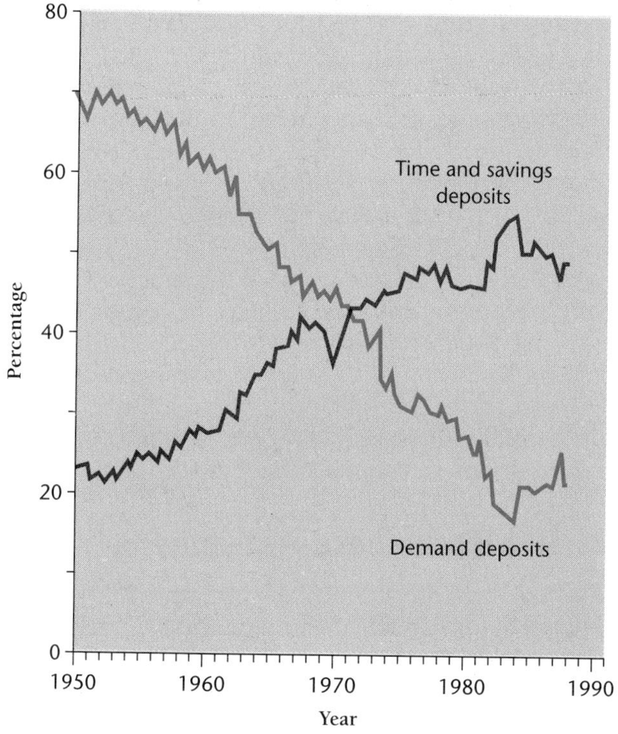

source: Federal Reserve *Historical Chart Book,* 1990.

deposits, in 1960 the Soviet Union began making, in British and other European banks, dollar deposits that were explicitly redeemable in U.S. dollars. Since 1960, the Eurodollar market has grown dramatically.

The tight constraints on bank CD rates in the late 1960s encouraged U.S. banks to borrow dollars from abroad and encouraged potential CD buyers to deposit their dollars abroad. To circumvent CD rate ceilings, dollars were deposited in foreign banks or foreign branches of U.S. banks, which then lent dollars to U.S. banks. With tax breaks, no reserve requirements, and little regulation of foreign currency trading, the Caribbean attracted foreign branches of most large U.S. banks. Many of these are shell banks, little more than small rented offices through which, on paper, billions of dollars pass.

Initially, Eurodollar deposits were not subject to reserve requirements, but since 1969 the Federal Reserve has subjected Eurodollars in foreign branches of U.S. banks to reserve requirements ranging from as high as 20 percent to as low as 3 percent. Regulation Q ceiling rates on CDs were partly lifted in 1970 and removed entirely in 1973. These developments reduced the competitive advantage of Eurodollars, although they remain a source of funds for many large banks.

The U.S. dollar often serves as a medium of exchange outside the United States in that many international transactions are conducted in U.S. dollars. Transactors who will be using U.S. dollars want to earn interest on their dollar holdings without the expense (or exchange-rate risk) of converting their dollars into another currency and then back into dollars. Eurodollar depositors include firms engaged in international trade, U.S. citizens seeking a high return on their deposits, and speculators betting that the value of the dollar will rise relative to other currencies.

Foreign banks multiply Eurodollar deposits in the same way that U.S. banks multiply U.S. deposits. A foreign bank that receives a million-dollar deposit may keep $100,000 and lend $900,000. This $900,000 can then be deposited in another foreign bank, with perhaps $90,000 kept on reserve and $810,000 lent. If all U.S. dollars abroad are held as bank reserves and banks decide to keep reserves equal to 10 percent of deposits, then every million U.S. dollars abroad can support ten million dollars in Eurodollar deposits.

Federal Funds and Repurchase Agreements

The development of the federal-funds market since the mid-1960s has provided another important tool for liability management by large banks. **Federal funds** are large, overnight loans of reserves deposited at the Federal Reserve Banks. Although these are loans among banks, they are called federal funds because it is the Federal Reserve that electronically credits one bank and debits another.

Before the mid-1960s, federal-funds loans were temporary arrangements in which banks that happened to end up with excess reserves could lend to banks that happened to be short that day. As shown in Figure 14.2, up until the mid-1960s the interest rate on these interbank loans, called the **federal-funds rate**, was generally very close to, but slightly below, the Federal Reserve discount rate (the interest rate charged on member bank borrowing from the Federal Reserve).

Since the mid-1960s, large banks have increasingly used the federal-funds market as a semipermanent source of funds. Big-city banks now borrow more or less continuously from other banks in order to relend to large corporate clients. Figure 14.2 shows that during credit crunches, when interest rates rise sharply, the federal-funds rate jumps as banks scramble to find money for their customers. The federal-funds rate can rise far above the discount rate because the Federal Reserve won't tolerate large, continuous borrowing through its discount window. Banks that need funds for their customers will, if necessary, pay a high federal-funds rate during credit crunches.

In a security **repurchase agreement,** a bank sells securities to a customer, usually a corporation, and agrees to repurchase the securities at a higher price on a given date — often the next day. In this way, the bank borrows money from a corporation, using some of its assets as collateral. This is another clever

Banks can raise money through the federal-funds market and repurchase agreements.

Figure 14.2 Short-Term Interest Rates

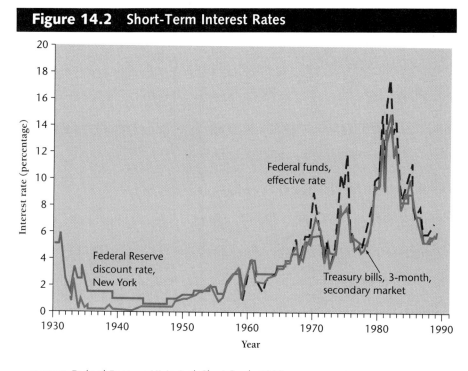

source: Federal Reserve *Historical Chart Book*, 1990.

arrangement that banks created to evade restrictions on traditional bank deposits. From their somewhat devious beginnings, repurchase agreements have become established as a commonplace way of making collateralized short-term loans.

ASSET SELECTION

Bank assets have changed dramatically over the years. Figure 14.3 shows that there has been a very large increase in the fraction of bank assets invested in loans and a corresponding decline in the percentage of bank assets invested in cash and securities. We'll begin our discussion of bank-asset choices by looking at the reasons behind this massive portfolio shift.

Bank Reserves

The Fed's reserve requirements must be satisfied by holding idle, non-interest-bearing reserves — either cash within the bank's own vaults or deposits with the Federal Reserve. Since World War II, bank reserves have fallen by nearly half, from 13 percent of bank assets in 1950 to 7 percent in 1989.

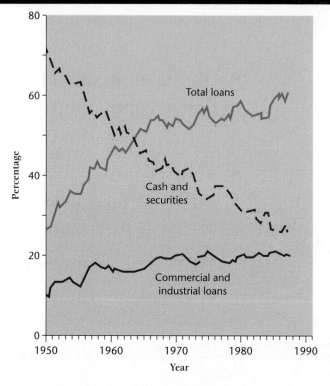

Figure 14.3   Commercial Bank Assets

source: Federal Reserve *Historical Chart Book*, 1990.

Bank reserves can be divided into required reserves and excess reserves (reserves in excess of that required by the Federal Reserve).

$$\text{Bank reserves} = \text{Required reserves} + \text{Excess reserves}$$

Banks hold excess reserves for precautionary purposes, to satisfy deficits between customer withdrawals and deposits. The advantage of holding excess reserves is the avoidance of a cash deficiency that compels the bank to incur expenses by raising cash quickly — by calling in loans, selling securities, or borrowing through the federal-funds market or the Fed's discount window. In the worst possible case, the bank's illiquidity could force it to close. Banks hold more excess reserves when they anticipate a deficit between withdrawals and deposits and when there is considerable uncertainty about their cash needs. The cost of holding excess reserves is the opportunity cost — the interest that could have been earned by investing this cash in loans or securities. When interest rates increase, banks want to hold less excess reserves.

Banks now hold very little excess reserves.

Although bank assets and liabilities have increased by a factor of 17 in the last 40 years, from $160 billion to $2,770 billion, excess reserves have been roughly unchanged, averaging slightly less than $1 billion. Interest rates in the 1970s and 1980s were much higher than in the 1950s and 1960s, and banks became very adept at minimizing their idle cash balances — for example, through the federal-funds market.

Almost all bank reserves today are required reserves, and these have declined sharply relative to bank assets since World War II. Reserve requirements have been reduced and, in addition, there has been a shift by depositors from checking accounts, which are subject to high reserve requirements, to time and savings deposits, which have virtually no reserve requirements. As banks have come to rely less on checking accounts for funds, there has been an accompanying decline in required and actual reserves.

Securities

The characteristics of various securities have been discussed earlier, particularly in Chapters 5, 6, and 7. Historically, banks have had an affinity for U.S. Treasury securities, because these are extremely liquid and thereby provide secondary liquidity reserves. In 1989, two-thirds of the securities held by banks were marketable Treasury securities. Where permitted by state charters, some banks and thrift institutions ventured into high-yield junk bonds in the 1980s. However, the Financial Institutions Reform, Recovery and Enforcement Act of 1989 prohibits all thrifts, whether state or federally chartered, from investing in low-rated or unrated securities.

Banks hold lots of Treasury securities.

There is no default risk in Treasury securities. The primary management decision for banks is the appropriate maturity or, more precisely, duration. As explained in earlier chapters, short-duration bonds are an implicit wager on rising interest rates (relative to the term structure) and long-duration bonds are an implicit bet on falling interest rates (again relative to the term structure). Banks adjust the duration of their bond portfolios to reflect their interest-rate forecasts and the exposure to interest-rate risk in their other assets and liabilities. We will look at interest-rate risk in depth later in this chapter.

Loans

Figure 14.3 chronicles a massive portfolio shift by banks from cash and securities to loans. Roughly one-third of the loans are for real estate — 60 percent to households, 40 percent to businesses. Another one-third are commercial and industrial loans. One-sixth are personal loans (for automobiles, education, and so on) and the remaining sixth go to farms, finance companies, and foreign banks.

The nation's largest and most prominent corporations do not need to borrow from banks because they have the size and reputation to raise funds by issuing securities directly in the money and capital markets. Yet large corporations like to keep their options open by maintaining access to many sources of funds, including bank loans. In fact, large companies often use established bank credit lines as implicit collateral for the short-term debt — called commercial paper — that they issue. Large, prominent companies are not at the mercy of commercial

| Highlight 14.4 | Credit-Card Bonds |

Credit cards offer users a convenient way of making purchases and an easy way to borrow money — though at interest rates that average close to 20 percent. The banks that issue credit cards raise the funds that they lend to credit-card borrowers through bank deposits, Eurodollars, and other sources. One relatively recent method of raising funds is to sell bonds, using as collateral loans to credit-card users ("credit-card receivables"). Bonds backed by credit-card debt are called credit-card bonds.

Citicorp is, by far, the largest issuer of credit-card bonds. As of April 1990, it had $10.5 billion in credit-card bonds outstanding, 36 percent of the total issued. The biggest buyers are other banks, looking for relatively secure short-term investments.

Each credit-card bond is backed by a specific, identified package of credit-card receivables. If a sufficient number of customers default on their credit-card borrowing, then the associated credit-card bond defaults too. The issuing bank is not obligated to use other funds to pay off its credit-card bonds and these bonds are not insured by the FDIC.

Credit-card receivables are notoriously risky, in that consumers put up no collateral and defaults average nearly 5 percent. But credit-card bonds are generally given the highest rating, triple-A, because they are insured by a bond-insurance company and because the issuing bank builds in a substantial cushion. In the spring of 1990, for example, Citicorp's credit-card bonds paid 9.5 percent interest and allowed a 2 percent servicing charge. Since Citicorp was charging consumers close to 20 percent interest on these credit-card loans, the annual loan default rate would have to rise to 20% − (9.5% + 2%) = 8.5% before the bonds were endangered.

In comparison to the historical 4.6 percent default rate experienced by Citicorp, these bonds offered about a 4 percent safety margin. If the default rate turns out to be 4.6 percent, the historical average, Citicorp keeps the 4 percent margin. A lower default rate gives Citicorp more profits; a higher default rate cuts into Citicorp's profits — up to an 8.5 percent default rate, at which point Citicorp has no profit and its credit-card bonds are on the brink of default.

Investors are apparently not convinced that credit-card bonds deserve triple-A ratings. The 9.5 percent yield on Citicorp's seven-year credit card bonds in spring 1990 was about a half-a-percentage point higher than the market yields on other seven-year triple-A corporate bonds.*

---

*Constance Mitchell, "Banks Pour Money into Bonds Backed by Credit-Card Loans," *Wall Street Journal*, March 26, 1990.

banks. If banks tried to charge excessive loan rates, large corporations would simply borrow elsewhere. Thus banks are compelled to offer large firms very competitive rates.

Smaller, lesser-known businesses do not have this easy access to money and capital markets and must rely on intermediaries for funds. These small- to medium-size companies are the cream of the banking loan market. Because of their dependence on banks and their presumed riskiness, they have to pay a substantial price for banking services. This is a financial market imperfection that arises because of the costs of gathering information on the creditworthiness of small- to medium-size businesses. Most investors don't want to buy securities issued by a firm they've never heard of in a town they've never seen. One of the primary virtues of banks is that they bridge this imperfection. As financial intermediaries with specialized knowledge of local firms, banks are able, for a price, to bring together borrowers and lenders.

Banks make many loans to households and to local businesses.

Not only have bank loans grown since World War II, but their character has changed as well. Short-term commercial loans that are implicitly renewable have been supplanted by loans that are explicitly long-term. In part, this development reflects a post-Depression wariness by borrowers. Too many businesses found that their implicitly renewable loans were not, in fact, renewed in the banking panic of the 1930s. They naturally prefer the security of a formal long-term agreement. For banks, this development reflects a thorough disillusionment with the Real Bills doctrine. If short-term commercial loans provide little security, then it is better to give borrowers the long-term loans they want.

Increasingly, banks have come to view themselves as broker-intermediaries whose primary function is to find money for their loan clients. In this perception, the difficult part is not deciding to whom loans should be offered, but rather ensuring that funds will be available when needed. Instead of investing what they have, banks now promise to lend what they think they can raise. In 1985, it was estimated that the nation's 15 largest banks had nearly a trillion dollars in contingent liabilities — commitments to make cash available, if needed.[2] These included lines of credit, bond insurance, and letters of credit (guarantees that an importer will pay for goods after they are delivered). The $1 trillion total was 10 percent larger than the total assets of these banks. Clearly, these banks did not anticipate having to make good on all of these commitments — and certainly not all at the same time — but they had given many a promise of funds if needed.

Banks try to find money for borrowers during credit crunches.

Bank liquidity thus has two faces: the capacity to meet deposit withdrawals and the capacity to satisfy those who need to borrow money. Depositor withdrawals are seldom a problem. Liquidity crises instead involve a scramble to find funds for borrowers. Liquidity management involves both the selection of a prudent amount of liquid assets and the development of reliably expandable liabilities.

Consider the 1966, 1969, 1973–1974, and 1979–1982 credit crunches. The interest-rate spikes in Figure 14.2 chronicle these crunches and, as noted, the federal-funds rate rose especially high as banks borrowed money for desperate

| Highlight 14.5 | **The Securitization of Borrowing** |

In December 1978, short-term business borrowing totaled $276 billion, of which 24 percent was commercial paper and 76 percent was loans from commercial banks. Ten years later, in December 1988, businesses borrowed $1,055 billion short-term, of which 43 percent was commercial paper and 57 percent bank loans. This shift from bank loans to commercial paper is a **securitization of borrowing,** the selling of securities directly to investors instead of relying on financial intermediaries to channel funds from investors to business borrowers.

Many of the businesses that now issue commercial paper instead of taking bank loans were the banks' most creditworthy customers. The loss of these customers has reduced the average quality of the loan portfolios held by banks. On the other side of the risk spectrum, there has been an explosive growth of junk-bond financing by businesses that traditionally borrowed from banks because they were perceived as not creditworthy enough to issue bonds.

Another form of securitization is in the pooling of loans that originate with financial intermediaries, for resale as pass-throughs or loan-backed debts. Mortgages are by far the most popular, but other securitized debts include automobile loans, credit-card receivables, and leases.

It is difficult to securitize loans that are nonhomogeneous and impractical for third parties to evaluate. New York pension-fund managers are rightfully nervous about lending money to Bill Myers to finance a skateboard emporium in Cucamonga, California. Because of their familiarity with local borrowers and the local economy, banks will continue to play a vital role in evaluating the creditworthiness of individuals and small businesses and in monitoring their timely repayment of loans.

customers. In each of these four episodes, banks sold some of their marketable securities in order to make more loans. In 1973–1974 and 1979–1982, banks also raised funds for their loan customers by issuing large amounts of short-term notes. When the Federal Reserve decides to tighten financial markets, banks are forced to ration credit, and some firms get crunched. But during these liquidity crises, banks scramble to find the funds that their loan customers, especially their most valued customers, are begging for.

MATCHING ASSETS AND LIABILITIES

Many savings-and-loan associations managed by honest and competent people were bankrupted in the 1980s by an unexpected increase in interest rates. They invested 80 percent or more of their assets in long-term, typically 30-year, fixed-rate mortgages, while their liabilities were almost entirely short-term, flexible-rate deposits that could be withdrawn whenever depositors were dissatisfied with deposit rates.

Unexpected interest-rate fluctuations can hurt financial intermediaries with mismatched assets and liabilities.

When interest rates rose, these S&L's were locked into what, in retrospect, were low-interest-rate mortgages, but they had to pay high interest rates to hold onto deposits. Their income was negative because they were earning less on their mortgages than they were paying to depositors. Looked at another way, their net worth was negative because the market value of their mortgages was less than their deposits: they could not have sold their mortgages for enough money to pay off their depositors.

These S&L's borrowed short and lent long, and lost. If their assets and liabilities had been mismatched in the other direction — borrowing long and lending short — they could have been bankrupted by an unexpected decline in interest rates. Most deposit intermediaries now try to protect themselves from interest-rate fluctuations by more closely matching their assets and liabilities. In some cases, they may be able to match a given pool of deposits to a given pool of loans, for example, issuing 5-year fixed-rate certificates of deposit to individuals, businesses, or even other banks and using the proceeds for 5-year fixed-rate loans. More often, there is not a perfect match, but the bank can estimate, on balance, its exposure to interest-rate risk. There are two primary techniques. One, gap analysis, focuses on how interest rates affect income; the other, duration analysis, considers the effect of interest rates on net worth.

Gap Analysis

Gap analysis estimates the effect of interest rates on income by estimating the fraction of assets and liabilities that are adjustable-rate, with interest rates that move up and down with market-interest rates within some target horizon, perhaps one year. As illustrated in Table 14.7, all items on both sides of the balance sheet are put into one of two categories: rate-sensitive (interest rates can change during the coming year) and fixed-rate (interest rates cannot change for at least one year).

Gap analysis estimates the net effect of interest rates on income.

A bank's **gap** is defined as

$$\text{Gap} = (\text{Rate-sensitive assets}) - (\text{Rate-sensitive liabilities}) \qquad (3)$$

If there is a change in the interest rates on a bank's rate-sensitive assets and liabilities, its annual income will change by the size of its gap multiplied by the size of the change in interest rates.

The bank in Table 14.7 has a gap of $10 million.

$$\text{Gap} = \$40 \text{ million} - \$30 \text{ million}$$
$$= \$10 \text{ million}$$

If interest rates increase by 2 percentage points (for example, from 7 percent to 9 percent), its annual income will increase by 2%($10,000,000) = $200,000.

As this example illustrates, a positive gap is an implicit wager that interest rates will increase; a negative gap is a bet that rates will fall. For some banks,

A positive gap is an implicit wager that interest rates will increase.

Table 14.7 A Bank's Gap Analysis (millions of dollars)

Assets		Liabilities	
Rate-sensitive	40	Rate-sensitive	30
(Variable-rate loans and short-term securities)		(Variable-rate deposits and short-term securities)	
Fixed-rate	60	Fixed-rate	70
(Reserves, fixed-rate loans, and long-term securities)		(Fixed-rate loans, long-term securities, and net worth)	

gap management involves adjusting the gap to be consistent with the bank's interest-rate forecasts — increasing the gap as when it predicts an increase in interest rates and decreasing the gap when it predicts a decline.

Gap analysis can also be used to gauge the exposure of a bank's profits to interest-rate risk. A bank that wants to protect its income during the next 12 months can adjust its assets and liabilities to obtain a gap of zero; the bank in Table 14.7 could sell $10 million of its short-term assets and use the proceeds to buy long-term assets.

The primary problem with gap analysis is that it focuses on the effect of interest rates on current income, but neglects the effect on the market value of the bank's fixed-rate assets and liabilities. As an extreme example, suppose that a more detailed look at the bank in Table 14.7 reveals the balance sheets shown in the top half of Table 14.8. The fixed-rate assets consist of $10 million in reserves and $50 million in 20-year zero-coupon bonds (with an 8 percent interest rate, paying $233 million after 20 years). The fixed-rate liabilities consist of $62 million in 5-year zeros (at 6 percent, paying $83 million after 5 years) and $8 million in net worth.

The bottom half of Table 14.8 shows that a 2-percentage-point increase in interest rates reduces the market value of its 20-year assets by $15.36 million and the market value of its 5-year liabilities by only $5.54 million, causing its net worth to fall by $9.82 million. Even though this bank has a positive gap and experiences an increase in its income during the next 12 months, it is bankrupted by the increase in interest rates, in that the market value of its assets is no longer adequate to pay off its liabilities.

Gap analysis gauges the effect of interest rates on the bank's income during the next year, but does not consider whether the market values of the fixed-rate assets and liabilities are equally sensitive to interest rates. To do this, we need to look at duration.

Duration Analysis

Because the assets and liabilities of a financial intermediary involve future cash flows, the present value of both sides of its balance sheet depends on interest

Table 14.8 A Peek Behind the Gap (millions of dollars)

Before Interest-Rate Increase

Assets		Liabilities	
Rate-sensitive		Rate-sensitive	
Variable-rate loans	40.00	Variable-rate deposits	30.00
Fixed-rate		Fixed-rate	
Reserves	10.00	5-year zeros	
20-year zeros		($83, @ 6%)	62.00
($233, @ 8%)	50.00	Net worth	8.00
	100.00		100.00

After Interest-Rate Increase

Assets		Liabilities	
Rate-sensitive		Rate-sensitive	
Variable-rate loans	40.00	Variable-rate deposits	30.00
Fixed-rate		Fixed-rate	
Reserves	10.00	5-year zeros	
20-year zeros		($83, @ 8%)	56.46
($233, @ 10%)	34.64	Net worth	−1.82
	84.64		84.64

rates. An increase in interest rates reduces the present value of the assets it holds and also reduces the present value of its obligations. Whether an increase in interest rates increases or reduces its net worth depends on whether its assets or liabilities are more sensitive to interest rates.

Chapter 7 explained how duration can be used to measure the sensitivity of present value to interest rates. Here, duration can be used to measure the interest-rate sensitivity of each side of a bank's balance sheet and determine whether, on balance, an increase in interest rates increases or reduces its net worth.

Duration measures the sensitivity of present value to interest rates.

Equation 8 in Chapter 7, reproduced here, tells us that if an asset's duration is D, then the percentage change in present value, %P, resulting from a 1-percentage-point change in the required return, ΔR, is approximately equal to:

$$\%P = -D\,\Delta R \qquad (4)$$

If, for example, an asset has a duration of 5 years, then a 1-percentage-point increase in the required return (for example, from 8 percent to 9 percent) will reduce its present value by approximately 5 percent.

The second rule we need to use is that the duration of a portfolio is a weighted average of the duration of the assets in the portfolio, with weights that reflect each asset's proportionate share of the portfolio. Consider the assets of the bank shown in Table 14.8. The variable-rate loans have a duration of essentially 0, since their market value is virtually unaffected by interest rates. Bank reserves also have a duration of zero. Remember that an asset's duration is its present-value-weighted average number of years until receiving the cash flow; thus the duration of a 20-year zero-coupon bond is 20 years. Therefore, the duration of this bank's assets is

$$\begin{bmatrix} \text{Duration of} \\ \text{total assets} \end{bmatrix} = \begin{bmatrix} \text{Duration} \\ \text{of loans} \end{bmatrix} \frac{\text{Loans}}{\text{Total assets}} + \begin{bmatrix} \text{Duration} \\ \text{of reserves} \end{bmatrix} \frac{\text{Reserves}}{\text{Total assets}}$$

$$+ \begin{bmatrix} \text{Duration} \\ \text{of bonds} \end{bmatrix} \frac{\text{Bonds}}{\text{Total assets}}$$

$$= (0)(0.40) + (0)(0.10) + (20)(0.50)$$

$$= 10$$

Similarly, on the liability side, the variable-rate deposits have a duration of essentially zero and the five-year zeros have a duration of 5 years. The duration of this bank's liabilities (other than net worth) is thus

$$\begin{bmatrix} \text{Duration of} \\ \text{total liabilities} \end{bmatrix} = \begin{bmatrix} \text{Duration} \\ \text{of loans} \end{bmatrix} \frac{\text{Loans}}{\text{Total liabilities}} + \begin{bmatrix} \text{Duration} \\ \text{of bonds} \end{bmatrix} \frac{\text{Bonds}}{\text{Total liabilities}}$$

$$= (0) \begin{bmatrix} \dfrac{30}{92} \end{bmatrix} + (5) \begin{bmatrix} \dfrac{62}{92} \end{bmatrix}$$

$$= 3.4$$

The change in the bank's net worth depends on its **duration gap**

$$\text{Duration gap} = (\text{Duration of assets}) - (\text{Duration of liabilities}) \left(\frac{\text{Liabilities}}{\text{Assets}} \right) \qquad (5)$$

The duration gap compares asset and liability duration.

The duration gap compares asset and liability duration, taking into account the fact that assets are somewhat larger than liabilities other than net worth. The size of the duration gap is an approximate estimate of the change in net worth, as a percentage of total assets, resulting from a 1-percentage-point increase in interest rates.

The bank in Table 14.8 has a positive duration gap

$$\text{Duration gap} = 10 - 3.4 \left(\frac{92}{100} \right)$$

$$= 6.9$$

which means that its assets are more sensitive to interest rates than its liabilities. Therefore, an across-the-board increase in interest rates reduces its net worth; a decline in interest rates increases its net worth.

In general, a positive duration gap is an implicit wager that interest rates will decline; a negative duration gap increases net worth if interest rates rise. A deposit intermediary can adjust its duration gap to reflect its interest-rate forecasts — a positive duration gap if it predicts a decrease in interest rates and a negative duration gap if it predicts an increase. A duration-gap calculation can also be used to estimate a bank's exposure to interest-rate risk. A bank that wants to protect its net worth from interest-rate fluctuations can adjust its assets and liabilities to obtain a duration gap of zero; the bank in Table 14.8 could sell some of its 20-year zeros and use the proceeds to buy shorter-term bonds.

A positive duration gap is an implicit wager that interest rates will decline.

Because the assets and liabilities of financial intermediaries are roughly equal, the duration gap formula in Equation 3 can be approximated by

$$\text{Duration gap} = (\text{Duration of assets}) - (\text{Duration of liabilities})$$

Thus whether the duration gap is positive or negative depends (roughly) on whether the intermediary's assets or liabilities have a longer duration. This approximation explains the following shorthand statement often made by financial analysts: a bank's net worth is protected from across-the-board changes in interest rates if its assets and liabilities have comparable durations; if asset and

---

The Volatility of Bank Stocks	**Highlight 14.6**

Any business is exposed to interest-rate risk if its asset and liability durations are not offsetting. Financial intermediaries are particularly vulnerable because they are so highly leveraged and because, historically, many thrifts had very long asset durations and relatively short liability durations.

Since shareholder equity is equal to net worth (the difference between the market value of the firm's assets and debts), a vulnerability to interest rates should be reflected in the effects of interest rates on the price of stock issued by banks and S&L's. An economist investigated this question using interest-rate and stock-price data for the years 1961–1983 and taking into account statistically the fact that stock prices also depend on the state of the economy.* He estimated that, if there were no change in the economy, an increase in long-term interest rates from 10 percent to 11 percent would reduce the per-share price of industrial stocks by 4 percent, of commercial-bank stocks by 9 percent, and of S&L's stocks by 24 percent. Thus, compared to industrial companies, banks are twice as sensitive to interest rates and S&L's six times as sensitive.

---

*G. J. Santoni, "Interest Rate Risk and the Stock Prices of Financial Institutions," *Federal Reserve Bank of St. Louis Review*, August–September 1984, pp. 12–20.

liability durations are mismatched, a relatively long asset duration is a bet that interest rates will fall, a relatively short asset duration is a bet that rates will rise.

Hedging with Financial Futures and Options

Financial futures and options can be used to hedge interest-rate risks.

A bank may find it undesirable to protect itself from interest-rate risk by restructuring its assets and liabilities. For example, attempts to replace long-term mortgages with short-term mortgages and to replace fixed-rate loans with variable-rate loans may meet with customer resistance. Efforts to encourage depositors to shift to longer-term certificates of deposit may also be unsuccessful without substantial interest-rate incentives. A bank may find it more profitable to accommodate customer preferences and then use financial futures and options to hedge the interest rate risk in its portfolio.

Chapter 8 explains a variety of financial futures and options contracts. All hedging strategies rely on the fact that, because changes in interest rates affect the values of financial futures and options in predictable ways, these instruments can be used to offset the effects of interest rates on a bank's other assets and liabilities. If a bank has a positive duration gap, an increase in interest rates will reduce its net worth; it can hedge this position by selling Treasury-bond futures, selling bond call options, or buying bond put options — all strategies that will make money if interest rates increase. If this is done in the appropriate amounts, portfolio losses caused by an increase in interest rates will be roughly offset by capital gains on its financial futures and options.

Relatively few banks use financial futures and options to hedge their portfolios against interest-rate risk. Successful hedging requires considerable expertise and regular monitoring, requiring an expense that many small- and medium-size banks don't want to incur. A few banks have made expensive errors, buying or selling inappropriate amounts, and some regulators discourage inexperienced banks from using futures and options.

Financial Supermarkets

Bank management is sometimes divided up into functions, such as liquidity management, loan management, investment management, and liability management. But these functions need to be coordinated. For example, if a bank's loans are structured to be very profitable if interest rates increase, but its securities are selected on the assumption that interest rates will decline, the bank's assets as a whole may be little affected by interest rates. Such a net position should be chosen deliberately, and not be the coincidental outcome of independent decisions. Coordination is needed so that the bank's overall portfolio reflects senior management's overall objectives.

Banking may be dominated by large, diversified institutions.

In the years ahead, small- and medium-size intermediaries may lose out in their competition with large, experienced, and well-known institutions, which can afford expensive expertise and equipment, can borrow in the money and capital markets, and have convenient branches to offer customers. The most attractive feature of small intermediaries may be that they are ready-made branches for the giants. To stay in business, many smaller institutions have welcomed mergers with larger institutions. For the next several years, the big will absorb the weak and get even bigger.

Since the mid-1960s, financial markets have endured great pressures and undergone remarkable changes. The clearing away of regulatory constraints and the aggressive evolution of financial intermediaries have been central to these changes. One aspect of these changes has been the creation and spread of innovative securities and markets to satisfy borrowers and lenders. Eurodollars and money-market mutual funds are good examples.

A second aspect has been the spread of institutions outside of their traditional roles. Most institutions began with very specific, focused objectives. Often this fine aim was accentuated by regulatory authorities that sharply constricted operations. In recent years, most institutions have been acting on the belief that they serve their customers best by offering them many different services. This is the financial analogue to the supermarket or the shopping center. It is more convenient and practical to use one firm for all of your financial services. There is also an element of business diversification. By offering several types of services, the financial intermediary avoids the risk that its specialty will be competed or regulated out of business, or adversely affected by other macroeconomic events. Commercial banks are the outstanding example of financial intermediaries that span markets. They are clearly the largest and most successful enthusiasts for this strategy. But other intermediaries are trying hard to imitate their example, if only for self-preservation.

The historic 1980 banking legislation substantially deregulated financial intermediaries. The general tenor of this law and of subsequent legislation and regulatory decisions has been to treat all financial institutions more equally. The fine details of this evolving new world are uncertain. But, overall, the distinctions between financial intermediaries are sure to blur further. No longer will we go to one intermediary for checking accounts, to another for a mortgage, to another for a car loan, to another for insurance, and to yet another to buy stock. More and more, we will have full-service intermediaries — financial supermarkets, open 24 hours a day, with branches all over the world.

These financial supermarkets may evolve from the largest bank, the humblest credit union, or from outside banking: Merrill Lynch with its vast finance expertise and retail network; Sears, Roebuck & Company, which has far more credit cards than any bank; General Motors or General Electric with their robust finance-company affiliates; IBM with its computers and financial strength; or AT&T with its communications apparatus. We can be pretty confident that there will be a rough-and-tumble scramble for dominant positions. There won't be room for hundreds of giants. Instead, there will be a nasty shakeout of the industry with lots of inefficient or unlucky firms broken or swallowed up by the successful ones.

One concern is that this same type of aggressive diversification, including branch banking and Eurodollars, was also very prevalent in the 1920s. Will the story end the same way? From a broader perspective, the innovations are part

of a very logical and appealing movement from mom-and-pop banking to financial supermarkets. There were excesses in the 1920s; the Federal Reserve followed
less-than-helpful monetary policies; and the Great Crash led to a web of regulations. As these melt or are ripped away, financial intermediaries are resuming
their longer-run evolution. Distinct types of intermediaries are giving way to
general-purpose financial institutions. It is hoped that they and the monetary
authorities will do better this time.

SUMMARY

Models and computers can be used to assess profits, risk, and liquidity under a
variety of plausible scenarios. Asset management is the allocation of funds into
reserves, loans, and securities. Liability management is the recognition that funds
can be raised by issuing liabilities as well as by selling assets. By aggressively
seeking funds, banks have become more flexible symmetrical intermediaries,
concerned both with profitably investing the funds of their depositor customers
and with finding funds at reasonable rates for their loan customers.

Banks can use gap and duration analyses to gauge the exposure of their
income and net worth to interest-rate risk. For instance, a positive gap and
negative duration gap is an implicit wager on rising interest rates. A bank that
wants to insulate its income and net worth from interest-rate surprises can
structure its assets and liabilities (possibly using financial futures and options)
to get a zero gap and zero duration gap.

The simultaneous management of assets and liabilities is a crucial part of
the movement toward financial supermarkets — unfettered diversified intermediaries offering customers a wide variety of borrowing and lending options.

IMPORTANT TERMS

certificates of deposit (CDs)
duration gap
Eurodollars
federal funds
federal-funds rate
gap
gap analysis

leverage
liability management
liquid assets
primary reserves
repurchase agreement
secondary reserves
securitization of borrowing

EXERCISES

1. Use the data in Table 14.6 to calculate commercial-bank net worth as a fraction of total
   assets and, from this, aggregate commercial-
   bank leverage.

2. Here are the balance sheets of a hypothetical
   bank.

Assets		Liabilities	
Cash	10	Deposits	70
Loans	70	Bonds	20
Securities	20	Net worth	10
	100		100

All data are in millions of dollars. What is this bank's degree of leverage? What will its return on its net worth be if the average interest rate on its deposits and bonds is 8 percent and the gross return on its assets is 8 percent? If the gross return on its assets is instead 10 percent? For what value of the gross return on assets is its return on net worth equal to -100 percent?

3. A thrift institution has a net worth equal to 2 percent of its assets, and the average interest rate on its deposits and bonds is 10 percent. What is its degree of leverage? What is the return on its net worth if the gross return on its assets is 10 percent? 8 percent?

4. The following balance sheet of a hypothetical savings-and-loan association shows the interest rate on its debts and the gross rate of return on its assets in parentheses. The assets and liabilities are in millions of dollars.

Assets		Liabilities	
Cash (0%)	5	Deposits (8%)	70
Mortgages (12%)	80	Bonds (10%)	25
Securities (8%)	15	Net worth	5
	100		100

a. What is its degree of leverage?
b. What is the average interest rate on its deposits and bonds?
c. What is the average gross rate of return on its assets?
d. What is its rate of return on net worth?

5. The following balance sheet of a hypothetical commercial bank shows the interest rate on its debts and the gross rate of return on its assets in parentheses. The assets and liabilities are in millions of dollars.

Assets		Liabilities	
Cash (0%)	5	Deposits (10%)	70
Loans (12%)	60	Bonds (10%)	20
Securities (10%)	35	Net worth	10
	100		100

a. What is its degree of leverage?
b. What is the average interest rate on its deposits and bonds?
c. What is the average rate of gross return on its assets?
d. What is its rate of return on net worth?

6. In 1987, Columbia Savings & Loan Association in California had $2.6 billion — 27 percent of its assets — in high-yield junk bonds.[3] During the preceding five years, the return on Columbia's net worth had ranged from 44 percent to 114 percent. If junk bonds pay no more than 18 percent, how could Columbia have such a high profit rate? Use the stylized balance sheet below to calculate the annual rate of return, both in dollars and as a percentage of net worth. (The assets and liabilities are in billions, with interest rates given in parentheses).

Assets		Liabilities	
Cash (0%)	$ 0.4	Deposits (11%)	$ 7.0
Junk (18%)	2.6	Bonds (11%)	2.2
Other (12%)	7.0	Net worth	0.3
	$10.0		$10.0

7. The U.S. League of Savings Associations estimated the percentages of all outstanding mortgages held by saving and loan associations in 1980 that paid various interest rates.[4]

Interest Rate	Percentage of Mortgages
5	1%
6	3%
7	8%
8	20%
9	30%
10	24%
11	10%
12	4%

Use these data to estimate the average interest rate on the mortgages held by savings-and-loan associations. Is this average interest rate higher or lower than the estimated 11 percent average cost of funds for S&L's in 1980?

8. A newspaper article describing the data used in the previous exercise said, "The tabulation breaks down 14 million outstanding mortgages, valued at about $5 billion, by the interest rate they carry."[5] What is the error in this statement?

9. Since World War II, there has been a dramatic shift in the composition of bank deposits — from checking accounts, which are subject to high reserve requirements, to time and savings deposits, which have virtually no reserve requirements. Why might banks want to encourage this shift? How could they do so?

10. Citibank is sometimes described as a financial supermarket. What advantages do you see, for customers and for the bank, of a financial-supermarket strategy?

11. Seventy percent of the mortgages issued by S&L's in 1984 were adjustable-rate; seventy percent of those issued in March 1986 were fixed-rate. In retrospect, many wished they had issued more fixed-rate mortgages in 1984 and fewer in 1986. Why?

12. In 1982, an economist estimated that the aggregate net worth of U.S. thrifts had fallen from $23 billion at the end of 1977 to −$44 billion at the end of 1981 and that 1,000 thrifts would be bankrupt by the end of 1983 if interest rates increased.[6] Why does an increase in interest rates reduce the net worth of thrifts?

13. A French company holding U.S. dollars that will be used to purchase goods at a price stated in terms of U.S. dollars can earn interest in the interim by making a Eurodollar deposit. Alternatively, it can convert its dollars into francs, make a franc deposit, and convert its francs back into dollars when it is time to pay for the goods. If they follow the latter course, will they gain or lose if the dollar appreciates relative to the franc while they are holding francs?

14. The federal-funds market has reduced the amount of reserves held by the banking system as a whole. What has this done to the deposit multiplier (the ratio of bank deposits to the monetary base)?

15. On October 5, 1979, Paul Volcker, the Chairman of the Federal Reserve Board of Governors, announced the imposition of an 8 percent reserve requirement on Federal Funds loans and repurchase agreements. Did this action ease or tighten credit conditions?

16. Walter Wriston, Citicorp's chief executive officer, was confident that the tight-money policies begun by the Federal Reserve in late 1979 would cause interest rates to fall. The bank suffered substantial losses when interest rates rose instead. How might Citibank's management have adjusted the bank's assets and liabilities to bet on falling interest rates?

17. Savings-and-loan associations borrow short-term and lend long-term. Why is this a disastrous strategy when interest rates rise unexpectedly? Why did I use the qualification "unexpectedly"?

18. In 1980, the chairman of a Massachusetts mutual savings bank said that matching a 2½-year savings certificate to a 2½-year mortgage note "would be a good trade-off."[7] Why is this strategy appealing to the savings bank? Why might it be unappealing to the savings bank's customers?

19. A bank's assets and liabilities have been divided into those with interest rates that can change within the next 12 months and those that can't.

Assets

Rate-sensitive	$500,000,000
Fixed-rate	300,000,000

Liabilities

Rate-sensitive	$200,000,000
Fixed-rate	600,000,000

Does this bank have a positive or a negative gap? Is it it implicitly betting that interest rates will increase, or decrease? If interest rates increase by 4 percentage points, by how much will its annual income rise or fall?

20. The commercial banks in the Tenth Federal Reserve District (including Wyoming, Colorado, Nebraska, Kansas, and Oklahoma) were separated into small banks (less than $300 million in assets) and large banks (more than $300 million in assets). The aggregate balance sheets for each group on December 31, 1983, were then divided into rate-sensitive and fixed-rate items.[8]

| | Small Banks | | Large Banks | |
	Assets	Liabil-ities	Assets	Liabil-ities
Rate-sensitive	54.8%	53.4%	49.8%	52.2%
Fixed-rate	45.2%	46.6%	50.2%	47.8%

Which group of banks had a positive gap, and which had a negative gap? Which group do you think showed an increase in income and which a decrease when interest rates increased during the first six months of 1984?

21. Using a 12-month horizon, a small mutual savings bank's assets and liabilities have been divided into rate-sensitive and fixed-rate.

Assets

| Rate-sensitive | $20,000,000 |
| Fixed-rate | 30,000,000 |

Liabilities

| Rate-sensitive | $40,000,000 |
| Fixed-rate | 10,000,000 |

Does this mutual savings bank have a positive or a negative gap? Will it make more money during the next 12 months if interest rates increase, or decline? If interest rates fall by 2 percentage points, by how much will its annual income change? How could this mutual savings bank obtain a zero gap?

22. Does an S&L that borrows short and lends long have a positive or a negative gap? Will its income rise or fall if interest rates decline?

23. In the early 1980s, California Federal Savings and Loan, the nation's fourth largest S&L and the principal subsidiary of CalFed, undertook a massive portfolio restructuring designed to insulate itself from interest-rate fluctuations.[9] For example, 90 percent of the mortgages it issued in 1985 were adjustable-rate. Overall, its total loan portfolio changed from 17 percent adjustable-rate in 1982 to 50 percent in 1984. CalFed also issued a variety of longer-term securities, to lengthen its liabilities at the same time that it was shortening its assets. In 1985, $14.2 billion of its $19.0 billion in assets and $16.7 billion of its liabilities were interest-sensitive within 10 years. CalFed divided these interest-sensitive assets and liabilities into subperiods.

Interest Sensitivity	Assets (millions)	Liabilities (millions)
Within 1 year	$8,766	$12,980
1 to 5 years	2,900	3,352
5 to 10 years	2,582	369

Use these data to write a one-paragraph report describing the exposure of CalFed's income to interest-rate risk.

24. A bank wants to bet that interest rates will decline within the next year. Should it increase or decrease its gap? Should it increase or decrease its duration gap?

25. A 1985 study of banks in the Tenth Federal Reserve District (including Wyoming, Colorado, Nebraska, Kansas, and Oklahoma) found

that between 1976 and 1983 these banks typically had positive gaps and negative duration gaps.[10] How is this possible? If a bank is in this situation, how will an increase in interest rates affect its current income? Its net worth?

26. A commercial bank has a negative gap and a negative duration gap. What will happen to its income and net worth if interest rates increase?

27. Here are the balance sheets of a hypothetical bank (all data are in millions of dollars).

Assets

Adjustable-rate mortgages	70
1-year Treasury bills	20
Reserves	10
	100

Liabilities

Money-market accounts	50
5-year zero-coupon CDs	40
Net worth	10
	100

Assume that the interest rates on the adjustable-rate mortgages and money-market accounts adjust continuously with market-interest rates. Is this bank's duration gap positive or negative? Will its net worth increase or decrease if market-interest rates fall by one percentage point?

28. The bank described in Table 14.8 wants to sell some of its 20-year zeros and use the proceeds to buy 5-year zeros, so that it will have a duration gap of zero. How much must it sell? What if it uses the proceeds to buy 1-year zeros?

29. Here are the balance sheets of an industrial corporation, with durations shown in parentheses.

Assets

Financial (duration = 1)	$ 10,000,000
Real (duration = 15)	90,000,000
	$100,000,000

Liabilities

Debt (duration = 10)	$ 50,000,000
Equity	50,000,000
	$100,000,000

Does this firm have a positive or a negative duration gap? Will the value of its equity increase or decrease if market-interest rates rise?

30. Use the data in the preceding exercise to estimate the effect on the value of this firm's equity of a 5-percentage-point increase in interest rates.

PART

IV

Government Monetary Policy

GOVERNMENT

MONETARY-POLICY

INSTRUMENTS

There have been three great inventions since the beginning of time: fire, the wheel, and central banking.

Will Rogers

The federal government is the largest single participant in financial markets. In September 1989, it had outstanding more than $130 billion in currency and reserves, $250 billion in short-term bonds, and $500 billion in long-term bonds. The federal government also held more than $300 billion in loans and mortgages. With this kind of clout, government financial decisions can move and shake financial markets.

As we saw in earlier chapters, U.S. monetary policy is determined by the Federal Reserve Board. In this chapter, we will look at three of its important policy tools: open-market operations, reserve requirements, and the discount rate. You will see how each of these policy instruments works and how each affects financial markets. In Chapter 16, we will look at how the Fed decides whether it will use these tools to ease or to tighten financial conditions. To begin, we need to look briefly at the Fed's balance sheet.

THE FED'S BALANCE SHEET

The Federal Reserve maintains careful records of its financial condition, and each Thursday releases a summary report of its balance sheet as of that Wednesday.

The Fed's balance sheet shows its assets and liabilities.

More detailed weekly records are published in the monthly *Federal Reserve Bulletin*. Table 15.1 shows the Fed's balance sheet for Wednesday, September 27, 1989. The Fed's balance sheet is much like any balance sheet, with assets on one side and liabilities on the other. However, some of the entries are unusual and probably a bit puzzling. We will discuss each item in turn.

Gold certificates. When the U.S Treasury buys gold, it issues gold certificates to the Fed and is credited with a deposit in its account at the Fed, upon which it can write checks to pay its bills. The gold certificate is an asset for the Fed since it is a claim on the Treasury's gold.

SDR certificates. As explained in Chapter 3, Special Drawing Rights (SDRs) are "paper gold" issued to governments by the International Monetary Fund (IMF) to settle international debts. As with gold certificates, the U.S. Treasury gives the Fed SDR certificates and is credited with a deposit at the Fed.

Treasury currency. There is a constant $300 million in U.S. Treasury notes that trace back to the Civil War greenbacks, and another $20 billion in coins issued by the Treasury. Some of this Treasury currency, mostly coins, is held by the Fed. When the Treasury mints coins, it deposits these in its Fed account and can write checks against this balance. The coins come into circulation when depository institutions request coins from their local Federal Reserve banks. They pay for the coins either with currency or by debiting their account balances at the Fed.

Loans to depository institutions. These are borrowings through the Fed's discount window, one of the policy tools discussed later in this chapter. These

Table 15.1 Federal Reserve Balance Sheet, September 27, 1989 (billions of dollars)

Assets		Liabilities	
Gold certificates	11.1	Federal Reserve notes	229.2
SDR certificates	8.5	Deposits by Deposit Institutions	36.0
Treasury currency	0.5	U.S. Treasury deposits	9.8
Loans to depository institutions	0.6	Foreign official accounts	0.3
Securities	228.2	Deferred-availability cash items	5.3
Cash items in process of collection	6.1	Miscellaneous	8.1
Assets denominated in foreign currencies	24.3		
Miscellaneous	9.4		
Total	288.7		288.7

source: *Federal Reserve Bulletin*, October 1989.

loans are a liability of the borrowing institution and an asset for the Fed.

Securities. The Fed's largest asset category, by far, is securities, of which some 97 percent are U.S. Treasury securities and the remainder are securities issued by federal agencies. The Fed's holdings of securities fluctuate with its open-market operations, another of the Fed's primary policy tools.

Cash items in process of collection. This category is related to deferred-availability cash items on the liability side of the Fed's balance sheet, and both relate to the Federal Reserve float, which will be explained in some detail later.

Assets denominated in foreign currencies. In recent years, the Fed has held an increasing amount of foreign currency and securities to facilitate international transactions and as a consequence of its efforts to stabilize exchange rates.

Federal Reserve notes. This is the currency issued by the Fed.

Deposits by deposit institutions. These are the deposits made by banks and other depository institutions with the Federal Reserve in partial fulfillment of their reserve requirements. These, too, are a policy tool.

U.S. Treasury deposits. The Treasury deposits money with the Fed and then pays its bills by writing checks against these deposits. The Treasury has accounts (called "tax and loan accounts") in commercial banks throughout the country that are used for the deposit of income taxes and Social Security taxes withheld by employers and for the proceeds from the sale of savings bonds. The Treasury withdraws funds from these accounts periodically (every few days from large banks, every few weeks from small banks) by a transfer from the commercial bank's reserve account with the Fed to the Treasury's account at the Fed. The Treasury then pays the government's bills by writing checks drawn on its Federal Reserve account.

Foreign official accounts. These are deposits with the Fed by foreign governments, central banks, and international agencies such as the World Bank.

Currency and the Monetary Base

Table 15.1 shows that the Fed's liabilities consist primarily of Federal Reserve notes and deposits by banks and other depository institutions. Federal Reserve finances are unique in that when the Fed wants to buy something, it can print money to pay for its purchases. To keep its balance sheets balanced, the Fed records these new Federal Reserve notes as a liability, which offsets the asset it acquires.

These Federal Reserve notes are very different from the liabilities of ordinary citizens and businesses. If you borrow money to buy a house, the mortgage liability is a real burden in that the requisite monthly payments come out of your income and reduce the funds available to buy food, clothing, and entertainment. The Fed's Federal Reserve–note liability is quite different. If you present a $10 Federal Reserve note for redemption, the Fed governors won't have to mine gold, sell furniture, or take second jobs to pay you off. The Fed will simply

The Fed's primary liabilities are Federal Reserve notes and bank reserves.

have two $5 bills printed up, or ten $1 bills, whichever you prefer. Clearly, the Federal Reserve's notes are a special kind of liability that any of us would enjoy having.

It is useful to have a record somewhere of how many Federal Reserve notes are in circulation and what the Fed purchased with them. Federal Reserve notes are included in the Fed's balance sheets to help financial analysts monitor the Fed's financial transactions, in order to understand and anticipate the effects on financial markets.

Federal Reserve notes make up about 90 percent of the nation's currency. The remaining 10 percent consists of $300 million in U.S. Treasury notes and about $20 billion in coins issued by the Treasury. Some Treasury currency is held by the Fed, and some Federal Reserve notes are held by the Treasury. In practice, these holdings are small (about half a billion dollars apiece), but they complicate our calculations of the amount of government money in private hands. A further difficulty is that an undetermined amount of currency has left the United States, or has been tucked into coin collections, buried in forgotten places, or lost at the beach or inside sofas. Ignoring this missing currency

$$
\begin{aligned}
\textbf{U.S. currency outstanding} = \ &\text{Federal Reserve notes} \\
&+ \text{Treasury notes and coin} \\
&- \text{Fed holdings of Treasury currency} \\
&- \text{Treasury holdings of Fed currency} \quad (1)
\end{aligned}
$$

Some of this outstanding currency is inside bank vaults and some is in private hands outside banks.

$$
\textbf{U.S. currency outstanding} = \text{vault cash} + \text{currency outside banks} \quad (2)
$$

The nation's monetary base consists of this outstanding currency plus the reserves of depository institutions with the Federal Reserve — since these reserves, just like the cash in bank vaults, support the banking system's deposit multiplication and can readily be converted into Federal Reserve notes. Therefore

$$
\textbf{monetary base} = \text{U.S. currency outstanding} + \text{reserve deposits with Fed} \quad (3)
$$

Since Equation 2 tells us that U.S. currency consists of vault cash and currency outside banks, we can also describe the monetary base as follows:

$$
\begin{aligned}
\textbf{monetary base} \\
= \ &(\text{vault cash} + \text{currency outside banks}) + \text{reserve deposits with Fed} \\
= \ &\text{currency outside banks} + (\text{vault cash} + \text{reserve deposits with Fed}) \\
= \ &\text{currency outside banks} + \text{bank reserves} \quad (4)
\end{aligned}
$$

Analysts are often particularly interested in the bank reserve part of the monetary base, since reserves support deposits in banks and other deposit institutions, and deposits are a major part of various monetary aggregates, such as M1 and M2.

Depository institutions can satisfy their reserve requirements either with vault cash or with deposits at the Federal Reserve. The advantage of vault cash is that it is near at hand for meeting withdrawals of customers who want cash.

The monetary base consists of outstanding currency and bank reserves.

The primary advantage of deposits at Federal Reserve banks is that these can be used for interbank transfers within the Federal Reserve.

When a private bank sends $100 million in Federal Reserve notes to its regional Federal Reserve bank, the bank is credited with a $100 million deposit, and the notes are either shredded or stored for future use. One hundred million dollars of bank reserves replaces $100 million of outstanding Federal Reserve notes, and the monetary base is unchanged. The T-accounts, showing the changes in the balance sheets of the the private bank and the Fed, are as follows.

Private Bank

Assets		Liabilities
Vault cash	−$100	
Deposits at Fed	+$100	

Federal Reserve

Assets	Liabilities	
	Federal Reserve notes	−$100
	Bank reserves	+$100

Changes in the Monetary Base

Other events on the asset or liability side of the Fed's balance sheets also affect the monetary base. Suppose, for example, that the Treasury writes a $100 million check drawn on its Fed account to pay for some gold bars, and the seller brings this check to a Federal Reserve Bank for redemption in Federal Reserve notes. The T-accounts are shown in Panel (a) of Table 15.2. Panel (b) shows what happens when the Treasury then issues a $100-million gold certificate to the Fed and is credited with a $100-million deposit in its Fed account. The net effect is that the Treasury has $100 million more in gold, the Fed has a $100-million gold certificate, and the monetary base has expanded by $100 million. This is an example of a change in the monetary base that is not instigated by the Fed.

Consider now the effects on the monetary base when the Treasury transfers $100 million from a commercial-bank account to its Fed account. The T-accounts are shown in Table 15.3. The bank loses $100 million in deposits and reserves, and the Fed transfers $100 million from bank reserves to the Treasury's account, reducing the monetary base by $100 million. This monetary contraction will be reversed when the Treasury writes $100 million in checks on its Fed account.

The monetary base is affected by changes in the Fed's assets and liabilities.

Table 15.2 The U.S. Treasury Buys Gold

(a) Payment for the Gold with a U.S. Treasury Check Drawn on the Fed

U.S. Treasury

Assets		Liabilities
Gold	+$100	
Deposits at Fed	−$100	

Federal Reserve

Assets	Liabilities	
	Federal Reserve notes	+$100
	Treasury deposits	−$100

(b) Issuance of a Gold Certificate to the Fed

U.S. Treasury

Assets		Liabilities	
Deposits at Fed	+$100	Gold certificates	+$100

Federal Reserve

Assets		Liabilities	
Gold certificates	+$100	Treasury deposits	+$100

Table 15.3   **The Treasury Transfers Money from a Private Bank to the Fed**

U.S. Treasury

Assets		Liabilities
Deposits at bank	−$100	
Deposits at Fed	+$100	

Private Bank

Assets		Liabilities	
Deposits at Fed	−$100	Treasury deposits	−$100

Federal Reserve

Assets		Liabilities	
		Bank reserves	−$100
		Treasury deposits	+$100

When the recipients cash their checks, Treasury deposits at the Fed will fall by $100 million and bank reserves will increase by $100 million. This example shows how the Treasury's receipts and outlays can have large, though temporary, effects on the monetary base.

Federal Reserve Float

Float arises from discrepancies in the dates on which payments and receipts are recorded. For example, bank float arises when a depositor's balances are credited before the bank itself receives credit for the funds. Suppose that Mary deposits a $2,000 paycheck in her local bank, and this bank immediately credits her account — allowing her to earn interest on this $2,000 and, if she wishes, to write checks against this amount. Because it takes time for Mary's paycheck to clear and thus for her bank to receive $2,000 in cash or credit from her employer's bank account, bank float is created. Mary's bank has implicitly lent $2,000 interest-free to Mary until her paycheck clears. If however, Mary's bank

Highlight 15.1	E. F. Hutton's Check Kiting

Trying to profit by a coordinated exchange of checks among bank accounts with insufficient funds is called kiting — and it is illegal. A desperate character might open checking accounts at three banks. A $50 check drawn on the first bank is used to pay for groceries. After a few days, a check drawn on a second bank is deposited in the first bank before the $50 grocery check shows up. After a few more days, a check drawn on a third bank is deposited in the second bank. Then, a few days later, a check drawn on the first bank is deposited in the third. And so it goes, running from bank to bank to avoid paying for groceries.

In 1983, the U.S. government began an investigation of allegations that the giant brokerage firm of E. F. Hutton (which has since been acquired by Shearson Lehman) had set up an elaborate overdraft system in the mid-1970s that generated millions of dollars in profits in the early 1980s. The government eventually estimated that E. F. Hutton's securities unit had made $4.35 billion in overdrafts at 400 banks around the country between July 1980 and February 1982, a period when interest rates topped 20 percent.

The officer of a small Massachusetts bank related the apparently typical procedure.* The local Hutton office would deposit a large check in the Massachusetts bank drawn on a bank in Phoenix or another distant city. Although these checks took several days to clear, "of course, we would credit the Hutton account right away." Hutton's New York office then wired this money from the Massachusetts bank to a money-market fund, where it could earn three or four days' worth of interest until it had to be wired to Phoenix to cover the original check.

> *I didn't realize they were engaged in such a grand, colossal scheme, or even something illegal. I thought it was aggressive cash management, where they were intentionally increasing the float in their favor. It never occurred to me that a major corporation would be involved in a check kite.*

Government investigators found one case in which E. F. Hutton officials wrote a check for $9.7 million on an account that had a balance of less than $3,500. A Hutton branch manager in Boulder, Colorado, testified that he had been subject to constant pressure from his superiors to overdraft accounts.†

In May 1985, E. F. Hutton's securities unit pleaded guilty to 2,000 felony counts of mail and wire fraud; in addition, it agreed to pay a $2 million fine, reimburse the government for $750,000 in legal expenses, and pay up to $8 million to the banks that it had defrauded. The government agreed not to prosecute any individual employees. Hutton also was fined $350,000 by Connecticut regulators and $65,000 by Massachusetts regulators. In addition, Hutton signed an agreement with the New York state attorney general to pay its New York customers in the future with checks to be drawn on New York banks instead of on California banks.

---

*"Locally, E. F. Hutton Isn't Talking," *Cape Cod Business Journal,* August 1985.
†Andy Pasztor, "House Panel: Ex-Hutton Chief Told of Overdrafts," *Wall Street Journal,* August 3, 1985.

imposes a waiting period and doesn't credit her for a $2,000 deposit until sometime after the check clears, then Mary is lending money interest free to her bank. The Fed now requires (with the exception of new accounts and large or questionable checks) that banks credit depositor accounts within one business day for local checks and four business days for other checks.

The Federal Reserve's check-clearing procedures create float for banks. Suppose you have a checking account in Ohio and go to Daytona Beach, Florida, for a vacation and you pay for a motel room there with a $100 check drawn on your Ohio bank. The motel deposits your check in a Daytona Beach bank. If the check had been drawn on the same bank in which it is deposited, it would have been cleared internally, with the bank simply crediting one account and debiting another. Because the check is drawn on another bank, the Daytona Beach bank will use a private clearinghouse or the Federal Reserve System to clear the check. To use the Federal Reserve System, the Daytona Beach bank sends your check to the district Federal Reserve Bank in Atlanta. From there, your check is sent to the Cleveland Federal Reserve Bank and on to your Ohio bank.

The Fed's check-clearing procedures can create float.

The Federal Reserve has a prearranged estimate of the time needed to deliver a check from a Reserve Bank to each bank in its district. This may be 0, 1, or 2 days. After this period has passed, the Daytona Beach bank is credited with $100 in reserves at the Atlanta Federal Reserve Bank. But $100 is not subtracted from the reserves of your Ohio bank until the bank actually receives your check and verifies its validity. Every day the check is delayed past the minimum period, two banks are credited with $100 in reserves, although the Fed has only $100. This is Federal Reserve float — an interest-free loan to banks from the Federal Reserve. (In Table 15.1, "deferred-availability cash items" are the checks that the Fed has received but not yet credited as bank reserves; "cash items in process of collection" are the checks that the Fed has not yet delivered and subtracted from bank reserves; and the difference is Federal Reserve float.) This $100 check will soon clear, but millions of new checks flow through the system daily. In 1979, the daily Federal Reserve float averaged $6.6 billion. With the 11.2 percent average federal funds rate that year, Federal Reserve float earned banks about $740 million in interest charges. Float can also cause fluctuations in bank reserves and the monetary base; for example, a snowstorm that causes a delay in the Fed's delivery of checks increases float, bank reserves, and the monetary base.

The 1980 banking deregulation laws directed the Federal Reserve to eliminate float or to begin charging banks interest on it. The Fed has subsequently reduced float by about 80 percent by improving its check-clearing procedures and revising its delivery estimates to reflect the average rather than the minimum time needed to deliver a check. The Fed charges interest on the remaining float by applying the federal-funds rate to an annual estimate of the size of the float and adding this cost to the amount it charges banks for its check-clearing services.

Formerly, banks could earn interest on Federal Reserve float when customers used paper checks. Probably the demise of this profitable opportunity will encourage the spread of electronically transferred funds, which have very little float.

THE MONETARY BASE, MONEY SUPPLY, AND INTERMEDIATION

Chapter 4 explained how banks are able to multiply deposits and create a money supply several times larger than the nation's monetary base. Checkable bank deposits can be used to carry out transactions by paying for goods, services, and assets. Deposit balances at financial intermediaries are matched on the asset side of their balance sheets by loans for the purchase of such things as cars, houses, and factories. Deposit intermediaries not only create deposits that can serve as money, but also create loans to finance spending.

Federal Reserve policies affect the size and use of the monetary base.

The Federal Reserve affects financial markets either through changes in the monetary base or through policies that affect the use of a given monetary base — either way, altering the amount of money available for lending, investing, and spending. For instance, when the Fed lends money through its discount window, this increases the monetary base; when the Fed lowers reserve requirements, this allows the monetary base to support a larger level of deposits and loans.

Easy-money policies make more funds available at lower interest rates.

The primary policy question for monetary authorities is easy money versus tight money. Easy-money policies make funds readily available and at lower interest rates, encouraging borrowing and spending, putting upward pressure on a nation's output and prices. Tight money has the opposite effects: higher interest rates, reduced borrowing, a contraction in spending, and restraint on inflation.

Monetary policies need not affect all sectors of the economy equally. A credit crunch may have little effect on defense contractors, but devastate the housing industry. The federal government can, if it wishes, pursue selective credit policies, such as giving low-cost loans to students or tax breaks to tobacco farmers. We will concentrate on three broad-based instruments of monetary policy: open-market operations, reserve requirements, and the discount rate.

OPEN-MARKET OPERATIONS

The Fed's purchases and sales of securities are called open-market operations.

Table 15.1 shows that the largest category of Fed assets is U.S. Treasury securities. The Fed's purchases and sales of securities are known as **open-market operations.** These transactions expand or contract the nation's monetary base and are, in practice, the predominant instrument of Fed monetary policy. We will look briefly at how these policies are implemented and at some of their consequences.

Securities Transactions

The Federal Reserve is able to use open-market operations to offset changes in the monetary base — for example, fluctuations that are caused by changes in U.S. Treasury deposits. The Fed can also use open-market operations to expand or contract the monetary base as part of a deliberate easing or tightening of credit conditions.

Open-market purchases increase the monetary base.

When the Fed purchases securities, it increases the monetary base; open-market sales contract the monetary base. Consider the details of an open-market purchase. Table 15.4 shows the T-accounts when the Fed purchases $100 million in Treasury securities from a bank and the bank leaves the sale proceeds deposited with a Federal Reserve Bank. There is a $100 million increase in bank reserves and in the monetary base.

If the Fed buys $100 million in Treasury securities from someone other than a bank, it pays for the securities with a Federal Reserve check. This check may be cashed, thereby increasing the amount of Federal Reserve notes in circulation, or it may be deposited in a bank and sent on to the Fed to be added to the bank's reserve account. Most likely, some of each will occur. In any case, the monetary base — currency outside banks plus bank reserves — will increase by $100 million.

The policy rule is very simple: The Fed buys securities when it wants to increase the monetary base and sells securities when it wants to reduce the monetary base. Such transactions ease or tighten financial markets. Open-market purchases expand the monetary base, either bank reserves or Federal Reserve notes, easing credit conditions. The purchase of securities increases bond prices (reducing interest rates), while the enlarged monetary base leads to more bank deposits and loans, expanding the money supply and credit. An open-market sale of securities has the opposite effects, reducing the monetary base and tightening financial markets. The sale of securities pushes their prices down and interest rates up; the contraction of the monetary base causes bank deposits and loans to shrink.

To the extent that various financial assets are good substitutes, open-market operations are a broadly based policy instrument with dispersed effects throughout financial markets. When Treasury-bill rates change, ripples are felt in the markets for bonds, loans, stock, and real assets.

The FOMC Directive

When the Federal Reserve System was established, open-market operations were not very well understood or considered to be very important. In the 1920s, open-market purchases were discovered and used, with ultimately ill effects, in an attempt to maintain the gold standard and Real Bills doctrine. As we saw in Chapter 12, it was thought that the inflow of European gold called for an expansion of the U.S. money supply, which could be directly accomplished by open-market purchases. In addition, the Fed wanted to buy Liberty Bonds from banks so that banks would hold commercial loans instead. The Fed soon learned

Table 15.4   The Fed Purchases Securities from a Private Bank

Private Bank

Assets		Liabilities
Deposits at Fed	+$100	
Treasury securities	−$100	

Federal Reserve

Assets		Liabilities	
Treasury securities	+$100	Bank reserves	+$100

that open-market operations are a fast and reliable way to ease or tighten financial markets. Today, they are the predominant monetary policy tool the Fed uses.

Before 1935, open-market transactions had been conducted by the individual district Reserve Banks with only informal coordination. The Banking Act of 1935 established the Federal Open Market Committee (FOMC) to plan and supervise open-market operations. Since it makes good sense to coordinate all monetary policy actions, a broad range of policy questions are now discussed and decided at the monthly FOMC meetings.

The monthly FOMC directive guides open-market operations.

Most policy actions are direct and specific: the discount rate is increased by a percentage point; reserve requirements on checking accounts are reduced by two percentage points. Open-market operations are, however, considerably fuzzier because, with imperfect foresight, the FOMC cannot spell out a precise daily plan for the coming month.

Instead, the FOMC issues a general directive describing its broad objectives. The structure of these directives and even much of their language vary little from month to month. As with State Department statements, it takes a trained eye to ferret out the slight nuances that reveal what it is that the FOMC is trying to say without actually saying it. Consider the following three paragraphs.

> *In light of the foregoing developments, it is the policy of the Federal Open Market Committee to foster financial conditions conducive to abatement of inflationary pressures, a sustainable rate of advance in economic activity, and continued progress toward equilibrium in the country's balance of payments. (October 1973)*

In light of the foregoing developments, it is the policy of the Federal Open Market Committee to foster financial conditions conducive to resisting inflationary pressures, supporting a resumption of real economic growth, and achieving equilibrium in the country's balance of payments. (March 1974)

In light of the foregoing developments, it is the policy of the Federal Open Market Committee to foster financial conditions conducive to stimulating economic recovery, while resisting inflationary pressures and working towards equilibrium in the country's balance of payments. (March 1975)

Any one of these statements in isolation would seem to be little more than a recitation of the virtues of motherhood, apple pie, and a stable economy. Taken together, they might appear to be only a monthly reaffirmation of these virtues. But experienced analysts correctly deduced a significant policy shift toward easy money.

In October 1973, on the eve of the 1974–1975 recession, inflation was of foremost concern to the FOMC (and was listed first among the three standard objectives). By March 1974, the recession was under way, with unemployment up sharply. The subtle shift in the directives from the "abatement" of inflation to "resisting" inflation, and from sustaining growth to "supporting a resumption" of growth, signaled an easing of monetary policy. The March 1974 paragraph was repeated verbatim through November 1974. Then, in December 1974 and January 1975, the phrase "cushioning recessionary tendencies" was inserted. In March 1975, economic recovery replaced inflation as the first of the three stated objectives. In late 1974 and early 1975 a credit crunch was eased, and interest rates tumbled sharply downward. The FOMC had indeed made a momentous decision, though it was reluctant to come right out and say it.

Now, admittedly, hindsight is a great help but, even with hindsight, it is not always easy to interpret Fed Policy. For example, in August 1980, *The Wall Street Journal* reported that financial markets were still puzzled by the Fed's announcement 10 months earlier that it was going to place "greater emphasis" on the supply of bank reserves,[1] a policy change that we will discuss in more detail in Chapter 18.

The Fed's open-market operations are carried out by the System's Account Manager, who is a vice-president of the Federal Reserve Bank of New York. The Account Manager trades securities over the counter through electronic links with 36 primary dealers, private firms allowed to trade directly with the Fed. When the Fed wants to make transactions, its Open Market Trading Desk notifies all 36 primary dealers virtually simultaneously and instructs them to submit their offers by a stated deadline. The Fed then accepts the best offers, with these securities debited or credited to the 12 Federal Reserve Banks, based on their shares of total Federal Reserve assets.

The Account Manager's general instructions come from a decoding of the most recent FOMC directive. This is coupled with a personal interpretation of financial market conditions and sifted through a daily telephone conference with two members of the FOMC. If, on a given day, financial markets seem tighter than desired, then the Account Manager makes open-market purchases, easing interest rates and increasing the monetary base. If there seems to be too much ease, then the Account Manager sells securities, firming up interest rates and shrinking the monetary base.

Dynamic and Defensive Transactions

Most open-market opera-
tions are defensive.

Most open-market operations, perhaps 80 percent to 90 percent, are defensive, made to offset short-term tremors in financial markets rather than to implement a policy change.[2] With daily fluctuations and aberrations in the economy, the Account Manager buys on some days and sells on others. Whether the Account Manager bought or sold on a particular day is consequently not a reliable guide to the overall thrust of monetary policy.

Many of the events that shake financial markets are easily anticipated. Other events surprise even the most knowledgeable market participants. Some events cause only small, almost insignificant blips in asset demands and supplies. Others threaten to become genuine crises.

The Account Manager often uses temporary security purchases, called repurchase agreements, to offset temporary financial disturbances. (Chapter 14 discussed how commercial banks borrow money from businesses using repurchase agreements.) In a Federal Reserve repurchase agreement, the Fed buys (or sells) securities to a primary dealer, who agrees to sell (or buy) them back at a set price on a certain date, usually within a week or two. Thus the securities are collateral for a short-term loan. The Fed uses repurchase agreements to cause an explicitly temporary expansion or contraction of the monetary base.

The public reliably increases its demand for cash before Christmas, Labor Day, Independence Day, and other holidays. Every other Wednesday, banks may need to borrow money to meet reserve requirements. Corporations predictably borrow money at the end of each quarter to pay taxes. The U.S. Treasury, large corporations, and foreign governments buy and sell large blocks of securities at irregular intervals. There are important seasonal variations in the cash needs of different parts of the country. Strikes, accidents, and bad weather can create temporary fluctuations in payment schedules and money demand. Rumors, hunches, and tea leaves lead powerful speculators to make staggering transactions. Some markets or agents can be flooded with funds or left high and dry.

Deposits and withdrawals from the Treasury's tax and loan accounts are another source of financial-market turbulence. The Treasury tries to synchronize its bill paying and withdrawals from its bank accounts, in order to avoid disrupting currency in circulation, bank reserves, and the monetary base. But there are inevitably misestimates and mistimings that disturb financial markets. As a consequence, every day the Fed's Account Manager tries to neutralize any dissynchronization in the Treasury's withdrawals and payments.

Federal Reserve float is another important source of daily fluctuations in the monetary base. Other events that disturb the Fed's balance sheet also cause the monetary base to fluctuate; for example, Treasury gold transactions, changes in

| **Does the Federal Deficit Increase the Money Supply?** | **Highlight 15.2** |

The President and Congress determine federal expenditures and tax rates. If expenditures exceed tax revenue, then the Treasury sells securities to make up the difference. Except for temporary lags between receipts and outlays, the monetary base is unaffected, since the money that the Treasury receives from its sales of securities is paid out again in its expenditures. It is the Federal Reserve that decides whether to increase or decrease the monetary base by purchasing or selling Treasury securities.

Three accounting identities allow us to see the relationship between federal deficits and monetary policy. The Treasury's budget constraint is

$$\frac{\text{Federal}}{\text{deficit}} = \frac{\text{Treasury}}{\text{bond sales}}$$

These bonds will be purchased either by the public or, through open-market operations, by the Fed.

$$\frac{\text{Treasury}}{\text{bond sales}} = \frac{\text{Increase in Treasury}}{\text{securities held by public}} + \frac{\text{Treasury securities}}{\text{purchased by Fed}}$$

The earlier discussion of the Fed's balance sheets showed that Federal Reserve purchases of securities leads to an equal increase in the monetary base:

$$\frac{\text{Treasury securities}}{\text{purchased by Fed}} = \frac{\text{Increase in monetary base}}{\text{from Fed purchases}}$$

Combining these three equations, we have the government's consolidated budget constraint, which simply states that the financing of the federal deficit must lead to additional Treasury securities held by the public or to an increase in the monetary base caused by the Fed's purchase of Treasury securities.

$$\frac{\text{Federal}}{\text{deficit}} = \frac{\text{Increase in Treasury}}{\text{securities held by public}} + \frac{\text{Increase in monetary base}}{\text{from Fed purchases}}$$

The consolidated government budget constraint is useful because it shows that government spending, taxation, bond sales, and monetary-base creation are interrelated. A federal deficit must implicitly be financed by an increase either in publicly held Treasury bonds or in the monetary base. To the extent that the deficit is financed by an increase in the monetary base (what is loosely called "printing money"), the deficit is said to have been **monetized**.

The consolidated government budget constraint can be misleading, though, in that it suggests that government policy is centralized when, in fact, the President, Congress, and the Federal Reserve Board each have considerable autonomy. In many countries, the treasury is allowed to print money and consequently decides how much of the government deficit is financed by money creation. In the United States, the Fed is a separate entity and makes its own decisions about purchasing and selling Treasury securities.

The Fed's decisions depend on its policy objectives and the state of the economy. Its decisions are affected by federal deficits only indirectly, to the extent that these deficits affect inflation, interest rates, unemployment, and other factors that matter to the Fed. In practice, during the 1980s, the federal deficit averaged about $150 billion a year and the annual increase in the monetary base was less than $15 billion. Thus, on average, the Fed monetized less than 10 percent of the annual federal deficit.

the amount of Treasury coins outstanding or in Treasury's holdings of Federal Reserve notes, or changes in discount-window loans.

For a given monetary base, shifts between bank reserves and currency outside banks cause changes in bank-created money. Other economic events cause fluctuations in monetary aggregates, interest rates, and other measures of financial-market conditions. Through it all, the Fed's Account Manager buys and sells securities, trying to smooth out the air pockets while keeping financial markets on whatever course the Open Market Committee has charted. In the next chapter, we will look at how the Open Market Committee chooses a monetary course.

RESERVE REQUIREMENTS

Deposit intermediaries can meet the Fed's reserve requirements with vault cash or deposits in Federal Reserve banks.

The second of the Fed's three primary policy tools is reserve requirements. Within limits established by Congress, the Federal Reserve Board sets **reserve requirements** for deposit intermediaries, mandating that they hold noninterest-bearing reserves (either vault cash or deposits in Federal Reserve Banks) equal to a specified fraction of their deposits. Ninety percent of all banks use vault cash to meet their reserve requirements, but the 10 percent which maintain deposits at Federal Reserve Banks account for 75 percent of all bank deposits.

Required reserves are monitored every two weeks.

Compliance with the Fed's reserve requirements is monitored every two weeks, as shown in Figure 15.1. Each maintenance period begins on a Thursday and ends on a Wednesday, using the institution's average daily deposits with Federal Reserve banks over this two-week period. The average daily balances in transaction accounts (also called checkable accounts) are calculated over a similar two-week period, ending two days earlier, on a Monday. Other reservable liabilities and the bank's vault cash are calculated over a two-week period ending on a Monday four weeks earlier.

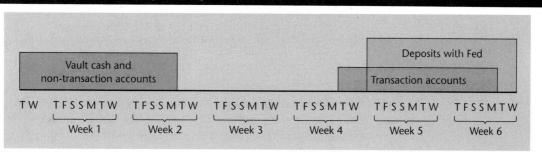

Figure 15.1 **The Timing of Required and Actual Reserve Calculations**

Reserve deficiencies or excesses of up to 2 percent of required reserves can be carried over to the next two-week maintenance period. If, after allowing for these carry-forward provisions, the bank still has a reserve deficiency, it is charged an interest rate equal to the Fed's discount rate plus a 2-percentage-point penalty on the amount of the deficiency until it is corrected.

The accounting lags in monitoring reserves allow deposit institutions and the Fed time to compile information on actual and required reserves so that they can better anticipate and meet reserve requirements. Institutions that turn out to have reserve deficiencies at the end of the maintenance period can borrow funds overnight from institutions with surplus reserves through the federal-funds market or else from the Federal Reserve through its discount window. Every other Wednesday is consequently a potentially hectic day in financial markets as banks scramble to obtain reserves to meet reserve requirements.

Reserve-Requirement Levels

Historically, the Fed's reserve requirements applied only to banks that chose to be members of the Federal Reserve system. Up until 1935, reserve requirements were set by Congress and seldom changed. The Banking Act of 1935 gave the Federal Reserve Board the authority to vary these requirements within broad limits specified by Congress, and the Fed began using reserve requirements to ease or to tighten financial markets. The landmark banking legislation of 1980 ordered the phasing in of the following reserve requirements for all depository institutions:

1. Three percent on the first $25 million of transaction-account balances (with that initial $25 million figure indexed to change annually by 80 percent of the percentage change in aggregate transaction balances).
2. Twelve percent on an institution's transaction-account balances above $25 million (this can be adjusted within the range 8 percent to 14 percent).
3. Three percent on nonpersonal time deposits (this can be adjusted within the range 0 percent to 9 percent). Nonpersonal deposits are those in which

a beneficial interest is held by a depositor, such as a corporation, that is not a natural person.

4. Three percent on Eurocurrency liabilities.

In addition, the Fed can require interest-earning supplemental reserves of up to 4 percent of transaction-account balances. The interest rate paid on these supplemental reserves can be no higher than the Fed's rate of return on its asset portfolio. The Garn-St Germain Act of 1982 further specified that the first $2 million of reservable liabilities subject to a 3-percent reserve requirement are exempt from reserve requirements (with the $2 million figure increased annually by 80 percent of the percentage change in aggregate reservable liabilities). Money-market deposit accounts (MMDAs) allowing up to six transfers per month by check, telephone, or automatic bill paying, with no more than three transfers by check, are considered savings accounts and are subject to time-deposit reserve requirements.

The most important reserve requirement is a 12-percent reserve requirement on transaction accounts.

The Fed's reserve requirements in January 1990 are shown in Table 15.5. An oversimplified approximation is that, except for some exemptions for small institutions, there is essentially a 12-percent reserve requirement on transaction accounts and virtually no reserve requirements on other accounts.

The Effect on Bank Profits

Reserve requirements reduce bank income by preventing banks from profitably investing these idle reserves. Suppose, for example, that a bank pays 5 percent annual interest on deposits subject to a 12-percent reserve requirement. On $100 in deposits, the bank must hold $12 in reserves and can invest $88. Since it must pay 5%($100) = $5 to obtain $88 in investable funds, it is effectively paying an interest rate of

$$\text{Effective cost of funds} = \frac{\$5}{\$88} = 0.0568(5.68\%)$$

Reserve requirements raise banks' effective cost of funds.

The 12-percent reserve requirement raises the effective cost of funds from 5 percent to 5.68 percent, in that the bank must earn at least 5.68 percent interest on the $88 that it is allowed to invest in order to pay 5 percent interest on the $100 deposit.

In general, if the deposit rate is R and the reserve requirement is k, then the effective cost of funds is given by

$$\text{Effective cost of funds} = \frac{R}{1 - k} \tag{5}$$

Some illustrative examples are shown in Table 15.6.

Before 1980, Federal Reserve member banks were at a competitive disadvantage compared to nonmember banks because their relatively high reserve requirements forced them to hold a sizable fraction of their assets as idle reserves. The 1980 banking legislation retained unprofitable reserve requirements but applied them equally to all depository institutions.

Table 15.5 Reserve Requirements at Depository Institutions, January 1990	
Type of Deposit	**Reserve Requirement**
Transaction accounts	
$0 million to $41.5 million*	3%
More than $41.5 million	12%
Nonpersonal time deposits	
Less than 1½ years*	3%
1½ years or more	0%
Eurocurrency liabilities	
All types*	3%

*The first $3.4 million of liabilities subject to 3-percent reserve requirements are exempt from reserve requirements.

For about one hundred years, from 1864 to 1966, reserve requirements depended on a bank's geographic location, with banks in large cities subject to higher reserve requirements than country banks. There is considerable arbitrariness in defining and measuring cities in a nation with suburbs, exurbs, and metroplexes, particularly when customers can bank by mail or phone. Between 1966 and 1972, reserve requirements were modified to reflect a bank's size as well as its geographic location. In 1972, geography was eliminated as a criterion. In 1980, the next logical step was taken, erasing the distinctions between member and nonmember banks and between banks and other deposit institutions.

A Liquidity Pool

Many observers believe that reserve requirements are intended to ensure bank liquidity. If so, then a policy of low reserve requirements for country banks seems backwards since, historically, country banks were most often recklessly managed and most often failed. They were the ones who most needed tough supervision and liquid assets.

Geographic reserve requirements were, in fact, the result of political compromise. Rural states were suspicious of the Eastern establishment and of a central banking authority. To win their support for the national banking system established during the Civil War, and later for the Federal Reserve System, Congress gave country banks low reserve requirements.

In practice, reserve requirements have little effect on the liquidity of individual banks. Consider a bank subject to 5-percent reserve requirements with the balance sheets shown in Panel (a) of Table 15.7. After satisfying its reserve requirements, the bank has $190 million in available funds, of which it invests 10 percent in liquid assets and the remaining 90 percent in illiquid assets. Panel

Required reserves have little effect on a bank's liquidity.

Table 15.6 Effective Cost of Funds, Taking into Account a 12-Percent Reserve Requirement

Deposit Rate	Effective Rate
5.00	5.68
7.00	7.95
9.00	10.23
11.00	12.50
13.00	14.77
15.00	17.05

Table 15.7 The Effect of a Deposit Withdrawal on Required Reserves and Liquid Assets

(a) Before Withdrawal

Assets		Liabilities	
Required reserves	$ 10,000,000	Deposits	$200,000,000
Liquid assets	19,000,000		
Illiquid assets	171,000,000		
Total	$200,000,000		$200,000,000

(b) After $20,000,000 Withdrawal

Assets		Liabilities	
Required reserves	$ 9,000,000	Deposits	$180,000,000
Liquid assets	0		
Illiquid assets	171,000,000		
Total	$180,000,000		$180,000,000

(b) shows the consequences of a $20 million decline in deposits. Since deposits have fallen by 10 percent, so have required reserves, from $10 million to $9 million. Only $1 million of the $20 million reduction in deposits can be paid out of required reserves; the remaining $19 million must come out of other assets — here, exhausting liquid assets.

Notice that a 10-percent decline in deposits causes a 10-percent decline in required reserves and a 10-percent decline in available funds other than required reserves. This is true regardless of the size of the reserve requirements. If there is a danger that deposits may drop by 10 percent, then 10 percent of available funds should be near at hand. Reserve requirements determine the amount of funds available for a bank to invest, but do not relieve it of the need to invest some of these funds in liquid assets.

Paradoxically, reserve requirements do enhance the liquidity of the banking system as a whole by providing a reservoir of funds that the Fed can tap in a liquidity crisis by reducing reserve requirements. For an individual bank, reserve requirements are an unprofitable burden, an implicit tax on earnings that is paid by the foregone interest on idle reserves. Required reserves do not provide liquidity or safety for an individual bank, which must take reserve requirements as fixed. For the banking system as a whole, required reserves are an emergency fund that can be mobilized by the Fed when there is a large withdrawal of deposits from the entire system.

A Powerful Tool

Reserve requirements are a powerful instrument of monetary policy. In a liquidity crisis, they offer an avenue for maintaining bank solvency. In noncrisis situations, they can be used to ease or tighten financial markets. If the Fed reduces reserve requirements, almost all of the freed reserves are invested by banks, easing credit conditions and stimulating the economy. If the Fed raises reserve requirements, banks curtail their lending and the economy contracts.

An increase in reserve requirements is a powerful tight-money policy.

In January 1990, required reserves totaled about $60 billion. A 10-percent reduction in reserve requirements (consisting primarily of a reduction in reserve requirements on transaction accounts from 12 percent to 10.8 percent) would increase the funds available to banks and other deposit intermediaries by $6 billion. Almost all of these newly freed reserves would be invested by banks, lent to borrowers, and recirculated through banks — just as if the Fed had increased the monetary base by $6 billion. (During the years 1986–1989, the monetary base increased by an average of about $15 billion a year.)

The deposit-multiplier model developed in Chapter 4 can be used to estimate the impact of reserve requirements on aggregate deposits. The basic model was given by Equation 6 in Chapter 4:

The deposit-multiplier model can be used to estimate the effect of reserve requirements on aggregate deposits.

$$D = \left(\frac{1}{\alpha + \beta}\right) B \tag{6}$$

where D is deposits, B is the monetary base, α is ratio of bank reserves to deposits (determined by reserve requirements and bank decisions to hold excess reserves), and β is the ratio of currency outside banks to deposits.

To illustrate the computations, we'll use the following numbers, which are approximately equal to those prevailing in January 1990:

$$D = \$3,000 \text{ billion}$$
$$B = \$300 \text{ billion}$$
$$\alpha = 0.02$$
$$\beta = 0.08$$

The deposit multiplier is 10.

$$D = \left(\frac{1}{0.02 + 0.08}\right)(\$300 \text{ billion})$$

$$= (10)(\$300 \text{ billion})$$

$$= \$3{,}000 \text{ billion}$$

The $60 billion in reserves held by banks and other deposit institutions in January 1990 was almost entirely required reserves; to simplify matters, we will assume that there are no excess reserves at all. This $60 billion in required reserves was only 2 percent of deposits, because deposit intermediaries had far more time and savings accounts subject to 0-percent or 3-percent reserve requirements than transaction accounts subject to 12-percent reserve requirements.

If reserve requirements are reduced by 10 percent (that is, from 12 percent to 10.8 percent) on checking accounts, so that α declines from 0.020 to 0.018, and there is no change in β, the deposit multiplier increases from 10 to

$$\frac{1}{0.018 + 0.08} = 10.20$$

and the level of deposits increases by $61 billion, to

$$D = \left(\frac{1}{0.018 + 0.08}\right)(\$300 \text{ billion})$$

$$= \$3{,}061 \text{ billion}$$

Another way to estimate the increase in deposits resulting from a reduction in reserve requirements is to note that a 10-percent reduction in reserve requirements reduces required reserves by 10%($60 billion) = $6 billion, effectively increasing the monetary base that is available for lending and depositing by $6 billion. Applying the initial deposit multiplier of 10, just as if there had been a $6 billion increase in the monetary base, gives a predicted deposit expansion of

(Change in deposits) = (Deposit multiplier)(Change in monetary base)
$$= 10(\$6 \text{ billion})$$
$$= \$60 \text{ billion}$$

which differs slightly from the actual value of $61 billion because the application of the deposit multiplier in this way is a linear approximation of a nonlinear equation.

Table 15.8 shows the effects of this decrease in reserve requirements on aggregate deposits, reserves, and bank investments. The only investments shown are those funded by deposits; other assets and liabilities are omitted. The deposit-multiplier model tells us that bank deposits increase from $3,000 billion to $3,061 billion. Required reserves decline from $60 billion to 0.018($3,061 billion) = $55 billion. Aggregate bank investments funded by deposits consequently increase by $66 billion — of which $5 billion comes from the decline

Table 15.8 The Effect of a Reduction in Reserve Requirements on Bank Deposits, Reserves, and Investments (billions of dollars)

(a) Before Decrease in Reserve Requirements

Assets		Liabilities	
Required reserves	$ 60	Deposits	$3,000
Investments	2,940		
Total	$3,000		$3,000

(b) After Decrease in Reserve Requirements

Assets		Liabilities	
Required reserves	$ 55	Deposits	$3,061
Investments	3,006		
Total	$3,061		$3,061

in required reserves and $61 billion comes from the consequent increase in deposits.

The important policy conclusion is that a seemingly slight reduction in reserve requirements can have a substantial effect on bank deposits and on the bank loans and other investments financed by these deposits. An increase in reserve requirements is an equally strong depressant. Raising reserve requirements by 10 percent would immobilize $6 billion in bank funds, almost all of which would come from curtailed bank investments. If there were no change in β (the ratio of currency outside banks to deposits), deposits would shrink by approximately $60 billion and bank loans and other investments would contract by more than $60 billion.

A Fed change in reserve requirements is widely publicized and usually interpreted as dramatic evidence of a change in monetary policy. Reserve-requirement changes are so powerful that they must be implemented with extreme caution. Frequent changes would be too disruptive to bank portfolio management. Between 1950 and 1980, reserve requirements were changed about once a year, usually by small amounts and often accompanied by cushioning changes in other policy instruments. As of January 1990, the only changes that were made in reserve requirements since 1980 had been a reduction between November 1980 and October 1983 in the maturity of nonpersonal time deposits subject to a 3-percent reserve requirement (from 4 years to 1½ years) and the automatic annual adjustment of the level of transaction accounts subject to a 3-percent reserve requirement and of the level of reservable liabilities exempt from reserve requirements.

Reserve requirements are changed infrequently and usually by small amounts.

| Highlight 15.3 | The Fed Learns from a Mistake |

In the mid-1930s, banks held very large amounts of excess reserves because
there were few attractive investment opportunities and they were fearful of
bank runs. The Federal Reserve was concerned because these reserves gave
banks flexibility, which weakened the Fed's control over the money supply;
for example, a sudden perceived improvement in the economy might have
persuaded banks to invest their excess reserves, thereby expanding bank
deposits and lending as described by the deposit-multiplier model. The
Fed thought that it could eliminate bank excess reserves and curtail bank
flexibility by raising reserve requirements, and consequently doubled requirements between August 1936 and May 1937.

Their reasoning was fallacious. The Fed assumed that banks are concerned solely with total reserves relative to deposits and do not care whether
these reserves are required or excess. This assumption is wrong, because
excess reserves can be fully used to meet deposit withdrawals or to meet
loan demands, while required reserves cannot. Banks consequently do care
about excess reserves relative to available funds. When reserve requirements
were increased in 1936 and 1937, banks maintained their large holdings
of excess reserves by curtailing investments — a policy that staggered
financial markets and precipitated a sharp recession. The Fed was subsequently forced to reduce reserve requirements.

What Should Be Included?

Economists and policymakers have long wrestled with the question of which
financial institutions and which liabilities should be subject to reserve requirements. We can apply these three principles:

1. High reserve requirements tend to increase the Fed's control over bank-
   deposit multiplication.
2. Required reserves are a pool of funds that can be tapped in a liquidity crisis.
3. Required reserves reduce the profits of institutions compelled to hold them.

Points 2 and 3 have already been discussed. Point 1 can be illustrated by the
extreme case of 100-percent reserves. Because reserves would equal deposits, the
monetary base, which consists of currency outside banks plus bank reserves,
would equal currency outside banks plus deposits. Thus, with 100-percent
reserves, the Fed would have complete control over currency plus aggregate
deposits, though not over the composition of deposits.

The question of which institutions should be subject to reserve requirements
has been debated for decades. In the 1970s, nationally chartered banks complained bitterly about the light reserve requirements on state-chartered banks

that did not belong to the Federal Reserve System. Member banks were subject to reserve requirements on all time and savings accounts, and the reserve requirements on checking accounts began at 7 percent and reached 16¼ percent when the bank's deposits exceeded $400 million. State-chartered banks had substantially lower reserve requirements. In addition, state-chartered banks in thirty states were allowed to use interest-earning assets to meet at least some of their reserve requirements; 36 states had no periodic monitoring of reserves; and 22 had no financial penalties for reserve deficiencies.[3] Some national banks made their feelings known by converting to state charters and dropping their Federal Reserve memberships.

> Before 1980, state-chartered banks had relatively light reserve requirements.

Banks also protested the light reserve requirements on other deposit intermediaries, such as savings-and-loan associations, and the absence of reserve requirements on nondeposit intermediaries. Banks were particularly annoyed by the spectacular growth of money-market funds, which offer extremely liquid, check-like accounts not subject to reserve requirements. In the 1970s, money-market funds lured hundreds of billions of dollars in deposits out of banks and forced banks to pay competitive interest rates (when not constrained by Regulation Q) to avoid losing even more deposits. Partly in response to bank complaints, the Fed imposed temporary reserve requirements on money-market funds in 1980 as part of a broad credit-tightening policy.

The 1980 Monetary Control Act mandates uniform reserve requirements on all deposit intermediaries, effectively reducing reserve requirements on banks that are members of the Federal Reserve System and raising requirements on nonmember banks and other deposit institutions. By eliminating reserve requirements on personal time and savings deposits, the Monetary Control Act also put banks and money-market funds on a proverbial level playing field. Bank transaction accounts are still subject to 12-percent reserve requirements, but this is largely offset by the fact that these accounts allow unrestricted checking,

There remains the issue of which liabilities should be subject to reserve requirements. The first principle enumerated above implies that the Fed should impose reserve requirements on all liabilities that it wishes to control. But with many liability candidates and an agnostic view that no particular monetary aggregate is all-important, Principle 1 offers little reason for discriminating among liabilities.

The second principle (an emergency liquidity pool) is also ambiguous. It could be argued that financial intermediaries need pools of reserves to provide protection in liquidity crises and that there should be stiffer reserve requirements on more volatile liabilities. However, it is difficult to assess the relative volatility of liabilities, and the danger of a liquidity crisis also depends on the liquidity of assets and the availability of other sources of funds. For example, volatile deposits are less worrisome when an institution can readily borrow elsewhere (as with banks) or when assets can be easily sold (as with money-market funds). In addition, the Fed can quell liquidity crises in more direct ways, such as timely loans. It is more logical to ensure lending arrangements during a crisis than to rely on high reserve requirements.

| Highlight 15.4 | **Using Liability Management to Evade Reserve Requirements** |

From a bank's standpoint, the lower the reserve requirements, the better. Banks have an incentive to raise funds through liabilities with low reserve requirements, and this encouragement inspired many innovations in bank liability management — and responses by the Federal Reserve. For example, Eurodollars were initially free of reserve requirements, and this feature enhanced their appeal in the mid-1960s. In 1969, the Fed imposed a 10-percent reserve requirement on new Eurodollar borrowing; in 1970, it raised this reserve requirement to 20 percent, successfully dampening the enthusiasm for Eurodollar loans. In subsequent years, Eurodollar reserve requirements were extended to average (rather than marginal) borrowings and substantially reduced.

Similarly, the formation of bank holding companies was encouraged by the absence of reserve requirements on debts issued by the holding company. In 1970, the Fed imposed a 5-percent reserve requirement on commercial paper issued by bank holding companies. In October 1979, the Fed put 8-percent reserve requirements on Federal Funds purchases, repurchase agreements, and even asset sales to foreign branches, and announced that it would extend reserve requirements to all liability management innovations by banks. The Fed withdrew this threat after passage of the 1980 Monetary Control Act and, today, only transaction accounts, Eurocurrency deposits, and nonpersonal time deposits of more than 1½ years are subject to reserve requirements.

The third principle recognizes that those liabilities subject to light reserve requirements are favored over those subject to burdensome requirements. The 1980 Monetary Control Act treats all depository institutions equally, but within deposit institutions, some liabilities are encouraged and others discouraged. An easy way of equalizing reserve requirements is to eliminate them altogether, and this has, in fact, been the long-run trend.

THE DISCOUNT WINDOW

Deposit intermediaries borrow from the Fed through its discount window.

Now we will look at the third of the Fed's three primary policy tools. The Federal Reserve lends money to deposit intermediaries through its **discount window**; the **discount rate** is the interest rate charged on these loans. Before the 1980 Monetary Control Act, with a brief exception in 1966, the discount window was open only to member banks, and bankers generally considered the discount window to be the primary advantage of Federal Reserve membership.[4]

When a bank borrows from the Fed, bank reserves and the monetary base are increased (see if you can draw up the T-accounts). The Fed may be able to anticipate some of this discount-window borrowing — for example, to meet reserve requirements every other Wednesday. In other cases, the borrowing may be caused by an unanticipated emergency.

When the Federal Reserve was created in 1913, it was intended that the Fed would be a reliable lender of last resort, using the discount window to avert bank runs by providing cash to temporarily illiquid banks. There was also some thought that discount lending could be used to adjust the nation's money supply to meet seasonal needs, particularly those arising from farming. The Federal Reserve Banks soon learned that the discount window can be used to manipulate the money supply for other purposes, such as financing government spending during World War I and keeping the money supply proportional to gold holdings. On the other hand, the Federal Reserve Banks were reluctant to lend money to unsound banks — those that needed funds to keep open. Thus the early use of the discount window was primarily to regulate the nation's money supply rather than to avert bank runs.

An increase in the discount rate discourages borrowing from the Federal Reserve and represents a tightening of monetary policy. When bank borrowing declines, fewer funds are available for lending and less money is in circulation, putting upward pressure on loan rates and on interest rates for substitute assets. To raise money, banks may sell some of their assets and use certificates of deposit, repurchase agreements, and federal funds, putting upward pressure on these interest rates, too. The repercussions of diminished borrowing from the Fed affect all bank assets and liabilities and virtually all financial markets.

> An increase in the discount rate tightens financial markets.

A decrease in the discount rate is an easy-money policy; it makes funds available for a wide variety of purposes and puts downward pressure on virtually all interest rates. In some extreme situations, such as the Great Depression, a lowering of discount rates may have little effect on economic activity. The Federal Reserve may make funds more easily available to banks, and yet banks may be reluctant to borrow if they do not see attractive lending opportunities: you can lead a horse to water, but you can't make it drink.

Short-Term Liquidity

In recent years, the discount window has been supplanted by open-market operations as the Fed's primary means of regulating the nation's money supply. The discount window is now used mainly as a safety valve to meet the temporary liquidity needs of individual banks.

Deposit institutions must calculate and satisfy reserve requirements every two weeks. If an institution's reserves happen to be inadequate, then it can temporarily borrow through the Fed's discount window to make up the difference, an action that is less disruptive (and expensive) than forcing the deficient bank to sell some of its securities.

Highlight 15.5 | **The Day the Stock Market Almost Disintegrated**

Chapter 10 recounted the stock-market crash of October 19, 1987, a day dubbed Black Monday when 604 million shares were traded on the New York Stock Exchange, the Dow Industrial Average fell 508 points (23 percent), and the aggregate market value of stocks fell by about $500 billion.

The next day, Terrible Tuesday, the stock market came close to a complete collapse. Many traders were drained of capital, and several large investment houses were rumored to have been bankrupted by the previous day's drop in stock prices. Banks were understandably wary of lending money to firms that might soon declare bankruptcy. Without cash or credit, potential buyers were far outnumbered by anxious sellers. The stock exchanges temporarily suspended trading on Tuesday in even the best-known stocks, including IBM for two hours and Merck for four hours.

Some observers blamed the Monday crash on excessively loose monetary policies and urged the Fed to reduce the money supply.* However, Alan Greenspan, recently appointed Chair of the Fed, was fearful of a wave of bankruptcies and of a complete loss of confidence in financial markets. People would be much less likely to invest in securities if they could not be certain of a reasonably efficient market in which securities can be sold quickly at a fair price. Before the stock market opened Tuesday, Greenspan called a press conference and announced the Fed's "readiness to serve as a source of liquidity to support the economic and financial system." During the day, the Fed pressured large banks to lend money to securities firms and promised to finance this lending with virtually unlimited discount-window loans. The ten largest New York banks lent a total of $5.5 billion to securities firms that week. After seesawing wildly, the Dow closed up 102 points on Terrible Tuesday and up another 187 points the next day. A financial collapse was averted, though memories of Black Monday and Terrible Tuesday have lingered for years,.

Felix Rohatyn, an experienced financier, said later that "Tuesday was the most dangerous day we had in 50 years. I think we came within an hour of the disintegration of the stock market."† Alan Greenspan deserves much of the credit for saving the market.

---

*Victor A. Canto and Arthur B. Laffer, "Monetary Policy Caused the Crash: Not Tight Enough," *Wall Street Journal,* October 22, 1987; also see the discussion in Paul R. Krugman, "Can We Avert the Next Financial Crisis," *Los Angeles Times,* October 29, 1989.

†Felix Rohatyn, quoted in James B. Stewart and Daniel Hertzberg, "How the Stock Market Almost Disintegrated a Day after the Crash," *Wall Street Journal,* November 20, 1987.

The discount window is also made available in emergencies. In June 1970, Penn Central, a large railroad thought to be conservatively managed, declared bankruptcy and defaulted on its loans. Many firms subsequently had great difficulty selling commercial paper to nervous investors and turned to their banks for help. The Fed supplied the funds to stop a corporate financial crisis by allowing these banks special discount-window loans. (It also suspended Regulation Q rate ceilings on some large certificates of deposit and in August 1970 it lowered reserve requirements.)

Similarly, when Franklin National Bank was on the verge of bankruptcy in 1974, it was allowed to borrow through the Fed's discount window until a shotgun merger could be consummated. The Continental Illinois collapse in 1985 (discussed in Chapter 11) and the stock-market crash of October 1987 were both mitigated by discount-window loans.

Since 1973, the Federal Reserve has allowed seasonal discount-window borrowing — for example, letting small banks in farming or resort areas meet their seasonal liquidity needs through the discount window. This seasonal borrowing is less expensive and disruptive than if the bank holds excess cash all year or sells bonds every busy season. Thus the Fed uses the discount window to offset temporary turbulence in financial markets rather than as a tool for implementing a general, longer-lasting easing or tightening of financial markets.

Misuse of the Discount Window

Populist politicians have often criticized the Federal Reserve and its discount window as a bank subsidy. If the discount rate charged banks is significantly below the rate of return that deposit institutions can earn on their investments, then the discount window increases bank profits by allowing them to borrow inexpensively. Another recurring criticism of the discount window is that it encourages banks to be illiquid. If the Federal Reserve can be counted on to bail banks out of liquidity crises, then there is little incentive to avoid such crises. Instead, banks will make excessively illiquid, high-yielding loans and borrow from the Federal Reserve whenever necessary. This is another of those seemingly permanent philosophical debates: does government assistance sap the self-reliance of its citizens? The differing views were illustrated by this joke told during the 1980 presidential election campaign:

> *What's the difference between a conservative and a liberal? If a man is drowning, the conservative will throw a life preserver 10 feet from the man and tell him, "Swim for it, it will do you good." The liberal, on the other hand, will throw the drowning man a wad of money and tell him to go buy himself a boat.*

The Federal Reserve employs a number of strategies to discourage excessive reliance on the discount window. When a bank uses the discount window repeatedly, it is reminded that the Fed does not have to lend money to a bank. The discount window is "a privilege, not a right," and this privilege must not be abused. In 1977, the Fed pointedly told some large banks to stop using the

The Fed's discount window is a privilege, not a right.

discount window unless there really were no good alternatives. In less drastic circumstances, the Fed discourages discount borrowing with fines, public criticism, and frequent, thorough audits (on the presumption that excessive borrowing suggests financial difficulties or mismanagement). Sometimes, the Fed adopts a formal rule: for example, that a bank is abusing the discount window if it borrows in 7 weeks of a 13-week period.

Another strategy to discourage excessive reliance on the discount window is to set the discount rate high enough to make borrowing truly a last resort rather than a regular, inexpensive source of funds. Since 1972, the Bank of England has followed a policy of setting the discount rate half a percentage point above the interest rate on short-term government securities. In recent years, the Federal Reserve has followed a similar, though less mechanical, policy. When short-term market-interest rates rise substantially, the Fed raises its discount rate to discourage banks from borrowing from the Fed at low interest rates for reinvestment at high interest rates. When market-interest rates fall, the Fed reduces the discount rate to avoid penalizing banks that have legitimate liquidity needs. With these semiautomatic adjustments, the discount rate has become a largely passive reflection of monetary conditions rather than an active tool for changing the money supply and interest rates.

Since 1986, the Fed has put each bank's discount-window borrowing into one of these three categories:

1. *Adjustment credit:* short-term, temporary loans to help depository institutions meet needs for funds that cannot be met through reasonable alternative sources.
2. *Seasonal credit:* temporary loans to smaller depository institutions to meet regular seasonal needs that cannot be met through special industry lenders.
3. *Extended credit:* loans to an institution in exceptional circumstances or experiencing difficulties adjusting to changing market conditions over a longer period of time.

The Fed lends money for adjustment, seasonal, and extended credit.

In 1985, 1986, and 1987, the discount rate on seasonal credit was set at a half percentage point above the rate on adjustment credit; in 1988, 1989, and 1990, this half-point surcharge was removed. The discount rate for the first 30 days of extended credit is equal to the discount rate on adjustment credit plus a minimum of half a percentage point after 30 days. In January 1990, for instance, the discount rate was 7 percent for adjustment credit, seasonal credit, and the first 30 days of extended credit; extended credit beyond 30 days was charged 9.2 percent, a 2.2-percent surcharge over the basic discount rate.

Figure 15.2 compares the Federal Reserve discount rate (before surcharges) with the Treasury-bill rate and the federal-funds rate. In recent years, changes in market-interest rates have typically preceded changes in the discount rate. Figure 15.3 shows excess reserves and discount-window borrowing. Comparison of these two figures reveals that use of the discount window picks up when market rates rise above the discount rate. Despite administrative reprimands, some profiteering apparently does go on; however, the fact that borrowings are

Figure 15.2 The Discount Rate, Federal Funds Rate, and Three-Month Treasury-Bill Rate

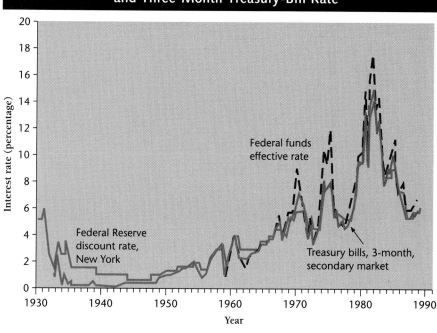

source: Federal Reserve *Historical Chart Book*, 1990.

relatively small in the face of substantial interest-rate differentials indicates that the Fed is largely successful in discouraging abuse of the discount window.

Policy Signals

Market-interest rates fluctuate continuously, while the Fed changes the discount rate infrequently, causing the gaps between market rates and the discount rate to widen and narrow. Many financial-market participants believe that these fluctuations provide useful information about the Fed's monetary-policy objectives. If market rates rise and the Fed promptly raises the discount rate, this action may be interpreted as a signal that the Fed is committed to a tight-money policy, since the increase in the discount rate suggests that the Fed expects interest rates to remain high or to go even higher.

If, on the other hand, market rates rise and the Fed does not raise its discount rate, this might be interpreted as a signal that the Fed expects the increase in interest rates to be temporary — perhaps because it will use some of its monetary policies to bring interest rates back down. Analogous interpretations can be affixed to a reduction in the discount rate, or a failure to reduce it, when market rates fall.

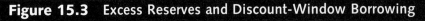

Figure 15.3 Excess Reserves and Discount-Window Borrowing

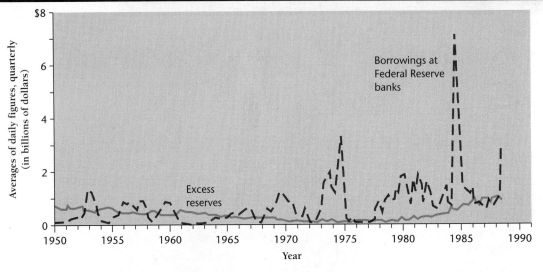

source: Federal Reserve *Historical Chart Book*, 1990.

Sometimes the announce-
ment of a policy change is
more important than the
policy itself.

Because the announcement of a change in the discount rate conveys information about Federal Reserve objectives, this is called the **announcement effect**:
the policy change, by itself, is not very important, but its announcement signals
intentions that are likely to be carried out in other ways. In recent years, discount-
rate changes have been more signal than substance. Changes in discount rates
are seldom large enough to affect financial markets very much. But as a perceived
policy signal, an unexpected change in the discount rate (or the absence of a
change) sometimes sends tremors through financial markets.

SUMMARY

The Fed can use Federal Reserve notes to buy assets or pay debts, recording
these notes on the liability side of its balance sheets. A small amount of Federal
Reserve notes are held by the U.S. Treasury, considerably more are in bank
vaults, and the bulk are held by the public. An open-market purchase of securities
by the Fed enlarges the monetary base, either through bank reserves or Federal
Reserve notes, easing credit conditions: bond prices rise, interest rates fall, and
bank deposits and loans expand. A Fed open market sale of securities has the
opposite effects, reducing the monetary base and tightening financial markets:
bond prices fall, interest rates increase, and bank deposits and loans contract.

The Fed uses open-market operations not only to implement policy changes,
but also to stabilize financial markets, offsetting daily fluctuations in bank reserves

and the monetary base caused by U.S. Treasury receipts and outlays, Federal Reserve float, and other economic events.

The most important reserve requirement today is 12 percent on transaction accounts (above a modest threshold), which depository institutions can meet with either vault cash or deposits with the Federal Reserve. Reserve requirements reduce bank income because these idle reserves cannot be profitably invested. An increase in reserve requirements is a very powerful tight-money policy; a reduction in reserve requirements eases credit conditions.

The Federal Reserve lends money to deposit intermediaries for adjustment, seasonal, and extended credit through its discount window. Deposit institutions are discouraged from borrowing what the Fed considers to be excessive amounts by the imposition of discount-rate surcharges, the threat of closer regulatory scrutiny and, in extreme cases, loss of access to the discount window.

An increase in the discount rate tightens financial markets; a reduction makes credit more readily available. In recent years, the Fed has not used the discount rate as a primary monetary-policy instrument to ease or tighten financial markets, but has instead kept the discount rate roughly aligned with market rates of interest, using the discount window to provide temporary liquidity during run-of-the-mill turbulence and extraordinary crises. Thus the Fed does not change the discount rate in order to cause changes in market-interest rates, but rather adjusts the discount rate in reaction to changes in market rates.

IMPORTANT TERMS

announcement effect
discount window
discount rate
float
monetary base

monetized
open-market operations
reserve requirements
U.S. currency outstanding

EXERCISES

1. Explain how the monetary base is affected by each of these economic events.
   a. The payment of taxes to the federal government each April 15.
   b. Holiday shopping in December.
   c. A snowstorm in Chicago and New York.

2. The text discusses the example of a check drawn on an Ohio bank that is deposited in a Daytona Beach bank. Under the rules that are used by Canada's private check-clearing system, the Ohio bank would retroactively debit the check-writer's account as of the date that the check was deposited in the Daytona Beach bank. Does the Canadian system have a great deal of float or very little?

3. Banks, money-market funds, and corporations transfer some $200 trillion each year using Fedwire, the Federal Reserve's electronic transfer service. The Fed credits the recipients of these wire transfers immediately, but does not debit the senders until the end of the day. Does this float create profits for the Fed or for Fedwire users?

4. In 1982 the FBI investigated a firm suspected

of a check-kiting scheme involving banks in California, the Caroline Islands, Guam, Hawaii, Massachusetts, and Ohio. What is check kiting and why do you suppose these banks were so widely scattered?

5. The Federal Reserve's reserve requirements are reported each month in the *Federal Reserve Bulletin*. Use the most recent issue to determine if there has been any change in reserve requirements from the January 1990 requirements described in the text.

6. Why is there sometimes a substantial increase in federal-funds market activity on Wednesdays?

7. The imposition of reserve requirements increases a bank's cost of funds by reducing the amount that it can profitably invest. Use Equation 5 in the text to determine the bank's cost of funds if
   a. its deposit rate is 6 percent and there is a 12-percent reserve requirement.
   b. its deposit rate is 5 percent and there is a 20-percent reserve requirement.

8. What rate of return must a bank earn on its investments to break even if it pays depositors 8-percent interest and these deposits are subject to a 12-percent reserve requirement? Three-percent reserve requirement? (Assume that the 8-percent figure includes all of the bank's administrative expenses.)

9. A bank has $500 million in transaction deposits subject to a 12-percent reserve requirement, and $500 million in other deposits subject to a 0-percent reserve requirement. What is its average reserve requirement (the ratio of total required reserves to total deposits)?

10. A savings-and-loan association has $200 million in transaction deposits subject to a 12-percent reserve requirement, and $800 million in other deposits subject to a 0-percent reserve requirement. Assuming that the bank holds no excess reserves, fill in the following balance sheet, showing the bank's reserves and available funds.

Assets

Reserves	
Investments	
Total	$1,100,000,000

Liabilities

Transaction accounts	$ 200,000,000
Other deposits	800,000,000
Net worth	100,000,000
Total	$1,100,000,000

What is this bank's average reserve requirement (the ratio of total required reserves to total deposits)? This bank's annual interest payments plus administrative expenses are equal to 10 percent of transaction deposits and 10 percent of other deposits, a total of 10%($1,000,000,000) = $100,000,000 annually. What rate of return must it earn on its investments for a 10-percent return on net worth?

11. What rate of return would the bank in Exercise 6 need to earn on its investments to break even if the Federal Reserve eliminated all reserve requirements? (Assume that the bank continues to hold no excess reserves.) What if the Fed maintained its reserve requirements, but paid 10 percent annual interest on all required reserves?

12. Explain how reserve requirements encourage banks to pay corporate depositors a higher interest rate on 5-year CDs than on 1-year CDs.

13. The 1980 Monetary Control Act reduced the maximum reserve requirement on transaction accounts from 16¼ to 12 percent. How much does this reduction increase the annual income of a bank with $1 billion in transaction accounts subject to these maximum reserve requirements, if it can earn a 10-percent annual rate of return on its investments?

14. If a bank can earn a 10-percent annual return on its investments, how many extra dollars does it earn each year from

a. having its first $41.5 million of transaction accounts subject to a 3-percent rather than a 12-percent reserve requirement?

b. having no reserve requirements on its first $3.4 million in deposits that would otherwise be subject to a 3-percent reserve requirement?

15. Do you think that the special reserve requirements described in Exercise 14 primarily benefit large or small banks? Explain your reasoning.

16. Panel (b) of Table 15.8 shows the effects on bank deposits, reserves, and investments of a 10-percent reduction in reserve requirements, from 2 percent to 1.8 percent. Construct a similar Panel (b), with data rounded to the nearest billion dollars, showing the consequences of a 10-percent increase in reserve requirements, from 2 percent to 2.2 percent.

17. Many brokerage firms offer cash-management accounts that allow money to be withdrawn by check or debit card. If it is a "sweep account," excess funds are automatically swept into a money-market fund at the end of each day, and funds are transferred from the money-market fund to the checking account as needed. If there are insufficient funds in the money-market fund, then the brokerage firm lends money, using the customer's stocks and bonds as collateral — just as with a margin account. Because funds are swept out of the checking account at the end of the day, the brokerage firm avoids reserve requirements. What is the advantage of avoiding reserve requirements? Isn't it prudent to keep reserves on hand to satisfy possible customer withdrawals?

18. James Tobin has proposed that transaction accounts be subject to 100-percent reserve requirements. How would this affect the interest rate that banks pay on transaction accounts?

19. An empirical study of the effect of reserve requirements on the prices of bank stocks found that the Monetary Control Act of 1980 significantly increased stock prices for Federal Reserve member banks relative to nonmember banks.[5] How would you explain this finding?

20. For the week ending September 29, 1989, the federal-funds rate was 9.02 percent and the Fed's discount rate was 7 percent on adjustment credit, seasonal credit, and the first 30 days of extended credit; extended credit beyond 30 days was charged 9.2 percent. Use a recent issue of the *Federal Reserve Bulletin* to determine the average federal funds and discount rates during the most recently reported week. Is the gap between the federal-funds rate and the basic discount rate as large as that prevailing in September 1989? Is the discount rate on extended credit beyond 30 days above or below the federal-funds rate?

21. After the Federal Reserve raised the discount rate from 6.5 percent to 7 percent on February 24, 1989, a *Wall Street Journal* reporter wrote that[6]

Although the discount rate isn't tied directly to the returns individuals get on their investments or what they pay to borrow, it can have a significant effect . . . because the discount rate plays a key role in financial markets as a signal of Fed policy.

Explain what the discount rate is and how it might signal Fed policy.

22. It is generally agreed that, other than the announcement effects, most changes in the discount rate would have little impact on the money supply or credit conditions. Why, then, does the announcement of an increase in the discount rate lead people to expect higher future interest rates?

23. In 1980 it was reported that[7]

The Federal Reserve Board today increased its bank discount rate by a full percentage point to a record 13 percent, a move local economists said is certain to send interest rates higher. . . . Bond prices plummeted in reaction.

Explain why bond prices might fall when an increase in the discount rate is announced. Describe a situation in which an increase in the discount rate would have little or no affect on bond prices.

24. If market-interest rates fell and the Fed did not reduce the discount rate, would you interpret this as a signal of easy or tight money? Explain your reasoning.

25. When member banks borrow heavily from Reserve Banks, there usually seems to be a credit crunch. Why? Doesn't member-bank borrowing expand the money supply, ease credit, and reduce interest rates?

26. Write a paragraph supporting or refuting the conclusion that the discount rate "is an absolute necessity for the sound management of a monetary system, and is a most delicate and beautiful instrument for the purpose."[8]

27. Discount-window borrowing is usually large when the discount rate is high and small when the discount rate is low. Shouldn't it be the other way around?

28. Here are some data for selected periods on adjustment borrowings through the Fed's discount window and the spread between the federal-funds rate and the Fed's discount rate.[9]

Period	Adjustment Borrowing (millions of dollars)	Federal-Fund Rate Minus Discount Rate (percent)
May 1981– October 1981	1,525	3.59
October 1981– November 1981	612	0.68
November 1981– July 1982	1,012	1.73
July 1982– October 1982	553	0.14
October 1982– November 1982	352	−0.06

Do these two variables seem to be positively or negatively related? How would you explain the observed empirical relationship?

29. Show the T-accounts when a bank uses the Fed's discount window to add $100 million to its reserves with the Fed.

30. Suppose that the Fed buys $1,000,000 in securities from private citizens and that, after the complete expansion of bank deposits and loans, there is an extra $500,000 in Federal Reserve notes outside banks and an extra $500,000 in bank reserves at the Fed. Assume that reserve requirements are 10 percent and that banks hold no excess reserves. Show the T-accounts for the Fed, banks, and the non-bank public.

31. The Monetary Control Act reduced reserve requirements, on average. If the Federal Reserve wanted to offset the expansionary or contractionary effects on financial markets, should it have bought Treasury bills or sold them?

32. Has the shift in the composition of bank deposits from transaction to savings accounts increased or diminished aggregate required reserves? If the Fed wanted to offset the effects of this change in required reserves on financial markets, should it have bought T-Bills or sold them?

33. Between 1929 and 1933, there was an outflow of gold from the United States, which the Federal Reserve did little to offset. After 1933, gold began flowing back into the United States and, even though the nation was still in the midst of the Great Depression, the Federal Reserve was concerned about a possible inflation and used monetary policies to offset this inflow. Did it raise or lower reserve requirements? Did it make open-market purchases, or sales?

34. Explain the error made by this 1986 investment newsletter.[10]

By 1995 those [federal] deficits are expected to top $775 billion. That's the amount of money the *government will spend each year — above and beyond the money it collects.*

Worse yet, that's the amount the Federal Reserve will have to cover by printing batches of new paper money.

35. In the 1960s, the U.S. government wanted to reduce long-term interest rates to stimulate corporate investment while raising short-term interest rates to improve the balance of payments. The Fed tried "Operation Twist," trading in short- and long-term government securities to twist the term structure. Should the Fed have bought shorts and sold longs, or vice versa? What are the implications, if any, of the Expectations Hypothesis for Operation Twist?

36. Use the Expectations Hypothesis to interpret this empirical observation.[11]

A good measure of the stance of monetary policy is the yield curve. . . . The yield curve is said to be inverted when short rates are above long rates, a consistently accurate prediction of tight money. During recessions and the early stages of economic recovery the yield curve is positive (i.e., short rates are below long rates), implying easy, or at least cheap, money. During the late stages of the recovery cycle, when inflation is strong and monetary policy has been forced to tighten sharply, short rates rise and the yield curve usually becomes inverted. . . . inverted yield curves have tended to precede downturns in economic activity.

37. Here is an excerpt from a syndicated newspaper column.[12]

For all their importance, interest rates remain a subject of immense confusion and mystery. The striking aspect of the current decline is that long-term interest rates have dipped far more than short-term rates. Since January, 1985, for example, rates on long-term Treasury bonds have fallen more than 3 percentage points while those on short-term Treasury bills have declined roughly 1 percentage point. . . .

The implication is that the Federal Reserve has so far played a secondary role in lowering rates. Its direct influence is concentrated on short-term rates.

According to the Expectations Hypothesis of the term structure, how can long-term rates fall more than short-term rates? How can the Fed affect long-term interest rates, even if it buys and sells only short-term Treasury bills?

38. Assume that the Expectations Hypothesis is correct and the Hicks Equation applies. The yield on one-year Treasury zeros is initially 10 percent and is expected to remain at 10 percent. The monetary authorities now sell a large quantity of one-year zeros, driving the yield up to 12 percent. However, it is still believed that one-year yields next year and thereafter will be 10 percent. What is the yield now on two-year zeros? On three-year zeros? Which yield changed the most?

39. Would the Fed have complete control over M1 if reserve requirements were 100 percent on demand deposits and 0 percent on time and savings deposits?

40. (requires calculus) Consider the following deposit-multiplier model.

$RR = kD$	(required reserves RR relative to deposits D)
$ER = \epsilon(1 - k)D$	(excess reserves ER relative to deposits D)
$C = \beta D$	(currency outside banks C relative to deposits D)
$RR + ER + C = B$	(reserves plus currency equals monetary base B)

Solve for $C + D$ as a function of B. Now take the derivative to determine the percentage change in $C + D$ resulting from a 1-percent change in ϵ. Is this elasticity positive or negative? Is this elasticity increased or reduced by high reserve requirements k? What is this elasticity when $k = 1$? In words, what is the policy implication of your results? (Note: The same qualitative results hold for the elasticity of $C + D$ with respect to β.)

THE

CONDUCT

OF

POLICY

We do not know enough to be able to achieve stated objectives by delicate, or even fairly coarse, changes in the mix of monetary and fiscal policy. In this area particularly the best is likely to be the enemy of the good. Experience suggests that the path of wisdom is to use monetary policy explicitly to offset other disturbances only when they offer a "clear and present danger."

Milton Friedman

The Federal Reserve was originally intended to be a lender of last resort to banks as financial markets rode a roller coaster over economic booms and busts. Since the 1930s, the Fed has been trying to smooth out the ride. In this chapter, we will discuss some of the operating procedures that the Fed uses to monitor the state of the economy and to determine an appropriate monetary policy.

We will consider several general issues, including the distinction between monetary and fiscal policies, the political pressures on the Fed, and the Fed's ability to implement timely policies. We will pay particular attention to the implications of the observation that the Fed is not able to achieve its objectives with great precision. Some observers, noting the historical instability of financial markets, endorse the use of admittedly imperfect policies. Others, worried about imperfections in even well-intentioned policies, propose that monetary policy be turned over to a dispassionate computer programmed to ignore the economy. We begin our consideration of these controversies with the distinction between monetary and fiscal policies.

MONETARY VERSUS FISCAL POLICIES

The Federal Reserve has broad control over the nation's **monetary policy**, using open-market operations, reserves requirements, and discount rates to alter the monetary base and monetary aggregates. Congress and the president determine the federal government's expenditures and tax rates, its **fiscal policy**. Any deficit between federal outlays and revenue is financed by the sale of Treasury debt; the Federal Reserve can use open-market operations to monetize as much or as little of this debt as it wishes.

In Chapters 19 and 20, a formal model will be used to compare the consequences of monetary and fiscal policies; here it suffices to note that monetary- and fiscal-policy decisions are made by different Government bodies, which do not always agree with each other's policies.

The Fed controls monetary policy; Congress and the president control fiscal policy.

Coordination and Conflict

Monetary and fiscal policies do not have identical effects on the economy. For the achievement of some objectives, monetary policy is appropriate; for others, fiscal policy is best. Most of the time, a combination of both is needed. For instance, if policymakers want to reduce military spending without depressing the economy, then reduced government spending (a contractionary fiscal policy) can be accompanied by open-market purchases (an expansionary monetary policy).

Monetary and fiscal policies have different effects on the economy.

In practice, this kind of coordination does not always occur, because the Fed, Congress, and the president do not always have the same objectives and because none is subservient to the others. For instance, Congress and the president may want to stimulate the economy in order to increase output and reduce unemployment at the same time that the Fed wants to cool the economy in order to fight inflation. The president cannot order the Fed to make open-market purchases, and the Fed cannot force Congress to reduce spending or increase taxes.

Because of its independent status, the Fed has been called the Supreme Court of Finance. It is not quite this, but there are definite similarities. The members are appointed by the president for very long terms (14 years), and at any time most of the Governors were chosen by the current president's predecessors. Congress has little control over the Fed's day-to-day operations, though it can impose general constraints, such as minimum and maximum levels for reserve requirements. The final similarity and difference between the Federal Reserve Board and the Supreme Court is that the president and Congress have tried to influence both, but have had more success with the Federal Reserve.

Political Pressures

The Fed usually gives the president the kind of monetary policy he wants. In the 1950s, the Fed was very cautious and, to avoid inflation, accepted three

The Fed usually accommodates the president's policy goals.

| Highlight 16.1 | **Threatening the Fed** |

In March 1990, the *Los Angeles Times* printed a front-page story with the headline "Interest Rates Peril Fed Chief's Job, Sources Say." The story began

> *President Bush is so upset over Federal Reserve Board Chairman Alan Greenspan's refusal to push interest rates down further that he is unlikely to reappoint him as Fed chairman when his term expires in August of 1991, sources said Thursday.**

The primary source for this story — identified only as a "longtime Bush adviser" — said that Bush was "mad as hell" about Greenspan's policies and added that "I can't believe he will reappoint him and I don't know a soul in the White House who thinks he will." Bush's press secretary immediately denied this story and said that Greenspan's reappointment hadn't even been discussed at the White House.

The story behind the story, according to a personal conversation with a *Times* reporter, was that Bush's advisers had criticized Greenspan for months for what they considered excessively high interest rates and now wanted to send an even stronger message. A member of the administration contacted a *Times* reporter and, on the usual condition of anonymity, leaked the story. (A reporter who violated the anonymity condition would lose all sources.)

Bush's press secretary routinely denied the story, but there was no doubt that the Fed received and understood the message: Bush and his advisers wanted lower interest rates and would keep pushing for lower interest rates. The *Times* reporters were well aware that they were not merely reporting economic events, but, instead, being used to deliver a message to the Fed; but the *Times* printed the story anyway because they thought that the message was newsworthy.

The Federal Reserve uses the same media techniques when it wants to send a message to the president, Congress, or financial markets. A staff member or one of the Fed's Governors contacts a trusted member of the press and, requiring anonymity, leaks information or expresses an opinion, perhaps about the state of the economy. The subsequent news story attributes these opinions to a "senior Fed official" or a "well-placed source." Often the unidentified well-placed source is the Federal Reserve Chairman!

---

*Jack Nelson, "Interest Rates Peril Fed Chief's Job, Sources Say," *Los Angeles Times,* March 9, 1990.

recessions during Dwight Eisenhower's eight years in office. John F. Kennedy became president in January 1961, having promised voters that he would reduce unemployment and get the country moving again. The Fed obligingly swung to a more expansionary monetary policy. In 1969, Richard Nixon took office, promising to stop inflation, and the Fed tightened the screws in a painful credit crunch. In 1977, Jimmy Carter became president, and his initially expansionary fiscal policies were supported by expansionary monetary policies. In 1981, Ronald Reagan became president and got the tight monetary policy that he apparently wanted to fight inflation.

Paul Samuelson once said that Federal Reserve governors were given two eyes so that they could watch both interest rates and the money supply.[1] The Fed actually appears to have three eyes: one for interest rates, one for monetary aggregates, and one for election returns.

It hasn't been all romance between the politicians and this three-eyed monster. Federal Reserve officials are repeatedly cajoled by the president and called before congressional committees. Often the president and Congress are upset because monetary and fiscal policies seem to be working at cross-purposes. Since 1965, there have been several occasions when expansionary fiscal policies were pitted against tight-money, contractionary monetary policies.

Since they are not elected officials, the members of the Federal Reserve Board are presumably less likely to manipulate the economy for personal political gain, though there still may be temptations to assist favored politicians. For instance, Federal Reserve Chairman Arthur Burns vehemently denied charges that the Fed pursued an easy-money policy in 1972 to assist Richard Nixon's reelection campaign. Former Fed Governor Sherman Maisel later wrote about the persistent pressure applied by the Nixon administration: "An election was approaching; from their point of view, the faster money grew, the better was monetary policy."[2]

It sometimes seems, particularly before elections, that the Federal Reserve is trying to cool the economy to fight inflation while the president is trying to stimulate the economy to reduce unemployment. For example, when Jimmy Carter ran for reelection in 1980 and lost, his advisers were bitterly critical of the Federal Reserve's tight-money policies, including an increase in the discount rate six weeks before the election. To some, these conflicts show that the system is working. When a president, prime minister, or king has controlled a nation's money supply, there has too often been irresponsible and ultimately destructive inflation. The political independence of the Federal Reserve allows it to follow unpopular but necessary policies.

In other eyes, including naturally those of the president and Congress, this separation thwarts useful coordination of monetary and fiscal policies. Monetary policy is too important to be trusted to unelected officials, who do not have to answer to the public. There is a long-standing suspicion that the Fed is run by bankers for the benefit of bankers, particularly East Coast bankers. This suspicion, together with the ill-founded assumption that bankers like high interest rates, forms one popular explanation of why the Fed has so often followed a tight-

The Fed has often been criticized for its tight-money policies.

| Highlight 16.2 | **The Political Business Cycle** |

An only slightly cynical explanation of the periodic conflict between expansionary fiscal policies and contractionary monetary policies is that economic events can have a decisive influence on elections. People think of their pocketbooks when they vote and judge the incumbent political party by the state of the economy. Casual observation and formal empirical studies indicate that high output and low unemployment sway votes to the incumbent party.*

There are two other, more subtle observations. First, changes in the levels of output and employment during the year preceding the election seem to be very important, perhaps more important than the levels themselves. Second, inflation tends to lag behind the economy in that the economy can be stimulated, thereby increasing output as well as reducing unemployment, with relatively little immediate impact on the rate of inflation.

The Political Business Cycle

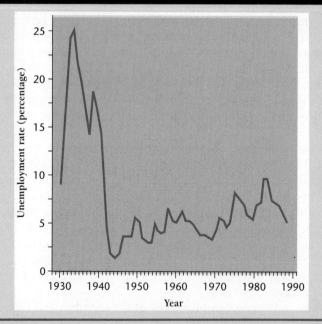

*See William D. Nordhaus, "The Political Business Cycle," *The Review of Economic Studies,* April 1975, pp. 169–190, and Ray Fair, "The Effect of Economic Events on Votes for President," *Review of Economics and Statistics,* May 1978, pp. 159–173.

These apparent phenomena explain why an incumbent party may try to stimulate the economy before an election and to cool off the economy after an election. This preelection stimulus and postelection restraint is called the **political business cycle**. The figure shows that the unemployment rate seems to decline before presidential elections and to rise afterwards. In 1932, the unemployment rate rose 7.7 percent and the incumbent president, Herbert Hoover, was soundly defeated. Since 1932, there has been only one instance in which the unemployment rate in a presidential election year was higher than during the preceding year: 1980, when the unemployment rate rose 1.3 percent and the incumbent, Jimmy Carter, lost decisively.

money policy. The late Texas Congressman Wright Patman, who served in the House from 1929 to 1976 and chaired the House Banking Committee for many of those 47 years, was a particularly vocal champion of this view, frequently berating Fed Governors for causing high interest rates. Periodically, Congress considers legislation to weaken the independence of the Fed or to turn monetary policy over to Congress or the president. Such proposals are often motivated by a feeling that the Fed's policy is wrong — usually, that it is too contractionary.

OBJECTIVES AND TARGETS

It is helpful to distinguish between the Fed's policy instruments (open-market operations, reserve requirements, and the discount rate) and its objectives, including the following:

A distinction can be made between the Fed's instruments and objectives.

1. *Low unemployment.* The involuntarily idleness of potentially productive people and factories is a waste of a nation's resources, a loss that is felt most keenly by the unemployed and the owners of idle businesses. There will always be some frictional unemployment — people looking for jobs because they have just entered the labor force or are temporarily between jobs. But persistent involuntary unemployment — people who are able and willing to work, but cannot find suitable jobs — has economic and social costs for these individuals and for the nation.
2. *Low inflation.* Constantly changing prices make rational economic planning difficult and undermine public confidence in the government's economic policies. When prices are increasing rapidly, people spend too much time trying to beat inflation by avoiding holding money and by rushing around to buy products quickly, before prices increase once again. Unfortunately, low inflation and low unemployment are generally conflicting goals, in that monetary policies that reduce inflation often increase unemployment.

3. *Stable financial markets.* People may be less willing to save, borrow, and invest when there is considerable turmoil in financial markets, with interest rates and asset prices fluctuating wildly. These fluctuations create risks not only for individuals, but also for businesses and financial institutions, which can be bankrupted by sudden unfortunate changes in the market value of their assets and liabilities.

4. *Stable foreign exchange markets.* Fluctuations in exchange rates create risks for those involved in import and export businesses. We saw in Chapter 3 how the appreciation and depreciation of a nation's currency affect the purchasing power of its citizens and the competitiveness of its industries. Large, unexpected changes in exchange rates can cause financial losses, and the fear of such losses can discourage commerce.

While the Federal Reserve is interested in the nation's unemployment, inflation, and so on, it does not directly control any of these. For monetary policies to be effective, there must be a reliable link between the Fed's actions and its goals. If the Fed wants to use open-market sales to reduce inflation, it should be confident that these sales will in fact affect inflation, and it needs some means of determining the appropriate amount of open-market sales.

Intermediate and Operating Targets

The lanes at bowling alleys have painted diamond markers some ten to twenty feet in front of the bowler. Many bowlers watch these diamonds as they release the ball, rather than lifting their heads to look at the distant pins. In the same way, the Federal Reserve has often used **intermediate targets** to help achieve its ultimate objectives.

The Fed often uses intermediate targets.

Thus the Fed might use a 5-percent increase in M1 during the next 12 months as an intermediate target, not because it particularly cares about the rate of growth of M1, but because it believes that, by hitting its 5-percent target for M1, it will be able to accomplish its objectives for unemployment, inflation, and other variables of real economic consequence. If the Fed uses M1 as an intermediate target, then it monitors M1 throughout the year and makes open-market purchases or sales when M1 deviates from its target 5-percent growth path.

The perfect intermediate target has two characteristics:

A perfect intermediate target is easy to hit and reliably related to the Fed's ultimate objective.

1. The Fed is able to hit the intermediate target consistently.
2. There is a reliable relationship between the intermediate target and the Fed's ultimate objectives.

Some potential intermediate targets are more successful by the first criterion, others by the second. None are perfect.

For example, suppose that the Fed's primary goal is low unemployment and that it chooses the interest rate on three-month Treasury bills as an intermediate target. The Fed can control the three-month Treasury-bill rate perfectly by calculating the Treasury-bill price that corresponds to the target interest rate and then making unlimited purchases or sales, as needed, at this price. However, there is not a perfect relationship between Treasury-bill rates and unemployment; for any particular value of Treasury-bill rates, unemployment can rise or fall, depending on other economic conditions. Thus, for an unemployment goal, Treasury-bill rates are a good intermediate target by the first criterion, but flawed by the second criterion.

In the 1970s, it seemed that M1 might be difficult to control (flawed by the first criterion), but that there was a reliable relationship between M1 and many of the Fed's objectives (good by the second criterion). Later in this chapter, we will look more closely at the advantages and disadvantages of interest rates and monetary aggregates as intermediate targets.

If the Fed uses an intermediate target, such as M1, that it does not control directly, then it may use **operating targets** to help achieve its intermediate targets. For instance, the Fed may want to reduce inflation and decide to use a 5-percent rate of growth of M1 as its intermediate target. Since M1 contains checkable deposits subject to reserve requirements, there may be a close relationship between bank reserves and M1. If so, the Fed might set an operating target of, say, 5-percent growth in bank reserves. It will then use open-market operations to keep bank reserves growing at 5 percent a year, hoping that this will ensure a 5-percent annual growth of M1 and that this growth rate for M1 will reduce inflation as desired. A perfect operating target is easy to hit and reliably related to the Fed's intermediate target. Unfortunately, there are no perfect operating or intermediate targets.

Operating targets can help achieve intermediate targets.

OBSTACLES TO EFFECTIVE POLICY

There are two fundamental reasons why all operating and intermediate targets are imperfect: uncertainty and policy lags. We will discuss the consequences of uncertainty first, and then of policy lags.

Policies are undermined by uncertainty and lags.

Uncertainty

Politicians are often impatient with economists who admit that they are not omniscient. It is said that Harry Truman once exclaimed in frustration, "Give me a onehanded economist! All my economists say 'on the one hand, . . . but on the other.'" If economists were certain about how the economy works and what the future holds, it would be easy to make policy decisions. Congress, the president, and the Fed could negotiate target values of unemployment, inflation, and other key variables and select policies that achieve these objectives. The problem is that they don't understand the past completely, cannot see the present clearly, and have only imperfect predictions about what is going to happen in the future.

We frankly do not have enough accurate, timely data to describe the economy's current condition, let alone know what conditions will be like five years or even five months from now. A policymaker who doesn't know much about

Highlight 16.3	A Case of Mysterious Excess Reserves

When bank reserves are scarce, the federal funds rate increases and the aggregate amount of excess reserves in the banking system declines. When funds are plentiful, the federal funds rate declines and excess reserves swell. During July 1980, however, the federal funds rate increased and, surprisingly, so did excess reserves. In the first week of August, excess reserves topped $1 billion, the highest level in 20 years, even though the federal funds rate had increased by nearly a percentage point, from an average of 8.68 percent during the week ending on July 25 to an average of 9.60 percent during the week ending on August 8. *The Wall Street Journal* reported that the spokesman for the New York Federal Reserve Bank who reported the August data "simply shook his head, saying that it was all 'quite mysterious' why banks would want to keep such large idle reserves."*

Finally, on August 25, the Fed announced that the case of the mysterious excess reserves had been solved. Federal Reserve statisticians estimate excess reserves by subtracting an estimate of required reserves from an estimate of total bank reserves and, for three consecutive weeks, they had underestimated required reserves by about $300 million — causing them to overestimate excess reserves by a like amount.

Aggregate required reserves is normally one of the Fed's most reliable data series. But in this instance the Fed had misinterpreted its own rules for calculating required reserves. In July 1980, the Fed removed a special 2 percent supplementary reserve requirement on large certificates of deposit (CDs) and the Fed's statisticians simultaneously reduced their estimate of aggregate required reserves on large CDs by 2 percent. But they forgot that each bank is subject to another rule, mandated by Congress, that fixes the minimum average reserve requirement on all savings and time deposits at 3 percent. Because of this special rule, required reserves must be calculated on a bank-by-bank basis. When the Fed's statisticians did this, they found their $300 million error and solved the excess reserve puzzle. Fortunately, the Fed's governors suspected that the reported sharp increase in excess reserves was misleading and did not overreact to this illusory signal that there was a glut of reserves.

---

*Edward P. Foldessy, "The Fed Clears Up Mystery of Data on Bank Reserves," *Wall Street Journal*, August 26, 1980.

the current state of the economy will almost certainly make some memorable policy errors. In June 1930, for example, in the midst of an economic depression that would continue for ten years, Herbert Hoover told a group that had come to Washington to urge an expansionary fiscal policy, "Gentlemen, you have come sixty days too late. The depression is over."[3]

Hoover was mistaken because he had very little information about output and employment. There were no gross-national-product data until the mid-1930s, and before 1940 the only regular unemployment figures were collected in the census, once every 10 years. Other economic data were scarce before World War II and often not very reliable.

Today, we have much better information about the current state of the economy. But we still don't have all the data we need, and we probably never will. Some data (including estimates of the gross national product) are available only quarterly. Some data, like real interest rates, are not officially available at all. Some, like weekly values of M1, are not very reliable. The weekly data on monetary aggregates are often substantially revised weeks or even months after their initial release. A Fed study found that, between 1968 and 1975, in a third of the cases the final estimate of the money growth rate differed from the preliminary estimate by more than 3 percentage points. How can the Fed accurately stabilize real interest rates or monetary aggregates if it barely sees them?

Forecasting Errors

Even more challenging, the Fed's policies must be aimed at the future, not the present, and economic forecasts are notoriously difficult, as evidenced by the embarrassingly inaccurate predictions that have been made in the past. Because the Great Depression was so calamitous, it is not surprising that it is also the source of many dramatically incorrect forecasts. In his final message to Congress, on December 4, 1928, President Calvin Coolidge boasted that

Economic forecasts are often inaccurate.

> *No Congress of the United States ever assembled, on surveying the state of the Union, has met with a more pleasing prospect than that which appears at the present time. . . . The country can regard the present with satisfaction and anticipate the future with optimism.*

Herbert Hoover took office in January 1929, and in July predicted that "The outlook of the world today is for the greatest era of commercial expansion in history." A few months later, the stock market crashed. But Herbert Hoover's optimism persisted. In his December 3, 1929, State of the Union message, he concluded that "The problems with which we are confronted are the problems of growth and progress." In March 1930, Hoover predicted that business would be normal by May. In early May, he declared that "we have now passed the worst"; in late May he predicted recovery by fall.

As the economy collapsed, politicians, businessmen, and economists kept predicting a quick return to prosperity. Charles Schwab, chairman of the board of Bethlehem Steel, said, "Never before has American business been as firmly entrenched for prosperity as it is today" (December 10, 1929). Andrew Mellon, Secretary of the Treasury, stated, "I see nothing in the present situation that is either menacing or warrants pessimism" (January 1, 1930). Robert Lamont, Secretary of Commerce, predicted that "Business will be normal in two months" (March 3, 1930). Even Irving Fisher, perhaps the greatest American economist, joined the chorus of optimists: "I expect to see the stock market a good deal higher than it is today within a few months" (October 15, 1929). Fisher lost his family fortune and a good deal of credibility. The politicians and businessmen didn't fare much better.

Unpredictable Behavior

Economic forecasting is much better now than in the 1930s, but it is not perfect and never will be, for economic decisions are made by humans — who are emotional, fallible, and unpredictable. An economist can tell you what is rational, what is reasonable, and what usually happens. But in any situation, fickle humans can turn around and do something entirely different. This is how Keynes explained the mayhem in the stock market and why he wrote that "There is nothing so disastrous as a rational investment policy in an irrational world."[4]

Similarly, in predicting the consequences of government policies, it is necessary to take into account, as best one can, how citizens will interpret these policies and how they will react to them. For example, government officials have long believed that the public sometimes overreacts to policy announcements. This is why incumbent presidents often announce potentially popular (but possibly unwise) policies only hours before a primary election or shortly before the presidential election itself. They are hoping to exploit the initial public enthusiasm before sober reflection sets in. With bad news, the best timing is months before the election or right after it. The Fed often announces unsettling financial news late on a Friday, after U.S. financial markets have closed, to give investors the weekend to calm down.

Citizens often react in surprising ways.

Citizens can react to policies in very unexpected ways. When the government announces an expansionary policy, one possible reaction is: "This will stimulate the economy; a boom is on the way." But another plausible response is: "If they are trying these stimulative policies, the economy must be in really bad shape; we must be sliding into a recession." Sometimes citizens react the first way, sometimes the second, and sometimes in other ways.

This fickleness can be very frustrating for government officials. In the Great Depression, President Hoover kept trying to buoy the economy with optimistic pronouncements, such as "Prosperity is just around the corner." This cheerleading was such an embarrassing failure that Simeon Fess, the National Chairman of the Republican Party, finally complained that[5]

Persons high in Republican circles are beginning to believe that there is some concerted effort on foot to utilize the stock market as a method of discrediting the administration. Every time an administration official gives out an optimistic statement about business conditions, the market immediately drops.

Expectations and the Reporting of Monetary Data

The public's reaction to government policies and pronouncements depends critically on its interpretation of these events. The weekly release of data on monetary aggregates is one example. In theory, an increase in the money supply should stimulate the economy and increase stock-market prices. Yet in the early 1980s, when the Fed reported a large increase in M1 and other monetary aggregates, stock prices often fell sharply.

The answer to this puzzle illustrates the critical role of expectations. During the early 1980s, the Fed was using M1 and other monetary aggregates as intermediate targets, trying to reduce inflation by keeping monetary aggregates within target guidelines. But the Fed does not directly control these monetary aggregates and does not know how fast they have been growing until data are gathered and analyzed. The Fed's weekly release of monetary data was a reporting of past increases in monetary aggregates, which, when they occurred, may well have reflected economic expansion. But by the time of the announcement, financial-market participants were looking ahead and trying to predict future Fed policy. If M1 had increased more than planned, they feared that the Fed would now use open-market sales to reduce the growth of monetary aggregates. Stock prices consequently declined, as theory says they should, in anticipation of this tightening of the monetary policy.

In the spring of 1970 President Nixon stated that, if he "had any money," he would buy stocks. Stock prices promptly fell by more than 10 percent. Investors seemed to feel that the economy must be in even worse shape than they had thought if the president had to tout stocks. In 1981, President Ronald Reagan was similarly disappointed by Wall Street's negative response to his tax program. We have all seen other government officials surprised by public reaction to their policies and predictions.

Policy Lags

Another reason policymakers cannot achieve their objectives with precision is that there are significant lags between when an economic problem occurs and when a policy response affects the economy. These delays are of three kinds:

Policies often involve a substantial lag.

1. *Recognition delays.* We don't have reliable data on many important economic variables until some time after the fact. For example, gross-national-product data are not available until several weeks after each quarter has ended; thus data for January through March are not available until mid-April. In addition, economic data are never final, but are always subject to revision. Because the data are inexact and the world is full of surprises, policymakers like to

see confirming data before making decisions; this is why a recession is not declared until output has declined for two consecutive quarters. Recognition delays mean that it may take a while for policymakers to realize that policy changes are needed. One study estimated that recognition delays average around five months.[6]

2. *Action delays.* It takes time for policies to be formulated and agreed upon. Government spending and tax laws are especially time consuming. Monetary policy has a relatively short action delay because Fed decisions are made by a small committee, strongly influenced by one individual — the Federal Reserve Chair.

3. *Transmission delays.* Most policies have far-reaching effects, and it takes some time for these ripples to work themselves out. Government expenditures and tax changes affect the income of households and businesses and thus their spending, which affects the income and spending of yet other households and businesses. It takes a long time for such ripples to fade away completely, but empirical models generally find that an increase in government spending has most of its effects within six months.[7]

Monetary policies have considerable transmission delays between their implementation and their ultimate effects. When the Fed makes an open-market purchase, it takes some time for the increase in the monetary base to complete its repeating cycle of loans, expenditures, and deposits. Milton Friedman concluded that there is a lag of about 12 to 18 months between changes in the rate of growth of the money supply and economic activity. John Kareken and Robert Solow interpret the data as indicating a shorter but still substantial lag.[8]

> *Monetary policy works neither so slowly as Friedman thinks [it does], nor as quickly and surely as the Federal Reserve itself seems to believe. . . . Though the full results of policy changes on the flow of spending may be a long time coming, nevertheless the chain of effects is spread out over a fairly wide interval. This means that some effect comes reasonably quickly, and that the effects build up over time so that some substantial stabilizing power results after a lapse of time of the order of six to nine months.*

Economic statistics are, as here, sometimes susceptible to a wide variety of interpretations. Friedman's lag of 12 to 18 months is based on a comparison of the rate of change of monetary aggregates with the level of economic activity. Kareken and Solow, and others, argue that a more useful comparison is between changes in the money supply and changes in economic activity, or between deviations of the money supply and of economic activity from their long-run trends. Friedman acknowledges that such comparisons reduce the lag down to about five months.[9]

These three virtually inescapable delays — recognition, action, and transmission — mean that there normally is a substantial lag between the time when economic stimulus or sedation is first needed and the time when policy changes actually affect the economy. If the recession or boom is brief, then it may be over by the time the counteractive policy is working. Increased government spending, tax cuts, or open-market purchases intended to cushion a recession may not stimulate the economy until the middle of the next boom. If so, then stabilization policy may be destabilizing!

Policymakers are usually competent and well-intentioned. But inherent policy lags may require policymakers to be clairvoyant, too. If government officials are mere mortals, who cannot see the future clearly, then the wrong policies may be chosen as often as not. Some economists argue that business cycles are very short, while monetary and fiscal policies take a long time to take effect. A recession or boom is over by the time the government has identified it, decided what to do about it, done it, and seen that the stabilization policy has had its effects.

To see how these delays can undermine policies, consider monetary policy during a recession, as depicted in the stylized Figure 16.1. From data that measure the recent performance of the economy, the Fed sees some signs of weakness. Is this a telling sign, a temporary blip, or a statistical quirk? The Fed decides to wait and gather more data. After a few weeks or months, there are some confirming data; but it is still not clear how severe and pronounced the weakness is. Should the Fed make large open-market purchases or wait a while longer?

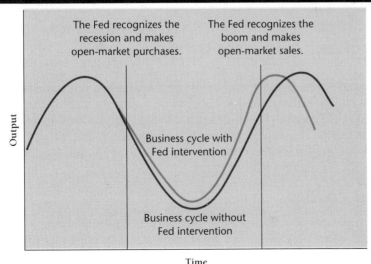

Figure 16.1 The Fed's Policies May Be Destabilizing When Business Cycles Are Short and Policy Lags Are Long

Lags can make fine-tuning impossible.

Time passes, and the Fed decides that the economy really is in a significant recession and should be given some substantial stimulus. Open-market purchases are used to increase the monetary base, reduce interest rates, and encourage spending. With time, the increase in the monetary base is spent, deposited in banks, lent out, spent again, redeposited, and lent out yet again. But by the time this monetary tonic is circulating through the economy, the recession may have already ended and the economy may be growing briskly. If so, then instead of softening the last recession, the monetary elixir exacerbates the next boom. By the time the Fed recognizes this excessive stimulus and starts draining money from circulation, the next recession may have already begun. The Fed will then cool off an already cold economy after having heated up a hot one; it would have been better had it kept its medicine locked up.

When policies have substantially lagged effects, the monetary authorities may find themselves repeatedly acting to offset the lingering effects of earlier policies. As a consequence, active policy may not be able to stabilize the economy completely.

The appendix to this chapter uses a simple mathematical model to show that perfect stabilization isn't feasible when the lagged effects of policies are stronger than the contemporaneous effects. Whether or not this is the case in practice depends on the horizon over which policymakers try to stabilize the economy. For a horizon of hours or days, the lagged effects of monetary and fiscal policies are surely greater than the contemporaneous effects, and policymakers therefore cannot hope to stabilize the economy hour to hour or day to day. For a horizon measured in months, the answer may be reversed. With an annual horizon, the lagged effects of most policies probably are smaller than the contemporaneous effects. Government policymakers may consequently be able to stabilize the economy year to year. Although fine-tuning the economy may be an unrealistic goal, smoothing out year-to-year performance may be possible.

RULES VERSUS DISCRETION

What kind of government policies should be followed in a very uncertain world? One answer is that the government should do nothing, except perhaps get out of the way; the government should pursue neutral policies that do not upset or distort the private economy. Implicit, and sometimes explicit, in this recommendation is the belief that the economy is inherently stable — that booms and busts are short-lived and self-correcting.

Neutral Policies

One operational difficulty with this advice is that of defining a neutral policy. The complete absence of a government might qualify as a neutral policy (though the actual process of shutting it down would hardly be neutral). But there are few, if any, responsible advocates of abolishing government entirely.

Would General Motors take over the national defense, financed by voluntary contributions?

If we are to have some government, it is very difficult to identify neutral policies. All government expenditures use resources that could be used for other purposes, and thus convey uneven benefits to the citizenry. For instance, expenditures on national defense divert bright scientists, skilled workers, and scarce materials from other uses and provide more benefits to the young than the old, to the healthy than the ill, to worriers than the carefree, and to those living in areas most likely to be attacked.

How are government expenditures to be financed? Taxes, bond sales, and money-printing are not neutral. In fact, one argument that has received considerable attention over the years is that it is precisely because monetary policy has important effects on the economy that the government should try to follow a neutral monetary policy. But even the foremost advocates (such as Friedrich von Hayek) have been unable to come up with a persuasive definition of a neutral monetary policy. Should the government regulate private money? Should it issue government money? How much? Should it hold this money (or some monetary aggregate) constant, or should it allow money to increase at a constant rate? How is the increased money supply to be put into circulation? These are but a sampling of the simple, but apparently unanswerable, questions. And the specific answers do make a difference: if money is not neutral, then no monetary policy can really be neutral.

Another conceptual difficulty for advocates of neutral policies is that individual and corporate income taxes increase with gross national product, reducing the government's budget deficit during booms (and increasing it during recessions). The government's consolidated budget constraint tells us that an increase in tax revenue presents policymakers with three options: the additional tax revenue can be spent on goods and services, used to purchase bonds, or used to reduce the monetary base (the Treasury can purchase bonds while the Fed simultaneously sells bonds, so that the bond supply is constant while the monetary base declines).

If the additional tax revenue raised during an economic boom is used to increase government spending or to purchase bonds, increasing bond prices and reducing interest rates, this will further stimulate the economy. If, however, the tax revenue is used to reduce the monetary base, this cools the expansion. Adjusting government spending or bond sales to variations in tax revenue is a pro-cyclical fiscal policy that magnifies economic booms and busts. Varying the money supply with tax revenue, in contrast, commits the government to an automatically counter-cyclical monetary policy.[10] None of these responses is neutral.

Fixed Rules

A variant on the neutral-money recommendation, one that is more operational, is that it really doesn't matter very much what the government does, as

It is difficult to identify neutral policies.

long as it is consistent about it. The seminal statement of this view was made by Henry Simons, a University of Chicago economist, in 1936.[11]

> In a free enterprise system we obviously need highly definite and stable rules of the game, especially as to money. The monetary rules must be compatible with the reasonably smooth functioning of the system. Once established, however, they should work automatically, with the chips falling where they may. . . . The responsibility for carrying out the monetary rules should be lodged in a federal authority . . . closely controlled in their exercise by a sharply defined policy. . . . Political control in this sphere should be confined exclusively to regulation of the quantity of money and near money.

In Simons' view, monetary authorities should be subservient to monetary rules. In monetary matters, as in other areas, we should be a nation governed by laws rather than by people.

Some argue that the Fed should follow fixed rules in place of discretionary policies.

This belief was roughly consistent with the broad antigovernment views then espoused by other members of what came to be called the Chicago School, which strongly extolled the virtues of unfettered markets and sharply criticized government interference. For many years, Milton Friedman was the most visible and effective proponent of the Chicago School.

Simons sidestepped the problem of defining a neutral monetary policy by arguing that the most important issue is that discretionary policy be replaced by fixed monetary rules. The actual rules are less important than the private sector's confidence that the rules will not be changed in mid-game. Nonetheless, there remains the practical question of making up the rules.

One of Simons' proposals was to fix the quantity of money, but this requires a precise definition of money, a definition that includes some assets and excludes other, very similar assets. In his 1936 essay, Simons expressed his frustration with "unfortunate character of our financial structure — with the abundance of what we may call 'near-moneys' — with the difficulty of defining money in such a manner as to give practical significance to the conception of quantity."[12]

This dilemma led Simons to urge the abolition of such near-moneys as bank deposits and short-term securities.[13]

> A liberal program of monetary reform should seek to effect an increasingly sharp differentiation between money and private obligations and, especially, to minimize the opportunities for the creation of effective money substitutes. . . . The abolition of private deposit banking is clearly the appropriate first step in this direction and would bring us in sight of the goal; but such a measure, to be really effective, must be accompanied, or followed closely, by drastic limitation on the formal borrowing powers of all private corporations and especially upon borrowing at short term.

Simons proposed requiring banks to hold 100-percent reserves against their deposits, restricting short-term business and consumer loans severely, and limiting government debt to cash and very-long-term bonds (ideally consols that never mature). An even more extreme proposal was to prohibit debt entirely.[14]

Ironically, Simons, a free-market economist, in his quest for a neutral monetary policy was led to advocate pervasive government regulation of financial markets.

The modern descendants of this Chicago tradition have generally eschewed such radical constraints on financial markets, but have continued to recommend passive monetary policy via fixed monetary rules. Milton Friedman, for instance, has long advocated that the Fed choose a monetary aggregate, such as M1 or M2, and simply keep this measure of the money supply growing at a constant 3 percent to 5 percent per year, regardless of the state of the economy.

Such advocates of passive policy are critics of discretionary demand-management policies. Their central criticism of monetary and fiscal stabilization policies is that, because of uncertainty and delays, policymakers have done a poor job and will continue to do so. Thus Edward Shaw wrote of the Fed.[15]

One passive policy rule is a fixed growth rate for M1 or M2.

> The antimanagement brief does not deny that monetary policy **could** perform miracles, promoting stable growth and fending off shocks to growth. But our experience contains no miracles. Management skills are not equal to the job of realizing the potentialities of monetary policy.

RATIONAL EXPECTATIONS AND THE NEW CLASSICAL ECONOMISTS

Classical economists assumed that an unfettered economy is always close to full employment and that full-employment output is unaffected by monetary and fiscal policies. They assumed that economic fluctuations about full employment are so brief and unimportant that they can be ignored. Robert Lucas, a University of Chicago economist, and other **new classical economists** have extended the classical models to allow for voluntary fluctuations in employment and output.

In new classical models, workers sometimes misjudge the price level and consequently miscalculate real wages. For example, if workers overestimate the price level, they underestimate the real value of the wages that firms offer. Some misinformed workers decide (mistakenly) that wage rates are not high enough to make work worth their while. As they leave their jobs, employment and output both decline. This voluntary unemployment is soon corrected, without the need for monetary or fiscal policies, when workers learn that they overestimated prices and underestimated real wages.

In new classical models, economic fluctuations are caused by errors in assessing prices.

Thus, according to the new classical economists, business cycles are caused by misjudgments regarding prices, mistakes that could be minimized if the government directed its attention to stabilizing prices. As Robert Lucas put it[16]

> The policy problem of reducing business cycle risk is a very real and important one, and one which I believe monetary and fiscal policies directed at price stability would go a long way toward achieving.

Only Surprise Policies Matter

Why are workers sometimes mistaken about the level of prices? If the economy were quiet and unchanging, there would be little reason for errors. Mistakes occur because of major events that are unforeseen or whose consequences are not accurately perceived. The new classical macroeconomists focus on government-instigated events, in reaction to the persistent Keynesian advocacy of active government stabilization policies. In this way, they agree with earlier classical economists that government intervention is unneeded and even counterproductive.

Citizens are aware of well-publicized, easily-accessible information. If the government were to announce, and the news services dutifully report, that the money supply will be decreased by 10 percent on February 8, people would anticipate this contractionary monetary policy. If a 10-percent decrease in the money supply reliably decreases prices 10 percent, people will be aware of this, too. They will fully anticipate this price deflation and it will not be a source of error in calculating real wages. These are **rational expectations,** based on the efficient utilization of available information.

If, as in the new classical models, all unemployment is voluntary, then with rational expectations, well-anticipated changes in the money supply do not cause mistakes in gauging the price level and consequently have no effect on employment or output! The only way that the Fed can affect employment and output is by using a surprise monetary policy, perhaps reducing the money supply after announcing that the money supply was going to be increased. But even this trick won't work very many times. A rational public will soon learn to expect the government to do the opposite of what it says. Policymakers will have to tell the truth every once in a while, just to keep the public guessing. In fact, any simple, consistent rules for conducting monetary policy will soon be learned by the public and rendered ineffective. The only monetary policy that can consistently alter employment and output is a random policy, using a secret coin flip to determine whether the money supply will be increased or decreased.

Of course, by definition, a random policy cannot be used to achieve purposeful objectives. Therefore, in a new classical model with full employment and rational expectations, a passive policy is best since active policies only affect the economy by surprising people and fooling them into making decisions they later regret.

Expectations and Government Policy

The foregoing analysis reflects the classical perception that the government does not do things for citizens, but rather to citizens. Here the government plays a precarious guessing game, trying to manipulate the public and fool it into making bad decisions. In such an environment, the best government policy is a passive one: keep the money supply growing at a stable well-publicized rate, allowing the private sector to make decisions on the basis of good information.

Rational expectations utilize information efficiently.

In new classical models with rational expectations, well-anticipated changes in the money supply do not affect employment or output.

While this model has some appealing features, the assumption that business cycles are caused by misinformation about prices is questionable. To obtain reasonably accurate up-to-date price information, all people need to do is listen to news reports or glance at newspaper headlines.

Some households do purchase bundles of goods and services that differ substantially from those included in the consumer price index reported in the news, but it does not seem plausible that their price errors are sufficient to cause the large, lengthy swings in unemployment that occur. For instance, between 1974 and 1975, unemployment increased by 2.8 million, from 5.6 percent to 8.5 percent of the labor force, while the CPI increased by 9.1 percent. It is hard to believe that this large increase in unemployment was due to a voluntary withdrawal from the labor force caused by widespread overestimates of inflation — to people thinking that prices were increasing much faster than they really were.

The new classical economists are ingenious and provocative; but even they admit that their models tell only a part of the story — that they contain some interesting insights, but are an incomplete explanation of business cycles. Robert Lucas has written that these models[17]

> *do succeed in their twin objectives. They provide examples of monetary economies in which money has . . . long-run neutrality . . . , yet retains the capacity to induce short-run disruptions of the sort documented by Friedman and Anna J. Schwartz. . . . Now it does not seem to me a critical or an economic insight to observe that one can detect differences between the world described in this paper and the United States, or that it utilizes "questionable ad hoc assumptions," or that it leaves facts unexplained. If ever there was a model rigged, frankly and unapologetically, to fit a limited set of facts it is this one. Ad hoc? If you only knew how hard it was.*

New classical models are an incomplete explanation of business cycles.

Lucas and others have shown that price errors can cause voluntary fluctuations in employment. Business cycles may be partly instigated and magnified by such errors. But that is not all there is to it. The Great Depression was not simply caused by a quarter of the labor force deciding to stay home because wages were too low to make work worthwhile. The drop in the unemployment rate to 3.5 percent in 1969 and the increases to 8.5 percent in 1975 and to 9.7 percent in 1982 were not due solely to mistakes about prices.

Keynes emphasized expectations, too; though he stressed largely inexplicable "mass psychology" and "animal spirits," rather than rational expectations. Expectations were central to his analysis of production decisions, investment plans, money demand, and the stock market. Yet the early Keynesian models used by his followers largely ignored expectations, partly for lack of a theory explaining expectations and partly for lack of good data measuring them. A major contribution of the rational-expectations literature is to reemphasize the point that expectations are important and are influenced by government policies. Policymakers, in turn, need to take into account private reactions of their policies; government policy does not operate in a vacuum.

The new classical economists are right that expectation errors can affect the economy, that private expectations are influenced by anticipated government policy, and that expectations should be taken into account in selecting policies. But monetary and fiscal policies, even when fully anticipated, do have real economic effects.

THE ECLECTIC VIEW

The question of passive or active policy, of rules versus authority, elicits a good deal of passion. The debate applies to many economic policies and is of deep personal concern to the protagonists as well as to the ordinary citizens whose lives will be affected by government policies.

One fundamental disagreement is whether or not the private economy is inherently stable. Can the Invisible Hand of market forces invoked by Adam Smith keep the economy on course, or should the government put a visible hand on the wheel? Classical economists believed that the economy was never far from full-employment equilibrium. After a rough roller coaster ride through booms and busts, culminating in the Great Depression, a lot of citizens with empty stomachs weren't so sure. Keynes legitimatized the view that the private economy is not inherently stable. The government should and could stabilize the economy, smoothing out or even eliminating business cycles. For 30 years, the Keynesian view had the upper hand. But Keynesian economics, too, did not deliver all that it had promised, and in the 1970s the pendulum swung back towards the classical skepticism of government.

The consensus among economists is that there is merit in both sides of this debate. Because of fundamental, inescapable errors and lags, it is, in fact, very difficult to fine-tune the economy. Very intelligent and well-intentioned experts have tried and have been found wanting. It is also true that in many ways government has become too big and meddlesome. But it is equally true that the good old days were not all that great, that the economy on occasion went through some fearsome, stressful times when a lot of decent, hard-working people suffered greatly.

Fixed policy rules do ensure less uncertainty about government actions, but may mean more uncertainty about the economy. A commitment not to let the economy disintegrate may well be more reassuring to households and businesses than an unshakable promise to ignore the economy. The federal government may not be able to eliminate business cycles completely, but when things turn sour — really obviously sour — policymakers need to be ready to step in and push the economy hard in the right direction.

It is also evident that many government regulatory agencies, such as the Securities Exchange Commission, have helped the public by increasing the quantity and accuracy of information available to it. Market forces do not always protect the needy or restrain corruption and banditry. The fundamental, and perhaps unsolvable, puzzle in economics is when to trust the market and when to trust government.

There are admittedly practical difficulties with implementing both points of view. If policymakers are to use discretionary policies, what signals should guide them? When should they alter government spending and tax rates? When should they tighten financial markets, and when should they ease up? Should they watch an interest rate, some measure of the money supply, some price index, some output level, some unemployment rate, or what? And when they do decide to act, what action should they take? If they want to tighten financial markets, should they raise the discount rate, raise reserve requirements, make open-market sales, or what? And how much of whatever they do, should they do?

These are difficult questions, and they apply to passive rules as well as discretionary policymaking. If we are going to encode some rules permanently in the law books and a computer to control fiscal and monetary policies automatically, which rules should they be? Human judgment is fallible, but it must be used, whether by exercising discretionary authority or by writing rules. Paul Samuelson has argued that when people "set up a definitive mechanism which is to run forever afterward by itself, that involves a single act of discretion which transcends, in both its arrogance and its capacity for potential harm, any repeated acts of foolish discretion that can be imagined."[18]

In the next two chapters, we will look at some very specific policies, passive and discretionary, that might be followed by the Fed, and at the actual policies employed since World War II. You will see that while fine-tuning may be impossible, the risks inherent in inflexible rules have consistently led the Fed to follow an eclectic approach, applying judgment to diverse measures of the condition of financial markets and the economy.

SUMMARY

The Federal Reserve Board is similar to a Supreme Court of finance, in that it has considerable autonomy and its actions do not always please the president and Congress. Broadly speaking, the Fed generally gives each president the kind of monetary policy he wants, but there are sometimes important conflicts, particularly before elections — when economic expansion usually has more appeal for the president than for the Fed.

The Federal Reserve has a variety of objectives, including low unemployment, low inflation, stable financial markets and stable exchange rates, but the Fed does not directly control any of these. If there were no lags and uncertainties, this would not matter, as the link between open-market operations and the Fed's objectives would be quick and sure. But with lags and uncertainties, the Fed cannot be sure of the effects of its policies, nor can it instantly revise its policies to fine-tune aggregate demand.

Because uncertainties and delays make the conduct of policy difficult, some observers recommend that the Fed follow simple mechanical rules instead of actively trying to stabilize the economy. Implicit in this recommendation is the classical belief that the private economy is inherently stable — that booms and recessions are short-lived and self-correcting.

The new classical economists believe that economic fluctuations are due to errors in assessing prices. Employment voluntarily expands when workers temporarily overestimate real wages, and contracts when they underestimate real wages. If there is both full employment and rational expectations, then well-anticipated government policies do not cause such mistakes and, consequently, do not affect employment and output.

IMPORTANT TERMS

fiscal policy
intermediate targets
monetary policy
new classical economists

operating targets
political business cycle
rational expectations

EXERCISES

1. Identify which of the following are monetary policies and which are fiscal policies.
   a. Reserve requirements are reduced.
   b. Personal income taxes are reduced.
   c. Military spending is reduced.
   d. The discount rate is reduced.
   e. The Fed buys Treasury bills.

2. The unemployment rate seems to go up at least as often as it goes down. Yet, the unemployment rate has risen in only one of the fourteen presidential election years from 1936 through 1988. Is this just a coincidence? If not, how would you explain this pattern?

3. Early in the 1984 presidential election campaign, a strategist for incumbent Ronald Reagan said that Paul Volcker, rather than Democratic candidate Walter Mondale, "may be our biggest political foe."[19] What did he mean by that?

4. In 1982, two staff writers for the *Los Angeles Times* wrote of government public-works projects to reduce unemployment: "Because of _____, such measures have usually not taken effect until after recovery was well under way."[20] What was the explanation omitted from this quotation? Give your own version of the argument that these staff writers may have learned in an economics course.

5. Leonall Anderson, a monetarist, argued that[21]

   Monetarist theories and empirical studies point to a relatively quick, but short-lived, response of output to a change in money growth, with a longer time period required for prices to respond fully. Post-Keynesian econometric models, on the other hand, produce an impact of money changes only over a much longer period.

   If monetary policies do have quick and short-lived effects, does this make them more or less useful for short-run economic stabilization? How would you explain Milton Friedman's recommendation that monetary policy not be used for short-run economic stabilization?

6. Populist politicians have often accused the Fed of being run by bankers for the benefit of bankers — in particular, of deliberately raising interest rates to increase bank profits. What is the critical flaw in this argument?

7. In December 1983, Milton Friedman showed a graph for 1980–83 purporting to show a close association between changes in M1 and changes in nominal GNP three months later.[22] Explain how this evidence either supports or undermines Friedman's recommendation that the Fed not use monetary policies to stabilize the economy.

8. Explain why "Simons advocated a system in which all financial wealth would be held in equity form, with no fixed money contracts, so that no institution that was not a bank could create effective money substitutes."[23]

9. Explain the economic logic behind this argument.[24]

Unemployment would be low when inflation was high only as long as the high rate of inflation was unexpected.

10. Explain this 1982 remark by Lyle Gramley, a Federal Reserve Board Governor, regarding proposals that the Fed target real interest rates: "we observe only nominal interest rates and then infer what real interest rates might be by guessing the price expectations of borrowers."[25] (Be sure to define real interest rates.)

11. How do new classical economists explain the rise in the unemployment rate to 10 percent in 1982?

12. On October 22, 1987, a celebrity economist recommended that monetary policy be gauged by the ratio of M1 to the monetary base B, with M1 a proxy for money demand and B for money supply.[26] When, as in September and October 1987, B grew faster than M1, the ratio M1/B fell, and he recommended that the Fed "tighten up" because the money supply was growing faster than demand. Can you think of any circumstance in which M1/B would fall even though the economy was slipping into recession?

13. Explain why, in new classical rational-expectations models, an increase in the money supply is just as likely to reduce output as to increase it.

14. It has been proposed that the Federal Reserve pay member banks interest on their excess reserves, total reserves, or deposits with Reserve Banks. How would such a plan affect bank behavior? How would it affect Fed control over monetary aggregates? Suppose that the Fed did pay interest on total bank reserves. If the Fed were to raise that interest rate, would this action ease or tighten financial markets?

15. Re-analyze the results of trying to peg gross national product at $5,000 billion when the dynamic model considered in the appendix is modified to

$$y_t = 200 + 4M_t + 2M_{t-1}$$

Explain why this policy of pegging gross national product is either more or less successful than with the appendix model.

Chapter 16 APPENDIX
THE DESTABILIZING EFFECTS OF LAGS

A simple model can illustrate how delays between the implementation of a policy change and its effects may make active stabilization policy infeasible. For concreteness, we will focus on monetary policy, but the moral we draw applies to fiscal policy as well.

Assume that the economy can be described by the following simple equation.

$$y_t = 200 + 2M_t + 4M_{t-1}$$

where y_t is the nominal gross national product in period t, M_t is the money supply in period t, M_{t-1} is the money supply in the preceding period, and all data are in billions of dollars. This model's key assumption is that there are substantial delays in the effects of monetary policy on the economy: this period's gross national product depends on the money supply in both the current and previous periods. Equivalently, an increase in the money supply affects the economy now and in the next period as well. Moreover, the lagged effects are assumed to be larger than the contemporaneous effects. Specifically, a $1 billion increase in the money supply increases gross national product by $2 billion this period and by $4 billion in the next period. The implication of this specification is that it is not feasible to use monetary policy to peg nominal gross national product!

Consider a case in which the money supply has been $800 billion for some time, and nominal gross national product is consequently $5,000 billion.

$$y_t = 200 + 2M_t + 4M_{t-1}$$
$$= 200 + 2(800) + 4(800)$$
$$= 5,000$$

Now a shock to the economy occurs, reducing the constant term from 200 to 190. Nominal gross national product will consequently fall by 10 (to 4,990) unless the monetary authorities act. In order to raise income by 10 in the current period, the money supply must be increased by 5 (since the increase in M_t is multiplied by 2). Hence, for period $t = 0$ (the time of the shock to the economy), the monetary authorities set $M_t = 805$.

In the next period ($t = 1$), the increase in the money supply is still affecting the economy, raising gross national product by another $4(5) = 20$, to 5,020 if the money supply is kept at 805.

$$y_t = 190 + 2M_t + 4M_{t-1}$$
$$= 190 + 2(805) + 4(805)$$
$$= 5,020$$

To keep gross national product at 5,000, the money supply must be reduced by 10 billion, to 795, to offset last period's increase by 5.

$$y_t = 190 + 2M_t + 4M_{t-1}$$
$$= 190 + 2(795) + 4(805)$$
$$= 5,000$$

So far, so good. But in the following period, the Fed must raise the money supply by 20 to offset the lagged effects of the preceding decrease by 10. And, in the next period, this increase of 20 will have to be offset by a decrease of 40. This unstable cycle of stop-and-go policies aimed at pegging nominal gross national product is summarized as follows:

Time Period t	Money Supply M_t
0	800
1	805

Time Period t	Money Supply M_t
2	795
3	815
4	775
5	855
6	695
7	1,015
8	375
9	1,655
10	−905

After nine periods of increasingly large swings between expansion and contraction, the situation becomes untenable, since a negative money supply is impossible.

Because the lagged effects are stronger than the contemporaneous effects, the monetary authorities must scramble in each period to offset the effects of last period's policy. The moral is that when there are substantial lags in the effects of policies, active policy may not be able to stabilize the economy completely. The monetary authority must settle for policies that offset shocks only partly, gradually, or not at all.

TARGETING

MONETARY AGGREGATES

During World War I, Will Rogers sent a telegram to the Secretary of War stating that he had figured out how to sink Germany's submarines. When he met with the Secretary, he suggested filling the German submarines with water. Asked how that could be done, Rogers replied, "I've given you the idea; now you work out the details."

In this chapter, we will consider a long-standing proposal that the Fed should focus its attention on a monetary aggregate, such as M1, and ignore interest rates and other economic indicators. You will see the logical underpinnings of this proposal and also learn why the Fed has resisted implementing it. We begin by examining why the Fed cannot peg both interest rates and monetary aggregates, and why a policy of stabilizing interest rates is sometimes counterproductive. Then we will look at a policy of targeting monetary aggregates.

THE CONFLICT BETWEEN INTEREST-RATE AND MONEY-SUPPLY TARGETS

The Federal Reserve can increase the nation's monetary base by buying securities and paying for them with Federal Reserve notes or by crediting banks with additional reserves. The Fed can reduce the monetary base by selling some of its security holdings and either retiring Federal Reserve notes or debiting bank reserve accounts.

Through its daily open-market operations, the Fed can fix either the size of the monetary base or the interest rates on the securities that it is buying and selling. But it cannot peg both the monetary base and interest rates. If the Fed is committed to pegging the monetary base at a given level, then it cannot buy or sell securities to stabilize interest rates. If interest rates begin to rise, for instance, the Fed cannot buy securities to restrain interest rates, because the monetary base would then rise above its target level.

Figure 17.1 uses a demand-and-supply graph to illustrate this point. The demand curve slopes downward because the demand for monetary base declines as the Treasury-bill rate increases. The cost of holding idle currency and reserves is the interest that could be earned by investing in Treasury bills. When the Treasury-bill rate increases, households, businesses, and banks all try to hold less of the monetary base.

Figure 17.1 shows that if the Fed holds the supply of monetary base constant when there is an increase in demand, the Treasury-bill rate will rise. Instead of pegging the monetary base, the Fed could announce that it is willing to buy or sell unlimited amounts of certain securities, such as Treasury bills, at given prices. The Fed thereby pegs the nominal interest rates on these securities at the levels that correspond to these fixed prices. If the demand for monetary base increases, then, as shown in Figure 17.1, the Fed can accommodate this increased demand by using open-market purchases to supply more monetary base, keeping the interest rate constant.

The target interest rate is pegged, as long as the Fed runs out of neither willpower nor securities. But when the Fed pegs an interest rate, it relinquishes control of the monetary base, since it must adjust its supply of the monetary base to accommodate fluctuations in private demand. Thus the Fed can peg the monetary base or interest rates, but not both.

The Fed can peg the monetary base or interest rates, but not both.

In practice, the Fed follows neither extreme path. It influences both the monetary base and interest rates, but pegs neither. Through its history, the Fed has sometimes paid more attention to interest rates and has sometimes emphasized various monetary aggregates. We will now look at the advantages and drawbacks of each of these targets.

INTEREST-RATE TARGETS

The basic argument for interest-rate targets is that these are the financial-market variables that influence fundamental economic decisions: whether to spend or save, whether to invest in financial or real assets. If the Fed wants to cool off the economy by discouraging consumption and productive investment, then it should tighten financial markets by increasing real interest rates. It is interest rates that affect saving and borrowing, and that are a barometer of the tightness of financial markets.

One criticism of interest-rate targets is that the Fed must deal with nominal interest rates, while consumption and investment decisions depend on real

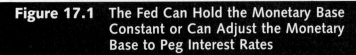

Figure 17.1   The Fed Can Hold the Monetary Base Constant or Can Adjust the Monetary Base to Peg Interest Rates

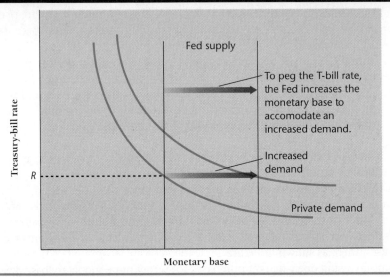

interest rates. Some argue that the Fed has no control over real interest rates, that an expansionary monetary policy may simply increase inflation and nominal interest rates equally, leaving real interest rates unchanged. In Chapter 5, we saw that real interest rates are by no means constant. In Chapter 22, we will see that whether or not monetary policy affects real interest rates depends on whether or not two classical assumptions — full employment and constant velocity — are appropriate.

A policy of stabilizing inter-est rates may destabilize the economy.

A second, less doctrinaire criticism of interest-rate targets is that a policy of stabilizing interest rates may destabilize the economy. Consider the case in which an increase in business and consumer spending causes an economic expansion. As saving declines and borrowing increases, interest rates are pushed upward. If the Fed uses open-market purchases to keep interest rates from rising, then it pumps more money into an already strong economy — putting gasoline on a fire, so to speak. In contrast, a policy of holding the money supply steady and allowing interest rates to rise stabilizes the economy by encouraging saving and discouraging borrowing.

Similarly, if business and household spending and borrowing decline, caus-ing a recession, interest rates sag. If the Fed makes no open-market transactions and allows interest rates to fall, this decline cushions the recession by encouraging borrowing and spending. If the Fed instead makes open-market sales to stabilize interest rates, this course of action will draw money out of the economy. By withdrawing money and propping up interest rates, the Fed discourages borrowing and spending, exacerbating the recession. Thus it is argued that stabilizing interest rates may destabilize the economy.

In rejoinder, interest-rate enthusiasts argue that they advocate monitoring interest rates, not mechanically pegging them and ignoring the condition of the economy. Interest rates are the channel by which monetary policy affects the economy and a barometer by which these effects can be measured. If the economy is in a recession that the Fed wants to end, then easy money and lower interest rates are appropriate.

VELOCITY

Classical economists assumed that there is a close relationship between a nation's money stock and the nominal value of its transactions. The great U.S. economist Irving Fisher observed that in every transaction the buyer exchanges a quantity of money equal to the price of the purchased item.[1] Applying this accounting identity to the nation as a whole, the **equation of exchange** states that

$$MV_T = P_T T \tag{1}$$

where M is the money supply, T is the number of transactions, P_T is the average price of these transactions, and V_T is **velocity**, the average number of times that money is exchanged during a given accounting period.

Velocity measures the frequency with which money is exchanged.

Suppose, for example, that there are $T = 500$ billion transactions a year, involving items with an average price of $P_T = \$100$. The total dollar value of these transactions is $P_T T = \$50$ trillion. If the money supply is $M = \$1$ trillion, then velocity is

$$V_T = \frac{P_T T}{M} = \frac{\$50 \text{ trillion}}{\$1 \text{ trillion}} = 50$$

This means that, on average, a dollar is used about fifty times a year. Equivalently, a dollar is held, on average, about a week between transactions.

Fisher believed that velocity — the average number of times the money stock is exchanged — is fixed by the institutional details of society's bill-paying habits: how often people are paid and how frequently they shop. Another prominent U.S. economist, John Burr Williams, argued that[2]

> Whatever cash most people have in their purses or their checking accounts they are compelled to have there in order to pay their bills when the time comes. In consequence it may be said that the velocity of circulation of most cash balances is habitually kept at the maximum figure that the ingenuity of producers and consumers can devise under the existing customs of the country concerning the frequency of pay days, salary days, rent days, and settlement days for charge accounts, and that nothing could substantially increase the velocity of circulation of such cash and deposits as actually do circulate at all in the proper meaning of

the term except to make pay days come daily instead of weekly, salary and rent days weekly instead of monthly, and tax days monthly instead of yearly.

The Quantity Theory

If V_T is, in fact, constant, then Equation 1 implies that the nominal value of transactions is proportional to the money supply. Other economists reached an even stronger conclusion by replacing the dollar value of all transactions $P_T T$ with the dollar value of a nation's gross national product Py.

$$MV = Py \qquad (2)$$

where P is an index of gross-national-product prices and y is real gross national product. Gross national product (GNP) is the most widely used measure of a nation's production of new goods and services. Velocity V now measures how frequently the money supply is used for gross-national-product transactions — for buying these newly produced goods and services.

The money supply can be measured by a variety of monetary aggregates — M1, M2, M3, and so on (as defined in Chapter 4). If M1 data are used in Equation 2, then velocity is usually identified as M1 velocity and labeled V1. Similarly, the use of M2 data yields M2 velocity, labeled V2.

If we use M1 to measure the money supply, then in 1990 the U.S. money supply was approximately \$800 billion and the dollar value of U.S. gross national product was about $Py = $ \$5,600 billion. Average daily M1 balances were about 14 percent of nominal GNP.

$$\frac{M1}{Py} = \frac{\$800 \text{ billion}}{\$5,600 \text{ billion}} = 0.14$$

M1 velocity was

$$V1 = \frac{Py}{M1} = \frac{\$5,600 \text{ billion}}{\$800 \text{ billion}} = 7$$

This means that, on average, in 1990 the currency and transaction-account balances in M1 were used about 7 times for gross-national-product transactions or, equivalently, that $365/7 = 52$ days passed between gross-national-product transactions.

If velocity is constant, then Equation 2 implies that the nominal (or dollar) value of gross national product is proportional to the money supply. If velocity is fixed at 7, for instance, then Equation 2 can be rearranged as

$$Py = 7M$$

The quantity theory assumes that velocity, the ratio of nominal GNP to the money supply, is constant.

If the money supply increases by 10 percent, from 800 to 880, then nominal GNP will increase by 10 percent also, from $7(800) = 5,600$ to $7(880) = 6,160$. This is a very strong assumption, which is known as the **quantity theory**: The quantity theory of money states that because velocity is constant, a change in the money supply causes a proportionate change in nominal gross national product.

If we also assume, as some economists do, that the economy is at full employment, then real gross national product y is constant. If both velocity V and real GNP y are constant, then Equation 2 tells us that a change in the money supply causes a proportionate change in the price level. Suppose that there is a 10 percent increase in the money supply. If velocity is constant, then nominal gross national product must increase by 10 percent. If real gross national product is constant, then the only way nominal gross national product can increase by 10 percent is if prices increase by 10 percent.

If velocity and real GNP are constant, an X% change in the money supply causes an X% change in prices.

The Imperfect Link Between Transactions and Output

A fundamental difficulty with the quantity theory is that there is an imperfect link between transactions and production. Money is used for many more transactions than for the newly produced goods and services included in a nation's gross national product. Purchases of old houses, used automobiles, gold, bonds, stocks, and other existing assets involve a transfer of ownership, not production, and are not included in gross national product. This imperfect mesh between production and transactions means that transactions are not necessarily fixed even if there is full employment and that the velocity of asset swaps cannot be considered institutionally determined.

A comparison of U.S. gross national product to M1 gives an M1 velocity of about 7, suggesting that a dollar is used on average about once every two months. This estimated interval between transactions is much too long, because the total value of transactions dwarfs the gross national product. The value of stock-market transactions alone is equal to a third of GNP; foreign-exchange transactions are several times GNP.

Annual transactions are much larger than GNP.

The total value of checking-account transactions in 1989 was about 800 times the average balance in these accounts: the average interval between transactions was less than half a day. This rapid turnover of checking-account deposits reflects the money management of large corporations and financial institutions, not typical households. In large New York City banks, annual transactions are more than 3,000 times the average balance. For households, annual transactions are, on average, about 50 times the average checking-account balance. For both households and businesses, total transactions are much larger than are gross-national-product transactions, and velocity is much higher than seven transactions a year.

Monetarism

During the Great Depression, the British economist John Maynard Keynes published *The General Theory of Employment, Interest and Money,* arguably one of the most influential books written in this century. In this book, he persuaded most economists to reject the classical economics that he and they had learned. Classical economists generally assumed that an economy's resources were fully employed. Keynes wrote that[3]

> professional economists after Malthus were apparently unmoved by the lack of correspondence between the results of their theory and the facts of observation . . . It may well be that the classical theory represents the way in which we should like our economy to behave. But to assume that it actually does so is to assume our difficulties away.

With the world economy a shambles in the 1930s, Keynes' arguments that involuntary unemployment was possible and that governments should use monetary and fiscal policies to bolster employment and output were persuasive. Early interpreters of Keynes were enthusiastic about the use of fiscal policies, but skeptical of the potency of monetary policy. In Keynesian models, open-market purchases by the Fed reduce interest rates, which stimulates spending. During the 1930s, these linkages seemed weak. Interest rates were already very low, and entrepreneurs were so worried about sales that lower interest rates might not have made much difference anyway. Early Keynesians looked to fiscal policy (government spending and tax cuts) as the most promising means of stimulating the economy.

Monetarists emphasize the effects of changes in the money supply on the economy.

An important dissenter was Milton Friedman, who argued that monetary disturbances are the major cause of economic fluctuations. For this argument, he was dubbed a "monetarist," and his views were labeled **monetarism**. In professional academic circles, he argued that money matters. In the public arena, what he was saying sounded more like "*only* money matters."

In Friedman's early years, many economists thought that his views reflected the quantity theory, Equation 2, with velocity constant. For if velocity is constant, then money, and only money, causes fluctuations in nominal gross national product. This interpretation was enhanced by the publication of a professional paper by Friedman titled, "The Quantity Theory of Money: A Restatement."[4]

With the passage of time, three important shifts occurred. The first shift was that Friedman's views became increasingly popular. More and more economists identified themselves as monetarists and, as this happened, the meaning of the term monetarist broadened. Monetarism meant so many different things to various people that economists wrote survey articles on "typical monetarist propositions."[5]

The second shift was that Keynesians acknowledged that, outside of deep depressions, monetary policy does affect the economy. For example, James Tobin, a leading Keynesian economist, has done the bulk of his work on monetary theory. In the 1970s and 1980s, it was the Keynesians who urged the government to use monetary policy to strengthen the economy.

The third shift reflected the fact that it became increasingly apparent that the simple quantity theory was untenable. Theoretical arguments and dozens of empirical studies indicate that velocity is not constant, but depends on interest rates and other factors.[6] When interest rates increase, households and businesses

| Velocity During Hyperinflations | Highlight 17.1 |

According to the simple quantity theory, velocity — the ratio of nominal gross national product to the money supply — is constant. Keynes argued that velocity is not constant, but increases when interest rates rise. Dramatic evidence of this effect occurs during rapid inflations. The nominal return on a physical asset is the income or services it yields plus its price appreciation, net of taxes and transaction costs. In a rapid inflation, physical assets have very high nominal rates of return, while cash pays no interest at all. The essence of a hyperinflation is a flight from currency, an extreme attempt to economize on money balances, which only pushes prices up even faster. During the German hyperinflation in 1922–1923, prices increased at a compounded rate of 322 percent per month. Workers were paid daily, or two or three times a day, and their children would bicycle back and forth between factories and home so that their parents' wages could be spent as soon as possible, before prices could increase once again. In the Hungarian hyperinflation between August 1945 and July 1946, prices increased at 19,800 percent per month. At one point, the government issued a 1,000,000,000,000,000,000,000-pengo note, which bought less than one U.S. penny. As the value of the cash fell, relative to real assets, the velocity of the Hungarian pengo increased by a factor of 300.

economize on their money holdings, because holding idle money forgoes the opportunity to profit from investments. As they reduce the amount of time that money is held between investments, velocity increases. In the opposite situation, when interest rates fall, the gains from active money management diminish, and households and businesses allow money to sit longer in their purses, cash registers, and checking accounts. In the early 1970s, Friedman accepted the evidence that velocity is affected by interest rates.[7] Friedman's subsequent policy recommendations seemed to rely less on the quantity theory and more on the classical assumption that the economy is never far from full employment.

Today, there is a great diversity among monetarists. Some believe that fluctuations in velocity are sufficiently small that the quantity theory is a useful approximation. Others acknowledge that velocity does vary and is significantly related to interest rates, but that these variations are predictable. While acknowledging that a change in the money supply does not automatically cause a proportionate change in nominal gross national product, they argue that the effects are at least predictable.

Monetarists have various degrees of belief in the classical assumptions that velocity is stable and the economy is at full employment.

Some monetarists make the classical assumption that the economy is always at or near full employment — so that changes in the money supply affect prices but not output. Others believe that changes in the money supply affect both output and prices, at least in the short run. Figure 17.2 is a stylized sketch to assist our understanding of these linkages.

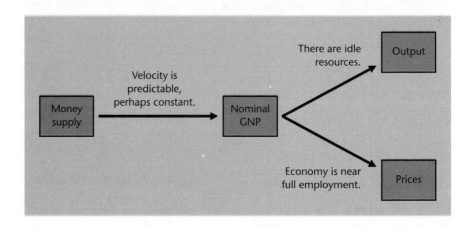

Figure 17.2 Monetarists Emphasize That the Money Supply Affects Nominal GNP, Perhaps Involving Mostly a Change in Prices

THE DEMAND FOR MONEY

The argument that velocity is not constant, but is influenced by interest rates and other factors can be clarified by reinterpreting velocity as one way of describing the demand for money. This idea goes back to Alfred Marshall, an economics professor at Cambridge University, and his former student A. C. Pigou, who together developed the **Cambridge cash-balances approach** by using demand-and-supply analysis to derive a quantity-theory equation. They argued that money is used as a store of wealth between the sale of some items and the purchase of others. Since purchases and sales depend on a nation's gross national product, they assumed that the demand for money M^D is proportional to nominal gross national product, Py.

Velocity reflects the demand for money.

$$M^D = kPy$$

If we assume that money demand M^D is equal to supply M, we derive

$$M = kPy$$

This equation is identical to the quantity theory equation $MV = Py$, with velocity $V = 1/k$.

Marshall's interpretation of this equation had profound consequences for economic theory. By emphasizing the role of money as a store of value rather than as a means of payment, Marshall shifted attention away from the institutional details that constrained the frequency of transactions. By reinterpreting the quantity theory equation as a statement that money demand is equal to money supply, he suggested that velocity is determined by people's preferences, and not rigidly fixed by a society's bill-paying customs.

Keynes's Reasoning

John Maynard Keynes was a student of Marshall and later joined him on the Cambridge faculty. Keynes, too, argued that money is a store of value, one of many possible ways of providing for future consumption. The opportunity cost of holding money is the higher rate of return that can be earned on other assets, including interest on bonds. Therefore, interest rates have a decisive influence on the decision to hold money rather than bonds, what he called investors' **liquidity preference.** In Keynes's words[8]

> *The rate of interest is the reward for parting with liquidity. . . . [It] is a measure of the unwillingness of those who possess money to part with their liquid control over it. . . . It is the "price" which equilibrates the desire to hold wealth in the form of cash with the availability of cash.*

This argument contradicted the classical assumption that velocity is fixed. If the demand for money depends on interest rates, then velocity depends on interest rates. In particular, an increase in interest rates reduces the demand for money and increases velocity. Figures 17.3 and 17.4 provide some evidence of these relationships.

Money demand depends on interest rates.

While noting that each individual's money is held in a single pool and "need not be sharply divided even in his own mind," Keynes found it helpful to identify three motives for holding money: the transactions motive, the precautionary motive, and the speculative motive. The first, the transactions motive, was very much in the Cambridge cash-balances tradition.[9]

> *One reason for holding cash is to bridge the interval between the receipt of income and its disbursement. The strength of this motive . . . will chiefly depend upon the amount of income and the normal length of the interval between its receipt and its disbursement . . . the value of current output (and hence on current income), and on the number of hands through which output passes.*

Keynes' second motive was precautionary.[10]

> *To provide for contingencies requiring sudden expenditure and for unforeseen opportunities of advantageous purchases, and also to hold an asset of which the value is fixed in terms of money to meet a subsequent liability fixed in terms of money, are further motives for holding cash.*
>
> *The strength of [the precautionary] motive will partly depend on the cheapness and the reliability of methods of obtaining cash, when it is required, by some form of temporary borrowing, in particular by overdraft or its equivalent. For there is no necessity to hold idle cash to bridge over intervals if it can be obtained*

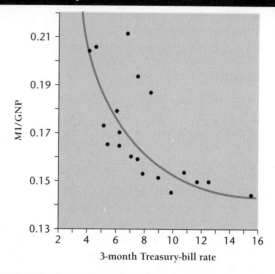

Figure 17.3   Money Demand Is Inversely Related to Treasury-Bill Rates, 1970–1988

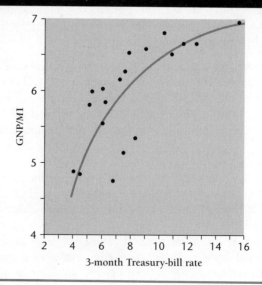

Figure 17.4   Velocity Is Positively Related to Treasury-Bill Rates, 1970–1988

without difficulty at the moment when it is actually required. Their strength will also depend on what we may term the relative cost of holding cash. . . . If deposit interest is earned or if bank charges are avoided by holding cash, this decreases the cost and strengthens the motive.

Early interpreters of Keynes stressed the third of his motives: for speculation about bond prices. Investors who are sufficiently bearish on bond prices so that the anticipated capital losses outweigh the interest income will hold money instead. When the Fed buys bonds, pushing bond prices up and interest rates down, the increased money supply is held by those speculators who are convinced that the now-lower interest rates do not provide enough income to offset the risk that interest rates will rise back to more normal levels, reducing bond prices and giving capital losses to bondholders. Thus an open-market purchase by the Fed "must raise the price of bonds sufficiently to exceed the expectations of some 'bull' and so influence him to sell his bond for cash and join the 'bear' brigade."[11]

The Modern Approach

Keynes's speculative motive doesn't live up to the billing of Keynes's approach as a "general theory," since it applies only when people expect bond prices to fall and can only be a temporary phenomenon since people will adjust their perceptions of what is a "normal" level of interest rates if low interest rates persist. Tobin generalized Keynes's argument by using the ideas of risk aversion and diversification (discussed in Chapter 11) to show that investors hold money when they are worried about bond prices.[12] In Keynes's approach, speculators switch from bonds to money when an anticipated decline in bond prices reduces the expected return on bonds below that on money. Tobin showed that even if bond prices are considered as likely to rise as fall, risk-averse investors will diversify by holding safe money as well as risky assets.

In the Keynes-Tobin dichotomy between money and bonds, money includes all assets with safe, fixed returns: cash, fixed-interest deposits, and Treasury bills. Tobin's portfolio arguments show why investors hold low-yielding fixed-interest assets and show how this demand is sensitive to interest rates.

To explain why people hold cash and checking-account balances rather than safe Treasury bills, economists rely on the opportunity-cost idea expressed by Keynes in explaining his precautionary motive. The primary advantage of money is that it can be used to pay for transactions; the disadvantage is that money earns little or no interest. The return on cash is zero. The highest return on checking accounts is around 5 percent. Meanwhile, Treasury bills, commercial paper, and the like may have returns of 10 percent, 15 percent, or even more. When these other interest rates are high, people economize on their money holdings in that, despite the inconvenience, funds needed for transactions can be invested temporarily to earn high rates of return. The appendix to this chapter uses a formal inventory model to analyze the costs and benefits of money economizing. The conclusions are plausible: money demand is positively related

Money can be used to pay for transactions, but earns little or no interest.

to the volume of transactions, negatively related to the interest rates on alternative assets, and positively related to the costs of transferring funds between money and interest-earning assets.

The fundamental reason money is held is the lack of synchronization between receipts and payments. If income and expenses were equal and occurred simultaneously, there would be no need to hold money. But, with imperfect synchronization, money is held, even if it pays little or no interest, in order to pay for day-to-day and extraordinary expenses.

High interest rates encourage people to economize on money holdings.

The higher the returns offered on alternative assets, the greater the incentive to economize on money holdings by investing temporarily and by adjusting the timing of income and disbursement. These pressures may incite institutional changes such as more frequent or flexible payment schedules, reduced lags between the payment and receipt of funds, higher yields on checking-account balances, and less costly transfer between money and other assets. Very high interest rates in the United States in the 1970s and 1980s spawned many such changes.

MONEY-SUPPLY TARGETS

Milton Friedman has long recommended that the Fed ignore the economy and keep the money supply growing at a steady annual rate — for example, that the Fed focus its efforts on keeping M2 growing at 3 percent to 5 percent a year. Because of his close association with monetarism, such rules — whether advocated by Friedman or by others — are often identified as monetarist policy recommendations.

Many monetarists recommend that the Fed focus on a monetary-aggregate target.

The specific numbers used in these rules can be rationalized in terms of the quantity theory equation,

$$MV = Py$$

which implies that the percentage increase in nominal gross national product Py is equal to the percentage increase in the money supply M plus the percentage increase in velocity V.

$$\%(Py) = \%M + \%V \tag{3}$$

If velocity is predictable, then hitting a money target will achieve nominal GNP objectives.

If the Fed could accurately predict the percentage change in velocity, then it could use Equation 3 to determine the percentage increase in the money supply (its intermediate target) consistent with a desired increase in nominal GNP. For example, a 4-percent increase in the money supply and a 3-percent increase in velocity would produce a 7-percent increase in nominal gross national product.

If real gross national product can be counted on to increase at a given rate, then the Fed will know how much of the target increase in nominal gross national product will be real and how much will be due to inflation. In particular, the quantity-theory equation implies that the percentage increase in prices is approximately equal to the percentage increase in the money supply plus the percentage increase in velocity minus the percentage increase in real gross national product.

$$\%P = \%M + \%V - \%y \qquad (4)$$

Classical economists assumed that velocity V and real gross national product y are approximately constant at any point in time, but may change gradually as time passes. Friedman estimated that real gross national product grows, on average, by about 2 percent to 3 percent a year while M2 velocity falls, on average, by about 1 percent to 2 percent. Therefore, Equation 4 implies that a 3-percent to 5-percent growth in M2 is consistent with a 0-percent rate of inflation.

If velocity and real output are predicted accurately, a money-supply target can achieve inflation objectives.

$$\begin{aligned} \%P &= \%M2 + \%V2 - \%y \\ &= (3\% \text{ to } 5\%) + (-1\% \text{ to } -2\%) - (2\% \text{ to } 3\%) \end{aligned}$$

The underlying assumptions are that velocity and real output deviate little from their long-run trend paths. Neither of these assumptions is strictly true. Velocity varies (for example, as interest rates change), and income fluctuates as the economy departs from full employment.

The Stability of Velocity

Figure 17.5 shows the velocity of M1 and M2 up until 1980, when these monetary aggregates were redefined. Figure 17.6 shows M1 and M2 velocity using the new definitions, with data estimated back to 1970. None of these velocities has been constant, in either the short run or in the long run.

Figure 17.5   M1 and M2 Velocity Before 1980

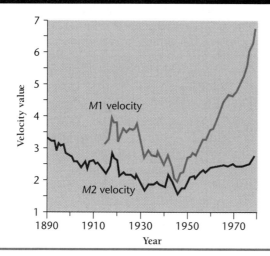

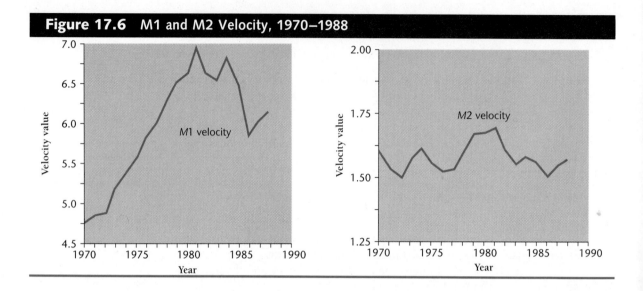

Figure 17.6   M1 and M2 Velocity, 1970–1988

Milton Friedman favored M2 velocity in his monumental A *Monetary History of the United States, 1867–1960,* written with Anna Schwartz and published in 1963. M2 velocity declined markedly between 1880 and 1915 (most likely because of the explosive growth of checking accounts). Friedman argued that the long-run trend of M2 velocity would continue to be downward, and his recommended 3-percent-to-5-percent growth rate for M2 assumes that M2 velocity falls by 1 percent to 2 percent a year. But there has been no consistent long-run trend since 1915. Using the current definition of M2, velocity has been trendless since 1970, though annual fluctuations of 3 percent to 5 percent have been common.

Many who follow monetary aggregates, including the Federal Reserve, have focused their attention on M1 rather than M2. M1 velocity has been reasonably stable during some periods, but erratic at other times. Figure 17.5 shows that M1 velocity was very high in the 1920s, when interest rates were high, and fell along with interest rates during the Great Depression. Between 1950 and 1980, rising interest rates lured money out of traditional checking accounts, restraining M1 and tripling M1 velocity. This 30-year upward trend was broken by sharp, unexpected declines in M1 velocity in 1982, 1983, 1985, and 1986. These sharp breaks are shown in Figure 17.7 by an examination of the annual percentage changes in velocity from 1970 through 1989.

Erratic velocity undermines a monetarist strategy.

These erratic swings in velocity undermine the credibility of a monetarist strategy. Suppose that the Fed had adopted an unwavering monetarist rule at the beginning of 1986, based on the historical 3-percent average annual increase in M1 velocity since 1950. Equation 3 implies that the predicted percentage increase in nominal gross national product is three percentage points larger than the percentage increase in M1.

Figure 17.7   Percentage Change in M1 Velocity, 1970–1989

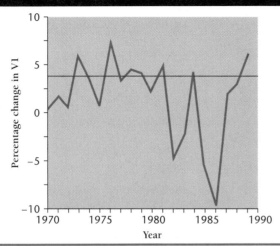

$$\%(Py) = \%M1 + \%V1$$
$$= \%M1 + 3\%$$

Aiming for a 6-percent increase in nominal gross national product (perhaps 2 percent real and 4 percent from inflation), the Fed might have committed itself to a 3-percent rate of growth of M1.

Now, what if (as actually happened) M1 velocity unexpectedly falls by 9 percent? This 12-percentage-point error in predicting velocity means a 12-percentage-point error in gross national product if the Fed refuses to budge from its 3-percent growth rate for M1. Instead of rising by 6 percent, nominal gross national product will fall by 6 percent.

$$\%(Py) = \%M1 + \%V1$$
$$= 3\% - 9\%$$
$$= -6\%$$

The Fed will have gotten the magnitude right and the sign wrong! In the unlikely event that this contraction affects only prices, not real gross national product, prices will fall by 8 percent instead of rising by 4 percent — hardly consistent with price stability.

There hasn't been an 8-percent deflation in the United States since the 1930s. If nominal gross national product fell by 6 percent, this would no doubt involve a substantial drop in real output. There would surely be an unexpected and unwanted economic recession if the Fed adhered to an M1 target and M1 velocity dropped unexpectedly, as it did in 1982, 1983, 1985, and 1986. If, on the other hand, M1 velocity increases unexpectedly, as it did in 1989, then strict

Highlight 17.2	The Effects of International Trade on Velocity

The Quantity Theory equation $MV = Py$ shows that velocity V is the ratio of nominal gross national product Py to a measure of the money supply M:

$$V = \frac{Py}{M}$$

When the Quantity Theory equation is reinterpreted in terms of money demand, it becomes clear that velocity is affected by economic events that alter money demand relative to nominal gross national product. Events that increase money demand reduce velocity; events that reduce money demand increase velocity.

The growing importance of international trade for the United States has implications for money demand and, therefore, for velocity. Gross national product (GNP) is intended to monitor domestic economic activity and consequently is an estimate of domestic production. GNP includes U.S. exports since these are produced in the United States, but excludes imported goods, since these are produced elsewhere. However, money demand in the United States depends on imports rather than exports, since U.S. consumers need dollars to buy German cars and Japanese cameras, but German and Japanese consumers do not need dollars to buy U.S. wheat and blue jeans.

Matters are even more complicated than this because U.S. workers are paid in dollars for blue jeans that the Japanese buy with yen, and Japanese workers are paid in yen for cameras that Americans buy with dollars. The important point is that money demand depends not just on domestic production — GNP — but on the size and relative magnitudes of exports and imports. As a consequence, velocity, the ratio of GNP to money demand, varies with exports and imports.

In 1969, U.S. imports were equal to 5.6% of GNP; in 1989, they were equal to 12.9%. In 1985, the difference between U.S. exports and imports was +$26.3 billion (+0.8% of GNP); in 1987, the difference was −112.6(−2.5% of GNP). Variations of this magnitude can cause substantial changes in velocity.

adherence to an M1 target will cause an unintentional increase in inflation. The erratic behavior of velocity is a primary reason why the Fed has resisted monetarist advice to target a monetary aggregate and ignore the economy.

Is It Controllable?

For a monetary aggregate, such as M1, to be a useful intermediate target, not only must there be a stable relationship between it and the Fed's objective, such as the rate of inflation, but the Fed must be able to hit its intermediate target with reasonable accuracy. The Fed cannot ensure a constant growth rate of M1 merely by maintaining a constant growth rate for the monetary base. During the 1970s, the annual growth rate of the monetary base was never more than 1.5 percent above or below the average growth rate for the decade; yet there were substantial fluctuations in monetary aggregates, output, and inflation.[13] Figures 2 through 6 in Chapter 4 show that there has been only the loosest connection between annual changes in the monetary base and in M1 and M2. If there is a stronger relationship, it involves considerable lags.

Monetary aggregates are influenced not only by the Fed, but also by the economic decisions of households, businesses, and financial institutions, and not only by current policies, but by past policies and events, too. It takes a considerable amount of time for an increase in the monetary base to cycle through the banking system and cause an eventual change in monetary aggregates. There are lots of slippages and external influences, substantial errors and delays, along the way. The very same errors-and-lags argument used in the previous chapter to explain why the Fed cannot fine-tune the economy also implies that the Fed cannot fine-tune monetary aggregates.[14]

The Fed cannot fine-tune monetary aggregates.

In December 1981, Anthony Solomon, respected President of the Federal Reserve Bank of New York, speculated that, "We may already be nearing the point where the Federal Reserve can influence the growth of these broad measures only indirectly by first influencing the behavior of the economy itself."[15] A most provocative reversal: the economy may be an intermediate target for monetary aggregates, rather than the other way around! Monetarists advised the Fed to stabilize the economy by stabilizing monetary aggregates, and the Fed responds that, as a practical matter, the only way it can get monetary aggregates to grow at a steady rate is somehow to keep the economy growing at a steady pace. It is apparently at least as difficult to stabilize monetary aggregates as it is to stabilize the gross national product.

A Plethora of Monetary Targets

Since 1975, the Fed has regularly announced annual target growth rates for most monetary aggregates. The Full Employment and Balanced Growth Act of 1978 (also called the Humphrey-Hawkins Act) requires the Fed to report semiannually to Congress on its monetary targets. Each February, the Fed announces its monetary targets for the current year, using a one-year period that begins in the fourth quarter of the preceding year and ends in the fourth quarter of the

| Highlight 17.3 | **The Monetary Base and Monetary Aggregates** |

Chapter 4 used a deposit-multiplier model to explain how, with fractional reserve banking, deposits and monetary aggregates are multiples of the monetary base B. Thus

$$M1 = mB$$

where the money multiplier m depends on bank reserves relative to deposits, currency outside of banks relative to deposits, and transaction accounts relative to other deposits. The percentage change in M1 is approximately equal to the percentage change in the money multiplier plus the percentage change in the monetary base:

$$\%M1 = \%m + \%B$$

If the money multiplier m is constant, then a change in the monetary base causes a given, proportional change in M1. However, the money multiplier is not constant. It changes as banks decide to hold more or less reserves and as households and business shift funds among currency, transaction accounts, and other deposits.

For instance, the Federal Reserve Bank of St. Louis (whose research group has a consistently monetarist orientation) reported that the monetary base grew at a 7.5 percent annual rate during the first seven months of July 1982 and at a 7.4 percent annual rate during the next three months.* If the money multiplier m had been constant, or had grown at a constant rate, during this period, M1 would have grown at a constant rate, too. But, in fact, the money multiplier declined at a 4.5 percent annual rate during the first seven months of the year and increased at a 5.8 percent annual rate during the next three months, giving very different growth rates for M1 over these two periods:

January 1982–July 1982: $\%M1 = \%m + \%B = -4.5\% + 7.5\% = 3.0\%$
July 1982–October 1982: $\%M1 = \%m + \%B = +5.8\% + 7.4\% = 13.2\%$

---

*Dallas S. Batten, *U.S. Financial Data*, Federal Reserve Bank of St. Louis, March 25, 1983, p. 1.

current year. These targets are ranges, such as a rate of growth of M2 that is between 6 percent and 9 percent. In July, the Fed informs Congress of its progress in achieving these objectives, its intention to maintain or alter these targets for the remainder of the year, and its tentative targets for the following year.

The Fed is not required to hit its targets and frequently doesn't. Because the Fed does not directly control monetary aggregates, it uses an empirical model to help predict how its monetary policies will affect monetary aggregates. This model has frequently gone awry, causing the Fed to miss its targets by substantial amounts. In the eleven years from 1976 through 1986 (after which the Fed stopped targeting M1), the Fed hit its target range for M1 only twice, in 1976 and 1984.

The Fed often misses its monetary targets.

Because of the imperfections of all monetary aggregates as intermediate targets, there is considerable debate among monetarists about which aggregate should be targeted. Edward Shaw, an advocate of a constant-money-growth rule, freely acknowledged the difficulties of selecting a money-supply target.[16]

> *If you suspect that growth in money was under tight restraint, you can tailor a definition to your suspicion. If you prefer to think that restraint was mild you can be right again — with a different definition. . . .*
>
> *The "supply of money" that central banks manipulate, that people hold most of the time and spend once in a while, that economists investigate is not, then, a simple concept. It can be a figure so transformed in the statistical beauty parlor as to be hardly recognizable by its closest friends.*

Friedman chose M2. Shaw picked M1. After Arthur Burns became Chairman of the Fed in 1970, he converted from M1 to M5 (which is closest to today's M3). Others prefer the monetary base.[17]

There are several alternative monetary targets, and it does make a difference which target is selected, because forcing one monetary aggregate to grow at a constant rate does not ensure that others will. Highlight 17.4 explains how unexpected shifts of funds by households, businesses, and banks often cause one monetary aggregate to grow faster than the Fed intends, while another grows more slowly. When this happens, the Fed must use subjective judgment in deciding whether it will respond to these changes and in assessing which of these divergent monetary aggregates it will believe.

Sometimes, one monetary aggregate grows rapidly while another grows slowly.

In dynamic, innovative financial markets, controlling one monetary aggregate almost ensures that new financial assets will develop and expand. After the Civil War, when the government tried to restrain bank notes, checking accounts took their place. The Fed's efforts to restrain traditional checking accounts in the 1970s fueled an explosion of check-like accounts. Financial-market innovations such as these increase the volume of transactions that can be carried out with a given monetary aggregate and, hence, increase velocity. For example, the introduction of NOW accounts reduced the appeal of traditional checking accounts and thereby increased M1 velocity, undermining the M1 target. Charles Goodhart, a senior economist at the Bank of England (which currently watches

Highlight 17.4	Interpreting Shifts Among Monetary Aggregates

Asset shifts can cause monetary aggregates to move in divergent ways, giving potentially misleading signals about the condition of financial markets and the economy. For instance, because many of the transaction accounts in M1 pay interest, some of the money in these accounts is kept there for savings, not for bill paying. On the other hand, money-market funds and cash-management accounts, which are not included in M1, can be used to pay bills, and some of the money in these accounts is kept there for bill-paying, not for savings. This blurring of the distinction between transaction and savings balances makes it difficult to interpret movements in monetary aggregates. Funds may switch from one type of account to another in response to changes in interest rates or the features of these accounts, causing changes in monetary aggregates, without reflecting any change in spending behavior and, thus, in gross national product.

Here is another example. As part of their banking relationship, many businesses maintain compensating balances in their corporate checking accounts in return for lines of credit and cash-management services. These funds are different from other checking-account balances in that they are not normally used to make transactions. In January 1988, the Fed surveyed 60 major banks to learn why there had been a sharp decline in checking-account balances during the preceding month. They found that many corporations had held excessive compensating balances earlier in the year and in December were allowed to reduce their checking-account balances.* This shift was of little or no economic significance, but the accompanying drop in M1 might have provoked open-market purchases by a more doctrinaire Fed.

Seemingly trivial differences in how business investment is financed can also cause monetary aggregates to diverge. If a business borrows money from a bank that has raised funds by selling repurchase agreements to an insurance company, these repurchase agreements are included in M2. If the bank instead raises money to lend the business by selling large certificates of deposit to the insurance company, these CDs are put in M3. If the business sells commercial paper directly to the insurance company, the commercial paper is included in L. If it sells bonds to the insurance company, it is ignored completely. These very similar transactions have virtually identical macroeconomic consequences for interest rates, employment, and prices, but very different effects on monetary aggregates.

---

*Bondweek, February 22, 1988.

its M5), offered Goodhart's Law: "Any definition of money which becomes an official target will lose all relationship with events in the real economy within two years."[18]

New near-moneys continue to be developed and attempts to control some are sure to spawn others. Some new moneys and near-moneys, such as electronic payments systems with overdraft privileges, will be exceedingly difficult to monitor. In a rapidly changing world, an up-to-date monetary rule is akin to the economics professor who gives the same exam year after year, but changes the answers each year. In the same spirit, the appropriate monetary rule might be "have the money supply grow at a constant rate year after year, but change the definition of the money supply each year." If so, is that really very different from a discretionary policy?

Herbert Stein, an economic advisor to several Republican presidents, has jokingly said that monetarism is "the theory that there is a stable and predictable relation between the price level as effect and the supply of money as cause. This theory has firm empirical support if the definition of the money supply is allowed to vary in an unstable and unpredictable way."[19] The continuing challenge for monetarism is to find a stable definition of the money supply that the Fed can control and that is reliably related to the Fed's ultimate objectives.

Destabilizing Policies?

We've seen a variety of cases in which the Fed might take regrettable actions if it myopically pegs a particular monetary aggregate. Here is one more example. During an economic boom, inflation reduces the purchasing power of currency, encouraging people to hold less money and buy more commodities before prices go higher still. The excess unwanted currency passes from hand to hand like a hot potato, as consumers try to spend it before it depreciates further. You learned in Chapter 5 that an increase in inflation expectations tends to raise nominal interest rates. If market-interest rates increase more than the interest rates on checking accounts, funds flow out of checking accounts, causing M1 to decline. If the Fed ignores the inflation and stabilizes M1, it makes open-market purchases, expanding the monetary base during an inflation — gasoline on the fire.

Monetary-aggregate targets can be destabilizing.

A final consideration is that economic events seldom affect all financial markets equally. Thus it is often useful to have specific detailed policies directed at particular financial markets or institutions. Before becoming Fed Chairman, Paul Volcker argued that[20]

> *There have been a number of occasions in the 1970s when the Federal Reserve had to pay the closest possible attention to particular financial problems and to the potential vulnerability of various credit markets. The recurrent concerns . . . about the capacity of thrift institutions to perform their role as intermediaries between savers and the mortgage market is one example. The potential disturbances growing out of the Penn Central Railroad and the Franklin and the Herstatt Bank affairs are another class of examples. The strain on the municipal bond markets and the concerns about the rising level of losses commercial banks were*

taking on loans a year or so ago are other cases in point. Their problems had to be dealt with — actually or potentially — by techniques that cannot be encompassed by any simple monetary rule.

The most reasonable conclusion for this chapter is that there is no simple, perfect policy for all times and all places. Doggedly pegging interest rates, M1, or some other specific target will sometimes be a good policy and, in other circumstances, be a poor policy. Instead of myopically focusing on one bit of data and ignoring everything else, it is more logical for the Fed to monitor many data.

The Fed monitors a variety of economic data.

The Fed is well aware that it is difficult to control monetary aggregates and that these can give an incomplete and possibly misleading description of the state of financial markets and of the economy. It instead follows a rather eclectic course, monitoring not only interest rates and monetary aggregates, but also output, employment, inflation, the balance of payments, and election returns. If the economy is in a serious recession that the Fed wants to soften, then easy money is called for. Rather than stubbornly pegging an interest rate or monetary aggregate as the economy falls apart, the Fed makes substantial open-market purchases, increasing the monetary base, reducing interest rates, and stimulating spending.

It tries to keep monetary aggregates and the economy growing at a reasonably steady pace, but it is not slavishly tied to any particular aggregate or to an eternally fixed growth rate. The Fed exercises subjective judgment and has made mistakes. In the next chapter, we will review the details of Fed policy since World War II. We will see that it has been tolerably successful in achieving its objectives, though it remains an unsettled issue whether it would have been more successful following other operating procedures.

SUMMARY

The quantity theory assumes that velocity, the ratio of nominal gross national product to some measure of the money supply, is constant — implying that gross national product changes proportionately with the money supply. Keynes successfully argued that the opportunity cost of holding money is the interest that can be earned on other assets; therefore, the demand for money is negatively related to interest rates and velocity is positively related to interest rates. Classical economists generally assumed not only that velocity is constant, but that the economy is at full employment. Monetarists are a diverse group, with varying degrees of faith in these two classical assumptions.

A policy of stabilizing interest rates may destabilize the economy. If, for example, an increase in business and consumer spending causes an economic expansion, interest rates will rise. If the Fed uses open-market purchases to keep interest rates from rising, then this increase in the monetary base will fuel an already strong economy.

Mechanically pegging some measure of the money supply is not an infallible policy either, for a variety of reasons. Velocity is not sufficiently stable. Lags and uncertainties make it difficult to control monetary aggregates. Shifts among assets cause monetary aggregates to move in divergent directions, giving contradictory signals about the state of financial markets and the economy. In practice, the Fed monitors not only interest rates and monetary aggregates, but many other economic indicators, before deciding whether monetary ease or restraint is appropriate.

IMPORTANT TERMS

Cambridge cash-balances approach
equation of exchange
liquidity preference
monetarism

quantity theory
square root rule
velocity

EXERCISES

1. A certain economy has 100 billion transactions a year, involving items with an average price of $120. If the money supply is $M = \$1$ trillion, what is the value of velocity? On average, how long is a dollar held between transactions?

2. An economy has a money supply $M = \$100$ billion and one billion transactions a week, involving items with an average price of $100. What is the value of velocity? On average, how long is a dollar held between transactions?

3. What will the rate of inflation be if the real gross national product increases by 2 percent, velocity increases by 2 percent, and the money supply increases by 4 percent?

4. The money supply is $1 trillion, and velocity is constant at 6. According to the quantity theory, what will happen to nominal gross national product if the money supply increases by 5 percent? If the economy is at full employment, how much of this increase in nominal gross national product will reflect an increase in output, and how much will simply be an increase in prices?

5. The money supply is $1 trillion, and the nominal gross national product is $5 trillion. What is the value of velocity? What will happen to nominal gross national product if velocity is constant and the money supply falls by 10 percent? What if both velocity and real gross national product are constant?

6. If nominal gross national product is 5,000 and the money supply is 400, what is the value of velocity? How many days, on average, is money held between GNP transactions? If the money supply increases by 4 percent, by what percentage (approximately) will
   a. nominal gross national product increase if velocity is constant?
   b. prices increase if velocity and real gross national product are both constant?

7. For many years, Milton Friedman recommended a 3-percent to 5-percent annual growth of M2. Why might this specific range be consistent with a 0-percent rate of inflation? If M2 velocity is constant and real gross national product increases by 2 percent a year,

what will happen to prices if M2 increases by 3 percent to 5 percent a year?

8. Explain the important omission from this statement in a publication by the Federal Reserve Bank of Cleveland: "The quantity theory of money states that over the long run, prices will rise in proportion to the rise in the money supply."[21]

9. During the 1945–1946 Hungarian hyperinflation, prices increased 19,800 percent per month. How fast must prices increase each day, compounded daily, to increase by 19,800 percent in a 30-day month?

10. From 1966 through 1969, the rate of inflation in Israel averaged 4 percent per year. The inflation record for 1970–1981 is shown below.

Year	Inflation Rate
1970	8%
1971	13%
1972	14%
1973	21%
1974	35%
1975	37%
1976	27%
1977	43%
1978	55%
1979	82%
1980	128%
1981	126%

The real Israeli money supply fell from 4 billion shekels in 1973 to 1.3 billion shekels in 1981. How is it mathematically possible for inflation to increase while the real money supply is decreasing? What do you suppose happened to velocity during this period?

11. Explain why velocity depends on interest rates if the demand for money depends on interest rates.

12. Critically evaluate the following quotation. Would you characterize it as a monetarist line of reasoning? If a producer, wholesaler, ship-per, and retailer were to merge, do you think that this would affect the demand for money?[22]

That the concept of total transactions is inherently uninteresting can be seen by reflecting on some simple questions. Who cares if a can of beans is sold once or twice or three times after leaving the packing plant but before being sold to the final consumer? Can it really be that the price of beans, and of goods in general, depends in an important way on how many times beans are sold on the way to the final consumer? Isn't it more likely that if, in the equation of exchange $[MV_T = P_T T]$, T should rise solely because of a change in the number of intermediate transactions, then V_T would also rise so that there would be little or no impact on the general price level?

13. The quantity theory assumes that velocity is a constant, depending essentially on institutional factors. Explain how each of the following would affect velocity, as measured by the monetary base and gross national product.
    a. A reduction in reserve requirements.
    b. An electronic funds transfer system.
    c. An increase in interest rates.

14. What explanations can you provide for the empirical evidence that M1 velocity moves pro-cyclically (increasing in booms, falling in recessions) and has also greatly increased over the past 30 years? In the 1974–1975 recession, M1 velocity actually increased. What might explain this unusual event?

15. According to the square root rule (Equation 6 in the Appendix) how would velocity be affected by an income redistribution from the rich to the poor?

16. In October 1985, an economist at the Federal Reserve Bank of Cleveland wrote that "The rapid growth of M1 typically indicates a strong economy. The recent growth of M1, however, has been associated with an unusually weak economy."[23] What happened to M1 velocity during this period?

17. If the Fed keeps M1 on a steady target although M1 velocity increases unexpectedly, what will happen to nominal gross national product?

18. If the Fed follows an eclectic approach, hoping to stabilize nominal gross national product, what will it do when M1 velocity declines?

19. The simple quantity theory assumes that velocity depends only on institutional factors. If there is an increased use of credit cards, what do you predict will happen to velocity, as measured by the monetary base and gross national product? Explain your reasoning.

20. Before the Fed's 1980 revisions, M2 included savings accounts in commercial banks but excluded savings accounts in savings-and-loan associations; M3 included savings accounts in both types of institutions. How do you suppose M2 velocity was affected by the relatively rapid growth of savings-and-loan associations in the 1950s and 1960s?

21. Before 1980, M1 included traditional checking accounts in commercial banks, but excluded NOW accounts and other check-like accounts. These other accounts were included in M2 or M3, depending on whether they were offered by commercial banks or thrift institutions. How did the shift of funds from commercial bank checking accounts to check-like accounts affect M1 velocity?

22. Before 1980, money-market funds were not included in the Fed's monetary aggregates. How did the shift of funds in the 1970s from commercial bank savings accounts (included in M2) to money-market funds affect M2 velocity?

23. In January 1986, Prudential-Bache's Director of Economics & Fixed Income Research predicted that "M1 could explode during the first few months of the year as a result of the elimination of minimum deposit requirements for Super NOW accounts."[24] What effect would such an explosion have on M1 velocity? What effect would you predict on gross national product if the funds going into Super NOW accounts come from time and savings accounts?

24. Is it contradictory for Milton Friedman to argue that money matters, but that we shouldn't use monetary policies to offset economic booms and recessions? Why did he recommend that M2 grow at 3 percent to 5 percent a year, rather than 0 percent?

25. Write a one-paragraph essay explaining why you agree or disagree with this analogy.[25]

    [Nonmonetarists argue that] whether monetary growth is excessive and inflationary can be judged only in relation to the behavior of many other indicators, such as interest rates and unemployment.

    To use an analogy, there is generally a fairly predictable relation between the amount of gas the driver feeds to his car and the speed of the car. But it does not follow that the safest way to drive a car is to use a constant pressure on the accelerator. . . .

26. Congress authorized nationwide NOW accounts, beginning on January 1, 1981. An Associated Press news story reported that funds pouring into these accounts during the first week of that year caused M1 to increase by $11.6 billion, to $417.6 billion. The story went on to report that business loans fell by $2 billion that week, "in line with analysts' expectations for a slowing in monetary expansion as the central bank's tight-credit policy of recent weeks, aimed at cooling inflation, restrains economic growth."[26] How could a rapid growth in M1 possibly be consistent with a tight-credit policy?

27. State the reasoning behind this quotation and explain why you either agree or disagree.[27]

    Sometimes Friedman and his followers seem to be saying: "We don't know what money is, but whatever it is, its stock should grow steadily at 3 to 4 per cent per year."

28. Give the logic behind this quotation and tell why you either agree or disagree with it.[28]

Perhaps we should abolish the Federal Reserve Board. Its functions could be handled by a new bureau of the Treasury, patterned on the Bureau of Alcohol, Tobacco and Firearms. Certainly monetary policy can be as dangerous as booze, butts and guns. . . .

[We could] require the Fed to slow money-supply growth steadily until it reached a rate compatible with the economy's ability to grow. If that were the law of the land all we would need would be a few capable clerks.

29. In Friedman and Schwartz's A *Monetary History of the United States, 1867–1960,* they argued that the Fed's 1942–1951 support of government security prices "converted all securities into the equivalent of money."[29] By the same reasoning, should all fixed-interest deposits be counted as money? Is this consistent with Friedman and Schwartz's preference for M2, which, at that time, excluded deposits in savings-and-loan associations?

30. In 1982, Congressional testimony on a constitutional amendment intended to compel Congress to balance the federal budget each year, Federal Reserve Chairman Paul Volcker spoke of "the difficulty of attempting to write a constitutional provision to induce discipline otherwise lacking, a provision that will serve us in fair weather and foul, and in economic circumstances that can be only dimly foreseen."[30] Do you think that he would have supported or opposed a constitutional amendment requiring the Federal Reserve to keep M1 growing at 3 percent to 5 percent a year? Put yourself in his place and write a 250-word essay defending your support or opposition to an M1 amendment.

31. In 1986, households and businesses shifted billions of dollars from saving accounts to checking accounts. If you were Chair of the Fed, would you predict that such a development would raise or lower interest rates?

32. The Federal Reserve has been announcing targets for monetary aggregates since 1975, but has generally used judgment rather than precise rules when monetary aggregates deviate from these targets. Between 1979 and 1982, the Fed paid more attention to its monetary targets, as explained by a Federal Reserve economist.[31]

Before 1979, the FOMC did not react automatically to short-run deviations of M1 from target. After the [1979] change in operating procedure, the FOMC continued to monitor the same set of economic indicators, but its automatic reaction was to resist short-run deviations of M1 from the target.

Would open-market purchases, or sales be in order if M1 began to exceed its target range?

33. "Until 1982, the M1 aggregate was considered to be the primary focus of the Federal Open Market Committee (FOMC), which had relied on the aggregate with an increasing degree of certitude through the 1970s."[32] What is the FOMC? Why might it focus more on M1 than on M2? Look at Figure 17.6 and speculate about why the FOMC paid increasingly less attention to M1 after 1982.

34. Why do you suppose that it is generally easier for the Fed to hit a target for the Federal funds rate than for M1?

35. Write a 250-word paragraph explaining and clarifying this argument by a Federal Reserve Board Governor.[33]

If the [FOMC] acted immediately to counter an observed change in money growth, and the change then proved to be temporary, the action could be destabilizing and require a subsequent offsetting adjustment . . . such attempts at fine tuning could produce perverse results.

Chapter 17 APPENDIX
AN INVENTORY MODEL OF MONEY DEMAND

To illustrate how the imperfect synchronization of income and expenses creates a demand for money, we will analyze a model in which there are two assets.[34] One is money, a means of payment that does not earn interest; the other is bonds, which cannot be used as a means of payment. Bonds earn an interest rate R but incur a transaction cost c whenever they are bought or sold.

Nominal income Y is received at evenly spaced intervals. Expenses occur continuously and uniformly, and exhaust each period's income. If we denote money holdings by M and bond holdings by B, then at the beginning of each period, total assets $M + B$ are equal to the income Y that has just been received. As payments are made during the period, assets decline to zero. This model is depicted in Figure 17.8.

One strategy is to hold only money throughout the period. This tactic avoids the transaction costs of buying and selling bonds but earns no interest. The polar opposite strategy is to put all wealth in bonds and then sell them continuously to pay expenses. This tactic maximizes interest income but incurs astronomical transaction costs. A better strategy is to hold some money and temporarily invest some funds in bonds.

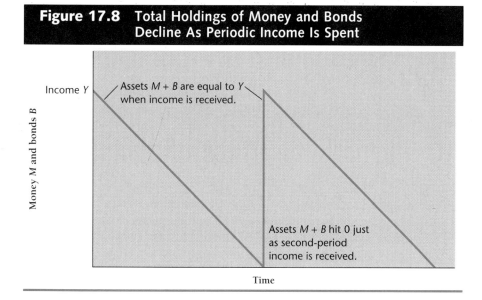

Figure 17.8   Total Holdings of Money and Bonds Decline As Periodic Income Is Spent

Income Y

Money M and bonds B

Assets $M + B$ are equal to Y when income is received.

Assets $M + B$ hit 0 just as second-period income is received.

Time

Consider the two-transaction strategy shown in Figure 17.9. A fraction α of income is invested at the beginning of each period (an investment equal to αY) and then withdrawn after $1 - \alpha$ of the period has elapsed (so as to pay the remaining expenses). Since an amount αY is invested for a time $1 - \alpha$ at an interest rate R, interest income is $(1 - \alpha)\alpha RY$. Net revenue is equal to interest income minus transaction costs $(1 - \alpha)R\alpha Y - 2c$, and this is maximized by choosing $\alpha = 0.5$ so that half of income is invested for half of the period. In Figure 17.9, interest revenue (before transaction costs) is proportional to the shaded area; a square maximizes this shaded area and therefore maximizes interest revenue.

Figure 17.10 shows the optimal timing of three transactions. Net revenue is maximized by investing $(\tfrac{2}{3})Y$ initially, withdrawing $(\tfrac{1}{3})Y$ after one-third of the period has elapsed, and then withdrawing the remaining $(\tfrac{1}{3})Y$ two-thirds of the way through the period.

In general, it can be shown that, with n transactions, the optimal strategy is to invest a fraction $(n - 1)/n$ of income initially and to withdraw $(1/n)Y$ after a fraction $(1/n)$ of the period has elapsed. Net revenue is $(n - 1)RY/2n - nc$; average holdings of bonds are equal to $(n - 1)Y/2n$; and average money holdings are $Y/2n$.

An increase in the frequency of transactions n raises transaction costs by c and raises interest revenue by $RY/2n(n + 1)$. The number of transactions should be increased until the additional transaction costs exceed the additional interest:

$$c > RY/2n(n + 1)$$

If n is treated as continuous, then marginal cost is c, marginal revenue is $RY/2n^2$, and n can be increased until marginal cost is equal to marginal revenue:

$$c = RY/2n^2$$

$$n = \sqrt{\frac{RY}{2c}} \qquad (5)$$

Average holdings are

$$M = \frac{Y/2}{n} = \sqrt{\frac{cY}{2R}} \qquad (6)$$

Equation 6 is known as the **square root rule**. The derivation assumes that n is continuous, and it is most useful as an approximation when n is large — a situation that generally occurs for households and businesses with large income.

The square root rule implies that the demand for money is positively related to both income and transaction costs, and negatively related to interest rates. The demand for money does not rise proportionately with income because there are economies of scale in the acquisition of bonds. Interest is proportional to the

Figure 17.9 With Two Transactions, Half of Income Should Be Invested in Bonds for Half of the Period

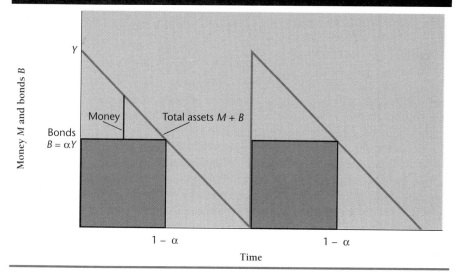

Figure 17.10 With Three Transactions, (²/₃)Y Should Be Invested in Bonds, with (¹/₃)Y Withdrawn After a Third of the Period Passes

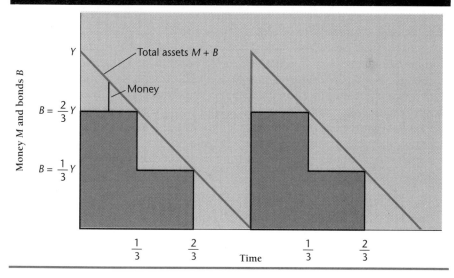

size of bond holdings, but transaction costs (trips to the bank, telephone calls, broker fees) do not rise proportionately with the size of the transaction. High-income agents consequently hold proportionately less money than low-income agents.

From Equation 6, we derive an equation for each agent's velocity

$$V = \frac{Y}{M} = \sqrt{\frac{2RY}{c}} \qquad (7)$$

showing that velocity is positively related to interest rates. Equation 5 suggests that, for the nation as a whole, velocity increases as income grows — a sharp contrast with the quantity theory (Equation 3), in which velocity is constant.

However, the inventory model applies to individual agents, and some caution must be exercised in extending it to the aggregate economy. If each agent's income increases with c and R constant, then velocity will indeed rise. However, aggregate national income could also increase because of population growth — an increase in the number of agents. If the income distribution is constant, then new agents hold the same money-to-income ratios as old agents, and aggregate velocity is constant. Also, if nominal income rises because of inflation, and transaction costs rise proportionately, thereby keeping c/Y constant, then velocity is again constant. Thus an increase in real per capita income should raise velocity, but an increase in population or the price level may leave velocity unchanged.

George Akerlof and Ross Milbourne have calculated aggregate income and interest-rate elasticities for a variety of parametric assumptions.[35] Their interest-rate elasticities are reasonably large when transaction expenses are moderate. Their aggregate income elasticities are significantly less than one.

The basic inventory model can be extended in a variety of directions. One change is to allow transaction costs to increase (but less than proportionately) with the size of transactions. This extension tends to reduce the number of transactions, increase average money holdings, and increase the interest elasticity of money holdings. A more complex modification is to introduce uncertainty regarding the size of future income and expenses, with some penalty cost if money balances turn out to be inadequate. This extension leads to the holding of extra, precautionary money balances, whose size is negatively related to interest rates, positively related to the cost of illiquidity, and positively related to the degree of uncertainty about future cash flow.

Such modifications do not upend the basic conclusions of inventory cash-management models.

1. Money demand is positively related to nominal income. Because of economies of scale in cash management, low-income agents hold relatively more money than high-income agents. As a nation's real per capita income increases, money demand rises less than proportionately, and velocity increases.

2. Money demand is negatively related to the nominal interest rates on alternative assets. When interest rates are high, agents economize on money balances, and velocity increases.

3. Money demand is positively related to the transaction costs incurred in switching back and forth between money and interest-earning assets. Institutional developments that reduce such transfer costs reduce money demand and increase velocity.

U.S. MONETARY POLICY

SINCE

WORLD WAR II

Experience over the first half of 1986 underscored the difficulty — I would say impossibility — of conducting monetary policy in current circumstances according to one or two simple, preset criteria.

Paul Volcker

In Chapter 12, we reviewed the Federal Reserve from its creation through the Great Depression, in order to explain the historical background of the regulatory structure constructed in the 1930s. Federal Reserve policies have evolved considerably since that time. The creators of the Federal Reserve strongly believed in the Real Bills doctrine (discussed in Chapter 12) and the gold standard (Chapter 3), both of which conflict with domestic stabilization. Federal Reserve Banks initially had few policy instruments, and power was too dispersed for stabilization policies to be very effective. There is also a suspicion that some of the early Federal Reserve Governors did not really understand the consequences of monetary policies.

In this chapter, we will review the Fed's policies since the Second World War. The purpose of this review is to learn about the procedures that the Fed has followed and to evaluate their effectiveness. We do not want to become armchair quarterbacks, using our almost perfect hindsight to pinpoint what the Fed should have done differently. But it is useful to try and imagine whether, given the circumstances and information then available, the Fed did a reasonable job. Did it usually accomplish its objectives? Were some operating procedures consistently more successful than others? Would we have been better off if the Fed had ignored financial markets and the economy?

INTEREST-RATE PEGGING AND THE FED-TREASURY ACCORD

During the Second World War, as during the First, the Federal Reserve was conscripted by the U.S. Treasury. The Treasury demanded that the Fed keep interest rates low to minimize the interest costs of financing the war. Despite its own reservations, in April 1942 the Fed agreed to peg the interest rates on Treasury securities at values ranging from 0.375 percent (⅜ of a percent) on three-month Treasury bills to 2.5 percent on the longest-term Treasury bonds.

The Fed pegged the interest rates on Treasury securities during and after World War II.

In World War I, the Federal Reserve had helped finance the war by lending money to banks through its discount window, so that banks could buy war bonds or lend money to people who did. In World War II, the Federal Reserve Banks themselves bought $20 billion in Treasury securities from 1942 to 1945 — 11 percent of the total issued.

When the Fed pegs interest rates, there is no uncertainty about interest rates, and the Expectations Hypothesis is appropriate, as explained in Chapter 7. If three-month Treasury bills are going to yield 0.375 percent year after year, then, to be competitive, longer-term bonds should yield 0.375 percent too. If, as in the 1940s, the Fed pegs longer-term interest rates at levels above 0.375 percent, ranging up to 2.5 percent, investors will choose the longer-term bonds. This is what happened. The Fed bought Treasury bills paying 0.375 percent and sold longer-term bonds paying higher interest rates. Despite the enormous Treasury sale of securities to finance the government's military spending, the Fed actually reduced its long-term bond holdings during World War II and exhausted its holdings of one- to two-year bonds in 1945.

While buying short-term bills and selling long-term bonds, the Fed, on balance, made large open-market purchases between 1941 and 1945, doubling the nation's monetary base, and with it M1. Despite wartime price controls, the price level increased by nearly 25 percent. After these controls were lifted, prices spurted upward. The price level in 1948 was 70 percent higher than in 1941.

After the war ended, the Treasury continued to insist that the Fed peg interest rates at low levels in order to minimize interest expenses for the Treasury as it rolled over the Treasury bills issued during the war. Government officials also argued that it would be wrong to let interest rates rise and bond prices fall, causing capital losses for the patriotic citizens who had purchased long-term Treasury bonds. The Treasury also reminded the Fed that it had precipitated a major recession in 1920–1921 when it abandoned the low interest rates maintained during World War I.

The Fed reluctantly acquiesced and kept interest rates very low until 1951. With the Treasury's consent, three-month Treasury-bill rates were around 0.5 percent through 1947, peeked over the 1-percent level in 1948, and in 1950 still averaged only 1.2 percent. Throughout this period, the postwar economy was very strong. Large wartime incomes and the forced saving caused by rationing had left citizens with lots of money and pent-up demands. Businesses were also big spenders as they built the factories and equipment to satisfy these consumer demands.

An Engine of Inflation

The Fed's policy of pegging interest rates fueled inflation.

By keeping interest rates very low, the Fed encouraged this economic boom. Most households and businesses did not want to hold securities paying 1-percent interest when the prices of consumer goods, housing, plant, and equipment were rising rapidly. They sold their securities to the Fed, and the money that the Fed used to buy these securities increased the nation's monetary base.

The Fed correctly recognized that pegging interest rates low fueled the economic boom and inflation, and it struggled for the freedom to switch to a more restraining monetary policy. It raised margin requirements on stock purchases to 100 percent, thereby eliminating loans for buying stock. It increased the discount rate three times, but banks weren't using the Fed's discount window very much. When banks wanted cash, they found it easier and cheaper to sell Treasury securities to the Federal Reserve. The Fed also kept reserve requirements high and, in 1948, it convinced Congress to give it the authority to raise them even higher. But banks offset this credit restraint by selling more Treasury securities to the Fed to acquire the needed reserves.

The economy cooled in 1949, but started overheating again in the spring of 1950. In June, fighting broke out in Korea, and more inflation was clearly on the horizon. The Fed was convinced that its policy of pegging interest rates low had made it an engine of inflation. In August 1950, as the Treasury was announcing the sale of another $13 billion of low-interest, short-term securities, the Federal Open Market Committee announced that it would henceforth do whatever was necessary to fight inflation.

The Accord

The Fed allowed short-term Treasury-bill rates to rise somewhat and, during the next six months, increased both reserve requirements and discount rates. On February 19, 1951, the Board of Governors publicly contradicted earlier announcements by both the Secretary of the Treasury and President Truman that interest rates on Treasury bonds would be held below 2.5 percent. Finally, after some posturing and peacemaking, on March 4, 1951, the Treasury-Fed Accord was announced.

> *The Treasury and the Federal Reserve System have reached full accord with respect to debt-management and monetary policies to be pursued in furthering their common purpose to assure the successful financing of the government's requirements and, at the same time, to minimize monetization of the public debt.*

The 1951 Accord established the Fed's independence.

Beneath this diplomatic language, a landmark precedent had been established. The **1951 Accord** acknowledged the independence of the Federal Reserve to choose the monetary policy it deemed appropriate.

THE 1950S: WATCHING NET FREE RESERVES AND INTEREST RATES

For the next several years, the Fed exercised its new freedom cautiously, perhaps fearing congressional action if there appeared to be too much conflict with the Treasury. The Fed's stated objective was now to maintain "an orderly market" for Government securities. It need not peg interest rates, but it dare not let them gyrate wildly. William McChesney Martin was the Chairman and spokesman for the Fed for almost 20 years, from 1951 to 1970, and although the Fed's policies did change and evolve over these twenty years, Martin provided a great deal of continuity.

The Fed adopted a **bills-only policy** in 1953, under which it restricted open-market operations to Treasury bills. (Brief exceptions were made in 1955 and 1958, when the Treasury had difficulty finding buyers for its security issues.) Apparently, the Fed followed this bills-only policy because it did not want even to suggest that it would support long-term Treasury-bond prices, as this might have been interpreted as a return to the pre-Accord policy of pegging interest rates.

In the 1950s, the Fed maintained an orderly bond market by not allowing interest rates to fluctuate wildly.

The Fed's main argument for a bills-only policy was that the Fed had to step back and allow the development of an independent, self-reliant market to allocate capital. However, the Expectations Hypothesis teaches us that long-term bond yields are affected by both present and future short-term interest rates and, therefore, by the Fed's current and anticipated Treasury-bill transactions. The Federal Reserve's monetary policy affects all interest rates, even if it buys and sells only short-term Treasury bills. The Fed eventually decided that a bills-only policy served no useful purpose, and abandoned it in 1961.

Figure 18.1 uses a variety of measures to trace monetary policy in the 1950s. (As explained in Chapter 10, Tobin's q is the ratio of the market value of corporate stock to the replacement cost of their assets.) The shaded areas identify the recessionary periods, as designated by the National Bureau of Economic Research. During the 1950s, the Fed watched net free reserves, interest rates, and M1 — in that order of importance. Net free reserves are bank excess reserves less borrowed reserves, which is the same as unborrowed reserves less required reserves. Net free reserves, which can be either positive or negative, measure the reserves available for lending after borrowed reserves have been paid back.

As you can see from Figure 18.1, net free reserves generally behaved in an appropriate counter-cyclical way during the 1950s, falling during booms and rising during recessions. But it is unclear how much of this pattern was cause and how much effect, since net free reserves automatically decline during economic booms when loan demand is brisk, and rise during recessions when loan demand is slack. Banks held enormous net free reserves during the Great Depression because there were no attractive investment opportunities, not because the Fed pursued an aggressively expansionary monetary policy. Nevertheless, it is true that in the 1950s the Fed did allow bank reserves to drop during booms

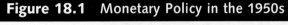

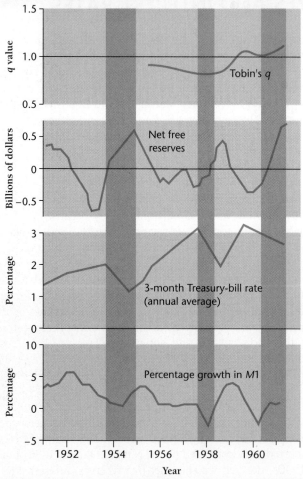

Figure 18.1 Monetary Policy in the 1950s

and rise during recessions. With effort, it could have pumped enough money into the economy during booms and pulled enough out during recessions to have caused a perverse pattern.

The monetary aggregate data in Figure 18.1 give a different picture. Monetary aggregates seem to have grown faster in booms than in recessions. Again, cause and effect are unclear — and for the same reason as with net free reserves. Remember our discussion in Chapter 4 of how banks create money. When bank excess reserves are depleted by loans, more funds are put into circulation, and more bank money is created. Thus in booms the same strong loan demand that reduces net free reserves also increases monetary aggregates. The conflicting movements in free reserves and monetary aggregates indicate that the Fed played a mostly passive role in the 1950s. Nonetheless, for those who emphasize monetary aggregates as barometers of monetary policy, Figure 18.1 suggests that the Fed's record was mediocre.

The interest-rate data in Figure 18.1 show that the Fed allowed interest rates to rise during booms, thereby exercising restraint, and allowed interest rates to fall during recessions, thereby encouraging recovery. The Board did seem a bit more concerned with fighting inflation than recession, and it might have been too cautious. But those who emphasize interest rates as a barometer of monetary policy give the Fed generally good marks in the 1950s.

Overall, in the 1950s, the Fed's performance was good by the free-reserves and interest-rate criteria and mediocre in terms of monetary aggregates, accurately reflecting the fact that the Fed was cautious, and paid more attention to the former than the latter. The major criticisms of Fed policy during the 1950s are: that it permitted three recessions in ten years because of an excessive fear of inflation and that it paid too little attention to monetary aggregates.

THE 1960S: ECONOMIC EXPANSION

John F. Kennedy was elected president in 1960, and economic growth was the new administration's major concern. Kennedy and his successor, Lyndon Johnson, were concerned by the nation's high unemployment rate and the resultant lost income and wasted resources. They also shared a keen desire to best the Soviet Union by demonstrating that the U.S. economy could grow faster and put a man on the moon sooner. An investment tax credit and liberalized depreciation rules were authorized in 1962. In 1964, a substantial reduction in personal and corporate income taxes took effect.

The Fed generally accommodated these expansionary programs. After an almost obsessive concern about inflation in the 1950s, the Fed changed to easy-money policies to accommodate economic expansion. This switch seemingly reflected the Fed's attention to election returns, or at least a sensible intention to avoid a fight with the president.

In the 1960s, the Fed accommodated the economic expansion desired by presidents Kennedy and Johnson.

Figure 18.2 shows the behavior of various monetary barometers. The 1960s were nearly recession-free — reflecting persistently expansionary monetary and fiscal policies. Monetary aggregates grew at a faster clip than in the preceding decade. Interest rates rose only moderately, considering the booming economy and the pickup of inflation to 4.7 percent in 1968 and 6.2 percent in 1969. The q data show that financial markets were generally supportive of business investment.

Credit Crunches

The two exceptions were the 1966 and 1969–1970 credit crunches caused by the Fed's increasing concern about inflation. In 1966, unemployment fell to 3.8 percent and consumer prices increased by 3.4 percent, the highest rate of

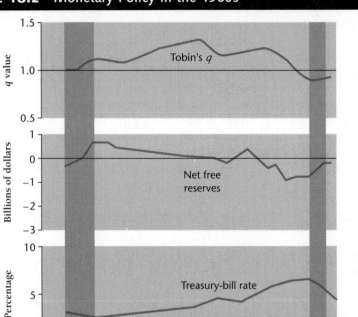

Figure 18.2 Monetary Policy in the 1960s

inflation since 1951. With the economy booming in 1966, banks were pressed with heavy loan demands, and the Fed decided to cool the economy by not supplying funds to satisfy these demands. Net free reserves fell, interest rates rose, q fell sharply, and the rates of growth of monetary aggregates declined. All of these data confirm the painful cries heard in 1966 when the monetary screws were tightened.

The interest-rate data in Figure 18.2 do not tell the complete story of this credit crunch, because the Fed did not raise deposit-ceiling rates in 1966 to keep pace with rising market-interest rates. Depositors withdrew their money — disintermediation — leaving banks and thrifts with insufficient funds to satisfy potential borrowers. Rather than increase interest rates to discourage loan applications, deposit institutions rationed credit by scaling down or rejecting applications.

The Fed has sometimes used credit crunches to combat inflation.

With their greater flexibility and resourcefulness, large banks scrambled for Eurodollars and other alternative sources of funds. Smaller banks and thrift institutions were the hardest hit, and the housing market suffered most. Judged by the aggregate data, the Fed turned in a deft performance. Inflation slowed from 3.4 percent in 1966 to 3.0 percent in 1967 without a recession. The unemployment rate stayed at 3.8 percent. But below the surface, the effects were very uneven. The sledgehammer blows to housing made "credit crunch" part of the national vocabulary.

Operation Twist

The Fed faced a dilemma during the booming 1960s in that economic growth called for low interest rates to persuade households and businesses to borrow and spend, but low U.S. interest rates encouraged investors to send funds abroad, seeking higher yields. To meet these conflicting objectives, the Fed tried what has become known as **Operation Twist** from 1961 to 1963 — an attempt to twist the term structure by raising short-term interest rates and lowering long-term interest rates. (The use of a code name reflected the high regard in which the military and the CIA were then held.)

The idea was that the Fed should sell short-term securities, thereby raising short-term interest rates, and use these funds to buy long-term bonds, thereby reducing their yields. Low long-term interest rates would encourage borrowing and spending, contributing to economic growth, while high short-term rates would keep funds from flowing abroad.

Economists who believed in the Expectations Hypothesis explanation of the term structure were openly skeptical. How, they asked, could long-term rates fall below short-term rates unless short-term rates were expected to decline greatly in the future? Apparently, the Fed would have to convince financial markets of an entirely unlikely scenario in which short-term rates rise temporarily and then decline drastically. In rebuttal, supporters of Operation Twist noted that when the future is uncertain, buying longs and rolling over shorts are imperfect substitutes, and changes in relative supplies can affect relative yields.

As it turned out, Operation Twist fizzled. The Fed made only modest sales of shorts and purchases of longs, purchases that were overwhelmed by the Treasury's sale of long-term bonds to finance its deficit. Over the postwar period as a whole, the average maturity of outstanding government debt steadily declined. But during 1961–1963 — the years in which Operation Twist was supposed to reduce the supply of long-term government bonds — the average maturity of privately held government debt actually increased. The Fed's Operation Twist was so timid that it allowed bond supplies to twist in the wrong direction.

Somewhat alarmed by the disarray in financial markets, the Fed switched to an easy-money policy in 1967. Reserve requirements and discount rates were reduced, and large open-market purchases were made. Bank reserves and monetary aggregates both jumped upward. Interest rates fell, and q increased. Vietnam War spending was by now overheating the economy. The unemployment rate fell to 3.6 percent in 1968 and 3.5 percent in 1969. Consumer prices increased by 4.7 percent in 1968 and by a shocking 6.1 percent in 1969.

In retrospect, the decision to cool the economy in 1966 by crunching a single sector was unwise. Similarly, the Fed can be criticized for trying to rescue that sector by stimulating the entire economy in 1967–1968. The fundamental problem was that distortions had been built into the economy by deposit-rate ceilings and by the unbalanced assets and liabilities of savings-and-loan associations and other thrift institutions. When these distortions were removed in the 1980s, the Fed was able to pursue more even-handed policies.

In 1969–1970, those regulations were still very much in place, and the monetary screws were again tightened. The 1968 election returns, which put Richard Nixon in the White House, may have influenced this Fed decision. All of the data agree that there was another, even tougher credit crunch. This time the monetary authorities stepped on the brakes long and hard enough to cause an unmistakable recession. The unemployment rate jumped to 4.9 percent in 1970 and to 5.9 percent in 1971.

Overall, the 1950s and 1960s were relatively successful decades for the Federal Reserve. The Fed awoke from a long slumber and engaged in active monetary policy. Its objectives were unmistakably influenced by political leaders. The Fed supported caution in the 1950s at the expense of prosperity, and risked inflation in the 1960s to support economic growth. As the 1960s ended, the Fed followed the politicians back to an emphasis on fighting inflation.

There were no major errors during these 20 years, and no calamities to compare with the monetary debacles before World War II. The Fed pretty much achieved its objectives, and criticism centered more on these objectives than on their implementation. The major imperfection in Fed policy was that, because of banking regulations enacted during the 1930s, its efforts to cool the economy affected some sectors of the economy much more than others.

THE 1970S: DISAPPOINTMENTS AND A REASSESSMENT

In 1970, Arthur Burns followed William McChesney Martin as Chairman of the Federal Reserve Board. He was expected to focus on controlling inflation and monetary aggregates, and he did — though some of his supporters were disappointed by his flexibility and pragmatism.

The 1970s often had high unemployment, inflation, and balance-of-payments deficits.

The early 1970s, like much of the rest of the decade, was characterized by high unemployment, rapid inflation, and large balance-of-payments deficits. The decade was spent in a fruitless search for a painless way to solve all three problems.

The Fed and the Nixon administration first tried what one official called "the old time religion" — a recession to cool the economy and reduce inflation. As the 1972 election grew near, monetary and fiscal policies turned sharply expansionary, and an impatient president imposed wage and price controls in late 1971. The Fed reduced reserve requirements and discount rates and made

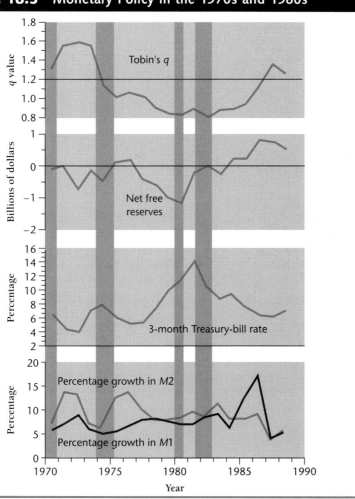

Figure 18.3 Monetary Policy in the 1970s and 1980s

large open-market purchases. Figure 18.3 shows that the monetary-aggregate data, now more closely watched, picked up steam. Interest rates tumbled, and q increased.

After the 1972 elections, monetary and fiscal policies again turned restrictive. The rates of growth of monetary aggregates slowed, interest rates rose, and q plunged. In 1973–1974, there was yet another credit crunch, reflecting a Fed decision to use a recession to cool inflation. The unemployment rate averaged 8.5 percent in 1975 — the highest level since the Great Depression — but, with oil and food shortages, consumer prices increased by 12.2 percent in 1974 and 7.0 percent in 1975.

As the 1976 presidential election approached, monetary and fiscal policies again turned expansionary. The growth of monetary aggregates increased, interest rates fell, and q increased slightly. Nonetheless, the Republican party had been tainted by the Watergate scandal and the Democratic candidate, Jimmy Carter, won the presidency. The new president wanted to reduce unemployment, and with help from the Fed, the economy continued strong in 1977 and 1978. The money supply grew at a brisk pace, and interest rates increased only modestly, considering the inflation rate of 7 percent in 1977 and 9 percent in 1978. As double-digit inflation loomed ahead, the President (reluctantly) and the Fed (aggressively) swung to contractionary policies. In 1978 there was another credit crunch, and in January 1980 a recession began.

Overall, the 1970s were similar to the 1950s and the 1960s in that the Fed was reasonably successful in pursuing the easy- or tight-money policies it chose. The major disappointment was that two substantial recessions had so little effect on inflation. Living standards in the United States were reduced by energy-related shocks to the economy, which could hardly have been offset by monetary policies.

The 1970s also saw the elevation of monetary aggregates as a closely watched barometer of monetary policy and the temporary neglect of bank-reserves data. The Fed continued to keep its second eye on interest rates and its third eye on election returns.

The Federal Reserve does not seem to have been guilty of clumsily destabilizing the economy, of exacerbating booms and recessions because of poor timing. The Fed pretty much stimulated and cooled the economy when it wanted to. The Fed is more open to the criticism that it knowingly helped put the economy on a four-year business cycle, coinciding with presidential elections. The only departure from this pattern was the 1976–1980 reversal when Jimmy Carter got things backwards — stimulating the economy after his 1976 election and cooling the economy before his 1980 defeat.

THE 1980S: THE TAMING OF INFLATION

As the 1970s came to an end, Paul Volcker took over as Federal Reserve Chairman. He faced the same problems that had greeted Arthur Burns at the beginning of the decade: high unemployment, rapid inflation, and large balance-of-payments deficits. The only changes were in degree: each problem was now worse. Volcker brought a fresh determination to stop inflation, but no miracles.

The value of the U.S. dollar fell to new lows in the fall of 1979 as currency traders grew increasingly nervous about inflation in the United States. At an International Monetary Fund meeting in Belgrade in late September, European central bankers told Volcker that they were skeptical of the Fed's efforts to reduce inflation and, more ominously, threatened to sell all of the U.S. dollars they were holding.[1] Volcker left the conference early, flew back to the United States and convened an extraordinary Saturday meeting of the Fed's Open Market Committee on October 6, 1979. Late that afternoon, Volcker announced to the press that the Fed would henceforth place[2]

> *greater emphasis in day to day operations on the supply of bank reserves and less emphasis on confining short-term fluctuations in the federal funds rate.*

Before this announcement, open-market operations were used to keep the average value of the federal-funds rate (over a month, a week, or even a day) within 0.5 percent or 1.0 percent of its target value. After October 6, 1979, the width of the Fed's target range was widened to 5 to 6 percentage points; if the federal-funds rate went outside this target band, the Open Market Committee met and, in practice, simply widened the band.

In October 1979, the Fed stated an intention to reduce inflation by slowing money growth.

While allowing interest rates to fluctuate more, the Fed targeted bank reserves more closely in order to stabilize monetary aggregates, as explained in a record of the FOMC meetings.[3]

> *The principal reason advanced for shifting to an operating procedure aimed at controlling the supply of bank reserves more directly was that it would provide greater assurance that the committee's objectives for monetary growth could be achieved.*

The details of these operating procedures are described in an accompanying highlight.

The Fed's increased attention to monetary aggregates and deemphasis of interest rates was called an experiment in monetarism. In retrospect, the main objective of the Volcker Fed in 1979 seems to have been to slow the growth of monetary aggregates in order to reduce the rate of inflation. It was less committed to the monetarist idea of maintaining a constant growth rate for monetary aggregates, no matter what the state of the economy. Nonetheless, there are some interesting lessons to be learned from the Fed's policies during this period.

Interest-Rate Instability

Without the Fed's steadying support, interest rates went through some truly breathtaking gyrations. In April 1980, the prime lending rate ran up to 20 percent and then retreated almost as rapidly as it had climbed that uncharted hill. The federal-funds rate jumped from less than 13 percent in mid-February to above 19 percent in early April and then fell below 10 percent in late May. On a single day, August 5, 1980, the federal-funds rate swung between 8.75 percent in the morning and 2 percent in the afternoon. The Fed meant what it said about letting interest rates fluctuate.

Interest rates fluctuated wildly in 1980.

Such wild interest-rate swings caused disarray, even despair, in financial markets, as both borrowers and lenders came to the historic conclusion that long-term bonds, traditionally a conservative investment, were now riskier than

| Highlight 18.2 | Targeting Nonborrowed Reserves |

The Federal Reserve used a nonborrowed-reserves control procedure between October 1979 and October 1982. After each meeting of the Open Market Committee, Fed staff members estimated the level of total bank reserves consistent with the Committee's targets for the growth of monetary aggregates, particularly M1, since Fed studies had indicated that, of the various monetary aggregates, M1 was most closely correlated with gross national product and prices.*

After determining a target path for total reserves for the three to five weeks between Committee meetings, the staff members subtracted an assumed level of borrowed reserves that had been determined by the Committee. The Open Market Desk was then instructed to use open-market operations to achieve a weekly nonborrowed reserves target equal to this difference between targeted total reserves and assumed borrowed reserves. Approximately once a week, the Fed staff adjusted its targets for total reserves and nonborrowed reserves in light of new information about the relationships between bank reserves and monetary aggregates.

Since the nonborrowed-reserves target is obtained by subtracting a desired level of borrowed reserves from an estimate of the level of total reserves consistent with desired levels of monetary aggregates, there was some ambiguity, even among Fed governors, about whether the operating procedure could best be described as targeting nonborrowed reserves or using nonborrowed reserves to hit a target for borrowed reserves.

The Fed procedure was based on the belief that its Trading Desk could hit its nonborrowed-reserve target with considerable accuracy and that the maintenance of such a target would control monetary aggregates automatically. The underlying theory was that if M1 started to grow faster than intended, banks would need funds to meet their reserve requirements. If the Fed held nonborrowed reserves steady, then banks would have to meet their reserve requirements by borrowing through either the federal-funds market or the Fed's discount window. Banks' reluctance to abuse their discount-window privileges would lead them to the federal-funds market, causing a substantial increase in the federal-funds rate and, with it, other short-term interest rates. As interest rates rose, funds would be taken out of transaction accounts and invested at these higher market-interest rates, causing M1 to decline. Thus it was intended that a policy of targeting nonborrowed reserves would achieve the Fed's targets for M1 and other monetary aggregates.

---

*Lyle Gramley, "Financial Innovation and Monetary Policy," *Federal Reserve Bulletin*, July 1982, p. 396.

stocks. Figure 18.4, using one measure of risk, the standard deviation of monthly returns, shows the striking increase in the riskiness of bonds after October 1979.

The president of the E. F. Hutton brokerage firm said, "This market has made traders queasy, uneasy, and at times shaken. The greatest problem of all is the volatility. Even in Government securities, prices have sometimes changed in a single day more than they did in an entire year in the past."[4] The chairman of Manufacturers Hanover bank said, "We ask ourselves, where's the roller coaster going in the next 12 months, but you can't even begin to think that far ahead anymore. You can't even think one month ahead."[5] The cautious left the long-term bond market, looking to short-term securities for price stability. The adventurous discovered long-term bonds now to be an exciting speculation, rivaling foreign currency and pork bellies.

Monetary-Aggregate Instability

And yet, as shown in Figure 18.5, monetary aggregates fluctuated almost as wildly as interest rates in 1980. Monetary aggregates fell at a record clip in April and soared at a record pace in August. For the rest of the year, monetary aggregates seemed to seesaw upwards, though the Fed revised its data frequently. Monetarist economists who had welcomed Volcker's demotion of interest-rate stability were, after one year, decrying the instability of monetary aggregates. Volcker responded that monetary aggregates aren't "something you control from week to week or even month to month. We always knew that, but we learned it in spades this year."[6] Overall, the standard deviation of the quarterly growth rate of M1 was 2.6 percent for the 10 quarters preceding October 1979 and 5.2 percent for the ten quarters afterwards.[7]

Monetary aggregates fluctuated in 1980.

One observer, Salomon Brothers' widely respected Henry Kaufman, blamed the instability of interest rates on the instability of monetary aggregates. Investors could no longer count on the Fed to stabilize interest rates, nor could they accurately gauge Fed intentions by movements in the federal-funds rate. Instead, they had to guess the future course of interest rates from conjectures about how the Fed would react to wild short-term swings in bank reserves and monetary aggregates.

For the year 1980 as a whole, the Fed did a pretty good job of controlling M1B, which is now called M1. M1B increased by only 6.3 percent in 1980, as compared to 7.4 percent in 1979 and 8.2 percent in 1978. Yet, at the same time that the rate of growth of M1B was slowing, the rate of inflation accelerated from 7.6 percent in 1978 to 11.3 percent in 1979 and to 13.5 percent in 1980. This reaffirms our earlier observation that there is not a close positive correlation between the money supply and prices.

Divergent Aggregates

The 1980 experience also confirms that it does make a difference which aggregate is targeted, since monetary aggregates do not all grow at the same rate. In 1980, the government monetary base increased by 4 percent, M1A by 3.9

Monetary aggregates diverged in 1980.

Figure 18.4 36-Month Standard Deviations of Monthly Bond and Stock Returns

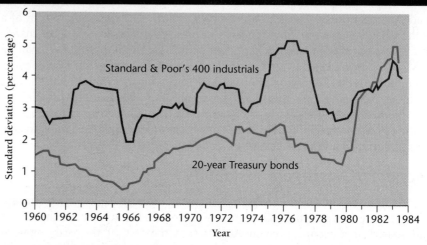

source: Michael F. Wilcox, of L. F. Rothschild, Unterberg, Towbin.

percent, M1B by 6.3 percent, M2 by 9.4 percent, and M3 by 10.0 percent. In 1981, it was more of the same. The Fed's target growth rates and actual monetary growth rates in 1981 were

	Target Range	Actual
M1A	3.0%–5.5%	−6.1%
M1B adjusted	3.5%–6.0%	2.3%
M1B unadjusted	6.0%–8.5%	6.3%
M2	6.0%–9.0%	10.0%
M3	6.5%–9.5%	11.4%

One out of five ain't bad! The disconcerting problem was that M1A and adjusted M1B were substantially *below* their targets while M2 and M3 were well *above* their targets. What should the Fed do? Some, watching the M1s, argued for monetary ease to avoid a recession. Others, watching M2 and M3, argued for more restraint to fight inflation.

The Fed concluded that the low level of M1 in 1981 was misleading because a lot of transaction money had temporarily gone into M2 in search of high interest rates. In 1982, the situation was reversed: M1 grew rapidly and M1 velocity suddenly dropped 5 percent below its predicted value. The Fed concluded that this increase in M1 was misleading, too, because these additional

Figure 18.5   **M1B and the Federal-Funds Rate Fluctuated Greatly in 1980**

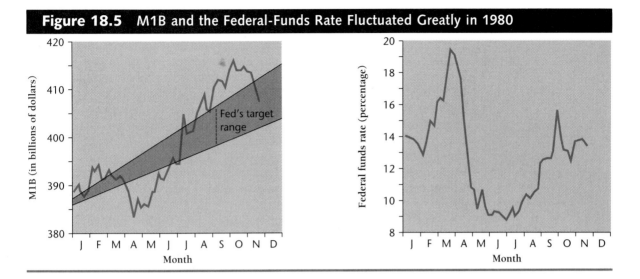

funds were precautionary savings rather than transaction funds. This flexible interpretation of seemingly arbitrary and ambiguous monetary aggregates led *The Wall Street Journal* to editorialize that "gearing monetary policy to movements in one or another of the Ms is as smooth and steady — and as reasonable — as a Keystone Kops chase."[8] They suggested a new monetary aggregate: M-w for "M-whatever."

A More Flexible Policy

In the summer of 1982, the unemployment rate hit 10.8 percent. The economy was in the worst recession since the 1930s, and some feared a complete economic collapse. Yet M1 was well above the Fed's target ranges. This was a crucial litmus test of the Fed's dedication to its M1 target.

The Fed was using M1 as an intermediate target to help achieve its goals for nominal gross national product. The targeted value of M1 was based on a predicted value of M1 velocity, the ratio of nominal gross national product to M1,

$$V1 = \frac{Py}{M1}$$

In 1982, gross national product was lower than the Fed wanted, but M1 was well above the Fed's target range, causing an unexpected drop in M1 velocity. One option for the Fed was to ignore the decline in velocity and stick to its M1 target, using contractionary monetary policies to restrain M1. Another option was to abandon the M1 target and react to the low level of gross national product, in effect targeting gross national product when there is a conflict between gross

With the economy in deep recession, the Fed allowed M1 to grow rapidly in 1982.

national product and M1. The Fed chose to ignore M1 and respond to the ailing economy by shifting to an expansionary monetary policy.

The Fed changed its formal operating procedures in October 1982, ending its three-year experiment in using nonborrowed reserves to control monetary aggregates. While the Open Market Desk continued to monitor bank reserves on a daily basis after October 1982, the Fed's reserve targets were no longer automatically adjusted to reflect deviations of monetary aggregates from their targeted paths. Instead, the Open Market Committee's bank-reserve targets are now based on the members' policy judgments, reflecting a variety of economic data in addition to monetary aggregates. The Open Market Desk is instructed to use flexible targets for nonborrowed reserves in order to achieve the Open Market Committee's target for borrowed reserves during each two-week reserve maintenance period.

When the Open Market Committee wants more reserve restraint, the Open Market Desk makes open-market sales, compelling banks to increase their borrowing through the Fed's discount window. Because of bankers' reluctance to abuse their discount-window privileges, this discount-window borrowing signals a tightening of credit availability and puts upward pressure on the federal-funds rate and other short-term interest rates.

The Fed made this change in 1982 because it accepted the argument that changes in monetary aggregates are often the result of financial-market developments — for example, shifts among various types of bank accounts — that do not significantly affect gross national product and prices and consequently do not need to be offset by open-market purchases or sales. The Fed would use discretion in deciding when to tighten and when to ease.

The Fed stopped targeting M1 after M1 velocity fell unexpectedly several times during the 1980s.

By the end of 1983, Volcker conceded that the erratic behavior of M1 velocity had persuaded the Fed to disregard changes in M1 for the foreseeable future. Preston Martin, vice chairman of the Fed, explained succinctly that short-term movements in M1 "are absolutely meaningless."

In 1985, M1 grew by 12 percent, while nominal gross national product increased by only 6.5 percent (3 percent real and 3.5 percent due to inflation) — so that velocity unexpectedly declined by 5.5 percent. The rapid 12-percent growth of M1 signaled to some observers a need for tightening, but Volcker concluded that "all other indicators are currently signaling either that monetary policy should be kept unchanged or even eased further."[9] Again the Fed chose to let the M1 signals be overruled by other indicators.

In 1986, M1 velocity declined by an incredible 9.5 percent. While M1 increased by more than 15 percent, nominal gross national product rose by about 5 percent (half real and half due to inflation). Again, monetarists warned of an imminent rapid increase in the rate of inflation, and again, the Fed chose to abandon its M1 targets and let its monetary policy be guided by other economic data. In February 1987, the Fed stopped targeting M1 entirely.

Overall, after increasing at an average rate of about 3.5 percent a year between 1948 and 1981, M1 velocity declined, on average, by about 4 percent a year between 1982 and 1987. This change in the behavior of velocity created

Increases in M1 May Be Contractionary! Highlight 18.3

Portfolio shifts among assets can cause changes in monetary aggregates that give misleading signals about the economy. One particularly striking case occurs when households or businesses transfer funds into transaction accounts (which are subject to 12-percent reserve requirements) from savings accounts, money-market funds, and other assets that are not subject to reserve requirements.*

The deposit-multiplier model analyzed in Chapter 4 showed that such a portfolio shift increases M1, signaling monetary expansion. Yet this relocation of funds may reflect no change whatsoever in spending behavior by households and businesses. They have simply decided to hold more funds in their transaction accounts and less elsewhere. Perhaps new features have increased the attractiveness of transaction accounts. Or investors may be nervous about the safety of uninsured money-market funds. Or, fearing an increase in interest rates, they have reduced their holdings of longer-term assets. In each case, the portfolio shift is not indicative of a change in spending, output, or employment.

In fact, since transaction accounts are subject to substantial reserve requirements, this portfolio shift actually reduces the amount of funds available for bank lending. Less of the monetary base circulates through financial markets, because more is sitting idle in bank vaults. When funds are transferred into transaction accounts from accounts that are exempt from reserve requirements, there is an increase in required reserves for the banking system, which tightens credit — despite the increase in M1.

The Fed is well aware of the fact that such a rearrangement of asset portfolios causes M1 to give a misleading signal about financial-market conditions.† When M1 grew rapidly in 1985 and 1986, the Fed believed that this increase was caused by just such a portfolio shift and consequently ignored the misleading signal given by M1.

---

*Iman Anabtawi and Gary Smith, "Money, Credit, and Banking in a Keynesian Macroeconomic Model," 1990.

†Bharat Trehan and Carl Walsh, "Examining the Recent Surge in M1," *Federal Reserve Bank of San Francisco Weekly Letter*, November 15, 1985, pp. 1–3.

Highlight 18.4	**P-Star**

In a statement before the Senate Banking Committee in February 1989, Fed Chairman Alan Greenspan suggested that some Governors were paying particular attention to P^* ("P-Star"), an indicator of potential inflation. This indicator is based on the Quantity Theory equation

$$MV^* = P^*y^*$$

where

M = current value of M2
V^* = average value of M2 velocity since 1955
y^* = estimate of real gross national product at full employment

The variable P^* is the value of the price level implied by the other three variables.

$$P^* = \frac{MV^*}{y^*}$$

P^* can be interpreted as the price level consistent with the current level of M2, an economy at full employment, and a value of M2 velocity equal to its historical average. If the actual price level tends, in practice, to converge to P^*, then the value of P^* relative to current prices may provide a useful indicator of inflationary or deflationary pressures. The Fed's interest in P^* was piqued by empirical studies by staff members indicating that inflation generally increases when the actual value of the price level is persistently below P^* and that inflation tends to decline when the current price level is persistently above P^*.

Several important assumptions are implicit in the use of P^* as an indicator of inflationary pressures. One is that M2 velocity will not deviate by very much or for very long from its historical average. Between 1955 and 1988, M2 velocity had an average value of 1.65 and ranged between 1.55 (6 percent below 1.65) and 1.80 (9 percent above 1.65). The average value of M2 velocity between 1983 and 1988 was 1.60. If M2 velocity does drift permanently away from its historical average, then P^* will be a persistently misleading barometer of inflationary pressures.

The estimate of full-employment output is a subjective matter, which depends critically on the value of the unemployment rate that is assumed to prevail when the economy is at full employment. A number of competing estimates are in use; these estimates are often revised significantly decades after the fact. The use of full-employment output in the calculation of P^* implicitly assumes the economy automatically returns to full employment without assistance from Federal Reserve monetary policy. The usefulness of P^* is an empirical question and, for now, some Fed Governors are watching P^* to see whether or not it proves to be a reliable indicator.

an enormous gap between the actual value of M1 and the value consistent with the historical relationship between M1 and gross national product.

To demonstrate this break with the past, the Federal Reserve Bank of San Francisco used data through 1980 to estimate how M1 is affected by changes in gross national product, interest rates, and other relevant factors.[10] This equation was then used to predict M1 using the values of these explanatory variables after 1980. Early in 1982, actual M1 began to rise above predicted M1, reflecting the unexpected decline in M1 velocity. By the end of 1986, actual M1 was nearly 25 percent higher than predicted M1, a gap of $125 billion. If the Fed had ignored this cumulative deterioration in the relationship between M1 and economic activity, and insisted on keeping M1 growing at a rate consistent with historical trends, there would have been a financial collapse rivaling the Great Depression.

M2 and M3 velocity also dropped unexpectedly in 1985 and 1986, but not as dramatically as M1 velocity. M2 velocity, which had been roughly trendless since 1960, fell by 2.25 percent in 1985 and by 4.25 percent in 1986. M3 velocity declined by about 0.75 percent between 1960 and 1980, and fell by 1.25 percent in 1985 and 3.25 percent in 1986. The Fed concluded that these velocity surprises reflected unanticipated shifts among assets (both within and outside the monetary-aggregate categories) that had little bearing on economic activity.

The Fed consequently followed an increasingly eclectic approach in 1987, 1988, and 1989, monitoring a wide variety of economic indicators. Alan Greenspan replaced Paul Volcker as Fed Chairman in 1987 and seems more tolerant of divergent opinions, perhaps because of the accumulated evidence that monetary policy cannot be guided reliably by one or two simple criteria. Individual members of the Open Market Committee have their own favorite indicators, including the unemployment rate, the nominal gross national product, the consumer price index, exchange rates, the term structure of interest rates, and the prices of gold, soybeans, and other commodities. All now use a variety of data to gauge the condition of financial markets and the economy. These policies accommodated sustained economic growth through 1990, with neither a recession nor excessive inflation.

The Fed was increasingly eclectic in 1987–1989.

SUMMARY

The U.S. Treasury insisted that the Fed peg interest rates on Treasury securities at low levels during and after the Second World War. In a booming economy, this policy compelled the Fed to make open-market purchases, buying Treasury securities at high prices to maintain low interest rates. The accompanying increase in the monetary base made the Fed an involuntary engine of inflation. The 1951 Accord between the Fed and the Treasury established the important principle that the Federal Reserve is an independent branch of government, free to follow the monetary policies it deems appropriate.

After the Accord, the Fed nonetheless continued for many years to "maintain orderly financial markets" by using open-market purchases to keep interest rates from fluctuating wildly. The Fed followed fairly cautious policies in the 1950s, monitoring net free reserves, interest rates, and M1 — in that order of importance. Fed policy during this period has been criticized for allowing three recessions in ten years because of exaggerated fears of inflation, and for paying too little attention to monetary aggregates.

In the 1960s, the Fed generally accommodated the wishes of presidents John Kennedy and Lyndon Johnson to reduce unemployment and increase the nation's output, although concern about inflation led to Fed-engineered credit crunches in 1966 and 1969–1970. During the 1970s, the economy was often characterized by high unemployment, rapid inflation, and large balance-of-payments deficits. The Fed watched monetary aggregates more closely and frequently tried to reduce inflation with a recession, though these anti-inflation efforts were often interrupted by presidential elections.

Between October 1979 and October 1982, the Fed under Paul Volcker paid less attention to stabilizing interest rates and more attention to reducing the growth of monetary aggregates sufficiently to wring inflation out of the economy. In this, it largely succeeded, though at the cost of the most severe recession since the Great Depression. With the inflation rate below 4 percent and the economy on the verge of collapse in the fall of 1982, the Fed changed to more expansionary policies that accommodated economic growth through the remainder of the decade. The divergent movements in monetary aggregates and erratic behavior of velocity, particularly M1 velocity, during the 1980s persuaded the Fed that it should not follow mechanical rules based on the behavior of one or two monetary aggregates. Instead, the Fed has followed an increasingly eclectic approach, using judgment and a variety of economic indicators to guide its policies.

IMPORTANT TERMS

1951 Accord   Operation Twist
bills-only policy

EXERCISES

1. The 1951 Accord established the principle that the Fed is not subservient to the Treasury and need not restrict open-market operations to doing whatever is necessary to maintain low interest rates. Explain how such a restriction might make the Fed, in its own words, an engine of inflation.

2. Explain why net free reserves can be negative and whether this is more likely to happen when credit is easy or tight.

3. Net free reserves are an imperfect indicator of the state of the economy. Identify some circumstances in which net free reserves can increase during an economic boom and some circumstances in which net free reserves can increase during a recession.

4. Interest rates often decline during a recession, as borrowing slackens and inflation diminishes. Explain why interest rates can increase during a recession, making interest rates an

imperfect indicator of the strength of the economy.

5. Alan Walter, a monetarist economics professor and personal economic advisor to British Prime Minister Margaret Thatcher, wrote in 1985 that[11]

Monetarists would normally agree that transaction money — the stuff with which people settle accounts — is the proper target. Financial assets, such as term savings accounts or certificates of deposit (CDs), are not transaction money. Nobody uses CDs to pay bills, so they should not appear in the money target.

Explain how some monetarists, including Milton Friedman, justify the targeting of monetary aggregates such as M2 and M3, which include time and savings accounts and certificates of deposit.

6. In the early 1960s the Federal Reserve argued that "the long-run rise in the volume of near money assets . . . has not reduced the effectiveness of monetary policy" and that M1 velocity had reached its "practical limit" of 3.0.
   a. Explain clearly what a velocity of 3.0 means.
   b. Why might there be a practical limit to velocity?
   c. Why would it matter to Fed policy whether or not velocity was at a practical limit?
   d. At the end of 1986, M1 velocity was 6.0. Did M1 or gross national product grow faster between 1960 and 1986?

7. Since World War II, time deposits have increased much more rapidly than transaction accounts. When there is this kind of shift in public preferences, how does it affect required reserves? In the absence of government policy actions, do you think that monetary conditions tighten or ease?

8. When the shift described in the previous exercise does occur, will the Fed tighten or ease monetary conditions if it acts to stabilize interest rates? M1?

9. In a November 1985 speech, Preston Martin, the vice-chairman of the Federal Reserve Board, said that "The Fed will continue to take a careful look at its M1 aggregate since declines in M1 velocity have 'cast doubt' on M1's reliability. . . . We may continue to deemphasize M1 and rely on the eclectic approach adopted this year."[12] What did he mean by "M1's reliability" and why does a decline in M1 velocity cast doubt on this?

10. What's wrong with the logic of this argument: "unless something politically improbable is done about the federal deficit, the deficit will continue to be financed largely with printed money flowing from the government."[13]

11. The text says that "The value of the U.S. dollar fell to new lows in the fall of 1979 as currency traders grew increasingly nervous about inflation in the United States." Explain why the value of the dollar is affected by inflation fears.

12. Compare these two news stories, the first from September 1980 and the second from May 1986.

September 1980[14]:

The nation's money surged upward again in the latest reporting period [M1 up by $1.2 billion in the previous week]. Analysts said that while the figures were not a surprise, fears of rising interest rates will grow unless the money supply declines in the next few weeks.

May 1986[15]:

The nation's money supply [M1] rose $4.2 billion in mid-April, the Federal Reserve reported Thursday.

Although the increase was larger than expected and pushed the money supply [more than $4 billion] above the Fed's growth target, there was virtually no reaction in the credit markets.

How do you explain the fact that a $1.2 billion increase that was not unexpected worried the financial markets in 1980, while an unexpected $4.2 billion increase was of no concern in 1986?

13. In a 1989 speech in Toronto, the president of the Federal Reserve Bank of Cleveland said[16]

A look at recent history reminds us vividly of the economic pain resulting from inflation. Every recession in the recent history of North America has been preceded by an outburst of cost and price pressures. . . . Today, in both Canada and the United States, people seem to be more aware than ever that the proper role of the central bank is to prevent these losses by stabilizing the price level.

Why did inflation so often precede recession?

14. In 1980, financial analysts voiced the novel opinion that bonds had become riskier than stocks, as indicated by the following quotations from the October 29, 1980 issue of *The Wall Street Journal*. Explain the reason for this remarkable shift in risk perceptions.[17]

"The long-term markets are in a state of disarray," says Sanford L. Weill, chairman and chief executive officer of Shearson Loeb Rhoades Inc., a large New York investment firm. "We have a lot of clients completely out of the long-term markets, period, because they've been burned so badly."

During the past two weeks alone, bond prices have fallen almost 8%. A decline of the same magnitude in the Dow Jones Industrial Average would represent a drop of 75 points.

"Stocks used to be twice as volatile as bonds," says Leon C. Cooperman, chairman of the investment policy committee at Goldman, Sachs & Co. "Now bonds are more volatile."

15. The news story in the previous exercise went on to report that

With a growing sense of gloom hanging over the bond market, many investment analysts said they're urging clients to switch away from long-term securities into the shortest possible maturities. "You can get almost as good yields at the short ends without the worry," says Data Resources' Mr. Eckstein.

Is there any worry in the shortest possible maturities?

16. Professor Robert J. Gordon of Northwestern asserted that "monetarism has been decimated by the collapse of velocity in 1982."[18] What is velocity and why would its collapse undermine monetarism?

17. The Congressional Budget Office argued that M1 velocity in 1984 might have been affected by a shift in the use of transaction balances to purchase imported products rather than U.S. products.[19] Explain why such a shift might either increase or decrease M1 velocity. (Remember that U.S. gross national product includes only goods and services produced in the United States.)

18. In a November 6, 1985, letter to Congressman Walter Fauntroy, Fed Chairman Paul Volcker wrote that, after an unexpected decline in M1 velocity during the first half of 1985, the Fed adjusted its M1 targets in July with "the expectation that velocity behavior would be closer to historical patterns in the second half of the year. . . . As a practical matter, however, the velocity of M1 continued to decline over the summer, continuing the unusual pattern of the earlier part of the year." A financial analyst commented that "the historic pattern may no longer bind M1 and GNP. Disinflation, falling interest rates, and financial deregulation are major structural changes in our economy which undoubtedly have affected M1 velocity. In [June 1985] we argued that the Fed should just forget about M1."[20] Explain how each of the three changes cited might reduce M1 velocity.

19. The record of the Federal Open Market Committee's meeting on May 17, 1988, states that "the members generally agreed that some further tightening of reserve conditions was needed to counter the risks of rising inflationary pressures in the economy."[21] If you were managing the Fed's open-market operations and received this directive, would you interpret it as an instruction to make more open-

market purchases, or sales? How would these transactions affect borrowed and unborrowed reserves?

20. In 1986 Prudential-Bache's chief economist wrote about "Monetarist Melancholia."[22]

    The only positive thing we can say about monetarists is that they've been wrong for so long that they're overdue to be right. Last year, M1 monetarists warned that a reaccelerating economy would stimulate reflation. Instead, the economy muddled and the CPI inflation rate fell from 4.0% in 1984 to 3.7% in 1985.

    Monetarists blame their forecasting error on an unexpected drop in velocity. . . . GNP is supposed to be a good proxy for the transactions which M1 is supposed to be financing. We don't believe that GNP is a good proxy for all transactions in our economy. . . .

    Even if they could forecast nominal GNP, monetarists have no model for predicting the breakdown between real growth and inflation. Traditionally, monetarists assume that the economy is at or close to full employment. So "excessive" monetary growth always leads (with a long and variable lag) to inflation. But in a world of gluts (in a world where too many goods are chasing too few consumers) the monetarist model is bound to fail. And it has.

    a. How is velocity measured, and how did the Fed know that it had collapsed?
    b. If velocity collapses and the Fed targets M1, what will happen to GNP?
    c. Why does a collapse in velocity undermine monetarism? Does an increase in velocity bolster monetarism?
    d. Why isn't the annual volume of transactions equal to gross national product?
    e. Explain how a monetarist model with full employment implies that monetary growth leads to inflation.

21. In 1982, an economist at Federal Reserve Bank of St. Louis presented data indicating that in 1981 and 1982 "rising market interest rates tended to shift funds [from checkable deposits subject to interest-rate ceilings] into time deposits [with no interest-rate ceilings], while falling market interest rates tended to shift funds into checkable deposits."[23] Explain why you find this empirical observation to be either plausible or implausible. Do you predict that a shift from checkable deposits to time deposits will ease financial markets or tighten them? Imagine that you are working for a Federal Reserve Bank, and write a paragraph justifying your prediction.

22. In 1988 and 1989, one Fed Governor, Manuel Johnson, paid particular attention to the shape of the term structure of interest rates, believing that an increase in long-term rates relative to short-term rates signals financial-market expectations that inflation will increase in the future. Provide a logical explanation for this belief.

23. In November 1985, two economists with the Federal Reserve Bank of San Francisco wrote that "The rapid growth of M1 relative to M3 thus appears to be a portfolio shift by the public out of term balances into, among other things, M1 balances. This explanation of the recent rapid M1 growth implies that the surge does not indicate stimulative monetary policy."[24] Why might the increase in M1, in fact, reflect a tightening of credit conditions?

24. On February 20, 1990, bond and stock prices fell after Fed Chair Alan Greenspan told a House Banking subcommittee that the likelihood of recession had faded. Two days later, bond and stock prices rose when he told the Senate Banking Committee that the sharp January increase in the Consumer Price Index was an aberration and that inflation might decline during the months to come. How would you explain these reactions by financial markets?

25. In 1986 an investment advisory service reported that stock prices usually decline when the Treasury-bill rate rises above the discount rate.[25] Explain why the success of this indicator depends on whether the Federal Reserve is targeting interest rates or monetary aggregates.

Macroeconomic Analysis

THE IS-LM MODEL

The ideas of economists and philosophers, both when they are right and when they are wrong, are more powerful than is commonly understood. Indeed, the world is ruled by little else. Practical men, who believe themselves to be quite exempt from any intellectual influences, are usually the slaves of some defunct economist. Madmen in authority, who hear voices in the air, are distilling their frenzy from some academic scribbler of a few years back. I am sure that the power of vested interests is vastly exaggerated compared with the gradual evolution of ideas.

John Maynard Keynes

In the next several chapters, we examine the ways in which the spending and financial decisions of households, businesses, and government are influenced by the economy and, in turn, affect the economy. To do this, we develop a simple model — the *IS-LM* model — to organize and clarify our thinking about the aggregate economic implications of changes in private or government spending and of changes in money supply and money demand. This model not only helps us understand the consequences of economic events, including monetary and fiscal policies, but also can be applied to a variety of interesting issues — for example, identifying conditions in which a policy of stabilizing interest rates destabilizes gross national product. We begin with a discussion of the important relationship between income and spending.

THE INTERACTION OF INCOME AND EXPENDITURES

The simultaneous interdependence of income and expenditures is a key to understanding economic booms and recessions. Income influences how much people spend, and spending, in the aggregate, influences how much income people earn. If people decide to spend less, others will earn less and consequently spend less, too. This fundamental income-expenditure interdependence explains how a recession can persist and grow like a snowball rolling downhill.

The Measurement of Production

Gross national product is the market value of newly produced goods and services.

A nation's **gross national product (GNP)** is the market value of the aggregate production of new goods and services — houses, automobiles, haircuts, financial advice — during a specified period of time, usually a year or a quarter of a year. GNP can be divided into **consumption goods,** which last only a short while — ice cream and strawberries — and **investment goods,** such as factories and apartment buildings, which last for a considerable period of time. GNP excludes the purchase and sale of items that were produced in earlier periods, such as the purchase of a used car, an old house, or a painting by Andy Warhol.

Gross national product is not a comprehensive measure of production because it excludes almost all activities that do not involve a financial transaction; for example, do-it-yourself projects and volunteer work. If you mow your lawn, coach a youth soccer team, or repair your car, you add nothing to GNP. Gross-national-product data also exclude prostitution, selling illegal drugs, and other covert activities. A plumber or waitress may hide perfectly legal activities, which are eligible for inclusion in the GNP, from tax authorities and GNP statisticians. This unreported underground economy makes the gross national product an incomplete tabulation of national output.

While GNP data attempt to gauge the ebb and flow of economic activity by measuring the production of new goods and services, there is much more to life, to a nation's well-being, than those things counted by GNP statisticians. Their data ignore the value of unpaid leisure activities — reading books, going to the beach, hiking in the woods. If you give up 40 hours a week of book-reading, beach-going, hiking, and daydreaming in order to shuffle papers in a dull office, government statisticians will increase GNP by your annual income; you will notice your lost leisure time, but they won't.

Nor do GNP statistics take into consideration any deterioration in the quality of life due to distasteful water, noxious fumes, disruptive noises, ugly environments, and unsettling fears of crime and war. Indeed, these unpleasant things actually increase GNP to the extent that we spend money to purify our water, cleanse the air, shield our ears, beautify our surroundings, and protect ourselves from domestic criminals and foreign aggressors.

GNP is a widely followed barometer of economic activity.

Despite its limitations, GNP is widely used as a barometer of economic activity. The amount of goods and services produced in an economy depends

The Effect of Exports and Imports on Gross National Product

Gross national product y can be divided among private consumption c, private investment i, government expenditures g, and exports x less imports z.

$$y = c + i + g + x - z$$

The distinction between private consumption and investment is intended to identify goods that are used up, or consumed, shortly after they are acquired as compared with those that have longer useful lives. Raspberries are clearly obtained for consumption, and a skyscraper is an investment. But there are many borderline cases. Should a pair of expensive jogging shoes be counted as consumption or investment? Because it is difficult to draw a line and even more difficult to get good data, all household expenditures — except for housing — are considered consumption in the national income accounts. (There is a consumption subcategory, consumer durables, that includes cars, refrigerators, and other obviously durable goods.)

Government activities — Congressional salaries, paper clips, and national defense — are included in GNP at cost, and no distinction is made between consumption and investment goods — between memos and highways, parades and medical research.

Because gross national product is intended to be an estimate of a nation's production of goods and services, an adjustment must be made for the fact that some of the expenditures in c, i, and g are for imports, goods produced in other countries. Subtracting imports z gives $c + i + g - z$, domestic expenditures on domestically produced goods. If we add in exports x, foreign expenditures on domestic goods, we have $c + i + g + x - z$, total expenditures on domestically produced goods.

In the late 1980s, gross national product averaged approximately 65 percent private consumption, 18 percent private investment, and 20 percent government spending (40 percent federal, 60 percent state and local) and -3 percent exports minus imports. The negative value for exports minus imports means that the United States imported more than it exported, and that its citizens purchased more than they produced — nearly a trillion dollars in all from 1984 through 1990. While U.S. citizens were buying Sony televisions and Toyota automobiles, foreigners accumulated U.S. dollars, bonds, and stocks, a trillion dollars in claims on future U.S. production. The most worrisome aspect of this trade deficit is not that we bought foreign products — apparently we thought these were good products, attractively priced — but that our standard of living will someday decline when foreigners use their financial claims to purchase our products.

on the amount of resources used and the productivity of those who use them. An efficient blend of fertile land, useful equipment, and skilled people can produce a gratifying quantity of goods and services. A nation's output can be disappointingly low when resources are lacking, misused, or left unused. It is particularly distressing when resources are squandered, with potentially productive factories and people left idle. Fluctuations in measured gross national product help us gauge the extent to which resources are utilized or wasted.

Income Depends on Spending, Spending Depends on Income

Gross national product can be identified by the types of goods and services produced (consumption goods, investment goods, and so on) or by the type of income earned for producing them. This dual perspective reflects the accounting identity that every person's expenditure is someone else's income.

Suppose that a sweater is bought for $20. Some of that $20 goes to the store's employees (as wage income) and some to its owners (as profit income on their investment in the store). If the store premises are rented, some of the $20 may provide rental income to the building's owners. Some of the $20 may go in interest income to those who have lent the store money; some goes to the supplier of the sweater and for electricity and other utilities. These payments, too, become income to workers or others. Ultimately, every penny of the $20 expenditure (and of everyone's expenditures) provides income to someone somewhere.

Thus, every dollar spent on goods and services provides income — wages, profits, interest, or rent. We can express this fundamental accounting identity as

$$y = e \tag{1}$$

where y is the economy's aggregate income, e is aggregate expenditures, and both are in real terms, adjusted for inflation.

The second half of this income-expenditure model that we are constructing is provided by the observation that planned expenditures are influenced by income, which we can represent mathematically as

$$e = a + by \tag{2}$$

Figure 19.1 graphs this equation using the specific values $a = 3,000$ and $b = 0.5$. (These are identified as planned expenditures because, as you will see shortly, businesses may be compelled to make unplanned inventory expenditures.)

The parameter b is the economy's aggregate **marginal propensity to spend out of income**, and is the slope of the line in Figure 19.1. A $1 increase in income increases spending by an amount b, presumably less than $1. In Figure 19.1, each $1 increase in income increases spending by $0.50. Sometimes it is assumed that only consumers respond to an increase in income; the parameter b is then called the **marginal propensity to consume**.

Aggregate expenditures are often separated into private consumption, private investment, and government spending — a separation motivated by Keynes's

Every expenditure gives someone income.

Planned expenditures are influenced by income.

Figure 19.1   Expenditures Depend on Output

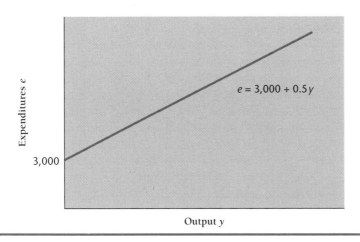

$e = 3,000 + 0.5y$

Expenditures e

3,000

Output y

belief that consumption is predictable, investment spending is volatile, and government spending is controllable. For our present purposes, there is no need to divide spending into three categories. All that really matters is that, in the aggregate, an increase in income increases spending. The source might be consumers who routinely spend a certain fraction of their incomes, businesses whose investment plans are stimulated by a strong economy, or a government whose expenditures rise to exhaust available tax revenue (and then some). The important point is that, overall, more income induces more spending.

Given the values of the parameters a and b, Equations 1 and 2 comprise a model that determines values for income and expenditures. We can do this graphically as in Figure 19.2, or mathematically by substituting Equation 2 into Equation 1:

$$y = e$$
$$y = a + by$$
$$y - by = a$$

$$y = \frac{a}{1 - b} \qquad (3)$$

For the specific values $a = 3,000$ and $b = 0.5$,

$$y = \frac{3,000}{1 - 0.5}$$

$$= 6,000$$

as shown in Figure 19.2.

Equation 3 and Figure 19.2 each determine the value of income, here 6,000, at which planned spending is exactly equal to income. In the national income

The income-expenditure model determines the value of income for which planned spending equals income.

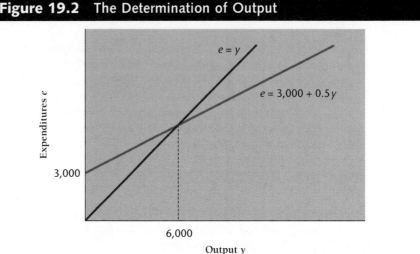

Figure 19.2   The Determination of Output

accounts, gross national product is an estimate of the nation's production of goods and services. The accountants set aggregate expenditures and income equal to aggregate output by assuming that everything that is produced is sold. Thus we can interpret y as measuring both output and income.

The Adjustment of Production to Spending

In our example, 6,000 is the level of production at which planned spending is exactly equal to output. Table 19.1 shows the level of planned spending for other values of output. When output is larger than 6,000, planned spending is less than 6,000; when output is smaller than 6,000, planned spending is larger than 6,000.

In situations where planned spending is not equal to output, inventories adjust to take up the slack. Businesses routinely make inventory investments in raw materials, goods that are still being processed, and finished goods that have not yet been sold. Much of their inventory accumulation is intentional, and therefore considered part of planned spending. It is helpful and prudent to have production materials on hand and to keep a stock of finished goods to meet customer demands. But some inventory accumulation may be unplanned and unwanted. When customers stop buying, unsold goods accumulate. If, on the other hand, planned spending exceeds output, then this excess spending causes an unplanned depletion of inventories — firms emptying their shelves and selling their demonstration and display items.

Production adjusts to demand, to offset unwanted inventory accumulation or depletion.

Figure 19.3 depicts these two cases, where output is either less than or greater than spending. Firms with unwanted inventory accumulation will reduce production to slow this accumulation. Businesses with empty shelves will increase production to meet demand. Thus there is a natural tendency for production to

Table 19.1 Income and Spending

Output y	Spending $e = 3{,}000 + 0.5y$	Spending vs. Output
4,000	5,000	$(e > y)$
5,000	5,500	$(e > y)$
6,000	6,000	$(e = y)$
7,000	6,500	$(e < y)$
8,000	7,000	$(e < y)$

adapt to demand, for the economy to gravitate to the point where production satisfies expenditures, with no unplanned inventory accumulation or depletion.

Multipliers

An autonomous change in spending, due perhaps to a change in tax rates, stock prices, or inflation expectations, can be portrayed in our model by changing a, the intercept of Equation 2. Planned spending is now higher at every level of income.

$$e = (a + \Delta a) + by$$

In our numerical example, perhaps the intercept increases from 3,000 to 3,100.

$$e = 3{,}100 + 0.5y$$

This increase in spending directly increases income by 100. There are also indirect effects, because more income induces more spending, which provides even more income. What is the total of these direct and indirect effects? In Figure 19.4, the expenditure function shifts upward, with the intercept rising by 100, putting the new solution at 6,200. Because of the indirect effects, output increases by 200, twice the size of the initial 100 increase in spending.

In general, we can use Equation 3 to determine the change in income mathematically by comparing the original value of income y with the new value $y + \Delta y$.

$$y = \frac{a}{1 - b}$$

$$y + \Delta y = \frac{a + \Delta a}{1 - b}$$

The change in income is

$$\Delta y = \frac{\Delta a}{1 - b}$$

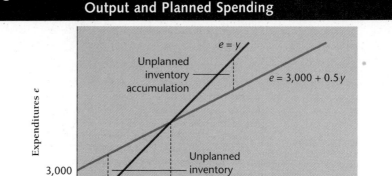

Figure 19.3   Inventories Are Affected by Gaps Between Output and Planned Spending

If we divide by Δa, we obtain the change in income per unit change in expenditure

$$\frac{\Delta y}{\Delta a} = \frac{1}{1 - b} \tag{4}$$

The interaction of income and spending multiplies the effect on income of a change in spending.

Equation 4 is called a **multiplier**, because the interaction of income and expenditure multiplies the effect on income of an autonomous change in spending. In our numerical example, $b = 0.5$ and the multiplier is 2.

$$\frac{\Delta y}{\Delta a} = \frac{1}{1 - b}$$

$$= \frac{1}{1 - 0.5}$$

$$= 2$$

Thus we found that when there is an initial increase of 100 in spending, income increases by 200, from 6,000 to 6,200.

This 200 increase no doubt takes some time, as the interaction of spending, income, and output proceeds. The initial 100 increase in spending causes a temporary depletion of inventories. Retail stores order more products from suppliers to replenish their inventories. Businesses expand production to fill these orders. The increased income earned in production leads to more spending, and the cycle repeats again — causing the eventual increase in production to be twice the size of the initial increase in spending.

Figure 19.4 An Autonomous Increase in Spending
Increases Output

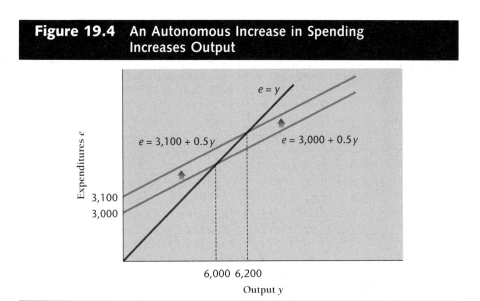

The value of the multiplier given by Equation 4 depends critically on the value of b, the marginal propensity to spend out of income (also called the marginal propensity to consume). Table 19.2 illustrates the fact that the larger the marginal propensity to spend is, the greater the multiplier becomes. When changes in income cause large changes in spending, the interaction of spending and income greatly magnifies the consequences of shocks to the economy.

The larger the marginal propensity to spend, the greater the multiplier.

Keynes reasoned that the "uncontrollable and disobedient psychology of the business world" sometimes causes autonomous drops in expenditures (sudden declines in a), which are multiplied through the income-expenditure linkage into sharp recessions.[1] This same linkage multiplies efforts by the government to end a recession by spending more. If the marginal propensity to spend is 0.5, the multiplier is 2, and a 100 increase in government spending raises national income by 200.

This analysis is based on Keynes's *General Theory*, which was written during the Great Depression. It focuses on the demand for goods and services (how much people want to buy) and ignores supply (how much producers want to sell). By assuming that people can buy as much as they please, we implicitly assume that there are idle resources, which firms would employ if only there were sufficient demand for their output. If people decide to buy more, producers will gladly expand production and employ more people. The extra wage and profit income further stimulate spending. Conversely, if people decide to spend less, businesses will cut back production and employ fewer people. Wages and profits slump, further reducing spending. Thus a nation's output and employment vary with the demand for goods and services.

Table 19.2   The Effect of the Marginal Propensity to Spend on the Multiplier

Marginal Propensity to Spend b	Multiplier $\dfrac{\Delta y}{\Delta a} = \dfrac{1}{1-b}$
0.0	1.0
0.1	1.1
0.3	1.4
0.5	2.0
0.7	3.3
0.9	10.0

The Role of Government

Keynes argued that governments should use monetary and fiscal policies to stabilize the economy.

Multiplier analysis is one of the most enduring and influential legacies of Keynes, in that it explains an economic phenomenon that classical models could not explain: how changes in consumer, business, and government spending can have pronounced effects on national income, production, and employment. Keynes's analysis was not only an explanation of business cycles; it was also a call for governments to use fiscal and monetary policies to stabilize the economy by offsetting the effects of economic shocks. If the economy slumps, the federal government can increase its own spending, or it can reduce tax rates, leaving households and businesses with more after-tax income that they can use to increase their spending. In an inflationary boom, the federal government can cool the economy by reducing spending or increasing taxes.

Such policies are sometimes blocked politically by concerns about the effects on the government's budget. If the federal government increases its spending or cuts taxes to strengthen the economy, its budget deficit increases. A balanced budget is generally favored by the public — and by many politicians seeking their votes.

American presidents from Franklin Roosevelt to Ronald Reagan have promised balanced budgets during their campaigns and then accepted budget deficits during their presidencies. From the outside, the government's budget deficit is an easy target for criticism, which predictably brings applause. But from the inside, presidents generally agree with economists that the aesthetic benefits of a balanced budget are often not worth what it would cost in higher unemployment and lost output. Keynes had particularly biting words for those who considered a balanced budget more important than the employment of idle resources. In *The General Theory*, he wrote[2]

> *If the Treasury were to fill old bottles with bank-notes, bury them at suitable depths in disused coal mines which are then filled up to the surface with town*

The Full-Employment Surplus

A budget deficit is sometimes interpreted as evidence that the government is using expansionary fiscal policies (high spending, low tax rates) to stimulate the economy, while a budget surplus shows that the government is following contractionary fiscal policies. The problem with this view is that budget surpluses and deficits depend not only on government spending and tax policies but also on the state of the economy.

To gauge whether the government has shifted to a more expansionary policy or a less expansionary policy, or has not really changed the thrust of its fiscal policy at all, we need to distinguish between the budget effects of policy changes and the budget effects of changes in the economy. With this in mind, in the early 1960s, the Council of Economic Advisers began estimating the **full-employment surplus** (now often called the "high-employment surplus" or the "structural surplus"): what the budget surplus (or deficit) would be if the economy were operating at full employment.

Presidents often embrace the full-employment surplus because it defuses vocal advocates of "fiscal responsibility." The president can plausibly argue that the budget would be balanced, or even in surplus, if the economy were only at full employment. The actual deficit is then blamed on the weakness of the economy rather than fiscal sins. For economists, the full-employment surplus is simply a way of gauging the overall thrust of government spending and tax policies. They do not recommend that the full-employment surplus should be zero or any particular number. The change in the full-employment surplus simply tells us whether the government's spending and tax policy is becoming more or less expansionary.

The graph on page 552 compares the actual federal surplus with the full-employment surplus and shows that there have been several periods in which the former gave a misleading impression of government fiscal policy. The budget deficits in the late 1950s and early 1960s were interpreted by some as evidence of fiscal irresponsibility, and they opposed any efforts to increase spending or cut taxes to stimulate the economy. John Kennedy's Council of Economic Advisers argued that these deficits were due to the weakness of the economy, not to overly aggressive fiscal policies in the 1950s by the Eisenhower administration. The substantial full-employment surpluses indicated a conservative and contractionary policy.

In the graph, a sharp drop in the full-employment surplus during the years 1964–66 indicates a significant shift to expansionary spending and tax policies — a shift that would have gone undetected had we looked only at the actual budget surplus. In 1971, 1975–76, and 1980–85, a weak economy again caused a substantial divergence between the actual and full-employment budgets.

In 1982, President Reagan ran into the now familiar problem of a large

Actual and Full-Employment Federal Budget Surplus

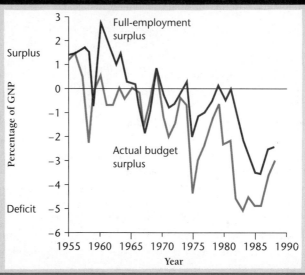

budget deficit caused, not by overly expansionary policies, but by a weak economy. For several months, government policy was virtually paralyzed as policymakers argued about the appropriate reaction to large budget deficits. Many counseled higher taxes and lower government spending to reduce the budget deficit. But the economy was already in a deep recession in 1982, with the employment rate above 10 percent. Higher taxes and lower spending would have pushed the economy in the wrong direction — to the brink of economic collapse.

The government's budget deficits were not really the problem; they were more a symptom of the problem, which was a terribly weak economy. If the unemployment rate had been, say, 4 percent lower, then gross national product would have been about 10 percent higher, some $300 billion in 1982. An additional $300 billion in national income would have generated nearly $100 billion more in federal tax revenue. Policymakers should have focused their attention on ways to end the recession, not ways to balance the budget. A strong economy would have produced hundreds of billions of dollars in extra output and income, enough to take the strain off a great many household, business, and governmental budgets.

The Reagan administration did, in fact, focus its attention on the economy, rather than the deficit, and increased spending while cutting tax rates substantially. With time, the economy did recover and return to an approximation of full employment. Concern grew that tax rates had been cut too far, because large budget deficits persisted, even at relatively low unemployment rates.

rubbish, and leave it to private enterprise on well-tried principles of laissez-faire to dig up the notes again . . . , there need be no more unemployment and, with the help of the repercussions, the real income of the community, and its capital wealth also would probably become a good deal greater than it actually is. It would, indeed, be more sensible to build houses and the like; but if there are political and practical difficulties in the way of this, the above would be better than nothing. . . . Thus we are so sensible, have schooled ourselves to so close a resemblance of prudent financiers, taking careful thought before we add to the "financial" burdens of posterity by building them houses to live in, that we have no such easy escape from the sufferings of unemployment.

Economists, businesspersons, and policymakers today generally accept Keynes's argument — not that deficits are good, but that government policies should be judged by their real effects on employment, output, and so on rather than by their financial effects on some accountant's balance sheet.

> Keynes believed that a balanced budget is less important than a strong economy.

THE *IS* CURVE

We have so far focused on the implications of the fact that output influences spending. Increased output means more income for households and more profits for firms. When households earn more, they spend more. When firms make more profits, their expansion plans turn bullish. Together, household and business spending increase.

This explanation of spending ignores financial markets and the influence of interest rates on spending — and interest rates surely do influence spending. For households and firms that borrow to finance spending, high interest rates are discouraging. For households and firms with cash to invest, high interest rates make bonds more attractive and commodities (particularly houses, buildings, and other long-lived physical assets) less so. Spending on houses, offices, factories, equipment, inventories, and other real assets depends on a comparison of their rates of return with the rates of return on financial assets. When financial assets offer relatively high yields, less is spent on real assets.

> High interest rates depress spending.

We can take into account this negative effect of high interest rates on spending by assuming that all bonds pay the same interest rate R and by expanding our expenditure equation to include this interest rate:

$$e = a + by + cR \qquad 0 < b < 1, c < 0 \qquad (5)$$

The parameter c measures the effect on spending of a change in the interest rate R, for a given level of income; c is negative because high interest rates depress spending.

The Shape of the *IS* Curve

We can depict graphically the dependence of expenditures on both output and the interest rate by identifying the combinations of y and R for which planned spending is equal to output. Figure 19.5 shows that as the value of the

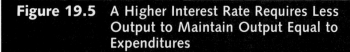

Figure 19.5 A Higher Interest Rate Requires Less Output to Maintain Output Equal to Expenditures

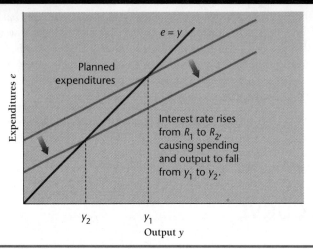

interest rate increases from R_1 to R_2, planned expenditures decline and the equilibrium level of output falls from y_1 to y_2.

The *IS* curve shows those values of y and r for which planned spending equals output.

Figure 19.6 plots the **IS curve**, showing these values of y and R and other combinations for which planned spending is just equal to output. (The letters *IS* refer to investment (I) and saving (S), since it can be shown that investment is equal to saving when expenditures equal output.) One point on the *IS* curve is at y_1 and R_1. Another is at y_2 and R_2, because an increase in the interest rate from R_1 to R_2 reduces equilibrium output from y_1 to y_2.

All points off the *IS* curve represent situations in which expenditures do not equal output. At points above the *IS* curve, R is too high; the excessive level of R reduces spending below output. At such a point, a decline in R will increase expenditures until spending is equal to output. Below the *IS* curve, R is too low; spending exceeds output, and here R must increase, reducing spending to a level compatible with output.

Designed by J. R. Hicks,[3] the *IS* curve is an ingenious graph, unlike most graphs in that it shows neither an historical record nor a causal relationship. The *IS* curve does not say that output determines the interest rate or that the interest rate determines output. Instead, output and the interest rate are determined simultaneously. The *IS* curve tells us which values of output and the interest rate are feasible values, in that output is equal to expenditures.

Shifts in the *IS* Curve

Economic events that increase spending shift the *IS* curve rightward.

If demand factors other than output and the interest rate alter expenditures, the *IS* curve shifts. In general, any event (other than a change in y or R) that increases spending shifts the expenditure function upward, as depicted in Figure

Figure 19.6 The IS Curve

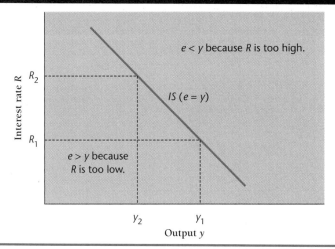

19.7, raising the level of output from y_1 to y_2 for a given interest rate R_1. This higher level of output for a given interest rate is shown in Figure 19.8 as a rightward shift of the *IS* curve. For an interest rate R_1, an increase in spending increases equilibrium output from y_1 to y_2.

An increase in government spending, for instance, raises aggregate expenditures, shifting the *IS* curve in an expansionary, rightward direction. The same is true of an autonomous increase in private spending, due perhaps to a tax cut or to more optimistic expectations about the economy. At any given interest rate, output must increase to maintain the equality of output and expenditures. Conversely, an autonomous decline in government or private spending shifts the *IS* curve in a contractionary, leftward direction.

The magnitudes of these *IS* shifts are given by the simple multiplier analyzed in Equation 4. When we move horizontally, as in Figure 19.8, the interest rate is held constant, and we can therefore use the Equation 4 multiplier, which omitted interest-rate changes. The difference between y_1 and y_2 is

$$\frac{\Delta y}{\Delta a} = \frac{1}{1 - b}$$

This horizontal shift was as far as we could go with Equation 4. To determine whether the interest rate in fact rises or falls, we need to look at financial markets, which we will do now.

THE *LM* CURVE

The *IS-LM* model assumes that there are two financial assets: money and bonds. Money consists of cash and checking accounts (M1) that earn a fixed interest

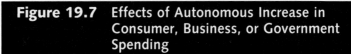

Figure 19.7 Effects of Autonomous Increase in Consumer, Business, or Government Spending

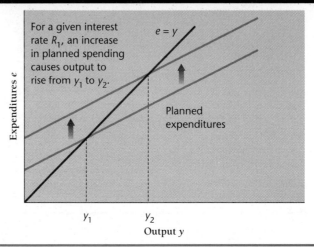

For a given interest rate R_1, an increase in planned spending causes output to rise from y_1 to y_2.

rate (perhaps zero); all bonds pay the same interest rate R. Financial markets offer households and businesses a choice between holding money and holding bonds. We can analyze that choice either by equating money demand and supply or by equating bond demand and supply. The first approach is the usual one, and we will follow it here.

Earlier chapters have shown that the Fed has only indirect and imperfect control over the supply of M1, but here we assume that the Fed can use open-market purchases and sales to increase or reduce M1 as it wishes. If we let M signify the nominal value of M_1 and P the price level, then M/P is the real value of the money supply.

We make two assumptions about money demand consistent with our discussion in Chapter 17. First, money demand is positively related to output, because as output and income expand, people want to hold more money to carry out the increased volume of transactions. Second, money demand is inversely related to the interest rate on bonds, because this interest is forgone by holding money instead of bonds.

We implement these assumptions by writing the real demand for money l as

$$l = f + gy + hR \qquad g > 0, h < 0 \qquad (6)$$

The parameter f is the constant intercept. The parameter g gauges the effect of an increase in income on the demand for money, and is positive. The parameter h gives the effect of an increase in the interest rate on the demand for money, and is negative.

Money demand is related positively to output and negatively to interest rates.

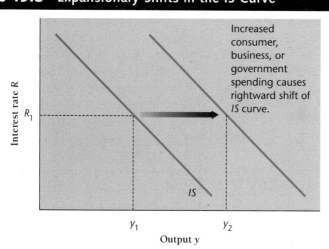

Figure 19.8   Expansionary Shifts in the IS Curve

Increased consumer, business, or government spending causes rightward shift of *IS* curve.

Interest rate R

R_1

IS

y_1 y_2

Output y

The Shape of the *LM* Curve

Analogous to the *IS* curve, we can derive an **LM curve** showing the combinations of y and R for which money demand is equal to supply. Figure 19.9 shows the money-demand and money-supply curves. The money-demand curve is downward sloping because money demand is negatively related to the interest rate. The money-supply curve is vertical because it does not depend on interest rates.

As output increases from y_1 to y_2, money demand increases (because people desire more money to carry out more transactions). If the interest rate did not change, money demand would be larger than supply, which is not an equilibrium. Since an increase in the interest rate reduces money demand, the interest rate must increase from R_1 to R_2 in order to keep money demand equal to the fixed supply.

Figure 19.10 shows these values of y and R and other values for which money demand is equal to supply. These combinations are called the *LM* curve, with L representing money demand and M money supply. One point on the *LM* curve is at y_1 and R_1. Another is at y_2 and R_2, because an increase in output from y_1 to y_2 increases the interest rate from R_1 to R_2.

At points above the *LM* curve, R is too high for money demand to equal supply; because an increase in R reduces money demand, these are points for which money demand is less than supply. From any point above the *LM* curve, a decline in R increases money demand until it is equal to the supply of money. Below the *LM* curve, R is too low; money demand is larger than the supply. Now, an increase in R, reducing money demand, is needed to equilibrate money demand and supply.

The *LM* curve shows those combinations of y and R for which money demand equals supply.

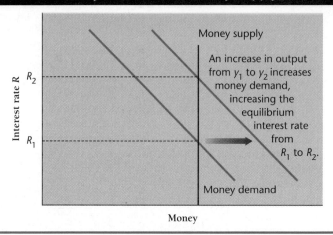

Figure 19.9   Money Demand and Money Supply

Figure 19.10   The LM Curve

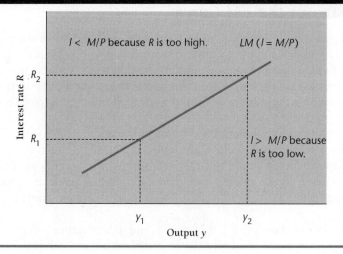

Shifts in the *LM* Curve

If factors other than output and the interest rate alter money demand or supply, the *LM* curve shifts. Figure 19.11 shows how, at a given level of output y_1, an increase in the real money supply requires a decrease in the interest rate from R_1 to R_2, increasing money demand to match the increased supply. Thus the *LM* curve shifts downward, as shown in Figure 19.12. It is probably easier to remember the direction of this shift if we describe it as rightward: an increase in the money supply is expansionary, shifting the *LM* curve rightward.

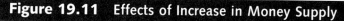

Figure 19.11   Effects of Increase in Money Supply

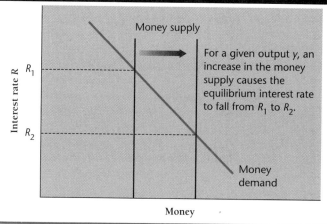

Money supply

For a given output y, an increase in the money supply causes the equilibrium interest rate to fall from R_1 to R_2.

Money demand

Money

Figure 19.12   An Increase in the Money Supply Shifts the LM Curve Rightward (Downward)

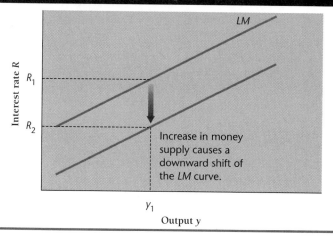

LM

Increase in money supply causes a downward shift of the *LM* curve.

Output y

Notice that the real money supply, M/P, can be increased either through an increase in the nominal money supply M or by a decline in the price level P. A halving of the price level, to take an extreme example, would double M/P as surely as if the Fed doubled the nominal level of M1. Thus an increase in M or a decrease in P shifts the *LM* curve rightward. A decrease in M/P — whether due to a decline in M or an increase in P — shifts the *LM* curve leftward.

Autonomous changes in money demand also shift the *LM* curve. Any event (other than a change in y or R) that reduces money demand has the same

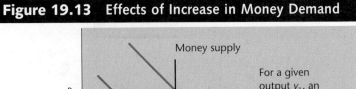

Figure 19.13 Effects of Increase in Money Demand

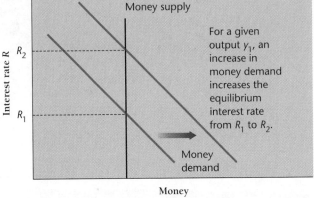

Figure 19.14 An Increase in the Money Demand Shifts the LM Curve Upward (Leftward)

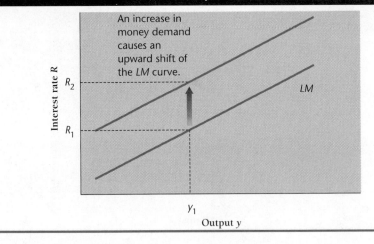

qualitative effects as an increase in the money supply — shifting the *LM* curve rightward. Figure 19.13 confirms this logic. At a level of output y_1, an increase in money demand, like a decrease in the money supply, requires an increase in interest rates from R_1 to R_2 in order to reduce money demand back down to the level of supply. Thus an increase in money demand shifts the *LM* curve upward, or leftward, as in Figure 19.14 — just like a contractionary reduction in the money supply. Conversely, a decrease in money demand will, like an increase in the money supply, shift the *LM* curve rightward. We can summarize these

Economic events that increase the real money supply or reduce money demand shift the *LM* curve rightward.

Figure 19.15   **The IS and LM Curves Determine Output and Interest Rates**

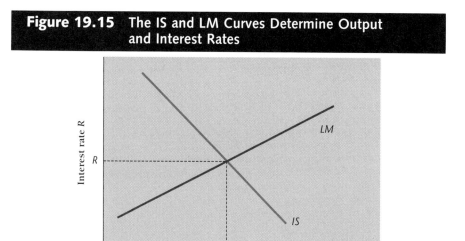

shifts by concluding that any event (other than a change in y or R) that increases the real money supply or reduces money demand shifts the LM curve in an expansionary, rightward direction.

IS AND LM CURVES TOGETHER

Figure 19.15 shows that the intersection of the IS and LM curves determines that particular combination of the interest rate and output at which output is equal to expenditures and money demand is equal to money supply. To apply these curves, as we will be doing in the next chapter, remember that the IS curve is negatively sloped and the LM curve positively sloped. Economic events that increase expenditures shift the IS curve in an expansionary, rightward direction; events that increase the real supply of money or reduce money demand shift the LM curve in that same direction. Contractionary events shift the IS and LM curves leftward.

SUMMARY

Income influences how much households and businesses spend; spending, in the aggregate, influences how much output is produced and how much income households and businesses earn. This interdependence of spending, income, and output helps us understand how economic events have multiplier or ripple effects on an economy, effects that can grow into economic booms and recessions.

The interaction of spending, income, and financial markets can be depicted by the IS and LM curves. With R and y the axes, the IS curve is negatively sloped and the LM curve positively sloped. The IS curve is shifted rightward by increases in expenditures; the LM curve is shifted rightward by increases in the real money supply or decreases in money demand.

IMPORTANT TERMS

consumption goods
full-employment surplus
gross national product (GNP)
investment goods
IS curve

LM curve
marginal propensity to consume
marginal propensity to spend out of income
multiplier

EXERCISES

1. Identify which of the following are included in the U.S. gross national product and which are excluded.
   a. Congressional salaries.
   b. The purchase of a car made in Germany.
   c. The purchase of 100 shares of IBM stock.
   d. The purchase of a new textbook.

2. Indicate which of the following transactions are counted as consumption, investment, government spending, or excluded from GNP.
   a. Disney builds a new amusement park in Washington, D.C.
   b. McDonald's rebuilds a California restaurant that collapsed during an earthquake.
   c. A collector pays $34 million for a Van Gogh painting.
   d. A college student publishes a book of his drawings which he sells for $12 each.
   e. A college student pays $12 for lunch at In-and-Out Burger.

3. Here is a simple income-expenditure model.
$$y = e$$
$$e = 800 + 0.8y$$
   a. What is the economic logic behind the first equation?
   b. What is the economic logic behind the second equation?
   c. What is the value of output y?
   d. What is the value of the multiplier?

e. By how much will output increase if expenditures increase by 20, from 800 to 820?

4. In the following income-expenditure model, expenditures have been separated into private consumption c, private investment i, and government spending g.
$$y = c + i + g$$
$$c = 140 + (\tfrac{2}{3})y$$
$$i = 400$$
$$g = 400$$
   a. What is the level of y?
   b. Policymakers want to increase investment spending sufficiently to raise the level of y to 3,000. How large an increase in i is needed?
   c. If, instead, policymakers were to increase government spending sufficiently to raise y to 3,000, how large an increase in g would be needed?

5. Use the following income-expenditure model to determine aggregate output y and to determine the effect on y of a decline in investment i from 600 to 500:
$$y = c + i + g$$
$$c = 300 + 0.6y$$
$$i = 600$$
$$g = 300$$

It has been proposed that government spending be a fixed fraction, say 10 percent, of national income. Determine the value of y and the effect on y of a decline in investment from 600 to 500, using the preceding model with $g = 0.1y$ in place of $g = 300$. Explain any differences from your previous answers.

6. If U.S. exports are larger than imports, are U.S. citizens purchasing more than they produce, or vice versa?

7. Business inventories fell by 2 percent in the summer of 1985. This could be a sign of economic weakness, indicating that firms are lightening up on supplies in anticipation of a slowdown in production. How could a drop in inventories also be interpreted as a sign of a vigorous economy?

8. Society has a choice between producing consumption goods and investment goods. How does this choice affect future generations? Give a specific example.

9. The size of the government deficit and the unemployment rate are positively correlated in that both tend to rise and fall together. Does this imply that government deficits cause unemployment? Is there any other logical explanation for the observed correlation?

10. Hong Kong's exports are larger than its GNP. How is this possible?

11. What could Abba Lerner have meant when he said that "The purpose of taxation is never to raise money, but to leave less in the hands of the taxpayer"?

12. In December 1983, with the unemployment rate at 8.2 percent, almost half the people polled by the *Los Angeles Times* agreed that "a balanced federal budget alone would bring economic prosperity or would be the most important factor in accomplishing it."[4] How might the federal budget be balanced? Do you agree that such action would bring prosperity?

13. The Reagan administration forecast a $130 billion deficit in 1989; the Congressional Budget Office predicted a $170 billion deficit. Which

do you suppose assumed a higher level of GNP? A higher level of interest rates?

14. Politicians frequently tell voters that "If any household or business let its spending exceed its income as frequently as the federal government does, it would soon be bankrupt."
   a. Why can't most households persistently spend more than their income? Cite an exception, a household that can purposely and legally let spending exceed income repeatedly, without going bankrupt.
   b. Why don't most businesses want their spending to exceed income indefinitely?
   c. How can the federal government get away with it?

15. In his final State of the Union address, in December 1932, with the unemployment rate nearing 25 percent, President Herbert Hoover told the nation that government could strengthen the economy by "the continual reduction of all government expenditures, whether national, state, or local. . . . Embraced in this problem is the unquestioned balancing of the federal budget." Explain why you either agree or disagree with this advice.

16. The Federal Reserve wants to stimulate investment spending. Should it aim for lower or higher interest rates? Why? Should it buy Treasury bills or sell them? Why?

17. Does the demand for money depend on nominal or real interest rates? Explain your reasoning.

18. Explain how the *IS* and *LM* curves are affected by an increase in each of the following.
   a. Output, y.
   b. Interest rate, R.
   c. Price level, P.

19. Explain how the *IS* and *LM* curves are affected by each of the following economic events.
   a. Increase in government spending.
   b. Tax cut for consumers.
   c. Increased business-profit expectations.
   d. Increased money supply.
   e. Increased demand for money.

20. How would the *IS* and *LM* curves be affected by increased service charges on credit cards?

21. How would the *IS* and *LM* curves be affected by an increased availability of money-market funds, which reduce the demand for cash and bank checking accounts?

22. If the marginal propensity to spend out of income is 0.6, then, according to the *IS-LM* model, a $1 billion increase in government spending increases aggregate output by which one of the following: zero, between $0 and $2.5 billion, $2.5 billion, more than $2.5 billion. Explain your answer.

23. The Gramm-Rudman bill mandated automatic spending cuts if Congress fails to achieve a series of declining deficit targets, starting with $171.9 billion in 1986 and $144 billion in 1987 and continuing down to $0 in 1991. If there had been a recession in 1987, due perhaps to a drop in U.S. exports, what effect would this recession have had on
    a. unemployment?
    b. tax revenue?
    c. the budget deficit?
    d. government spending under Gramm-Rudman?

Would the provisions of Gamm-Rudman have eased or worsened this hypothetical recession?

24. The government wants to use tax changes to reduce consumption, while using interest-rate changes to increase investment. Should it raise or lower taxes? Should it increase or reduce interest rates? Which branches of government can affect taxes and interest rates directly?

25. The following news story summarizes an argument that international aid costs the United States very little. Explain why this argument is unpersuasive.[5]

> [U.S. Treasury Secretary G. William] Miller's message is that, because 25% of U.S. manufactured exports are purchased by developing nations, international aid to these nations eventually helps the U.S. "These purchases of U.S. goods and services have major beneficial effects on U.S. employment and profits — yielding gross-national-product growth of $3 for each dollar we pay to the banks (or agencies) [to distribute abroad] — and this in turn leads to increased tax receipts," which largely offset the U.S. contributions, Miller says.

THE EFFECTS OF

ECONOMIC EVENTS

ON AGGREGATE DEMAND

The theory of economics does not furnish a body of settled conclusions immediately applicable to policy. It is a method rather than a doctrine, an apparatus of the mind, a technique of thinking, which helps its possessor to draw correct conclusions.

John Maynard Keynes

The ideas underlying the *IS-LM* model were developed by John Maynard Keynes during the Great Depression, a time when there was an abundance of idle resources. To apply this model in other circumstances, we need to take into account the possibility that output is limited by available resources and that, as resources become fully utilized, there is upward pressure on wages and prices.

The *IS* and *LM* curves determine the level of output if there are no resource constraints and the price level is fixed. We can therefore consider this *IS-LM* output level to be aggregate demand, the amount that would be produced at a given price level if there were no supply constraints. In Chapter 21, we will develop a model of aggregate supply — the quantity that, together with aggregate demand, determines the level of production and prices.

In this chapter, however, we continue to focus on aggregate demand, since this is often the target of monetary and fiscal policies. We will consider how various economic events affect the *IS* and *LM* curves and, as a consequence, aggregate demand. Which events — and which combinations of events — on balance raise aggregate demand, and which reduce it? We begin by looking at changes in private spending.

PRIVATE EXPENDITURES

Chapter 19 explained that changes in private expenditures shift the *IS* curve in easily remembered ways. An increase in spending causes an expansionary rightward shift, as shown in Figure 20.1. A decrease in spending causes a contractionary, leftward shift. The rightward *IS* shift depicted in Figure 20.1 causes aggregate demand and interest rates to increase, for reasons that will be explained shortly. First, we need to recognize that there are many diverse reasons why private spending might expand or contract.

Consumer Spending and Saving

An increase in household spending shifts the *IS* curve rightward.

Households use some of their income to buy goods and services, and save the remainder for future purchases. They put their savings into bonds, stocks, and other assets, which are not part of the gross national product because they are not newly produced goods and services. If households decide to spend more and save less — perhaps because of a stock-market boom or inflationary fears — the *IS* curve shifts rightward, as in Figure 20.1, raising aggregate demand and interest rates. If households save more and spend less — perhaps because they are concerned about losing jobs or about the solvency of the Social Security system — their diminished spending causes a contractionary, leftward shift of the *IS* curve.

Business Borrowing and Investment

An increase in business investment spending shifts the *IS* curve rightward.

Businesses expand, buying additional plants and equipment, when they think that these real assets can be used profitably. Their profit expectations depend on difficult and subjective interpretations of future economic conditions. The business that orders 1,000 personal computers must be concerned not only with how productively these computers can be employed now, but also with their usefulness during the next several years. Will the manufacturer provide support, or go bankrupt? Will third-party developers introduce improved software and other enhancements? Will better machines soon be available?

The business contemplating the construction of an office building or a manufacturing plant must think decades ahead. Will overbuilding cause a collapse of the office market? Will the population move into or out of this region of the country? Will unfavorable changes in exchange rates devastate sales? With limited knowledge of the future, businesses may swing from unfounded pessimism to excessive optimism, and then back again. These mercurial mood shifts can move the *IS* curve to and fro, with repercussions on aggregate demand. Increases in business-investment spending shift the *IS* curve rightward, as in Figure 20.1; diminished investment spending shifts the *IS* curve leftward.

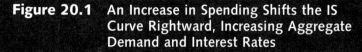

Figure 20.1   **An Increase in Spending Shifts the IS Curve Rightward, Increasing Aggregate Demand and Interest Rates**

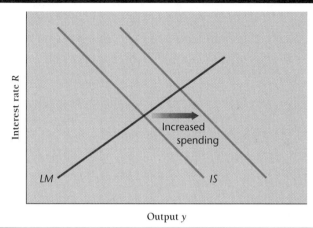

Output y

Exports and Imports

Gross national product monitors the utilization of a nation's resources and, hence, aggregate production. Since imported goods are produced elsewhere, imports are excluded from gross national product. Exports are included, because these represent domestic production.

Changes in exchange rates, tastes, or other factors that affect exports and imports can alter aggregate demand through shifts in the *IS* curve. A devaluation of a nation's currency, making its currency and its products cheaper, should increase its exports, shifting the *IS* curve rightward. This predictable effect leads some nations to follow policies designed to devalue their currencies — in effect, trying to spur sales by reducing prices. For nations, as for individual businesses, a lower price is a generally reliable way of selling more products. But, for nations and businesses, it may not be advantageous to sell products at a minimal profit, or even a loss. At the extreme, a nation that cared only about maximizing sales could guarantee full employment of its resources by giving away its national output, in essence becoming the unpaid servant of other countries.

Exports can also be stimulated by the development of superior products or by the dropping of trade barriers. Conversely, the prohibition of imports compels the increased purchase of domestically produced goods, shifting the *IS* curve rightward. Such barriers to imports increase domestic aggregate demand, as intended, but at the cost of forcing people to buy products evidently inferior to the forbidden imports.

Changes in exports and imports affect aggregate demand, as indicated by these examples, through shifts in the *IS* curve. However, some government

Increased exports or reduced imports shift the *IS* curve rightward.

| Highlight 20.1 | **Providing for Future Generations** |

In their immediate macroeconomic consequences for aggregate demand, there is no real difference between additional household spending on consumer goods and additional business spending on investment goods. Both shift the *IS* curve rightward, increasing aggregate demand and interest rates. But the difference between consumption and investment goods, between enjoying the present and providing for the future, can be very important to future generations.

Consider two countries whose real per-capita gross national products grow annually by 1.25 percent and 2 percent, respectively. There will be little change in their relative positions over any short period of time; but if these differing growth rates continue over many years, their relative positions will change dramatically. Assume that real per capita GNP in 1870 is $1,800 in the first country and $1,400 in the second. After 100 years of 1.25-percent and 2.0-percent growth, real per capita GNP in 1970 will be $7,000 in the first country and $11,000 in the second. Their relative positions have been reversed. The first country began with a real per capita GNP 30 percent higher than the second; 100 years later, the second country had a real per capita GNP 60 percent higher than the first. This is a true story: the two countries are Great Britain and the United States.

policies designed to manipulate aggregate demand by altering exports and imports are of questionable benefit. It would often be better to use monetary and fiscal policies to influence domestic household and business spending directly, rather than indirectly by subsidizing exports or restricting imports.

GOVERNMENT FISCAL POLICY

Table 20.1 shows the federal budget for 1989. The budget deficit that year was $1,195.2 billion − $1,046.7 billion = $148.5 billion. The government's outlays include purchases of goods and services and also **transfer payments**: Social Security benefits, interest payments, and other disbursements for which the recipients do not have to produce any goods or provide any services. Taxes are also transfer payments, this time from citizens to the government. When you pay income taxes, you do not personally receive any goods or services by return mail.

Government purchases of goods and services *g* are part of aggregate national expenditures. Transfer payments are not expenditures and are not included in *g*, because they are not purchases of goods and services. If households use Social Security benefits or unemployment compensation to buy food and clothing, these

Table 20.1 The Federal Budget in 1989 (billions of dollars)	
Disbursements	
Purchases of goods and services	$ 402.9
Transfer payments to persons	472.6
Grants-in-aid to state and local governments	119.4
Interest on federal debt	171.1
Subsidies of government enterprises	29.2
	$1,195.2
Receipts	
Personal income taxes	$ 460.4
Social insurance contributions	422.5
Excise and other taxes	58.7
Corporate profit taxes	105.1
	$1,046.7

expenditures are included in consumption c; if businesses use interest payments or tax rebates to buy buildings and equipment, these are included in investment i. Thus government spending affects aggregate expenditures directly; taxes and other transfers affect spending indirectly through their effects on private consumption and investment.

Government spending affects aggregate spending directly; taxes do so indirectly.

Spending and Taxation

The government's **fiscal policies**, spending and taxation, affect aggregate demand by shifting the *IS* curve. These effects may be the consequence of policies enacted for other purposes — an increase in defense spending to fight a war, an increase in taxes to reduce a budget deficit. Keynes advocated the deliberate use of fiscal policies to enlarge or contract spending and, with it, aggregate demand — bolstering aggregate demand during recessions and diminishing demand during inflationary booms.

Keynes urged the use of fiscal policy to stabilize aggregate demand.

An increase in government spending or a reduction in tax rates shifts the *IS* curve rightward, as in Figure 20.2, raising aggregate demand and interest rates. A reduction in government spending or increase in tax rates shifts the *IS* curve leftward, reducing aggregate demand and interest rates. Let's now consider why interest rates are affected by shifts in the *IS* curve.

Demand-Side Crowding Out

The multiplier model introduced in Chapter 19 tells us that, neglecting interest rates, an autonomous increase in spending increases the output by this:

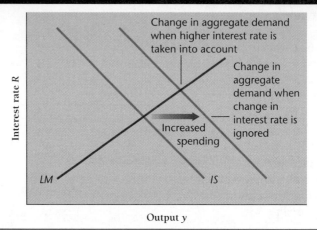

Figure 20.2   The Induced Rise in Interest Rates Reduces the Effect of Increased Spending on Aggregate Demand

$$\frac{\Delta y}{\Delta a} = \frac{1}{1 - b}$$

where b is the marginal propensity to spend. In Figure 20.2 we depict this increase in y as a rightward shift in the *IS* curve. As the figure shows, the interest rate is, in fact, affected by the increase in spending. The interest rate rises along the upward-sloping *LM* curve, and as a result the increase in y is less than that predicted by the simple multiplier formula.

The economic explanation is as follows. An increase in private or government spending directly raises aggregate expenditures and, further, has the multiplier effects attributable to the interaction of spending and income. An increased level of income and transactions also increases the demand for money, yet there has been no change in the money supply.

With money demand up and money supply unchanged, money is tight, putting upward pressure on interest rates. To increase their cash balances, people sell bonds, causing bond prices to fall and, consequently, the interest rates on bonds to rise. This increase in interest rates persuades people to economize on their money holdings, so that they will make do with the fixed money supply. Thus the increase in y raises money demand, and this is offset by an increase in R, which reduces money demand. That is why the *LM* curve is positively sloped: if the money supply is constant, then a higher level of income requires a higher interest rate.

Higher interest rates diminish not only money demand, but also private expenditures, especially for investment goods. When interest rates go up, households and businesses are less inclined to take out loans to buy houses, factories, and equipment and more inclined to buy high-yielding bonds instead. The

An increase in spending increases money demand, pushing interest rates upward.

tightening of the money market and the accompanying higher interest rates discourage private spending, partly offsetting the initial increase in spending. Hence, the *IS-LM* intersection in Figure 20.2 is to the left of the simple multiplier.

An increase in government spending, for instance, increases aggregate demand, but not by as much as we thought when we neglected interest-rate changes in Chapter 19. This upward pressure that increased government spending exerts on interest rates causes the **demand-side crowding out** discussed in the financial press: when the Treasury sells bonds to finance government spending, private borrowers are crowded out of financial markets as interest rates soar and private spending crashes.

Government spending increases interest rates, causing demand-side crowding out.

We cannot be certain that private spending goes down in Figure 20.2. Expenditures are discouraged by the increase in interest rates, true enough, but the higher level of income encourages households and businesses to increase their spending. On balance, we cannot be sure whether the negative effects of higher interest rates are weaker or stronger than the positive effects of higher income. Whether private spending goes up or down depends on whether output goes up by more than government spending or by less. If it goes up by more, then private spending must, on balance, increase with government spending. In most empirical models, this is, in fact, the case. These models predict that government spending actually encourages private spending.

The Quantity Theory

It can be seen in Figure 20.2 that the effect of an increase in private or government spending on aggregate demand is smaller the steeper the *LM* curve is. The extreme case is a vertical *LM* curve — a special case assumed by the simple **quantity theory**. Chapter 17 explained how the simple quantity theory assumes that velocity and, hence, money demand do not depend on interest rates. If the simple quantity theory is correct, the *LM* curve is vertical: any value of the interest rate is consistent with money demand equals money supply, because neither demand nor supply depends on the interest rate.

The quantity theory implies a vertical LM curve and complete demand-side crowding out.

More formally, the quantity-theory equation is

$$MV = Py$$

or

$$\frac{M}{P} = \frac{1}{V}y$$

where M/P is the real money supply and $(1/V)y$ can be interpreted as money demand. Since velocity V is given, there is only one level of y consistent with the equality of money demand and money supply, and this value does not depend on the interest rate.

Figure 20.3 shows that an increase in government (or private) spending has no effect on aggregate demand if the *LM* curve is vertical. When the *IS* curve moves in an expansionary, rightward direction, income rises, so the demand for

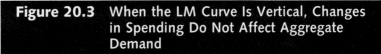

Figure 20.3   When the LM Curve Is Vertical, Changes in Spending Do Not Affect Aggregate Demand

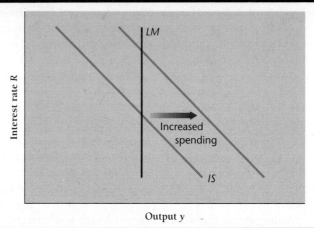

money expands and the interest rate increases. But the quantity theory implies that the higher interest rate does not reduce money demand. According to the quantity theory, if the money supply does not change, there is only one level of y consistent with money equilibrium — the initial level! The interest rate must rise sufficiently to reduce private expenditures by as much as government expenditures have increased. Thus, the quantity theory implies complete demand-side crowding out, because aggregate demand is not affected by government (or private) spending.

FINANCIAL MARKETS

Financial-market events affect the economy by shifting the *LM* curve. In our model, there are two financial assets: bonds paying a market interest rate R and money M1 that pays a fixed interest rate, perhaps zero. We assume for now that the Fed sets targets for M1 and is able to achieve its objectives. Thus the Fed determines the supply of M1 and the financial decisions of households, businesses, and banks determine the demand for M1.

The Demand for Money

Chapter 19 explained that an increase in money demand, like a decrease in money supply, is contractionary, shifting the *LM* curve leftward, as shown in Figure 20.4. A decrease in money demand would be expansionary, shifting the *LM* curve in the opposite, rightward direction.

Figure 20.4 An Increased Demand for Money Shifts the LM Curve Leftward, Increasing Interest Rates and Decreasing Aggregate Demand

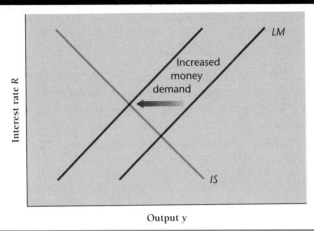

The demand for money can change for a wide variety of reasons. Changes in money demand in response to variations in y and R are taken into account by the slope of the LM curve and involve movements along a stationary LM curve. All other factors that affect money demand cause a shift in the LM curve.

Suppose, for example, that, the public becomes increasingly fearful that several prominent corporations will go bankrupt, leading to a wave of bond defaults. A consequent shift in public preferences from bonds to money moves the LM curve leftward, as in Figure 20.4, putting upward pressure on the bond rate R and reducing aggregate demand. An easing of these fears of default would have the opposite effects, reducing the demand for money, shifting the LM curve rightward, in turn reducing the interest rate and increasing aggregate demand.

We can remember these effects not only by shifting the LM curve in the appropriate direction, but by thinking through the economic logic. Consider, for example, the increased demand for money depicted in Figure 20.4. If people want more money, but the money supply is fixed, then this excess demand makes money "tight." As people sell bonds to raise cash, bond prices will fall and interest rates will increase. The increase in interest rates, in turn, depresses household and business spending, particularly for long-lived investment goods, reducing aggregate demand.

This increase in interest rates and the drop in expenditures reduce the demand for money — in fact, just offsetting the initial increase, because aggregate money demand must equal the fixed supply. Each individual need not maintain a constant money demand, however. Those who initially wanted more money may wind up with more money, while others are persuaded by higher interest

An increased demand for money shifts the LM curve leftward, increasing interest rates and reducing aggregate demand.

rates and lower expenditures to hold less money. What is certain is that, in the aggregate, people must be reconciled to holding the fixed money supply.

Financial Innovations

Many changes in money demand are the result of financial innovations. An increased use of credit cards reduces the demand for money, shifting the *LM* curve rightward, reducing the interest rate and increasing aggregate demand. Thus the spread of credit cards has expansionary implications for the economy. The introduction of interest-paying NOW accounts, in contrast, increases the demand for M1, shifting the *LM* curve leftward, with contractionary effects on aggregate demand.

The development of money-market funds, brokerage cash-management accounts, and electronic funds-transfer systems all reduce money demand by making it easier for households and businesses to economize on their money holdings. The *IS-LM* model tells us that these financial innovations had real economic repercussions. A reduced demand for money shifts the *LM* curve rightward, reducing interest rates and increasing aggregate demand for goods and services.

MONETARY POLICY

The Fed has a variety of tools for conducting its **monetary policies**, including open-market operations, reserve requirements, and the discount rate. In practice, day-to-day manipulation of M1 is accomplished by open-market purchases and sales of Treasury securities. An open-market purchase increases the money supply, shifting the *LM* curve in the expansionary, rightward direction depicted in Figure 20.5. The interest rate declines, encouraging spending and thereby increasing aggregate demand. Open-market sales by the Fed shift the *LM* curve leftward, increasing the interest rate and reducing aggregate demand

Open-market purchases increase the money supply and reduce interest rates, increasing aggregate demand.

Again, we can think through the economic logic. When the Fed makes open-market purchases, the money supply is increased, making money "easy." The Fed's bond purchases simultaneously push bond prices up and interest rates down. The decline in interest rates encourages household and business spending, expanding aggregate demand. Together, the decline in interest rates and expansion of expenditures must increase money demand enough to match the enlarged supply.

Mixed Monetary and Fiscal Policy

The government can combine monetary and fiscal policies to achieve its objectives.

So far, we have separated monetary and fiscal policies because monetary policy affects the *LM* curve and fiscal policy affects the *IS* curve. But there is no reason the federal government must do only one or the other. It can pursue a combination of monetary and fiscal policies that are both expansionary, policies that are both contractionary, or policies that push in opposite directions.

Figure 20.5 **An Increased Money Supply Shifts the LM Curve Rightward, Reducing Interest Rates and Increasing Aggregate Demand**

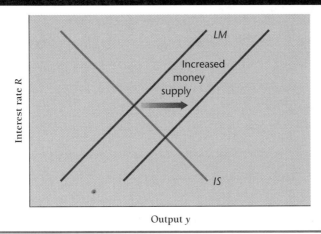

During the 1960s, the expansionary fiscal policies (increased spending and reduced tax rates) followed by the Kennedy and Johnson administrations were accompanied by expansionary monetary policies. As shown in Figure 20.6, the *IS* and *LM* curves both moved rightward, increasing aggregate demand greatly (and, as intended, cutting the unemployment rate in half). By itself, the expansionary fiscal policy would have increased interest rates and caused some demand-side crowding out, but the Fed followed an accommodating monetary policy, supplying the additional money demanded and restraining interest rates. The early years of the Reagan administration were very different, as explained in Highlight 20.2.

Should the Fed Peg the Money Supply or Interest Rates? (Optional)

The *IS* and *LM* curves can also be used to clarify our analysis of a question introduced in Chapter 17. We know that the Fed cannot simultaneously peg both interest rates and the money supply. Are there some identifiable circumstances in which pegging one or the other will better achieve the Fed's objectives?

Suppose that the Fed is interested in a target level of aggregate demand y*. If there were no lags or uncertainty, the link between open-market transactions and aggregate demand would be quick and sure, and it would not matter whether the Fed used an interest rate or the money supply as an intermediate target. As shown in Figure 20.7, knowing the position of the *IS* curve and the shape of the *LM* curve, the Fed could use open-market operations to place the *LM* curve

Highlight 20.2   Contradictory Monetary and Fiscal Policies

Soon after taking office, in January 1981, Ronald Reagan persuaded Congress to approve a historic tax cut and to increase government spending, particularly for national defense. This expansionary fiscal policy shifted the IS curve rightward, as during the Kennedy-Johnson administrations. But the Volcker Fed in the 1980s was much more concerned about inflation than was the Fed in the early 1960s, and with good reason.

During the 1960s, the annual rate of inflation reached a maximum of 5.5 percent in 1969 and was below 3.2 percent from 1960 through 1967. In sharp contrast, the inflation rate was 13.5 percent in 1980 and 10.3 percent in 1981. Instead of accommodating the Reagan administration's expansionary fiscal policies, the Volcker Fed offset them and then some, because the Fed was determined to slow down the economy and break the inflationary fever.

The Volcker Fed followed contractionary monetary policies during the early years of the Reagan administration, shifting the LM curve enough leftward, as shown in the accompanying figure, to reduce aggregate demand and cause the most severe recession since the 1930s. As shown, interest rates soared. Together, this particular combination of fiscal and monetary policies dealt the budget deficit the worst possible triple whammy: increased federal spending, reduced tax rates, and a recession to reduce tax revenue even more. No wonder the Reagan administration ran up unprecedented budget deficits.

Expansionary Fiscal Policies and Contractionary Monetary Policies

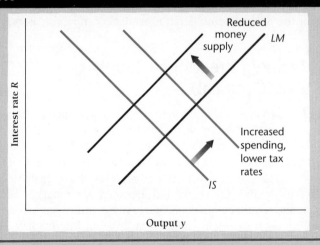

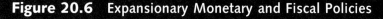

Figure 20.6 Expansionary Monetary and Fiscal Policies

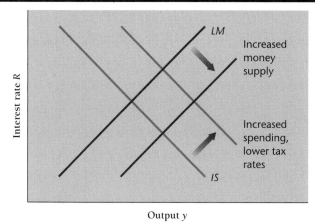

Output *y*

where aggregate demand does indeed equal y^*. These open-market operations could equally well be described as designed to hit a target interest rate R^* or a target money supply $M1^*$.

Now suppose that there is uncertainty about the position of the IS curve. The Fed cannot be sure where the IS curve will be and does not know the level of aggregate demand until some time after the fact. It chooses to use either the interest rate or M1 as an intermediate target because these can be monitored more easily than aggregate demand. Now it makes a difference which it targets.

The IS curve in Figure 20.7 is what the Fed anticipates, but the actual IS curve may be somewhat to the right of this (labeled IS+ in Figure 20.8) or somewhat to the left (labeled IS−). If the Fed pegs the money supply at $M1^*$, the LM curve is stationary, and the actual level of aggregate demand will be at one of the circled IS-LM intersections, depending on whether the IS curve turns out to be more expansionary or more contractionary than predicted. Notice that, in either case, the Fed allows the interest rate to fluctuate.

If the Fed instead targets the interest rate, it will use open-market operations to shift the LM curve to the boxed points on the IS curve where the interest rate remains at R^*. (To reduce the clutter, the actual shifts of the LM curve are not shown.) Notice that there is less variation in aggregate demand if the Fed pegs the money supply than if it pegs the interest rate. If spending is stronger than anticipated and IS+ results, then if the Fed uses open-market purchases to keep the interest rate from rising, these open-market purchases increase aggregate demand further. If spending is weak and IS− results, then the Fed makes open-market sales to keep the interest rate from falling and thereby pushes aggregate demand even lower.

Figure 20.8 analyzes IS uncertainty. The Fed also makes errors in estimating money demand, causing the LM uncertainty shown in Figure 20.9. The curve

When there is IS uncertainty, targeting interest rates rather than the money supply de-stabilizes aggregate demand.

Figure 20.7 With No Uncertainty, Targeting R* or
M1* Gives Aggregate Demand y*

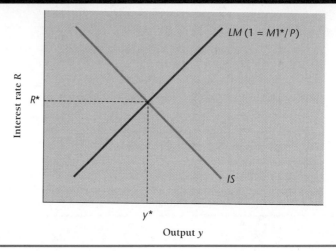

Figure 20.8 When There Is IS Uncertainty, Targeting
R* Causes a Larger Error in Aggregate
Demand

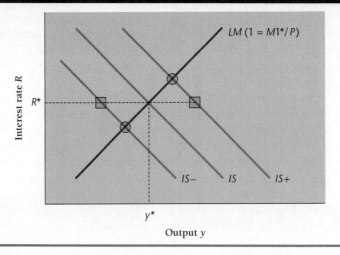

LM+ illustrates the case in which money demand is smaller than expected and the Fed holds the money supply constant, allowing the *LM* curve to move rightward. The circled intersection with the *IS* curve shows that aggregate demand is higher than intended. If money demand is instead unexpectedly strong and the Fed targets the money supply, the *LM* curve slides leftward, as shown by *LM−*, and the level of aggregate demand at the circled intersection with the *IS* curve is smaller than desired. If the Fed instead targets the interest rate, it adjusts the money supply to fluctuations in money demand, holding the *LM* curve steady. The boxed intersection with the *IS* curve shows that hitting the interest-rate target R^* allows the Fed to offset unforeseen changes in money demand automatically and to hit its target for aggregate demand exactly.

> When there is *LM* uncertainty, interest-rate targets stabilize aggregate demand.

We can summarize by saying that, in comparison with a policy of targeting the money supply, a policy of targeting interest rates tends to stabilize aggregate demand in the face of *LM* uncertainty, but tends to destabilize aggregate demand when there is *IS* uncertainty. Unfortunately, matters are more complicated than this, because there is actually both *IS* and *LM* uncertainty. *IS* and *LM* surprises may be positively correlated, negatively correlated, or uncorrelated, and this, too, affects the success of policies, making a simple conclusion impossible.

There is no perfect policy for all times and places. Myopically focusing monetary policy on M1, an interest rate, or some other single economic indicator will, in some circumstances, be a poor policy. The Fed instead diversifies its policies by watching a variety of economic data.

Figure 20.9   When There Is LM Uncertainty, Targeting R* Causes a Smaller Error in Aggregate Demand

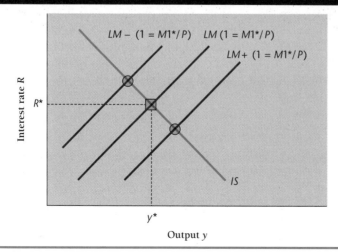

| Highlight 20.3 | The Fed's Preference for Secrecy |

The Federal Reserve's policy deliberations take place in secrecy and so do most of its actions. For many years, the Fed's Open Market Committee wouldn't announce when it was meeting, let alone what was discussed or decided, and refused even to confirm or deny reports of its open-market operations. Verbatim minutes of Open Market Committee meetings were not published until five years after the meeting.

Today, the timing of Open Market Committee meetings is public knowledge, but they are still closed meetings and the only public record is a brief summary published several weeks later in the *Federal Reserve Bulletin*. Verbatim minutes are no longer kept, lest they be made public under the Freedom of Information Act, and internal memos remain confidential for five years. The Fed continues to conduct its open-market operations in secrecy. Since 1983, it has agreed to confirm outside reports of its operations, but it still refuses to say whether its purchases and sales of Treasury securities are defensive transactions or represent a shift in monetary policy.

A small army of financial analysts — Fed watchers — tries to discern the Fed's actions and intentions by monitoring zigs and zags in financial data and mulling over nuances in speeches by Federal Reserve Governors. Often, the Fed watchers are wrong. For example, on Wednesday, November 22, 1989, the federal-funds rate dropped sharply, leading Fed watchers to conclude that the Fed was easing credit. In fact, the rate decline had been an unintended consequence of the Fed's efforts to make technical adjustments in the money supply; the following Monday, the Fed made conspicuous open-market purchases, pushing the federal-funds rate upward, and sending an unambiguous signal that it was not easing credit conditions.[*]

Fed Chairman Alan Greenspan argues that a public announcement of policy changes "would reduce our flexibility to implement decisions quietly at times to achieve a desired effect, while minimizing possible financial market disruptions."[†] After a mini-crash in the stock market on Friday, October 13, 1989, in which the Dow Jones Industrial Average fell by 190.58 points (6.9%), the second largest drop in history, Fed Vice Chairman Manuel Johnson told reporters from the *New York Times* and *Washington Post* that the Fed would provide funds to prevent a financial crisis. Both newspapers reported these assurances on the front page of their Sunday editions, citing a "senior Fed official." Fed Chairman Greenspan was furious

---

[*]Douglas R. Sease, "Bonds Fall on Move by the Fed," *Wall Street Journal,* November 28, 1989.

[†]David Wessel and Tom Herman, "Should Fed Hide Its Moves, Leaving Markets Confused?" *Wall Street Journal,* November 29, 1989.

about these stories. The next day, in a telephone conference call to the members of the Open Market Committee, the President of the New York Federal Reserve Bank reportedly "delivered a long tirade" about this public discussion of Fed policy.‡

Most economists consider it implausible that a risk-averse public is better off having to guess what the Fed is doing. One observer, William Greider, author of *Secrets of the Temple,* a probing look behind the Fed's veil, suggests that its passion for secrecy is intended to create an almost religious aura:

> *The central bank, notwithstanding its claims to rational method, enfolded itself in the same protective trappings that adorned the temple — secrecy, mystique, an awesome authority that was neither visible nor legible to mere mortals. . . . Its decrees were cast in a mysterious language people could not understand, but its voice, they knew, was powerful and important.*§

Another explanation is that, if the Fed does not announce its actions and intentions, then it won't be blamed for its mistakes. It was, for example, after Senator William Proxmire criticized Fed Chairman Arthur Burns publicly, that the Fed stopped keeping and reporting verbatim mintues of Open Market Committee meetings.‖ Some Fed critics quote the extreme language of Henry Ford, Sr., "It is well enough that the people of the nation do not understand our banking and monetary system for, if they did, I believe there would be a revolution before tomorrow morning."#

A more moderate view is that the Fed might be reluctant to tighten credit, particularly before elections, if it had to publicly announce a policy that irritated the incumbent president. Thus, one full-time Fed watcher argues that "If the Fed officially announced every single policy shift, it would attract excessive political attention — and that might intimidate the Fed and cause it to not fight inflation as much as it should."** Whether or not it would be able to resist such political pressure, the Fed has so far resisted efforts to make its deliberations and actions public.

---

‡Alan Murray, "Oct. 13's Stock Slide Shows Fed Official's Differences," *Wall Street Journal,* November 19, 1989.

§William Greider, Secrets of the Temple (New York: Simon & Schuster, 1987), p. 240.

‖Greider, p. 345.

#Quoted in Greider, p. 55.

**David M. Jones, quoted by Wessel and Herman.

THE AGGREGATE DEMAND CURVE

We can summarize the demand side of the economy by using the *IS-LM* model to derive an aggregate demand relationship between *y* and *P*. When this is combined with a supply-side relationship between *y* and *P*, we will be able to determine output and prices. In the remainder of this chapter, we will derive the aggregate demand relationship between *y* and *P*. Aggregate supply is described in the next chapter.

The *IS* and *LM* curves describe spending and financial markets — the demand side of the economy. So far, we have held the price level constant. Therefore, we can say that the *IS* and *LM* curves determine, for a given price level, the interest rate *R* and output *y* consistent with income equal to expenditures and with money demand equal to money supply.

An increase in the price level reduces the real money supply, shifting the *LM* curve leftward.

Changes in the price level affect the real money supply *M/P* and the position of the *LM* curve. If the price level increases, for instance, the real money supply *M/P* declines and the *LM* curve shifts leftward, as in Figure 20.10, giving new values of *y* and *R*. Thus there are many possible *LM* curves, one for each possible value of the price level, and each giving a different level of aggregate demand.

The aggregate demand curve shows how a change in the price level affects aggregate demand.

The **aggregate demand curve** shows how a change in the price level affects the level of *y* consistent with an *IS-LM* intersection; that is, with the demand-side requirements that income equal expenditure and money demand equal supply. The aggregate demand curve can be derived by observing that the initial *IS-LM* intersection in Figure 20.10 for a price level P_1 gives an aggregate demand

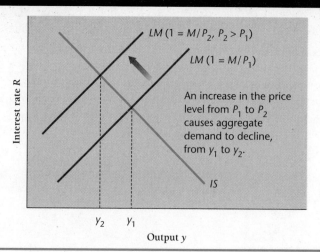

Figure 20.10   An Increase in the Price Level Reduces the Real Money Supply, Shifting the LM Curve Leftward

$LM (1 = M/P_2, P_2 > P_1)$

$LM (1 = M/P_1)$

An increase in the price level from P_1 to P_2 causes aggregate demand to decline, from y_1 to y_2.

IS

Interest rate *R*

y_2 y_1

Output *y*

y_1 and interest rate R_1. An increase in the price level to P_2 reduces the real money supply and shifts the *LM* curve leftward, reducing aggregate demand to y_2 and raising the interest rate to R_2. Figure 20.11 summarizes this inverse relationship between prices and aggregate demand, showing that as the price level increases from P_1 to P_2, aggregate demand falls from y_1 to y_2.

Although the change in the interest rate from R_1 to R_2 is not shown in Figure 20.11, do not be misled into thinking that the interest rate has been held constant. The interest rate has been omitted from this two-dimensional graph, but its change has been taken into account in the *IS* and *LM* curves that underlie the aggregate demand curve.

The aggregate demand curve shown in Figure 20.11 is easy to remember because it looks like any standard demand curve — for hot dogs, cottage cheese, or jogging shoes. The logic, however, is quite different. The demand curve for hot dogs involves a change in one price, the price of hot dogs, with all other prices held constant. The resultant change in relative prices twists our spending patterns: when the price of hot dogs goes up, we buy fewer hot dogs and more hamburger, fish, and chicken. The aggregate demand curve in Figure 20.11, in contrast, involves a change in all prices. Aggregate expenditures decline, not because we are shifting from hot dogs to hamburgers, but because the real money supply is tightened, pushing interest rates upward and expenditures downward.

Shifts in the Aggregate Demand Curve

Any economic event (other than a change in the price level) that shifts the *IS* curve or the *LM* curve also shifts the aggregate demand curve. Figure 20.12

Economic events (other than the price level) that shift the *IS* or *LM* curve also shift the aggregate demand curve.

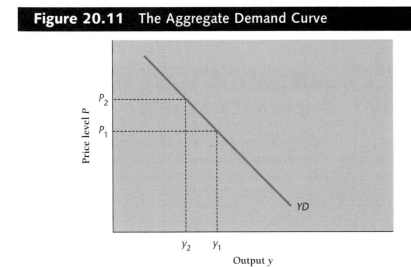

Figure 20.11   The Aggregate Demand Curve

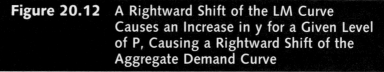

Figure 20.12   A Rightward Shift of the LM Curve
Causes an Increase in y for a Given Level
of P, Causing a Rightward Shift of the
Aggregate Demand Curve

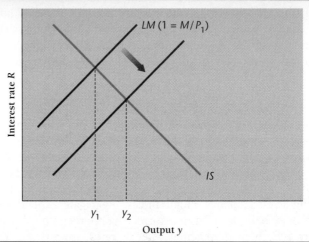

shows a rightward movement in the *LM* curve, due either to an increase in the nominal money supply or to a drop in money demand. At any given price level, income increases from y_1 to y_2. Figure 20.13 shows the corresponding shift in the aggregate demand curve. Similarly, any event that increases expenditures, shifting the *IS* curve rightward, also shifts the aggregate demand curve rightward. In general, an expansionary rightward movement of the *IS* curve or the *LM* curve causes an expansionary rightward movement of the aggregate demand curve. Contractionary, leftward movements of the *IS* and *LM* curves move the aggregate demand curve leftward.

DO PRICE ADJUSTMENTS MAKE THE ECONOMY INHERENTLY STABLE?

Classical economists assumed that the price level has a stabilizing effect on aggregate demand, without really explaining why. They believed that when the economy booms, prices will rise and soon stifle demand, automatically stopping the boom. They assumed that when aggregate demand slumps, threatening a recession, prices fall and soon bolster demand, keeping the economy strong. Thus aggregate demand is stabilized automatically through price adjustments.

This argument has considerable appeal, but the reasons for a negatively sloped aggregate demand curve are much more subtle than they appear at first glance. It is easy to see how we, as individual consumers, might buy more steak

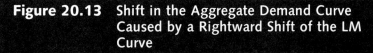

Figure 20.13 Shift in the Aggregate Demand Curve Caused by a Rightward Shift of the LM Curve

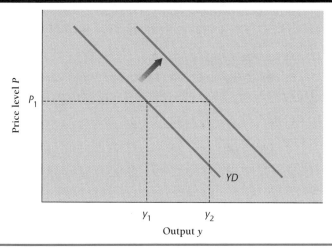

if its price were lower. But that response assumes that other prices are unchanged. We buy more steak because its price falls relative to other prices. But the stabilization of aggregate demand involves a rise or fall in all prices. If all prices fall, will we buy more of everything?

If our dollar incomes were constant while all prices fell, then our real incomes would increase and we probably would spend more. We could afford a higher standard of living, and we would probably choose to enjoy one. But if all prices fall, so will aggregate nominal income. Lower prices make things less expensive, but lower prices also reduce the income of those who sell these now less-expensive things. Sellers lose what buyers gain and, in the aggregate, we are all both sellers and buyers. If prices drop 10 percent, then aggregate nominal income also drops 10 percent and aggregate real income is unchanged. Why, if our real income is unchanged, will we buy more commodities? Won't we buy the same quantity of commodities, so that real spending, like real income, is constant?

The Keynes Effect

Keynes pondered this question and concluded that any stimulus to aggregate demand is indirect and, surprisingly, works through financial markets. Lower prices increase the real value of the money supply, shifting the *LM* curve to the right just as if the monetary authorities had printed more money. When prices decline 10 percent, the existing money supply becomes larger relative to people's needs for money to carry out transactions. Not needing so much money, people

The Keynes effect refers to the effect of prices on the real money supply.

buy securities, pushing bond prices up and interest rates down. These lower interest rates provide a stimulus to expenditures on goods and services.

After identifying how lower prices might logically raise aggregate demand, Keynes went on to argue that this was a slim reed on which to hang a faith that recessions would quickly cure themselves. Keynes saw at least four reasons why recessions might persist for an uncomfortably long period. First, prices and wages might not fall quickly. In 1933, the unemployment rate was 25 percent and GNP was less than half the size of full-employment GNP. It is hard to imagine a more depressed economy. Yet, prices and wages did not fall freely to replenish aggregate demand. Wages fell by about 1 percent in 1933, while prices dropped by 2 percent, not nearly enough to have a significant effect on the economy. In 1934, the unemployment rate was still 22 percent, yet wages went up by 18 percent and prices by 7 percent!

Keynes's second argument was that, during the Great Depression, even had prices fallen, there would have been little stimulus to aggregate demand. In theory, a lower price level increases the real money supply, reducing interest rates and stimulating spending (particularly investment spending). But interest rates were already very low. In 1933, the interest rate on prime business loans was 1.5 percent and the Treasury-bill rate was 0.5 percent. Interest rates had very little room left to fall. (They certainly would not turn negative as long as cash offered a safe 0 percent return.) In 1934, the prime rate was still 1.5 percent, while the Treasury-bill rate dropped to 0.3 percent, hardly enough to unleash a torrent of investment spending.

Third, Keynes did not think that interest rates mattered very much to such a depressed economy. Who would invest in new plant and equipment when so much was already sitting idle? Total investment was, in fact, only $1.4 billion in 1933, not even enough to offset the deterioration of existing capital; the nation's capital stock actually fell by $4.4 billion in 1933. Entrepreneurs did not need a slightly more favorable interest rate; they needed customers.

Keynes's fourth explanation of why falling prices don't quickly end recessions was that deflationary expectations might actually reduce expenditures. People who expect prices to fall may well hoard cash, postpone expenditures, and wait for lower prices. This drop in demand weakens the economy even further and puts additional downward pressure on prices. There could be a self-fulfilling deflationary spiral, with the economy getting progressively worse instead of better.

The Pigou Effect

While Keynes tried to overthrow classical economics, A. C. Pigou tried to defend it. After reading *The General Theory* and Keynes's explanation of how falling prices might bolster aggregate demand through financial markets, Pigou suggested another possible avenue.

Pigou noted that the real value of money and bonds hinges on the price of commodities. A lower price level increases the real purchasing power of accumulated financial assets, and when people find their real wealth enlarged, they are likely to spend more and save less. Thus, as the price level decreases, the *IS* curve should shift rightward.

The Pigou effect is often illustrated by extreme cases. Wassily Leontieff, a Harvard professor, put it this way: "If wages are low enough, this dime in my hand will employ everyone in the nation; and my only requirement on them is that they do not show up at my office for work. . . ."[1] If prices fell low enough, you could buy Cleveland for a dime, and you might be tempted to spend a nickel.

But, in practice, if prices do not fall so drastically, is the Pigou effect of any practical importance? Between 1929 and 1933, the Consumer Price Index fell by about 25 percent. The total amount of cash and government bonds outstanding was about $20 billion, and economists estimate that an extra $1 billion in wealth increases spending by about $0.05 billion. If so, then even a 50 percent fall in prices would have increased the real value of these financial assets by $20 billion and increased spending by only $1 billion. That would have been a very light brake on the collapse of GNP from $105 billion in 1929 to $56 billion in 1933.

There are also redistributional consequences that may reverse the Pigou effect. Most financial assets are someone else's financial liabilities. If you buy a corporate bond and the price level declines, the real value of that bond increases. You are wealthier, but the corporation's shareholders are that much poorer. If you take out a mortgage to buy a house and prices decline, the real value of the mortgage increases, making the lender richer and pushing you closer to bankruptcy. The now richer creditors may spend more, but the now poorer debtors will probably spend less. There is no guarantee that aggregate expenditures will, on balance, increase as Pigou predicted.

Indeed, Irving Fisher believed that the Great Depression was exacerbated by lower prices. He argued that debtors are forced to reduce their spending in order to meet their more burdensome debt payments, while creditors are under no similar compulsion to spend their new wealth. Fisher argued that, on balance, lower prices probably reduce spending so that the *IS* curve, contrary to Pigou, actually shifts leftward.

Pigou, himself, did not have much faith in the Pigou effect. He criticized Keynes for leaving a hole in his theory, but he admitted that it was of little practical importance. Pigou saw that prices did not fall freely and that their decline was not painless. He witnessed many bankruptcies and even a few riots during deflations. He agreed with Keynes that the real money supply, *M/P*, could be increased more quickly and less painfully by monetary policy, increasing *M*, than by a deflation.

> The Pigou effect refers to the effect of prices on real wealth.

SUMMARY

Increases in spending shift the *IS* curve rightward, increasing aggregate demand and interest rates. Demand-side crowding out refers to the fact that, while an increase in government spending directly enlarges aggregate demand, it also increases money demand, pushing interest rates up and thereby discouraging private spending, especially private investment spending. When this crowding out is taken into account, the effect of increased spending on aggregate demand is not as large as indicated by the income-expenditure multiplier. If the quantity theory holds, so that velocity and money demand do not depend on interest rates, the *LM* curve is vertical and there is complete crowding out.

Financial innovations that allow households and businesses to get along with smaller money holdings reduce the demand for money. An increased money supply or diminished money demand shifts the *LM* curve rightward, reducing interest rates and thereby increasing aggregate demand. The government need not use only monetary policy or only fiscal policy to achieve its policy objectives; it can use a combination of the two.

In comparison with a policy of targeting the money supply, a policy of targeting interest rates tends to stabilize aggregate demand in the face of *LM* uncertainty, but to destabilize aggregate demand when there is *IS* uncertainty. Matters are more complicated when there is both *IS* and *LM* uncertainty

The aggregate demand curve summarizes the *IS-LM* model of the demand side of the economy. With *P* and *y* the axes, the aggregate demand curve is negatively sloped because an increase in the price level reduces the real money supply, pushing interest rates up and discouraging spending. Expansionary shifts in the *IS* or *LM* curve shift the aggregate demand curve in an expansionary, rightward direction.

IMPORTANT TERMS

aggregate demand curve

demand-side crowding out

fiscal policies

monetary policies

quantity theory

transfer payments

EXERCISES

1. Use the *IS-LM* model to predict whether aggregate demand and interest rates will be increased or decreased by each of the following economic events.
   a. Consumer spending declines.
   b. Business investment increases.
   c. The Fed makes an open-market sale of Treasury securities.
   d. The demand for money increases.
   e. The price level increases.

2. Which increases aggregate demand more, an increase in consumer spending or an increase in money demand?

3. The *IS-LM* model tells us that an increase in spending does not raise aggregate demand as much as indicated by the simple multiplier, $1/(1 - b)$. Explain in your own words why this is so.

4. It has been proposed that 100 percent reserve requirements be imposed on banks. Others advocate the abolition of reserve requirements. Which of these proposals do banks favor? How would these very different proposals affect the nation's money supply, aggregate demand, and interest rates?

5. The Tax Reform Act of 1986 phased out the

tax deductibility of interest paid on credit-card balances. If this leads people to use credit cards less and to hold fewer bonds and larger checking account balances, what will be the effect on M1? Aggregate demand? Interest rates?

6. How would a drop in consumer spending affect aggregate demand? Is this effect relatively large or small if the *LM* curve is vertical? What economic assumption underlies a vertical *LM* curve?

7. An economics midterm asked this question:

In a 1980 speech, Paul Volcker cautioned that a drop in the interest rate does not always imply that the Federal Reserve has adopted a more expansionary monetary policy. Using the IS/LM *model, explain his comment.*

The answer key gave this answer:

Volcker was emphasizing that a drop in the interest rate will result from either a rightward shift in the LM *curve due to a more expansionary monetary policy or a leftward shift in the* IS *curve due, for instance, to a drop in the autonomous level of investment expenditures. In the latter case, it would be incorrect to infer from a drop in the interest rate that the Fed has adopted a more expansionary monetary policy.*

An accompanying graph showed that output y would rise in the former case and fall in the latter. What is wrong with this answer? In particular, why can we not infer from the direction of change in y whether or not the Fed is responsible for the change in *R*?

8. In its February 22, 1982 "Business Outlook," *Business Week* wrote that "To many, if not most, economists and money-market analysts, the problem with the administration's program is that it fails to resolve the conflict between an expansive fiscal policy and a restrictive monetary policy." Use the *IS-LM* model to analyze the consequences of such a conflict.

9. The government wants to use some combination of monetary and fiscal policies to increase

defense spending and business investment while reducing consumer spending and keeping aggregate demand constant. Ignoring exports and imports, identify which of the following should be increased and which should be decreased.
   a. Government spending.
   b. Personal income taxes.
   c. The money supply.

10. The government wants to raise aggregate demand enough to reduce the unemployment rate by 2 percentage points. What are the appropriate monetary and fiscal policies if they want all of the increase in output to be
   a. government purchases.
   b. private consumption.
   c. private investment.

11. Congress and the president want to reduce consumption and increase investment, leaving aggregate demand unchanged. What combination of monetary and fiscal policies is appropriate?

12. Much of the Reagan years in the 1980s were characterized by high federal spending and low tax rates. If the Fed had wanted to hold aggregate demand steady during this period, should it have raised or lowered reserve requirements? What would have been the net effect of Reagan and Fed policies on aggregate demand and interest rates?

13. The government wants to stimulate the economy. Would an expansionary monetary or fiscal policy increase the federal deficit more? Explain.

14. The president wants to reduce consumption and government spending, increase investment spending, and hold aggregate demand constant. What combination of policies would you recommend?

15. Congress has authorized a $500 billion expenditure over the next 5 years to repair many of the interstate highways. If the Federal Reserve monetizes the effect of this spending on the federal deficit, will this reinforce or counter

the effect of the increased federal spending on aggregate demand? On interest rates?

16. Circle the appropriate words of the pairs in parentheses.[2]

    The monetary-fiscal mix during the Reagan administration has been bizarre. To reduce the federal deficit, encourage private investment, and hold aggregate spending constant, Congress needs to (raise/lower) taxes while the Fed (buys/sells) Treasury bills.

17. Predict how the combination of policies recommended in the preceding exercise will affect
    a. the monetary base.
    b. bank deposits.
    c. M1.
    d. interest rates.
    e. reserve requirements.
    f. velocity.
    g. business investment.
    h. bond prices.
    i. the government deficit.

18. Will a surprise drop in velocity cause the Fed to miss its aggregate demand target more if it pegs an interest rate or the money supply? Explain your answer.

19. Explain how the aggregate demand curve is affected by an increase in each of the following.
    a. output y.
    b. interest rate R.
    c. price level p.
    d. government spending.
    e. tax cut for consumers.
    f. increased demand for money.

20. Explain what Keynes meant when he wrote: "It is, therefore, on the effect of a falling wage- and price-level on the [real supply of] money that those who believe in the self-adjusting quality of the economic system must rest the weight of the argument."[3]

AGGREGATE SUPPLY

Now, as I have often pointed out to my students, some of whom have been brought up in sporting circles, highbrow opinion is like a hunted hare; if you stand in the same place . . . it can be relied upon to come round to you in a circle.

Dennis Robertson

The *IS-LM* model describes the demand side of the economy, determining the level of aggregate demand consistent with any given price level. In this chapter, we will look at the supply side: labor demand, labor supply, and production decisions. Once we have a supply-side relationship between price level and output, we can put an aggregate supply curve together with our aggregate demand curve and determine output and prices.

The supply side is complicated by the fact that there are three very different, competing views of the labor market. Classical economists assumed a labor-market equilibrium in which all unemployment is voluntary. In Keynesian disequilibrium models, some unemployment is involuntary, and this involuntary unemployment increases in recessions and diminishes in booms. The new classical models allow for business cycles — fluctuations in employment and output — while maintaining the classical assumption that all unemployment is voluntary. Since these three views have very different implications for macroeconomic policy, we will examine each, beginning with the classical model.

THE CLASSICAL MODEL OF THE LABOR MARKET

Classical economists believed that labor demand and supply depend mainly on real wages.

Classical economists believed that labor demand and labor supply depend mainly on the real wage rate, W/P, where W is the nominal wage rate ($/hour) and P is the price level ($ per commodity). The units for the real wage rate are commodities per hour.

Firms use labor, plants, and equipment to produce output and make profits. In the short run, plants and equipment are fixed, so that the crucial decision is how much labor to employ in order to produce output. Microeconomics tells us that competitive profit-maximizing firms will hire labor up to the point where the marginal product of labor (measured in commodities per hour) is equal to the real wage rate (also measured in commodities per hour). Since the marginal product of labor declines as employment increases, the lower the real wage rate, the greater the labor demand. This inverse relationship between labor demand and the real wage rate is graphed in Figure 21.1.

Household labor supply also depends on the real wage rate, since this is the price (in commodities per hour) that workers receive for their labor. A decision to supply labor is a choice between work and leisure, with the reward for work being its wages or, more accurately, the commodities that can be purchased with those wages. People choose between enjoying leisure or enjoying the commodities that can be earned by working. The labor supply curve shown in Figure 21.1 indicates that an increase in the real wage rate increases the supply of labor.

Figure 21.1   The Classical Labor-Market Equilibrium

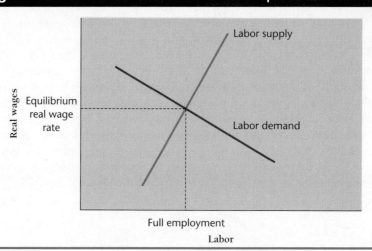

Voluntary Unemployment

Classical economists assumed that the labor market is in equilibrium, in that freely adjusting wages keep labor demand equal to labor supply. There is full employment at the equilibrium real wage in Figure 21.1. Because demand equals supply, everyone who wants to work at the prevailing wage has a job.

In classical equilibrium models, all unemployment is voluntary.

Those who do not have jobs are voluntarily unemployed in that they do not want to work for the prevailing wages. The unemployed choose to be unemployed, deciding that they have better things to do with their time than work. If the labor market is in equilibrium, all unemployment is voluntary, though admittedly the unemployed may wish they were smarter or more skilled so that they could qualify for jobs that command higher wages. Robert Lucas, a prominent new classical economist, wrote that[1]

> the unemployed worker at any time can always find some job at once, and a firm can always fill a vacancy instantaneously. That neither does so by choice is not difficult to understand given the quality of the jobs and the employees which are easiest to find.
>
> Thus there is an involuntary element in all unemployment, in the sense that no one chooses bad luck over good; there is also a voluntary element in all unemployment, in the sense that however miserable one's current work options, one can always choose to accept them.

To the classical economist, the statistically unemployed choose to be unemployed. They may be disappointed with their job offers because they have not yet faced up to the reality of their bad luck, or, as Thomas Malthus wrote long ago, "These are the unhappy persons who in the great lottery of life have drawn a blank."[2]

Employment Does Not Depend on the Demand Side

Notice that in Figure 21.1 full employment and the real wage rate are uniquely determined by the intersection of the labor demand and supply curves. The demand for labor depends only on the real wage rate and on the productivity of labor. The supply of labor depends on the real wage rate and on how highly people value leisure relative to the goods and services that can be earned by working.

Labor productivity and preferences are predetermined, at least in the short run. Productivity depends on intelligence, education, motivation, and training and is not going to be significantly affected by economic fluctuations in prices and interest rates. Similarly, how highly people value expensive cars relative to dozing at the beach is not going to change overnight with the latest tremor in the CPI or the bond market.

Thus, classical economists assumed that the demand side of the economy does not affect labor demand and supply curves and hence does not affect the

In classical models, employment is not affected by
aggregate demand.

level of employment and the real wage rate. If, for instance, there is an increase in aggregate demand that causes prices to rise 20 percent, nominal wages will also increase 20 percent in order to maintain the equilibrium real wage. If the price level falls 20 percent, nominal wages will immediately drop 20 percent. Real wages and employment will be unchanged.

The Classical Aggregate Supply Curve

The aggregate supply curve
describes the supply-side relationship between output
and the price level.

The **aggregate supply curve** describes the supply-side relationship between production and the price level. How much a nation produces depends on its utilization of plants, equipment, raw materials, and labor — of which labor is the most variable. Thus production depends primarily on the level of employment. In the classical model, there is full employment and the nation consequently produces its full-employment level of output which, like real wages and employment, depends on productivity and worker attitudes.

Since employment and output are at their full-employment levels in the classical model, irrespective of the price level, the aggregate supply curve is vertical, as shown in Figure 21.2. Aggregate demand has no effect on output and employment, in that no matter where the aggregate demand curve is, prices immediately adjust to the level appropriate for full employment. An increase in aggregate demand, such as that depicted in Figure 21.2, raises the price level, increases nominal wages proportionately, and has no effect on employment and output. Output is determined by supply, and demand adapts to it. This is **Say's law**: supply creates its own demand.

The classical aggregate supply curve is vertical.

The aggregate supply curve shifts gradually as time passes and a nation's population, productivity, and leisure preferences evolve. The classical model suggests that efforts to increase output be directed at the supply side of the economy, including programs to train and retrain workers and incentives to enlarge and improve the nation's structures and equipment.

Since aggregate demand affects only prices and interest rates, the Fed is advised to ignore output and employment and direct monetary policies toward stabilizing prices. For example, the continuing growth of the labor force and increases in worker productivity might be increasing full-employment output by 3 percent a year, sliding the vertical aggregate supply curve rightward at this rate. If the Fed can slide the aggregate demand curve rightward by 3 percent a year, then prices will be stable.

If the quantity theory applies, then we have (from Chapter 17)

$$MV = Py$$

Where M is the money supply, V is velocity, P is the price level, and y is real GNP. The (approximate) percentage changes are given by

$$\%M + \%V = \%P + \%y$$

or

$$\%P = \%M + \%V - \%y$$

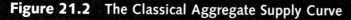

Figure 21.2   The Classical Aggregate Supply Curve

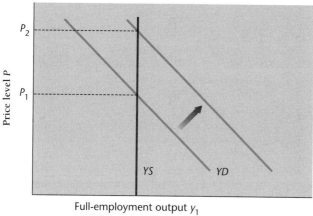

In 1963, Milton Friedman estimated that full-employment output in the United States is increasing by about 2.5 percent a year and that M2 velocity is falling by about 1.5 percent a year.[3] These values

$$\%P = \%M - 1.5\% - 2.5\%$$
$$= \%M - 4\%$$

led to his recommendation that the Fed should keep M2 growing at 3 percent to 5 percent a year. Implicit in this advice is the classical assumption that departures from full employment are small and brief.

MARKET DISEQUILIBRIA

Many wages and prices in modern industrial economies do not seem to be governed by the classical model of supply and demand. Instead, we observe minimum wage laws, multiyear wage contracts, implicit long-term wage commitments, price floors and ceilings, regulatory constraints, and average-cost pricing rules. Although demand and supply imbalances exert pressure on wages and prices, there is considerable inertia.

Wages and prices are often sticky.

Wage declines in the United States are so rare that they are startling news when they do occur. In 1980, several deeply troubled companies (Chrysler, Braniff, and Uniroyal) did persuade their employees to forgo part of previously negotiated pay increases. Even then, wages did not actually fall; they just did not go up as much as previously agreed. At the time, *The Wall Street Journal* wrote that[4]

Highlight 21.1   Reagan's Supply-Side Economics

The imposition of taxes provides an incentive to avoid the activity that is being taxed. Gasoline taxes discourage the purchase of gas-guzzling cars. Import taxes discourage the purchase of imports.

In the late 1970s, some supply-side economists argued that high tax rates in the United States were discouraging work, production, and investment. For instance, high-income taxpayers were in a 70-percent tax bracket, paying 70 cents in taxes on every additional dollar of income. Supply-side economists argued that a reduction in tax rates would encourage people to work more, particularly those who are very productive — as gauged by their high incomes.

A Reduction in Income-Tax Rates Increases Labor Supply

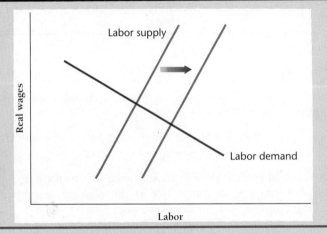

The accompanying figure shows that an enhanced desire to work increases the supply of labor, reducing equilibrium real wages and increasing equilibrium employment. (The newly enthusiastic workers bid down before-tax wages, persuading employers to hire them.) As full-employment output increases, the aggregate supply curve shifts rightward, as in the next figure, increasing output and reducing prices.

In 1980, supply-side economists persuaded presidential candidate Ronald Reagan that he could promise voters the enticing combination of lower taxes, increased output, and lower prices. The more enthusiastic claimed that output would increase so much that a tax cut would actually increase federal tax revenue, reducing the federal deficit.

Most economists (including many of Reagan's long-time advisers) were skeptical of these supply-side effects and particularly dubious of the claim that lower tax rates would reduce the federal deficit. Lower tax rates do make work more rewarding, encouraging the sacrifice of leisure in favor of work. But lower tax rates also allow workers to keep more of what they

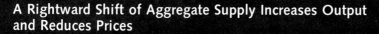

A Rightward Shift of Aggregate Supply Increases Output and Reduces Prices

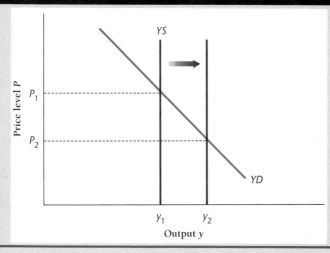

are already earning; they may consequently decide that they do not need to work as much in order to provide food and shelter. It is unclear whether a cut in tax rates will increase or reduce labor supply.

In addition, very few people have the option of being paid for working a few extra minutes or hours every week. Most people settle into a workstyle and lifestyle that suits them. They become efficient secretaries, plodding bureaucrats, workaholic professors, or whatever. Few will be persuaded by slightly lower tax rates to change their occupation or work habits dramatically.

A final difficulty is that the increase in employment depicted in the first figure requires wages to decline by more than prices. In theory, workers should accept a decline in real before-tax wages readily, since they do want to work more and the tax cut has caused their after-tax wages to increase. In practice, though, wages seldom decline. Unions don't like to negotiate wage decreases; employers do not like to cut the salaries of executives and other nonunion employees. If wages don't fall, as shown in the figure, employment won't increase, since it is lower wages that are supposed to persuade firms to hire more people.

Income-tax rates were substantially reduced during the Reagan years, but whatever supply-side effects occurred were swamped by the demand-side effects of its fiscal policies (low taxes, higher spending) and the Fed's monetary policies (very contractionary until 1982 and then expansionary). The federal deficit didn't disappear, but increased to record levels. So overwhelming were the demand-side effects that some called Reagan a born-again Keynesian.

A student of economic theory wouldn't find anything remarkable about such sacrifices. It would be normal to expect pay to rise when companies are prospering and to be scaled back when times are rough. In reality, though, it doesn't usually work that way.

Wages, salaries and benefits tend to rise every year in the U.S., through good times and bad. . . . Unless conditions get desperate, managements don't even suggest that employees take pay cuts or give up benefits that have been promised.

The asymmetry in wage changes — that wages rise more easily than they fall — means that average wages do not decline unless unemployment is extraordinarily high. In U.S. manufacturing industries, annual average hourly wages have not declined in any year since 1933. In that year, the national unemployment rate was 25 percent and manufacturing wages declined by about 1 percent, from 44.4 to 43.7 cents per hour.

In most years, wages increase even if there is considerable unemployment. We have all seen specific instances in which prices and wages rose even though there were excess supplies of commodities and labor. We have seen auto workers, teachers, and administrators unemployed while the wages of their employed brethren rose sharply. We have seen car makers, colleges, and electrical utilities increase prices after sales have declined. We have seen people wait in line for hours hoping to buy an admissions ticket or to get a job. We have heard qualified and responsible people told that there are no job openings, that no mortgage loans are being made, and that no apartments are available.

Writing during the Great Depression, Keynes was openly scornful of the classical full-employment model.[5]

The classical theorists resemble Euclidean geometers in a non-Euclidean world who, discovering that in experience straight lines apparently parallel often meet, rebuke the lines for not keeping straight — as the only remedy for the unfortunate collisions which are occurring. Yet, in truth, there is no remedy except to throw over the axiom of parallels and to work out a non-Euclidean geometry. Something similar is required today in economics. We need to throw over the . . . classical doctrine and to work out the behavior of a system in which involuntary unemployment in the strict sense is possible.

Involuntary Unemployment

A person is involuntarily unemployed if he or she is qualified for a job and willing to work for the prevailing real wage, but is not offered the job. Consider, for instance, people with Ph.D.s who would like to be French professors. If the market for French professors is at a full-employment equilibrium, then people without teaching jobs choose to be unemployed, turning down job offers because, at the prevailing wage, they prefer leisure to work. Their unemployment is, however, involuntary if they are willing to work for the wages paid others with similar skills, but are told, "Sorry, we have no openings now, but we'll keep your application on file." The same test can be applied to unemployed auto workers, carpenters, and financial managers.

Involuntary unemployment necessarily involves a market disequilibrium, a disparity between demand and supply. Keynes and his major interpreters argue that most labor markets are in continual disequilibrium. At any time, some labor markets have excess supply (unemployment); some have excess demand (vacancies); and some are close to equilibrium. Everywhere, wages are set for extended periods of time and do not immediately respond to every jiggle in labor demand and supply. In the United States, most nonunion wages are set annually, while union contracts are typically of two- to three-year duration. Wage scales often have a rigid structure (frequently based on seniority) that appears to have little relation to the demands and supplies for different types of labor. Nominal wage cuts are strongly resisted and rarely occur.

Figure 21.3 shows a situation in which there is an excess supply of labor because the actual wage is higher than the full-employment level. If firms employ only as much labor as they demand, then actual employment is demand determined, as shown in Figure 21.3. The excess labor supply represents people who are qualified for these jobs and would like to work for prevailing wages, but find that all jobs are filled.

Wages in excess-supply markets may rise more slowly than wages in excess-demand or equilibrium markets, but wages do not decline except in drastic circumstances. Instead of rapid wage cuts to restore equilibrium, unemployment persists for some time.

Market disequilibria can cause involuntary unemployment.

Figure 21.3   A Labor Market With Excess Supply

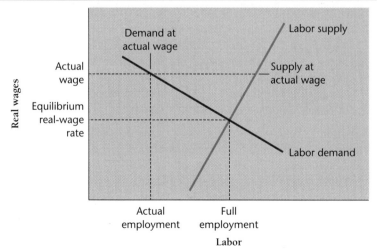

Employment Is a Commitment

Minimum-wage laws, labor unions, and powerful employers are part of the story. More fundamental is the nature of labor and employment. Buying and selling labor is not like trading soybeans. Decisions to offer and accept employment involve substantial commitments by both sides. An employer invests considerable resources in selecting, hiring, and training each employee. It is also expensive for an employee to find an attractive job and become proficient at it.

There is a substantial bond between employer and employee that neither side is eager to break. An employer does not want to lose experienced and proven employees, particularly those with skills specifically honed to the needs of the firm. Employees want to stay and utilize their acquired skills and avoid the daunting financial and social costs of relocation. Half of all workers in the United States are in jobs that will last 15 years or more.[6]

In such an environment, it is not surprising that businesses do not engage in impersonal daily hirings and firings — the way commodity firms buy and sell soybeans — in response to fluctuating market conditions. An employer who impulsively slashed wages and fired workers whenever business was slow or when new job applicants were available would find it difficult to attract employees. Workers demand and get stability in wages and employment.

> A job usually entails substantial commitments by employer and employee.

What Is Full Employment?

Labor is not homogeneous, traded in one vast labor market. There are many labor markets, varying by occupation and geographic location among other features. Labor demand and supply are in a continual state of flux in these diverse markets. There are always some markets with excess demands and others with excess supplies, making the concept of full employment amorphous. An influential British labor economist, William Beveridge, suggested that[7]

> *Full employment means always having more vacant jobs than unemployed [workers]. It means that the jobs are at fair wages, of such a kind, and so located that the unemployed . . . can reasonably be expected to take them; it means by consequence, that the normal lag between losing one job and finding another will be very short. The proposition . . . means that the labour market should always be a seller's market rather than a buyer's market.*

This definition bears little resemblance to the classical labor-market equilibrium. While, as Lucas points out, an unemployed French teacher who is told that all teaching jobs are filled could probably get a job cleaning houses or delivering newspapers, Keynes viewed that bleak choice as a socially wasteful form of involuntary unemployment. If markets really worked, the wages of employed French teachers would immediately drop, and more jobs teaching French would open up. If there really were full employment, the French teachers without jobs would be those who freely decided that the wages were not high enough to make teaching worth their while, rather than applicants without seniority or tenure who are simply told that there are no openings.

Most wages are not very flexible in the short run. Explicit and implicit contracts between employers and employees keep wages firm even when there are qualified people available who would work for lower wages. Classical economists were right in arguing that excess labor supplies and demands do exert pressures on wages. But Keynes was right in arguing that wage adjustments are neither perfect nor instantaneous. In a hypothetical long run in which the world stands still while wages adjust, wages will eventually find their equilibrium levels. But in a world that does not stand still, wages are often not at equilibrium levels. (And, as Keynes remarked, "In the long run, we are all dead.")

Not every person who is counted as unemployed is an involuntary victim of sticky wages and seniority rules. Some of the unemployed are too choosy, asking for jobs and wages for which, realistically, they are not qualified. Such people are voluntarily unemployed. On the other hand, some of the employed are trapped in bad jobs and unable to pursue careers for which they are qualified. They have to settle for less because sticky wages and tenure rules protect the jobs of less-qualified people. The reported unemployment rate both overstates and understates the extent to which labor markets are not in equilibrium.

Higher Prices Increase Employment

What does the aggregate supply curve look like in a Keynesian model? There may be occasions when almost all labor markets are either in equilibrium or have excess demand. If so, output is near the full-employment level and the aggregate supply curve is essentially vertical. In this situation, higher prices have little effect on employment and output.

However, because nominal wages rise more easily than they fall, there are often labor markets with excess supplies, and output is consequently not at the full-employment level. In this case, output may increase with prices, making the aggregate supply curve positively sloped, not vertical. We will now look at this possibility more carefully.

In excess-supply labor markets, the real wage rate W/P is too high because the nominal wage rate does not fall to clear the market. In this situation, an increase in the price level will reduce real wages W/P, increasing employment, and bring the market closer to equilibrium. To the classical economist, such behavior reveals irrationality. If people accept jobs as their real wages decline, they must have money illusion, paying too much attention to nominal wages and too little to prices. To Keynes, seeing labor-market disequilibria rather than equilibria, unemployment is involuntary, and an increase in the price level is the easiest way to reduce real wages.

In disequilibrium models, higher prices may increase employment.

For most workers, the only viable alternative to their current job is not leisure, but another job somewhere else. Keynes concluded that workers are keenly concerned with their wages relative to the wages of others with similar skills — a line of reasoning that explains why workers resist a reduction in

| Highlight 21.2 | **Measuring Unemployment** |

The unemployment rate is a widely publicized barometer of the extent to which labor resources are being underutilized. These data require a separation of the population into those working and not working and, of those not working, a division between those who want jobs and those who do not.

To estimate the size of these three groups among the entire working-age population, the Census Bureau conducts a monthly survey of about 55,000 households.* Some people of working-age (16 years or older) are neither working nor looking for work, including homemakers, students, the retired, and people who are not interested in working. The subtraction of these people from the working-age population leaves the available civilian labor force — people who are ready, able, and willing to work.

People who have paid jobs of any sort — full time or part time, glamorous or menial — are counted as employed. (People with jobs who are not actually at work because of vacation, illness, natural disasters, bad weather, or labor disputes are nevertheless counted as employed.) People in the labor force who do not have paid jobs are labeled unemployed. The Bureau of Labor Statistics uses these data to estimate the overall unemployment rate, which is the ratio of the number of unemployed people to the civilian labor force. The Bureau also compiles a large number of detailed unemployment rates for specific segments of the population.

The dividing line between the unemployed included in the labor force and the homemakers, students, and bums who are excluded is that the former tell the census interviewer that they are either waiting to be recalled from a temporary layoff or that they actively looked for a job during the preceding four weeks.

For several reasons, the monthly unemployment data may give a misleading count of the number of people without jobs who are available for work. The survey questions about whether a person is actively seeking work are particularly vague and subjective. Embarrassment (or fear of losing unemployment benefits) undoubtedly prompts some who are not really interested in work to pretend that they are. Some people have frankly unrealistic job hopes, halfheartedly looking for pleasant jobs with short hours and high pay. (Should I be counted as unemployed if I am sitting by my pool, waiting for the Los Angeles Dodgers to call?) Also, a significant number of the unemployed are students, homemakers, and retirees looking

---

*For more details on the collection of employment and unemployment data, see U.S. Department of Labor, Bureau of Labor Statistics, *How the Government Measures Unemployment* (Washington, D.C.: U.S. Government Printing Office, 1977).

for part-time jobs. Should they be counted in the same way as a family's primary breadwinner, who is desperately looking for a full-time job?

On the other hand, some wasteful unemployment does not appear in the unemployment statistics. People wanting full-time jobs but forced to settle for temporary part-time employment are counted as fully employed. So are people who have jobs for which they are overqualified. A history Ph.D. waiting on tables and an auto worker pumping gas are counted as fully employed. Those who become so discouraged that they quit looking for work are not counted as unemployed; instead, they are no longer included in the labor force. In December 1982, with the unemployment rate at 10.8 percent, the Bureau of Labor Statistics estimated the number of such discouraged workers to be almost two million. Had they been counted as unemployed, the unemployment rate would have been almost two percentage points higher.

Movements in and out of the labor force — from looking for work to not looking, or vice versa — can cause misleading short-term changes in unemployment data. During a recession, the reported unemployment rate sometimes drops for a month or two, not because more people find jobs, but because more people stop looking for jobs. Similarly, the unemployment rate occasionally increases in the midst of an economic boom because many people enter the labor force looking for the jobs that they have heard are plentiful.

nominal wages but accept a decline in real wages that is caused by higher prices. In the words of Nobel Laureate James Tobin[8]

> *Labor markets are decentralized, and there is no way money wages can fall in any one market without impairing the relative wage status of the workers there. A general rise in prices is a neutral and universal method of reducing real wages, the only method in a decentralized and uncontrolled economy. Inflation would not be needed, we may infer, if by government compulsion, economy-wide bargaining, or social compact, all money wage rates could be scaled down together.*

If nominal wages are less flexible than prices, then changes in prices can cause changes in real wages, employment, and output. The aggregate supply curve is not vertical, but positively sloped as in Figure 21.4. An increase in prices causes a decline in real wages and an increase in employment and output.

Product Market Disequilibria

The positively sloped aggregate supply curve in Figure 21.4 can be derived in another way, by observing that whether a firm decides to expand and hire

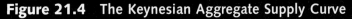

Figure 21.4   The Keynesian Aggregate Supply Curve

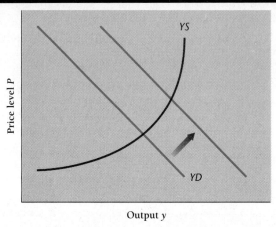

Output y

more people or to cut back and let people go usually depends on how well its product is selling. Consider, for example, the following newspaper item.[9]

> *Osborne Computer Corp., once one of the hottest stars in the personal computer field, laid off nearly all of its non-management workers Friday.*
>
> *The company, founded 2½ years ago by Adam Osborne, was selling 10,000 briefcase-sized Osborne I computers each month at its peak. But competitors have deeply eroded the company's market.*

Isn't the demand for a company's product the most important determinant of its labor demand? In the classical model, the answer is no. Every firm can sell all it wants at the prevailing price, and firms know this price before they make any employment and production decisions. Firms need only compare worker productivity with the real wage rate to determine how many people can be profitably employed. Firms do not worry about sales because everything they produce gets sold at the quoted price.

In reality, many product markets, as well as labor markets, are "fixprice" rather than "flexprice." Most businesses set their prices to cover average costs and provide what they consider to be a normal profit. This sort of pricing rule is almost inevitable in regulated industries and is widely used by other businesses as well.

Long-run profitability is a large part of the underlying logic: if the product cannot be sold for a reasonable profit, then it should not be produced. On the other hand, setting the price at what is perceived to be an excessive level alienates customers, invites government regulation, and encourages entry into the industry by new competitors. Thus many businesses avoid both destructive price wars and price gouging by setting their prices to cover costs and give a reasonable profit, while using advertising and product innovations to compete for customers.

This behavior makes good sense, but it is not an auction market in which prices equate demand and supply. Instead, product prices are predetermined by production costs and, in the short run at least, sales are determined by customer demand. For example, electric utilities set rates, then supply whatever electricity users demand. Similarly, General Motors announces car prices and adjusts its production to car demand. When a car maker reduces prices, it usually does so in the form of a rebate, which it makes the basis for a major advertising campaign — hardly the behavior that would be observed in an auction market. This same price stickiness is also true of most services. Barbershops, law firms, hospitals, and colleges are all fixprice markets, not because their prices are constant, but because their prices are not immediately responsive to market forces.

At times, demand does exceed supply in fixprice markets, and there are shortages of electrical power, automobiles, or hospitals. In such cases, higher prices are not used to auction off electricity, cars, or hospital beds. Instead, rationing, waiting lists, and other devices are used to allocate the supply. When this happens, sales are supply constrained. Such shortages are unusual because most firms build in some excess capacity so that they can quickly adjust production to meet demand. In this way, they avoid disappointing their customers (and losing them to their competitors). When demand is strong, firms increase employment and output, and perhaps raise prices. When demand is weak, there are layoffs and some restraint on prices. Thus there is a positive association between output and prices — a positively sloped aggregate supply curve — as shown in Figure 21.4.

Many firms respond to demand changes by adjusting production rather than prices.

When production adjusts to demand, the demand for labor depends not just on real wages, but also on the demand for products that businesses sell. When product demand increases, businesses expand output and increase their demand for labor; if the tightened labor market puts upward pressure on wages, businesses pass these costs along in higher prices. When demand sags, businesses cut back production and reduce their demand for labor, restraining wages and prices.

The Aggregate Supply Curve

Therefore, we have two somewhat different disequilibrium explanations for a positively sloped aggregate supply curve. An increase in aggregate demand may raise prices, causing real wages to decline, employment to expand, and output to increase. Or an increase in aggregate demand may expand output, causing employment, wages, and prices to rise. In the first case, it is the increase in prices that leads to the increase in output; in the second, it is the increase in output that pushes prices up. Figure 21.4 shows the positive correlation between prices and output common to both disequilibrium models.

There are two disequilibrium interpretations of a non-vertical aggregate supply curve.

The supply curve in Figure 21.4 has two extreme regions, one nearly vertical and the other nearly horizontal. Along the vertical portion, the economy is operating at full capacity; on the horizontal portion, prices are unaffected by demand.

| Highlight 21.3 | Guns and Butter in the 1960s |

The unemployment rate was 3 percent during the Korean War (1951–53) and near 4 percent during the peacetime prosperity of 1955–57. But prosperity faded during the last three years of the Eisenhower administration. The unemployment rate averaged 6.8 percent in 1958, the highest since the Great Depression, and stayed above 5 percent during the entire period 1958–60.

John F. Kennedy became president in 1961, with a campaign pledge to get the country moving again — in particular, to reduce the unemployment rate to 4 percent. The cornerstone of his economic program was a substantial reduction in personal and corporate income taxes. But Kennedy couldn't sell his proposed tax cut to a Congress that was fearful of large budget deficits. The economy stayed in the doldrums with a 6.7 percent unemployment rate in 1961. In 1962, government spending increased by 8 percent and the unemployment rate fell to 5.5 percent — encouraging, but still far from the administration's 4 percent target.

Lyndon Johnson, succeeding to the presidency after Kennedy's assassination in November 1963, managed to coax substantial tax legislation out of a still-reluctant Congress — roughly a 20 percent reduction in personal income taxes and a 10 percent cut in corporate taxes. Government spending increased for a variety of health, education, and welfare programs as Johnson waged what he called a War on Poverty to achieve a Great Society. Together, lower taxes and higher government spending reduced the full-employment budget surplus (used to gauge the thrust of fiscal policy, as explained in Chapter 19) from 1.2 percent in 1963 to 0.2 percent in 1964 and 0.1 percent in 1965. The Fed followed an accommodating monetary policy, and the unemployment rate fell steadily, until it reached 4.1 percent in the fourth quarter of 1965 — almost exactly on target. These two years of economic recovery convinced many skeptics that monetary and fiscal demand-management policies could end recessions and maintain full employment.

The Vietnam War was heating up in late 1965, and Lyndon Johnson wanted guns and butter — guns to fight a war and butter to achieve the Great Society. As military spending increased, the full-employment surplus fell to a 1.9 percent deficit by 1967. The Fed, meanwhile, allowed the money supply to expand faster than prices in 1967 and 1968. The unemployment rate fell to 3.5 percent; output strained the economy's full-employment capacity; and inflationary pressures surfaced. The economy was having trouble delivering more guns and more butter, and in 1969 the Fed switched to a contractionary monetary policy in order to fight inflation.

The horizontal portion of the aggregate supply curve is an extreme case that Keynes focused on in *The General Theory*. Here, the aggregate demand curve determines output, but has little or no effect on prices. Product demand creates its own supply, turning Say's law upside down! Classical economists studied the supply side of the economy, confident that demand will adapt. Keynes studied the demand side of the economy in the 1930s, believing that this is what determines output.

Today, Keynesians look at both aggregate demand and supply, believing that the U.S. economy is generally in the intermediate range depicted in Figure 21.4, though sometimes closer to one extreme or the other. When the economy is severely depressed, output may vary with little or no change in prices. When the economy is extremely strong, however, output cannot easily expand, and prices are bid up rapidly as people futilely try to acquire more commodities.

When the economy is not on the vertical portion of the aggregate supply curve, monetary policy can have real effects on output and employment. Expansionary monetary policies — open-market purchases, reductions in reserve requirements, lowering of the discount rate — shift the *LM* curve rightward, reducing the interest rate and increasing aggregate demand. The aggregate demand curve shifts rightward, as in Figure 21.4, causing output (and employment) to expand and prices to increase.

When the economy is on the nonvertical part of the aggregate supply curve, monetary policies have real economic effects.

Since monetary policies have real effects on the economy, Keynesians urge the Fed during economic recession to use expansionary policies to increase output and reduce unemployment. When the Fed uses contractionary monetary policies to slow inflation, Keynesians warn that these policies may cause a recession, diminishing output and increasing unemployment.

NEW-CLASSICAL EXPLANATIONS OF BOOMS AND RECESSIONS

The classical model of the labor market has considerable theoretical appeal. Demand and supply curves — surely the heart of economics — are brought together, market-clearing prices are determined, and free exchanges executed. It is a clear, consistent, and even elegant theory. Its only vulnerability is its apparent inability to explain the business cycles that are such a pervasive aspect of economic life — breaking up families, bankrupting businesses, and toppling governments. The Great Depression in the 1930s was, for many, the final proof of the inadequacy of the classical model. A generation of economists turned away and embraced Keynes's alternative analysis.

By the 1970s, memories of the Great Depression had faded, dissatisfaction with government policies had grown, and there was a resurgence of interest in classical macroeconomics. In response, the **new classical economists** offered a market-equilibrium explanation of economic fluctuations. We will now look at their reasoning and its provocative implications.

New-classical economists have a market-equilibrium explanation of economic fluctuations.

Rational Mistakes

Classical economists assumed that agents are perfectly informed and certain of the future. But, clearly, a pervasive characteristic of human existence is how little we really know about the future. A second, though less obvious, characteristic is that information is not free. Rational economic agents will, as in other activities, weigh the costs and benefits of acquiring information and choose to be imperfectly informed when they believe that the gains from acquiring additional information are less than the expense.

The new classical economists argue that fully rational people sometimes base their labor-supply decisions on inaccurate information, since perfect information is exorbitantly expensive. They consequently sometimes make voluntary employment or unemployment errors, until they realize their miscalculation. In this way, temporary mistakes can cause business cycles.

Typically, individuals sell few things — mostly their labor — but buy an enormous variety of goods and services, some of which are purchased weekly, monthly, or even less frequently. It is very difficult, and expensive, for households to maintain up-to-date information about the prices of these products. The spirit of this argument can be captured by assuming that labor knows its nominal wage rate W, but not the commodity price level P. Instead, it bases its labor-supply decisions on a possibly incorrect price estimate P^* and, hence, a possibly incorrect real wage calculation, W/P^*. Since producers sell relatively few products, they are assumed to know these prices and their wage rates: firms do not make errors in gauging the real wage rate.

This simple and plausible modification of the classical model gives it the flexibility to explain economic fluctuations, without abandoning the classical assumption that all unemployment is voluntary. The key observation is that if workers underestimate the price level ($P^* < P$), they overestimate their real wages ($W/P^* > W/P$). When workers overestimate the price level ($P^* > P$), they underestimate real wages. Consider the implications.

Surprise Unemployment

We will look at the overestimation of real wages first. An underestimate of the price level ($P^* < P$) causes an overestimate of real wages ($W/P^* > W/P$) and a consequent increase in the supply of labor, as shown in Figure 21.5. By assumption, employers are perfectly informed about wages and prices, and the labor demand curve does not shift in this fashion. Because the labor supply has expanded, the real wage rate is bid down and both employment and output increase. Employers capitalize on employee misperceptions by hiring more labor at lower real wages.

The new employees willingly agree to this bargain because their underestimate of prices leads them to believe that real wages have actually increased. This is surprise employment, in that when workers go to the store to spend their wages they will be surprised by the high prices and withdraw from the labor force.

Targeting Nominal GNP

The classical full-employment assumption suggests that nominal GNP is a suitable target for a nation's monetary authority. If we denote nominal GNP by Y and the price level by P, then real GNP y is given by $y = Y/P$. Suppose that an economy's resources will be fully utilized, producing full-employment output, regardless of unexpected fluctuations in aggregate demand. The Fed can then combine the full-employment level of real GNP y_f with a target price level P^* to give a nominal GNP target

$$Y^* = P^* y_f$$

The (approximate) percentage changes are given by

$$\%Y^* = \%P^* + \%y_f$$

If real GNP is expected to increase by 2 percent and the Fed desires a 3 percent inflation, then a 5 percent increase in nominal GNP is appropriate. (The quantity-theory equation $MV = Py$ with stable velocity gives a money supply target corresponding to the Fed's nominal GNP target.)

Critics of nominal GNP targeting are skeptical of the crucial assumption that the Fed need not be concerned with fluctuations in real GNP. Consider an oil embargo (a leftward shift of the aggregate supply curve) that increases prices and reduces real GNP. Suppose that, in the absence of Fed action, real GNP would decline by 1 percent (instead of increasing by 2 percent) and that prices would increase by 10 percent (rather than 3 percent), so that nominal GNP would increase by $(-1\%) + (10\%) = 9\%$, which is 4 percentage points above the Fed's 5 percent target. If the Fed follows a nominal GNP target rule, it will use contractionary monetary policies to reduce nominal GNP by 4 percent. The implicit assumption is that this contractionary monetary policy does not have significant real economic effects. Critics argue that, because monetary policies do have real effects, nominal GNP targeting may, as in this example, sometimes mislead the Fed into following policies that make recessions more severe.

The reverse situation occurs when workers underestimate their real wages, as shown in Figure 21.6. Here, households believe the price level to be higher than it actually is. Because they think that real wages are low, they voluntarily withdraw from the labor force. As the labor supply schedule shifts leftward, employers must pay higher real wages to keep their reluctant workers. Real wages rise, though labor believes that real wages have declined, and both employment and output contract. This is voluntary, surprise unemployment because workers will be surprised when they learn how low commodity prices are and will then return to the jobs they mistakenly left.

Voluntary unemployment occurs when workers overestimate prices and underestimate real wages.

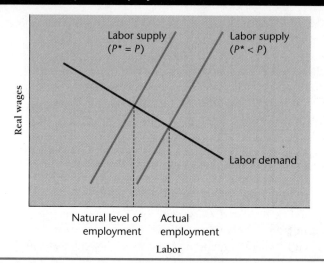

Figure 21.5 Surprise Employment

This is the new classical market-equilibrium explanation of business cycles. Booms in economic activity occur when workers underestimate the price level; recessions occur when they overestimate it. These business cycles are self-correcting because households soon correct any price misperceptions. Some workers may be fooled some of the time, but they will not be fooled all of the time. The natural state of affairs, or the long-run equilibrium toward which the economy will automatically gravitate, has $P^* = P$, since the perceived price level will not be permanently higher or lower than the actual price level.

When workers perceive prices correctly, the natural level of employment is attained.

When $P^* = P$, the labor supply is accurate and the **natural level of employment** is attained. This natural level coincides with the classical notion of full employment with perfect information. The important extension by the new classical economists is that they permit voluntary (though mistaken) departures from the natural level of employment. There is always full employment, in the sense that everyone who wants a job has one; but there are booms and recessions as real-wage perceptions fluctuate. One of these market equilibria is at the natural level of employment, where perceptions are accurate.

The New-Classical Interpretation of the Aggregate Supply Curve

Imperfectly perceived prices give a nonvertical aggregate supply curve.

This new classical model has interesting implications for the aggregate supply curve. Accurately perceived price changes do not cause errors in gauging real wages, and consequently do not alter labor supply, employment, or output. For a correctly perceived price change, output is constant and the aggregate supply curve is vertical. But an imperfectly perceived price change does cause output

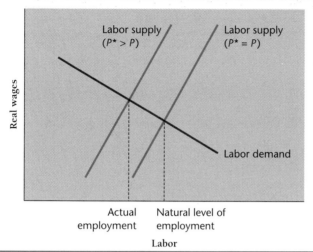

Figure 21.6 Surprise Unemployment

fluctuations, implying a nonvertical aggregate supply curve. Figure 21.7 shows two aggregate supply curves, one for correct price estimates and one for incorrect estimates. (These two curves are sometimes labeled long-run and short-run, because workers may make mistakes in the short run, but not the long run; we avoid these labels to leave open the possibility that workers are correct in the short run.)

Suppose that there is an increase in aggregate demand, as shown in Figure 21.7. If the accompanying increase in prices is correctly gauged, wages increase proportionately and there is no change in employment or output. The economy moves up the vertical supply curve in Figure 21.7. This is the natural level of output corresponding to the natural level of employment in Figures 21.5 and 21.6.

What if the price increase is not fully recognized by households — if, for instance, price expectations are constant and households do not realize that prices have increased? Perceived real wages will be above actual real wages and, as explained in the preceding section, labor supply expands, thereby increasing employment and output. The economy moves up the nonvertical aggregate supply curve in Figure 21.7. Employment and output are temporarily above their natural levels because of price errors.

Figure 21.8 shows the new-classical interpretation of recessions. If the aggregate demand curve moves leftward, there is downward pressure on prices. If this price decline is correctly perceived, wages drop proportionately to keep the labor market in equilibrium; real wages, employment, and output are unchanged. The economy moves down the vertical aggregate supply curve with output still at the natural level. If, however, households do not realize that prices

Figure 21.7 New-Classical Aggregate Supply Curves

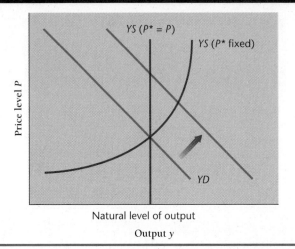

Figure 21.8 A New-Classical Recession

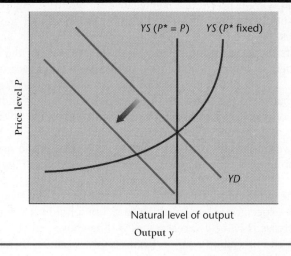

have fallen, they underestimate their real wages and reduce their labor supply. Employment and output drop below their natural levels as the economy slides down the nonvertical aggregate supply curve in Figure 21.8.

It is important to recognize that the new-classical explanation of a nonvertical aggregate supply curve is very different from the Keynesian disequilibrium interpretation. In the Keynesian interpretation, a nonvertical aggregate supply curve is the consequence of imperfectly adjusting wages and prices. According to the new classical economists, a nonvertical aggregate supply curve describes an

---

George Bush's Economic Advisers

After his January 1989 inauguration as U.S. President, George Bush chose a Council of Economic Advisers with a definite new-classical view of the economy. In their 1990 Annual Report,* the Council concludes that, "Because it is not possible for people to be 'fooled' indefinitely about the rate of inflation, higher inflation cannot permanently lower the unemployment rate." The Council pointedly contrasted their views with those expressed in 1962 by President John Kennedy's Council of Economic Advisers. The Kennedy Council argued that "discretionary policy is essential" to achieve the goals of the Employment Act of 1946: "maximum employment, production, and purchasing power." The Bush Council argued that "discretionary macroeconomic policies can be detrimental to good economic performance. Instead, policies should be designed to work well with a minimum of discretion."

Interestingly, although Bush's Council urges that government spending and taxation be guided by systematic rules, they are wary of conducting monetary policy according to simple rules. While endorsing a credible commitment to low rates of inflation, they state that, "In the 1960s and 1970s, a rule that specified a fixed growth rate of the money supply was proposed and might have been appropriate; changes in the financial sector in the 1980s, however, have rendered such a simple rule unworkable. . . . Substantial movements in the velocities of the monetary aggregates in recent years have made rigid monetary targeting inappropriate."

Economic Report of the President (Washington, D.C.: Government Printing Office, February 1990).

---

equilibrium adjustment of wages and prices to inaccurate price information. It is price expectations rather than market prices that are sluggish.

Rational Expectations

Chapter 16 introduced the idea of **rational expectations**, based on the efficient utilization of available information. If we assume, as the new classical economists usually do, that workers have rational expectations, then government policies with foreseeable effects on prices do not cause fluctuations in employment or output. If the Fed announces an increase in reserve requirements and workers correctly anticipate that this tightening of financial markets will cause prices to decline by 10 percent, the aggregate supply curve is vertical. Labor supply does not change, nominal wages fall by 10 percent, and employment is unaffected. The only policies that can raise or lower employment are unpredictable ones.

Rational expectations are based on efficient utilization of available information.

In new classical models with rational expectations, well-anticipated monetary policies do not affect employment and output.

Since any changes in employment and output that do occur are attributable to mistakes that workers later regret, the new classical economists do not endorse the use of monetary policy to expand or contract employment and output. The Fed can increase employment only by fooling people into working for lower real wages than they think they are being paid. This is not a legitimate role for government officials. Instead, the Fed should follow policies conducive to stable prices, so that workers will not misjudge prices.

SUMMARY

Private preferences, government policy, and the nation's endowment of people, capital, land, and technology, determine an economy's aggregate demand and aggregate supply curves. The intersection of these curves determines output and the price level (with the interest rate implicitly determined by the underlying *IS* and *LM* curves).

The logic behind the aggregate demand and supply curves is very important. We should resist the temptation to view these as ordinary demand and supply curves, with their intersection giving some sort of macroeconomic market equilibrium. There is a superficial resemblance between aggregate demand and supply curves and the microeconomic demand and supply curves for, say, Idaho potatoes. But these are not ordinary demand and supply curves.

The aggregate demand and supply curves give a simple summary of a number of complex interrelationships. The aggregate demand curve shows, for different price levels, the levels of output such that income is equal to expenditures and money demand is equal to supply. These income levels need not be the desired levels, since workers and factories may be involuntarily idle. The aggregate supply curve shows the price levels at various levels of output. Firms may not be selling all they would like at these price levels, and labor demand need not equal labor supply. The intersection of the aggregate demand and supply curves shows the levels of output and prices that prevail, not necessarily those that simultaneously equilibrate all markets.

If there is a classical full-employment equilibrium, then markets are in equilibrium. Output is unaffected by price changes, and hence the aggregate supply curve is vertical with output always at the full-employment level. Thus classical economists focused their attention on the supply side of the economy, believing a nation's resources determine how much is produced. Spending and financial markets — aggregate demand — affect only interest rates and the price level.

The aggregate supply curve is positively sloped, not vertical, in Keynesian models with market disequilibria. Because wages are sticky downward, there can be an excess supply of labor. This unemployment is involuntary in the sense that the unemployed are willing and able to work at the prevailing wage but cannot get jobs because of explicit or implicit commitments by employers not to auction off the jobs of those who are employed. It may be easier to reduce real wages by increasing prices than by cutting wages. If so, then an increase in the price level reduces real wages, increasing employment and output.

The prices of many goods and services are also sticky, with businesses adapting production to demand. When demand increases, firms hire more workers and increase production; labor markets tighten, putting upward pressure on wages, which, as with other production costs, are passed along in higher prices. In these disequilibrium models, there is a role for monetary policy in raising or lowering aggregate demand, increasing or reducing employment, and pushing or restraining prices.

The new classical economists have a market-equilibrium explanation of a nonvertical aggregate supply curve. They point out that economic fluctuations can be caused by errors in assessing prices. When workers underestimate prices, they overestimate real wages, causing labor supply, employment, and output to increase. Recessions occur when workers overestimate prices and underestimate real wages. As time passes, workers correct their mistakes, and the natural level of employment is reestablished. There is no need or justification for active monetary policy in these models, since departures from full employment are temporary and caused by regrettable mistakes.

IMPORTANT TERMS

aggregate supply curve
natural level of employment
new-classical economists

rational expectations
Say's law

EXERCISES

1. In the classical model, what do labor demand, labor supply, and employment depend on?
2. In the classical model of the labor market, what happens to wages, employment, and output if prices fall by 10 percent?
3. In the classical model, what happens to prices and employment if the Fed reduces reserve requirements?
4. A 1987 *Los Angeles Times* headline stated that a new defense department order for airplanes would create 5,000 jobs. An economics professor responded "Nonsense. This will actually cost 5,000 jobs." Explain his reasoning, using the classical model of the labor market.
5. The Economic Recovery Act of 1981 reduced personal income taxes over a three-year period. Some economists argued that, in anticipation of lower income taxes in the future, people would work less in 1981 (and more in 1984, when taxes were lower) but spend more

in 1981 (in anticipation of larger after-tax income in the future). If so, how would 1981 output, employment, wages, and prices be affected? Assume a classical full-employment model.
6. Explain why you agree or disagree with the following argument in support of the conclusion that a lot of unemployment is voluntary.[10]

   Job losers are barely over half of all the unemployed, and are mostly adults. Many others are unemployed because of actions they took more or less voluntarily: They quit their last job, just joined the labor force, or just rejoined it.

7. How will an increase in government spending affect output, prices, the interest rate, money supply, money demand, and velocity? Does your answer depend on whether or not the aggregate supply curve is vertical?
8. Indicate whether the Bureau of Labor Statistics

counts each of these persons employed, un-employed, or out of the labor force.

a. Tom Weathers is a college student.

b. David Drier is a U.S. congressman.

c. After losing his job as a stockbroker, Bill Barnes washes dishes at the Buffalo Inn.

d. Bob Brown works for a Houston real estate firm, but is actively seeking a job in Boston where his girlfriend lives.

e. Classes are over, and Professor Smith takes a three-month vacation.

9. Okun's Law says that, in any given year, real gross national product would be 3 percent higher if the unemployment rate were 1 percentage point lower (for example, 7 percent instead of 8 percent). In 1982, the unemployment rate was 9.7 percent and real gross national product was $3,073 billion. In 1983, the unemployment rate was 9.6 percent and real gross national product was $3,310 billion. Use Okun's Law to estimate how much higher real gross national product would have been in these two years had the unemployment rate been 5 percent.

10. For each of the following macroeconomic events, predict whether output, prices, and employment will rise or fall (assuming that the aggregate supply curve is not vertical).

a. To balance its budget, the government reduces spending.

b. To balance its budget, the government increases taxes.

c. To take advantage of new tax breaks, consumers save more.

d. An import tax persuades Californians to buy Fords instead of Hondas.

11. An economy can be described by aggregate demand and supply curves.

a. Why is the demand curve downward sloping?

b. Why might the supply curve be vertical? Why might it be upward sloping and not vertical?

c. The Council of Economic Advocates has recommended a large reduction in government spending. What will happen to output and prices if the aggregate supply curve is not vertical?

d. With elections fast approaching, the president needs to raise output and reduce prices. What does he need to do to demand and supply? What policy change did President Reagan hope would do the trick?

12. The Economic Recovery Act of 1981 substantially reduced tax rates on personal income. Assume that the labor market is in equilibrium and that this reduction in income tax rates increases the supply of labor. If so, what will happen to equilibrium

a. real before-tax wages?

b. employment?

c. output?

d. prices?

e. nominal wages?

What will happen to employment and output if nominal wages do not change?

13. Indicate whether each of the following economic events will raise or lower output, prices, and interest rates. Assume that the aggregate supply curve is not vertical.

a. Congress cuts defense spending.

b. The Fed abolishes reserve requirements.

c. A vast oil field is discovered in Iowa.

d. Congress prohibits car imports.

e. Fearing a banking collapse, people hoard cash.

f. Deciding the end is near, households increase their spending dramatically.

g. The Fed sells Treasury bills.

14. For each of the following macroeconomic events, predict whether output and prices will rise or fall (assuming that the economy is not at full employment).

a. Worried about the upcoming election, the government increases its spending.

b. Fearing the collapse of the Social Security system, consumers save more.

c. To balance its budget, the government levies a special $2,000 tax on every household.

d. Energy prices skyrocket after all nuclear power plants are shut down permanently.

e. There is a worldwide craze for products made in the United States.

15. The Fed wants to stimulate investment spending without fueling inflation and thus wants to lower interest rates without raising prices. What combination of monetary and fiscal policies is appropriate?

16. Classical economists believed that a nation could increase its investment spending by reducing consumption. Keynes argued that reduced consumption spending might diminish investment. Why does increased investment require reduced consumption in the classical model? How can consumption and investment both increase in the Keynesian model?

17. Congress is considering reducing taxes on wage income and simultaneously increasing cigarette taxes. If there is no net change in tax revenue, how will output, employment, and prices be affected in a classical full-employment model?

18. Some members of the Reagan administration advised sharply higher income-tax rates to reduce the budget deficit. Assuming a classical full-employment model and taking into account both the demand-side effect on consumption and the supply-side effect on labor supply, how do higher income-tax rates affect output, employment, and prices?

19. Does Say's Law state that "supply creates its own demand" or that "demand creates its own supply"? Explain the reasoning behind this law.

20. In the new classical models, if the Fed unexpectedly raises reserve requirements, causing a change in prices that some workers do not notice, will they underestimate or overestimate their real wages? Will employment expand or contract? What will bring an automatic end to this boom or recession?

INFLATION

There is no sight in the world more awful than that of an oldtime economist, foam-flecked at the mouth and hell-bent to cure inflation by monetary discipline. God willing, we shan't soon see his like again.

Paul Samuelson

Inflation is a sustained, continuing rise in prices.

This chapter focuses on **inflation,** a sustained rise in the price level, which is often measured by the annual rate of change in the Consumer Price Index. It is important to distinguish between a high price level and a rapid rate of inflation. On January 15, 1991, the price of a certain house was $100,000 and, during the preceding 12 months, the price had increased at an annual rate — its rate of inflation — of 20 percent. The price of the house and the rate of increase of the price are two separate data: the price level can increase even while the rate of inflation is falling. In our example, if the price of this house a year later, on January 15, 1992, were $110,000, there would have been a $10,000 increase in the price level, but a decrease in the rate of inflation from 20 percent to 10 percent. Sometimes, people say that the rate of inflation is increasing when they really mean that the price level is increasing.

We will begin this chapter by discussing the causes of inflation and then address its consequences: how inflation affects citizens' well-being and economic behavior. One conclusion we will draw is that people should react differently to a high price level and a high rate of inflation. For example, if you are considering buying a house, a high price makes the house less appealing, but that house is more attractive if its price is rising rapidly.

THE CLASSICAL LINK BETWEEN MONEY AND INFLATION

Inflation is often associated with rapid increases in the money supply. Nobel Laureate Milton Friedman said, plainly enough, "Inflation is always and everywhere a monetary phenomenon."[1] The economic logic linking money and inflation can be found in classical analysis by assuming full employment and institutionally determined velocity. The simple quantity-theory equation

$$MV = Py \tag{1}$$

can be rewritten as

$$P = \left(\frac{V}{y}\right) M \tag{2}$$

If velocity V and output y are fixed in the short run, then the price level P depends solely on the money supply. Government spending, budget deficits, militant unions, and oil embargoes do not affect the price level in the classical model.

Money is said to be "neutral" in the classical model, since the money supply only determines the price level and does not affect the level of output. A 10 percent increase in the money supply raises the level of prices by 10 percent; a 10 percent reduction in the money supply reduces the price level by 10 percent. Either way, employment and output stay at their full-employment levels.

As time passes, there may be gradual changes in velocity (due to the evolution of society's bill-paying habits) and in output (due to changes in the nation's work force, capital stock, and technology). The percentage change in prices — the rate of inflation — depends on the rate of increase in the money supply relative to the rate of growth of velocity and the rate of growth of output:

$$\%P = \%M + \%V - \%y \tag{3}$$

If, for example, output grows at 2 percent a year and improvements in society's bill-paying habits increase velocity by 3 percent a year, then a 5 percent rate of money growth implies a 6 percent rate of inflation

$$\%P = 5\% + 3\% - 2\% = 6\%$$

and a 10-percent money growth implies an 11 percent inflation rate,

$$\%P = 10\% + 3\% - 2\% = 11\%$$

Summarizing, in classical models, with full employment and institutionally determined velocity, the level of the money supply determines the price level, and the rate of the growth of the money supply relative to the rates of growth of velocity and output determine the rate of inflation.

Inflation is often associated with rapid increases in the money supply.

With full employment and fixed velocity, the money supply determines the price level and the rate of inflation.

Short-Run Correlations

Figure 22.1 shows some annual data on the rate of inflation and the rate of growth of M1. There is not much correlation between the two. In years when M1 has increased by 4 percent to 6 percent, the rate of inflation has been anywhere from 3 percent to 11 percent. The current rate of inflation depends on more than the current rate of change of the money supply.

Remember, too, that a high correlation between the rate of inflation and some monetary aggregate, such as M1, does not necessarily confirm the assertion that inflation is due to the government's printing presses having run amok. Monetary aggregates include private money (such as checking accounts) in addition to government currency. Monetary aggregates can increase much faster (or more slowly) than the monetary base. Figure 22.2 shows that, as with M1, there is not a close correlation between changes in the monetary base and the current rate of inflation.

There is not a close relationship between inflation and the rates of growth of M1 and the monetary base.

The Long Run

In the classical model, the explanation of inflation is quite simple — too simple, it turns out. The classical link between money and inflation is, like most classical propositions, more appropriate for the long run than for the short run. When Friedman said that inflation is always and everywhere a monetary phenomenon, he did not mean that literally every jog in the consumer price index is due to a corresponding wiggle in the money supply. Instead, he meant that major inflations, involving rapid and sustained price increases, are generally accompanied by rapid and sustained increases in the money supply. This long-run argument is reasonable. If the money supply grows at 20 percent a year for several years, then (applying the quantity-theory equation $MV = Py$) either output must grow rapidly, velocity must fall rapidly, or prices must increase rapidly.

Rapid sustained increases in the money supply cause inflation.

In the short run, some or all of these three things may happen — but not in the long run. Output can increase very rapidly as an economy emerges from a recession, but the long-run growth of output is limited by a society's resources. It is difficult to imagine real output growing at 20 percent a year forever. Similarly, velocity does fluctuate considerably in the short run, but it is hard to imagine it falling by 20 percent a year forever. That leaves prices. If the money supply grows by 20 percent a year, year after year, it is almost certain that there will be rapid inflation.

Conversely, if the money supply consistently grows at 2 percent annually, then a rapid, sustained inflation requires a large, continual decline in output or a rapid, continuing increase in velocity (so that money circulates progressively faster). Output can decline substantially in the short run and velocity can increase considerably, but long-run movements sufficient to sustain a triple- or even double-digit inflation are implausible. The higher the rate of inflation and the longer it persists, the more certain it is that the money supply is increasing rapidly.

Figure 22.1 Annual Percentage Changes in M1 and the Consumer Price Index, 1970–1988

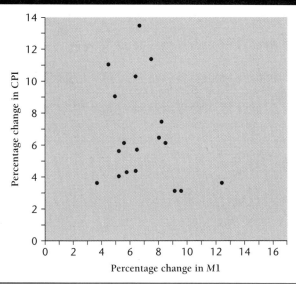

Figure 22.2 Annual Percentage Changes in the Monetary Base and the Consumer Price Index, 1970–1988

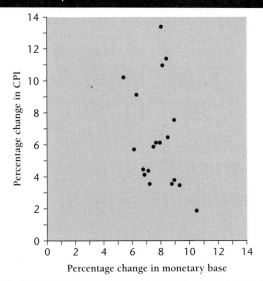

THE CAUSES OF INFLATION IN THE SHORT RUN

In the short run, velocity is not fixed and the economy is not always at full employment; the data in Figures 22.1 and 22.2 demonstrate that there is not a close correlation between increases in the money supply and inflation. Not every increase in the money supply raises prices proportionately, and prices can rise without a corresponding increase in the money supply.

In macroeconomic models, prices are determined by the intersection of aggregate demand and supply curves, as shown in Figure 22.3. (Chapters 19–21 discuss the details behind these curves.) The aggregate demand curve reflects spending and financial markets. It is shifted in an expansionary rightward direction by an increase in household, business, or government spending and by an increase in the supply of money or a decline in money demand (which makes money plentiful). The aggregate demand curve is shifted in a contractionary leftward direction by a decline in spending, a decrease in the money supply, or an increase in money demand.

The aggregate supply curve describes how much is produced at various price levels or, equivalently, the price level at various levels of production. One explanation of its positive slope is that as firms increase production, they incur cost increases that they pass along in higher prices. (In classical full-employment models, the aggregate supply curve is vertical because production is at the full-employment level, regardless of the level of prices.) The aggregate supply curve is shifted rightward if production increases for a given price level or, equivalently if the price level declines for a given level of production.

In macroeconomic models, changes in aggregate demand or supply affect prices.

Any shift in the aggregate demand or aggregate supply curves affects the price level. The money supply affects prices to the extent that it changes the location of the aggregate demand curve, but other events affect aggregate demand, too. An expansionary monetary policy is no more or less inflationary than an equally expansionary fiscal policy or equally expansionary changes in private spending or money demand. In Figure 20.3, price changes are due to shifts in the aggregate demand and supply curves, regardless of whether these shifts are caused by monetary policy, fiscal policy, or private actions.

Classical economists usually assumed that the full adjustment of prices to economic events occurs very quickly. They assumed, for instance, that if the nation's money supply were doubled overnight, people would wake in the morning to find prices doubled, too, and economic activity proceeding otherwise undisturbed. A continuing inflation in the classical model requires continuing increases in the money supply, day after day.

Prices adjust sluggishly and imperfectly.

However, many prices are set in individual markets by contracts, regulatory authorities, average-cost rules, and other procedures that are not very sensitive to demand and supply shifts. Because prices adjust sluggishly and imperfectly, inflation reflects both old and new economic events. Changes in the money supply and other economic events have continuing effects on prices; conversely,

Figure 22.3 The Price Level Is Determined by Aggregate Demand and Supply

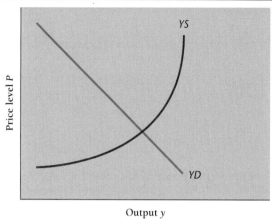

Output *y*

price changes are influenced not only by current events but also by the gradual playing out of the consequences of past events.

For instance, there was a large increase in oil prices in 1973–74 that reduced the demand for cars, particularly large cars. There were ripple effects on steel, rubber, auto workers, Detroit housing, and many other markets. There were also effects on the markets for coal, oil-drilling equipment, insulation, Sun Belt housing, and innumerable others. No omniscient auctioneer announced the new prices that simultaneously cleared thousands of markets. Instead, prices were set in separate markets by a variety of procedures, and it took years for the effects of higher oil prices to work themselves out.

Low Unemployment and High Inflation

To understand inflation, we need to look at the pricing behavior that underlies the aggregate supply curve. Many businesses set prices using **average-markup** or target-return pricing formulas. In these pricing rules of thumb, average costs at normal production levels are calculated, and the price is set at some normal markup over these costs, so as to earn a target profit rate. A simple representation is

$$Py^* = (1 + a)(Wn^* + Cm^*) \tag{4}$$

where P is the price, y is the number of items produced, W is the hourly wage rate, n the number of hours of paid employment, C the price of other, nonlabor expenses (such as raw materials and taxes), m the quantity of these nonlabor inputs, and a is the markup that provides profits. $Wn^* + Cm^*$ is total cost and Py^* is total revenue. (Asterisks affixed to y, n, and m indicate that these are calculated at normal operating levels.)

Many businesses use average-markup pricing rules.

This markup equation can be rewritten on a per-unit basis as

$$P = (1 + a)\left(\frac{Wn^*}{y^*} + \frac{Cm^*}{y^*}\right) \tag{5}$$

or

$$P = (1 + a)\left(\frac{W}{y^*/n^*} + \frac{C}{y^*/m^*}\right) \tag{6}$$

Equation 5 says that the price is a markup over unit labor cost Wn^*/y^* and other per-unit costs Cm^*/y^*. Equation 6 shows that costs depend on wages relative to labor productivity y/n^* and on other costs C relative to their productivity $y/m)^*$. These rules assume that the firm produces at its planned or normal operating level and sells all of what it is producing; actual profits depend on actual sales and output.

In the short run, as production fluctuates, companies do not adjust their markup or their estimates of normal productivity. Economic fluctuations affect prices mainly through costs W and C. When demand increases, production expands and additional resources are utilized; if resource costs increase, businesses pass these costs along via higher prices.

Some inputs are raw materials traded in markets with very flexible prices. When industrial demand for such materials expands, their costs increase quickly. In most industries, labor is by far the most important production expense and, normally, the most important source of cost pressures. But most wages are not

When aggregate demand increases, higher production costs lead firms to increase prices.

Figure 22.4   The Pressure on Prices Can Be Gauged by the Gap Between Actual and Full-Employment Output

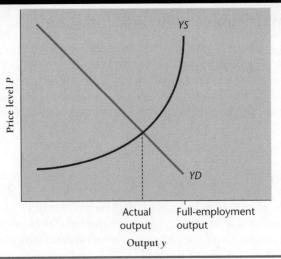

Figure 22.5   **When Actual Output Exceeds Full-Employment Output, the Upward Pressure on Costs and Prices Shifts the Aggregate Supply Curve Upward**

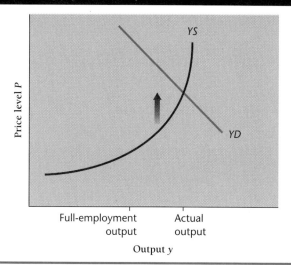

very flexible. An increased demand for labor does not immediately translate fully into higher wages; a reduced demand for labor seldom causes wages to decline.

An aggregate overview is provided by Figure 22.4, in which the intersection of the aggregate demand and aggregate supply curves determine current output and the current price level. At this intersection, there may well be market pressures that have not yet been translated into price changes. Some markets have excess supplies and are exerting a downward pull on prices; others have excess demands and are pushing prices upward. We can gauge the overall pressure on prices by comparing actual output with the economy's **full-employment output**, defined here as that level of production at which excess demands are balanced by excess supplies, so that overall there is no substantial demand-supply pressure on prices. When actual output is above full-employment output, there are many excess demands, few excess supplies, and considerable upward pressure on costs and prices. When an economy's actual output is below its full-employment potential, there are few markets with excess demands and many with excess supplies, so that markets are exerting downward pressure on costs and prices.

Figure 22.5 shows how higher input costs translate into higher prices. Output is temporarily above the economy's full-employment potential. Factories are operating at greater-than-normal capacity, perhaps at levels that cannot be sustained without excessive wear and tear on workers and machines. These high production levels require lots of labor, fuel, and other inputs. The strong demands

Full-employment output is that level of output at which there is little demand-supply pressure on prices.

Figure 22.6   When Actual Output Is Below Full-Employment Output, the Downward Pressure on Costs and Prices Shifts the Aggregate Supply Curve Downward

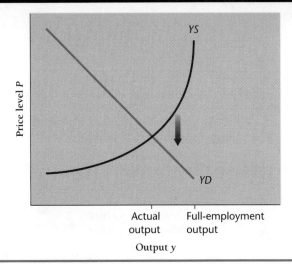

for these inputs push their prices upward, though sooner for many raw materials than for labor, which may be bound by long-term contracts. As firms find their input costs increasing, they cover these costs by raising their prices. The aggregate supply curve shifts upward, because firms charge higher prices at a given level of output. These higher prices reduce demand and pull output back towards the full-employment level. Figure 22.6 shows the opposite picture, in which actual output is far below full-employment potential.

Demand-supply pressures shift the aggregate supply curve over time.

These examples show why it is important to remember that the intersection of the aggregate demand and aggregate supply curves does not show an aggregate market equilibrium, but only where the economy is at a given time. From this position, prices may rise or fall, because the labor market and other markets are in disequilibrium with excess demand or supply. This inflation or deflation does not require continuing increases in the money supply, but only the playing out of old disequilibria. Of course, prices are affected not only by continuing adjustments to old pressures, but also by new economic events — by labor-force growth, capital accumulation, technological improvements, monetary and fiscal policies, changes in private preferences, and so on.

The unemployment rate is one measure of inflationary pressures.

The gap between actual and full-employment output is closely related to the rate of unemployment, suggesting that we can gauge inflationary pressures by the size of the unemployment rate, particularly since labor is the biggest cost for most employers. The amount of excess supply and demand in labor markets should influence how fast wages increase and, with markup-pricing rules, wage increases lead to price increases.

Figure 22.7 shows that there has been a close relationship between the annual percentage changes in wages and in prices. Each of the three exceptions occurred at times when the cost of nonlabor inputs changed dramatically. In 1952–53, raw-materials prices fell at an 8 percent annual rate; in 1973–75 and 1979–80, raw-materials prices rose by 16 percent and 15 percent per year, respectively, mostly because of higher energy prices. Price increases are roughly equal to wage increases less normal productivity growth, except when there are unusual changes in the costs of other inputs.

The Phillips Curve

The idea that changes in wages and prices depend on the unemployment rate was first tested by A. W. Phillips, using British data for the years 1861–1957.[2] Ever since, the label **Phillips curve** has been applied to the idea that there is a tradeoff between unemployment and inflation. Increases in aggregate

The Phillips curve describes a tradeoff between unemployment and inflation.

Figure 22.7 **Wages and Prices**

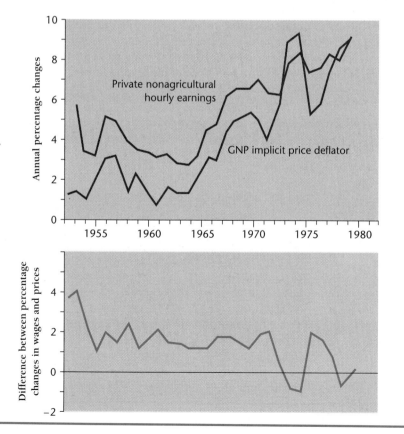

demand tighten labor markets as unemployment falls and vacancies grow, thereby causing wages and prices to increase. The hard-nosed cure for inflation is a recession. Like a bloodletting, the economy has to be weakened to be made well. In 1980, Paul Volcker, the Chairman of the Federal Reserve Board, was asked if stringent monetary and fiscal policies intended to reduce inflation would cause a recession. "Yes," he replied, "and the sooner the better."[3]

Contractionary monetary and fiscal policies reduce output and employment. With slacker labor and commodity markets, there is less upward pressure on wages and prices. Arthur Okun put it this way.[4]

> When markets are exceedingly weak no businessman will dare raise his prices for fear of losing his markets, and no workers — organized or unorganized — will demand significant wage increases for fear of losing their jobs. The problem of curing inflation is difficult and demanding because we will not take this decapitation cure for the headache of rising prices.

As shown in Figure 22.8, U.S. data for the years 1954 through 1969 confirm a Phillips curve relationship between unemployment and inflation. Using similar data through 1960, President Kennedy's Council of Economic Advisers selected a 4-percent unemployment rate as a target full-employment goal, anticipating that this would be accompanied by roughly a 3-percent inflation rate. (Of particular historical interest was the period 1955–57, during which the unemployment rate had been close to 4 percent and the inflation rate did not exceed 3.3 percent.) Below a 4-percent unemployment rate, these advisers feared that the rate of inflation might rise to a politically intolerable level.

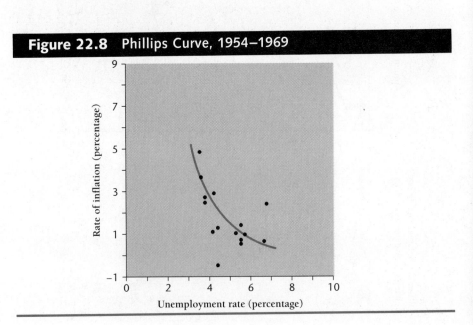

Figure 22.8   Phillips Curve, 1954–1969

As indicated in Table 22.1, the level of unemployment fell to around 4 percent in 1965–1967, with about 3 percent inflation. In 1968–69, the rate of unemployment dropped further and the pace of inflation quickened. Concern turned from unemployment to inflation. After Richard Nixon's inauguration in early 1969, he tried the hard-nosed recession cure for inflation for a while and then, with an election approaching, tried wage and price controls. Neither approach eradicated inflation, as households and politicians can testify.

High Unemployment and High Inflation

Table 22.1 and Figure 22.9 show that from the mid-1970s through the early 1980s the U.S. experienced **stagflation**: high unemployment and rapid inflation. Where did the Phillips curve tradeoff go? At levels of unemployment where prices were stable in the 1950s there was close to double-digit inflation in the 1970s. Why? Three answers are frequently offered: nonlabor costs, changes in the composition of the labor force, and inflation expectations. We will discuss the first two briefly and the third in more depth.

Stagflation is high unemployment and rapid inflation.

Markup prices (Equations 4–6) depend on material costs, which can increase even when there is considerable unemployment. Dramatic, unprecedented increases in material expenses, especially for fuel (which leaped upward in 1973–74 and again in 1978–81), created inflationary pressures that, with imperfect markets, took years to work themselves out.

A second explanation of the coexistence of rapid inflation with relatively high unemployment concerns the composition of the labor force. In 1970, George Perry first noted that over the postwar period there had been a dramatic movement into the labor force of male teenagers and of females, who are disproportionately represented among the unemployed, as shown in Table 22.2.[5] Perry argues that the females and teenage males who entered the labor market in the 1960s and 1970s tended to be relatively unskilled and to work fewer hours. The reported unemployment rate thus understated the tightness of labor markets, since some of the unemployed were unable or unwilling to take the full-time jobs available. Perry argued that the Phillips curve shifted outward, so that an aggregate unemployment rate of 6 percent in the 1970s and 1980s meant tighter labor markets and more inflation than in the 1950s. Perry concludes that, to some extent, these structural changes are curing themselves as the population ages and as women who now enter the labor market are better prepared and more committed to full-time work.

INFLATION EXPECTATIONS

The third explanation of the outward shift in the Phillips curve emphasizes the effect of inflation expectations on wages. This argument is clearest in the case of a competitive labor market. The real wage rate W/P is equal to the nominal wage rate W divided by the price level P. If the price level increases by 10 percent,

Table 22.1   Unemployment and Inflation, 1952–1989

Year	Unemployment Rate (%)	Change in Consumer Price Index (%)
1952	3.0	1.9
1953	2.9	0.8
1954	5.5	0.7
1955	4.4	−0.4
1956	4.1	1.5
1957	4.3	3.3
1958	6.8	2.8
1959	5.5	0.7
1960	5.5	1.7
1961	6.7	1.0
1962	5.5	1.0
1963	5.7	1.3
1964	5.2	1.3
1965	4.5	1.6
1966	3.8	2.9
1967	3.8	3.1
1968	3.6	4.2
1969	3.5	5.5
1970	4.9	5.7
1971	5.9	4.4
1972	5.6	3.2
1973	4.9	6.2
1974	5.6	11.0
1975	8.5	9.1
1976	7.7	5.8
1977	7.1	6.5
1978	6.1	7.6
1979	5.8	11.3
1980	7.1	13.5
1981	7.6	10.3
1982	9.7	6.2
1983	9.6	3.2
1984	7.5	4.3
1985	7.2	3.6
1986	7.0	1.9
1987	6.2	3.6
1988	5.5	4.1
1989	5.3	4.8

Figure 22.9 Unemployment and Inflation, 1954–1989

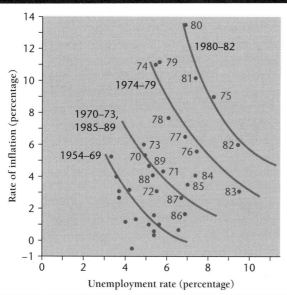

then nominal wages must also rise by 10 percent to keep real wages from falling. Wage contracts set for one, two, three, or even more years are influenced by the anticipated rate of inflation over the duration of the contract. If wage adjustments reflect an attempt to maintain market-equilibrium real wages, then workers will want, and employers will grant, annual wage increases equal to the expected rate of inflation.

The argument is less persuasive in a labor market with excess supply (unemployment). Real wages must decline to clear a market with excess supply, but there is usually strong resistance to cutting nominal wages. If the anticipated rate of inflation is zero, nominal wages may be constant. If the anticipated rate of inflation is 5 percent, will wages also rise by 5 percent? If so, then real wages will be unchanged and the market will be no closer to equilibrium. It is more likely that wages will rise slightly or not at all, so that real wages decline and the excess labor supply is reduced.

This is Keynes's conclusion based on reasoning and observation. Real wages are reduced and employment increased more easily through price increases than through wage cuts. While nominal wages seldom decline, real wages often sag in excess-supply labor markets during inflations. College French teachers would be in open revolt if their salaries were slashed, but throughout the 1970s they accepted wage increases that did not keep up with inflation.

Inflation and inflation expectations do affect wages even in excess-supply labor markets; for example, many union contracts have built-in cost-of-living adjustments. However, Keynesians do not assume that every 1-percentage-point

| Highlight 22.1 | A Policy Dilemma for the Fed |

Oil prices quadrupled in 1973–1974 and then doubled in 1978–1981, in each case instigating inflationary spirals in the United States. As businesses raised prices to cover their increased energy costs, workers demanded wage increases to match these price hikes, and businesses raised prices to cover the increased wages. The annual rate of inflation in the United States increased from 3.4 percent in 1972 to 8.7 percent in 1973 and then 12.9 percent in 1974. After falling back below 5 percent in 1976, the rate of inflation averaged nearly 12 percent between 1978 and 1981.

Figure 22.3 shows that economic events that affect aggregate demand cause unemployment and inflation to move in opposite directions. An increase in aggregate demand (a rightward shift of the aggregate demand curve) increases prices and output, reducing unemployment. A decline in aggregate demand (a leftward shift of the aggregate demand curve) restrains prices and reduces output, increasing unemployment. The surges in energy prices in the 1970s, in contrast, were supply-side events that caused stag-flation — higher rates of both unemployment and inflation. An increase in energy prices causes firms to increase their prices, shifting the aggregate supply curve in Figure 22.3 upward: prices rise and output falls.

Such energy shocks pose a cruel dilemma for a nation's monetary authorities. If the Federal Reserve uses contractionary monetary policies to offset inflationary pressures, it makes an imminent recession even more severe. If the Fed uses expansionary monetary policies to avoid a recession, it adds to the already substantial inflation momentum. In practice, after each of the energy shocks in the 1970s, the Fed restrained the money supply enough to allow interest rates to reach levels that caused a recession.

In the summer of 1989, after nearly seven years of expansion, the U.S. economy seemed on the verge of its first recession since 1982. For months, many private and government economists had interpreted signs of a slowing economy as evidence of a looming recession and encouraged the Fed to lower interest rates to bolster the economy. Then, in early August, the situation was dramatically altered by a supply-side shock. Iraqi troops invaded Kuwait and seized their rich oil fields, prompting an embargo of Iraq and threatening a major war in the Mideast.

In anticipation of higher oil prices and increased inflation, interest rates jumped upward, and bond prices slumped. Higher interest rates and the prospect of increased unemployment sent stock prices tumbling. During the three days following the Iraqi invasion, stock prices fell by 7 percent in the United States and by more than 10 percent in Japan.

Again, the Fed faced a cruel dilemma. A tight-money policy to restrain inflation would surely tip the U.S. economy into recession. An easy-money policy to support the economy would guarantee rapid inflation.

Table 22.2	Changes in the Structure of the Labor Market					
	Percent of Labor Force			Unemployment Rate		
	1955	1969	1979	1955	1969	1979
Males (25–64)	55.9	48.9	44.1	2.9	1.7	3.3
Males (16–19)	3.7	4.8	5.0	10.7	11.4	15.8
Females	31.7	37.8	43.2	4.9	4.7	6.8

increase in the expected rate of inflation automatically increases wages in excess-supply labor markets by a full percentage point.

Since employers pass wage increase along as price increases, an anticipated inflation that affects the rate of increase of wages also affects the rate of increase of prices. There consequently may have been more inflation in the 1970s at a 6 percent unemployment rate than in the 1950s or 1960s simply because inflation expectations had increased. As the rate of inflation increased, the economy shifted from a low-inflation-expectations Phillips curve to high-inflation-expectations Phillips curves. By this interpretation, the rate of inflation is, in part, a self-fulfilling prophecy. If people expect a rapid inflation, there will be generous wage increases, which firms then pass along in the higher prices that people expect. If people expect little or no inflation, wage increases will be modest and firms will restrain prices. In the words of Nobel Laureate Robert Solow, "Perhaps it is simply that we have inflation because we expect inflation, and we expect inflation because we've had it."[6]

The Phillips curve depends on inflation expectations.

Credible Policy

Those who emphasize the role of inflation expectation in sustaining a rapid inflation stress the need to reduce inflation expectations. For example, Harvard economics professor Martin Feldstein wrote in 1980[7]

> Since the unemployment cost of reducing inflation depends crucially on the credibility of such a policy, it is important that the government and the Fed remain steadfast now in their determination to fight inflation even as the unemployment rate continues to rise. The perception that the government would accept 8% to 9% unemployment . . . for three to four years in order to eliminate inflation would almost certainly bring inflation down so fast that it would be unnecessary to pay such a high cost.

To establish credibility, government leaders stick out their jaws and talk tough, inwardly hoping that public faith will make tough action unnecessary. In practice, this posturing has not been very successful. It took the Reagan administration, with Martin Feldstein as Chairman of the Council of Economic Advisers, three

A reduction in inflation expectations may reduce inflation.

years of 8-percent to 10-percent unemployment to bring the inflation rate down to a politically acceptable level.

William Fellner was a particularly vigorous advocate of the view that the war against inflation can be won by destroying inflationary expectations.[8] In his view, labor and businesses keep pushing for higher wages and prices because they are convinced that policymakers do not have the stomach for a prolonged recession. Each new administration says that it is willing to pay the recession cost of stopping inflation, but labor and business know that politicians are timid and that an election is always right around the corner. So citizens ignore the recession threat and press for higher wages and prices, confident that inflationary government policies will soon return. People keep their inflation expectations, thereby helping to maintain the inflation they expect.

A more benign interpretation is that citizens became confident that, with the government's help, prolonged recessions would not occur. In the old days, when prosperity seemed temporary and a major recession seemed likely, employees and employers were more timid about raising wages and prices. It is economically dangerous for an employer to agree to an expensive wage contract on the eve of a recession; it is more sensible to insist on modest wage increases and to endure a strike if necessary. It is easier to agree to higher wages and to charge higher prices if there is little danger of economic collapse and the government can be counted on to accommodate inflationary pressures.

Put somewhat differently, modern governments would like to guarantee endless prosperity. An economically secure future encourages businesses to expand and helps voters sleep soundly at night. But unions and businesses have little reason for restraint in setting wages and prices if the government guarantees full employment no matter what they charge. For a credible war on inflation, the government must abandon its commitment to full employment and, indeed, insist that any sign of inflation will bring the punishment of recession.

Fellner argued that, as in every war, the government must be resolute and not show the enemy any signs of weakness. Here, as the comic-strip character Pogo said, "We have met the enemy, and they is us." The government must convince us that, this time, it really means it and that it is we who must surrender by reducing our inflation expectations. Reviewing the credibility record in the 1970s, James Tobin asked[9]

> Isn't this what Arthur Burns [the Chairman of the Fed] has done without spectacular results? Fellner and others would answer, I paraphrase, that the threat has not been credible enough precisely because Keynesian economists and politicians undermine it by advocating accommodation. In similar vein, two Presidents have complained that they could win the war in Southeast Asia if only political opposition at home would cease to impair their credibility to the enemy. The analogy underscores the difficulty of the threat approach in a democracy. In any case, I do not see how, in our decentralized system of wage- and price-setting, there is any incentive for a firm or union or individual worker to be the first to de-escalate. I note also that when Dr. Burns disciplines his class for inflationary offenses, the innocent are punished more than the guilty.

Tax Incentives and Inflation Insurance

Just as high taxes now penalize cigarette and alcohol consumption, so taxes can be used to penalize large wage or price increases. Such a system would discourage, but not rigidly control, inflation. For example, the Wallich-Weintraub Tax-based Incomes Policy (TIP) proposed a penalty tax on any of the roughly 1,000 largest U.S. corporations whose average wage increase exceeded some norm, say 5 percent per year.*

Abba Lerner offered an even more flexible proposal. He suggested that the government establish a market for price increases. Certificates could be printed that give the owner the right to raise wages or prices by some specified amount. The government could auction off these certificates like oil leases. Productive companies that want to pay higher wages will pay for this privilege; businesses that are unwilling to pay this inflation-licensing fee are not allowed to raise their wages. In this way, businesses are given the freedom to pay whatever wages they want, but are forced to pay for their socially undesirable behavior, just as polluters can be required to pay cleanup expenses.

Yet another proposal is for the government to offer real wage insurance. Workers who settle for the modest wage increases that would be appropriate if inflation is low will be compensated (via tax refunds) if inflation turns out to be high. Again, the hope is that inflation can be reduced by persuading people to act as if they expect inflation to be reduced.

———————————

*See Sidney Weintraub, *Capitalism's Inflation and Unemployment Crisis* (Reading, Mass.: Addison-Wesley, 1978).

This persuasion approach to policymaking has had its darker and lighter moments. One unfortunate consequence has been political pressure on administration economists to shade their forecasts — to make unduly optimistic inflation predictions in an attempt to reduce people's inflation expectations: "No one ever sold a used car by admitting that he didn't know if it would work or not." But economists are not salespeople. The false-smile approach to economic policy only undermines the credibility of economists and their political mentors.

Anti-inflation psychology was behind Gerald Ford's distribution of WIN ("Whip Inflation Now") buttons that citizens were to wear to work each day. This was a bizarre application of the advertising-campaign approach to reducing inflation expectations. These buttons are destined to become collector's items, even though the Gerald R. Ford Library is not stockpiling them. It was also proposed that subliminal messages be broadcast during the Super Bowl to convince people that inflation was slowing.

| Highlight 22.3 | **Establishing the Fed's Credibility** |

Arthur Burns was Chairman of the Fed during most of the inflation-filled 1970s. In his public speeches and Congressional testimony, he repeatedly talked of the need to reduce the rate of inflation, often with words unusually passionate for a central banker. In a September 1973 speech at the Minneapolis Federal Reserve Bank, he said that*

> The time will surely come when monetary policy can again be less restrictive, but that time has not yet arrived. . . .
> The principal source of my optimism, however, lies not in these general indicators of progress in dealing with economic and financial problems, but in my faith in our Nation and its good people. Our country has been blessed with rich natural resources and our people have been endowed with the vision and energy to strive for a better life.

He concluded an August 1974 statement to the Joint Economic Committee of Congress with these words.†

> This illustrious Committee has on past occasions provided timely and courageous leadership to the Congress and to the Nation. The opportunity has arisen once again for the Joint Economic Committee to help our country find its way out of the great peril posed by raging inflation. Our people are weary, and they are anxiously awaiting positive and persuasive steps by their government to arrest inflation and to restore general price stability. The Federal Reserve pledges to you its full cooperation in your search for ways to restore a stable and lasting prosperity.

Some thought that the Fed was more talk than action. Burns often spoke of the need to maintain or restore prosperity and of the role fiscal policy could play in slowing inflation, suggesting less than an all-out commitment by the Fed to reduce the rate of inflation. There was also evidence, mentioned in Chapters 16 and 18, that the Fed was susceptible to political pressure, particularly before presidential elections. Workers, businesses, and financial analysts were not convinced of the Fed's willingness to endure a long, severe recession to stop inflation.

In March 1978, Jimmy Carter appointed G. William Miller, a businessman, to replace Arthur Burns as Fed Chair. By the summer of 1979, the rate of inflation had reached double digits and the value of the U.S. dollar had fallen to new lows. Miller was perceived by many to be insuf-

*Arthur F. Burns, "Objectives and Responsibilities of the Federal Reserve System," September 8, 1973 speech, *Federal Reserve Bulletin*, September 1973, pp. 655–657.

†Arthur F. Burns, statement before the Joint Economic Committee, August 6, 1974; reprinted in *Federal Reserve Bulletin*, August 1974, pp. 561–567.

ficiently independent of the administration and Congress and, perhaps worse, too indecisive.

In August 1979, with financial markets in disarray, Carter replaced Miller with Paul Volcker, the widely known and respected president of the New York Federal Reserve Bank. Two months later, Volcker established a take-no-prisoners approach. Over and over, he said that the Fed would do whatever was necessary to stop inflation — warning that those who were betting on inflation in their wage agreements and investment strategies would lose their bets.

And he meant what he said. Volcker stuck to his anti-inflation objectives during the 1980 presidential election, despite bitter complaints and severe pressure from the Carter administration. He was unmoved by three years of protests, lectures, and scolding by congressional committees. Volcker stayed the course until October 1982. The rate of inflation finally dropped below 4 percent, while the unemployment rate reached double digits, the highest level since the Great Depression, and there were genuine fears that the economy was on the brink of financial collapse. Only then did the Fed relax its grip.

Tests of Volcker's credibility occurred in 1982, 1983, 1985, and 1986, when M1 grew rapidly. Monetarists warned of imminent inflation. Volcker observed the unanticipated declines in M1 velocity and concluded that inflation was not a threat. Most importantly, the public had learned from the 1979–1982 experience that Volcker would not hesitate to apply the monetary brakes — as long and as hard as necessary — if the rate of inflation did begin increasing. Financial markets shrugged off the rapid growth of M1 because Volcker had established the credibility of the Fed's commitment to restrain inflation.

Alan Greenspan replaced Volcker as Fed Chair in August 1987. Any questions about his competence were quickly answered by his deft handling of the October 1987 stock-market crash. His reputation grew during the next two years as the Fed's eclectic approach guided the economy between the shoals of inflation and recession. When Greenspan appeared before congressional banking committees in 1990, there were mostly empty chairs and perfunctory questions, the Chairman of the Senate Banking Committee explaining that "The job is in the best possible hands."‡

---

‡Tom Redburn, "How Times Have Changed: Fed Chief off the Hot Seat," *Los Angeles Times,* February 23, 1990.

The Natural Rate of Unemployment

Figure 22.10 shows three short-term Phillips curves, each for a different anticipated rate of inflation, and a long-run Phillips curve for which wages and prices have adjusted to eliminate market disequilibria and the expected rate of inflation is equal to the actual rate of inflation. This long-run Phillips curve assumes that in a long-run market equilibrium, a 1-percent increase in the expected rate of inflation increases the actual rate of inflation by 1 percent.

The long-run Phillips curve is vertical.

Look at the short-run Phillips curve for a 5-percent expected rate of inflation. When the economy is to the left of the long-run Phillips curve, at Point 1 for instance, the actual rate of inflation is higher than the 5-percent expected rate of inflation. Inflation expectations will increase, to correspond more accurately with actual inflation, moving the economy towards the short-run Phillips curve with a 10-percent expected rate of inflation, and closer to the long-run Phillips curve where the actual and expected rates of inflation are equal. When, on the other hand, the economy is to the right of the long-run Phillips curve, the actual rate of inflation is lower than the expected rate; inflation expectations decline and the economy moves leftward towards the long-run Phillips curve.

This model is consistent with U.S. historical experience. The data from the 1950s and 1960s shown in Figure 22.8 provide estimates of a short-run Phillips curve appropriate for low-inflation expectations. When the unemployment rate fell in the 1960s, the economy temporarily moved along this short-run, low-inflation-expectations curve. But as inflation expectations increased in the 1970s in line with actual inflation, the economy shifted to higher and higher Phillips curves. There was more inflation as people came to expect that there would be more inflation.

A decline in unemployment may cause more inflation in the long run than in the short run.

The same mechanism works in reverse. When the economy is thrown into a recession, it moves down a short-run Phillips curve if inflation expectations remain high. For example, the economy might slide down the curve in Figure 22.10 with a 10-percent expected rate of inflation. Large increases in unemployment initially cause relatively small decreases in inflation, but as inflation expectations decline, the economy moves to lower Phillips curves, such as those with 5 percent and then 0-percent expected rates of inflation. There is less inflation because people expect less inflation. In sum, in booms, a given decline in unemployment brings more inflation in the long run than in the short run, as people become accustomed to the inflation and integrate it into their wage agreements. In recessions, a given increase in unemployment reduces inflation more in the long run than in the short run as people revise their inflation expectations downward.

Most economists believe that there is no long-run tradeoff between unemployment and inflation. In the long run, all unemployment is voluntary and unaffected by prices. This is the classical paradigm in which wages and prices adjust to equate labor demand and supply. An increase in the anticipated rate of inflation simply raises the rate of increase of wages, percentage point for percentage point, and has no effect on real wages. There is only one level of

Figure 22.10   Short-Run and Long-Run Phillips Curves

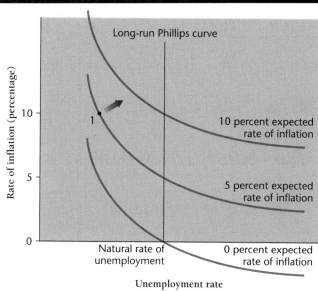

The long-run Phillips curve intersects the axis at the natural rate of unemployment.

unemployment — where the long-run Phillips curve intersects the axis — that is consistent with long-run equilibrium. Milton Friedman called this unique, presumably frictional, unemployment rate the **natural rate of unemployment.**

There is substantial disagreement about whether short-run departures from the long-run full-employment equilibrium reflect misjudgments about prices or the sluggish adjustment of wages and prices. By the new-classical interpretation (previously discussed in Chapters 16 and 21), monetary and fiscal policies can reduce unemployment below the natural rate only by creating an unanticipated inflation. When workers do not realize that real wages are being eroded by inflation, the labor supply expands, real wages fall, and astute firms expand employment. When these new employees realize how much prices have increased and how their real wages have fallen, they return to their voluntary unemployment. Similarly, economic events that reduce inflation more than workers realize cause temporary voluntary recessions as workers leave their jobs, erroneously believing that real wages are too low to make work worthwhile. Thus, by the new classical interpretation, variations in unemployment about the natural rate are the voluntary consequences of misestimates of inflation. If workers have rational expectations, then monetary and fiscal policies with foreseen consequences do not cause inflation mistakes and consequently do not affect employment or output, even in the short run.

Keynesian economists, in contrast, argue that fluctuations in employment and unemployment are not just voluntary responses to price misperceptions. Sluggish wages and prices can cause market disequilibria, including involuntary unemployment. Fluctuations in unemployment affect the rate of inflation, and these effects are larger to the extent that the inflation is anticipated.

These are two quite different interpretations of short-run Phillips curves. In the first, it is unanticipated inflation that causes voluntary fluctuations in unemployment; in the second, it is changes in involuntary unemployment that cause fluctuations in inflation. The way to distinguish between these two interpretations is to ask whether unemployment can be affected by a change in aggregate demand whose inflationary consequences are anticipated correctly. The new-classical answer is "no"; the Keynesian answer is "yes."

There is disagreement about whether low unemployment causes rapid inflation, or vice versa.

THE CONSEQUENCES OF INFLATION

Inflation has long been viewed as a disease, causing the decay of a society and exposing the weakness of its government. In 1812, Madame de Staël wrote of how inflation in Austria during Napoleon's rule had quickly corrupted the Austrians.[10]

> I no longer found the same honesty in the people that had struck me four years earlier; paper money stimulates the imagination with hopes of rapid and easy gain, and the hazards of chance upset the steady, even flow of existence, the basis for honesty in the common people. During my stay in Austria a man was hanged for forging counterfeit money just after the old notes had been replaced; on his way to the gallows he cried out that it was not he who had stolen but the state.

Many think that inflation reduces everyone's real income.

In the 1970s and 1980s, politicians repeatedly told U.S. voters that inflation is "public enemy number one" and "the cruelest tax of all," that it arbitrarily and capriciously robs us while we sleep. In the 1980 election campaign against President Jimmy Carter, Ronald Reagan repeatedly asked voters, "Are you better off now than you were four years ago?" Most people apparently answered with a resounding "No!"; otherwise, he wouldn't have kept asking. Yet, the economic statistics indicate that, in economic terms at least, most people really were better off. During Jimmy Carter's four years as president, real per capita GNP increased 10 percent; real per capita after-tax income increased 8 percent; and real per capita consumption increased 9 percent.

More generally, the 1970s are widely believed to have been near-disastrous economically, with rampant inflation steadily reducing everyone's standard of living. The 1970s were not uninterrupted prosperity by any means — recessions repeatedly reduced output below its full-employment potential — but neither were they one long downhill slide. Even when inflation and population growth are taken into account, as Table 22.3 shows, real per capita output, income, and consumption all increased in the 1970s — in fact, almost as much as in the 1960s and much more than in the good, old, low-inflation 1950s. The fraction of the population below the poverty level fell from 12.6 percent in 1970 to 11.7 percent in 1979. For the elderly, thought to be especially vulnerable to inflation, the poverty rate fell from 24.6 percent in 1970 to 15.2 percent in 1979. No matter how we look at it, inflation did not impoverish us.

Table 22.3	Percentage Growth in Three Real Per Capita Measures of Economic Well-Being		
	Gross National Product	After-Tax Income	Consumption
1950–1959	15.1	12.7	11.3
1960–1969	31.5	31.6	29.7
1970–1979	26.9	25.0	28.6

What accounts for this substantial gap between perception and experience? One plausible explanation is the asymmetrical interpretation of income and price increases. An increase in income is typically viewed as a just reward for hard labor and meritorious accomplishment; an increase in prices, on the other hand, is perceived as unfair and reprehensible. If income and prices increase proportionately, there is no change in real income, but people in this situation often feel that they have lost something, that the increase in prices has taken away what is rightfully theirs.

When income and prices go up together, people may feel that they are having to struggle to keep their income rising as fast as prices — that they must earn more income to offset the higher prices, wearing themselves out trying to swim upstream. In fact, it may be the higher prices that enable them to earn higher income; or, put somewhat differently, it may be their higher wages that are causing the higher prices. Money illusion, in which people concentrate on their nominal incomes and ignore prices, seems to have given way to inflation illusion, in which people watch prices and do not pay enough attention to their incomes.

Inflation's Winners and Losers

According to a widely held belief, an increase in prices automatically reduces everyone's standard of living. This is not true; a price increase does raise the cost to buyers, but it also increases the income of sellers. One person's higher price is another's higher income. A price increase does not mysteriously obliterate a nation's resources; it only transfers more dollars from buyers to sellers. And we are all both buyers and sellers. We buy commodities and sell our labor to firms which, in turn, pay us wages out of the revenue they receive from selling commodities. Were all wages and prices increased by the same amount — say 10 percent — real incomes would be unchanged.

In practice, wages and prices do not all change equally.[11] Within every inflation, some prices increase much more than others. As a result, some people gain while others lose. For example, in 1973, the Consumer Price Index rose 8.8 percent, but farm income increased 31 percent. This relative increase in farm prices transferred income to farmers from the rest of the nation. The tremendous increase in oil prices in 1973–1974 and 1979–1980 similarly transferred

Inflation does not reduce everyone's real income, but may create winners and losers.

hundreds of billions of dollars out of the United States to oil-exporting nations. In 1981, the United States imported almost $100 billion of oil, about $1,500 per household. Many of the complaints about inflation in the 1970's were misdirected. The pain many felt was not due to inflation, but to relative price shifts in favor of farmers and oil owners.

Inflation does reduce the real value of financial assets denominated in dollars. George borrows $100 from Mary, and agrees to pay her $105 a year later. As prices rise, that $105 is worth less and less to Mary. Suppose that she was planning to spend the $105 on wine now selling for $5 a bottle. At $5 a bottle, the real value of George's IOU is 21 bottles of wine. If the price of wine rises 5 percent, to $5.25 a bottle, the $105 IOU is worth only 20 bottles; the 5-percent inflation has reduced Mary's wealth by one bottle of wine.

Where did that bottle go? It didn't disappear. There was simply a transfer of wealth from Mary to George. Mary's loss was George's gain. He had a debt of $105, which was the equivalent of 21 bottles of wine. When prices increased 5 percent, his real debt dropped by 5 percent. The real burden of his debt decreased by the amount that Mary's wealth decreased.

Price increases hurt creditors and help debtors.

This is what always happens. Increases in prices hurt creditors and help debtors. Conversely, deflations help creditors and hurt debtors. In 1810, David Ricardo wrote[12]

> *The depreciation of the circulating medium has been more injurious to moneyed men. . . . It may be laid down as a principle of universal application, that every man is injured or benefited by the variation of the value of the circulating medium in proportion as his property consists of money, or as the fixed demands on him in money exceed those fixed demands which he may have on others. . . . [The farmer] more than any other class of the community is benefited by the depreciation of money, and injured by the increase in its value.*

Ricardo's moneyed men, with sizable financial assets, are hurt by inflation and resist it. Farmers, owning land that appreciates with inflation, have traditionally favored inflationary government policies that will allow them to repay their large debts with less valuable currency. When there was inflation during the Civil War, William McCormick wrote to his brother in England of reports that "creditors were seen running away from their debtors and their debtors pursued them in triumph and paid them without mercy."

When William Jennings Bryan campaigned against the gold standard in 1896, he was appealing for inflationary policies that would make it easier for farmers to pay off their mortgages. In the 1930s, Franklin Roosevelt promised inflation for similar reasons. In an October 22, 1933, radio speech that was printed on the front page of the *New York Times* the next day, he said

> *Finally, I repeat what I have said on many occasions, that ever since last March the definite policy of the government has been to restore commodity price-levels. . . . The object has been to make possible the payment of public and private debts more nearly at the price-level at which they were incurred.*

Here was a shrewd and successful politician promising inflation!

For the conservatively moneyed families who owned safe bonds, the Great Depression was only a rumor. The deflation of the 1930s just made them richer. Many wisely used their cash to buy depressed land, especially property with foreclosed mortgages. In the 1970s the reverse was true. Homeowners who had borrowed at single-digit interest rates to buy houses appreciating at double-digit rates profited handsomely from inflation. This time, the people with their money conservatively invested in bonds were the losers. As with wages and prices, there is often an asymmetrical interpretation of this transfer. Those who profit from an inflation (or deflation) credit their financial expertise; those who lose, blame the inflation. In most cases, it would be more accurate to say that some were lucky, and others unlucky.

Inflation Expectations and Nominal Interest Rates

In the earlier example, Mary agreed to a 5-percent nominal rate, which a 5-percent inflation reduced to a 0-percent real return (measured in bottles of wine). If wine prices instead increase by 10 percent, her real return is −5 percent: She lends $100 (which could have been used to purchase 20 bottles of wine) and gets back $105 (which can buy only approximately 19 bottles).

If Mary anticipates a 10-percent inflation, she won't be enthusiastic about lending money at a 5-percent nominal interest rate, since she could instead buy 20 bottles of wine and keep them for a year, for a 0-percent real return. That's not much, but it's better than lending money at 5 percent while wine prices go up 10 percent. If George wants to borrow money from Mary, he will have to offer her at least a 10-percent nominal return. Otherwise, she will stockpile wine instead of lending him money. If a 20-percent inflation is anticipated, he will have to offer at least a 20-percent interest rate. And with prices rising so rapidly, he may well be willing to pay such high interest rates.

In general, the nominal interest rates people agree to take into account the expected inflation rate, with a higher expected rate of inflation tending to increase nominal interest rates. We saw in Chapter 5, however, that there is not a simple, fixed relationship between the expected rate of inflation and nominal interest rates. An increase in the expected rate of inflation does not, for example, automatically raise nominal interest rates by an equal amount, leaving real interest rates constant. Later in this chapter, we will use our macro model to see how real interest rates are affected by inflation expectations.

> Nominal interest rates are affected by inflation.

Other Inflation Transfers

In addition to financial assets, a wide variety of contracts and legal regulations are stated in nominal terms, with real values and costs that are altered by inflation. Among these are taxes, fines, pensions, leases, alimony, and child-support payments. In each case, inflation reduces both the burden on the payer and the benefit to the payee.

Highlight 22.4   Inflation Affects Taxes

Because the tax code is not indexed to the price level, inflation alters the real burden of taxes. For example, taxes are levied on nominal rather than real interest income. If you invest $100 when there is no inflation and receive a 3-percent return, you pay a tax on this $3 in interest income — a $1 tax in a 33-percent tax bracket. Your real after-tax return is 2 percent. Now, suppose that a 9-percent inflation raises the nominal interest rate to 12 percent, keeping the real before-tax return at 3 percent. You must pay a tax on the entire $12 in interest income, even though $9 of this income was intended merely to offset the effect of inflation on the real value of your $100. In a 33-percent tax bracket, you pay a $4 tax, keeping $8 — not enough to offset the 9-percent inflation. Your real after-tax rate of return is −1 percent!

Similarly, capital gains due to inflation are taxed even though there may have been no change in the real value of the assets. If you buy a piece of land for $100,000 (use your imagination) and all prices double, you will be no better or worse off. But if you sell the land at the doubled price — $200,000 — you must pay a tax on the $100,000 nominal capital gain.

Taxable corporate profits are typically overstated during inflationary periods, because generally accepted accounting procedures cause production costs to be understated. In profit calculations, the cost of a machine that can be used for ten years is spread over the ten years, with the annual depreciation expense intended to show how much capital is being used to produce output. In theory, the firm should use the current value of its capital — what it would cost to replace the machine. But, in practice, firms calculate their capital expenses each year on the basis of the original cost of plants and equipment, which is like figuring labor costs on the basis of wage rates ten or twenty years ago. The result is that inflation causes capital costs to be understated, profits to be overstated, and businesses with lots of old capital to pay relatively more taxes.

Firms also overstate their profits during inflations if they use FIFO (First In, First Out) inventory accounting. Businesses keep an inventory of unsold items that, though identical, were produced at different times and at different costs. When one of these items is sold, which cost should be used in figuring profits? With the FIFO accounting method, the cost of the good produced earliest and still in inventory is used. During inflations, FIFO accounting understates current production costs and overstates profits. The U.S. government estimated that reported corporate profits would have been $50 billion lower in 1979 if all firms had been using LIFO (Last In, First Out) accounting.

On the other hand, to the extent that firms borrow money, they, along with other debtors, benefit from inflation. A fully indexed tax code would include these gains as income and would also index capital costs. The net effects of an indexed tax system on an individual firm depend on its debt and capital. John Shoven and Jeremy Bulow estimated that, with a full inflation adjustment for depreciation, inventories, and debt, General Motors' 1974 taxable income would have been only $410 million, rather than the reported $950 million. This is because General Motors has little debt. For AT&T, which has lots of debt, they estimated that taxable income would have increased from $3.2 billion to $8.2 billion. Inflation with unindexed taxes hurt General Motors shareholders, but benefited AT&T shareholders.

Perhaps the most important cost of inflation is that, because it is often unexpected, it capriciously creates winners and losers. It is not that prices increase, but rather that they change (up or down) unexpectedly. Agreements that seem satisfactory turn into bad deals, with the winners celebrating their foresight while the losers damn the price changes. These haphazard, indiscriminate wealth transfers undermine the social fabric and encourage the belief that society is unfair. Instead of working and consuming, citizens turn their attention to speculation on the course of prices and to bitterness over bad guesses.

Keynes was well aware of this social cost of fluctuating prices. In the 1930s, it was deflation that worried Keynes. Years earlier, after World War I, he had warned against inflation for similar reasons.[13]

The sight of this arbitrary rearrangement of riches strikes not only at security, but at confidence in the equity of the existing distribution of wealth. Those to whom the system brings windfalls, beyond their deserts and even beyond their expectations or desires, become "profiteers," who are the object of the hatred of the bourgeoisie, whom the inflation has impoverished, not less than of the proletariat. As the inflation proceeds and the real value of the currency fluctuates wildly from month to month, all permanent relations between debtors and creditors, which form the ultimate foundation of capitalism, become so utterly disordered as to be almost meaningless; and the process of wealth-getting degenerates into a gamble and a lottery.

Lenin was certainly right. There is no subtler, no surer means of overturning the existing basis of society than to debauch the currency. The process engages all the hidden forces of economic law on the side of destruction, and does it in a manner which not one man in a million is able to diagnose.

Shoe-Leather Costs

Even if all contracts in an economy were indexed, there would still be one asset that loses value in an inflation: currency. When prices are rising rapidly, the one thing you certainly don't want to be hoarding is dollars. Instead, you want to hold financial or real assets that are appreciating in value.

In the 1922–23 German hyperinflation, workers were paid several times a day. Their children would bike to the factory gates to collect these wages and then pedal furiously back to town to spend the money as quickly as possible. When the United States experienced double-digit inflation and double-digit interest rates, many people spent many hours trying to minimize the length of time they were caught holding idle cash, either at home, at their businesses, or in their checking accounts. They made daily trips to banks, shuffling funds back and forth. Businesses put billions of dollars into overnight and even hourly loans.

This hectic cash management is one consequence of inflation that is not just a transfer, but a social cost. Citizens devote precious time and energy to economizing on their cash holdings, investing temporarily in interest-earning assets and rushing to buy commodities before prices go up. This scurrying about consumes time, energy, and shoe leather, so it is known as the shoe-leather cost of inflation.

Inflation encourages hectic cash management.

Most economists believe that shoe-leather costs during moderate inflations can hardly be large enough to merit newspaper headlines and political upheaval. Tobin put it this way:[14]

> *According to economic theory, the ultimate social cost of anticipated inflation is the wasteful use of resources to economize holdings of currency and other non-interest-bearing means of payments. I suspect that intelligent laymen would be utterly astounded if they realized that this is the great evil economists are talking about. They have imagined a much more devastating cataclysm, with Vesuvius vengefully punishing the sinners below. Extra trips between savings banks and commercial banks? What an anti-climax!*

MACROECONOMIC EFFECTS OF INFLATION

There are macro as well as micro consequences of the money avoidance caused by inflation. An increase in the expected rate of inflation makes financial assets less attractive and real assets more attractive, and thus may cause an increase in the interest rates on financial assets. Inflation-induced expenditures on real assets raise aggregate demand and prices, too. Can an increase in inflation expectations be a self-fulfilling prophecy? We will use our macro model to examine the effect of inflation expectations on interest rates and prices.

Inflation in the *IS-LM* Model

Since the nominal rate of return on money is zero, the difference between the yield on bonds and the yield on money is the nominal interest rate R. The demand for money is inversely related to R, since an increase in R makes money less attractive relative to alternative assets. Consumption expenditures depend on the real interest rate — the nominal interest rate less the rate of inflation —

Repressed Inflation in the Soviet Union	**Highlight 22.5**

In 1989, U.S. politicians and citizens were alarmed by a federal budget deficit that was equal to three percent of gross national product (GNP). That same year, the government of the Soviet Union had a budget deficit that amounted to more than 10 percent of its GNP. The Soviet deficit was aggravated by the payment of large worker-incentive bonuses and by an anti-alcoholism campaign that drastically reduced tax revenue from vodka sales because production shifted from authorized government stores to private stills.*

Almost all of the U.S. budget deficit was financed by the sale of Treasury bonds. In the Soviet Union, an ideological opposition to high interest rates prevented the Soviet government from offering bonds that investors — at home or abroad — would want to buy; instead, the Soviet deficit was financed by an enormous increase in the money supply.

Unable to acquire private property, either directly or through stock, and unwilling to buy low-interest bonds, a Soviet citizen's most attractive investment is generally state-subsidized consumer goods. And this is where they have invested, waiting in lines for hours for an opportunity to stockpile goods — even unpalatable food, unreliable televisions, and shoes that are the wrong size (that they hope to barter for something useful).

Soviet president Mikhail Gorbachev's chief economic adviser has a sign on his desk quoting Lenin: "Inflation is the greatest danger to communism." The Soviets' ruble-financed deficits should have led to inflation, but with prices controlled by the government, there was instead repressed inflation — stable prices and acute shortages, with store shelves stripped virtually bare soon after deliveries are received. In 1990, there was a 400-billion ruble overhang — money that Soviet citizens held, not for carrying out day-to-day transactions, but simply because they had nothing better to do with these rubles.

The situation was exacerbated in the spring of 1990 when Gorbachev announced that as part of efforts to decontrol the economy, bread prices would double on July 1, 1990, and that other food prices would be increased sharply six months later. Overall, Gorbachev announced that 60 percent of all food products would have their prices doubled, 25 percent would have their prices increased by lesser amounts, and 15 percent would be decontrolled. To ease the burden on consumers, an elaborate set of special payments to the young and the poor was established (for example, an extra 30 to 39 rubles a month to children, an additional 35 rubles to students) that increased the government's deficit and printing of rubles even more.

*Many of the details in this example are from Michael D. Intriligator, "Problems of Economic Reform in the Soviet Union," April 1990.

The announcement of impending price increases sparked panic buying by Soviet citizens holding soon-to-be depreciated rubles. Sales of basic food-stuffs — flour, macaroni, and cereals — increased by a factor of six to eight, and would have been even higher had more been available.† Every store in Leningrad was completely emptied of these basic foods. Trucks carrying supplies were mobbed by customers before they could unload. Stores even sold out of perishable produce (that citizens hoped to freeze) and the shoddiest-made, least-popular consumer goods (that people hoped to barter). Even questionable products seemed a better investment than a currency that was certain soon to lose half of its value.

†Michael Parks, "Rising Costs Spark Soviet Buying Spree," *Wall Street Journal,* May 26, 1990.

since this measures how many future commodities can be gained by consuming less and saving more. Investment decisions also hinge on real interest rates, since firms compare the real rates of return on physical capital with the real yields on financial assets and with the real interest rates on loans to finance expansion.

Money demand depends on nominal interest rates; spending depends on real interest rates.

Thus the demand for money that underlies the *LM* curve depends on nominal interest rates, while the spending decisions that underlie the *IS* curve depend on real interest rates. We will draw the *IS-LM* curves with the nominal interest rate on the vertical axis, as in Figure 22.11. For any given nominal interest rate, an increase in the expected rate of inflation reduces the real interest rate, increasing expenditures on real assets, shifting the *IS* curve rightward to an intersection with the *LM* curve at Point 1. (In fact, the magnitude of the vertical shift of the *IS* curve is just equal to the change in inflation expectations.)

This spending stimulus increases aggregate demand, as shown in Figure 22.12, putting upward pressure on output and the price level. The higher price level pushes the *LM* curve leftward (Figure 22.11), until it intersects the *IS* curve at Point 2, where *P* and *y* are both higher. If the aggregate supply curve is not vertical, then the increase in the nominal interest rate (comparing Point 2 with the initial position) must be less than the initial vertical shift of the *IS* curve. Therefore, the nominal interest rate does not increase by as much as inflation expectations, and the real interest rate declines. Overall, an increase in inflation expectations increases nominal interest rates while reducing real interest rates. Lower real interest rates stimulate spending so that output, employment, and prices all increase.

The classical, full-employment model comes to a different conclusion, as shown in Figures 22.13 and 22.14. If the aggregate supply curve is vertical, with output fixed at the full-employment level, then a rightward shift in the *IS* curve to Point 1 must cause an equal leftward shift in the *LM* curve to Point 2, so that the *IS* and *LM* curves intersect at the initial level of output. The increase in the

Figure 22.11 An Increase in the Expected Rate of Inflation Shifts the IS Curve Upward, Leading to an Increase in the Price Level and a Leftward Shift of the LM Curve

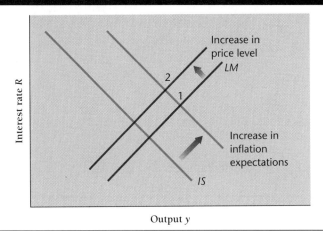

nominal interest rate is equal to the vertical shift of the *IS* curve, which is equal to the increase in inflation expectations. Thus the real interest rate is unchanged. In the classical full-employment model, the nominal rate of interest increases by the amount of the increase in inflation expectations. Inflation expectations do not affect output, employment, or real interest rates.

Money and Interest Rates

These results allow us to distinguish the effects of monetary policy on nominal and real interest rates. In Chapter 20, the *IS-LM* model indicated that an increase in the money supply lowers interest rates and increases output. Yet some observers believe that an increase in the money supply actually raises interest rates! Inflation expectations provide an answer to this puzzle.

Figure 22.15 shows that an increase in the money supply shifts the *LM* curve rightward, to an intersection at Point 1. If inflation expectations increase, then the accompanying drop in anticipated real interest rates increases spending, shifting the *IS* curve rightward to an *IS-LM* intersection at Point 2.

The increase in inflation expectations reinforces the expansionary monetary policy. If the aggregate supply curve is not vertical, then output and prices both increase. The price increase shifts the *LM* curve back to Point 3, where output, employment, and prices are all higher. The real interest rate has fallen.

We cannot be certain whether the nominal interest rate goes up or down. It depends on whether the drop in the real interest rate is smaller or larger than the increase in inflation expectations. What we can say is that, if an increase in

**Figure 22.12   The Effect of Increased Inflation
Expectations on Prices and Output**

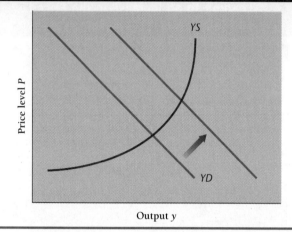

**Figure 22.13   If the Aggregate Supply Curve Is
Vertical, an Increase in the Expected Rate
of Inflation Must Be Fully Offset by an
Increase in the Price Level**

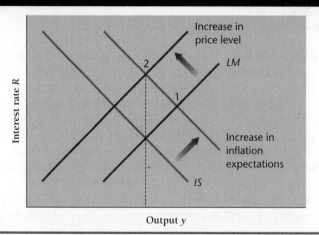

Figure 22.14 **The Effect of Increased Inflation Expectations on Prices and Output If the Aggregate Supply Curve Is Vertical**

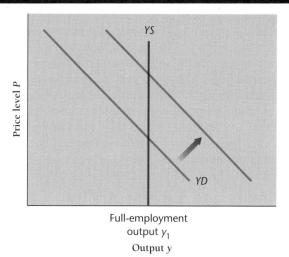

Full-employment output y_1

Output y

Figure 22.15 **An Increase in the Expected Rate of Inflation Shifts the IS Curve Upward, Leading to an Increase in the Price Level and a Leftward Shift of the LM Curve**

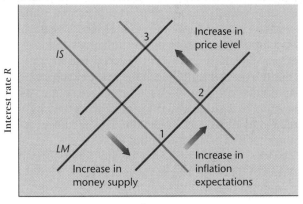

Output y

the money supply increases inflation expectations (reducing real yields), then the resultant stimulus to spending reinforces the expansionary effects of the increase in the money supply. Prices increase; nominal interest rates may increase; real interest rates decline; and real output increases.

An increase in the money supply may increase nominal interest rates and reduce real interest rates.

The conclusion is different if there is full employment. In Chapter 21, we saw that, in the classical model, an open-market purchase raises prices with no effect on output or interest rates. In the previous section of this chapter, we noted that, in the classical model, any increase in inflation expectations raises nominal interest rates but does not change real interest rates or output. Therefore, in a classical, full-employment model, the monetary authorities can alter the price level, the rate of inflation, and nominal interest rates, but cannot affect real output and real interest rates. Attempts to reduce real interest rates by increasing the money supply are futile: inflation increases, nominal interest rates increase, and real interest rates are unchanged.

Money Neutrality and Superneutrality

Money may be neutral, but not superneutral.

There are two separate classical propositions here — one regarding the price level and the other the rate of inflation. The first proposition, **money neutrality**, is that a one-time increase in the money supply will raise the price level proportionately, with no real effects on the economy. The second proposition, **money superneutrality**, is that a continuing increase in the money supply will cause a sustained inflation, with no real effects on economic activity. Neither of these classical propositions holds if there is less than full employment. And it is not certain that they would hold even in a long-run full-employment equilibrium.

James Tobin has pointed out that money could be neutral in the long run, but not superneutral. His basic argument is that, since cash has a fixed nominal rate of return (zero), which cannot rise with inflation, anticipated inflation encourages people to hold less cash and more of other assets, financial and real, whose nominal returns do increase during inflations. People trying to avoid holding cash during inflations will accept reduced real rates of return on alternative assets. Thus the inevitable decline in the real yield on cash during inflations causes a similar decline in the real yields on all substitute assets. Diminished real interest rates, in turn, have real effects on the economy, encouraging investment spending and capital accumulation. This argument is so closely associated with Tobin that it is called the **Tobin effect.**

Real interest rates tend to rise during deflation and fall during inflation.

We have already seen some evidence of the Tobin effect in the decline of real yields on Treasury bills during the inflationary 1970s (Figure 5.4). A more comprehensive study of nearly 200 years of U.S. data on interest rates, during both inflations and deflations, came to the same conclusion.[15] As shown in Figure 22.16, nominal interest rates tend to rise somewhat during inflation (but not as much as inflation increases) and to rise during deflations, too! Real interest rates fall during inflation (when money is unattractive) and rise during deflations (when money is attractive).

An example of the latter occurred during the Great Depression. Remember that the classical cure for a slump is lower prices, which should raise aggregate

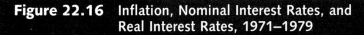

Figure 22.16 Inflation, Nominal Interest Rates, and Real Interest Rates, 1971–1979

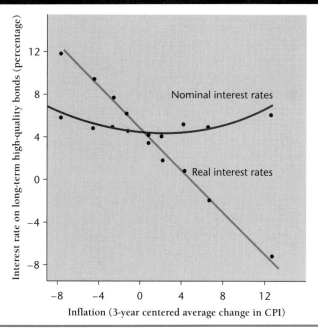

demand. However, an anticipated deflation raises real interest rates, encouraging people to hoard cash and postpone spending. With a 1.5 percent interest rate for prime business loans, the 2 percent deflation in 1933, as modest as it was, raised the real interest rate on prime loans to a discouraging 3.5 percent. A faster deflation in the 1930s would have made real rates even higher and discouraged spending even more. With a 10 percent deflation, for instance, even cash has a 10 percent real return. Why buy commodities whose prices are declining by 10 percent, when you can hold cash instead?

SUMMARY

Inflation is a continuing increase in the price level. In a classical model (with full employment and the simple quantity theory), the level of the money supply determines the price level and the rate of growth of the money supply determines the rate of inflation. The rate of inflation is equal to the rate of growth of the money supply plus the rate of growth of velocity minus the rate of growth of full-employment output, and the last two are assumed to be predetermined. To cure inflation, the monetary authorities need only keep the rate of growth of the money supply in line with output and velocity growth. The cure is relatively painless, since output stays at the full-employment level.

Highlight 22.6	**Hyperinflation**

Figures 22.11 and 22.12 showed that an increase in inflation expectations raises aggregate demand, the opposite of the effects of an increase in the price level, which reduces aggregate demand by reducing the real money supply. This is an example of why it is important to distinguish between the price level and the rate of inflation.

This inflation-expectations effect suggests that there is the potential for an unstable inflationary spiral. As in Figure 22.12, an increase in inflation expectations puts upward pressure on prices. If prices increase rapidly, inflation expectations may rise further, causing additional price increases. This chase could degenerate into a vicious self-fulfilling cycle. Is hyperinflation around the corner? In the past, hyperinflations have been rare but very destructive, destroying confidence in government and wasting the energy (and shoe leather) of citizens trying to avoid holding money. For example, after World War I, the victorious Allies demanded large reparation payments from Germany. In January 1923, French and Belgian troops, on the claim that Germany was behind in its payments, occupied the Ruhr district. The German government called a general strike and printed hundreds of billions of marks to pay the strikers. Jonas Prager tells what happened.*

> Between May and June 1923, consumer prices more than quadrupled; between July and August, they rose more than 15 times; in the next month over 15 times, and between September and October, by ten times the previous month's increase.
>
> The German economy was thoroughly disrupted. Businessmen soon discovered the impossibility of rational economic planning. Profits fell as employees demanded frequent wage adjustments. Workers were often paid daily and sometimes two or three times a day, so that they could buy goods in the morning before the inevitable afternoon price increase. The work ethic suffered; wage earners were both more reluctant to work and less devoted to their jobs. Bankers were on the phone hour after hour, quoting the value of the mark in dollars, as calls continuously came in from merchants who needed the exchange rate to adjust their mark prices.
>
> In an age that preceded the credit card, businessmen traveling around the country found themselves borrowing funds from their customers each stage of the way. The cash they'd allocated for the entire trip barely sufficed to pay the way to the next stop. Speculation began to dominate production.

In late 1923, the hyperinflation was ended with dramatic suddenness. The old currency, reichsmarks, was replaced by rentenmarks. One renten-

---

*Wall Street Journal, letter to the editor, May 12, 1980.

mark was worth a trillion reichsmarks. The government announced that rentenmarks were sound money, backed by first mortgages on the land and other physical assets of the nation. This was a meaningless public-relations ploy; what was important was that reparations, strike payments, and business loans ended, and the government printing presses stopped.

However, the memories lingered. A generation of eminent German and Austrian economists were permanently scarred by these hyperinflations. Even after emigration to America, they retained a lifelong distrust of government and a commitment to sound money.

Inflation in the long run is a largely monetary phenomenon in that a sustained monetary growth that causes aggregate demand to grow faster than full-employment output will almost certainly cause inflation. Conversely, long-run inflation without money growth will be limited by a persistent tendency of money demand to outstrip supply.

There is only a loose relationship between money and inflation in the short run because both output and velocity can vary considerably from year to year. The price level is determined by aggregate demand and supply. It is not important how much of this aggregate demand is attributable to government monetary policy, fiscal policy, or various facets of private behavior. Short-term inflation reflects both current events and the working out of old disequilibria.

In many markets, prices are set by regulatory authorities or according to rules of thumb based on production costs, so as to yield a reasonable profit at normal production levels. Costs consequently give a preview of prices. Some costs, particularly for raw materials, are very sensitive to demand and supply. Other costs, particularly wages, do not respond immediately to demand and supply.

Although rough and approximate, the unemployment rate can be used to gauge the overall tightness of labor markets. Wages hardly ever fall, even if there is lots of unemployment, but wage increases do tend to be smaller when the unemployment rate is high. Since wage increases cause firms that set prices by mark-ups to raise prices, there is an inverse relationship, known as the Phillips curve, between unemployment and the rate of inflation. According to this logic, inflation can be cured by contractionary monetary and fiscal policies.

Many years of economic slack after 1974 did not reduce inflation. One explanation is based on nonlabor costs, including rising energy prices; a second is the large increase in the number of relatively inexperienced workers in the labor force. A third explanation focuses on the self-fulfilling nature of inflation expectations. When people expect rapid inflation, they set wages and prices to keep up with their expectations, and thus fulfill their prophecy. An anti-inflation medicine should include sufficient promises, threats, or bribes to convince people that rapid inflation will soon end.

The new classical economists believe that any short-run relationship between unemployment and inflation is attributable to inflation errors. People who are voluntarily employed become voluntarily unemployed when they overestimate inflation and underestimate their real wages. Since these errors are soon corrected, there is no long-run tradeoff between unemployment and inflation. This new-classical argument assumes that the only difference between the short run and the long run is temporary misperceptions about prices. Keynesians argue that the main difference between the short-run and the long-run is that it takes time for wages and prices to adjust to changes in demand and supply; in their models, monetary and fiscal policies can have real effects on the economy even if people know the rate of inflation.

Higher prices reduce the real value of cash and nominally denominated obligations, transferring wealth from creditors to debtors. Anticipated inflation tends to increase nominal interest rates; but macroeconomic models tell us that if the aggregate supply curve is not vertical, nominal interest rates generally rise by less than the anticipated rate of inflation. Inflation expectations reinforce the real effects of monetary policies. Increasing the rate of growth of the money supply increases prices, reduces real interest rates, and increases output. Nominal interest rates may go up or down.

If the aggregate supply curve is vertical, one-time increases in the money supply raise the price level proportionately (money neutrality); an increase in the rate of growth of the money supply increases the rate of inflation and nominal interest rates without affecting real interest rates and output (superneutrality).

IMPORTANT TERMS

average-markup
full-employment output
inflation
money neutrality
money superneutrality

natural rate of unemployment
Phillips curve
stagflation
Tobin effect

EXERCISES

1. Explain how the price level can increase even while the rate of inflation is decreasing.

2. Provide a logical justification for the conclusion that "inflation is always and everywhere a monetary phenomenon."

3. What will the rate of inflation be if the money supply increases by 5 percent, velocity falls by 2 percent, and real output increases by 3 percent?

4. Using aggregate demand and aggregate supply curves, show what happens over time to an economy initially at its full-employment output level after an expansionary monetary policy increases aggregate demand, output rises above the potential level (as people work overtime and harder), and prices rise, a little at first and then more later as wage contracts are renegotiated.

5. Using aggregate demand and aggregate supply curves, show what happens to an economy initially at its full-employment output level after sharply higher energy prices cause firms

to raise prices, reduce output, and lay off workers, who, as time passes, agree to work for lower wages.

6. How do new-classical economists explain the observation that the rate of inflation generally increases during booms and declines during recessions? In particular, how would they account for the historical data for 1960–1966 and 1980–1983 shown in Table 22.1?

7. Answer the following question: "I've read somewhere that there is an inverse relationship between unemployment and inflation. Does this mean that less unemployment causes more inflation or that more inflation causes less unemployment?"

8. What is the rate of inflation at the natural rate of unemployment? What is the expected rate of inflation at the natural rate of unemployment?

9. In 1810, David Ricardo wrote that the farmer "more than any other class of the community is benefited by the depreciation of money, and injured by the increase in its value." Why?

10. Why are nominal interest rates on bonds always positive, no matter what the rate of inflation or deflation?

11. Explain why you agree or disagree with the contention that "The [anticipated] real interest rate is always positive . . . People will never willingly save, lend, or invest if the expected return is negative."[16]

12. In the summer of 1980, *The Wall Street Journal* reported that "Apprehension about inflation nearly wrecked the bond markets earlier this year."[17] Why would expectations of inflation cause a crash in bond prices?

13. In 1980, the 3-month Treasury-bill rate dropped to 7 percent, while almost everyone was forecasting approximately 11-percent inflation. In 1983, the 3-month Treasury-bill rate was 9 percent, while everyone forecast approximately 5 percent inflation. In both cases the inflation forecasts turned out to be

accurate. What were the realized real rates of return in each of these cases?

14. Between August 1945 and July 1946, the number of Hungarian pengos (the unit of Hungarian currency) in circulation increased by a factor of 12,000,000,000,000,000,000,000,000,000, while the price level increased by a factor of 4,000,000,000,000,000,000,000,000,000. Did the real money supply increase or decrease? Why?

15. Explain Keynes's conclusion[18]

This progressive deterioration in the value of money through history is not an accident, and has behind it two great driving forces — the impecuniosity of Governments and the superior political influence of the debtor class.

16. In 1988, the 33 percent tax bracket began at $43,150 for a single person and $71,900 for a married couple filing a joint return. In 1989, the 33 percent tax bracket began at $44,900 for a single person and $74,850 for a married couple filing a joint return. Make an educated guess about the reason for this change.

17. A switch from LIFO to FIFO accounting increased Chrysler's profits by $40 million in 1970. How can such an accounting change increase a firm's profits? Why might a company nonetheless prefer LIFO accounting?

18. Brazilian accountants developed NIFO (Next In, First Out) accounting, in which the reported cost of an inventory good used in any given year is equal to an estimate of the cost of its replacement. Why might Brazilian firms find this accounting system advantageous?

19. The *IS-LM* model with a nonvertical aggregate supply curve tells us that a Fed open-market purchase reduces interest rates while raising output, employment, and prices. Would an increase in inflation expectations offset or reinforce the Fed's policy action?

20. It has been argued that most of the dramatic increase in nominal interest rates in the late 1970s reflected an increase in the expected

rate of inflation, rather than an increase in real rates of return. How do changes in inflation expectations get translated into changes in nominal interest rates?

21. Many economists were puzzled by the failure of interest rates to fall as much as inflation during 1981–1983. One explanation offered was that while inflation had fallen, inflation expectations had not. Use the *IS-LM* model to show how high inflation expectations imply high nominal interest rates. A very different explanation was that disinflation inherently raises real interest rates. Use the *IS-LM* model to show how a drop in inflation expectations raises real interest rates.

22. Economists have vigorously debated whether a large federal deficit causes high real interest rates. Consider an economy with a nonvertical aggregate supply curve, no budget deficit, and a 2 percent real interest rate on T-bills. Identify an economic event that will cause
    a. high real interest rates and a large federal deficit.
    b. high real interest rates and a large federal surplus.

23. Give a logical macroeconomic answer to the following.[19]

    The notion is that expanding the money supply would spark a boom by lowering interest rates. This is perhaps the weakest link in the whole Keynesian universe. If expanding money lowers interest rates, how come we have recently experienced both record money growth and record interest rates?

24. What is the crucial assumption underlying the following advice?

    The impending huge federal deficit poses a dilemma for the Federal Reserve. If the Fed decides that the deficit must be financed by the public, interest rates will rise and private investment will be crowded out. On the other hand, if the Fed monetizes the deficit by purchasing Treasury securities, it will be fueling the fires of inflation. The only way out of this dilemma is for Congress to recognize the simple lesson that there is no free lunch.

25. Nominal interest rates on ten-year Treasury bonds dropped by about 3 percentage points in 1985, a fall many attributed to a crumbling of inflation expectations. Why do lower inflation expectations affect interest rates? How do they affect aggregate demand? If Congress wants to offset the effect of lower inflation expectations on aggregate demand, should it raise or lower taxes? If the Fed wants to offset the effect of lower inflation expectations on nominal interest rates, should it buy or sell Treasury securities? Do such actions by Congress and the Fed have similar or contradictory effects on aggregate demand?

26. In the early 1980s, the United States went through a period of disinflation, a dropping of people's inflation expectations from the double-digit levels of a few years earlier. Imagine that it is 1982 and you are forecasting a coming disinflation. Predict the changes in each of the following and (briefly) explain your reasoning.
    a. Nominal interest rates.
    b. Velocity.
    c. The international value of the dollar.
    d. Fed policy.

27. In 1983, the Fed's tight-money policies reduced inflation expectations dramatically. In the *IS-LM* model, spending depends on the real interest rate, while money demand depends on the nominal interest rate. Holding the price level constant, so that we can examine shifts in the aggregate demand curve, what are the effects of a decrease in inflation expectations on aggregate demand, the nominal interest rate, and the real interest rate when the monetary authorities peg
    a. the money supply.
    b. the real interest rate.
    c. the nominal interest rate.
    d. aggregate demand.

28. Here is some advice on how to get rich by predicting interest rates:

    The answer is simple, and to figure it out, all you have to do is to be able to read a figure that you can find in the financial section of many major newspapers. . . . This figure is called the average maturity index of money funds and it will give you the most accurate prediction available regarding what interest rates are going to do in the near future.[20]

    What is the logical basis for this advice that the average maturity of money-market fund portfolios is an interest rate predictor? If the average maturity lengthens, is that a prediction that interest rates are headed up or down? What is the flaw in the conclusion that you can use the maturity index to predict interest rates profitably?

29. "Whenever the Federal Reserve decides that inflation is too high or the dollar needs strengthening, it takes actions that make everybody's borrowing expensive and more difficult. That hurts profits, which pushes stock prices down."[21] Why, even if profits were unaffected, would this tightening by the Fed reduce stock prices?

30. Explain the logic behind this argument:

    The short-run view encouraged concentration on the possibilities of raising the level of output, relative to potential, by demand expansion, even though that might be inflationary. Such a policy would not work in the long run. It worked by surprise — by the actual inflation rate exceeding what people had expected, which made employers willing to hire more workers. But people could not be surprised indefinitely; they would catch on and then the inflation would lose its power to lower unemployment.[22]

THE

MACROECONOMICS

OF A

LARGE, OPEN ECONOMY

Things are seldom what they seem
Skim milk masquerades as cream.

W. S. Gilbert

In 1989, the U.S. exported $360 billion in merchandise to the rest of the world and imported $470 billion in merchandise, and this was but a small part of the total international trade of goods and services among nations. Purchases and sales of financial assets likewise hurdle international boundaries. Individuals, businesses, banks, and governments borrow and invest worldwide. Japanese investors buy U.S. stock, U.S. banks lend money to Poland's government, and the Saudi government buys U.S. Treasury bills.

The linkage of world markets for goods, services, and financial assets means that economic events in one nation have worldwide repercussions. When interest rates rise in the United States, interest rates rise in Europe. When Latin American economies stumble, U.S. banks fail. When the Japanese stock market sneezes, Wall Street shudders.

In this chapter, we will analyze an open economy, like that of the United States, which affects and is affected by foreign economies. We will begin by looking at data concerning international transactions. Then we will look at some simple rules for predicting the international consequences of economic events. The concluding section analyzes a formal macroeconomic model of a large, open economy.

THE BALANCE OF PAYMENTS

International transactions take many different forms. Americans buy French wine, and the Soviet Union buys American grain. Americans visit China, and English people tour the United States. Americans invest in the German stock market, and Koreans buy Treasury bills. The U.S. government gives aid to Ecuador, and Japanese firms pay dividends to U.S. stockholders. Americans buy Swiss francs, and Brazilians buy dollars. With an exhaustive compilation of all such transactions, the totals must balance. Every use of funds is someone else's source of funds. Sources equal uses, assets equal liabilities, and balance sheets always balance. Statisticians, economists, and politicians have, however, traditionally scrutinized selected subsets of a complete accounting.

Every use of funds is also a source of funds.

The Current Account

Table 23.1 shows some selected U.S. data for 1989. There has long been considerable interest in a nation's merchandise **trade balance**: its exports of commodities minus imports. In 1989, the United States had a trade deficit of $110 billion; it imported $110 billion more in merchandise than it exported. A nation's trade balance is often interpreted as a rough barometer of the competitiveness of its industries. By this standard, U.S. businesses are having extreme difficulties competing with foreign businesses.

A nation's trade balance is its exports minus imports.

Long ago, when trade surpluses and deficits were financed by precious metals, the so-called mercantilists watched trade data because they believed that a nation's wealth consisted of its holdings of gold and silver. Adam Smith, in his appropriately named *The Wealth of Nations,* argued that this was a very incomplete accounting. Gold and silver may have value, but the sale of commodities for gold does not increase a nation's wealth. It merely substitutes one item for another — food for gold, clothing for silver. The true wealth of a nation is the quantity and productivity of its resources: its people, its land, and its capital. Only a miserly nation could be happy perpetually forgoing consumption in order to hoard metal.

Mercantilists believed that a nation's wealth was its gold and silver.

By the same logic, spending U.S. dollars on German cars, Japanese televisions, and French wine is not a complete loss. Instead of buying U.S. goods, we buy foreign goods. The foreigners who accept these dollars will presumably use them to buy the U.S. goods that we spurned. If they don't, so much the better. Would you rather drive a Mercedes-Benz or count pieces of paper?

One of the most worrisome aspects of the enormous U.S. trade deficit is that foreigners will someday cash in their dollars, buying much of the U.S. gross national product, leaving little for U.S. citizens. We will have traded our children's food and clothing for our VCRs and BMWs.

The **goods-and-services balance** is similar to the trade balance, but it includes services as well as goods. These services include interest and dividend

The goods-and-services balance includes services as well as goods.

Table 23.1   U.S. International Transactions 1989 (billions of dollars)

	Receipts	Payments	Cumulative Net
Current Account			
Merchandise			
Exports	+360		
Imports		−470	−110 = Trade balance
Net services	+20		−90 = Goods-and-services balance
Net transfers		−20	−110 = Current-account balance
Capital Account			
Foreign assets in U.S.			
Foreign official assets	+10		
Other foreign assets	+190		
U.S. assets abroad			
U.S official reserve assets		−30	
Other U.S. gov't assets		0	
U.S. private assets		−100	
Statistical discrepancy	+40		+110 = Capital-account balance

payments, tourist expenditures, purchases and sales of military equipment, and foreign expenses of operating military bases abroad. This conglomeration is a bit unusual. Domestic interest and dividend expenses are not considered to be a purchase of services, and domestic military equipment is generally considered goods rather than services. The contrary international treatment is probably intended to preserve the trade balance as a barometer of the relative competitiveness of a nation's industries.

The current-account balance adds net transfer payments to the goods-and-services balance. These transfers include foreign aid and private gifts to or from individuals and organizations. Thus the **current account** includes international purchases of currently produced goods and services and international transfer payments. Figure 23.1 shows some historical data on the U.S. trade and current-account balances.

The current-account balance is important because it must be financed by the sale or acquisition of financial assets — an increase or decrease in foreign claims against the United States, either U.S. dollars or assets that can be converted into dollars. In 1989 the United States had a current account deficit of $110 billion that was financed by a $110 billion increase in foreign holdings of U.S. currency, bonds, stock, and other claims.

The current account includes international purchases of newly produced goods and services and international transfer payments.

The current-account balance must be financed by the sale or purchase of assets.

The Capital Account

The international purchases and sales of assets are collected in a nation's **capital account**. These transactions are labeled capital outflows and inflows, terms that can be confusing since they convey an image of something unilaterally leaking out of a country or pouring in. These data describe transactions, the exchange of one item for another. A U.S. capital outflow is a U.S. purchase of foreign assets, such as an exchange of U.S. dollars for German bonds or Japanese stock; dollars flow out of the United States in return for foreign assets. A U.S. capital inflow is a foreign purchase of U.S. assets, such as Germans buying Treasury bills and Japanese buying IBM stock; cash flows into the United States in return for U.S. assets.

> The capital accounts include international purchases and sales of assets.

A current-account deficit must be financed by a capital-account surplus (and vice versa). Table 23.1 shows a 1989 current account deficit for the United States of $110 billion. U.S. expenditures on goods and services and transfer payments exceeded revenue by $110 billion, necessitating a $110 billion increase in foreign claims against the United States — a capital-account surplus of $110 billion.

> A current-account deficit must be financed by a capital-account surplus.

Three other balance-of-payment figures (not shown in Table 23.1) can be used to show other aspects of these foreign claims. The *basic balance* nets out purchases and sales of long-term securities, leaving short-term claims against the United States. The *net-liquidity balance* nets out illiquid short-term transactions, leaving short-term liquid claims. The *official settlements balance* nets out private short-term liquid assets, leaving official short-term liquid claims against the government. These various calculations measure different facets of U.S. international transactions, describing how much Americans are buying and selling, how much they are giving away, and how much they are borrowing and lending.

It is natural to think that it is the current-account imbalance that determines the offsetting capital-account imbalance. If we want Taiwanese shoes, Japanese televisions, and German cars, then we must pay for them with U.S. dollars and Treasury bills. However, because of the unique position of the U.S. dollar as world money, some observers use the capital-account imbalance to explain the current account. If the rest of the world wants U.S. dollars and Treasury bills, they must pay for them with shoes, televisions, and automobiles.

Financing Balance-of-Payments Deficits

From World War II up until 1975, the United States routinely exported more goods and services than it imported. The United States shared some of its output with the rest of the world. Much of this export surplus was financed by gifts to foreign individuals, organizations, and governments. Subtracting these gifts left a current-account balance that fluctuated between surplus and deficit, roughly balancing over the years.

Although the current account was in rough balance, the United States acquired long-term investments while supplying gold and dollars, "world

Figure 23.1   U.S. International Transactions

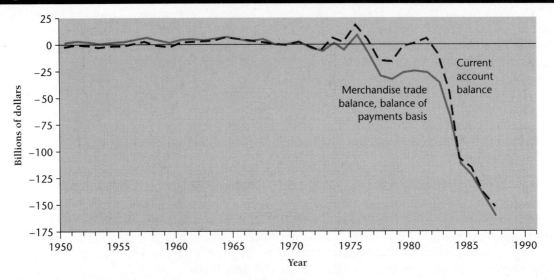

source: From Federal Reserve *Historical Chart Book*, 1989.

The U.S. dollar is an international medium of exchange.

money," to carry out international trade. The U.S. dollar has, in many ways,
replaced gold as the international medium of exchange. Thirty-three nations peg
the value of their currencies to the dollar, including Afghanistan, Iraq, Peru, the
Sudan, and Vietnam. About two-thirds of the reserve assets of the world's central
banks are U.S. dollars. Central banks in large industrial countries hold dollars
almost entirely; developing countries have about half of their reserves in dollars.

Since 1975, the United States has run persistent current-account deficits,
mostly the result of large trade deficits. The United States has financed these
current-account deficits by selling U.S. currency, bonds, and stocks to foreign
citizens, businesses, and governments. Before 1975, the United States traded
liquid assets for illiquid ones; since 1975, the U.S. has traded liquid and illiquid
assets for merchandise.

The fact that the United States has supplied dollars and other assets to the
rest of the world does not imply that the United States is in financial difficulty.
If anything, it is a healthy sign that the U.S. supply of world money is growing
with international commerce. These balance-of-payments deficits occur because
the world wants to use liquid U.S. assets as world money. The international
accumulation of U.S. dollars reflects the strength, not the weakness, of the dollar.
Conversely, the U.S. dollar's share of international monetary reserves has declined
from a peak of almost 90 percent in 1976. The tentative emergence of a multicurrency reserve system in the late 1970s, with central banks acquiring German
marks and Japanese yen, reflected a perceived weakness of the U.S. dollar.

| The Dollar as World Money | Highlight 23.1 |

If Coca-Cola is the international soft drink and Big Mac the international hamburger, then the U.S. dollar is the international money. Foreigners own more than a trillion dollars in U.S. financial assets. At the end of 1989, U.S. banks alone held more than $700 billion in foreign deposits denominated in dollars. Foreign banks hold hundreds of billions in Eurodollar deposits denominated in dollars. The worldwide preference for assets denominated in dollars rather than francs, yen, or rubles reflects a faith in the value of the dollar and its near-universal acceptability in international transactions — ranging from oil to grain to foreign exchange — where prices are quoted in dollars and trades are settled in dollars.

More than $150 billion in U.S. currency is held outside the United States, including 40 percent of the $100 bills. The U.S. dollar is the official currency in Liberia and Panama and is freely used alongside the shekel in Israel. The dollar is an unofficial medium of exchange in many countries, often accepted at a premium above the official exchange rate. In Brazil, Mexico, and other countries with rapid inflation, the dollar is said to be the poor man's Swiss bank — the easiest way to keep one's savings in a sound currency. In the Soviet Union and other Eastern European countries, the dollar is used for black market trades — those outside government-approved stores — because the dollar can be converted into other currencies and the domestic currency cannot. Nobody outside the Soviet Union wants rubles; everyone wants dollars.

International transaction data are sometimes misinterpreted because of an understandable confusion about the various balance-of-payments statistics. Some may read of a deficit in the net-liquidity balance or the official-settlements balance and mistakenly interpret that as a goods-and-services or current-account deficit. Another confusing factor is the unique position of the United States as a supplier of world money. When small countries have deficits, they must use their foreign-currency holdings — their international reserves — to pay their bills, because their domestic currencies are of little use to other nations. When their foreign-currency holdings are exhausted, they are unable to run further deficits. For the United States, the situation is different. When the United States has a deficit in its liquidity balance, other nations acquire more U.S. dollars, dollar deposits, and other liquid assets. Foreign nations are willing to hold U.S. dollars because, as a world money, they can be used to pay bills.

In a world of fixed exchange rates, balance-of-payments data were studied by governments and speculators for evidence of unrealistic exchange rates. With freely floating exchange rates, there is considerably less motive for this scrutiny, since governments no longer have the responsibility for making exchange-rate adjustments and need not put themselves at the mercy of speculators.

As the world moved toward floating exchange rates in the 1970s, the U.S. government adopted the recommendation of a presidential advisory committee that balance-of-payments data be deemphasized. The data are now called U.S. "international transactions" rather than the balance of payments, and the basic, net-liquidity, and official-settlements balances are no longer officially reported. Only the goods-and-services and current-account balances are given, and the pejorative words "deficit" and "surplus" are avoided in press releases.

INTERNATIONAL LINKAGES

In an economically interdependent world, events in one country may have worldwide economic consequences. Exchange rates, like interest rates and stock prices, are notoriously difficult to forecast, but analysts do the best they can using several economic tools. In this section, we will discuss several international linkages that can be used to help understand and predict changes in exchange rates and other international repercussions of economic events. Then we will look at a formal model for analyzing several linkages simultaneously.

International Reserves and the Monetary Base

A current-account imbalance need not affect the monetary base.

A current-account deficit or surplus need not cause a change in a nation's monetary base. A country can pay for its imports by issuing more of its own currency, true enough; but it can choose to pay for its imports in other ways, too. When the United States had a $110 billion current-account deficit in 1989, this deficit did not cause a $110 billion increase in outstanding Federal Reserve notes. United States individuals and businesses who pay for imports do not need extra dollars from the Federal Reserve to do so, and the dollars they use need not leave the United States. Importers may exchange their dollars for marks, yen, and other foreign currencies. They (or those who sell them foreign exchange) may deposit their dollars in U.S. banks or exchange them for Treasury bills. If dollars leave the United States, it will be because foreigners want more dollars, not because the United States has a current-account deficit.

Central banks alter the monetary base when they use their currency to buy or sell foreign exchange. A Fed use of dollars to purchase yen increases the U.S. monetary base, the same as if the Fed had bought Treasury bills. If the Fed purchases yen from a U.S. bank, the bank is credited with additional reserves; if the seller is not a U.S. bank, then the Fed pays for the yen with a check, which, sooner or later, is deposited in a U.S. bank and then credited to the bank's reserves with the Fed. Either way, the monetary base expands by the size of the Fed's foreign-exchange purchase.

The use by the Fed of open-market purchases or sales of Treasury securities to offset the effects of its foreign-exchange transactions on the U.S. monetary base is known as a **sterilized intervention**. For instance, if the value of the dollar is falling relative to the Japanese yen, the Fed might intervene, buying dollars with yen — either from its holdings of yen or by borrowing yen from other central banks. This purchase of dollars reduces the monetary base, but the Fed can put these dollars back into circulation by using them to buy Treasury bills. Since there is no change in the monetary base, this is a sterilized intervention. The net effect is that the Fed has swapped yen for Treasury bills.

A Fed purchase of foreign exchange can be sterilized, with no effect on the U.S. monetary base, by an open market sale.

Purchasing-Power Parity

Chapter 3 introduced the concept of the **law of one price**: the domestic price of a foreign item should equal the domestic price of a comparable domestic item; otherwise, no one will buy the more expensive item. If the domestic price is P_d, the foreign price P_f, and the exchange rate (domestic currency per foreign currency) is e, then purchasing-power parity requires

$$P_d = eP_f \qquad (1)$$

Suppose, for instance, that a U.S. sweater costs P_d = $50, a comparable English sweater costs P_f = £20, and the exchange rate is 1.50 dollars per pound. The U.S. price of the British sweater is

$$eP_f = (£20)(1.50 \text{ dollars/pound}) = \$30$$

The law of one price is violated because the U.S. sweater is far more expensive than the comparable British sweater. In the absence of trade restrictions, British sweaters will be imported to the United States and sales of the overpriced U.S. sweater will collapse. Comparable U.S. and British sweaters can be sold side by side only if purchasing-power parity is established by a rise in British sweater prices, a drop in U.S. sweater prices, or a devaluation of the dollar relative to the pound.

Purchasing-power parity explains exchange rate movements by applying the law of one price to price indexes reflecting the average prices of a wide variety of goods and services. According to purchasing-power parity, the percentage change in the exchange rate is equal to the difference between the percentage changes in domestic and foreign prices:

Purchasing-power parity says that the percentage change in an exchange rate is determined by the difference between the two nations' rates of inflation.

$$\%e = \%P_d - \%P_f \qquad (2)$$

Equation 2 implies that the exchange rate should rise (a depreciation of the domestic currency) when the domestic rate of inflation exceeds the foreign rate of inflation. The domestic currency should appreciate when the domestic country has the lower rate of inflation.

There are several reasons why deviations from the law of one price and purchasing-power parity can persist for some time. Transportation costs, import or export taxes, and other trade barriers may make it difficult for people to buy relatively inexpensive foreign products. For some products, ranging from Coca-Cola to Stealth bombers, people may believe that there are no good substitutes for the real thing. Nonetheless, the logic underlying purchasing-power parity can help us understand and anticipate some of the international consequences of economic events.

Suppose that the United States follows an expansionary monetary policy, which increases U.S. prices. Purchasing-power parity tells us that the dollar should depreciate, or foreign prices should rise. If a foreign government does not want the value of its currency to change relative to the dollar, then it, too, will have to adopt expansionary policies, ensuring that the other nation will experience as much inflation as the United States does.

Similar logic applies to other economic events. A decrease in money demand or an increase in private or government spending is expansionary and raises domestic prices (and output too, if the economy is not at full employment). Purchasing-power parity implies that either the value of the dollar will fall or foreign prices will rise. The more committed governments are to stable exchange rates, the more certain we can be that either the Fed will have to act to offset the inflationary consequences of this economic event or other nations will be provoked into inflationary policies.

Interest Rates

The anticipated rates of return on comparable domestic and foreign assets should be similar.

Chapter 7 explained how comparable domestic and foreign assets should be priced to yield similar rates of return, taking into account anticipated changes in exchange rates. If R_d is the rate of return (in domestic currency) on a domestic asset, R_f is the rate of return (in foreign currency) on a comparable foreign asset, and the anticipated percentage change in the exchange rate is %e, then the two assets have the same anticipated rate of return only if the following (approximate) relationship holds:

$$R_d = R_f + \%e \tag{3}$$

Suppose, for instance, that U.S. Treasury bonds yield $R_d = 10$ percent and that the dollar is expected to depreciate by 2 percent relative to the British pound during the coming year (%e = 2%), perhaps because the annual rate of inflation in the United States is 2 percent higher than that in Britain. Unless comparable British bonds yield $R_f = 8$ percent, investors will flock to the more attractive of the two bonds and neglect the other. Both types of bonds will be willingly held — and someone must hold them — only if they are priced to give comparable rates of return.

Equation 3 implies that changes in asset prices and yields in one country should cause corresponding changes in other countries, or changes in exchange rates. If Fed open-market sales of Treasury bills cause United States interest rates to rise from 10 percent to 12 percent, then interest rates must rise in England, too, or else currency traders will buy dollars and sell pounds (increasing the value of the dollar relative to the pound) until the anticipated future depreciation of the dollar relative to the pound is 4 percent rather than 2 percent. To hold the current exchange rate constant, the governments must reduce U.S. interest

U.S. Interest Rates Are Affected by Foreign Interest Rates	**Highlight 23.2**

At its meeting on December 19, 1989, the Federal Reserve's Open Market Committee discussed the state of the U.S. economy and reached a consensus that although a recession did not appear imminent, there were troubling signs of economic weakness. They voted to reassure financial markets and bolster the economy by using open-market operations to lower interest rates somewhat. The following morning, the Fed's trading desk bought Treasury bills, reducing interest rates. However, during the next 2½ months, long-term Treasury bond rates rose by ¾ of a point.

The reason? The dramatic reunification of East and West Germany and the anticipated need for huge amounts of capital to modernize Eastern Europe caused large increases in European interest rates. At the same time, concerns about Japan's rising rate of inflation caused Japanese interest rates to rise sharply. Interest rates on U.S. Treasury bonds had to rise, too, for these securities to be competitive with European and Japanese bonds.

This incident illustrates how the linkages among world interest rates can constrain and blunt the Federal Reserve's monetary policies and how financial events now have international repercussions. The Open Market Committee used to focus almost exclusively on U.S. economic data. Now they study detailed statistics for all of its major trading partners.

rates or raise British interest rates — for instance, through Fed purchases of Treasury securities or Bank of England sales of British securities.

Foreign Exchange Demand and Supply

Another apparatus that analysts use to understand exchange-rate movements is demand and supply, as illustrated by the market for British pounds relative to U.S. dollars shown in Figure 23.2. The exchange rate e is the price of the foreign currency in dollars — dollars per pound. The U.S. demand curve describes the willingness of U.S. citizens to exchange dollars for pounds; it is downward sloped because pounds are less attractive as they become more expensive. The supply curve in Figure 23.2 describes the willingness of foreigners, primarily the British, to sell pounds for dollars. The supply curve is upward sloping because the more dollars they can get for their pounds, the more pounds they are willing to sell.

Demand and supply can help explain exchange rate movements.

As shown in Figure 23.3, an increase in the U.S. demand for pounds causes an increase in the equilibrium exchange rate — an increase that can be described as an appreciation of the pound relative to the dollar or as a depreciation of the dollar relative to the pound. An increase in the foreign supply of pounds causes a drop in the equilibrium exchange rate — a depreciation of the pound and appreciation of the dollar.

An increased U.S. demand for a foreign currency causes foreign currency to appreciate relative to the dollar.

Highlight 23.3   **A Managed Float by the Group of Five**

Figure 23.1 shows that the United States had a very large trade deficit in 1980. According to the law of one price, the value of the dollar should have declined, making U.S. goods less expensive and foreign goods more so, until the deficit was eliminated. But between 1980 and 1985, the value of the dollar increased by 40 percent relative to other currencies!

The accompanying graph makes this point another way, tracing the value of the dollar and U.S. prices relative to foreign prices since 1973, when the United States changed from fixed to flexible exchange rates. (The foreign data are weighted by the amount of trade conducted with the United States.) According to purchasing-power parity, movements in exchange rates should match movements in relative prices; but the graph shows that, for the United States at least, there were prolonged discrepancies between relative prices and exchange rates.

U.S. Violations of Purchasing-Power Parity

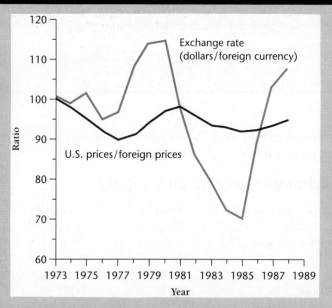

source: Economic Report of the President, January 1989.

In 1973, the U.S. had a small, $1 billion trade surplus. Between 1973 and 1980, U.S. prices increased at a slightly slower rate than the prices of its trading partners. The dollar should consequently have appreciated slightly relative to these other currencies; instead, it depreciated by 15 percent, making foreign products considerably more expensive in 1980 than in 1973. Yet the U.S. ran a $25 billion trade deficit in 1980.

Between 1980 and 1985, U.S. prices continued to increase more slowly than the prices of its trading partners. The graph shows that instead of depreciating more to eliminate the U.S. trade deficit, the value of the dollar increased by more than 40 percent, making foreign goods increasingly inexpensive. The U.S. trade deficit increased to $122 billion.

One reason for this perverse movement of exchange rates was that while foreign goods became more attractive, so did U.S. financial assets. Real interest rates were very high in the United States during the years 1980–1985. For instance, between 1980 and 1985, the interest rates on U.S. bank deposits averaged 11.5 percent. With an average inflation rate of 6.9 percent, these deposits provided an alluring real return of 11.5 percent − 6.9 percent = 4.6 percent. In Germany, in contrast, the average bank deposit rate between 1980 and 1985 was 6.5 percent, the average inflation rate 4.2 percent, and the real interest rate 2.3 percent. In Japan, the average deposit rate was 4.1 percent, the inflation rate 3.9 percent, and the real rate of return only 0.2 percent.* Because of its high real interest rates, the United States exported financial assets and imported merchandise.

In September 1985, U.S. government representatives met in New York with their counterparts from France, Great Britain, Japan, and West Germany. This Group of Five agreed to make concerted efforts to lower the value of the dollar, making U.S. goods less expensive, to help balance the U.S. trade deficit. These nations agreed to pursue monetary and fiscal policies conducive to a devaluation of the dollar and, further, to intervene in foreign-exchange markets, selling dollars as needed to drive their value down. In 1986, they met again in Tokyo, along with Canada and Italy, making a Group of Seven pledged to the depreciation of the U.S. dollar.

The intervention of central banks in foreign-exchange markets to manipulate exchange rates is called a **managed float**. With a **crawling peg**, the central bank pegs the exchange rate, but periodically adjusts the peg to correct substantial demand-supply imbalances. With a **dirty float**, the central bank allows the exchange rate to fluctuate with demand and supply, but occasionally enters the market, often surreptitiously. The accompanying graph shows that after the Group of Five agreed to a managed float, there was indeed a dramatic drop in the value of the dollar, though the U.S. trade deficit continued to increase through 1987 and then to shrink very slowly.

---

*These data are from International Monetary Fund, *International Financial Statistics Yearbook, 1989*, pp. 108, 117.

Figure 23.2   The Market for British Pounds

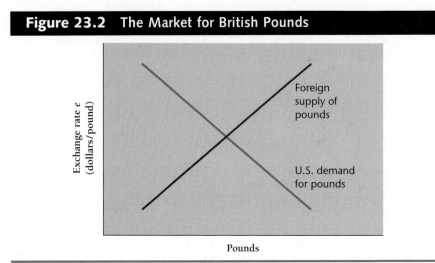

With this demand-supply graph in mind, Table 23.2 lists the anticipated exchange-rate effects of several economic events. This table shows the shift in demand relative to supply because most events that cause U.S. citizens to demand more pounds also persuade foreigners to supply more pounds.

For instance, an increase in the U.S. price level makes U.S. products more expensive relative to British products. U.S. citizens now demand more pounds to buy British goods, while the British want fewer dollars to buy U.S. goods and consequently supply fewer pounds to acquire dollars. The demand for pounds goes up and the supply of pounds goes down; more briefly, we can say that the demand for pounds increases relative to the supply. A look at Figure 23.2 or 23.3 confirms that an increase in demand relative to supply increases the value of the pound, as noted in Table 23.2. As an exercise, you should look at the other nine events in Table 23.2 and reason out the consequences listed there.

A TWO-COUNTRY MACRO MODEL (Optional)

Sometimes it is said that floating exchange rates free nations to follow their own economic objectives. This is true in the sense that each nation's price level can move separately, with the exchange rate adjusting to eliminate foreign-exchange demand-supply imbalances. But it is also true that each nation's economic policies affect other nations.

In order to analyze the international transmission of economic events, we will briefly examine a macroeconomic *IS-LM* model of a world economy consisting of two large nations, modeled symmetrically. For concreteness, we can

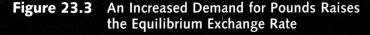

Figure 23.3   **An Increased Demand for Pounds Raises the Equilibrium Exchange Rate**

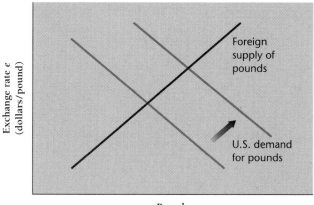

think of the domestic country as the United States and the foreign country as either a large trading partner or as the entire rest of the world.

The model has two separate labor markets, one in each country. People work in the country in which they live, for a real wage equal to the nominal wage divided by the price level in that country. Each country has a nonvertical aggregate supply curve, so that an increase in its output causes an increase in its price level.

We use the law of one price $P_d = eP_f$ as a simplifying approximation, assuming that the products produced in the two countries are perfect substitutes. There is consequently a single, worldwide *IS* equation:

$$a + by_d + cy_f + dr = y_d + y_f \qquad (4)$$

where y_d and y_f are domestic and foreign output, r is the interest rate, and a, b, c, and d are parameters. This *IS* equation is analogous to our earlier model of a single, closed economy: world spending is equal to world output, with world spending positively related to output in each nation and negatively related to the interest rate. There is a single real interest rate because domestic and foreign securities are assumed to be perfect substitutes and are consequently priced to yield a common real rate of return r.

The nations' two moneys are not good substitutes, since private citizens hold only their own domestic currency. Thus there are two separate *LM* equations (with parameters f, g, h, i, j, and k).

$$f + gy_d + h(r + \pi_d) = \frac{M_d - F_f}{P_d} \qquad (5)$$

Table 23.2 Demand-Supply Predicted Effects on Value of Pound Relative to Dollar

Economic Event	Demand for Pounds Relative to Dollar	Value of Pound Relative to Dollar
Increase in U.S. price level	Increase	Increase
Increase in U.K. price level	Decrease	Decrease
Increase in U.S. income	Increase	Increase
Increase in U.K. income	Decrease	Decrease
Increase in U.S. interest rates	Decrease	Decrease
Increase in U.K. interest rates	Increase	Increase
Increase in expected U.S. inflation	Increase	Increase
Increase in expected U.K. inflation	Decrease	Decrease
Fed buys pounds	Increase	Increase
Bank of England buys dollars	Decrease	Decrease

$$i + jy_f + k(r + \pi_f) = \frac{M_f - F_d}{P_f} \tag{6}$$

These private money demands correspond to those of the closed-economy model. Both state that the demand for money is positively related to income and negatively related to the nominal return on securities (the international real return plus the domestic rate of inflation). Governments hold foreign exchange, denoted by F. The total money supply is M and the amount available to the public is $M - F$, the amount of money outstanding less the amount held by the foreign government. Thus the amount of money in private circulation can be increased either by the domestic government issuing more currency or by the foreign government using some of its foreign exchange. An increase in the domestic price level reduces the real money supply.

International Effects of Fiscal and Monetary Policies

The present model is more complicated than our earlier closed-economy model, in that there are now two outputs and two price levels to take into account, which makes a graphical solution tedious. Table 23.3 summarizes the results of a detailed analysis.[1] The signs in this table show whether each economic event has a positive, negative, or indeterminate effect on the indicated variable.

Consider first an increase in government or private spending by either country. A rightward shift of the domestic IS curve increases domestic output, domestic prices, and world interest rates. This increase in world interest rates reduces money demand in the foreign country. To maintain money demand equal to supply, its output and prices must increase, too, so as to bolster money

Do Budget Deficits Cause Trade Deficits?

In 1989, the U.S. federal government's budget deficit was $150 billion, and the nation's trade deficit was $110 billion. Many believe that there is a close relationship between budget and trade deficits. Japanese purchases of U.S. Treasury securities simultaneously help finance the federal budget deficit (the U.S. Treasury sells bonds to raise funds) and the U.S. trade deficit (the United States uses Treasury bonds to pay for Hondas and Toyotas). Some national-income-accounting equations can help us see whether there is an inexorable link between budget and trade deficits.

Chapter 19 explained that a nation's gross national product y can be divided among private consumption c, private investment i, government spending g, and exports x less exports z,

$$y = c + i + g + x - z$$

Exports are included and imports are netted out because gross national product is intended to be an estimate of a nation's production. $c + i + g + x - z$ is total expenditures on domestically produced goods.

The nation's trade deficit is the difference between its imports and exports.

$$\text{trade deficit} = z - x$$

The expenditure equation can be rearranged as

$$c + i + g - y = z - x = \text{trade deficit}$$

The left-hand side of this equation is the difference between a nation's expenditures on goods and services and its production of goods and services; the right-hand side is its trade deficit. This equation shows that a nation can live beyond its means — buying more goods and services than it produces — by running a trade deficit, importing more than it exports. It must of course finance this trade deficit with currency, bonds, and other claims that foreigners may someday redeem for goods and services. Thus a trade deficit can represent a swapping of future goods and services for current goods and services.

The link between a nation's trade deficit and the government's budget deficit is less clear-cut. If we let t represent the government's tax revenues, net of Social Security and other transfer payments from the federal government, then the government's budget deficit is

$$\text{budget deficit} = g - t$$

Private saving is equal to income minus taxes and consumption,

$$\text{private saving} = y - t - c$$

Now, subtracting tax revenue *t* from both sides of the expenditure equation and rearranging, we have

$$(y - t - c) + (z - x) = \quad i \quad + (g - t)$$

private   +   trade   =   private   +   budget
saving   deficit   investment   deficit

This national-income-accounting identity states that a nation's private saving plus its trade deficit finance investment spending and the budget deficit.

If saving and investment are constant, an increased budget deficit requires an increased trade deficit. In practice, however, saving and investment are not constant, but are instead affected by the same factors that affect budget and trade deficits. Do economic events that reduce the budget deficit also reduce the trade deficit? Not necessarily. A stronger economy (due, for example, to increased private spending) generally increases imports, worsening the trade deficit, and also increases tax revenues, reducing the budget deficit.

Our overall conclusion is that if the budget deficit increases, without a corresponding increase in private saving or decline in investment, then the trade deficit must increase, too. Between 1981 and 1989, for example, the budget deficit increased (in real terms) by about $70 billion. For the trade deficit to be constant, private saving would have had to increase by $70 billion more than investment spending. In fact, saving increased by $30 billion *less* than investment, and the trade deficit increased by $100 billion.

demand. Thus output and prices increase in both countries, along with the world interest rate. The exchange rate may rise or fall, depending on whether U.S. prices increase more or less than foreign prices.

These consequences of increased spending are very similar to those for a closed economy. An increase in world spending expands output, employment, and prices. The enlarged output increases money demand, while higher prices diminish real money supplies, pushing the world interest rate up.

An increase in world spending increases output, employment, prices, and interest rates.

Table 23.3 also shows the consequences of an increase in the U.S. money supply, due either to an open-market purchase by the Fed or to a decision by the foreign country to use some of its dollar holdings to purchase securities (a sterilized intervention in the foreign-exchange market). The domestic consequences are the same as for a closed economy. An open-market purchase reduces the interest rate on securities, stimulating spending and thereby raising domestic output, employment, and prices. But, surprisingly, foreign output, employment, and prices decline!

An open-market purchase increases domestic output but reduces foreign output.

This result is unexpected, but the logic is straightforward. An expansionary monetary policy reduces interest rates at home and abroad. This interest-rate

Table 23.3 International Effects of Monetary and Fiscal Policies

Variable Affected	Increase in U.S. or Foreign Spending	Increase in U.S. Money Supply	Increase in Foreign Money Supply
U.S. output	+	+	−
Foreign output	+	−	+
U.S. prices	+	+	−
Foreign prices	+	−	+
Exchange rate ($ per foreign currency)	?	+	−

decline increases the demands for both domestic and foreign money. The in-creased U.S. money demand is satisfied by the increased money supply. Because the foreign money supply is unchanged, its increased money demand must be offset by a decline in foreign output (reducing money demand) and an accom-panying decline in prices (increasing the real value of the foreign money supply). Put somewhat differently, the lower interest rates brought about by U.S. monetary policies increase the demand for foreign money, which has the same effects on the foreign economy as a contraction of the foreign money supply. Since U.S. prices are up and foreign prices are down, the law of one price is maintained by an increase in the exchange rate; that is, a depreciation of the dollar. Table 23.3 also shows the analogous consequences of an increase in the foreign money supply.

Policy Conflict and Coordination

Floating exchange rates free nations to follow their own domestic economic objectives, in the sense that their domestic price levels can move separately, with offsetting exchange-rate adjustments. But it is not true that domestic policies do not affect other nations.

We've seen that an expansionary monetary policy in the United States reduces U.S. interest rates, expands output, and increases prices. A depreciation of the dollar may hold constant the foreign prices of U.S. goods and the U.S. prices of foreign goods, thereby leaving the balance of trade unchanged. To the extent that U.S. and foreign assets are substitutes (and these days they are very much so), foreign interest rates will also decline. This will increase the demand for money in the foreign country which, like an reduction in the money supply, is contractionary. Thus, an expansionary monetary policy can export unemploy-ment. Similarly, a contractionary monetary policy can export inflation.

The foreign nation may not want the recession caused by expansionary U.S. monetary policies. If so, it may be provoked into making its own open-market purchases to keep its output and employment from falling. Monetary policies may be internationally contagious! By the time both nations are content, world money supplies may have been enlarged considerably.

Some national objectives may be incompatible. For example, the United States may want low interest rates, but the foreign country wants high interest rates. The United States then follows an easy-money policy and the foreign nation follows a tight-money policy. As long as investors have international mobility in choosing securities, the two nations will quarrel and at least one will be frustrated.

Here is one final example. Consider a situation in which the foreign country decides to use open-market operations to peg its exchange rate versus the dollar. Table 23.3 reminds us that this commitment means that the foreign country must make open-market sales if the dollar starts to appreciate, and open-market purchases if the dollar depreciates. Now suppose that the Fed makes an open-market purchase. If unanswered, U.S. output and prices will rise and the dollar will depreciate. The foreign country responds with an open-market purchase to stabilize the exchange rate, putting enough of its money into circulation to cause

its prices to rise as much as U.S. prices. Thus an expansionary U.S. monetary policy induces expansionary monetary policies by foreign nations desiring stable exchange rates. Inflation is exported!

The general conclusion is that there are international consequences of economic events, in that events in one country affect employment, output, and prices in other countries. An expansionary fiscal policy stimulates all countries, while an expansionary monetary policy depresses foreign economies. If other nations do not welcome these international economic ripples, then expansionary fiscal policies tend to provoke contractionary policies abroad, while expansionary monetary policies induce expansionary policies in response. In such cases, there may well be international economic conflicts and a need for some coordination and cooperation.

SUMMARY

From data on international transactions, specific details can be culled to measure such categories as exports versus imports and borrowing and lending among nations. These various balances of trade and payment are useful and informative but are sometimes interpreted carelessly.

Between 1950 and 1975, the United States acquired long-term claims against the rest of the world and sold gold and short-term liquid claims against the United States. Since 1975, the United States has run current-account deficits, supplying dollars and dollar-denominated assets as the world's money.

Current-account deficits and surpluses can, but need not, affect a nation's monetary base. A central bank purchase or sale of foreign exchange does affect the monetary base, though such intervention can be sterilized by offsetting bond purchases or sales.

Domestic prices, foreign prices, and exchange rates are roughly linked through the law of one price and purchasing-power parity. Although purchasing-power parity does not hold exactly, especially in the short run, this concept is helpful in remembering the direction in which relative prices tend to move.

Another way to help understand and anticipate exchange-rate movements is to consider the demand and supply of a currency. Events that cause an increased demand relative to supply cause the equilibrium value of that currency to appreciate.

An expansionary fiscal policy increases output, employment, and prices, both at home and abroad, and tightens world financial markets. The effect on the exchange rate is uncertain because foreign prices may go up more or less than domestic prices. Expansionary monetary policies increase domestic output and prices, reduce interest rates, and depreciate the domestic currency. To the extent that lower interest rates increase foreign money demand, there is a contractionary effect on its output and prices. In an interdependent world, each nation should take into account foreign economic events and foreign reactions to domestic economic events.

IMPORTANT TERMS

capital account
crawling peg
current account
dirty float
goods-and-services balance

law of one price
managed float
purchasing-power parity
sterilized intervention
trade balance

EXERCISES

1. In what sense does a nation's balance of payments balance?

2. Are U.S. citizens more likely to buy German cars if the dollar appreciates relative to the deutschemark, or if it depreciates?

3. According to purchasing-power parity, why does a rapid inflation in the United States cause the value of the dollar to fall?

4. If the value of the dollar is fixed relative to other currencies by a gold standard, what happens if there is a rapid inflation in the U.S.?

5. Why do some central banks resist the appreciation of their currency? Does a country receive benefits from a currency appreciation?

6. Use foreign exchange demand and supply to predict whether a reduction in U.S. interest rates causes the dollar to appreciate or depreciate.

7. Use demand and supply to predict the effect on the value of the yen relative to the dollar of the imposition of quotas severely restricting imports of Japanese goods to the United States.

8. The Fed has increased reserve requirements substantially. Use *IS-LM* analysis and the demand and supply of British pounds to predict the effect on the value of the pound relative to the dollar.

9. Use *IS-LM* analysis and the demand and supply of deutschemarks to predict the effect on the value of the dollar relative to the deutschemark of an increased use of credit cards in the United States.

10. Explain how an open-market sale by the Fed would "defend the dollar."

11. Recently the Fed announced an increase in the discount rate, and the stock market fell while the dollar rose on international exchange markets. Can economic theory explain this?

12. Elaborate on the reasoning underlying the following newspaper story.[2]

    The U.S. is doing surprisingly well lately with the current account in its international-payments book. *That account covers trade in goods and services plus certain unilateral transfers . . . this basic measure of international competitiveness has a moderating influence on both the price spiral and joblessness, and private analysts say it indicates that the White House incumbent probably won't be embarrassed by an acute weakness of the U.S. dollar any time soon. . . .*

A relatively strong dollar helps restrain inflation, economists note, by making imported goods relatively cheap in dollar terms. Moreover, if the dollar stays fairly steady, the Federal Reserve Board won't have to jack up interest rates to make the dollar attractive for foreigners to hold. If a return to last spring's super-steep interest rates can be averted, then a sharp rise in unemployment might also be avoided.

13. In the early 1960s, the United States had high unemployment and balance-of-payments deficits. In the late 1960s, the United States had high inflation and balance-of-payments deficits. Why did the Fed find it easier to respond to the problems of the late 1960s?

14. Income taxes have been reduced in order to increase a nation's output. Will the central bank have to buy or sell foreign currencies to keep the value of its currency constant? Explain your reasoning.

15. In 1987 an economist with the Federal Reserve Bank of San Francisco wrote that "The failure of the trade balance to turn around has been held responsible for dampening GNP growth. . . . Unfortunately, the discussion of the relationship between the trade balance and economic growth has generally failed to specify clearly the driving forces behind the expected trade improvement."[3] Give an example of a macroeconomic event that would improve the U.S. trade balance while dampening GNP. Identify a macroeconomic event that would improve the U.S. trade balance, while stimulating GNP.

16. If a nation imposes high taxes on imported goods, will the value of its currency appreciate, or depreciate? Explain your reasoning.

17. Write a rebuttal to this argument.[4]

[U.S.] exports to Mexico fell by a staggering 60 percent, and our $4 billion trade surplus with Mexico turned into a $4 billion deficit in 1982. Based on an estimate that every $1 billion increase in U.S. exports creates 24,000 new jobs in the U.S. economy, the Mexican debt problem alone appears to have cost the U.S. 200,000 jobs in 1982. Clearly, in this case, any aid to help Mexico service its external debts will not only help promote world financial stability, but will also benefit the U.S. economy.

18. A news article reported that "The Europeans, particularly the French, have complained that high U.S. interest rates force them to increase their own interest rates to prevent an outflow of capital from Europe."[5] Why do Europeans object to high interest rates if these do, indeed, succeed in keeping investors at home?

19. How would an increase in reserve requirements affect the foreign-exchange value of the dollar? If our trading partners did not want the value of the dollar changed in this way, should their central banks increase or reduce their money supplies?

20. Explain whether purchasing-power parity supports or refutes the following argument.[6]

International currency stabilization will, however, only be possible when national economies are stable — when the industrial countries have succeeded in combining reasonably high employment with tolerably stable prices. Until then all talk of international currency reform will be in a vacuum and can safely be ignored except by those whose employment depends on the discussion.

21. It has been estimated that the central banks of France, Germany, Italy, Japan, Switzerland, the United Kingdom, and the United States lost more than $10 billion on their foreign exchange transactions between 1973 and 1979.[7] How did they do this? Why do they gamble in the foreign-exchange casino?

22. After World War II, the Allied occupation

forces replaced the German reichsmark with the deutschemark, with ten reichsmarks worth one deutschemark. In 1990, a newspaper story about the coming monetary unification of East and West Germany wrote that "Few Germans who were around at the time will forget the day in 1948 when they lost 90% of their money."[8] Did the 1948 currency conversion have real economic effects?

23. Explain the economic logic behind the following *Wall Street Journal* news stories.

    The U.S. dollar spurted higher against most major currencies, carried aloft by higher American interest rates and speculation that the Federal Reserve System hadn't eased credit conditions as some analysts had believed. Gold's price dipped $8 an ounce, to $618.40. (July 13, 1980)

    The U.S. dollar plunged on a drop in U.S. and [Eurodollar] interest rates and the price of gold recovered some of its losses from earlier this week. (July 17, 1980)

24. Some economists say that it is no accident that the U.S. experienced record trade and budget deficits in the early 1980s. Explain how each of the following economic events affects the trade deficit (imports minus exports) and the budget deficit (federal government spending minus revenue).
    a. A Fed open-market sale.
    b. A sharp increase in the value of the dollar.

25. A vast oil field has been discovered in New Hampshire, shifting the U.S. aggregate supply curve rightward. How will this economic event affect the United States money supply if the world is on a gold standard? How will it affect the value of the U.S. dollar if exchange rates are floating?

26. Use Table 23.3 to determine the effects of reduced government spending in one country, accompanied by open-market operations by a second nation designed to hold its output and prices steady, on employment, output, prices, interest rates, and the exchange rate.

27. The Reagan administration tried to reduce the U.S. trade deficit with Japan by encouraging U.S. exports to Japan.
    a. To encourage exports, should the U.S. government aim to raise or lower the value of the dollar relative to the yen?
    b. If this policy is successful, how will it affect output and employment in both of these countries?
    c. If the monetary authority in each nation acts to offset these trade effects on output and employment, will it try to raise or lower interest rates?
    d. If investors anticipate the exchange-rate change assumed in (a), will U.S. interest rates tend to be higher or lower than Japanese interest rates?

28. In a classical market-equilibrium model, predict how the abolishment of compulsory retirement ages in the United States would affect U.S.
    a. output.
    b. employment.
    c. wages.
    d. prices.
    e. interest rates.
    f. the value of the dollar.

29. Money-market funds made bonds more accessible to small investors and thereby reduced the demand for money. How did this institutional development affect U.S. output, prices, and interest rates? Did this development cause the U.S. dollar to appreciate, or to depreciate? If foreign nations wanted to offset this effect on the value of the dollar, what could they have done about it?

30. If the Fed increases reserve requirements, will the following go up or down?
    a. Interest rates.
    b. Output.
    c. Unemployment.
    d. Investment spending.
    e. The value of the dollar.

References

Chapter 1

1. Lil Phillips, "Phindex Shows Horrific Inflation," *Cape Cod Times,* July 10, 1984.
2. John A. Johnson, "Sharing Some Ideas," *Cape Cod Times,* July 12, 1984.
3. *Barron's,* July 30, 1984.
4. "Inflation to Smile About," *Los Angeles Times,* January 11, 1988.
5. Robert L. Rose, "Retirement Planning Should Begin with Early Look at Social Security," *Wall Street Journal,* April 30, 1985.
6. Gerald Krefetz, *How to Read and Profit From Financial News* (New York: Ticknor & Fields, 1984), p. 1.

Chapter 2

1. W. S. Jevons, "Barter," in *Money and the Mechanism of Exchange* (New York: D. Appleton, 1892), pp. 1–7.
2. Paul Einzig, *Primitive Money,* 2nd ed. (Oxford: Pergamon Press, 1966), p. xi.
3. Art Pine, "Fixed Assets, or: Why a Loan in Yap Is Hard to Roll Over," *Wall Street Journal,* March 29, 1984.
4. John Kenneth Galbraith, *Money* (Boston: Houghton Mifflin, 1975), p. 8.
5. Peter W. Barnes, "Treasury Officials Have Money to Burn but Generally Don't," *Wall Street Journal,* August 20, 1980.
6. Richard N. Cooper, "The Gold Standard: Historical Facts and Future Prospects," *Brookings Papers on Economic Activity,* I, 1982, pp. 1–45.
7. David Ricardo, *The Works and Correspondence of David Ricardo,* Vol. IV, Pamphlets 1815–23, Piero Sraffa, ed. (Cambridge: Cambridge University Press, 1951), pp. 59, 62.
8. Galbraith, *Money,* p. 59.

Chapter 3

1. Jack L. Hervey, "Dollar Drop Helps Those Who Help Themselves," *Chicago Fed Letter,* March 1988, pp. 1–3.
2. *Houston Chronicle,* November 16, 1980.
3. William Tuohy, "The Pound: Pride Goeth Before a Fall," *Los Angeles Times,* January 17, 1985; Paul Lewis, "Weak Pound: An Opportunity," *New York Times,* January 18, 1985.
4. Lester Thurow, *Los Angeles Times,* May 26, 1985.
5. "On the Hamburger Standard," *The Economist,* September 6, 1986.
6. "Junk Currencies," *The Economist,* April 2, 1988, p. 66.
7. Galbraith, *Money,* p. 310.

8. "A Financial North Star" (editorial), *Wall Street Journal,* February 26, 1990.
9. "Why Europeans Care About U.S. Interest Rates," *Boston Globe,* July 14, 1981.
10. William Tuohy, "The Pound: Pride Goeth Before a Fall," *Los Angeles Times,* January 17, 1985.
11. Andrew Reinbach, "Topping Out," *U.S. Real Estate Week,* March 9, 1987, p. 7.
12. Edward Yardeni, "Money & Business Alert," Prudential-Bache Securities, April 22, 1987.

Chapter 4

1. Charles Mackay, *Memoirs of Extraordinary Popular Delusions and the Madness of Crowds* (London: Richard Bentley, 1841. Reprinted Boston: L. C. Page, 1932), p. 37.
2. Galbraith, *Money,* pp. 73–74.
3. A. B. Hepburn, *A History of Currency in the United States* (New York: Macmillan, 1915), p. 102.
4. Quoted in Herman E. Krooss and Martin R. Blyn, *A History of Financial Intermediaries* (New York: Random House, 1971).
5. William M. Gouge, *A Short History of Paper Money and Banking in the United States* (1835. Reprinted New York: Augustus M. Kelly, 1968).
6. H. Parker Willis and George W. Edwards, *Banking and Business* (New York: Harper and Brothers, 1925), pp. 96–97 and *New York Times,* March 22, 1931, Section IV, p. 10.
7. John Maynard Keynes, *A Treatise on Money,* Vol. 1 (London: Macmillan, 1930), pp. 41–43.
8. See, for example, John Wenninger and Charles M. Sivesind, "Defining Money for a Changing Financial System " Federal Reserve Bank of New York *Quarterly Review* (Spring 1979), pp. 1–8.
9. *Wall Street Journal,* December 29, 1979.

Chapter 5

1. James A. Wilcox, "Tax-Free Bonds," *Federal Reserve Bank of San Francisco Weekly Letter,* March 14, 1986.
2. Robert J. Samuelson, "Interest Rates Are Lower — Does that Equal 'Right'?" *Los Angeles Times,* March 13, 1986.
3. Stephen C. Leuthold, "Interest Rates, Inflation, and Deflation," *Financial Analysts' Journal* (January–February 1981), pp. 28–41.
4. Lawrence H. Summers, "The Non-Adjustment of Nominal Interest Rates: A Study of the Fisher Effect," in James Tobin, ed., *Macroeconomics, Prices, and Quantities,* Essays

in Memory of Arthur M. Okun (Washington, D.C.: Brookings Institution, 1983), pp. 201–241.

5. *New Yorker,* September 22, 1986, p. 111.

6. *London Times,* quoted in the *New Yorker,* March 11, 1985, p. 138.

7. Jane Bryant Quinn, "A Savings Program for College Tuition," *Cape Cod Times,* September 6, 1987.

8. Gerald Krefetz, *How to Read and Profit from Financial News* (New York: Ticknor & Fields, 1984), p. 43.

9. Krefetz, pp. 44–45.

10. Debra Whitefield, "Money Talk," *Los Angeles Times,* June 4, 1987.

11. Carmella M. Padilla, "It's a . . . a . . . a . . . All-Terrain Vehicle, Yeah, That's It, That's the Ticket," *Wall Street Journal,* July 17, 1987.

12. Family Real Estate advertisement, *Claremont Courier,* November 1, 1986.

13. James Flanigan, "Tax Reform: Time for Logical Deductions," *Los Angeles Times,* March 15, 1987.

14. Karen Slater, "Premium Municipal Bonds Touted for Overall Return," *Wall Street Journal,* June 3, 1988.

15. William E. Fruhan, Jr., "How Fast Should Your Company Grow?," *Harvard Business Review,* January-February 1984, p. 87.

Chapter 6

1. Edward I. Altman and Scott A. Nammacher, "The Default Rate Experience on High Yield Corporate Debt," Morgan Stanley & Co., March 1985.

2. Securities and Exchange Commission, "Report to Congress on the Accounting Professions and the Commission's Oversight Role," 1980.

3. Robert N. Anthony, "Games Government Accountants Play," *Harvard Business Review,* September–October 1985, p. 161.

4. M. Weinstein, "The Effect of a Rating Change Announcement on Bond Prices," *Journal of Financial Economics,* December 1977, pp. 329–350. G. Hettenhouse and W. Satoris, "An Analysis of the Information Value of Bond-Rating Changes," *Quarterly Review of Economics and Business,* Summer 1976, pp. 65–78, agree, but Louis H. Ederington, Jess B. Yawitz, and Brian E. Roberts, "The Information Content of Bond Ratings," NBER Working Paper No. 1323, April 1984, disagree.

5. Paul Asquith, David W. Mullins, and Eric D. Wolff, "Original Issue High Yield Bonds: Aging Analysis of Defaults, Exchanges, and Calls," *Journal of Finance,* September 1989, pp. 923–52.

6. Theodore J. Forstmann, "Violating Our Rules of Prudence," *Wall Street Journal,* October 25, 1988.

7. W. B. Hickman, *Corporate Bond Quality and Investor Experience* (New York: National Bureau of Economic Research, 1958).

8. G. Pye, "Gauging the Default Premium," *Financial Analysts' Journal,* January–February 1974, pp. 49–52.

9. Edward Altman and Scott Nammacher, "The Default Experience on High Yield Corporate Debt," *Financial Analysts' Journal,* July–August 1985, pp. 25–41.

10. Fraine and Mills.

11. Gail Bronson and Jeffrey H. Birnbaum, "Soaring Interest Rates Pit Manufacturers Against Retailers on Timing of Payments," *Wall Street Journal,* December 8, 1980.

12. *Wall Street Journal,* October 6, 1980.

13. World Bank, *World Development Report 1989* (Oxford: Oxford University Press, 1989), p. 23.

14. B. Steinberg, "How the Debt Bomb Might Be Defused," *Fortune,* May 2, 1983, p. 130.

15. Andrew Tobias, *The Only Investment Guide You'll Ever Need* (New York: Harcourt Brace Jovanovich, 1978), p. 3.

16. Standard & Poor's, *Debt Ratings Criteria: Municipal Overview,* 1986, p. 23.

17. Standard & Poor's, *Debt Ratings Criteria: Industrial Overview,* 1986, p. iii.

18. Galbraith, "A Classic Case of 'Euphoric Insanity,'" *New York Times,* November 23, 1986.

19. *Federal Reserve Bulletin,* September 1989, p. A40.

20. Irwin L. Kellner, "Why Interest Rates Are High," *The Manufacturers Hanover Economic Report,* March 1983, pp. 1–3.

Chapter 7

1. Robert J. Shiller, "Conventional Valuation and the Term Structure of Interest Rates," National Bureau of Economic Research Working Paper #1610, 1985 (and several references therein).

2. For example, B. G. Malkiel, *The Term Structure of Interest Rates* (Princeton, N.J.: Princeton University Press, 1966); C. R. Nelson, *The Term Structure of Interest Rates* (New York: Basic Books, 1972).

3. Gary Smith, *Money and Banking* (Reading, Mass.: Addison-Wesley, 1982), pp. 98–99.

4. Another study found that the standard deviations increased less than proportionately for bonds with durations of one to five years during the period 1950–79: Jonathan E. Ingersoll, Jr., "Is Immunization Feasible?" in George G. Kaufman, G. O. Bierwag, and Alden Toevs, eds. *Innovations in Bond Portfolio Management: Duration Analysis and Immunization* (Greenwich, Conn.: JAI Press, 1983), p. 175.

5. Jane Bryant Quinn, "Woman's Day Money Facts," *Woman's Day,* April 27, 1982, p. 29.

6. Tom Herman and Matthew Winkler, "Curve on Yields Poses Dilemma for Bond Buyer," *Wall Street Journal,* November 11, 1988.

7. "Personal Investing," *New York Times Financial Planning Guide,* May 19, 1985.

8. Martin Baron, "'Lions,' 'Tigers,' 'Cats,' Await Small Investor," *Los Angeles Times,* November 21, 1982.

9. Edward Yardeni, "Money & Business Alert," Prudential-Bache Securities, November 20, 1985, p. 1.
10. Jack Clark Francis, *Management of Investments,* 2nd ed. (New York: McGraw-Hill, 1988), p. 500.
11. Constance Mitchell, "U.S. Needs a Few Good Investors As It Tries to Sell 40-Year Bonds," *Wall Street Journal,* April 6, 1990.
12. Karen Slater, "Jumping on the Bondwagon," *Wall Street Journal,* December 2, 1985.
13. Robert Guenther, "Banking Outside the U.S. Is Becoming Less Foreign," *Wall Street Journal,* July 11, 1990.
14. Quoted in Steven Mintz, "Strategies," *Investment Management World,* May–June 1986, p. 22.
15. Frederick R. Macaulay, *Some Theoretical Problems Suggested by the Movement of Interest Rates, Bond Yields, and Stock Prices in the United States Since 1856,* New York: Columbia University Press, 1938.
16. "Business Bulletin," *Wall Street Journal,* March 13, 1986.
17. Krefetz, p. 27.
18. David M. Gordon, "Reining In on the Federal Reserve," *Los Angeles Times,* September 30, 1986.
19. Paul Watro, "Bank Earnings: Comparing the Extremes," Federal Reserve Bank of Cleveland, 1987.
20. Eric N. Berg, "Fixed-Rate Mortgages Held Threat to Lenders," *New York Times,* March 10, 1986.
21. Alice Priest Shafran, "Streetsmarts for Househunters," *Sylvia Porter's Personal Finance Magazine,* September 1986, p. 37.
22. Jeffrey H. Birnbaum, "J. C. Penney Switches to Long-Term Debt to Fight Burgeoning Interest Expenses," *Wall Street Journal,* October 14, 1980.
23. Barbara Donnelly, "Pros Offer Methods for Sizing Up Bonds," *Wall Street Journal,* May 11, 1989.

Chapter 8

1. David Dreman, *The New Contrarian Investment Strategy* (New York: Random House, 1982), p. 233.
2. Kathryn M. Welling, "Let the Buyer Beware," *Barron's,* November 7, 1977, p. 13.
3. *Wall Street Journal,* June 17, 1981.
4. George Anders, "Portfolio Insurance Provided Cold Comfort," *Wall Street Journal,* October 28, 1987.
5. Fischer Black and Myron Scholes, "The Pricing of Options and Corporate Liabilities," *Journal of Political Economy,* 1973, pp. 637–654.
6. Quoted in Richard J. Teweles and Frank J. Jones, *The Futures Game,* 2nd ed. (New York: McGraw-Hill, 1987), p. 11.
7. Eric N. Berg, "Contrarians on Campus," *New York Times,* November 18, 1984.
8. Hume & Associates, "The TED Spread," 1986.
9. Hume & Associates, "The GSR Trade," 1986.
10. Bill Sing, "Possibility of a Bear Market Doesn't Mean Inves-

tors Have to Hibernate," *Los Angeles Times,* October 10, 1987.
11. Anise C. Wallace, "Chasing Option and Dividend Income," *New York Times,* August 4, 1985.
12. H. J. Maidenberg, "Stock Options — Traders' New Game," *New York Times,* September 2, 1973.

Chapter 9

1. Dan Dorfman, "Fed Boss Banking on Housing Slump to Nail Down Inflation," *Chicago Tribune,* April 20, 1980.
2. Quoted in Arthur Schlesinger, Jr., "Inflation Symbolism vs. Reality," *Wall Street Journal,* April 9, 1980.
3. "Housing Squeeze Tightens More Here," *Houston Chronicle,* April 3, 1980.
4. Don G. Campbell, "S&Ls Turn to Mortgage Acceleration to Help Bail Themselves Out," *Los Angeles Times,* September 12, 1982.
5. Andrew Carron, of the Brookings Institution, quoted in "While Congress Fiddles, More Thrifts Burn," *The Economist,* February 27, 1982, p. 73.
6. Dennis Jacobe, director of research at the U. S. League of Savings Associations, quoted in Eric N. Berg, "Fixed-Rate Mortgages Held Threat to Lenders," *New York Times,* March 10, 1986.
7. Franco Modigliani, "Comment," in James Tobin, editor, *Macroeconomics: Prices and Quantities* (Washington, D.C.: Brookings Institution, 1983), p. 243. One example is an April 11, 1987 *Wall Street Journal* column (David B. Hilder, "ARMs Race On, but Borrowers Face Choices") in which negative amortization is said to be a "drawback."
8. "Nibbling Down Affordable Mortgages," *Business Week,* March 14, 1983, p. 153.
9. David Henry, "Lender of Last Resort," *Forbes,* May 18, 1987, pp. 73–75.
10. David Pauly, "Bracing for the Great Car Glut," *Newsweek,* September 15, 1986, p. 59.
11. Robin Gross and Jean V. Cullen, *Help! The Basics of Borrowing Money* (New York: Times Books, 1980), p. 45.
12. R. J. Turner, *The Mortgage Maze,* Arlington, Va.: Alexandria House Books, 1982, p. 64.
13. Don G. Campbell, "Early Loan Payoff Gains Popularity," *Los Angeles Times,* October 20, 1985.
14. Douglas R. Sease, "Buying a Car? Here's How to Figure Savings in Latest Offers from GM, Ford, and Chrysler," *Wall Street Journal,* May 3, 1982.
15. Turner, pp. 242–43.
16. "How to Save on a Car Loan," *Consumer Reports,* April 1978, pp. 201–202.
17. "Hot Tips," *Sylvia Porter's Personal Finance,* February 1986, p. 18.
18. Irwin T. Vanderhoof, "The Use of Duration in the Dynamic Programming of Investments," in George G. Kaufman, G. O. Bierwag, and Alden Toevs, eds., *Innovations in Bond*

Portfolio Management: Duration Analysis and Immunization (Greenwich, Conn.: JAI Press, 1983), p. 46.

19. Don G. Campbell, "Biweekly 'Yuppie Mortgages' Interest State Lenders," *Los Angeles Times,* April 26, 1987.

20. Don G. Campbell, "Creating a Market for Biweeklies," *Los Angeles Times,* April 26, 1987.

21. First Federal Savings of the Palm Beaches, letter dated July 11, 1986.

Chapter 10

1. The classic references are John Burr Williams, *The Theory of Investment Value* (Cambridge, Mass.: Harvard University Press, 1938) and Benjamin Graham and David L. Dodd, *Security Analysis* (New York: McGraw-Hill, 1934).

2. Williams, pp. 57–58.

3. John Maynard Keynes, *The General Theory of Employment, Interest, and Money* (New York: Macmillan), 1936, p. 154.

4. Andrew Tobias, *The Only Investment Guide You'll Ever Need* (New York: Harcourt Brace Jovanovich, 1978), p. 37.

5. Vartanig G. Vartan, "Dow Off by 11.44 to 806.91 as Fears on Fed Heighten," *New York Times,* November 2, 1977.

6. For example, see Charles P. Kindleberger, *Manias, Panics, and Crashes* (New York: Basic Books, 1978).

7. A wonderful account is given by Frederick Lewis Allen, *Only Yesterday* (New York: Harper, 1931).

8. Allen, p. 333.

9. Edmund Wilson, "Hull-House in 1932: III," *New Republic,* February 1, 1933, p. 320.

10. *Wall Street Journal,* January 19, 1987.

11. Goldman, Sachs, "Portfolio Strategy," October 22, 1987, p. 1.

12. James B. Stewart and Daniel Hertzberg, "Speculative Fever Ran High in the 10 Months Prior to Black Monday," *Wall Street Journal,* December 11, 1987.

13. John Dorfman, "An Appraisal: Enormous Volume Could Be a Good Sign, Some Say," *Wall Street Journal,* October 19, 1987.

14. Felix Rohatyn, a general partner in Lazard Frères & Co., quoted in James B. Stewart and Daniel Hertzberg, "How the Stock Market Almost Disintegrated a Day After the Crash," *Wall Street Journal,* November 20, 1987.

15. Robert J. Shiller, "Investor Behavior in the October 1987 Stock Market Crash: Survey Evidence," Yale University, November 1987. Also see "What Really Ignited the Market's Collapse After Its Long Climb," *Wall Street Journal,* December 16, 1987.

16. Some classic references are Eugene F. Fama, "The Behavior of Stock Market Prices," *Journal of Business,* January 1965, pp. 34–105, and Eugene F. Fama and Marshall E. Blume, "Filter Rules and Stock Market Trading," *Journal of Business,* 1966, pp. 226–241.

17. R. Ball and P. Brown, "An Empirical Evaluation of Ac-

counting Income Numbers," *Journal of Accounting Research,* Autumn 1968, pp. 159–178. But see O. Maurice Joy and Charles P. Jones, "Earnings Reports and Market Efficiencies: An Analysis of Contrary Evidence," *Journal of Financial Research,* 1979, pp. 51–64, and Eugene H. Hawkins, Stanley C. Chamberlin, and Wayne E. David, "Earnings Expectations and Security Prices," *Financial Analysts' Journal,* September–October 1984, pp. 24–38.

18. Avner Arbel and Bikki Jaggi, "Market Information Assimilation Related to Extreme Daily Price Jumps," *Financial Analysts' Journal,* November–December 1982, pp. 60–66.

19. David Dreman, *The New Contrarian Investment Strategy* (New York: Random House, 1982), pp. 108–113.

20. Mark Hulbert's ratings, cited in Peter Brimelow, "Rating the Advisers," *Barron's,* July 15, 1985, pp. 6–7.

21. Irwin Friend, Marshall Blume, and Jean Crockett, *Mutual Funds and Other Institutional Investors: A New Perspective,* Twentieth Century Fund Study (New York: McGraw-Hill, 1971).

22. Patricia C. Dunn and Rolf D. Theisen, "How Consistently Do Active Managers Win?" *Journal of Portfolio Management,* Summer 1983, pp. 47–50.

23. Mark Kritzman, "Can Bond Managers Perform Consistently?" *Journal of Portfolio Management,* Summer 1983, pp. 54–56.

24. For a first-person account, see R. Foster Winans, "The Crash of a Wall Street Reporter," *Esquire,* September 1986, pp. 233–241.

25. *Wall Street Journal,* January 2, 1987.

26. Robert Goerner, "Viva Vino," *Performing Arts,* January 1984, p. 15.

27. Richard Ney, interviewed on the television program "Firing Line," December 10, 1975.

28. Randall Smith, "Chrysler May Consider a Different Direction in Place of Its Bond-Heavy Pension Strategy," *Wall Street Journal,* January 21, 1987.

29. Allen Parkman, "Using Economic Analysis in Your Practice," *ABA Journal,* February 1, 1987, pp. 54–58.

30. Michael H. Sherman, "Cash Signals a Lack of Confidence," *Investment Management World,* March–April 1986, p. 23.

31. Peter L. Bernstein, "Diversification: Old, New, and Not-So-New," *Financial Analysts' Journal,* March–April 1985, pp. 22–24.

32. James Flanigan, "Stock Market Clock May Soon Strike Midnight," *Los Angeles Times,* March 14, 1986.

33. Cited in Dreman, p. 130.

34. James Flanigan, "Wall Street's Disaster Was All Too Real," *Los Angeles Times,* December 13, 1987.

35. Sidney Cottle, Roger F. Murray, and Frank E. Block, *Graham and Dodd's Security Analysis,* 5th ed. (New York: McGraw-Hill, 1988).

36. Burton Crane, *The Sophisticated Investor* (New York: Simon and Schuster, 1959), p. 18.

37. *Consumers Digest,* "Get Rich Investment Guide," Volume 3, No. 4, 1982, p. 63.

38. 1986 advertisement for *Penny Stock Advisor,* Coral Springs, Florida.

39. "Money & Business Alert," Prudential-Bache Securities, November 20, 1985.

40. Kidder, Peabody & Co., "Portfolio Consulting Service," May 20, 1987.

41. Quoted in *Business Week,* December 1, 1986, p. 50.

42. John Fedders, quoted in Julie Kosterlitz, "The Thomas Reed Affair," *Common Cause,* January–February 1983, p. 17.

Chapter 11

1. Leo Gould, *You Bet Your Life* (Hollywood, California: Marcel Rodd, 1946).

2. Harry Markowitz's classic book is *Portfolio Selection,* New York: Wiley, 1959; James Tobin applied mean-variance analysis to macroeconomic theory in "Liquidity Preference as Behavior Towards Risk," *Review of Economic Studies,* February 1958, pp. 65–86.

3. Adam Smith, *The Wealth of Nations,* 1776. Reprinted London: Methuen, 1920, Vol. 1, Ch. 10, p. 109.

4. Carmen Brutto, quoted in *New York Times,* February 17, 1976.

5. William S. Peters, "The Psychology of Risk in Consumer Decisions," in George Fisk, ed., *The Frontiers of Management and Psychology,* New York: Harper, 1964, pp. 209–223.

6. J. H. Evans and S. H. Archer, "Diversification and the Reduction of Dispersion: An Empirical Analysis," *Journal of Finance,* December 1968, pp. 761–767.

7. John R. Dorfman, "Company Offers Gold at a Big Discount in Phone Solicitations — but With a Catch," *Wall Street Journal,* October 12, 1987.

8. Alexandra Peers, "Psych 101: Investor Behavior," *Wall Street Journal,* November 13, 1987.

9. Thomas C. Noddings, *Advanced Investment Strategies,* Homewood, Illinois: Dow Jones-Irwin, 1978, p. 51.

10. Hans R. Stoll and Robert E. Whaley, "Program Trading and Expiration-Day Effects," *Financial Analysts' Journal,* March–April 1987, pp. 16–28.

11. Stanley J. Cohen and Robert Wool, *How to Survive on $50,000 to $150,000 a Year,* Boston: Houghton Mifflin, 1984, p. 36.

12. Roger G. Ibbotson and Rex A. Sinquefield, *Stocks, Bonds, Bills and Inflation: 1986 Yearbook,* Ibbotson Associates, Inc., Chicago, Illinois, 1986.

13. Barbara Quint, *Money,* September 1976.

Chapter 12

1. See Herman E. Kroos and Martin R. Blyn, *A History of Financial Intermediaries* (New York: Random House, 1971), pp. 134–136.

2. Condy Raguet, *A Treatise on Currency and Banking,* 1839; Reprinted. (New York: Augustus M. Kelley, 1967), p. 92.

3. Kroos and Blyn, p. 134.

4. Both quoted in Krooss and Blyn, p. 119.

5. Milton Friedman and Anna Jacobsen Schwartz, *A Monetary History of the United States, 1867–1960,* National Bureau of Economic Research (Princeton: Princeton University Press, 1963), pp. 269–270.

6. For example, John K. Galbraith, *Money* (Boston: Houghton Mifflin, 1975), pp. 131, 175–180.

7. For example, Krooss and Blyn, p. 170.

8. Galbraith, *Money,* p. 194.

9. Galbraith, *Money,* pp. 186–187.

10. Krooss and Blyn, p. 13.

11. Arthur Okun, "Rules and Roles for Fiscal and Monetary Policy" in *Fiscal and Monetary Policy: The Eclectic Economist Views the Controversy,* J. J. Diamond, ed. (Chicago: De Paul University, 1971), p. 59.

12. R. Alton Gilbert and Geoffrey E. Wood, "Coping with Bank Failures: Some Lessons from the United States and the United Kingdom," *Federal Reserve Bank of St. Louis Review,* December 1986, pp. 5–14.

13. Fred Schwed, Jr., *Where Are the Customers' Yachts?* (New York: Simon and Schuster, 1940), p. 91.

14. *Time,* November 18, 1929, p. 45.

Chapter 13

1. Arthur F. Burns, "Maintaining the Soundness of Our Banking System," Speech to American Bankers Association Convention, Honolulu, Hawaii, October 21, 1974.

2. Frank Wille, "Dissenting Statement, FDIC Approves Merger in Alice, Texas," News Release, FDIC, August 18, 1975.

3. Editorial, "The Centralizing of the System," *Financier,* April 1980, pp. 5–6.

4. Economic Policy Commission, American Bankers Association, *The Guaranty of Bank Deposits* (New York: ABA, 1933), p. 43.

5. Quoted in Arthur M. Schlesinger, Jr., *The Coming of the New Deal* (Boston: Houghton Mifflin, 1958), p. 443.

6. "A Guide to the Federal Home Loan Bank System," FHLB System Publication Corporation, March 1987, p. 18.

7. "A Guide to the Federal Home Loan Bank System," p. 21.

8. "Who's Killing the Thrifts?" *Newsweek,* November 10, 1986.

9. James Ring Adams, "The Big Fix," *American Spectator,* March 1989, pp. 21–24.

10. Charles McCoy and Paulette Thomas, "Hundreds of S&Ls Fall Hopelessly Short of New Capital Rules," *Wall Street Journal,* December 7, 1989.

11. Paulette Thomas, "As S&L Bailout Plan Draws Nearer Passage, Flaws Become Clearer," *Wall Street Journal,* July 21, 1989.

12. For example, R. Alton Gilbert, "Bank Failures and Public Policy," *Federal Reserve Bank of St. Louis Review,* November 1975, p. 12. See also K. E. Scott and T. Mayer, "Risk and Regulation in Banking: Some Proposals for Federal Deposit Insurance Reform," *Stanford Law Review,* May 1971, pp. 857–902.

13. Federal Deposit Insurance Corporation, *The First Fifty Years: A History of the FDIC, 1933–1983,* Washington, D.C., 1984, pp. 97–98.

14. See "The Examiners: Now the Customers Check Out the Banks; So Do Other Banks," *Wall Street Journal,* September 9, 1976.

15. Gary Smith, *Investments* (Glenview, Ill.: Little, Brown–Scott, Foresman, 1990), pp. 190–195.

16. For example, Edward J. Kane, National Bureau of Economic Research, Working Paper #2317, 1987.

17. Richard F. Janssen and Edward P. Foldessy, "After a Near-Disaster, Savings Banks Vow to Take Tougher Stance in Making Loans," *Wall Street Journal,* May 20, 1980.

18. H. Parker Willis, John M. Chapman, and Ralph W. Robey, *Contemporary Banking,* New York: Harper, 1933, p. 560.

19. Federal Reserve Board of Governors, *Annual Report,* 1956, pp. 52–55.

20. Dan Dorfman, "Fed Banking on Housing Slump to Nail Down Inflation," *Chicago Tribune,* April 20, 1980.

21. James Tobin, "Deposit Interest Ceilings as a Monetary Control," *Journal of Money, Credit and Banking,* February 1970, pp. 4–14.

22. Michael Weinstein, "ATM Makers Perceive Opportunities Despite Signs of Saturation," *American Banker,* December 19, 1984, p. 14.

23. John Duffy, executive vice president of Security Pacific Corporation, *Wall Street Journal,* September 3, 1980.

24. Richard Flamson, chief executive officer of Security Pacific Corporation, *Wall Street Journal,* September 3, 1980.

25. Herbert Stein, "Backstage at the Fed," *Wall Street Journal,* April 4, 1986.

26. *Wall Street Journal,* June 12, 1980.

27. James Tobin 1970, pp. 4–14.

28. Quoted in Jonathan D. Aronson, *Money and Power: Banks & the World Monetary System,* Beverly Hills, CA: Sage Publications, 1977.

29. "A Guide to the Federal Home Loan Bank System," FHLB System Publication Corporation, March 1987.

30. "Banking Deregulation Benefits Many People but Stirs Some Worry," *Wall Street Journal,* September 30, 1985.

31. "A Guide to the Federal Home Loan Bank System," FHLB System Publication Corporation, March 1987, p. 59.

32. Charles S. Sanford, Jr., President, Bankers Trust Company, "Glass-Steagall: An Anti-Competitive Rule," speech to the American Bankers Association Investment and Funds Management Conference, Atlanta, Georgia, February 15, 1984.

33. G. Christian Hill, "Strategy That Failed Seems Likely to Alter S&Ls Future Tactics," *Wall Street Journal,* May 16, 1980.

34. Bruce Horovitz, "Behind the Scenes of a Bank Takeover by FDIC," *Los Angeles Times,* January 5, 1986.

35. James Bates and Daniel Akst, "Regulators Close Center National Bank," *Los Angeles Times,* April 12, 1986.

36. James R. Booth, "The Securitization of Lending Markets," *Federal Reserve Bank of San Francisco Weekly Letter,* September 29, 1989.

37. Pomona First Federal Savings, "Interest," Fall 1989, p. 3.

38. Michael Quint, "Accounting Proposal Irks Bankers," *New York Times,* November 21, 1989.

39. G. Christian Hill and Michael Allen, "High Yields for Deposits Fall, Thanks to Thrift Rescue," *Wall Street Journal,* August 24, 1989.

40. Eric N. Compton, *The New World of Commercial Banking* (Lexington, Mass.: D. C. Heath, 1987), p. 105.

41. James McMahon, vice president of the Western Independent Bankers group, *New York Times,* October 19, 1980.

Chapter 14

1. *New York Times,* May 25, 1980.

2. "Concerns Mount Over Banks' Liabilities," *New York Times,* June 25, 1985.

3. David B. Hilder, "More Thrifts Grow Big by Investing in Areas Other Than Mortgages," *Wall Street Journal,* May 6, 1987.

4. Don G. Campbell, "S&Ls Turn to Mortgage Acceleration to Help Bail Themselves Out," *Los Angeles Times,* September 12, 1982.

5. Campbell.

6. "While Congress Fiddles, More Thrifts Burn," *The Economist,* February 27, 1982.

7. Richard F. Janssen and Edward P. Foldessy, "After a Near-Disaster, Savings Banks Vow to Take Tougher Stance in Making Loans," *Wall Street Journal,* May 20, 1980.

8. Karlyn Mitchell, "Interest Rate Risk Management at Tenth District Banks," *Federal Reserve Bank of Kansas City Economic Review,* May 1985, pp. 3–19.

9. The data in this exercise are from CalFed's 1985 *Annual Report,* pp. 7, 28–29.

10. Mitchell.

Chapter 15

1. Kenneth Bacon, staff reporter, *Wall Street Journal,* August 4, 1980, p. 1.

2. John Wood, "A Model of Federal Reserve Behavior," *Monetary Process and Policy,* George Horwich, ed. (Homewood, Ill.: Irwin, 1967).

3. G. J. Santoni, "The Monetary Control Act, Reserve Taxes and the Stock Prices of Commercial Banks," *Federal Reserve Bank of St. Louis Review,* June–July 1985, pp. 12–20.

4. Peter S. Rose, "Banker Attitudes Toward the Federal Reserve System: Survey Results," *Journal of Bank Research* (Summer 1977), pp. 77–84.

5. Santoni.
6. Alexandra Peers, "How Discount-Rate Rise Will Affect Consumer Fees — and When," *Wall Street Journal,* February 27, 1989.
7. *Houston Chronicle,* February 15, 1980.
8. *Report of the Committees on Finance and Industry* (London: His Majesty's Stationery Office, 1931), p. 97.
9. Federal Reserve Bank of St. Louis, *U.S. Financial Data,* December 10, 1982, p.1.
10. *Investment Newsletter,* "Capital Gains," 1986.
11. J. Anthony Boeckh and Richard Coghlan, "The Inflation Risk and Prospective Returns for the 1980s," in J. Anthony Boeckh and Richard T. Coghlan, editors, *The Stock Market and Inflation* (Homewood, Ill.: Dow Jones-Irwin, 1982), pp. 146–147.
12. Robert J. Samuelson, "Interest Rates are Lower — Does that Equal 'Right'?" *Los Angeles Times,* March 13, 1986.

Chapter 16

1. Paul Samuelson, "Money, Interest Rates and Economic Activity: Their Interrelationships in a Market Economy," in American Bankers Association, *Proceedings of a Symposium on Money, Interest Rates, and Economic Activity,* 1967, p. 44.
2. Sherman Maisel, *Managing the Dollar* (New York: Norton, 1975), p. 278.
3. A. M. Schlesinger, Jr., *The Crisis of the Old Order* (Boston: Houghton Mifflin Co., 1957), p. 231.
4. John M. Keynes, *The General Theory of Employment, Interest, and Money* (London: Macmillan, 1936).
5. *New York World,* October 15, 1930.
6. John Kareken and Robert Solow, "Lags in Monetary Policy," in Commission on Money and Credit, *Stabilization Policies* (Englewood Cliffs, N.J.: Prentice-Hall, 1963).
7. Gary Fromm and Lawrence Klein, "A Comparison of Eleven Econometric Models of the United States," *American Economic Review,* 63 (May 1973).
8. Kareken and Solow, p. 2.
9. Milton Friedman, "The Lag in the Effect of Monetary Policy," *Journal of Political Economy* (1961), pp. 447–466.
10. For a formal analysis see Gary Smith, "Monetarism, Bondism, and Inflation," *Journal of Money, Credit, and Banking,* May 1982.
11. Henry C. Simons, "Rules vs. Authorities in Monetary Policy," in *Journal of Political Economy* (February 1936), pp. 13–14, 29–30.
12. Simons, p. 16.
13. Simons, p. 30.
14. Simons, *Economic Policy for a Free Society* (Chicago: University of Chicago Press, 1948).
15. Edward S. Shaw, "Money Supply and Stable Economic Growth," in H. H. Jacoby, *United States Monetary Policy* (New York: Praeger, 1964), p. 89.

16. Robert E. Lucas, Jr., "Unemployment Policy," *American Economic Review,* 68, May 1978, p. 357.
17. Robert E. Lucas, Jr., "Tobin and Monetarism: A Review Article," *Journal of Economic Literature* (June 1981), pp. 562–63.
18. Paul Samuelson, "Reflections on Central Banking," reprinted in *The Collected Scientific Papers of Paul Samuelson,* Volume 2, Joseph Stiglitz, ed. (Boston: M.I.T. Press, 1966), p. 1362.
19. Laurie McGinley, "The Fed Is Bracing for Political Criticism As Campaign Goes On," *Wall Street Journal,* February 1, 1984.
20. *Los Angeles Times,* November 22, 1981.
21. L. C. Anderson, "The State of the Monetarist Debate," *Federal Reserve Bank of St. Louis Review,* September 1973, p. 4.
22. Milton Friedman, "Lessons From the 1979–1982 Monetary Policy Experiment," *American Economic Review,* Papers and Proceedings, May 1984, pp. 397–400.
23. Charles P. Kindleberger, *Manias, Panics and Crashes* (New York: Basic Books, 1978), p. 73.
24. Herbert Stein, *Presidential Economics* (New York: Simon & Schuster, 1984), p. 250.
25. Lyle Gramley, "Financial Innovation and Monetary Policy," *Federal Reserve Bulletin,* July 1982, p. 396.
26. Victor A. Canto and Arthur B. Laffer, "Monetary Policy Caused the Crash: Not Tight Enough," *Wall Street Journal,* October 22, 1987.

Chapter 17

1. For example, see Irving Fisher, *The Purchasing Power of Money* (New York: Macmillan, 1911).
2. John Burr Williams, *The Theory of Investment Value* (Cambridge, Mass.: Harvard University Press, 1938), p. 52.
3. John Maynard Keynes, *The General Theory of Employment, Interest and Money* (London: Macmillan, 1936), p. 33.
4. Milton Friedman, "The Quantity Theory of Money: A Restatement," in *Studies in the Quantity Theory of Money* (Chicago: University of Chicago Press, 1956), pp. 3–21.
5. For example, see Thomas Mayer, *The Structure of Monetarism* (New York: W. W. Norton, 1978).
6. A frequently cited survey is David Laidler, *The Demand for Money: Theories and Evidence,* third ed. (New York: Dun-Donnelly, 1985).
7. See Friedman's comments in *Milton Friedman's Monetary Framework,* Robert J. Gordon, ed. (Chicago: University of Chicago Press, 1974).
8. Keynes, p. 167.
9. Keynes, pp. 195–196.
10. Keynes, p. 196.
11. Keynes, p. 171.
12. James Tobin, "Liquidity Preference as Behavior Towards Risk," *Review of Economic Studies,* February 1958, pp. 65–86.

13. Lyle Gramley, "Financial Innovation and Monetary Policy," *Federal Reserve Bulletin,* July 1982, p. 396.

14. In a number of empirical macro models, attempts to peg monetary aggregates lead to unstable policies. See John H. Ciccolo, "Is Short-Run Monetary Control Feasible?" New York: Federal Reserve Bank of New York, 1974, and Lawrence Radecki, "Short-run Monetary Control: An Analysis of Some Possible Dangers," *Federal Reserve Bank of New York Quarterly Review,* Spring 1982, pp. 1–10. Also see Henry C. Wallish and Peter M. Keir, "The Role of Operating Guides in U.S. Monetary Policy: An Historical Review," *Federal Reserve Bulletin,* September 1979, especially p. 688.

15. "Solomon Sees Fed Policy Changes," *Los Angeles Times,* December 29, 1981.

16. Edward S. Shaw, "Money Supply and Stable Economic Growth," in H. H. Jacoby, *United States Monetary Policy* (New York: Praeger, 1964), pp. 74, 76.

17. Karl Brunner, Alan Meltzer, the St. Louis Fed, and even Milton Friedman have all expressed support for targeting the monetary base; see, for example, Milton Friedman, "Monetary Policy for the 1980s," in *To Promote Prosperity: U.S. Domestic Policy in the Mid-1980s,* edited by John H. Moore (Stanford: Hoover Institution Press, 1984), pp. 23–60.

18. Anthony Harris, "Competition vs. Monetarism, Study in Policy Schizophrenia," *Financier,* October 1981, p. 48.

19. Herbert Stein, "Verbal Windfall," *New York Times Magazine,* September 9, 1979, p. 14.

20. Paul Volcker, "A Broader Role for Monetary Targets," *Federal Reserve Bank of New York Quarterly Review,* Spring 1977, p. 27.

21. Federal Reserve Bank of Cleveland, *Economic Trends,* November 1989, p. 2.

22. William Poole, *Money and the Economy: A Monetarist View* (Reading, Mass.: Addison-Wesley, 1978), p. 19.

23. William T. Gavin, "The M1 Target and Disinflation Policy," *Economic Commentary,* Federal Reserve Bank of Cleveland, October 1, 1985, p. 1.

24. Edward Yardeni, "Money & Business Alert," Prudential-Bache Securities, January 15, 1986.

25. Franco Modigliani, *New York Times,* November 6, 1977.

26. Associated Press, "NOW Account Funds Cause M1B to Surge $11.6 Billion," *Houston Chronicle,* January 17, 1981.

27. James Tobin, "The Monetary Interpretation of History, A Review Article," *American Economic Review,* June 1965, pp. 464–485.

28. Lindley H. Clark, Jr., *Wall Street Journal,* Sept. 30, 1980.

29. Milton Friedman and Anna Schwartz, *A Monetary History of the United States, 1867–1960* (Princeton, N.J.: Princeton University Press, 1963), p. 563.

30. Paul A. Volcker, statement before the Subcommittee on Monopolies and Commercial Law of the Committee on the Judiciary, U.S. House of Representatives, May 5, 1982,

printed in the *Federal Reserve Bulletin,* May 1982, pp. 298–301.

31. Federal Reserve Bank of Cleveland, *Economic Trends,* January 1990, p. 2.

32. William T. Gavin, "The M1 Target and Disinflation Policy," *Economic Commentary,* Federal Reserve Bank of Cleveland, October 1, 1985.

33. Wallish and Keir, p. 688.

34. James Tobin, "The Interest-Elasticity of Transactions Demand for Cash," *Review of Economics and Statistics,* August 1956, pp. 241–247; William J. Baumel, "The Transactions Demand for Cash: An Inventory Theoretic Approach," *Quarterly Journal of Economics,* November 1952, pp. 545–556.

35. George Akerlof and Ross Milbourne, "New Calculations of Income and Interest Elasticities in Tobin's Model of the Transactions Demand for Money," *Review of Economics and Statistics,* November 1978, pp. 541–546.

Chapter 18

1. Lindley H. Clark, Jr., "Speaking of Business: The Elderly Economist," *Wall Street Journal,* February 12, 1980.

2. *Federal Reserve Bulletin,* October 1979, p. 830.

3. "Record of Policy Actions of the Federal Open Market Committee," *Federal Reserve Bulletin,* December 1979, p. 974.

4. *Wall Street Journal,* October 30, 1980.

5. *Wall Street Journal,* October 14, 1980.

6. Quoted in Kenneth Bacon, "Better Economic News Helps Smother Flames of Fed-Carter Dispute," *Wall Street Journal,* October 6, 1980.

7. John T. Wooley, *Monetary Politics* (London: Cambridge University Press, 1984), p. 105.

8. *Wall Street Journal,* August 26, 1981.

9. Paul Volcker, July 1985, quoted in Edward Yardeni, *Money & Business Alert,* Prudential-Bache Securities, January 27, 1988.

10. Michael C. Keeley and Gary C. Zimmerman, "Interest Checking and M1," *Federal Reserve Bank of San Francisco Weekly Letter,* November 21, 1986.

11. Alan Walters, "The Right Stuff," *Economist,* May 4, 1985, pp. 23–25.

12. Preston Martin, speech to an Agricultural Outlook Conference, quoted in Prudential-Bache Securities, *Money & Business Alert,* December 4, 1985.

13. Lucien O. Hooper, "Coping With Indefiniteness," *Financial World,* April 18–May 1, 1984.

14. *Wall Street Journal,* September 15, 1980.

15. Associated Press, "Money Supply Climbs $4.2 Billion," *Los Angeles Times,* May 2, 1986.

16. W. Lee Hoskins, "Breaking the Inflation-Recession Cycle," *Economic Commentary,* Federal Reserve Bank of Cleveland, October 15, 1989, p. 1.

17. *Wall Street Journal,* October 29, 1980.
18. Robert J. Gordon, *Economist,* November 15, 1982.
19. Congressional Budget Office, "The Economic and Budget Outlook: An Update," August 1985, pp. 40–41.
20. Edward Yardeni, "Money & Business Alert," Prudential-Bache Securities, January 8, 1986, p. 1; the quotations from the Volcker letter are also from Yardeni.
21. "Record of Policy Actions of the Federal Open Market Committee," *Federal Reserve Bulletin,* August 1988, p. 540.
22. Yardeni, "Money & Business Alert," Prudential-Bache Securities, February 16, 1986.
23. Jude L. Naes, Jr., "U.S. Financial Data," Federal Reserve Bank of St. Louis, October 29, 1982, p. 1.
24. Bharat Trehan and Carl Walsh, "Examining the Recent Surge in M1," *Federal Reserve Bank of San Francisco Weekly Letter,* November 15, 1985, pp. 1–3.
25. James D. Bowyer, "Money," *United,* April 1986, p. 16.

Chapter 19

1. John Maynard Keynes, *The General Theory of Employment, Interest and Money* (New York: Macmillan, 1936), p. 317.
2. Keynes, p. 122.
3. J. Hicks, "Mr. Keynes and the 'Classics': A Suggested Interpretation," *Econometrica,* April 1937, pp. 147–59.
4. *Los Angeles Times,* December 8, 1983.
5. *Wall Street Journal,* September 17, 1980.

Chapter 20

1. Quoted in Paul Samuelson, "A Brief Survey of Post-Keynesian Developments," in *Keynes' General Theory: Reports of Three Decades,* Robert Lekachman, ed. (New York: St. Martin's Press, 1964), p. 333.
2. James Tobin, *New York Times,* May 7, 1988.
3. John Maynard Keynes, *The General Theory of Employment, Interest, and Money* (London: Macmillan, 1936), p. 266.

Chapter 21

1. Robert Lucas, "Unemployment Policy," *American Economic Review,* Papers and Proceedings, May 1978, p. 354.
2. T. R. Malthus, *An Essay on the Principle of Population* (London: J. Murray, 1817).
3. Milton Friedman and Anna Jacobsen Schwartz, *A Monetary History of the United States, 1867–1960,* National Bureau of Economic Research (Princeton, N.J.: Princeton University Press, 1963).
4. *Wall Street Journal,* October 22, 1980.
5. Keynes, pp. 16–17.
6. Robert E. Hall, "Employment Fluctuations and Wage Rigidity," *Brookings Papers on Economic Activity,* 1980:1, p. 99.
7. William H. Beveridge, *Full Employment in a Free Society* (New York: W. W. Norton, 1945), p. 18.
8. James Tobin, "Inflation and Unemployment," *American Economic Review,* Papers and Proceedings, May 1972, p. 3.
9. *Los Angeles Times,* September 9, 1983.
10. *Fortune,* October 1976.

Chapter 22

1. Milton Friedman, "What Price Guideposts?" in *Guidelines, Informal Controls, and the Marketplace,* G. Schultz and R. Aliber, editors (Chicago: University of Chicago, 1969).
2. A. W. Phillips, "The Relation Between Unemployment and the Rate of Change of Money Wages in the United Kingdom, 1861–1957," *Economica,* November 1958, pp. 283–99. The Phillips' curve was actually discovered by Irving Fisher, "A Statistical Relation Between Unemployment and Price Changes," *International Labour Review,* June 1926, pp. 785–92.
3. Arthur Schlesinger, Jr., "Inflation Symbolism vs. Reality," *Wall Street Journal,* April 9, 1980.
4. *New York Times,* February 22, 1970.
5. George Perry, "Changing Labor Markets and Inflation," *Brookings Papers on Economic Activity,* 1970, pp. 411–41; also see Charles Schultze, "Has the Phillips Curve Shifted? Some Additional Evidence," *Brookings Papers on Economic Activity,* 1971, pp. 452–67.
6. Robert Solow, *Technology Review,* December–January 1979, p. 31.
7. *Wall Street Journal,* May 20, 1980.
8. William Fellner, "The Valid Core of Rationality Hypotheses in the Theory of Expectations," *Journal of Money, Credit, and Banking,* November 1980, pp. 763–87.
9. James Tobin, "How Dead Is Keynes?" *Economic Inquiry,* 15 (October 1977), pp. 459–68.
10. Madame de Staël, *Ten Years of Exile* (New York: Saturday Review Press, 1972), p. 143.
11. For some formal evidence of how different prices matter to different households, see R. Michael, "Variations Across Households in the Rate of Inflation," *Journal of Money, Credit, and Banking,* February 1979, pp. 32–46; and R. P. Hagemann, "Inflation and Household Characteristics: An Analysis of Group Specific Price Indexes," U.S. Department of Labor, Bureau of Labor Statistics, Working Paper No. 110, December 1980.
12. David Ricardo, *The Works and Correspondence of David Ricardo,* Volume III, P. Sraffa, ed. (Cambridge: Cambridge University Press, 1951), pp. 136–37.
13. John Maynard Keynes, *Economic Consequences of the Peace* (New York: Harcourt, Brace and Rowe, 1920), pp. 235–36.

14. James Tobin, "Inflation and Unemployment," *American Economic Review* (1972), p. 15. But see M. S. Feldstein, "The Welfare Cost of Permanent Inflation and Optimal Short-Run Economic Policy," *Journal of Political Economy* (1979), pp. 749–68. For a list of inflation costs, see Stanley Fischer and Franco Modigliani, "Towards an Understanding of the Real Effects and Costs of Inflation," *Weltwirtschaftliches Archiv,* 1978, pp. 810–33.

15. S. C. Leuthold, "Interest Rates, Inflation and Deflation," *Financial Analysts' Journal,* January–February 1981, pp. 28–41.

16. G. J. Santoni and Courtenay C. Stone, "Navigating Through the Interest Rate Morass: Some Basic Principles," *Federal Reserve Bank of St. Louis Review,* March 1981, p. 18.

17. Peter B. Roche and Tom Herman, *Wall Street Journal,* July 18, 1980.

18. John Maynard Keynes, *Monetary Reform* (New York: Harcourt, Brace and Company, 1924), p. 12.

19. *Wall Street Journal,* September 3, 1974.

20. William E. Donoghue, *William E. Donoghue's Complete Money Market Guide,* excerpted in Consumer's Digest, *Get Rich Investment Guide,* Volume 3, Number 4, 1982, pp. 226–227.

21. James D. Bowyer, "To Sell or Not to Sell," *United,* April 1986.

22. Herbert Stein, *Presidential Economics* (New York: Simon & Schuster, 1984), p. 222.

Chapter 23

1. For the details, see Gary Smith, *Macroeconomics* (New York: W. H. Freeman, 1985), pp. 532–544.

2. Richard Janssen, *Wall Street Journal,* August 22, 1980.

3. Carl Walsh, "The Trade Balance and the Economic Outlook," *Federal Reserve Bank of San Francisco Weekly Letter,* March 6, 1987, p. 1.

4. Hang-Sheng Cheng, "Bailing Out Banks?" *Federal Reserve Bank of San Francisco Bulletin,* July 29, 1983.

5. John M. Legeo, "U.S. Officials Contend European Policies Largely to Blame for High Interest Rates," *Wall Street Journal,* March 1, 1982.

6. John Kenneth Galbraith, *Money* (Boston: Houghton Mifflin), 1975, p. 310.

7. Dean Taylor, "Official Intervention in the Foreign Exchange Market or, Bet Against the Central Bank," UCLA working paper No. 185, October 1980.

8. Tyler Marshall, "German Reunification Gets Bogged Down Over Money," *Los Angeles Times,* April 17, 1990.

Glossary

1951 Accord Accord between the Fed and the Treasury that established the important principle that the Federal Reserve is an independent branch of government and is free to follow monetary policies that it deems appropriate.

adjustable-rate loans A loan on which the rate rises and falls with market interest rates, protecting lending institutions whose deposit rates move with market interest rates. These flexible-rate loans are also known as variable-rate, renegotiable-rate, rollover, and so on, and have a variety of terms and conditions. If the monthly payments are fixed while the loan rate fluctuates, negative amortization may occur.

aggregate demand curve Summarizes the *IS-LM* model of the demand side of the economy. With price level *P* and output *y* on the axes, the aggregate demand curve is negatively sloped because an increase in the price level reduces the real money supply, which pushes interest rates up and discourages spending. Expansionary shifts in the *IS* or *LM* curves shift the aggregate demand curve in an expansionary rightward direction.

aggregate supply curve A positively sloped curve showing the price level at various levels of output. Firms may not be selling all they would like at these price levels, and labor demand need not equal labor supply. The intersection of the aggregate demand and aggregate supply curves shows the levels of output and prices that prevail, not necessarily those levels that simultaneously equilibrate all markets. If there is a classical full-employment equilibrium, then employment and output are unaffected by price changes; hence, the aggregate supply curve is vertical with output always at the full-employment level.

amortized loan A loan that is paid off gradually rather than with a single balloon payment at the end. The periodic payments include principal as well as interest. The most common amortized loan involves constant monthly payments over the life of the loan, with *n* monthly payments *X* set so that their present value at the stated monthly loan rate *R* is equal to the amount borrowed *P*: $X = RP/\{1 - 1/(1 + R)^n\}$.

announcement effect Occurs when the announcement of a policy change, unimportant by itself, signals intentions that are likely to be carried out in other ways. In recent years, discount-rate changes have been more signal than substance. Changes in discount rates are seldom large enough to affect financial markets very much, but because the announcement of a change in the discount rate conveys information about Federal Reserve objectives, an unexpected change in the discount rate (or the absence of a change) sometimes sends tremors through financial markets.

arbitrage A virtually risk-free exploitation of price discrepancies. For example, simultaneously buying stock on one exchange for $20 a share and selling it on another for $22 a share until this price discrepancy is eliminated.

automated teller machines (ATMs) Machines that allow customers to make deposits and withdrawals and obtain account information without actually entering the deposit institution. The first ATMs were installed in the outside walls of banks to allow for after-hours transactions; much of the subsequent growth in ATMs has occurred off bank premises.

average markup A formula that businesses use to set prices, also known as target-return pricing. In this pricing rule of thumb, average costs at normal production levels are calculated and the price is set at some normal markup over these costs, in order to earn a target profit rate.

balloon loans A loan on which the periodic payments include little or no repayment of the principal; thus, the last payment (the balloon payment) must be relatively large. Before the Great Depression, most home mortgages were three- to five-year balloon loans on which only interest was paid until maturity, at which time a balloon payment equal to the size of the loan was due. Today, conventional mortgages are amortized, so that the principal is paid off during the term of the loan.

Bank Holding Company Act The 1956 act, amended in 1970, that defines a bank as an institution that both accepts deposits that can be withdrawn on demand and makes commercial loans. A financial institution that did only one of these activities technically was not a bank but was what some call a "nonbank" bank, and hence was not regulated by the Federal Reserve. The Competitive Banking Equality Act of 1987 closed the nonbank bank loophole by defining a bank as any FDIC-insured institution, but it exempted nonbank banks established before March 5, 1986.

bankers' acceptances A promissory note issued by a firm that the bank stamps "accepted" to guarantee that the bank will repay the note if the firm does not. Bankers' acceptances are used in international trade and are often resold in secondary markets.

barter The trading of goods and services for other goods and services; for example, corn for potatoes or wood for leather.

basis The difference between the futures price and the spot price of an item. For precious metals, financial assets, and other things that can be stored and sold short, the basis is determined by the cost of carry. Because the cost of carry is usually positive, futures prices are generally above spot prices and increase with the amount of time until delivery.

basis points Term used by financial market participants to describe hundredths of a percentage point, because interest rates generally change by only a fraction of a percent each day; e.g., an increase from 8.50 percent to 8.58 percent is 8 basis points.

bearer bonds Bonds for which proof of ownership is demonstrated by possession of the security. (*Cf.* **registered bonds.**)

big board The New York Stock Exchange, on which the stocks of many prominent U.S. corporations are traded.

bills-only policy Policy which the Fed followed during much of the 1950s of restricting its open market operations to Treasury bills.

bimetallic standard A standard under which a nation uses two metals with fixed prices as money. For instance, in the Mint Act of 1792, the U.S. Congress established a bimetallic standard with the price of gold fixed at $19.39 per troy ounce and the price of silver at $1.292 an ounce.

book value The net worth (assets minus liabilities) of a company, often calculated on a per share basis, that is shown on the firm's balance sheets. The market price of the stock may be above or below book value because investors value a firm for the profitability of its assets, whereas accountants look at depreciated cost.

Bretton Woods agreement A 1944 agreement that established fixed exchange rates, with the participating nations' agreement to make whatever currency transactions were required to maintain these exchange rates. This system worked tolerably well through the 1950s but came apart in the 1960s. Since 1973, the major exchange rates have been allowed to fluctuate.

buying on margin Buying stock with borrowed money, thus creating leverage that multiplies the gains or losses when the return on the stock is not equal to the interest rate on the loan. The Federal Reserve sets margin requirements (currently 50 percent), the minimum margin that brokerage firms must require of their customers. With an x percent margin requirement, a stock buyer must pay at least x percent of the cost of the stock, borrowing the rest from the brokerage firm.

call option An option that gives its holder the right, but not the obligation, to buy an asset at a fixed price on or before a specified date. For example, a call option could give the owner the right to buy a share of ABC stock for $100 at any time within six months.

Cambridge cash-balances approach Developed by Alfred Marshall, an economics professor at Cambridge University, and his former student A. C. Pigou, using demand and supply analysis to derive a quantity theory equation. By reinterpreting the quantity theory equation as a statement that money demand is equal to money supply, they suggested that velocity is determined by people's preferences and is not rigidly fixed by a society's bill-paying customs.

capital account   A tabulation of a nation's international purchases and sales of assets. A capital *outflow* for the United States is a U.S. purchase of foreign assets; e.g., an exchange of U.S. dollars for German bonds and Japanese stock. A U.S. capital *inflow* is a foreign purchase of U.S. assets; e.g., Germans buying Treasury bills and Japanese buying IBM stock. A capital-account *surplus* finances a current-account deficit, and a capital-account *deficit* accompanies a current-account surplus.

capital gains   The profit made when an asset is sold for more than its purchase price. A *capital loss* occurs if the sale price is less than the purchase price.

capital market   The market in which purchases and sales of securities with more than a year to maturity take place. (*Cf.* **money market**.)

capital risk   An unanticipated change in an asset's price caused by an unexpected change in interest rates. The longer an asset's duration, the more sensitive its price is to interest rate fluctuations, and the larger the capital risk.

cash flow   Refers to payments consisting of more than one future payment. The present value of a cash flow is equal to the sum of the present values of the individual payments.

certificates of deposit (CDs)   Bank-issued deposit certificates that cannot be redeemed before a fixed expiration date. Large negotiable CDs are issued by banks in denominations of $100,000 or more and can be sold in the short-term bond market.

closed-end investment company   A company having a fixed number of shares outstanding. The shares of closed-end funds are traded on the stock exchanges or over-the-counter, at a market price that need not equal the fund's net asset value.

collateral   Real estate, automobiles, stocks, bonds, and other assets put up by a borrower as security for a loan. These assets become the property of the lender if the borrower defaults.

collateralized mortgage obligations (CMOs)   Bond-like instruments that finance some mortgage pools.

CMOs have fixed interest rates and are divided into several classes. The last class of securities, called the accrual class or Z class, is similar to zero-coupon bonds in that the payment of interest and principal does not begin until the prior three classes have been repaid.

commercial bank   A deposit intermediary that accepts deposits and makes loans.

commercial loan theory of banking   *See* **Real Bills doctrine**.

commercial paper   Short-term bonds issued by low-risk companies.

commodity money   A commodity that is used as a medium of exchange, for example, tobacco in colonial Virginia.

common stock   Corporate stock, the holders of which are the legal owners of the firm; the name indicates that the shareholders own the firm "in common." Stockholders elect (normally with one vote per share) a board of directors that hires the top executives, supervises the management of the firm, and decides the dividends to be paid to shareholders.

compensating balance   A balance, equal to 10 or 20 percent of the size of a loan, deposited in low-interest or no-interest checking accounts, that a firm may be required to maintain by the bank that gave the firm a line of credit, allowing it to borrow funds as needed.

compound interest   Describes the earning of interest on interest, a powerful arithmetic that causes seemingly slight differences in annual returns to grow to large differences in wealth over many years. Over short horizons, this monthly, daily, or even continuous crediting of interest increases the effective return on a bank deposit or other investment by crediting interest on interest. An amount P invested at an annual rate of return R, compounded m times a year, grows to $P(1 + R/m)^m$ after 1 year and to $P(1 + R/m)^{mn}$ after n years.

consol   Also called a *perpetuity*, it pays a perpetual cash flow that continues period after period. For a required rate of return R, the present value of a consol paying X each period is $P = X/R$.

constant dividend growth model   If the dividend

D_1 grows at a constant rate g and the investor's required return is $R > g$, then the present value of a stock simplifies to this central equation of fundamental analysis, $P = D_1/(R - g)$.

Consumer Price Index (CPI)   A widely followed price index that attempts to measure changes in the cost of living for typical U.S. households.

consumption goods   Goods that last only a short while, such as ice cream and strawberries. Gross national product can be divided into consumption goods and investment goods. (*Cf.* **investment goods**.)

continuous compounding   Interest calculations that assume that the frequency of compounding is infinitely large (and the time between compounding infinitesimally small), giving

$$\lim_{m \to \infty} (1 + R/m)^m \to e^R$$

where $e = 2.718 \ldots$ is the base of natural logarithms.

corporate bonds   Fixed-income securities of various maturities issued by corporations to purchase new plants and equipment, pay current bills, and finance the takeover of other companies.

cost of carry   The cost of buying a commodity now and holding it until the delivery date of a futures contract. This cost includes storage, spoilage, insurance, and foregone interest, less any cash flow from the item while it is being held.

coupon rate   The annual coupon as a percentage of a bond's face value; e.g., a bond that pays $1000 at maturity and $45 every six months has a 9 percent coupon rate.

coupons   The periodic (usually semiannual) interest payments on a bond, made in addition to a final payment when the bond matures. Called "coupons" because, traditionally, they were cut from the bond certificate and redeemed through a local bank or securities dealer.

covering   Occurs when, instead of taking delivery, the buyer of a futures contract reverses the position by selling the contract before the delivery date; a contract writer can reverse this position by repurchasing the contract.

crawling peg   A float in which the central bank pegs the exchange rate, but periodically adjusts the peg to correct substantial demand-supply imbalances. (*See also* **managed float** and **dirty float**.)

creative financing   Novel ways of financing sales, usually involving a loan from the seller. Buyers and sellers turn to creative financing when money is tight and it is difficult to get mortgages from financial institutions.

credit scoring   System used by some banks to quantify an individual's creditworthiness based on the economic and demographic characteristics and default frequencies of past borrowers.

crowding out   Occurs when government spending displaces private spending. (*See also* **demand-side crowding out** and **supply-side crowding out**.)

currency appreciation   A nation's currency appreciates as foreign currency becomes less expensive. Before World War I, a British pound cost $4.76; in 1989, it cost $1.50. Over this period, dollars appreciated relative to the pound, and the pound depreciated relative to the dollar.

currency depreciation   A nation's currency depreciates as foreign currency becomes more expensive.

currency outstanding   *See* **U.S. currency outstanding**.

current account   A nation's net international purchases of currently produced goods and services plus its net international transfer payments. The current-account balance must be financed by the sale or acquisition of financial assets — an increase or decrease in foreign claims against the nation. Thus a current-account deficit must be financed by a capital-account surplus (and vice versa).

daily limits   Specified limits on the daily change in the settlement prices of some futures contracts, which are set by exchanges.

daily settlement   The daily transfer of funds from winners to losers required by futures exchanges, using end-of-the-day settlement prices. Also called *marking to market*.

debit cards   Similar in appearance to credit cards and used in stores as are credit cards, but actually representing an electronic checking account in that funds are automatically transferred from the customer's bank account to the merchant's account.

debt In contrast to equity, debt involves a legally binding contract to pay a specified amount of money.

default Occurs when a borrower violates the terms of the debt contract; for example, by not making a scheduled coupon payment on time. A default is not necessarily a complete loss; it may be a temporary suspension of coupon payments or a prelude to a partial payment. In the first month after default, a bond typically trades at 40 percent of its face value.

demand-side crowding out Refers to the fact that, although an increase in government spending directly enlarges aggregate demand, it also increases money demand, pushing interest rates up and thereby discouraging private spending, especially private investment spending. When this crowding out is taken into account, the effect of increased spending on aggregate demand is not as large as indicated by the income-expenditure multiplier.

deposit multiplier The ratio of deposits to the monetary base. Fractional reserve banking multiplies the monetary base into a much larger amount of deposits. The ratio of the change in deposits to a change in the monetary base will not equal the deposit multiplier unless the deposit multiplier is constant.

dirty float A float in which the central bank allows the exchange rate to fluctuate with demand and supply, but occasionally enters the market, often surreptitiously. (*See also* **crawling peg** and **managed float**.)

discount basis Basis on which interest rates are sometimes calculated, relative to the amount paid back rather than the amount loaned; for example, the calculation of Treasury-bill rates relative to face value rather than purchase price. Banks are no longer allowed to calculate consumer-loan rates on a discount basis.

discount rate The interest rate that Federal Reserve Banks charge on loans to deposit institutions.

discount window Window through which deposit institutions can borrow money from the Federal Reserve. The discount window was intended to defuse bank runs by making Federal Reserve Banks reliable lenders of last resort, a source of emergency cash for banks.

disintermediation Occurred when interest rates rose above deposit-rate ceilings — instead of depositing money in financial intermediaries, savers withdrew money and purchased Treasury bills and other market securities. During periods of disintermediation when deposits shrink, intermediaries must look elsewhere for funds or cut back on their lending.

diversified portfolio Because a single asset may be risky, a portfolio of several imperfectly correlated (or, better, negatively correlated) assets can be used to reduce risk. Counting on asset gains and losses to offset each other is of no interest to those who are risk-neutral or risk-seeking, but is very attractive to risk-averse investors.

divisibility The extent to which a fraction of an asset can be purchased or sold for a like fraction of the price of the whole asset.

Dow Jones Industrial Average The widely followed average of the stock prices of thirty prominent blue-chip companies, using a divisor that changes from time to time to offset substitutions and stock splits, thereby maintaining a logically consistent daily index of stock prices. In contrast, market-value indexes such as the S&P 500 and the NYSE indexes, weight each stock's price by the number of shares outstanding.

dual banking system System in the United States in which banks can be chartered (and supervised) by either the federal or state government. Presently, about one-third of all banks are federally chartered.

duration The present-value weighted average number of years until the cash flow of an asset is received. Approximately equal to the percentage change in the asset's present value resulting from a one-percentage-point change in the required return. The duration of a bond with coupons is less than its maturity and decreases as the coupons increase.

duration gap Compares a bank's asset and liability

duration, taking into account that assets are some-what larger than liabilities other than net worth.

$$\text{duration gap} = (\text{duration of assets})$$
$$- (\text{duration of liabilities})\left(\frac{\text{liabilities}}{\text{assets}}\right)$$

The size of the duration gap is an estimate of the change in net worth, as a percentage of total assets, resulting from a one-percentage-point increase in interest rates.

Edge Act   The 1919 act that allows bank holding companies to establish interstate subsidiaries (Edge Act corporations) for accepting deposits and making loans related to international business transactions.

efficient market   A market in which there are no obviously mispriced securities and, therefore, no transactions that can be counted on to make abnormally large profits. The efficient-market hypothesis does not assume that a stock's price is equal to some objective measure of its intrinsic value, or even that all investors agree on that value — only that investors cannot consistently make unusually large profits trading on information. The weak, semi-strong, and strong forms of the efficient market hypothesis state that abnormal profits cannot be made from information about past stock prices, any public information, and any information, respectively.

electronic funds transfer system   A computerized network in which transactions are electronically recorded and funds instantly transferred from the buyer's account to that of the seller.

equation of exchange   The U.S. economist Irving Fisher observed that in every transaction the buyer exchanges a quantity of money equal to the price of the purchased item. Applying this accounting identity to the nation as a whole, the equation of exchange states that $MV_T = P_T T$, where M is the money supply, T is the number of transactions, P_T is the average price of these transactions, and V_T is velocity, the average number of times that money is exchanged during a given accounting period.

equity   A claim on the company's profits after interest and other expenses have been paid and, in the event of liquidation, a claim on the company's assets after its debts have been settled. Contrast to corporate debt and other fixed-income securities.

Eurodollars   U.S. dollar deposits in foreign banks or foreign branches of U.S. banks.

excess reserves   Reserves held by depository institutions beyond those required by the Federal Reserve.

exchange rate   The price of one currency in terms of another; for example, the U.S. dollar price of German marks.

exchange rate risk   Uncertainty about future exchange rates and consequently about the rate of return on an investment denominated in one currency (such as francs) in terms of another (such as dollars). The rate of return, measured in domestic currency, on an investment denominated in foreign currency is equal to the foreign rate of return plus the rate of appreciation of the foreign currency relative to the domestic currency.

exercise date   The date on which an option contract expires.

exercise price   The price at which an option contract can be exercised. Also called the *striking price*.

exercise value   The minimum value of an option — the amount an option holder could save by exercising the option instead of buying or selling the asset at its market price. The exercise value of a call option is equal to the difference $P - E$ between the value of the asset P and the option's exercise price E if $P > E$ (and zero otherwise). The exercise value of a put is equal to $E - P$ if $P < E$ (and zero otherwise).

Expectations Hypothesis   Explains the term structure of interest rates by interest-rate expectations — specifically the Hicks Equation. If securities are priced so that a strategy of rolling over short-term bonds is expected to do as well as a strategy of holding long-term bonds, then when no change in one-year rates is anticipated, comparable assets of differing maturities will all be priced to have the same yield. Longer-term rates will be above the current one-year rate if rates are expected to rise in the future, and below if rates are expected to decline.

expected value A weighted average of the possible returns, using probabilities as weights to reflect the likelihood of each outcome; denoted by the Greek symbol μ, $\mu = x_1 P[x_1] + x_2 P[x_2] + \ldots + x_n P[x_n]$. The expected value is the long-run average if the frequency with which each outcome occurs corresponds to its probability.

Federal Deposit Insurance Corporation (FDIC) Established in the 1930s to insure deposits against bank failure, it has eliminated the panicky bank runs that plagued banks in the past.

federal funds Large, overnight loans of reserves deposited at the Federal Reserve banks. Although these are loans among banks, they are called federal funds because it is the Federal Reserve that electronically credits one bank and debits another.

federal funds rate The interest rate on interbank loans through the federal funds market.

Federal Home Loan Bank (FHLB) system Created in the 1930s to supervise and assist S&L's. All federally chartered S&L's must join the FHLB system; qualified state-chartered S&L's may join if they wish. There are twelve district federal home loan banks that, since 1951, have been privately owned by the member institutions. The Federal Home Loan Bank Board supervised the FHLB system until 1989 when it was replaced by two new organizations: the Office of Thrift Supervision, which now charters, regulates, and supervises S&L's, and the Federal Housing Finance Board, which now oversees the twelve federal home loan banks.

Federal Home Loan Mortgage Corporation (Freddie Mac) Established in 1970 by the Federal Home Loan Board, owned by the twelve federal home loan banks and individual thrift institutions. Freddie Mac is similar to both Fannie Mae and Ginnie Mae in that it puts together pools of mortgages, financing its purchases by the sale of pass-through mortgage participation certificates and bond-like instruments called Guaranteed Mortgage Certificates (GMCs) and Collateralized Mortgage Obligations (CMOs).

Federal National Mortgage Association (FNMA, or Fannie Mae) Established in 1938 to funnel funds to mortgage borrowers. In 1968, it was split into two separate organizations: a private corporation that retained the name Fannie Mae, and a government corporation, the Government National Mortgage Association (Ginnie Mae). Fannie Mae sells short- and medium-term bonds, using the proceeds to buy mortgages from mortgage bankers and other mortgage originators. Although privately owned, Fannie Mae is subject to government supervision; in return, Fannie Mae borrows some money directly from the federal government and is able to borrow privately at relatively low rates because it is a quasi-governmental agency.

Federal Open Market Committee (FOMC) Consists of the seven Fed Governors and five of the twelve Federal Reserve bank presidents; most monetary policy decisions are made at its monthly meetings.

Federal Reserve Board (Fed) Comprised of seven governors, appointed by the president to overlapping fourteen-year terms, it is the primary monetary authority in the United States.

Federal Savings and Loan Insurance Corporation (FSLIC) Established by Congress in 1933 with the FDIC to insure deposits in S&L's. In 1989 the insolvent FSLIC was replaced with a new deposit-insurance fund for thrifts, the Savings Association Insurance Fund (SAIF), which is administered by the FDIC.

fiat money Something that has little value as a commodity but, because of law or tradition, is accepted as a medium of exchange; for example, Yap stones and U.S. Federal Reserve notes.

financial assets Paper claims, such as bank deposits, bonds, and stocks. In the United States and other countries with well-developed financial markets, many savers invest in financial assets that are issued by borrowers to raise funds to lend to others or to acquire physical assets.

Financial Institutions Reform, Recovery, and Enforcement Act of 1989 (FIRREA) An act that imposes higher, asset-based capital requirements on deposit institutions, which are to be strictly enforced by promptly closing insolvent institutions. An insured deposit intermediary must either be chartered as a bank or be a Qualified Thrift Lender with 70 percent of its assets in residential mortgage-related assets. The insolvent FSLIC was replaced by SAIF, administered by the FDIC. The Office of Thrift Supervision (OTS) was established with the power to charter, regulate, and supervise all thrifts, whether state or federally chartered. The Resolution Trust Corporation, a division of the FDIC, raises funds through bond sales to terminate insolvent thrifts by subsidizing acquisitions or paying off depositors.

financial intermediaries Intermediaries such as commercial banks, credit unions, insurance companies, and mutual funds, that borrow from some economic agents and lend to others.

financial markets Established means for trading bonds, stocks, and other financial assets. These come in many different forms (such as the New York Stock Exchange and the over-the-counter market) and involve a variety of agents (including brokers and dealers).

fiscal policy The federal government's expenditures and tax rates, which are determined by Congress and the president. Any deficit between federal outlays and revenue is financed by the sale of Treasury debt; the Federal Reserve can use open-market operations to monetize as much or as little of this debt as it wishes. (*Cf.* **monetary policy**.)

fixed-income securities A security in which the amount of money to be repaid is specified in the promissory note.

float Arises from discrepancies in the dates on which payments and receipts are recorded. The Federal Reserve's check-clearing procedures create float for banks when one bank is credited with reserves from a cashed check before another bank's reserves are debited. Federal Reserve float is an interest-free loan to banks from the Federal Reserve.

forward contract A private agreement to deliver a certain item on a specified date at a price agreed to today, but not paid until delivery. Futures contracts are similar, but are standardized and traded on organized exchanges. (*Cf.* **futures contract**.)

forward prices Prices agreed to today but not paid until the specified future delivery date. A U.S. importer who has agreed to pay a certain amount of yen for a product six months from now and wants to guarantee the dollar cost of the product can pay dollars now for a six-month forward contract for yen.

forward rates The implicit future rates of return embedded in the term structure of interest rates, in the sense that these are the future interest-rate values for which the strategies of buying long-term securities and rolling over short-term securities do equally well. An investor whose interest-rate expectations are not equal to these implicit forward rates has reason for preferring shorts to longs, or vice versa.

fractional reserve banking A system of banking in which depository institutions keep only a fraction of their deposits as reserves. If these deposits are a medium of exchange, then the depository institutions create money.

full-employment output The level of production at which excess demands are balanced by excess supplies, so that overall there is no substantial demand-supply pressure on prices. The overall pressure on a nation's prices can be gauged by comparing actual output with the economy's full-employment output. When actual output is above full-employment output, there are many excess demands, few excess supplies, and considerable upward pressure on costs and prices. When an economy's actual output is below its full-employment potential, there are few markets with excess demands and many with excess supplies, so that markets are exerting downward pressure on costs and prices.

full-employment surplus Often called the *high-employment surplus* or *structural surplus*, it is an estimate of what the government's budget surplus (or deficit) would be if the economy were operating at full employment.

fundamental analysis Analysis used by investors to compare the price of a security to the present value of the anticipated cash flow. This approach leads to a study of a firm's dividends, earnings, and assets.

future value   Value of an investment after it has earned a specified rate of return for a given number of years. If an amount P earns an annual rate of return R for n years, the investment grows to $F = P(1+R)^n$.

futures contract   An agreement to deliver a certain item on a specified date at a price agreed to today, but not paid until delivery. For example, a mill might agree to pay a farmer $3 per bushel for 100,000 bushels of wheat delivered six months from now — thus eliminating the mill's uncertainty about the cost of wheat and the farmer's uncertainty about revenue. Unlike forward contracts, futures contracts are standardized and traded on organized exchanges. Futures can be used for hedging a position (e.g., a farmer can sell wheat futures); for speculation (e.g., a wager on the price of silver); or for arbitrage (e.g., stock index arbitrage).

gap (of a bank)   Defined as

gap = (rate-sensitive assets)
    − (rate-sensitive liabilities)

If the interest rates on a bank's rate-sensitive assets and liabilities change, the bank's annual income will change by the size of its gap multiplied by the size of the change in interest rates.

gap analysis   Techniques by which banks gauge their exposure to interest-rate risk. Gap analysis focuses on how interest rates affect income; in contrast, *duration analysis* considers the effect of interest rates on net worth. Gap analysis estimates the effect of interest rates on income by estimating the fraction of assets and liabilities that are adjustable-rate, with interest rates that move up and down with market interest rates during some target horizon, perhaps one year.

Garn-St Germain Depository Institutions Act   Established in 1982 in response to the S&L crisis, this act hastened the deregulation of banking. Banks and thrifts were authorized to offer money-market deposit accounts with no interest-rate ceiling and no reserve requirement so that they could compete with money-market funds. Federal thrifts were allowed to diversify their assets away from home mortgages by making business loans and by increasing their consumer loans and loans secured by nonresidential real estate. The act affirmed the power of the FDIC and FSLIC to arrange interstate mergers if necessary, and to allow banks to make interstate acquisitions of closed banks or thrifts with assets of at least $500 million.

Generally Accepted Accounting Principles (GAAP)   The Securities and Exchange Commission (SEC) requires that financial statements conform to these principles, which are adopted by the Financial Accounting Standards Board (FASB). The FASB is an independent group that is supported financially by the accounting industry and periodically publishes its opinions on accounting practices that it considers acceptable.

Glass-Steagall Act   This 1933 act prohibits U.S. commercial banks from engaging in investment-banking activities, i.e., helping businesses and state and local governments raise money through the sale of securities. To comply with the law, banks were forced to specialize in either commercial or investment banking. Foreign banks can operate both as commercial and investment banks in the United States, unconstrained by Glass-Steagall.

gold standard   A standard under which a nation's money is either gold or convertible into gold at a fixed price. Between 1834 and 1933, with the exception of the Civil War and an occasional financial panic, the United States was effectively on a gold standard in which the government bought and sold gold at the fixed price of $20.67 per ounce. Consistent with this commitment, the U.S. twenty-dollar gold piece contained a little less than an ounce of gold.

goods-and-services balance   Similar to a nation's trade balance but encompassing services as well as goods, including interest and dividend payments, tourist expenditures, purchases and sales of military equipment, and foreign expenses of operating military bases abroad.

Government National Mortgage Association (GNMA, or Ginnie Mae) Government corporation that resulted from the split in 1968 of the Federal National Mortgage Association (FNMA, or Fannie Mae) into two separate organizations. It is part of the Department of Housing and Urban Development (HUD) and administers government mortgage subsidy programs that had previously been handled by Fannie Mae; for example, using Treasury money to make HUD-subsidized mortgages. In 1970, Ginnie Mae created the revolutionary idea of selling pass-through GNMA certificates to finance the purchase of mortgages from private institutions.

graduated-payment mortgages (GPM) Mortgage for which the monthly payments are initially low and then increase over time to ease the financial burden on young homeowners who expect nominal income to grow steadily. Ideally, the mortgage payments will be a constant fraction of income, rather than a constant dollar amount.

Gresham's Law Axiom that bad money drives out good. A medium of exchange that is more valuable in some nonmonetary use will be withdrawn from circulation; for example, silver dollars containing more than a dollar's worth of silver, or a rare quarter worth more than 25 cents to a collector.

gross national product (GNP) The market value of the aggregate production of new goods and services, e.g., houses, automobiles, haircuts, financial advice, during a specified period of time, usually a year or a quarter of a year. GNP excludes the purchase and sale of items that were produced in earlier periods, such as the purchase of a used car, an old house, or a painting by Andy Warhol. Gross national product is not considered a comprehensive measure of production because it excludes most activities that do not involve a financial transaction; for example, do-it-yourself projects and voluntary activities.

Hicks equation In accordance with the Expectations Hypothesis, the term structure of interest rates is such that long-term rates are the product of the current and anticipated future short-term rates:

$$(1 + R_n)^n = (1 + R_1)(1 + R_1^{+1}) \ldots (1 + R_1^{n-1})$$

high-powered money Label sometimes applied to the monetary base because, with fractional reserve banking, government money can support a much larger quantity of deposit money.

holding companies Some banks have evaded restrictions on branching and other activities by setting up holding companies, which can control a variety of banking and nonbanking subsidiaries. Some holding companies are established to administer several banks; others are conglomerates that control a variety of nonfinancial businesses as well as banks.

hyperinflation An extremely rapid rate of inflation. In Germany from 1922–1923, prices increased at a rate of 322 percent a month; in Hungary from 1945–1946, prices increased by 19,800 percent a month.

idiosyncratic risk Also called *micro risk, unsystematic risk,* or *diversifiable risk;* it arises from events specific to individual companies and can be diversified away.

income Encompasses the benefits received while owning an asset. This includes the cash flow generated by the investment, e.g., the interest from a bond, dividends from a stock, and rent from an apartment building, and the services provided by an asset, e.g., transportation from a car, shelter from a house, and pleasure from fine art.

income risk Uncertainty about the rates of return that the cash flow from an investment will earn when it is reinvested. The purchase of long-term assets is profitable if interest rates fall unexpectedly; rolling over short-term assets does well if interest rates rise unexpectedly.

index arbitrage The attempt to earn risk-free profits whenever the basis, or spread, between the price of a stock-index futures contract and the index itself differs from the cost of carry (the Treasury-bill rate minus the dividend yield on the stocks in the index) by more than the transactions costs that arbitrage entails. Arbitrageurs buy stocks and sell futures if the futures price is too high and do the reverse if it is too low.

inflation A persistent, continuing increase in the prices of goods and services. Inflation is often measured by the change in the Consumer Price Index (CPI), which monitors the cost of a standard amount of goods and services.

inflation risk   Created by uncertainty about future prices. The purchasing power of the proceeds from an investment depends on the course of prices. An unexpected increase or decrease in the rate of inflation erodes and swells, respectively, the purchasing power of fixed nominal cash flows. Although inflation and interest rates do not move in unison, a strategy of rolling over short-term assets at least offers the likelihood that nominal interest rates will increase if inflation does.

interest-rate parity equation   States that, for the basis to equal the cost of carry, the difference between the dollar futures and spot prices of a foreign currency should approximately equal the difference between U.S. and foreign interest rates.

intermediate targets   Targets often used by the Federal Reserve to help achieve its ultimate objectives. For example, the Fed might use M1 as an intermediate target, aiming for a 5 percent increase in M1 during the next 12 months, not because it particularly cares about the rate of growth of M1, but because it believes that by hitting its 5 percent target for M1, it will be able to accomplish its objectives regarding unemployment, inflation, and other variables of real economic consequence.

International Monetary Fund (IMF)   Established at Bretton Woods to lend foreign exchange to nations that need to buy their currency in order to stabilize exchange rates, the IMF now lends foreign exchange to nations that need help paying for imports.

intrinsic value   The present value of a stock's prospective cash flow, discounted by the investor's required return, taking into account the returns available on alternative investments, its risk, and other salient considerations. A stock is worth buying if its intrinsic value is larger than its price, but not otherwise.

investment bank   A firm that helps businesses and state and local governments issue and trade securities.

investment company   A company that pools investor funds and buys a portfolio of securities, provid-

ing diversification and, it hopes, superior management. These may be either open-end or closed-end.

investment goods   The components of gross national product, such as factories and apartment buildings, that last for a considerable period of time. (*Cf.* **consumer goods.**)

IS curve   A positively sloped curve that shows those values of y and R for which planned spending is just equal to output. The *IS* curve is shifted in an expansionary rightward direction by an increase in private or government spending caused by any event other than a change in y or R.

junk bonds   The generic label for low-quality debts, i.e., unrated bonds or low-rated bonds issued by companies that either are not well known or are known to be risky. Some of these bonds are *new junk*, sold to finance risky ventures, and some are *fallen angels*, bonds issued by companies that were once financially secure and now are not.

L (liquidity)   A monetary aggregate that includes M3, savings bonds, short-term liquid Treasury securities, commercial paper, and bankers' acceptances.

law of one price   An axiom that the domestic price of a foreign item will equal the domestic price of a comparable domestic item. Otherwise, no one will buy the more expensive item.

leverage   Occurs when a relatively small investment reaps the benefits or losses from a much larger investment; for example, the use of borrowed money to finance an investment. Leverage is said to be a two-edged sword because it multiplies gains and losses. If a fraction x of an investment is your own money, then your degree of leverage is $1/x$. If you pay a rate B on the borrowed money and earn a rate of return R on the total investment, then the rate of return on your own money is $B + (1/x)(R - B)$.

liability management   The aggressive search by banks for attractive sources of funds. Since the early 1960s, as deposit rates have become increasingly flexible, banks have come to view the garnering of funds as important as their allocation.

limited liability   Refers to the fact that, although

stockholders are the legal owners of a corporation, they are not personally responsible for its debts; their potential loss is limited to the amount of money they have invested in the firm's stock.

liquid assets Cash or assets that can be readily converted into cash, needed to accommodate withdrawal risks, through both deposits and loans. In addition to return and risk, banks must maintain an effective balance between illiquid assets and liquid assets.

liquidity Gauges how easily an asset can be converted into a medium of exchange. Liquidity can be measured by how far ahead one has to look for a buyer in order to obtain a competitive price.

liquidity constrained Households or businesses that have a limited ability to borrow against future income.

liquidity preference The preference to keep wealth in the form of ready cash. John Maynard Keynes argued that money is a store of value, one of many possible ways of providing for future consumption. The opportunity cost of holding cash is the higher rate of return that can be earned on other assets, including interest on bonds. Therefore, interest rates have a decisive influence on the decision to hold cash rather than bonds.

liquidity-premium hypothesis The hypothesis that, if investors are more concerned with capital risk than income risk, they have a natural preference for short-term assets and require relatively high returns on long-term bonds — higher than predicted by the simple Expectations Hypothesis. According to this theory, the term structure is normally upward sloping.

LM curve A negatively sloped curve that shows those combinations of y and R for which money demand is equal to supply. The LM curve is shifted in an expansionary rightward direction by an increase in the real money supply or reduction in money demand caused by any event other than a change in y or R.

London Interbank Offered Rate (LIBOR) Measures the interest rate that international banks charge one another for large Eurodollar loans (i.e., loans denominated in U.S. dollars). LIBOR is commonly used as an international benchmark to fix the minimum interest rate that bank syndicates must charge on Eurodollar loans, often to foreign governments.

M1 A monetary aggregate that includes currency outside banks, traveler's checks, commercial-bank checking accounts, and other transaction accounts.

M2 A monetary aggregate that includes M1, overnight Eurodollars and repurchase agreements, money-market deposit accounts, money-market mutual fund shares, savings deposits, and small (less than $100,000) time deposits.

M3 A monetary aggregate that includes M2, large time deposits (greater than $100,000), term Eurodollars, term repurchase agreements, and institutional money-market fund shares.

macro risk See **systematic risk.**

managed float The intervention of central banks in foreign-exchange markets to manipulate exchange rates. (See also **crawling peg** and **dirty float.**)

margin The initial amount that must be put up by an investor who borrows money from a broker to buy stock. The investor must also keep the account's equity (market value minus loan) above the broker's maintenance margin requirement. (See also **buying on margin.**)

marginal propensity to consume The effect of an increase in income on planned consumption spending.

marginal propensity to spend out of income The effect of an increase in income on planned spending.

marginal tax rates The extra tax levied on an additional dollar of a person's income, determined by the person's tax bracket. The Tax Reform Act of 1986 compressed fifteen tax brackets (ranging from 11 percent to 50 percent) into two rates, 15 percent and 28 percent, with a 5 percent surcharge on some incomes in the 28 percent bracket, raising the effective marginal tax rate for these persons to 33 percent. The marginal tax rate is appropriate for comparing and evaluating investment decisions (and it is generally higher than the average tax rate).

market segmentation hypothesis   Hypothesis that investors have diverse preferences and specialize in different maturities. Some investors, such as life insurance companies and pension funds, have long horizons and prefer long-term bonds to minimize income risk while other investors, particularly those most concerned with real rates of return, prefer to roll over short-term assets. If the market is sharply segmented, then the interest rates on different maturities might depend solely on demand and supply within that segment of the market, allowing very different interest rates on bonds with only slightly different maturities.

marking to market   The daily transfer of funds from winners to losers required by futures exchanges, using end-of-the-day settlement prices. Also called the *daily settlement.*

McFadden Act   Largely motivated by a fear that Bank of America would span the nation, this 1927 act prohibits interstate branching and allows each state to regulate branching within its borders.

mean (μ)   The expected value of a probability distribution, i.e., the probability-weighted average of the possible outcomes. The mean of a set of data is the average value of the observations.

medium of exchange   Commonly exchanged items that the recipients intend to trade for other items; for example, gold in nineteenth-century America and modern Federal Reserve notes.

micro risk   *See* **unsystematic risk.**

monetarism   The view that monetary disturbances are the principal cause of economic fluctuations. Although often identified with Milton Friedman and the Quantity Theory, monetarists are a diverse group with varying adherences to the classical beliefs that, in the short run or the long run, the Quantity Theory holds and the economy is always at full employment.

monetary aggregates   Aggregates, including M1, M2, M3, and L, through which the Fed monitors the nation's monetary assets.

monetary base   The outstanding amount of government money, which is held either as bank reserves or as currency outside of banks.

monetary policy   The policy of using open-market operations, reserves requirements, and discount rates to alter the monetary base and monetary aggregates; the Federal Reserve has broad control over the nation's monetary policy. (*Cf.* **fiscal policy**.)

monetized   The extent to which the federal deficit is financed by an increase in the monetary base (what is loosely called "printing money"). A federal deficit must implicitly be financed by an increase either in publicly held Treasury bonds or in the monetary base.

money illusion   Focusing on nominal rather than real data; for example, using nominal wages to choose between work and leisure.

money market   Market in which purchases and sales of securities that mature in less than a year take place. (*Cf.* **capital market**.)

money neutrality   The proposition that a one-time increase in the money supply raises the price level proportionately, with no real effect on the economy. (*Cf.* **money superneutrality**.)

money superneutrality   The proposition that a continuing increase in the money supply causes a sustained inflation, with no real effect on economic activity. (*Cf.* **money neutrality**.)

money-market deposit accounts (MMDAs)   Authorized in 1982 to allow deposit institutions to compete with money-market funds. Depositors can make an unlimited number of withdrawals in person or by mail, and are allowed a maximum of three checks per month or a total of six monthly withdrawals by check, telephone, or automatic bill paying. These accounts have no reserve requirements and, unlike money-market funds, are federally insured.

money-market funds   Mutual funds that purchase short-term securities such as bank CDs and Treasury bills, thereby providing a very liquid investment for small investors. Shareholders can quickly and easily withdraw their money by giving written or telephoned instructions. Most funds allow shareholders to write checks payable to a third party, typically with a $500 minimum.

moral-hazard   A problem that occurs when one of the parties to a contract alters his or her behavior so as to profit from the contract at the other party's expense. For example, a homeowner who has fire insurance may become less careful about avoiding a fire; a person with medical insurance may be less frugal about medical expenses.

multiplier   The equation, $\Delta y/\Delta A = 1/(1 - b)$, giving the change in income per unit change in expenditure, shows how the interaction of income and expenditure multiplies the effect on income of an autonomous change in spending.

mutual fund   *See* **open-end investment company.**

The National Association of Security Dealers Automated Quotation (NASDAQ)   A nationwide, computerized price-quotation network for many over-the-counter securities.

National Credit Union Administration   Administration that initiated nationwide credit union deposit insurance in 1970.

natural level of employment   The natural state of affairs, or the long-run equilibrium toward which the economy automatically gravitates, where the perceived price level is equal to the actual price level. In the new classical market-equilibrium explanation of business cycles, labor demand is always equal to supply, but labor supply fluctuates when workers misperceive prices. Booms in economic activity occur when workers underestimate the price level; recessions occur when they overestimate it.

natural rate of unemployment   The unique, presumably frictional, unemployment rate where the vertical long-run Phillips curve intersects the axis. Most economists believe that, in the long run, all unemployment is voluntary and unaffected by prices. In the long run, an increase in the anticipated rate of inflation simply raises the rate of increase of wages, percentage point for percentage point, and has no effect on real wages. There is only one level of unemployment — where the long-run Phillips curve intersects the axis — that is consistent with long-run equilibrium.

negative amortization   The increase in the unpaid balance when the monthly loan payment is insufficient to cover the interest charge. This can occur in many business and personal loans (such as a line of credit from a bank, loans from a stockbroker, or credit card balances) where there is no set repayment schedule. It also can occur with adjustable-rate loans if the monthly payment does not increase when interest charges do.

negotiable order of withdrawal (NOW) accounts   Established by a favorable court decision in 1972 in Massachusetts, permitting these checking accounts to pay 5¼ percent interest at a time when interest-paying checking accounts were illegal.

new classical economists   Classical economists assumed that the economy was always close to full employment and that full-employment output was unaffected by monetary and fiscal policies. They assumed that departures from full employment are so brief and unimportant that they can be ignored. Robert Lucas and other new classical economists have extended the classical models to allow for voluntary fluctuations in employment and output caused by workers' misperceptions of real wages.

no-loads, or **no-load funds**   Investment companies that do not charge load fees. All closed-end funds are no-loads.

nominal data   Economic data, such as wage rates, income, or wealth, that are recorded in dollars (or marks in Germany and yen in Japan). (*Cf.* **real data.**)

nominal rate of return   The rate of return that compares the dollars received from an investment with the dollars invested, without adjusting for the purchasing power of the dollars. (*Cf.* **real rate of return.**)

nonbank bank   As defined by the Bank Holding Company Act, a financial institution that either accepts deposits that can be withdrawn on demand or makes commercial loans, but not both. Nonbanks were not regulated by the Federal Reserve until 1987, when the Competitive Banking Equality Act closed the nonbank bank loophole by defining a bank as any FDIC-insured institution; however, it exempted nonbank banks established before March 5, 1986.

nontraded goods   Goods and services that are not governed by the law of one price because of prohibitive import and export expenses. For example, a haircut and a round of golf can cost much more in Japan than in the United States because it is impractical for the Japanese to have their hair cut in Iowa and play golf in Georgia.

normal distribution The widely used bell-shaped Gaussian probability distribution. For many assets, this is a reasonable, useful approximation for describing investor uncertainty about the asset's return. A normal distribution is symmetrical about its mean with about a ⅔ probability of being within one standard deviation of its mean and about a 95 percent probability of being within two standard deviations.

open interest The total daily amount of outstanding option and futures contracts. Those who own contracts are said to be "long"; those who have written these contracts are "short."

open-end investment company An investment company whose shares increase as more money is invested in the fund and decline as money is withdrawn. Each day or several times a day, the fund calculates its net asset value (NAV) and stands ready to issue or redeem shares at this price.

open-market operations The Fed's purchases and sales of securities. These transactions expand or contract the nation's monetary base and are, in practice, the predominant instrument of Fed monetary policy.

operating targets Targets used by the Fed to help achieve its intermediate targets. For instance, the Fed may want to reduce the rate of inflation and decide to use a 5 percent rate of growth of M1 as intermediate target. Since M1 contains checkable deposits subject to reserve requirements, there may be a close relationship between bank reserves and M1. If so, the Fed might set an operating target of, say, 5 percent annual growth in bank reserves, hoping that this will ensure a 5 percent annual growth of M1 and that this growth rate for M1 will reduce inflation as desired.

Operation Twist The Fed faced a dilemma during the booming 1960s in that economic growth called for low interest rates to persuade households and

businesses to borrow and spend, but low U.S. interest rates encouraged investors to send funds abroad, seeking higher yields. To meet these conflicting objectives, the Fed (halfheartedly) tried what has become known as Operation Twist — an attempt to twist the term structure of interest rates by buying long-term securities and selling short-term securities.

option contract A contract that gives one of the parties the right, but not the obligation, to buy or sell an item in the future at a price that is specified now. A mill might pay a farmer $20,000 for an option giving it the right to buy 100,000 bushels of wheat six months from now at $3 a bushel. If the market price of wheat drops below $3, then the mill will not exercise its option. Since options do not have to be exercised, but merely valued on the expiration date, contracts can be written on intangibles such as the S&P 500 stock index.

over-the-counter (OTC) Refers to the trading of securities that are not listed on organized exchanges, by dealers who make a market by quoting prices at which they are willing to buy and sell a security. The prices of many OTC securities are reported on the National Association of Securities Dealers' Automatic Quotations system (NASDAQ).

pass-through securities Created when banks and other institutions that originate mortgage loans sell these mortgages to GNMA and other agencies that form mortgage pools. The originating institution sends the mortgage interest and principal payments to GNMA, which passes them through to those who own GNMA certificates. GNMA guarantees the payment of interest and principal and, in return, levies a fee on each mortgage pool it creates.

perfect substitutes Securities that (neglecting yields) are equally attractive, taking into account such factors as liquidity, transaction costs, and risk. Such securities should be priced to give the same anticipated yield. The closer substitutes securities are for each other, the more their yields will move in unison.

Phillips curve A curve that shows an inverse relationship between the unemployment rate and the rate of inflation. Increases in aggregate demand tighten labor markets as unemployment falls and vacancies grow, causing wages and prices to increase. The hard-nosed cure for inflation is a recession.

points   A loan fee equal to a specified percentage of the loan paid at the time the loan is made. For example, for a $100,000 loan at 12 percent plus 5 points, the borrower receives $95,000 (i.e., $100,000 less the 5 percent points charge), but pays 12 percent interest on the full $100,000 loan. Points were originally devised to circumvent usury ceilings, which restrict stated rather than effective interest rates on loans.

political business cycle   The preelection stimulus and postelection restraint of the economy by an incumbent party.

Ponzi scheme   An investment in which the money of new investors is used to pay off earlier ones. Such schemes require an ever-expanding group of participants and collapse when new players cannot be found.

portfolio insurance   A flexible procedure for limiting losses by selling securities continuously as prices drop (buying as prices rise). Enough investors following these mechanical rules could destabilize financial markets.

prepayment penalties   Money that the borrower must pay the lender if the loan is repaid early. These protect lenders if interest rates fall and the borrower refinances the loan.

present value   The amount that an investor is willing to pay for a cash flow, determined by discounting the cash flow by the investor's required rate of return. For a single payment F after n years and a required rate of return R, the present value is given by $P = F/(1 + R)^n$.

primary market   Market in which the initial issuance of a security is said to occur; e.g., a household deposits money in a savings account, the U.S. Treasury raises money by selling bonds, and a business incorporates by issuing stock. In each case, a financial record of the transaction is created that shows the existence of a debt or of equity. Later trades of these certificates occur in the **secondary market**.

primary reserves   Cash, deposits with the Fed, and deposits in other banks with which a bank can maintain liquidity.

prime rate   Traditionally, the interest rate charged on six-month commercial loans to customers (usually businesses) that are deemed to have the lowest risk of default. Large businesses are generally reluctant to tie their lending rate to the prime rate, which is set unilaterally by banks, and insist instead on a benchmark rate, such as LIBOR, that is determined in competitive financial markets.

probabilities   Used to quantify uncertainty by describing which outcomes are likely and which are unlikely. Probabilities cannot be negative and must add to one. With coins, dice, and cards we may be able to reason the probabilities from the physical characteristics of the experiment; investment probabilities are inherently subjective.

probability distribution   Distribution used to specify probabilities for ranges of outcomes when there are an infinite number of possible outcomes; i.e., a 10 percent chance that the return will be between $200 and $300, a 30 percent chance that it will be between $100 and $200, etc. In a graphical representation of a probability distribution, the area under the curve shows the probability for that range of outcomes.

program trading   Originally, the buying or selling of a diversified portfolio of stocks; now associated with index futures since these are the easiest way to trade baskets of stocks. (*See also* **index arbitrage** and **portfolio insurance**.)

purchasing-power parity   Based on the law of one price, it holds that the percentage change in an exchange rate is approximately equal to the difference in the two nations' rates of inflation. If, for example, the United States has a 5-percent inflation and Germany has a 2-percent inflation, the dollar should depreciate by 3 percent relative to the mark.

put option   Option in which the owner has the right to sell an asset at a fixed price on or before a specified date; the option becomes increasingly valuable if the price of the underlying asset declines.

quantity theory   Assumption that velocity, the ratio of nominal gross national product to some measure of the money supply, is constant — implying that gross national product moves proportionately with the money supply. Keynes successfully argued that the opportunity cost of holding money is the interest that can be earned on other assets; therefore, the demand for money is negatively related to interest rates and velocity is positively related to interest rates.

random walk hypothesis   The weak form of the efficient-market hypothesis; states that each change in a stock's price is unrelated to previous changes — much as each flip of a coin is unrelated to previous tosses or each step by a drunkard is unrelated to previous steps.

rates of return   The return from an investment consists of income (the benefits received while owning the asset), and capital gains (the profits made when the asset is sold).

rational expectations   Expectations based on the efficient utilization of available information. If, as in the new classical models, all unemployment is voluntary with economic fluctuations due to errors in assessing prices, then rational expectations imply that well-anticipated changes in the money supply do not cause mistakes in gauging the price level and, consequently, have no effect on employment or output.

real assets   Tangible physical assets, such as land, houses, livestock, and precious metals. (*Cf.* **financial assets**.)

Real Bills doctrine   Also known as the commercial loan theory; it states that bank loans should be short-term, self-liquidating, and productive. This doctrine was intended to ensure bank liquidity and also appropriately regulate the money supply. In practice, this strategy helps liquidity but does not guarantee it, and causes the money supply to move with the business cycle.

real data   Economic data such as wage rates, income, and wealth that are recorded in terms of purchasing power. Real data are constructed by deflating nominal data by a price index. A **real interest rate** is a nominal interest rate minus the rate of change of some price index.

real rate of return   Measurement of the percentage increase in purchasing power provided by an investment. Approximately equal to the nominal (dollar) percentage return minus the percentage rate of inflation.

registered bonds   The owner of which registers with the bond's trustee and receives coupon payments without the physical presentation of the bond certificate. Since 1983, all U.S. Treasury securities have been registered. (*Cf.* **bearer bonds**.)

regulated investment company   Companies that satisfy the criteria established by the Investment Company Act of 1940 — a designation that exempts them from corporate taxes. Among these criteria, the company must register with the SEC and comply with its disclosure requirements, own a diversified portfolio, and distribute at least 90 percent of its interest and dividend income as it is received.

Regulation Q   An act limiting interest rates on some types of deposits. Because it was believed that competitive pressures to pay high-interest rates on deposits had led banks to make high-interest, high-risk loans, the Banking Acts of 1933 and 1935 prohibited institutions other than commercial banks from offering checking accounts; prohibited the payment of interest on checking accounts; and, under Regulation Q, gave the Federal Reserve the power to set the maximum interest rates that banks could pay on other types of deposits. In 1980, these deposit-rate ceilings were phased out by the Depository Institutions Deregulation and Monetary Control Act.

repurchase agreement (repo)   A security agreement in which a bank sells securities to a customer, usually a corporation, and agrees to repurchase the securities at a higher price on a given date, often the next day. In this way, the bank borrows money from a corporation, using some of its assets as collateral.

required rate of return The rate used to determine the present value of a cash flow; it depends on the returns available on alternative investments and on other characteristics — such as the riskiness of the cash flow — that make the investment relatively attractive or unattractive.

reserve requirements Government requirements compelling banks to hold some fraction of their deposits as reserves, either as cash in their vaults or as deposits with the Federal Reserve that earn no interest.

reversing Action in which the buyer of a futures contract, rather than taking delivery, can reverse (or cover) the position by selling the contract before the delivery date. A contract writer can reverse this position by repurchasing the contract.

risk An uncertain situation. The risk of a promised cash flow or anticipated asset return is often gauged by the standard deviation. Risk-averse investor require high expected returns of risky investments.

risk averse Describes a person who sacrifices expected return to reduce risk and prefers a diversified portfolio containing dissimilar assets. Diversification reduces risk most effectively if the asset returns are uncorrelated or, even better, negatively correlated. A risk-averse person would certainly buy insurance if the expected return were zero, and may purchase insurance with a negative expected return.

risk neutral Describes a person who chooses the alternative with the highest expected return, placing all eggs in one basket. A risk-neutral person does not like insurance or lottery tickets because both have negative expected returns.

risk seeking Describes a person who accepts fair bets and will even sacrifice expected return to increase risk; for example, one who buys a lottery ticket if the expected value is zero and maybe buys one with a negative expected return. The risk seeker shuns diversification.

Say's Law Axiom that supply creates its own demand. In the classical full-employment model, the aggregate supply curve is vertical and aggregate demand has no effect on output and employment. Output is determined by supply and, through price changes, demand adapts to it.

secondary market Market in which assets are traded after their initial issuance in the primary market. After a company issues bonds or stock in the primary market, these notes and shares may pass from hand to hand in the secondary market, either on an exchange or over-the-counter.

secondary reserves Held in addition to a bank's primary reserves to maintain liquidity. Secondary reserves include Treasury bills and other very safe, short-term assets that can be converted into cash almost immediately. (*See also* **primary reserves**.)

Securities and Exchange Commission (SEC) Established by Congress as a federal agency to enforce the provisions of the Securities Act of 1933 and the Securities Exchange Act of 1934, which were passed in the aftermath of the stock-market crash of 1929 and subsequent economic depression. The SEC oversees the public sale of securities in the primary market and trading in the secondary market, and has a wide range of powers designed to ensure the fairness and integrity of these markets including prohibiting fraud and compelling the disclosure of pertinent information.

securitization The conversion of illiquid loans into marketable loan-backed securities. For example, more than half of all residential mortgages are now resold in the secondary mortgage market, and these mortgages are securitized in that investors no longer have to be mortgage bankers or S&L's to invest in mortgages.

securitization of borrowing The sale of securities directly to investors without relying on financial intermediaries to channel funds from investors to business borrowers.

semi-strong form A form of the efficient-market hypothesis stating that abnormal returns cannot be consistently earned using any publicly available information, including past prices and such data as interest rates, inflation, and corporate earnings. Thus, fundamental analysis cannot beat the market.

settlement price A price, equal to the closing price

for actively traded contracts, set by a futures exchange at the end of each trading day to reckon each trader's profit or loss that day. Those having losses must make cash payments (daily settlements) to the brokerage accounts of those having profits before the beginning of the next trading day.

smart cards Cards used like debit cards to make immediate payments for goods and services, but having embedded microprocessors that record its user's transactions and financial situation.

Special Drawing Rights (SDRs) "Paper gold" used within the IMF to allow balance of payments deficit nations to purchase foreign exchange from surplus nations.

specialist A designated person at the NYSE who collects orders and acts as both a broker (trading for others) and a dealer (trading for oneself). As a broker, the specialist executes a transaction when someone is willing to buy at a price at which another is willing to sell. Specialists also act as dealers in order to maintain a "fair and orderly" market by buying or selling, as needed, for their own accounts.

speculative bubble Sometimes, asset prices lose touch with intrinsic values as people hope to profit not from the asset's cash flow, but from selling the asset at ever-higher prices. During these speculative bubbles, it seems foolish to sit on the sidelines while others become rich; in retrospect, it looks like mass hysteria. When the bubble bursts, buyers cannot be found and prices fall precipitously.

speculator One who buys an asset not for the long-run cash flow but to sell a short while later for a profit, in contrast to an investor who is willing to hold an asset for keeps.

spot prices The current market price of an item for immediate delivery.

square root rule In inventory models of money demand, average money holdings are equal to the square root of $cY/2R$ where c is the cost of a money-bond transaction, Y is nominal income, and R is the nominal interest rate.

stagflation High unemployment and high inflation, in contradiction to the Phillips curve idea that there is an inverse relationship between unemployment and inflation. The United States experienced stagflation from the mid-1970s through the early 1980s.

standard deviation The square root of the variance; it gauges the spread of a distribution and gauges risk by measuring how certain we are that the return will be close to its expected value. The standard deviation has the same units (dollars or percent) as the data, whereas the units for the variance are dollars-squared or percent-squared.

sterilized intervention Occurs when a central bank uses open-market purchases or sales to offset the effects of its foreign-exchange transactions on the monetary base. For instance, if the value of the dollar is falling relative to the Japanese yen, the Fed might support the dollar by buying dollars with yen. This purchase of dollars reduces the monetary base, but the Fed can put these dollars back into circulation by using them to purchase Treasury bills. Because there is no change in the monetary base, this is a sterilized intervention.

striking price Also called the *exercise price*; it is the price at which an option contract can be exercised.

strong form A form of the efficient-market hypothesis that holds that there is no information, public or private, that allows some investors to beat the market consistently. This hypothesis is contradicted by evidence that a few do profit by using information not available to other investors, often in violation of federal laws.

supply-side crowding out Occurs if the government takes more from the economy at full employment, when output is a fixed pie, so that the private sector has less.

swap An agreement to sell a currency at a stated price and then repurchase it at a stated price on a specified future date. The difference between the sale and repurchase prices is the swap rate. For instance, a New York bank might swap deutschemarks for dollars with a German bank by agreeing to sell deutschemarks at a price of 0.50 dollars/mark on February 1 and to repurchase the deutschemarks at a price of 0.52 dollars/mark on March 1; thus the New York bank temporarily borrows dollars and the German bank borrows marks.

systematic risk   Also called *macro risk, market risk,* or *nondiversifiable risk*; it concerns macroeconomic events such as unanticipated changes in interest rates, inflation, and the unemployment rate that affect all securities. With this risk, there is no safety in numbers — mere diversification cannot protect investors from recession or high interest rates.

T-accounts   Accounts that show the changes on a balance sheet caused by some financial event.

tax-exempt bonds   Bonds on which the interest is free of income taxes. The term usually refers to state and local bonds, also called *municipals* or *munis*, that are exempt from federal income taxes. A bond that is exempt from both state and federal taxes (e.g., a California bond held by a Californian) is double tax-exempt. Bonds that are exempt from federal, state, and city income taxes are triple tax-exempt.

term structure of interest rates   Describes the yields to maturity on zero-coupon bonds that have different maturities but are otherwise identical; a yield curve compares the yields to maturity on coupon bonds of various maturities. The Expectations Hypothesis says that the relationship between short-term and long-term interest rates reflects the anticipated future course of interest rates.

Tobin effect   Argument of James Tobin, who pointed out that money could be neutral in the long run, but not superneutral. Because cash has a fixed nominal rate of return (zero), its real rate of return must become increasingly negative as inflation increases. To avoid holding cash during inflations, people will accept reduced real rates of return on alternative assets. Diminished real interest rates, in turn, have real effects on the economy, encouraging investment spending and capital accumulation.

Tobin's *q*   The ratio of the market value of a firm to the replacement cost of its assets. A *q* value larger than one indicates that the firm's profit rate exceeds the shareholders' required return on their stock and that the firm will benefit shareholders if it retains additional earnings for expansion. A firm with a *q* of less than one is worth more dead than alive.

trade balance   A nation's exports of commodities minus its imports; often interpreted as a rough barometer of the competitiveness of its industries.

transfer payments   A government's outlays including Social Security benefits, interest payments, and other disbursements for which the recipients do not have to produce any goods or provide any services. Taxes are also transfer payments, but are from the citizens to the government. Government purchases of goods and services affect aggregate expenditures directly; taxes and other transfers affect spending indirectly by affecting private consumption and investment.

Treasury bills (T-bills)   Federal government securities with maturities of less than one year, which are sold to raise money for government expenditures. There are no periodic interest payments; the investor's return is equal to the difference between the bill's purchase price and its face value, which is received when the bill matures. Unlike virtually all other securities, the financial press traditionally calculates T-bill returns on a discount basis, relative to the bill's face value rather than the purchase price, and thereby understates the investor's actual rate of return.

unit banking   Laws permitting a bank to have only one geographic location. In 1975, there were still 15 states (mostly in the Midwest) that completely prohibited bank branches; by 1987, 11 of these 15 states had passed laws allowing branch banks.

U.S. currency outstanding   Currency held by the private sector. U.S. currency outstanding is equal to Federal Reserve notes plus Treasury notes and coin, minus Fed holdings of Treasury currency, minus Treasury holdings of Fed currency. Because some of this outstanding currency is inside bank vaults and some is in private hands outside banks, U.S. currency outstanding is also equal to vault cash plus currency outside banks.

variance   The average squared deviation of the outcomes about their mean; i.e., a measure of whether the possible (or actual) values are close to the mean or widely scattered. For a probability distribution, the probabilities are used as weights in calculating this average; for empirical data, the observed frequencies are used. (If the data are a small sample, statisticians usually divide by $n - 1$ rather than by n.)

velocity   The ratio of the nominal value of some measure of transactions to some measure of the money supply; velocity is the average number of times that this money is exchanged for these transactions during a given accounting period. M1 velocity, for example, is the ratio of nominal gross national product to M1.

weak form   The form of the Efficient Market Hypothesis that holds that past data on stock prices are of no use in predicting future price changes.

yield curve   Similar to the term structure, it compares the yields to maturity on coupon-paying bonds with different maturities.

yield to maturity   The discount rate at which the present value of the bond's coupons and principal is equal to its price. A bond's price is higher than its face value when its yield to maturity is below the coupon rate, and is less than its face value when its yield is above the coupon rate.

zero-coupon bonds (zeros)   Bonds that pay no coupons; as with T-bills, the buyer receives a single, lump sum at maturity. A series of zeros maturing at six-month intervals can be created by stripping away the coupons from conventional bonds. The implicit annual rate of return R on a zero costing P that pays an amount F in n years is given by the compound interest formula $P(1 + R)^n = F$.

Index

Year	United States Population	Real Gross National Product (1982$)	Year	Unemployment Rate	Consumer Price Index	Annual Rate of Inflation	Interest Rate on One-Year Treasury Bills
1950	152.271	1,203.7	1950	5.3	24.1	5.9	1.15
1951	154.878	1,328.2	1951	3.3	26.0	6.0	1.51
1952	157.553	1,380.0	1952	3.0	26.5	0.8	1.81
1953	160.184	1,435.3	1953	2.9	26.7	0.7	2.04
1954	163.026	1,416.2	1954	5.5	26.9	−0.7	1.37
1955	165.931	1,494.9	1955	4.4	26.8	0.4	1.40
1956	168.903	1,525.6	1956	4.1	27.2	3.0	2.60
1957	171.984	1,551.1	1957	4.3	28.1	2.9	3.32
1958	174.882	1,539.2	1958	6.8	28.9	1.8	2.66
1959	177.830	1,629.1	1959	5.5	29.1	1.7	3.42
1960	180.671	1,665.3	1960	5.5	29.6	1.4	5.28
1961	183.691	1,708.7	1961	6.7	29.9	0.7	2.74
1962	186.538	1,799.4	1962	5.5	30.2	1.3	3.34
1963	189.242	1,873.3	1963	5.7	30.6	1.6	3.14
1964	191.889	1,973.3	1964	5.2	31.0	1.0	3.87
1965	194.303	2,087.6	1965	4.5	31.5	1.9	4.13
1966	196.560	2,208.3	1966	3.8	32.4	3.5	4.99
1967	198.712	2,271.4	1967	3.8	33.4	3.0	4.90
1968	200.706	2,365.6	1968	3.6	34.8	4.7	5.67
1969	202.677	2,423.3	1969	3.5	36.7	6.2	6.53
1970	205.052	2,416.2	1970	4.9	38.8	5.6	8.23
1971	207.661	2,484.8	1971	5.9	40.5	3.3	4.66
1972	209.896	2,608.5	1972	5.6	41.8	3.4	4.03
1973	211.909	2,744.1	1973	4.9	44.4	8.7	5.99
1974	213.854	2,729.3	1974	5.6	49.3	12.9	7.65
1975	215.973	2,695.0	1975	8.5	53.8	6.9	6.79
1976	218.035	2,826.7	1976	7.7	56.9	4.9	5.84
1977	220.239	2,958.6	1977	7.1	60.6	6.7	5.34
1978	222.585	3,115.2	1978	6.1	65.2	9.0	7.40
1979	222.055	3,192.4	1979	5.8	72.6	13.3	10.70
1980	227.757	3,187.1	1980	7.1	82.4	12.5	12.49
1981	230.138	3,248.8	1981	7.6	90.9	8.9	14.66
1982	232.520	3,166.0	1982	9.7	96.5	3.8	14.86
1983	234.799	3,279.1	1983	9.6	99.6	3.8	8.83
1984	237.001	3,501.4	1984	7.5	103.9	3.9	10.12
1985	239.279	3,618.7	1985	7.2	107.6	3.8	9.22
1986	241.625	3,717.9	1986	7.0	109.6	1.1	7.88
1987	243.934	3,853.7	1987	6.2	113.6	4.4	5.86
1988	246.329	4,024.4	1988	5.5	118.3	4.4	7.07
1989	248.777	4,142.6	1989	5.3	124.0	4.6	9.27